WORLD ETHICS

Wanda Torres Gregory
Simmons College

Donna Giancola
Suffolk University

THOMSON ™

WADSWORTH

Australia • Canada • Mexico • Singapore • Spain • United Kingdom • United States

THOMSON

WADSWORTH

Publisher: Holly J. Allen
Philosophy Editor: Steve Wainwright
Assistant Editor: Lee McCracken
Editorial Assistant: Anna Lustig
Technology Project Manager: Susan DeVanna
Marketing Manager: Worth Hawes
Marketing Assistant: Justin Ferguson
Advertising Project Manager: Bryan Vann
Signing Representative: Carolyn Gogolin
Print/Media Buyer: Robert King

Permissions Editor: Stephanie Keough-Hedges
Production Service: Penmarin Books
Text Designers: John Edeen/Lisa Delgado
Copy Editor: Kevin Gleason
Cover Designer: Yvo Riezebos
Cover Image: ' Ar tists Rights Society (ARS),
    New York/ADAGP, Paris
Cover and Text Printer: Thomson/West
Compositor: G&S Typesetters, Inc.

3 4 5 6 7 07

For more information about our products,
contact us at:
Thomson Learning Academic Resource Center
1-800-423-0563
For permission to use material from this text,
contact us by:
Phone: 1-800-730-2214
Fax: 1-800-730-2215
Web: http://www.thomsonrights.com.

Library of Congress Control Number: 2002104138

ISBN-13: 978-0-534-51271-2
ISBN-10: 0-534-51271-2

Wadsworth/Thomson Learning
10 Davis Drive
Belmont, CA 94002-3098
USA

Thomas Learning
60 Albert Street, #15-01
Albert Complex
Singapore 189969

Australia
Nelson Thomson Learning
1120 Birchmount Road
Toronto, Ontario M1K 5G4
Canada

Australia
Nelson Thomson Learning
102 Dodds Street
South Melbourne, Victoria 3205
Australia

Canada
Nelson Thomson Learning
1120 Birchmount Road
Toronto, Ontario M1K 5G4
Canada

Europe/Middle East/Africa
Thomson Learning
Berkshire House
168-173 High Holborn
London WC1V7AA
United Kingdom

Latin America
Thomson Learning
Seneca, 53
Colonia Polanco
11560 Mexico D.F.
Mexico

Preface

In the West, the study of ethics is becoming increasingly global in its perspectives. The move from an exclusive focus on classics in the European tradition to an inclusive, multicultural scope reflects an awareness that ethics spans the world. Such cognizance promises to bring with it an earnest recognition of differences and a genuine acknowledgment of diversity. New prospects for dialogues and comparisons also arise from this heightened consciousness and attitude of sensitivity.

This book is an attempt to participate in the move to a global-minded ethics. It is a multicultural sourcebook in ethics that includes historical traditions and contemporary movements from around the world. Its aim is to provide a comprehensive, though certainly not exhaustive, survey of world ethics by offering a broad and diverse selection of primary texts containing predominantly ethical reflections. The readings focus on ethical theories rather than applied ethics or approaches to moral issues, and although most of their authors are philosophers, we incorporate contributions from various disciplines and fields besides philosophy. All the authors are major figures who have made a significant impact in their areas of expertise. Primacy has been given to seminal or classic thinkers over the more recent and lesser-known representatives influenced by them.

The primary rationale behind this book is the belief that students gain a richer and deeper understanding of ethical concepts when these are considered from a multicultural and multidisciplinary perspective. In turn, the study of a world ethics contributes to a more concrete sense of the importance and relevance of ethical reflections for humans across cultures and disciplines; the philosophical spirit of ethics is not exclusive to members of the European tradition or to philosophers. Moreover, students themselves generally come from diverse cultures and pursue majors in studies other than philosophy. The study of an ethics that incorporates these backgrounds and interests enables students to identify themselves and their views, concerns, and interests within a context of moral reasoning. The goal of preserving the philosophical spirit of ethics while helping students develop their critical thinking skills is best attained through the study of ethical theories. Students may have a firmer grasp of the ethical concepts in debates about specific moral issues when these are first grounded in explicit theoretical reflections. In the long run, they can also benefit from having direct access to original texts, even when they find these initially difficult to read or understand.

The special features of this book cover matters of content as well as method. Here are the highlights:

- Fifty-nine multicultural selections offer ethics instructors a wide range of choices for course design.
- To facilitate students' understanding of historical and cultural continuities, the readings are divided into four major parts: The first two are on historical traditions, European and Asian; the third part gathers, under the rubric "Contemporary Cultural Perspectives," a variety of African, African-American, Latin American, and Native American approaches to ethical questions; and the last part is on feminism.

Each major part contains a broad array of viewpoints so that students may develop a better sense of important internal differences.

- Two tables of contents—one cultural, the other thematic—enable instructors to take flexible approaches. The cultural or main table of contents lists the selections in historical order within each of the four major parts. The twenty headings in the thematic table identify as many different approaches in ethics.
- A major timeline places all the contributors in chronological order of birth.
- A general introduction covers five topics: a definition of ethics; fundamental ethical concepts; an outline of themes, with basic definitions of various approaches; multiculturalism in ethics, with brief introductions to the Asian traditions, contemporary cultural perspectives, and feminists; and the basics of critical thinking.
- Following the introduction is a general list of suggested sources, including Web sites, on the traditions and perspectives.
- An introduction preceding each selection presents a brief biography of the author, a background view of his or her general philosophy, and a summary of the basic points in the reading.
- Each reading is followed by study questions and a short annotated bibliography of secondary sources.

Acknowledgments

We would like to express our gratitude to everyone who helped us complete this book. Our first thanks go first to Peter Adams, former Philosophy Editor at Wadsworth, for his unwavering support and expert guidance. We are grateful to Steve Wainwright, Wadsworth's current Philosophy Editor, for his able assistance in the final stages of production. We would also like to acknowledge the Wadsworth staff for their efficient and diligent performance.

We are grateful to our reviewers for their conscientious reading and invaluable commentaries: Susan Armstrong, Humboldt State University; Mary Ann Cutter, University of Colorado, Colorado Springs; Frank Fair, Sam Houston State University; Daniel Holbrook, Washington State University; Rosalind Ekman Ladd, Wheaton College; Jonathan Mandle, SUNY-Albany; Carol Nicholson, Rider University; Lynn Pasquerella, University of Rhode Island; Frank Ryan, Kent State University; H. Benjamin Shaeffer, Humboldt State University; David Sosa, University of Texas-Austin; Anita Superson, University of Kentucky; Barbara Swyhart, California University of Pennsylvania; Valerie Tiberius, University of Minnesota; and Julie Van Camp, California State University, Long Beach.

Our gratitude also goes to our students, Undine Pawlowski from Suffolk University, and Courtney Knapp and Christina Fullam from Simmons College, who assisted us with the technical tasks.

Finally, Wanda is deeply thankful to Sue Stafford and Diane Raymond for being such caring mentors and inspiring colleagues, and to her family for their unconditional, loving support.

WANDA TORRES GREGORY
DONNA GIANCOLA

Contents

Thematic Contents

Timeline

Lao Tzu, Seventh century B.C.E.
The Buddha, 563–483 B.C.E.
Confucius, 551–479 B.C.E.
The *Bhagavad Gita,* Sixth–second centuries B.C.E.
Socrates, 470/69–399 B.C.E.
Plato, 428/27–348/47 B.C.E.
Aristotle, 384–322 B.C.E.
Mencius, 371–289 B.C.E.
Epicurus, 341/42–270 B.C.E.
Hsün Tzu, c. 310–210 B.C.E.
The Dhammapada, Third century B.C.E.
Epictetus, c. 50–c.138
Augustine, 354–430
Santideva, 685–763
Al-Ghazali, 1058–1111
Maimonides, 1135–1204
Thomas Aquinas, 1225–1274
David Hume, 1711–1776
Immanuel Kant, 1724–1804
John Stuart Mill, 1806–1873
Søren Kierkegaard, 1813–1855
Karl Marx, 1818–1883
Friedrich Nietzsche, 1844–1900
Black Elk, 1863–1950
W. E. B. Du Bois, 1868–1963
Mohandas Gandhi, 1869–1948
G. E. Moore, 1873–1958
Martin Buber, 1878–1965
Ruth Benedict, 1887–1948
Paul Mbuya Akoko, 1891–1981
Oruka Rang'inya, 1900–1979
Jean-Paul Sartre, 1905–1980
Emmanuel Levinas, 1906–1995; Léopold Sédar Senghor, 1906–2001
Simone de Beauvoir, 1908–1986
Kwame Nkrumah, 1909–1972
A. J. Ayer, 1910–1989
Aimé Césaire, 1913–
Paulo Freire, 1921– ; John Rawls, 1921–
Frantz Fanon, 1925–1961; Malcolm X, 1925–1965
Thich Nhat Hanh, 1926–
Mary Daly, 1928–
Martin Luther King, Jr., 1929–1968; Annette Baier, 1929–

Alasdair Macintyre, 1929–; Nel Noddings, 1929–
Luce Irigaray, 1930–
Enrique Dussel, 1935– ; Sara Ruddick, 1935–
Carol Gilligan, 1936– ; Rosemary Radford Ruether, 1936–
Alison Jaggar, 1942–
Angela Davis, 1944– ; María Lugones, 1944–
Sarah Lucia Hoagland, 1945– ; Elizabeth Spelman, 1945–
bell hooks, 1952–
Cornel West, 1953–

Introduction

What Is Ethics?

The word *ethics* has its roots in the Greek word *ethos*, meaning "custom" or "habit." The Latin word *mores*, from which we get the word *morality*, is basically synonymous with the word *ethos*. In their common usage, the words *ethics* and *morality* appear to reflect their etymology. Ordinarily, they refer to the social or cultural standards and principles by which we customarily judge things as "right," "wrong," "good," and "bad." Usually, we focus on human beings and their actions as the main objects of our moral or ethical evaluations. We have an extensive vocabulary for expressing such judgments about people and their conduct—with terms such as *ethical, moral, unethical, immoral,* and *amoral,* to cite the most obvious. Our daily lives seem to reveal an understanding of such concepts as we apply them in our personal interactions and to our social institutions. We learn given moral codes, standards, and principles, and many of us try to lead our lives according to the ethical guidelines we adopt. Most of us embrace our moral beliefs with conviction and uphold our ethical ideals with passionate certainty. Yet, disagreements, inconsistencies, conflicts, dilemmas, and unsolved problems abound when it comes to moral or ethical matters. Adopting ethics or morals without investigation can prevent us from unraveling such conflicts and problems because we may not see what lies beneath.

The discipline called ethics differs from the ordinary, commonsense approach, for it begins with an explicit awareness of the moral dimensions of our lives. Rather than assuming ethical or moral matters as given, it focuses on these with an attitude of questioning, making deliberate efforts to reflect on the issues, problems, and concepts involved. In its pursuits, ethics searches for answers through rigorous methods of examination, and it subjects its own claims to intense scrutiny. Its ultimate aim is to provide systematic explanations and well-grounded arguments regarding ethical questions. Thus, ethics may be defined as the thoughtful analysis and evaluation of the standards and principles by which we issue judgments in terms of moral values.

Though the modes of investigation proper to ethics are more rigorously methodical than those we consistently use in everyday life, its subject matter is familiar to everyone. It poses the fundamental questions humans have always asked themselves, such as "What kind of a life should I live?" "Is there an ultimate good?" "Why should I be moral?" "How do I know what is the right thing to do?" "Are humans basically good or evil?" "What kind of society is just?" And although ethics is predominantly a philosophical field of inquiry, it is not the exclusive province of philosophers. Writers, scientists, politicians, religious leaders, judges, educators, students, and laypersons—in short, people from all walks of life—have adopted the philo-sophical spirit in their reflections on moral questions. Nor is ethics a matter of abstract theorizing and sheer speculation having little or no relevance for our real lives. Rather, it offers us ways of thinking about the moral features of our own existence— our assumptions, beliefs, judgments, ideals, concepts, values, and conduct—in a se-rious and careful manner. Significantly, then, such modes of thought always open up paths for self-awareness and self-reflection.

Some Fundamentals of Ethics

Many ethical claims are *prescriptive* statements: statements about what *ought* to be. They can take many forms, such as commands ("You ought to tell the truth"), rules ("No stealing"), judgments ("You did wrong"), and exhortations ("Help your neighbor"). Correspondingly, they can play different roles—imperative, regulative, adjudicative, persuasive—in the exchange between the speaker or writer and her audience. Yet, in their basic character, prescriptive statements deal, explicitly or im-plicitly, with moral values.

Although the central claims in ethics are prescriptive statements, ethics also in-cludes *descriptive* statements: statements about what *is*. They may be drawn from many sources, including general observations, personal narrations or confessions, formal reports, studies, empirical findings, and scientific conclusions. Their role in ethics tends to be secondary, for they are normally used in a supportive function. For example, an ethical theorist might claim that humans are naturally good and pre-scribe moral guidelines reflecting that belief. To support his claim about our innate goodness, he could quote studies in social science regarding children's behavior or simply note certain constant features in human actions.

Some philosophers distinguish between ethics and moral theory as being dif-ferent fields of inquiry. However, in this book, we treat the two as synonymous. Tra-ditionally, ethics has been subdivided into *normative* ethics and *theoretical* ethics. Normative ethics focuses on human conduct and issues norms or moral precepts, principles, and standards. Theoretical ethics is also called *metaethics*—from the Greek prefix *meta*, meaning "above," "beyond," or "about." It focuses on ethical sys-tems as such, while it raises questions concerning meaning, logic or method, epis-temology (the theory of knowledge), and metaphysics (the theory of the ultimate na-ture of reality). Metaethics addresses such questions as "Is the concept 'good' definable?" "How do we reach moral conclusions?" "Is morality a matter of knowl-edge and truth?" "Do we have a free will, or is our behavior determined by certain causal laws?" Ethics embraces both normative and theoretical questions. Occasion-ally, ethicists combine these as they develop their particular positions. Thus, in this book we generally use the term *ethics* without explicitly distinguishing between the normative and theoretical subdivisions.

Themes in Ethics

Though there are a wealth of topics and a wide range of views in ethics, general questions and similar approaches do recur over time and across traditions. The thematic table of contents of this book identifies some of those constant themes and positions and names their proponents who appear in the book. Following this table of contents is a framework designed to give you a basic sense of these common problems and views in ethics. It is a deliberately oversimplified summary of general points offering you one of many ways of organizing and classifying the material. Thus, it also leaves out the many possible combinations and intersections between ethical theories.

One of the classic problems in ethics is skepticism (from the Greek word *skepsis*, meaning "doubt"). Skeptics may doubt the rationality, universality, or objectivity of morality. In this, they also may raise epistemological points concerning the difficulty or impossibility of attaining knowledge and truth in ethics. Moral skepticism most commonly takes the following forms:

- *Relativism* doubts the existence of universal, absolute moral values. Its basic claim is that morality is created by humans. So, morality is relative to particular individuals, societies, or cultures.
- *Subjectivism* doubts the objectivity of moral statements. Its basic claim is that moral statements are merely descriptions of our subjective states. Thus, morality is relative to individuals and is really a matter of personal opinions.
- *Emotivism* doubts that reason plays a significant role in morality. Its basic claim is that ethical judgments are just the expression of our emotions. Morality is subjective in a radical sense because it is really a matter of personal feelings.

Other ethical theories respond to skepticism by claiming instead that morality is universal, objective, or rational. Some of these responses will also affirm that moral knowledge and truth are possible.

A classical debate in ethics revolves around the issue of whether the central point of concern is the agent or her actions. The six main perspectives are:

- *Deontology* (from the Greek word *deon*, meaning "duty") assigns primary importance to the concept of moral obligation or duty and focuses on our intentions in acting.
- *Teleology* (from the Greek word *telos*, meaning "end") concentrates on the ends or goals of our actions.
- *Consequentialism* focuses on the consequences or effects of our actions.
- *Hedonism* (from the Greek word *hedone*, meaning "pleasure") and *utilitarianism* combine teleological and consequentialist perspectives. Their supposition is that behavior is or should be aimed at producing the good life, and they focus on such consequences of our actions as pleasure, happiness, or utility.
- *Virtue ethics* centers on the agent and attaches significance to the person's character and traits. It asks what are the main virtues, what characterizes a virtuous person, and how can we become virtuous.

Many ethical theories ask metaphysical questions about human nature. Some propose that humans are naturally good, others that we are innately evil. Many theories also consider the question of free will versus determinism. In addition, ethical theories differ in their scope. Whereas some concentrate on the morality of the individual, others focus on the broader dimensions of human actions and interactions. Chief among these perspectives are:

- *Egoism* proposes that morality is or ought to be based on the interests of the individual human ego or self. It is generally critical of ethical theories that value altruism, the concern for others.
- *Existentialist ethics* are theories that take the question of the meaning of human existence as the basis for their reflections on morality.
- *Ethics of care* approaches look at the interpersonal dimension of our relationships. They consider the quality of our attitudes and dispositions toward others to be important.
- *Social ethics* take explicitly critical views of established social structures and provide moral codes of conduct for groups, societies, or states as a way of solving the problems they see.
- *Theories of justice* reflect on the nature of justice to provide patterns for an ideal, just society.
- *Environmental ethics* propose that morality goes beyond the strictly human realm and include our relation to nonhuman beings, nature, or the universe.
- *Religious ethics* propose that morality is a matter of our relation to the divine and develop ethical theories based on religious beliefs or spiritual views.
- *Theories critical of religion* insist that morality is not a religious matter and develop explicitly critical views of religious institutions, beliefs, or principles.

Multiculturalism in Ethics

In Europe and North America, the study of ethics generally has been limited to the contributions made by the members of the European (Anglo-European or Euro-American) traditions (covered in Part 1). Moreover, the classic representatives of that tradition have been predominantly white males. However, the countries that once referred to themselves as "the West" are now opening their eyes to the world in a new way. They are beginning to move away from their Eurocentrism by acknowledging the existence of multiple, global perspectives, even within the borders of their own countries. Europe and North America are not the only places where people have reflected on ethical questions. Latin American and Caribbean countries, along with the Asian and African continents, contain a multitude of historical and contemporary perspectives. Nor are white males the only persons who have engaged in ethical inquiries. Women and peoples of color have also undertaken philosophical pursuits into moral matters. Some women have adopted feminist perspectives, while some exponents of various cultural perspectives have taken race or ethnicity as their starting points of ethical reflection. The study of ethics in the United States today is thus becoming increasingly multicultural in its explicit awareness and recognition of other ethical theories from around the world. This book is part of that recent development. In the main table of contents, you will find different traditions and contemporary movements in ethics. They are divided according to these cultural perspectives so that you may get a sense of the historical and thematic continuities within each division. The thematic table of contents also gives you a sense of the points of comparison and contrast within and between the traditions and movements.

In what follows, we briefly summarize the main features shared by the groups that until recently were neglected in the Anglo-European tradition in ethics—Asians, exponents of various cultural perspectives on race or ethnicity, and feminists. At the end of this introduction, you will also find a list of suggested secondary sources for each group.

The Asian Traditions

Part 2 presents representatives of various philosophies or religions from the Asian continent. The selections drawn from Taoism, or Daoism, and Confucianism originate in China; those from Hinduism and Buddhism, in India; and those from Islam, in the Middle East. However, the geographical distribution of the principal philosophies and religions in the Asian continent is much wider and more complex than this pattern might suggest. For example, Buddhism is followed in a number of countries of South and East Asia, including China.

Most Asian philosophies integrate into them the religious or spiritual dimension of life; they do not treat ethics as a separate mode of philosophical inquiry. Rather, moral philosophy emerges as part of a larger framework of metaphysical theories, religious beliefs, and cultural practices. Ethical questions are posed and answered in terms that intertwine conceptions of the ultimate nature of reality, the divine, and society. Unlike some of the dominant European theories that view the moral agent as an individual in isolation from her world, most Asian philosophies emphasize the interconnectedness of humans as belonging within greater wholes.

Given that morality is generally viewed as a spiritual matter, moral doctrines in the Asian traditions are developed as spiritual teachings, rather than systems of thought that are detached from religious concerns. More than moral theories or bodies of truths about ethical subjects, they are practical guides into the living realization of a spiritual truth. The majority of these teachings incorporate prescriptive codes detailing vows, rituals, observances, and disciplines that are designed to ensure the fulfillment of moral precepts. The moral philosopher often takes on the role of a spiritual guide who imparts his ethical wisdom to followers. The figure of the sage who embodies the moral ideals in his character and life is also frequently central to these ethical doctrines.

Asian philosophies develop models of moral life that are presented as ways to spiritual perfection. Thus, although ethical issues vary widely across the Asian traditions, the question of how to live a life in accordance with spiritual principles is one of the most common concerns. Accordingly, some representatives from the Asian traditions take the cultivation of moral character as their central point and offer virtue ethics. Others develop deontological ethics that define duty in terms of sacred obligations. However, it is not unusual to find a combination of both types of ethical approaches. Because Asian traditions rarely detach moral matters from the larger contexts of human existence, some of their moral theories also focus on social or environmental issues.

Contemporary Cultural Perspectives

Part 3 presents representatives from countries, ethnic groups, and races other than those that have predominated in the Anglo-European tradition in ethics. We have classified them according to those geographical, cultural, or racial aspects that have most defined and distinguished these peoples as specific groups: African, African-American, Latin American and Caribbean, and Native American.

Social and political concerns predominate in the ethical reflections of contemporary peoples of color, and their critical moral theories factor in their historical backgrounds of colonialism, as well as prevailing conditions of oppression, exploitation, and poverty. Such critiques question many of the dominant ideas and structures of the society on which they focus, scrutinizing its moral assumptions and ideals, social standards, and institutions with the objective of uncovering forms of domination. When they propose ethical solutions, these critiques often demand radical changes in the morality or fabric of society. Ethical issues concerning social justice and equality are thus usually of prime importance.

These ethicists also apply this same critical approach to the European tradition in ethics, analyzing and questioning its dominant concepts, theories, and methods of moral reasoning. Thus, at times, the cultural, racial, or social prejudices underlying dominant ideas in ethics are the subject of critical discussion. For instance, such critiques may be leveled against the Eurocentric, racist, or classist character of certain moral theories; beliefs in moral universals, fixed natures, and unchanging essences may be charged with concealing and perpetuating these tendencies. However, rather than rejecting the European tradition in its totality, a variety of these ethicists attempt to appropriate some of its aspects in new ways. The nineteenth-century European philosophies of G. W. F. Hegel, in his analysis of the master-slave relation, and of Karl Marx, in his critique of capitalism, are two notable sources of such influence.

There is also a great element of self-reflection in the ethics of many contemporary peoples of color. The question of identity—cultural, national, racial, or existential—may take a central place, and the quest for original, new, or revitalized elements of self-definition can become a main goal. At times, the question of identity is framed within more general discussions concerning the definition of philosophy in relation to a given race, culture, or nation. For example, there is much controversy over issues such as whether there is a distinctively Latin American philosophy, whether it is defined by its themes or its forms, and whether it underestimates the historical, national, or racial differences between Latin Americans.

Contemporary Feminist Philosophers

Part 4 presents a sample of feminist approaches to ethics. Though offering a multitude of diverse and opposing perspectives, these writers stand together in taking issue with the moral practices and theories that have prevailed in the patriarchal or male-dominated spheres of society and thought. With their common focus on women's experiences, they look critically at social practices that devalue, silence, and subjugate women, as well as theoretical systems that neglect, dismiss, and depreciate them as inferior. In this sense, these approaches are characterized by their confrontation with the male-biased assumptions and male-centered applications of traditional morality and moral theory. In their critiques, feminists have questioned not only the moral values, standards, and institutions but also the ethical problems, concepts, and methods that have reigned in these patriarchal traditions. At the same time, there are many different efforts to construct new ethical codes and theories based on feminist principles. Thus, in giving voice to women, feminist approaches to ethics aim not only to alleviate women's experiences of oppression but also to change or overcome the structures that oppress them.

Feminism has a long history of activism, extending much farther back in the past than its first notable expression in the United States, the women's suffrage movement of the 1840s. Theories directly concerned with women's social and political roles were formed as early as the eighteenth and nineteenth centuries, by thinkers such as Mary Wollstonecraft, Harriet Taylor, and John Stuart Mill. However, feminist philosophy is a relatively new academic field that emerges in Anglo-European countries primarily as an intellectual response to the issues of the women's rights movement of the 1960s. When it arrives on the scene of Anglo-European philosophy, feminist philosophy brings to mind the concrete problems suffered by women within patriarchal structures, and it comes with an active sense of commitment to solve those problems. As they incorporate practical concerns into their theoretical approaches to the many issues affecting women, feminists often combine different disciplines into their philosophies. While they confront the patriarchal modes of thought, feminists have also dipped into the wealth of theories offered by the philosophical tradition, often by recasting them in ways that try to address women's issues.

The feminist selections in this book reflect the characteristics noted above. Covering perspectives such as the ethics of care, environmental ethics, existentialist ethics, lesbian ethics, and social ethics, they address many moral issues concerning women. A main question pursued by feminists focuses on gender differences in moral understanding, concerns, values, and choices. The development of an ethics based on "feminine" or "female" characteristics, such as caring, is one answer to that question. It is also a matter of controversy whether a feminine ethics is a feminist ethics or whether it perpetuates patriarchal morality. Differences in race, ethnicity, class, and sexuality among women have also become major moral issues in the feminist agenda as the assumption that there is a universal "woman" with essential features and uniform moral experiences is put into question. Thus, as feminists critically examine the Anglo-European tradition in ethics, they begin to subject their own approaches to scrutiny.

Critical Thinking in Ethics

In its philosophical spirit, ethics follows a certain way of thinking: critical thinking. As its etymology indicates, the term *critical* (from the Greek word *krinein*, meaning "to discern" or "to judge") refers to a serious, careful manner of sifting and weighing our ideas. The common usage of the term to designate a negative attitude of faultfinding, hostility, and harsh censuring fails to capture this original meaning. Rather, critical thinking involves a disposition to "think about" and "think through" matters; to question, reflect, analyze, and assess things in a reasoned manner.

As a theoretical discipline, ethics is based on reasoning, explanation, and argumentation. These are essentially methods of critical thinking, not mere forms of expressing personal opinions and quarreling with others:

- To *reason* is to draw or develop explanations or inferences.
- An *explanation* is a line of thought that tries to make a point clear and understandable by pointing to its characteristics or causes.
- *Inferences* are lines of thought that proceed through arguments.
- An *argument* is formed by premises and conclusions.
- A *conclusion* is a statement about a certain issue; more specifically, it is an answer to a question, a point that we wish to establish about a given matter.
- Conclusions demand support. They require *premises* or reasons offered in defense of the point we wish to make. Premises, in turn, may need their own support. Thus, arguments may acquire highly complex forms, with long chains of premises, subconclusions, and conclusions.

Especially when it comes to ethical issues, people often have strong, ardent beliefs that they defend with fervor against others. Many live their lives according to these convictions and are willing to die for them. In fact, sometimes moral disputes have ended in violence and death. Being human, ethicists are no more immune than others to these tendencies in their personal lives. However, the methods of reasoning, explanation, and argumentation in ethics set strict guidelines for how we think about and discuss moral matters.

Theoretical claims in ethics require explanation or argumentation. Moreover, explanations and arguments must meet certain rational standards of quality. In everyday life, weak explanations and faulty arguments may still convince or persuade people into acceptance, perhaps because they are influenced by their emotions or are careless in their thinking. In ethics, however, there are logical and empirical standards of evaluation that are based on the ideals of critical thinking:

- *Logical* standards focus on the form or structure of reasoning. They pose questions such as: Does this make sense? Is this coherent or consistent? Does this follow a clear line of reasoning?
- *Empirical* standards focus on the content or subject matter of reasoning. They pose questions such as: Does this address the issue? Is this supported by experience? What assumptions does this make? What are its implications and consequences?

As you read the selections in this book, you will gain a more concrete sense of how ethics follows a critical way of thinking. It is also important that you exercise critical thinking skills in your own reading of the texts. Read and reread them with a questioning and reflective attitude. This book has been designed to assist you in such philosophical endeavor. The selections contain sets of questions to get you started on the path of critical thinking. We hope you will raise many more questions on your own.

General Suggestions for Further Reading

The European Traditions

GENERAL REFERENCE

Asby, W., ed. *A Comprehensive History of Western Ethics: What Do We Believe?* (Amherst, NY: Prometheus Books, 1997).

Becker, L. C., and C. B. Becker, eds. *A History of Western Ethics* (New York: Garland Publishers, 1992).

———. *Encyclopedia of Ethics.* Vols. I and II (New York: Garland Publishers, 1992).

Bourke, V. J. *A History of Ethics* (Garden City, NY: Doubleday, 1968).

Cavalier, R. J., J. Gouinlock, and J. P. Sterba, eds. *Ethics in the History of Western Philosophy* (New York: St. Martin's Press, 1989).

Hastings, J. et al., eds. *Encyclopaedia of Ethics.* Vols. 1–10 (New York: Scribner; Edinburgh: T. & T. Clark, 1924–1927).

Jones, W. T., F. Sontag, M. O. Beckner, and R. J. Fogelin, eds. *Approaches to Ethics* (New York: McGraw Hill, 1969).

MacIntyre, A. *A Short History of Ethics: A History of Moral Philosophy from the Homeric Age to the Twentieth Century,* 2d ed. (Notre Dame, IN: University of Notre Dame Press, 1998).

Singer, P., ed. *A Companion to Ethics* (Oxford; Cambridge, MA: Blackwell Reference, 1991).

The Asian Traditions

GENERAL REFERENCE

Asian Studies WWW Virtual Library

http://www.coombs.anu.edu.au/WWWVL-AsianStudies.html

Gupta, B., and J. N. Mohanty, eds. *Philosophical Questions East and West* (Lanham, MD: Roman & Littlefield, 2000).

Hastings, J., et al., eds. *Encyclopaedia of Ethics.* Vols. 1–10 (New York: Scribner, 1924–1927).

Hunt, A. D., M. T. Crotty, and R. B. Crotty. *Ethics of World Religions.* Rev. ed. (San Diego, CA: Green Haven Press, 1991).

Koller, J. *Oriental Philosophies,* 2d ed. (New York: Charles Scribner's Sons, 1985).

Scharfstein, Ben-Ami. *A Comparative History of World Philosophy, from the Upanishads to Kant* (Albany: State University of New York Press, 1998).

Solomon, R. C., and K. Higgins, eds. *From Africa to Zen: An Invitation to World Philosophy* (Lanham, MD: Rowman & Littlefield, 1993).

CHINESE

Carr, B., and I. Mahalingam, eds. *Companion Encyclopedia of Asian Philosophy* (London; New York: Routledge, 1997). Part IV, "Chinese Philosophy."

Chan, Wing-Tsit. *A Sourcebook in Chinese Philosophy* (Princeton, NJ: Princeton University Press, 1963).

Deutsch, E., and R. Bonteke, eds. *A Companion to World Philosophies* (Malden, MA; Oxford: Blackwell, 1997). T. Weiming, "Chinese Philosophy: A Synoptic View"; S. Kwong-Loi, "Ideas of the Good in Chinese Philosophy."

Philosophy Information of China

http://www.pitt.edu/subjects/area/eastasian/elib/html/cphil.htm

Singer, P., ed. *A Companion to Ethics* (Oxford; Cambridge, MA: Blackwell, 1991). C. Hansen, "Classical Chinese Ethics."

Yu-Lan, Fung. *A History of Chinese Philosophy.* Vol. I. Trans. D. Boddes (Princeton, NJ: Princeton University Press, 1952).

ISLAMIC

Carr, B., and I. Mahalingam, eds. *Companion Encyclopedia of Asian Philosophy* (London; New York: Routledge, 1997). Part VI, "Islamic Philosophy."

Deutsch, E., and R. Bonteke, eds. *A Companion to World Philosophies* (Malden, MA; Oxford: Blackwell, 1997). T. Albertini, "Islamic Philosophy: An Overview"; M. Wahba, "The Concept of the Good in Islamic Philosophy."

Esposito, J. L. *Islam: The Straight Path* (New York: Oxford University Press, 1988).

Glassé, C. *The Concise Encyclopedia of Islam* (New York: HarperCollins, 1991).

Houvannisian, R., ed. *Ethics in Islam* (Malibu, CA: Undena Publications, 1985).

Islamic Thought (MSA@ University of Buffalo)

http://wings.buffalo.edu/sa/muslim/isl/thought.html

Nasr, H. S. *Ideals and Realities of Islam* (London: Unwin Hyman, Ltd., 1985).

INDIAN

Buddhist Studies WWW Virtual Library

http://www.ciolek.com/WWWVL-Buddhism.html

Carr, B., and I. Mahalingam, eds. *Companion Encyclopedia of Asian Philosophy* (London; New York: Routledge, 1997). Part II, "Indian Philosophy." Part III, "Buddhist Philosophy."

Deutsch, E., and R. Bonteke, eds. *A Companion to World Philosophies* (Malden, MA; Oxford: Blackwell, 1997). N. Smart, "Survey of Buddhist Thought"; P. D. Premasiri, "Ideas of the Good in Buddhist Philosophy"; J. N. Mohanty, "A History of Indian Philosophy" and "The Idea of the Good in Indian Thought."

Dharmasiri, G. *Fundamentals of Buddhist Ethics* (Antioch, CA: Golden Leaves, 1989).

Herman, A. L. *An Introduction to Indian Thought* (Englewood Cliffs, NJ: Prentice-Hall, 1976).

Hindu Resources Online

http://www.hindu.org

Hopkins, E. W. *Ethics of India* (New Haven, CT: Yale University Press, 1924).

Maitra, S. K. *The Ethics of Hindus* (New Delhi: Asian Publication Services, 1978).

Singer, P., ed. *A Companion to Ethics* (Oxford; Cambridge, MA: Blackwell, 1991). P. Bilimoria, "Indian Ethics."

Contemporary Cultural Perspectives

AFRICAN

African Philosophy Resources

http://www.augustana.ab.ca/~janzb/afphilpage.htm

Appiah, A. K., ed. *In My Father's House: Africa in the Philosophy of Culture* (Oxford: Oxford University Press, 1992).

English, P., and K. M. Kalumba, eds. *African Philosophy: A Classical Approach* (Upper Saddle River, NJ: Prentice-Hall, 1996).

Hord, L. F. (Mzee Lasana Okpara), and J. S. Lee, eds. *I Am Because We Are: Readings in Black Philosophy* (Amherst: University of Massachusetts Press, 1995).

Mosley, A., ed. *Selected Readings in African Philosophy* (New York: Macmillan, 1995).

Odera Oruka, H., ed. *Sage Philosophy: Indigenous Thinkers and Modern Debate on African Philosophy* (Leiden, NY: E. J. Brill, 1990).

AFRICAN-AMERICAN
African Philosophy Resources

http://www.augustana.ab.ca/~janzb/afphilpage.htm

Gordon, L. R., ed. *Existence in Black: An Anthology of Black Existential Philosophy* (New York: Routledge, 1997).

Harris, L., ed. *Philosophy Born of Struggle: Anthology of Afro-American Philosophy from 1917* (Dubuque, IA: Kendall/Hunt Publishing Company, 1983).

Hord, L. F. (Mzee Lasana Okpara), and J. S. Lee, eds. *I Am Because We Are: Readings in Black Philosophy* (Amherst: University of Massachusetts Press, 1995).

Pittman, J. P., ed. *African-American Perspectives and Philosophical Traditions* (New York; London: Routledge, 1997).

LATIN AMERICAN AND CARIBBEAN
Davis, H. E. *Latin American Thought: A Historical Introduction* (New York: Free Press, 1974).

Gracia, J. E., ed. *Latin American Philosophy in the Twentieth Century: Man, Values, and the Search for Philosophical Identity* (New York: Prometheus Books, 1986).

Schutte, O. *Cultural Identity and Social Liberation in Latin American Thought* (Albany: State University of New York Press, 1993).

Solomon R. C., and K. M. Higgins, eds. *From Africa to Zen: An Invitation to World Philosophy* (Lanham, MD: Rowman & Littlefield, 1993). J. Valadez, "Pre-Columbian and Modern Philosophical Perspectives in Latin America."

The WWW Virtual Library: Latin American Studies

http://lanic.utexas.edu/las.html

NATIVE AMERICAN
Bol, M. C., ed. *The Stars Above, the Earth Below* (Niwot, CO: Roberts Rinehart Publishers for Carnegie Museum of Natural History, 1998).

Dunsmore, R. *Earth's Mind: Essays in Native Literature* (Albuquerque: University of New Mexico Press, 1997).

Tedlock, D., and B. Tedlock, eds. *Teachings from the American Earth: Indian Religion and Philosophy* (New York: Liveright, 1975).

Thorton, R., ed. *Studying Native Americans: Problems and Prospects* (Madison: University of Wisconsin Press, 1998).

WWW Virtual Library – American Indians

http://www.hanksville.org/NAresources/indices/NAculture.html

Feminist Philosophers

GENERAL REFERENCE AND READERS
Andolsen, H. B., C. E. Gudorf, and M. D. Pellauer, eds. *Women's Consciousness, Women's Conscience: A Reader in Feminist Ethics* (San Francisco: Harper & Row, 1985).

Card, C., ed. *Feminist Ethics* (Lawrence: University Press of Kansas, 1991).

Cole, B. E., and S. Coultrap-McQuin, eds. *Explorations in Feminist Ethics: Theory and Practice* (Bloomington: Indiana University Press, 1992).

Frazer, E., J. Hornsby, and S. Lovibond, eds. *Ethics: A Feminist Reader* (Oxford; Cambridge, MA: Blackwell, 1992).

Feminist Theory Web site

http://www.cddc.vt.edu/feminism

Gender Inn: The Women's Studies Database

http://www.uni-koeln.de/phil-fak/englisch/datenbank/e_index.htm

Held. V., ed. *Philosophy in a Feminist Voice: Critique and Reconstructions* (Princeton, NJ: Princeton University Press, 1998). V. Held, "Feminist Reconceptualizations in Ethics."

Jaggar, A., and I. M. Young, eds. *A Companion to Feminist Philosophy* (Malden, MA; Oxford: Blackwell, 1998).

Pearsall, M., ed. *Women and Values: Readings in Recent Feminist Philosophy* (Belmont, CA: Wadsworth, 1986).

Singer, P., ed. *A Companion to Ethics* (Oxford; Cambridge, MA: Blackwell, 1991). J. Grimshaw, "The Idea of a Female Ethic."

Tong, R. *Feminine and Feminist Ethics* (Belmont, CA: Wadsworth, 1993).

General Web Site Sources

Ethics Updates

http://ethics.acusd.edu

The Internet Encyclopedia of Philosophy

http://www.utm.edu/research/iep/e/ethics.htm

Philosophy in Cyberspace

http://www.geocities.com/Athens/Acropolis/4393/ethics.htm

Stanford Encyclopedia of Philosophy

http://plato.stanford.edu

Part 1

The European Traditions

G. E. MOORE (1873–1958)
Selections from "The Subject-Matter of Ethics"

MARTIN BUBER (1878–1965)
Selections from *I and Thou*

RUTH BENEDICT (1887–1948)
Selections from "Anthropology and the Abnormal"

A. J. AYER (1910–1989)
Selections from "Critique of Ethics and Theology"

JEAN PAUL SARTRE (1905–1980)
Selections from *Existentialism and Human Emotions*

JOHN RAWLS (1921–)
Selections from *A Theory of Justice*

EMMANUEL LEVINAS (1906–1995)
Selections from "The Face" and "Responsibility for the Other"

ALASDAIR MCINTYRE (1929–)
Selections from "The Virtues, the Unity of a Human Life and the Concept of a Tradition"

Socrates (470/69–399 B.C.E.)

Socrates was among the first philosophers of the ancient Greek world to place the human being at the center of philosophy. His predecessors, called pre-Socratics or natural philosophers, were concerned mainly with the origin and nature of the universe. Socrates, however, insisted on the primacy of moral inquiry. For him, "the unexamined life is not worth living." By this he implies that each person should reflect carefully on the moral conceptions and principles guiding his or her own life. One of the mottoes inscribed on the walls of the temple of Delphi, where priestesses called Pythians would interpret the oracles from Apollo, the god of the sun, read: "Know thyself." In its traditional meaning, it was a maxim urging people to keep to their particular places within society and to carry out their corresponding duties. Socrates gave it new meaning as an injunction to look within oneself, to scrutinize one's very soul. Moral inquiry is thus a matter of deep personal reflection leading to self-knowledge. For Socrates, such is the essence of moral or ethical wisdom.

Socrates believed his sacred duty as a philosopher was to serve his city-state, Athens, by helping others through the process of moral self-examination. He wrote no philosophical treatises, but spent most of his time engaged in intellectual conversations with his fellow citizens. Plato, his most famous disciple, wrote philosophical dialogues in which Socrates was a main character. Plato's earlier dialogues (*Euthyphro, Apology, Crito*) reflect or perhaps repeat Socrates' own thoughts while illustrating the Socratic method.

In his approach, Socrates constantly searches for the definition of a term — say, justice. His search is an attempt to determine what justice is as such, not merely an expression of interest in examples of just acts. For Socrates, it is a matter of seeking out the essence (*ousia*) of justice. The other Greek words he uses are *idea* and *eidos*, which usually mean "visible form" or "shape" or "outward appearance." For Socrates, these terms mean the common form, appearance, or aspect of particular things — their universal characteristics. For example, this common form is what allows us to identify all just acts as just and to distinguish them from unjust acts. In this pursuit, Socrates submits his interlocutors to intensive cross-examination to determine whether they have a direct understanding of the term, not just a superficial acquaintance with the word.

Though offering paralyzing rebuttals in his interrogations, Socrates himself gives no explicit answers. In fact, he never professed to be anyone's teacher. He held claim only to a distinctively human kind of wisdom whereby "what I do not know I do not think I know either." The recognition of one's own ignorance is the starting point for all knowledge. Knowing *that* one does not know is the first step toward knowing *what* something is. The process of learning involves breaking away from previous beliefs and conventional doctrines that do not withstand the test of reason. Thus, the way to knowing what something *is* is by knowing what it is *not*. This is called "negative wisdom."

Socrates once compared himself to a midwife (his mother's occupation). He assists others by "delivering" them from their own ignorance. It is up to the individual "to labor" for truth. Ultimately, self-knowledge cannot be taught. Like the midwife who in Socrates' times also had to decide if the child was a "bastard" or not, Socrates' further role is to submit their beliefs to critical scrutiny and prove to them that they are not wise. Socrates also characterized himself as a gadfly who arouses Athens from its sleep by stinging, urging, and reproaching Athenians into venturing on the way to moral wisdom. Thus, Socrates annoyed and embarrassed many of his fellow citizens, some of them quite influential, who claimed to have knowledge and wisdom.

Socrates lived to see himself ridiculed in Aristophanes' comedy *The Clouds.* There he is portrayed as the leader of a school called the "Thinkery" that, for a fee, taught nonsense to its students. Decades after the first performance in 423 B.C.E., the Assembly of Athens sentenced Socrates to death by ingesting hemlock. He was charged with corrupting the young and with disbelief in the ancient Greek gods. In the eyes of his accusers, he was a "busybody" who investigated all things "beneath the earth and in the heavens," confusing others by "making the weaker argument stronger." Like Aristophanes' satire, this charge depicts Socrates as a Sophist. Sophists were itinerant teachers who called themselves wise (*sophos*) and for a fee taught their students how to achieve virtue (*arete*), which for the Greeks meant "excellence." They were masters in rhetoric—the art of persuasive speaking—who claimed they could teach people to argue for any position. Because Plato represented them as dangerous charlatans in his dialogues, there is much debate about whether the identification of Socrates as a Sophist was accurate.

In his defense in front of the Athenian Assembly (portrayed in Plato's *Apology*), Socrates maintained that he was following a divine command to urge others to care first and foremost for the improvement of their souls. The virtuous person is the one who strives for moral excellence, a state that can be reached only through the examined life. Thus, for Socrates, virtue is knowledge. This is a paradoxical identification. It seems to imply that one cannot *be* morally good without *knowing* what is good. Yet the possibility of attaining such wisdom appears to go beyond the limits of human knowledge. Socrates' role is all the more perplexing because he disclaimed having this kind of knowledge or being a teacher of virtue. In the meantime, we must live our lives, making moral decisions, acting on them, and dealing with the consequences. It could be, then, that moral wisdom is rather a matter of *becoming* morally good by striving for self-knowledge. The search for universals would thus give impulse and direction to the life of the examiner.

Plato seems to have written the *Euthyphro* some time within twelve years after Socrates' death, in what is considered Plato's early period—during which he appears to remain close to Socrates' philosophy without developing his own particular views. It is not clear whether Euthyphro, who seems to be a priest, was an actual person. Nor is it certain whether the dialogue between Euthyphro and Socrates really took place. Its setting is outside the law courts presided over by the archon (essentially a very powerful magistrate), where they happen to meet. Socrates explains he is there to answer the indictment brought against him by Meletus, who charged him with corrupting the young and with unholiness or impiety before the gods. Euthyphro is there to prosecute his father for murdering one of his workers. His relatives criticize him for being an impious or unholy son, but Euthyphro claims to have exact knowledge of the divine laws and of what are holiness and unholiness. Socrates asks him to define these terms, conventionally understood as reverence and irreverence toward the Greek gods and their divine laws. Thus begins the Socratic search for the essence of piety.

The search that ensues is not a mere conceptual exercise; it touches on matters directly affecting their lives. The question of each individual's holiness depends upon the accuracy of his own knowledge of holiness. That is why Socrates asks Euthyphro whether he is not afraid of being unholy in his actions while claiming to have exact knowledge. You will detect the typical Socratic irony when he asks Euthyphro to tutor him in piety so that he may defend himself in court. It corresponds to Euthyphro's own pretense of knowledge. Socrates reveals Euthyphro's ignorance through his method of examination. Euthyphro's various definitions fail to capture the essence of piety.

You will note that Euthyphro's last two definitions refer to the gods, to their likes and dislikes. He resorts to those very gods he claims to revere as a pious or holy man. Socrates asks him a crucial question that concerns the status of holiness: "Is that which is holy loved by the gods because it is holy or is it holy because it is loved by the gods?" In other words, does holiness stand on its own or does it stand or fall with the inclinations of the gods? In the first instance, what is holy is holy in and of itself, intrinsically so, independent of the gods. In the second case, the gods determine what is holy, so that holiness is defined entirely by the gods. At the heart of Socrates' question is the relationship between morality and religion. Is there a moral good that is objective and autonomous? Or does it depend on the subjective will of the gods; that is, on divine command? In this sense, Socrates' dictum about the examined life also applies to religious beliefs. Thus, reason calls religion into question.

EUTHYPHRO

Persons of the Dialogue:
Socrates, Euthyphro

SCENE: THE PORCH OF THE KING
ARCHON

Euthyphro Why have you left the Lyceum, Socrates? and what are you doing in the Porch of the King Archon? Surely you cannot be concerned in a suit before the King, like myself?

Socrates Not in a suit, Euthyphro; impeachment is the word which the Athenians use.

Euth. What! I suppose that some one has been prosecuting you, for I cannot believe that you are the prosecutor of another.

Soc. Certainly not.

Euth. Then some one else has been prosecuting you?

Soc. Yes.

Euth. And who is he?

Soc. A young man who is little known, Euthyphro; and I hardly know him: his name is Meletus, and he is of the deme of Pitthis. Perhaps you may remember his appearance; he has a beak,

Reprinted by permission of the publishers and Trustees of the Loeb Classical Library from: Plato: Volume I, Euthyphro, *Loeb Classical Library Volume # L036, trans. by H. N. Fowler, 383–392, 393, 394, Cambridge, MA: Harvard University Press, 1914, 1953. The Loeb Classical Library ® is a registered trademark of the President and Fellows of Harvard College.*

and long straight hair, and a beard which is ill grown.

Euth. No, I do not remember him, Socrates. But what is the charge which he brings against you?

Soc. What is the charge? Well, a very serious charge, which shows a good deal of character in the young man, and for which he is certainly not to be despised. He says he knows how the youth are corrupted and who are their corruptors. I fancy that he must be a wise man, and seeing that I am the reverse of a wise man, he has found me out, and is going to accuse me of corrupting his young friends. And of this our mother the state is to be the judge. Of all our political men he is the only one who seems to me to begin in the right way, with the cultivation of virtue in youth; like a good husbandman, he makes the young shoots his first care, and clears away us who are the destroyers of them. This is only the first step; he will afterwards attend to the elder branches; and if he goes on as he has begun, he will be a very great public benefactor.

Euth. I hope that he may; but I rather fear, Socrates, that the opposite will turn out to be the truth. My opinion is that in attacking you he is simply aiming a blow at the foundation of the state. But in what way does he say that you corrupt the young?

Soc. He brings a wonderful accusation against me, which at first hearing excites surprise: he says that I am a poet or maker of gods, and that I invent new gods and deny the existence of old ones; this is the ground of his indictment.

Euth. I understand, Socrates; he means to attack you about the familiar sign which occasionally, as you say, comes to you. He thinks that you are a neologian, and he is going to have you up before the court for this. He knows that such a charge is readily received by the world, as I myself know too well; for when I speak in the assembly about divine things, and foretell the future to them, they laugh at me and think me a madman. Yet every word that I say is true. But they are jealous of us all; and we must be brave and go at them.

Soc. Their laughter, friend Euthyphro, is not a matter of much consequence. For a man may be thought wise; but the Athenians, I suspect, do not much trouble themselves about him until he begins to impart his wisdom to others; and then for some reason or other, perhaps, as you say, from jealousy, they are angry.

Euth. I am never likely to try their temper in this way.

Soc. I dare say not, for you are reserved in your behaviour, and seldom impart your wisdom. But I have a benevolent habit of pouring out myself to everybody, and would even pay for a listener, and I am afraid that the Athenians may think me too talkative. Now if, as I was saying, they would only laugh at me, as you say that they laugh at you, the time might pass gaily enough in the court; but perhaps they may be in earnest, and then what the end will be you soothsayers only can predict.

Euth. I dare say that the affair will end in nothing, Socrates, and that you will win your cause; and I think that I shall win my own.

Soc. And what is your suit, Euthyphro? are you the pursuer or the defendant?

Euth. I am the pursuer.

Soc. Of whom?

Euth. You will think me mad when I tell you.

Soc. Why, has the fugitive wings?

Euth. Nay, he is not very volatile at his time of life.

Soc. Who is he?

Euth. My father.

Soc. Your father! my good man?

Euth. Yes.

Soc. And of what is he accused?

Euth. Of murder, Socrates.

Soc. By the powers, Euthyphro! how little does the common herd know of the nature of right and truth. A man must be an extraordinary man, and have made great strides in wisdom, before he could have seen this way to bring such an action.

Euth. Indeed, Socrates, he must.

Soc. I suppose that the man whom your father murdered was one of your relatives—clearly he was; for if he had been a stranger you would never have thought of prosecuting him.

Euth. I am amused, Socrates, at your making a distinction between one who is a relation and one who is not a relation; for surely the pollution is the same in either case, if you knowingly associate with the murderer when you ought to clear yourself and him by proceeding against him. The real question is whether the murdered man has been justly slain. If justly, then your duty is to let the matter alone; but if unjustly, then even if the murderer lives under the same roof with you and eats at the same table, proceed against him. Now the man who is dead was a poor dependant of mine who worked for us as a field labourer on our farm in Naxos, and one day in a fit of drunken passion he got into a quarrel with one of our domestic servants and slew him. My father bound him hand and foot and threw him into a ditch, and then sent to Athens to ask of a diviner what he should do with him. Meanwhile he never attended to him and took no care about him, for he regarded him as a murderer; and thought that no great harm would be done even if he did die. Now this was just what happened. For such was the effect of cold and hunger and chains upon him, that before the messenger returned from the diviner, he was dead. And my father and family are angry with me for taking the part of the murderer and prosecuting my father. They say that he did not kill him, and that if he did, the dead man was but a murderer, and I ought not to take any notice, for that a son is impious who prosecutes a father. Which shows, Socrates, how little they know what the gods think about piety and impiety.

Soc. Good heavens, Euthyphro! and is your knowledge of religion and of things pious and impious so very exact, that, supposing the circumstances to be as you state them, you are not afraid lest you too many be doing an impious thing in bringing an action against your father?

Euth. The best of Euthyphro, and that which distinguishes him, Socrates, from other men, is his exact knowledge of all such matters. What should I be good for without it?

Soc. Rare friend! I think that I cannot do better than be your disciple. Then before the trial with Meletus comes on I shall challenge him, and say that I have always had a great interest in religious questions, and now, as he charges me with rash imaginations and innovations in religion, I have become your disciple. You, Meletus, as I shall say to him, acknowledge Euthyphro to be a great theologian, and sound in his opinions; and if you approve of him you ought to approve of me, and not have me into court; but if you disapprove, you should begin by indicting him who is my teacher, and who will be the ruin, not of the young, but of the old; that is to say, of myself whom he instructs, and of his old father whom he admonishes and chastises. And if Meletus refuses to listen to me, but will go on, and will not shift the indictment from me to you, I cannot do better than repeat this challenge in the court.

Euth. Yes, indeed, Socrates; and if he attempts to indict me I am mistaken if I do not find a flaw in him; the court shall have a great deal more to say to him than to me.

Soc. And I, my dear friend, knowing this, am desirous of becoming your disciple. For I observe that no one appears to notice you—not even this Meletus; but his sharp eyes have found me out at once, and he has indicted me for impiety. And therefore, I adjure you to tell me the nature of piety and impiety, which you said that you knew so well, and of murder, and of other offences against the gods. What are they? Is not piety in every action always the same? and impiety, again—is it not always the opposite of piety, and also the same with itself, having, as impiety, one notion which includes whatever is impious?

Euth. To be sure, Socrates.

Soc. And what is piety, and what is impiety?

Euth. Piety is doing as I am doing; that is to say, prosecuting any one who is guilty of murder, sacrilege, or of any similar crime—whether he be your father or mother, or whoever he may be— that makes no difference; and not to prosecute them is impiety. And please to consider, Socrates, what a notable proof I will give you of the truth of my words, a proof which I have already given to others:— of the principle, I mean, that the impious, whoever he may be, ought not to go unpunished. For do not men regard Zeus as the best and most righteous of the gods?—and yet they admit that he bound his father (Cronos) because he wickedly devoured his sons, and that he too had punished his own father (Uranus) for a similar reason, in a nameless manner. And yet when I proceed against my father, they are angry with me. So inconsistent are they in their way of talking when the gods are concerned, and when I am concerned.

Soc. May not this be the reason, Euthyphro, why I am charged with impiety—that I cannot away with these stories about the gods? and therefore I suppose that people think me wrong. But, as you who are well informed about them approve of them, I cannot do better than assent to your superior wisdom. What else can I say, confessing as I do, that I know nothing about them? Tell me, for the love of Zeus, whether you really believe that they are true.

Euth. Yes, Socrates; and things more wonderful still, of which the world is in ignorance.

Soc. And do you really believe that the gods fought with one another, and had dire quarrels, battles, and the like, as the poets say, and as you may see represented in the works of great artists? The temples are full of them; and notably the robe of Athene, which is carried up to the Acropolis at the great Panathenaea, is embroidered with them. Are all these tales of the gods true, Euthyphro?

Euth. Yes, Socrates; and, as I was saying, I can tell you, if you would like to hear them, many other things about the gods which would quite amaze you.

Soc. I dare say; and you shall tell me them at some other time when I have leisure. But just at present I would rather hear from you a more precise answer, which you have not as yet given, my friend, to the question, What is 'piety'? When asked, you only replied, Doing as you do, charging your father with murder.

Euth. And what I said was true, Socrates.

Soc. No doubt, Euthyphro; but you would admit that there are many other pious acts?

Euth. There are.

Soc. Remember that I did not ask you to give me two or three examples of piety, but to explain the general idea which makes all pious things to be pious. Do you not recollect that there was one idea which made the impious impious, and the pious pious?

Euth. I remember.

Soc. Tell me what is the nature of this idea, and then I shall have a standard to which I may look, and by which I may measure actions, whether yours or those of any one else, and then I shall be able to say that such and such an action is pious, such another impious.

Euth. I will tell you, if you like.

Soc. I should very much like.

Euth. Piety, then, is that which is dear to the gods, and impiety is that which is not dear to them.

Soc. Very good, Euthyphro; you have now given me the sort of answer which I wanted. But whether what you say is true or not I cannot as yet tell, although I make no doubt that you will prove the truth of your words.

Euth. Of course.

Soc. Come, then, and let us examine what we are saying. That thing or person which is dear to the gods is pious, and that thing or person which is hateful to the gods is impious, these two being the extreme opposites of one another. Was not that said?

Euth. It was.

Soc. And well said?

Euth. Yes, Socrates, I thought so; it was certainly said.

Soc. And further, Euthyphro, the gods were admitted to have enmities and hatreds and differences?

Euth. Yes, that was also said.

Soc. And what sort of difference creates enmity and anger? Suppose for example that you and I, my good friend, differ about a number; do differences of this sort make us enemies and set us at variance with one another? Do you not go at once to arithmetic, and put an end to them by a sum?

Euth. True.

Soc. Or suppose that we differ about magnitudes, do we not quickly end the difference by measuring?

Euth. Very true.

Soc. And we end a controversy about heavy and light by resorting to a weighing machine?

Euth. To be sure.

Soc. But what differences are there which cannot be thus decided, and which therefore make us angry and set us at enmity with one another? I dare say the answer does not occur to you at the moment, and therefore I will suggest that these enmities arise when the matters of difference are the just and unjust, good and evil, honourable and dishonourable. Are not these the points about which men differ, and about which when we are unable satisfactorily to decide our differences, you and I and all of us quarrel, when we do quarrel?

Euth. Yes, Socrates, the nature of the differences about which we quarrel is such as you describe.

Soc. And the quarrels of the gods, noble Euthyphro, when they occur, are of a like nature?

Euth. Certainly they are.

Soc. They have differences of opinion, as you say, about good and evil, just and unjust, honourable and dishonourable: there would have been no quarrels among them, if there had been no such differences—would there now?

Euth. You are quite right.

Soc. Does not every man love that which he deems noble and just and good, and hate the opposite of them?

Euth. Very true.

Soc. But, as you say, people regard the same things, some as just and others as unjust,—about these they dispute; and so there arise wars and fightings among them.

Euth. Very true.

Soc. Then the same things are hated by the gods and loved by the gods, and are both hateful and dear to them?

Euth. True.

Soc. And upon this view the same things, Euthyphro, will be pious and also impious?

Euth. So I should suppose.

Soc. Then, my friend, I remark with surprise that you have not answered the question which I asked. For I certainly did not ask you to tell me what action is both pious and impious: but now it would seem that what is loved by the gods is also hated by them. And therefore, Euthyphro, in thus chastising your father you may very likely be doing what is agreeable to Zeus but disagreeable to Cronos or Uranus, and what is acceptable to Hephaestus but unacceptable to Here, and there may be other gods who have similar differences of opinion.

Euth. But I believe, Socrates, that all the gods would be agreed as to the propriety of punishing a murderer: there would be no difference of opinion about that.

Soc. Well, but speaking of men, Euthyphro, did you ever hear any one arguing that a murderer or any sort of evil-doer ought to be let off?

Euth. I should rather say that these are the questions which they are always arguing, especially in courts of law: they commit all sorts of crimes, and there is nothing which they will not do or say in their own defence.

Soc. But do they admit their guilt, Euthyphro, and yet say that they ought not to be punished?

Euth. No; they do not.

Soc. Then there are some things which they do not venture to say and do: for they do not venture to argue that the guilty are to be unpunished, but they deny their guilt, do they not?

Euth. Yes.

Soc. Then they do not argue that the evil-doer should not be punished, but they argue about the fact of who the evil-doer is, and what he did and when?

Euth. True.

Soc. And the gods are in the same case, if as you assert they quarrel about just and unjust, and some of them say while others deny that injustice is done among them. For surely neither

God nor man will ever venture to say that the doer of injustice is not to be punished?

Euth. That is true, Socrates, in the main.

Soc. But they join issue about the particulars—gods and men alike; and, if they dispute at all, they dispute about some act which is called in question, and which by some is affirmed to be just, by others to be unjust. Is not that true?

Euth. Quite true.

Soc. Well then, my dear friend Euthyphro, do tell me, for my better instruction and information, what proof have you that in the opinion of all the gods a servant who is guilty of murder, and is put in chains by the master of the dead man, and dies because he is put in chains before he who bound him can learn from the interpreters of the gods what he ought to do with him, dies unjustly; and that on behalf of such an one a son ought to proceed against his father and accuse him of murder. How would you show that all the gods absolutely agree in approving of his act? Prove to me that they do, and I will applaud your wisdom as long as I live.

Euth. It will be a difficult task; but I could make the matter very clear indeed to you.

Soc. I understand; you mean to say that I am not so quick of apprehension as the judges: for to them you will be sure to prove that the act is unjust, and hateful to the gods.

Euth. Yes indeed, Socrates; at least if they will listen to me.

Soc. But they will be sure to listen if they find that you are a good speaker. There was a notion that came into my mind while you were speaking; I said to myself: 'Well, and what if Euthyphro does prove to me that all the gods regarded the death of the serf as unjust, how do I know anything more of the nature of piety and impiety? for granting that this action may be hateful to the gods, still piety and impiety are not adequately defined by these distinctions, for that which is hateful to the gods has been shown to be also pleasing and dear to them.' And therefore, Euthyphro, I do not ask you to prove this; I will suppose, if you like, that all the gods condemn and abominate such an action. But I will amend the definition so far as to say that what all

the gods hate is impious, and what they love pious or holy; and what some of them love and others hate is both or neither. Shall this be our definition of piety and impiety?

Euth. Why not, Socrates?

Soc. Why not! certainly, as far as I am concerned, Euthyphro, there is no reason why not. But whether this admission will greatly assist you in the task of instructing me as you promised, is a matter for you to consider.

Euth. Yes, I should say that what all the gods love is pious and holy, and the opposite which they all hate, impious.

Soc. Ought we to enquire into the truth of this, Euthyphro, or simply to accept the mere statement on our own authority and that of others? What do you say?

Euth. We should enquire; and I believe that the statement will stand the test of enquiry.

Soc. We shall know better, my good friend, in a little while. The point which I should first wish to understand is whether the pious or holy is beloved by the gods because it is holy, or holy because it is beloved of the gods.

Euth. I do not understand your meaning, Socrates.

Soc. I will endeavour to explain: we speak of carrying and we speak of being carried, of leading and being led, seeing and being seen. You know that in all such cases there is a difference, and you know also in what the difference lies?

Euth. I think that I understand.

Soc. And is not that which is beloved distinct from that which loves?

Euth. Certainly.

Soc. Well; and now tell me, is that which is carried in this state of carrying because it is carried, or for some other reason?

Euth. No; that is the reason.

Soc. And the same is true of what is led and of what is seen?

Euth. True.

Soc. And a thing is not seen because it is visible, but conversely, visible because it is seen; nor is a thing led because it is in the state of being led, or carried because it is in the state of being carried, but the converse of this. And now I think, Euthyphro, that my meaning will be intelligible; and my meaning is, that any state of action or passion implies previous action or passion. It does not become because it is becoming, but it is in a state of becoming because it becomes; neither does it suffer because it is in a state of suffering, but it is in a state of suffering because it suffers. Do you not agree?

Euth. Yes.

Soc. Is not that which is loved in some state either of becoming or suffering?

Euth. Yes.

Soc. And the same holds as in the previous instances; the state of being loved follows the act of being loved, and not the act the state.

Euth. Certainly.

Soc. And what do you say of piety, Euthyphro: is not piety, according to your definition, loved by all the gods?

Euth. Yes.

Soc. Because it is pious or holy, or for some other reason?

Euth. No, that is the reason.

Soc. It is loved because it is holy, not holy because it is loved?

Euth. Yes.

Soc. And that which is dear to the gods is loved by them, and is in a state to be loved of them because it is loved of them?

Euth. Certainly.

Soc. Then that which is dear to the gods, Euthyphro, is not holy, nor is that which is holy loved of God, as you affirm; but they are two different things.

Euth. How do you mean, Socrates?

Soc. I mean to say that the holy has been acknowledged by us to be loved of God because it is holy, not to be holy because it is loved.

Euth. Yes.

Soc. But that which is dear to the gods is dear to them because it is loved by them, not loved by them because it is dear to them.

Euth. True.

Soc. But, friend Euthyphro, if that which is holy is the same with that which is dear to God, and is loved because it is holy, then that which is dear to God would have been loved as being dear

to God; but if that which is dear to God is dear to him because loved by him, then that which is holy would have been holy because loved by him. But now you see that the reverse is the case, and that they are quite different from one another. For one (θεοφιλὲς) is of a kind to be loved because it is loved, and the other (ὅσιον) is loved because it is of a kind to be loved. Thus you appear to me, Euthyphro, when I ask you what is the essence of holiness, to offer an attribute only, and not the essence—the attribute of being loved by all the gods. But you still refuse to explain to me the nature of holiness. And therefore, if you please, I will ask you not to hide your treasure, but to tell me once more what holiness or piety really is, whether dear to the gods or not (for that is a matter about which we will not quarrel); and what is impiety? . . .

Soc. Then we must begin again and ask, What is piety? That is an enquiry which I shall never be weary of pursuing as far as in me lies; and I entreat you not to scorn me, but to apply your mind to the utmost, and tell me the truth. For, if any man knows, you are he; and therefore I must detain you, like Proteus, until you tell. If you had not certainly known the nature of piety and impiety, I am confident that you would never, on behalf of a serf, have charged your aged father with murder. You would not have run such a risk of doing wrong in the sight of the gods, and you would have had too much respect for the opinions of men. I am sure, therefore, that you know the nature of piety and impiety. Speak out then, my dear Euthyphro, and do not hide your knowledge.

Euth. Another time, Socrates; for I am in a hurry, and must go now.

Soc. Alas! my companion, and will you leave me in despair? I was hoping that you would instruct me in the nature of piety and impiety; and then I might have cleared myself of Meletus and his indictment. I would have told him that I had been enlightened by Euthyphro, and had given up rash innovations and speculations, in which I indulged only through ignorance, and that now I am about to lead a better life.

Study Questions

1. What are Euthyphro's three definitions of piety? What are Socrates' objections to each?
2. Given Socrates' reasons for rejecting Euthyphro's definitions, what does he demand in general for the definition of an essence?
3. How are the Socratic principles of moral wisdom and negative wisdom illustrated in the dialogue?
4. What does Euthyphro learn, if anything?
5. What seems to be Socrates' own answer to the question about the status of holiness?
6. What does Socrates seem to be criticizing of the religion of his time? Would this apply to religion in general?

Suggestions for Further Reading

Allen, R. E. *Plato's "Euthyphro" and the Earlier Theory of Forms* (New York: Humanities Press, 1970). Background introduction to the *Euthyphro* in Chapter I. Detailed commentary on the dialogue in Chapter II.

Brickhouse, T. C., and N. D. Smith. *Plato's Socrates* (New York; Oxford: Oxford University Press, 1994). Chapter 4 examines the Socratic ethics.

Guthrie, W. K. C. *Socrates* (New York: Cambridge University Press, 1972). Chapter III examines the philosophical significance of Socrates' ideas.

Plato. *Apology, Crito*. Two early dialogues that further develop Socrates' life and philosophy.

Vlastos, G., ed. *The Philosophy of Socrates* (South Bend, IN: University of Notre Dame, 1980). Essay 8 examines Socrates' definition of piety.

Plato (428/27–348/47 B.C.E.)

Alfred North Whitehead, a twentieth-century philosopher, once characterized the general tradition of European philosophy as "a series of footnotes to Plato." Written mainly in the form of dialogue, Plato's philosophical works pursue the central problem of being and becoming (permanence and change) in great depth and detail through a wide range of theoretical perspectives—from ethics, politics, and religion to art, physics, and mathematics. By laying the foundation and setting the direction for subsequent systems of European thought, Plato's writings place him among the world's greatest philosophers.

Plato was born into a wealthy Athenian family distinguished by its important political roles and connections. Naturally drawn to a political life because of his aristocratic lineage and social status, Plato soon became disenchanted as a young man with the actual workings of Athenian public affairs, which he had hoped would lead his city-state "from an unjust way of life to a just one." Convinced that there would be no end to the evils of humankind until philosophers became rulers or rulers became philosophers, he turned to philosophy in search of a way to discern the universal features of justice in the city-state and the individual. Plato counted the indictment and death sentence of Socrates, his most influential teacher, among the injustices committed in Athens. After the death of Socrates in 399 B.C.E., Plato left Athens and traveled for a time, visiting intellectual and political centers in Megara, Italy, Sicily, and possibly Cyrene and Egypt. In memory of Socrates, Plato wrote his early, middle, and late dialogues, in which he recounts his teacher's life and perhaps faithfully reproduces his moral philosophy.

When he was around forty years old, Plato returned to Athens from Sicily and established a school called the Academy, one of the oldest and most enduring European centers for study and research in fields such as aesthetics, astronomy, epistemology, ethics, metaphysics, mathematics, politics, and psychology. During the next twenty years, Plato wrote his middle dialogues, including what is considered one of the most important books in European philosophy: the *Republic*. In the dialogues from that period, Plato began to move beyond Socrates by putting forth his own philosophy, in which he developed theories of reality (metaphysics) and knowledge (epistemology) as a larger context for ethics. After this period, Plato returned twice to Syracuse, Sicily, in an unsuccessful attempt to educate Dionysius II, whom he had hoped to train as a philosopher-king. Upon this failure, Plato returned to the Academy, where he continued teaching until his death. During this last period of his life, he wrote his late dialogues, in which his philosophy achieves its full-blown independence from Socratic thought.

Plato's lifelong focus on the problem of being and becoming was greatly influenced by Socrates' search for essence (*ousia*) or for the common form, appearance, or aspect (*eidos* or *idea*) of particular things; that is, for their universal characteristics. He also incorporated Socrates' famous method of cross-examination through dialogue into his own writings. However, Plato's philosophy was neither exclusively nor permanently indebted to the Socratic doctrine and method, for he was exposed to other philosophies, pondered other problems, and developed various theories as answers to his particular questions.

Plato's guiding concern with the problem of being and becoming led him to consider different metaphysical doctrines that emphasized either the permanent or the changing character of the cosmos. His particular metaphysics developed through intellectual encounters with the philosophical legacies of Socrates' predecessors, such as Heraclitus, who searched for the permanent law underlying the changing cosmos, and Parmenides, who denied the reality of a changing cosmos while affirming the oneness of being. In addition, his thought was engaged with the philosophies of some of his own contemporaries, in particular with the Pythagoreans, who believed that the cosmos was mathematical in nature. Plato's philosophy was also involved in constant battle with the doctrines of the Sophists, such as Protagoras, Gorgias, and Antiphon. These self-proclaimed wise (*sophos*) men professed to teach virtue or excellence (*arete*), mainly by teaching rhetoric, the art of persuasive speaking, in exchange for a fee. Plato interpreted much of their doctrines as leading to relativism—the denial of an ultimate, absolute, objective, independent reality—and skepticism—doubt concerning the very possibility of knowledge or of certain kinds of knowledge.

Plato's famous theory of the Ideas or Forms shows how his philosophy appropriated, modified, and contested the various doctrines to which he had been exposed. He eventually impressed on the Greek term *idea*, or *eidos*, a philosophical meaning that differed from those assigned by Socrates and others. For Plato, the

Ideas are real entities that are objective (existing independently of our minds), perfect, permanent, unchanging, nonmaterial or invisible, and intelligible (capable of being grasped by our intellect). Ideas are the essences of things existing in the material or visible world. Though there are multiple things in that world, they are united into kinds or classes. Ideas are what give things their unity and identity. For example, the Idea of a table makes each material table a table as such. Each table, regardless of its material and style, shares or partakes of the Form of table. Whereas material tables are imperfect, impermanent, and changing, the Form of table is a perfect, unchanging, and eternal pattern, model, or ideal. Ideas pervade the world of being, the realm of the permanent and unchanging, while material things come and go in the world of becoming, the realm of the impermanent and changing.

The world of becoming is inferior because it is less real than the world of being. In relation to the world of being, the world of becoming stands as a dependent copy to an independent original. When we intellectually grasp the world of being, we attain knowledge (*episteme*), but when we perceive the world of becoming through our senses, we merely have opinion (*doxa*). *Episteme* is knowledge of the Ideas and, as such, it is itself permanent and unchanging—eternally true. The objects of *doxa* constantly change and are subject to perceptions, so opinions are sometimes true and other times false. Thus, a firm understanding of the world of becoming can be guaranteed only by having knowledge of the Ideas in the world of being.

Plato's theory of the Ideas can serve as a broader context for understanding his moral philosophy in the *Republic*. The central question pursued in this dialogue composed of ten books is: What is justice? True to the Socratic search for the definition of moral terms through cross-examination, Plato seeks to determine what justice is as such through this grand dialogue between Socrates and other characters. However, unlike Socrates, Plato not only undertakes the task of writing down a definite answer to this question, but sees it as the way toward grasping the Idea or Form of justice. In this sense, Plato's *Republic* offers a theory of justice, an account of what is justice. It proposes that there is a real, objective, perfect, permanent, unchanging, invisible, and intelligible justice: an Idea or Form, an eternal model of justice. Such an Idea can be grasped adequately only through knowledge; that is, it is a matter of *episteme,* not of *doxa.* Acquiring such knowledge involves, among other things, learning what justice is not, by abandoning inadequate beliefs about justice, and by discerning between justice and injustice.

Because the Idea of justice pervades the world of being, it is pertinent to ask how does justice occur in the world of becoming? More specifically, what constitutes just acts as such, and what constitutes a just way of living for the human being? Plato answers these questions with his theories of the state and of the soul; that is, he offers an account of how actual political organizations or societies and living persons can attain justice. He sees the internal structure and functions of the state and its kinds as parallel to and grounded in those of the soul. Justice in both the soul and the state is a matter of order and the harmonious working of the parts within a whole. Each individual must strive to bring harmony to his or her soul in order to live in an ordered society. Thus, justice is a virtue or excellence through which the personal, ethical, and political are closely interconnected.

For Plato, the Idea of the good is the highest Form in the world of being. This supreme goodness, like the sun, gives life and illuminates all that is. Like the eye that cannot see without the light of the sun, the soul cannot attain knowledge without the Idea of the good. The moral ideal for the human being, the good person, is to direct the soul toward the light of the Form of the good. Moral virtue, then, is ultimately a matter of knowledge. The lovers of wisdom (philosophers) are those who, in cultivating the highest faculty of the soul (reason), turn toward the world of being where the supreme goodness shines in all its light. In this way their souls can achieve the highest virtue or excellence (wisdom). Thus, at the level of the state, philosophers should be the ruling class guiding their society toward goodness.

In the first two of the six selections that follow, Thrasymachus and Glaucon (in the selection known as the "Ring of Gyges"), respectively, argue that injustice is superior to justice. In the third selection, Socrates discusses with Glaucon the division of the soul into the appetitive, spirited, and rational parts (corresponding, respectively, to the classes of laborers, guardians, and rulers in the state). Socrates also defines justice as the harmony of the soul and identifies it with virtue. In the fourth selection, Socrates gives an explanation of the good through an analogy with the sun. In the fifth, Socrates tells the famous allegory of the cave to illustrate the importance of knowledge in the education of the soul. In the final selection, he refutes the claim that injustice is superior to justice.

REPUBLIC

Selection 1

[Thrasymachus] . . . [You] fancy that the shepherd or neatherd fattens or tends the sheep or oxen with a view to their own good and not to the good of himself or his master; and you further imagine that the rulers of states, if they are true rulers, never think of their subjects as sheep, and that they are not studying their own advantage day and night. Oh, no; and so entirely astray are you in your ideas about the just and unjust as not even to know that justice and the just are in reality another's good; that is to say, the interest of the ruler and stronger, and the loss of the subject and servant; and injustice the opposite; for

the unjust is lord over the truly simple and just: he is the stronger, and his subjects do what is for his interest, and minister to his happiness, which is very far from being their own. Consider further, most foolish Socrates, that the just is always a loser in comparison with the unjust. First of all, in private contracts: wherever the unjust is the partner of the just you will find that, when the partnership is dissolved, the unjust man has always more and the just less. Secondly, in their dealings with the State: when there is an income-tax, the just man will pay more and the unjust less on the same amount of income; and when there is anything to be received the one gains nothing and the other much. Observe also what

Plato. Republic, *Books I, II, IV, VI, VII, and XII. In* The Dialogues of Plato, *trans. B. Jowett, 3rd. ed. New York: Oxford University Press, 1892.*

happens when they take an office; there is the just man neglecting his affairs and perhaps suffering other losses, and getting nothing out of the public, because he is just; moreover he is hated by his friends and acquaintance for refusing to serve them in unlawful ways. But all this is reversed in the case of the unjust man. I am speaking, as before, of injustice on a large scale in which the advantage of the unjust is more apparent; and my meaning will be most clearly seen if we turn to that highest form of injustice in which the criminal is the happiest of men, and the sufferers or those who refuse to do injustice are the most miserable—that is to say tyranny, which by fraud and force takes away the property of others, not little by little but wholesale; comprehending in one, things sacred as well as profane, private and public; for which acts of wrong, if he were detected perpetrating any one of them singly, he would be punished and incur great disgrace—they who do such wrong in particular cases are called robbers of temples, and man-stealers and burglars and swindlers and thieves. But when a man besides taking away the money of the citizens has made slaves of them, then, instead of these names of reproach, he is termed happy and blessed, not only by the citizens but by all who hear of his having achieved the consummation of injustice. For mankind censure injustice, fearing that they may be the victims of it and not because they shrink from committing it. And thus, as I have shown, Socrates, injustice, when on a sufficient scale, has more strength and freedom and mastery than justice; and, as I said at first, justice is the interest of the stronger, whereas injustice is a man's own profit and interest.

Thrasymachus, when he had thus spoken, having, like a bathman, deluged our ears with his words, had a mind to go away. But the company would not let him; they insisted that he should remain and defend his position; and I myself added my own humble request that he would not leave us. Thrasymachus, I said to him, excellent man, how suggestive are your remarks! And are you going to run away before you have fairly taught or learned whether they are true or not?

Is the attempt to determine the way of man's life so small a matter in your eyes—to determine how life may be passed by each one of us to the greatest advantage? . . .

Selection 2

[Glaucon] They say that to do injustice is, by nature, good; to suffer injustice, evil; but that the evil is greater than the good. And so when men have both done and suffered injustice and have had experience of both, not being able to avoid the one and obtain the other, they think that they had better agree among themselves to have neither; hence there arise laws and mutual covenants; and that which is ordained by law is termed by them lawful and just. This they affirm to be the origin and nature of justice;—it is a mean or compromise, between the best of all, which is to do injustice and not be punished, and the worst of all, which is to suffer injustice without the power of retaliation; and justice, being at a middle point between the two, is tolerated not as a good, but as the lesser evil, and honoured by reason of the inability of men to do injustice. For no man who is worthy to be called a man would ever submit to such an agreement if he were able to resist; he would be mad if he did. Such is the received account, Socrates, of the nature and origin of justice.

Now that those who practise justice do so involuntarily and because they have not the power to be unjust will best appear if we imagine something of this kind: having given both to the just and the unjust power to do what they will, let us watch and see whither desire will lead them; then we shall discover in the very act the just and unjust man to be proceeding along the same road, following their interest, which all natures deem to be their good, and are only diverted into the path of justice by the force of law. The liberty which we are supposing may be most completely given to them in the form of such a power as is said to have been possessed by Gyges the ancestor of Croesus the Lydian. According to the tradition, Gyges was a shepherd in the service of the king of Lydia; there was a great storm, and an earthquake made an opening in the earth at the place where he was feeding his flock. Amazed at the sight, he descended into the opening, where, among other marvels, he beheld a hollow brazen horse, having doors, at which he stooping and looking in saw a dead body of stature, as appeared to him, more than human, and having nothing on but a gold ring; this he took from the finger of the dead and reascended. Now the shepherds met together, according to custom, that they might send their monthly report about the flocks to the king; into their assembly he came having the ring on his finger, and as he was sitting among them he chanced to turn the collet of the ring inside his hand, when instantly he became invisible to the rest of the company and they began to speak of him as if he were no longer present. He was astonished at this, and again touching the ring he turned the collet outwards and reappeared; he made several trials of the ring, and always with the same result—when he turned the collet inwards he became invisible, when outwards he reappeared. Whereupon he contrived to be chosen one of the messengers who were sent to the court; where as soon as he arrived he seduced the queen, and with her help conspired against the king and slew him, and took the kingdom. Suppose now that there were two such magic rings, and the just put on one of them and the unjust the other; no man can be imagined to be of such an iron nature that he would stand fast in justice. . . .

Selection 3

[Socrates] . . . [M]ight a man be thirsty, and yet unwilling to drink?

[Glaucon] Yes, he said, it constantly happens.

And in such a case what is one to say? Would you not say that there was something in the soul bidding a man to drink, and something else forbidding him, which is other and stronger than the principle which bids him?

I should say so.

And the forbidding principle is derived from reason, and that which bids and attracts proceeds from passion and disease?

Clearly.

Then we may fairly assume that they are two, and that they differ from one another; the one with which a man reasons, we may call the rational principle of the soul, the other, with which he loves and hungers and thirsts and feels the flutterings of any other desire, may be termed the irrational or appetitive, the ally of sundry pleasures and satisfactions?

Yes, he said, we may fairly assume them to be different.

Then let us finally determine that there are two principles existing in the soul. And what of passion, or spirit? Is it a third, or akin to one of the preceding?

I should be inclined to say—akin to desire.

Well, I said, there is a story which I remember to have heard, and in which I put faith. The story is, that Leontius, the son of Aglaion, coming up one day from the Piraeus, under the north wall on the outside, observed some dead bodies lying on the ground at the place of execution. He felt a desire to see them, and also a dread and abhorrence of them; for a time he struggled and covered his eyes, but at length the desire got the better of him; and forcing them open, he ran up to the dead bodies, saying, Look, ye wretches, take your fill of the fair sight.

I have heard the story myself, he said.

The moral of the tale is, that anger at times goes to war with desire, as though they were two distinct things.

Yes; that is the meaning, he said.

And are there not many other cases in which we observe that when a man's desires violently prevail over his reason, he reviles himself, and is angry at the violence within him, and that in this struggle, which is like the struggle of factions in a State, his spirit is on the side of his reason;—but for the passionate or spirited element to take part with the desires when reason decides that she should not be opposed, is a sort of thing which I believe that you never observed occurring in yourself, nor, as I should imagine, in any one else?

Certainly not.

Suppose that a man thinks he has done a wrong to another, the nobler he is the less able is he to feel indignant at any suffering, such as hunger, or cold, or any other pain which the injured person may inflict upon him—these he deems to be just, and, as I say, his anger refuses to be excited by them.

True, he said.

But when he thinks that he is the sufferer of the wrong, then he boils and chafes, and is on the side of what he believes to be justice; and because he suffers hunger or cold or other pain he is only the more determined to persevere and conquer. His noble spirit will not be quelled until he either slays or is slain; or until he hears the voice of the shepherd, that is, reason, bidding his dog bark no more.

The illustration is perfect, he replied; and in our State, as we were saying, the auxiliaries were to be dogs, and to hear the voice of the rulers, who are their shepherds.

I perceive, I said, that you quite understand me; there is, however, a further point which I wish you to consider.

What point?

You remember that passion or spirit appeared at first sight to be a kind of desire, but now we should say quite the contrary; for in the conflict of the soul spirit is arrayed on the side of the rational principle.

Most assuredly.

But a further question arises: Is passion different from reason also, or only a kind of reason; in which latter case, instead of three principles in the soul, there will only be two, the rational and the concupiscent; or rather, as the State was composed of three classes, traders, auxiliaries, counsellors, so may there not be in the individual soul a third element which is passion or spirit, and when not corrupted by bad education is the natural auxiliary of reason?

Yes, he said, there must be a third.

Yes, I replied, if passion, which has already been shown to be different from desire, turn out also to be different from reason.

But that is easily proved:—We may observe even in young children that they are full of spirit almost as soon as they are born, whereas some of them never seem to attain to the use of reason, and most of them late enough.

Excellent, I said, and you may see passion equally in brute animals, which is a further proof of the truth of what you are saying. And we may once more appeal to the words of Homer, which have been already quoted by us,

He smote his breast, and thus rebuked his soul;

for in this verse Homer has clearly supposed the power which reasons about the better and worse to be different from the unreasoning anger which is rebuked by it.

Very true, he said.

And so, after much tossing, we have reached land, and are fairly agreed that the same principles which exist in the State exist also in the individual, and that they are three in number.

Exactly.

Must we not then infer that the individual is wise in the same way, and in virtue of the same quality which makes the State wise?

Certainly.

Also that the same quality which constitutes courage in the State constitutes courage in the individual, and that both the State and the individual bear the same relation to all the other virtues?

Assuredly.

And the individual will be acknowledged by us to be just in the same way in which the State is just?

That follows of course.

We cannot but remember that the justice of the State consisted in each of the three classes doing the work of its own class?

We are not very likely to have forgotten, he said.

We must recollect that the individual in whom the several qualities of his nature do their own work will be just, and will do his own work?

Yes, he said, we must remember that too.

And ought not the rational principle, which is wise, and has the care of the whole soul, to rule, and the passionate or spirited principle to be the subject and ally?

Certainly.

And, as we were saying, the united influence of music and gymnastic will bring them into accord, nerving and sustaining reason with noble words and lessons, and moderating and soothing and civilizing the wildness of passion by harmony and rhythm?

Quite true, he said.

And these two, thus nurtured and educated, and having learned truly to know their own functions, will rule over the concupiscent, which in each of us is the largest part of the soul and by nature most insatiable of gain; over this they will keep guard, lest, waxing great and strong with the fulness of bodily pleasures, as they are termed, the concupiscent soul, no longer confined to her own sphere, should attempt to enslave and rule those who are not her natural-born subjects, and overturn the whole life of man?

Very true, he said.

Both together will they not be the best defenders of the whole soul and the whole body against attacks from without; the one counselling, and the other fighting under his leader, and courageously executing his commands and counsels?

True.

And he is to be deemed courageous whose spirit retains in pleasure and in pain the commands of reason about what he ought or ought not to fear?

Right, he replied.

And him we call wise who has in him that little part which rules, and which proclaims these commands; that part too being supposed to have a knowledge of what is for the interest of each of the three parts and of the whole?

Assuredly.

And would you not say that he is temperate who has these same elements in friendly harmony, in whom the one ruling principle of reason, and the two subject ones of spirit and desire are equally agreed that reason ought to rule, and do not rebel?

Certainly, he said, that is the true account of temperance whether in the State or individual.

And surely, I said, we have explained again and again how and by virtue of what quality a man will be just.

That is very certain.

And is justice dimmer in the individual, and is her form different, or is she the same which we found her to be in the State?

There is no difference in my opinion, he said.

Because, if any doubt is still lingering in our minds, a few commonplace instances will satisfy us of the truth of what I am saying.

What sort of instances do you mean?

If the case is put to us, must we not admit that the just State, or the man who is trained in the principles of such a State, will be less likely than the unjust to make away with a deposit of gold or silver? Would any one deny this?

No one, he replied.

Will the just man or citizen ever be guilty of sacrilege or theft, or treachery either to his friends or to his country?

Never.

Neither will he ever break faith where there have been oaths or agreements?

Impossible.

No one will be less likely to commit adultery, or to dishonour his father and mother, or to fail in his religious duties?

No one.

And the reason is that each part of him is doing its own business, whether in ruling or being ruled?

Exactly so.

Are you satisfied then that the quality which makes such men and such states is justice, or do you hope to discover some other?

Not I, indeed.

Then our dream has been realized; and the suspicion which we entertained at the beginning of our work of construction, that some divine power must have conducted us to a primary form of justice, has now been verified?

Yes, certainly.

And the division of labour which required the carpenter and the shoemaker and the rest of the citizens to be doing each his own business, and not another's, was a shadow of justice, and for that reason it was of use?

Clearly.

But in reality justice was such as we were describing, being concerned however, not with the outward man, but with the inward, which is the true self and concernment of man: for the just man does not permit the several elements within him to interfere with one another, or any of them to do the work of others,—he sets in order his own inner life, and is his own master and his own law, and at peace with himself; and when he has bound together the three principles within him, which may be compared to the higher, lower, and middle notes of the scale, and the intermediate intervals—when he has bound all these together, and is no longer many, but has become one entirely temperate and perfectly adjusted nature, then he proceeds to act, if he has to act, whether in a matter of property, or in the treatment of the body, or in some affair of politics or private business; always thinking and calling that which preserves and co-operates with this harmonious condition, just and good action, and the knowledge which presides over it, wisdom, and that which at any time impairs this condition, he will call unjust action, and the opinion which presides over it ignorance.

You have said the exact truth, Socrates.

Very good; and if we were to affirm that we had discovered the just man and the just State, and the nature of justice in each of them, we should not be telling a falsehood?

Most certainly not.

May we say so, then?

Let us say so.

And now, I said, injustice has to be considered.

Clearly.

Must not injustice be a strife which arises among the three principles—a meddlesomeness,

and interference, and rising up of a part of the soul against the whole, an assertion of unlawful authority, which is made by a rebellious subject against a true prince, of whom he is the natural vassal,—that is all this confusion and delusion but injustice, and intemperance and cowardice and ignorance, and every form of vice?

Exactly so.

And if the nature of justice and injustice be known, then the meaning of acting unjustly and being unjust, or, again, of acting justly will also be perfectly clear?

What do you mean? he said.

Why, I said, they are like disease and health; being in the soul just what disease and health are in the body.

How so? he said.

Why, I said, that which is healthy causes health, and that which is unhealthy causes disease.

Yes.

And just actions cause justice, and unjust actions cause injustice?

That is certain.

And the creation of health is the institution of a natural order and government of one by another in the parts of the body; and the creation of disease is the production of a state of things at variance with this natural order?

True.

And is not the creation of justice the institution of a natural order and government of one by another in the parts of the soul, and the creation of injustice the production of a state of things at variance with the natural order?

Exactly so, he said.

Then virtue is the health and beauty and well-being of the soul, and vice the disease and weakness and deformity of the same?

True.

And do not good practices lead to virtue, and evil practices to vice?

Assuredly.

Still our old question of the comparative advantage of justice and injustice has not been answered: Which is the more profitable, to be just and act justly and practise virtue, whether seen or unseen of gods, and men, or to be unjust and act unjustly, if only unpunished and unreformed?

In my judgment, Socrates, the question has now become ridiculous. We know that, when the bodily constitution is gone, life is no longer endurable, though pampered with all kinds of meats and drinks, and having all wealth and all power; and shall we be told that when the very essence of the vital principle is undermined and corrupted, life is still worth having to a man, if only he be allowed to do whatever he likes with the single exception that he is not to acquire justice and virtue, or to escape from injustice and vice; assuming them both to be such as we have described?

Yes, I said, the question is, as you say, ridiculous. Still, as we are near the spot at which we may see the truth in the clearest manner with our own eyes, let us not faint by the way.

Certainly not, he replied. . . .

Selection 4

. . . Still, I must implore you, Socrates, said Glaucon, not to turn away just as you are reaching the goal; if you will only give such an explanation of the good as you have already given of justice and temperance and the other virtues, we shall be satisfied.

Yes, my friend, and I shall be at least equally satisfied, but I cannot help fearing that I shall fail, and that my indiscreet zeal will bring ridicule upon me. No, sweet sirs, let us not at present ask what is the actual nature of the good, for to reach what is now in my thoughts would be an effort too great for me. But of the child of the good who is likest him, I would fain speak, if I could be sure that you wished to hear—otherwise, not.

By all means, he said, tell us about the child, and you shall remain in our debt for the account of the parent.

I do indeed wish, I replied, that I could pay, and you receive, the account of the parent, and not, as now, of the offspring only; take, however, this latter by way of interest, and at the same time have a care that I do not render a false account, although I have no intention of deceiving you.

Yes, we will take all the care that we can: proceed.

Yes, I said, but I must first come to an understanding with you, and remind you of what I have mentioned in the course of this discussion, and at many other times.

What?

The old story, that there is a many beautiful and a many good, and so of other things which we describe and define; to all of them 'many' is applied.

True, he said.

And there is an absolute beauty and an absolute good, and of other things to which the term 'many' is applied there is an absolute; for they may be brought under a single idea, which is called the essence of each.

Very true.

The many, as we say, are seen but not known, and the ideas are known but not seen.

Exactly.

And what is the organ with which we see the visible things?

The sight, he said.

And with the hearing, I said, we hear, and with the other senses perceive the other objects of sense?

True.

But have you remarked that sight is by far the most costly and complex piece of workmanship which the artificer of the senses ever contrived?

No, I never have, he said.

Then reflect: has the ear or voice need of any third or additional nature in order that the one may be able to hear and the other to be heard?

Nothing of the sort.

No, indeed, I replied; and the same is true of most, if not all, the other senses—you would not say that any of them requires such an addition?

Certainly not.

But you see that without the addition of some other nature there is no seeing or being seen?

How do you mean?

Sight being, as I conceive, in the eyes, and he who has eyes wanting to see; colour being also present in them, still unless there be a third nature specially adapted to the purpose, the owner of the eyes will see nothing and the colours will be invisible.

Of what nature are you speaking?

Of that which you term light, I replied.

True, he said.

Noble, then, is the bond which links together sight and visibility, and great beyond other bonds by no small difference of nature; for light is their bond, and light is no ignoble thing?

Nay, he said, the reverse if ignoble.

And which, I said, of the gods in heaven would you say was the lord of this element? Whose is that light which makes the eye to see perfectly and the visible to appear?

You mean the sun, as you and all mankind say.

May not the relation of sight to this deity be described as follows?

How?

Neither sight nor the eye in which sight resides is the sun?

No.

Yet of all the organs of sense the eye is the most like the sun?

By far the most like.

And the power which the eye possesses is a sort of effluence which is dispensed from the sun?

Exactly.

Then the sun is not sight, but the author of sight who is recognised by sight.

True, he said.

And this is he whom I call the child of the good, whom the good begat in his own likeness, to be in the visible world, in relation to sight and the things of sight, what the good is in the intellectual world in relation to mind and the things of mind.

Will you be a little more explicit? he said.

Why, you know, I said, that the eyes, when a person directs them towards objects on which the light of day is no longer shining, but the moon and stars only, see dimly, and are nearly blind; they seem to have no clearness of vision in them?

Very true.

But when they are directed towards objects on which the sun shines, they see clearly and there is sight in them?

Certainly.

And the soul is like the eye: when resting upon that on which truth and being shine, the soul perceives and understands and is radiant with intelligence; but when turned towards the twilight of becoming and perishing, then she has opinion only, and goes blinking about, and is first of one opinion and then of another, and seems to have no intelligence?

Just so.

Now, that which imparts truth to the known and the power of knowing to the knower is what I would have you term the idea of good, and this you will deem to be the cause of science, and of truth in so far as the latter becomes the subject of knowledge; beautiful too, as are both truth and knowledge, you will be right in esteeming this other nature as more beautiful than either; and, as in the previous instance, light and sight may be truly said to be like the sun, and yet not to be the sun, so in this other sphere, science and truth may be deemed to be like the good, but not the good; the good has a place of honour yet higher.

What a wonder of beauty that must be, he said, which is the author of science and truth, and yet surpasses them in beauty; for you surely cannot mean to say that pleasure is the good?

God forbid, I replied; but may I ask you to consider the image in another point of view?

In what point of view?

You would say, would you not, that the sun is not only the author of visibility in all visible things, but of generation and nourishment and growth, though he himself is not generation?

Certainly.

In like manner the good may be said to be not only the author of knowledge to all things known, but of their being and essence, and yet the good is not essence, but far exceeds essence in dignity and power.

Selection 5

[Socrates] And now, I said, let me show in a figure how far out nature is enlightened or un-enlightened:—Behold! human beings living in an underground den which has a mouth open towards the light and reaching all along the den; here they have been from their childhood, and have their legs and necks chained so that they cannot move, and can only see before them, being prevented by the chains from turning round their heads. Above and behind them a fire is blazing at a distance, and between the fire and the prisoners there is a raised way; and you will see, if you look, a low wall built along the way, like the screen which marionette players have in front of them, over which they show the puppets.

[Glaucon] I see.

And do you see, I said, men passing along the wall carrying all sorts of vessels, and statues and figures of animals made of wood and stone and various materials, which appear over the wall? Some of them are talking, others silent.

You have shown me a strange image, and they are strange prisoners.

Like ourselves, I replied; and they see only their own shadows or the shadows of one another, which the fire throws on the opposite wall of the cave?

True, he said; how could they see anything but the shadows if they were never allowed to move their heads?

And of the objects which are being carried in like manner they would only see the shadows?

Yes, he said.

And if they were able to converse with one another, would they not suppose that they were naming what was actually before them?

Very true.

And suppose further that the prison had an echo which came from the other side, would they not be sure to fancy when one of the passers-by spoke that the voice which they heard came from the passing shadow?

No question, he replied.

To them, I said, the truth would be literally nothing but the shadows of the images.

That is certain.

And now look again, and see what will naturally follow if the prisoners are released and disabused of their error. At first, when any of them is liberated and compelled suddenly to stand up and turn his neck round and walk and look towards the light, he will suffer sharp pains; the glare will distress him, and he will be unable to see the realities of which in his former state he had seen the shadows; and then conceive some one saying to him, that what he saw before was an illusion, but that now, when he is approaching nearer to being and his eye is turned towards more real existence, he has a clearer vision,—what will be his reply? And you may further imagine that his instructor is pointing to the objects as they pass and requiring him to name them,—will he not be perplexed? Will he not fancy that the shadows which he formerly saw are true than the objects which are now shown to him?

Far truer.

And if he is compelled to look straight at the light, will he not have a pain in his eyes which will make him turn away to take refuge in the objects of vision which he can see, and which he will conceive to be in reality clearer than the things which are now being shown to him?

True, he said.

And suppose once more, that he is reluctantly dragged up a steep and rugged ascent, and held fast until he is forced into the presence of the sun himself, is he not likely to be pained and irritated? When he approaches the light his eyes will be dazzled, and he will not be able to see anything at all of what are now called realities.

Not all in a moment, he said.

He will require to grow accustomed to the sight of the upper world. And first he will see the shadows best, next the reflections of men and other objects in the water, and then the objects themselves; then he will gaze upon the light of the moon and the stars and the spangled heaven; and he will see the sky and the stars by night better than the sun or the light of the sun by day?

Certainly.

Last of all he will be able to see the sun, and not mere reflections of him in the water, but he will see him in his own proper place, and not in another; and he will contemplate him as he is.

Certainly.

He will then proceed to argue that this is he who gives the season and the years, and is the guardian of all that is in the visible world, and in a certain way the cause of all things which he and his fellows have been accustomed to behold?

Clearly, he said, he would first see the sun and then reason about him.

And when he remembered his old habitation, and the wisdom of the den and his fellow-prisoners, do you not suppose that he would felicitate himself on the change, and pity them?

Certainly, he would.

And if they were in the habit of conferring honours among themselves on those who were quickest to observe the passing shadows and to remark which of them went before, and which followed after, and which were together; and who were therefore best able to draw conclusions as to the future, do you think that he would care for such honours and glories, or envy the possessors of them? Would he not say with Homer,

'Better to be the poor servant of a poor master,'

and to endure anything, rather than think as they do and live after their manner?

Yes, he said, I think that he would rather suffer anything than entertain these false notions and live in this miserable manner.

Imagine once more, I said, such an one coming suddenly out of the sun to be replaced in his old situation; would he not be certain to have his eyes full of darkness?

To be sure, he said.

And if there were a contest, and he had to compete in measuring the shadows with the prisoners who had never moved out of the den, while his sight was still weak, and before his eyes had become steady (and the time which would be needed to acquire this new habit of sight might be very considerable), would he not be

ridiculous? Men would say of him that up he went and down he came without his eyes; and that it was better not even to think of ascending; and if any one tried to loose another and lead him up to the light, let them only catch the offender, and they would put him to death.

No question, he said.

This entire allegory, I said, you may now append, dear Glaucon, to the previous argument; the prison-house is the world of sight, the light of the fire is the sun, and you will not misapprehend me if you interpret the journey upwards to be the ascent of the soul into the intellectual world according to my poor belief, which, at your desire, I have expressed—whether rightly or wrongly God knows. But, whether true or false, my opinion is that in the world of knowledge the idea of good appears last of all, and is seen only with an effort; and, when seen, is also inferred to be the universal author of all things beautiful and right, parent of light and of the lord of light in this visible world, and the immediate source of reason and truth in the intellectual; and that this is the power upon which he who would act rationally either in public or private life must have his eyes fixed.

I agree, he said, as far as I am able to understand you.

Moreover, I said, you must not wonder that those who attain to this beatific vision are unwilling to descend to human affairs; for their souls are ever hastening into the upper world where they desire to dwell; which desire of theirs is very natural, if our allegory may be trusted.

Yes, very natural.

And is there anything surprising in one who passes from divine contemplations to the evil state of man, misbehaving himself in a ridiculous manner; if, while his eyes are blinking and before he has become accustomed to the surrounding darkness, he is compelled to fight in courts of law, or in other places, about the images or the shadows of images of justice, and is endeavouring to meet the conceptions of those who have never yet seen absolute justice?

Anything but surprising, he replied.

Any one who has common sense will remember that the bewilderments of the eyes are of two kinds, and arise from two causes, either from coming out of the light or from going into the light, which is true of the mind's eye, quite as much as of the bodily eye; and he who remembers this when he sees any one whose vision is perplexed and weak, will not be too ready to laugh; he will first ask whether that soul of man has come out of the brighter life, and is unable to see because unaccustomed to the dark, or having turned from darkness to the day is dazzled by excess of light. And he will count the one happy in his condition and state of being, and he will pity the other; or, if he have a mind to laugh at the soul which comes from below into the light, there will be more reason in this than in the laugh which greets him who returns from above out of the light into the den.

That, he said, is a very just distinction.

But then, if I am right, certain professors of education must be wrong when they say that they can put a knowledge into the soul which was not there before, like sight into blind eyes.

They undoubtedly say this, he replied.

Whereas, our argument shows that the power and capacity of learning exists in the soul already; and that just as the eye was unable to turn from darkness to light without the whole body, so too the instrument of knowledge can only by the movement of the whole soul be turned from the world of becoming into that of being, and learn by degrees to endure the sight of being, and of the brightest and best of being, or in other words, of the good.

Very true. . . .

Selection 6

[Socrates] . . . Was not some one saying that injustice was a gain to the perfectly unjust who was reputed to be just?

[Glaucon] Yes, that was said.

Now then, having determined the power and quality of justice and injustice, let us have a little conversation with him.

What shall we say to him?

Let us make an image of the soul, that he may have his own words presented before his eyes.

Of what sort?

An ideal image of the soul, like the composite creations of ancient mythology, such as the Chimera or Scylla or Cerberus, and there are many others in which two or more different natures are said to grow into one.

There are said to have been such unions.

Then do you now model the form of a multitudinous, many-headed monster, having a ring of heads of all manner of beasts, tame and wild, which he is able to generate and metamorphose at will.

You suppose marvellous powers in the artist; but, as language is more pliable than wax or any similar substance, let there be such a model as you propose.

Suppose now that you make a second form as of a lion, and a third of a man, the second smaller than the first, and the third smaller than the second.

That, he said, is an easier task; and I have made them as you say.

And now join them, and let the three grow into one.

That has been accomplished.

Next fashion the outside of them into a single image, as of a man, so that he who is not able to look within, and sees only the outer hull, may believe the beast to be a single human creature.

I have done so, he said.

And now, to him who maintains that it is profitable for the human creature to be unjust, and unprofitable to be just, let us reply that, if he be right, it is profitable for this creature to feast the multitudinous monster and strengthen the lion and the lion-like qualities, but to starve and weaken the man, who is consequently liable to be dragged about at the mercy of either of the other two; and he is not to attempt to familiarize or harmonize them with one another—he ought rather to suffer them to fight and bite and devour one another.

Certainly, he said; that is what the approver of injustice says.

To him the supporter of justice makes answer that he should ever so speak and act as to give the man within him in some way or other the most complete mastery over the entire human creature. He should watch over the many-headed monster like a good husbandman, fostering and cultivating the gentle qualities, and preventing the wild ones from growing; he should be making the lion-hearted his ally, and in common care of them all should be uniting the several parts with one another and with himself.

Yes, he said, that is quite what the maintainer of justice will say.

And so from every point of view, whether of pleasure, honour, or advantage, the approver of justice is right and speaks the truth, and the disapprover is wrong and false and ignorant?

Yes, from every point of view.

Come, now, and let us gently reason with the unjust, who is not intentionally in error. 'Sweet Sir,' we will say to him, 'what think you of things esteemed noble and ignoble? Is not the noble that which subjects the beast to the man, or rather to the god in man; and the ignoble that which subjects the man to the beast?' He can hardly avoid saying Yes—can he now?

Not if he has any regard for my opinion. . . .

Study Questions

1. What views of human nature transpire in Thrasymachus' and Glaucon's arguments about injustice? in Socrates' final argument about injustice?
2. How are knowledge and moral action related in Plato's notions of justice and the good? What does it take to be just? to be good? Where does one's moral worth lie?
3. How are the personal and the political dimensions related in Plato's moral theory?
4. What is the human condition described in the allegory of the cave? What does the education of the soul entail? How does this relate to morality?
5. What is implied in Plato's conception of the Idea of the good regarding the cosmos and the soul?
6. Can Plato's theory of justice be put into practice? What would doing so entail?

Suggestions for Further Reading

Crombie, I. M. *An Examination of Plato's Doctrines, Vol. I: Plato on Man and Society* (London: Routledge and Kegan Paul, 1966). See Chapters 1 and 2 for a general introduction to Plato's life, writings, and thought; see Chapter 3 for a detailed discussion of the *Republic* and Chapter 6 for a general view of his ethics.

Irwin, T. *Plato's Ethics* (Oxford: Oxford University Press, 1995). A detailed exposition of Plato's ethics, particularly as developed in his *Republic*.

Gould, J. *The Development of Plato's Ethics* (London: Cambridge University Press, 1955). Chapters 10–13 develop an analysis of Plato's *Republic*.

Kraut, R., ed. *The Cambridge Companion to Plato* (New York: Cambridge University Press, 1992). See Kraut's "Introduction to the Study of Plato" and "The Defense of Justice in Plato's *Republic*."

Taylor, A. E., *Plato: The Man and His Work* (London: Methuen, 1963). See especially Chapter XI on the *Republic*.

White, N. *A Companion to Plato's Republic* (Indianapolis, IN: Hackett, 1979). Provides a six-chapter interpretation of Plato's *Republic* and explanatory summaries of each of its books.

Aristotle (384–322 B.C.E.)

Born in Stagira, in Macedon, Aristotle was the son of a court physician to the king of Macedon. After his father's death, Aristotle went to Athens to study in Plato's Academy, where he remained for twenty years, until Plato's death. Some years later, Aristotle was invited by Philip of Macedon to tutor his young son, Alexander, later known as Alexander the Great. When Alexander assumed power upon his father's death, Aristotle returned to Athens and founded his own school, the Lyceum, where he directed and carried out philosophical lectures and scientific research. Since he had the habit of teaching while he strolled up and down the colonnades, Aristotle and his followers came to be known as the "Peripatetics" (from the Greek *peripatein,* meaning "to walk about"). Following the death of Alexander in 323 B.C.E., the anti-Macedonian sentiments of the Athenians flared and threatened to consume Aristotle's own life when he was charged with "impiety" on account of his associations with the Macedonian court. Recalling Socrates' earlier death sentence, Aristotle fled Athens "lest the Athenians sin twice against philosophy," but he died a year later in Chalcis, a Macedonian stronghold.

During the early Middle Ages, Aristotle's works were translated, studied, and preserved by Arab philosophers. Later, Thomas Aquinas, the medieval Christian theologian, came to refer to him as "the Philosopher." This grand disciple of Plato stands side by side with his teacher as one of the main pillars of European philosophy. Though he was a prolific writer, only a fraction of his works are extant, and most of what remains are his lecture notes. In spite of their terse style, these writings reveal the breadth and depth of his interests and activities, for in his wonder toward the natural world Aristotle inquired into all things. He strove to attain knowledge not only through philosophical reflections (on topics such as logic, metaphysics, psychology, politics, ethics, rhetoric, and poetry), but also through scientific investigations (in fields such as biology, botany, anatomy, zoology, physics, and astronomy). Known for his classification of knowledge into three sciences—theoretical (aimed toward knowledge for its own sake), practical (aimed toward action), and productive (for making something)—Aristotle himself explored all these fields.

Though he was Plato's most gifted student, Aristotle eventually developed his own philosophy, often with explicit criticisms of his teacher's philosophical methods and ideas. Aristotle saw these departures and critiques necessary because "although both [Plato and the truth] are dear, it is right to give preference to the truth." Unlike Plato, who sought after truth in an eternal, unchanging realm beyond the natural world, Aristotle turned first toward the world given in experience. Plato believed that real and objective entities (Ideas or Forms) in a permanent world provide universal patterns for individual things in the changing world. Like Plato, Aristotle believed that our understanding of individual things requires that we know their universal forms. However, disagreeing with Plato, Aristotle insisted that these forms are inherent within, not beyond, individual things. Arguing that sense experience is the starting point of knowledge, he emphasized that their principles of intelligibility are found within the world in which we live. He understood change itself as a movement from potentiality to actuality; that is, as the actualization of a thing's potential. However, a full account of the "whys" of something requires that we search for its four explanations or causes (*aitia*): the material cause (the stuff of which it is made), the formal cause (what defines and distinguishes it as a particular kind of thing), the efficient cause (its source of change), and the final cause (what it is for), its end (*telos*). Because Aristotle believed that things have final causes, he is said to have a "teleological" conception of the universe in which everything (including the natural world as a whole) has a "what for," a function or end. Thus, unlike Plato, who claimed that we can attain knowledge only by directing our minds to the permanent world of the Ideas, Aristotle believed it is possible to achieve knowledge about the natural world itself.

Following Aristotle's own classification of knowledge, his *Nicomachean Ethics* develops a practical science, a system of knowledge aimed toward action, specifically by providing a guide for living the good life. The goal of political science is to develop a course of action for the good of the city-state; that is, for the social good. Ethics, as the science for the good of the individual, is a branch of political science offering a knowledge that not only is geared toward our living but is also rooted in direct and concrete observations of human life. Thus, Aristotle offers a practical moral philosophy, not an exact science of absolute ethical principles.

From the very start, Aristotle's *Nicomachean Ethics* assumes a teleological understanding of the human being. Although all our actions are aimed at a good or end, some goods are means to further goods. Aristotle believes that there is an ultimate end, a supreme good for the sake of which all other ends are pursued. Unlike Plato, who identified the highest good with the transcendent Form of the good and pointed to knowledge as the means to achieving it, Aristotle insists it is found in the practical realm of human life. This highest good must be attainable through action and must be final (not a means to another end) and self-sufficient (lacking in nothing).

According to Aristotle, the highest good is happiness or, better said, well-being (*eudaimonia*). He defined the human being as a "rational animal," claiming that we are distinctive among living things in our soul's ability to reason and the activities of our reason. Our function or end as humans is intrinsically tied to our rationality. Our well-being consists then in exercising the rational part of our soul well. Aristotle thus defines happiness as an "activity of the soul in accordance with virtue." It is a matter of attaining excellence or virtue (*arete*), of becoming virtuous and thus fully actualizing our potentiality as human beings.

In Aristotle's virtue ethics, there are different kinds of virtues, moral and intellectual. Moral virtue is an excellence in character that is attained through habit, whereas intellectual virtue is an excellence in thought that is acquired through instruction. We can all become morally virtuous by training ourselves to listen to and obey reason in the control of our appetites and desires. Thus, in what is called the "doctrine of the golden mean," Aristotle sees moral virtue as a kind of moderation, whereby we develop the habit of rationally aiming at the appropriate midpoint in our feelings and actions for each situation. Although it is difficult enough to determine the right midpoint for each circumstance in order to achieve moral excellence, it is much more difficult to attain intellectual excellence. Very few of us are able to live a life devoted exclusively to the exercise of reason in pure speculation or contemplation (*theoria*). Yet, the kind of happiness attainable in such life of wisdom is higher than what most humans can reach through moral excellence because it is almost divine.

NICOMACHEAN ETHICS

Book I • The Good for Man

SUBJECT OF OUR INQUIRY

All human activities aim at some good: some goals subordinate to others

1. Every art and every inquiry, and similarly every action and pursuit, is thought to aim at some good; and for this reason the good has rightly been declared to be that at which all things aim. But a certain difference is found among ends; some are activities, others are products apart from the activities that produce them. Where there are ends apart from the actions, it is the nature of the products to be better than the activities. Now, as there are many actions, arts, and sciences, their ends also are many; the end of the medical art is health, that of shipbuilding a vessel, that of strategy victory, that of economics wealth. But where such arts fall under a single capacity—as bridle-making and the other arts concerned with the equipment of horses fall under the art of riding, and this and every military action under strategy, in the same way other arts fall under yet others—in all of these the ends of the master arts are to be preferred to all the subordinate ends; for it is for the sake of the former that the latter are pursued. It makes no difference whether the activities themselves are the ends of the actions, or something else apart from the activities, as in the case of the sciences just mentioned.

The science of the good for man is politics

2. If, then, there is some end of the things we do, which we desire for its own sake (everything else being desired for the sake of this), and if we do not choose everything for the sake of something else (for at that rate the process would go on to infinity, so that our desire would be empty and vain), clearly this must be the good and the chief good. Will not the knowledge of it, then, have a great influence on life? Shall we not, like archers who have a mark to aim at, be more likely to hit upon what is right? If so, we must try, in outline at least, to determine what it is, and of which of the sciences or capacities it is the object. It would seem to belong to the most authoritative art and that which is most truly the master art. And politics appears to be of this nature; for it is this that ordains which of the sciences should be studied in a state, and which each class of citizens should learn and up to what point they should learn them; and we see even the most highly esteemed of capacities to fall under this, e.g. strategy, economics, rhetoric; now, since politics uses the rest of the sciences, and since, again, it legislates as to what we are to do and what we are to abstain from, the end of this science must include those

Aristotle. Nicomachean Ethics, *trans. W. D. Ross, Books I, II, and X. In* The Works of Aristotle, *Vol. IX, ed.* W. D. Ross. *Oxford: Clarendon Press, 1925.*

of the others, so that this end must be the good for man. For even if the end is the same for a single man and for a state, that of the state seems at all events something greater and more complete whether to attain or to preserve; though it is worth while to attain the end merely for one man, it is finer and more godlike to attain it for a nation or for city-states. These, then, are the ends at which our inquiry aims, since it is political science, in one sense of that term.

NATURE OF THE SCIENCE

We must not expect more precision than the subject-matter admits of. The student should have reached years of discretion

3. Our discussion will be adequate if it has as much clearness as the subject-matter admits of, for precision is not to be sought for alike in all discussions, any more than in all the products of the crafts. Now fine and just actions, which political science investigates, admit of much variety and fluctuation of opinion, so that they may be thought to exist only by convention, and not by nature. And goods also give rise to a similar fluctuation because they bring harm to many people; for before now men have been undone by reason of their wealth, and others by reason of their courage. We must be content, then, in speaking of such subjects and with such premisses to indicate the truth roughly and in outline, and in speaking about things which are only for the most part true, and with premisses of the same kind, to reach conclusions that are no better. In the same spirit, therefore, should each type of statement be *received;* for it is the mark of an educated man to look for precision in each class of things just so far as the nature of the subject admits; it is evidently equally foolish to accept probable reasoning from a mathematician and to demand from a rhetorician scientific proofs.

Now each man judges well the things he knows, and of these he is a good judge. And so the man who has been educated in a subject is a good judge of that subject, and the man who has received an all-round education is a good judge

in general. Hence a young man is not a proper hearer of lectures on political science; for he is inexperienced in the actions that occur in life, but its discussions start from these and are about these; and, further, since he tends to follow his passions, his study will be vain and unprofitable, because the end aimed at is not knowledge but action. And it makes no difference whether he is young in years or youthful in character; the defect does not depend on time, but on his living, and pursuing each successive object, as passion directs. For to such persons, as to the incontinent, knowledge brings no profit; but to those who desire and act in accordance with a rational principle knowledge about such matters will be of great benefit.

These remarks about the student, the sort of treatment to be expected, and the purpose of the inquiry, may be taken as our preface.

WHAT IS THE GOOD FOR MAN?

It is generally agreed to be happiness, but there are various views as to what happiness is. What is required at the start is an unreasoned conviction about the facts, such as is produced by a good upbringing

4. Let us resume our inquiry and state, in view of the fact that all knowledge and every pursuit aims at some aide, what it is that we say political science aims at and what is the highest of all goods achievable by action. Verbally there is very general agreement; for both the general run of men and people of superior refinement say that it is happiness, and identify living well and doing well with being happy; but with regard to what happiness is they differ, and the many do not give the same account as the wise. For the former think it is some plain and obvious thing, like pleasure, wealth, or honour; they differ, however, from one another—and often even the same man identifies it with different things, with health when he is ill, with wealth when he is poor; but, conscious of their ignorance, they admire those who proclaim some great ideal that is above their comprehension. Now some thought that apart from these many goods there is an-

other which is self-subsistent and causes the goodness of all these as well. To examine all the opinions that have been held were perhaps somewhat fruitless; enough to examine those that are most prevalent or that seem to be arguable.

Let us not fail to notice, however, that there is a difference between arguments from and those to the first principles. For Plato, too, was right in raising this question and asking, as he used to do, 'Are we on the way from or to the first principles?' There is a difference, as there is in a race-course between the course from the judges to the turning-point and the way back. For, while we must begin with what is known, things are objects of knowledge in two senses—some to us, some without qualification. Presumably, then, *we* must begin with things known to *us*. Hence any one who is to listen intelligently to lecturers about what is noble and just and, generally, about the subjects of political science must have been brought up in good habits. For the fact is the starting-point, and if this is sufficiently plain to him, he will not at the start need the reason as well; and the man who has been well brought up has or can easily get starting-points. And as for him who neither has nor can get them, let him hear the words of Hesiod:

Far best is he who knows all things himself;
Good, he that hearkens when men counsel
    right;
But he who neither knows, nor lays to heart
Another's wisdom, is a useless wight.

Book II • *Moral Virtue*

MORAL VIRTUE, HOW PRODUCED, IN WHAT MEDIUM AND IN WHAT MANNER EXHIBITED

Moral virtue, like the arts, is acquired by repetition of the corresponding acts

1. Virtue, then, being of two kinds, intellectual and moral, intellectual virtue in the main owes both its birth and its growth to teaching (for which reason it requires experience and time), while moral virtue comes about as a result of habit, whence also its name (ἠθική) is one that is formed by a slight variation from the word ἔθος (habit). From this it is also plain that none of the moral virtues arises in us by nature; for nothing that exists by nature can form a habit contrary to its nature. For instance the stone which by nature moves downwards cannot be habituated to move upwards, not even if one tries to train it by throwing it up ten thousand times; nor can fire be habituated to move downwards, nor can anything else that by nature behaves in one way be trained to behave in another. Neither by nature, then, nor contrary to nature do the virtues arise in us; rather we are adapted by nature to receive them, and are made perfect by habit.

Again, of all the things that come to us by nature we first acquire the potentiality and later exhibit the activity (this is plain in the case of the senses; for it was not by often seeing or often hearing that we got these senses, but on the contrary we had them before we used them, and did not come to have them by using them); but the virtues we get by first exercising them, as also happens in the case of the arts as well. For the things we have to learn before we can do them, we learn by doing them, e.g. men become builders by building and lyre-players by playing the lyre; so too we become just by doing just acts, temperate by doing temperate acts, brave by doing brave acts.

This is confirmed by what happens in states; for legislators make the citizens good by forming habits in them, and this is the wish of every legislator, and those who do not effect it miss their mark, and it is in this that a good constitution differs from a bad one.

Again, it is from the same causes and by the same means that every virtue is both produced and destroyed, and similarly every art; for it is from playing the lyre that both good and bad lyre-players are produced. And the corresponding statement is true of builders and of all the rest; men will be good or bad builders as a result of building well or badly. For if this were not so, there would have been no need of a teacher, but all men would have been born good or bad at their craft. This, then, is the case with the virtues also; by doing the acts that we do in our transactions with other men we become just or unjust, and by doing the acts that we do in the presence of danger, and by being habituated to feel fear or confidence, we become brave or cowardly. The same is true of appetites and feelings of anger; some men become temperate and good-tempered, others self-indulgent and irascible, by behaving in one way of the other in the appropriate circumstances. Thus, in one word, states of character arise out of like activities. This is why the activities we exhibit must be of a certain kind; it is because the states of character correspond to the differences between these. It makes no small difference, then, whether we form habits of one kind or of another from our very youth; it makes a very great difference, or rather *all* the difference.

Now neither the virtues nor the vices are *passions,* because we are not called good or bad on the ground of our passion, but are so called on the ground of our virtues and our vices, and because we are neither praised nor blamed for our passions (for the man who feels fear or anger is not praised, nor is the man who simply feels anger blamed, but the man who feels it in a certain way), but for our virtues and our vices we *are* praised or blamed.

Again, we feel anger and fear without choice, but the virtues are modes of choice or involve choice. Further, in respect of the passions we are said to be moved, but in respect of the virtues and the vices we are said not to be moved but to be disposed in a particular way.

For these reasons also they are not *faculties;* for we are neither called good or bad, nor praised or blamed, for the simple capacity of feeling the passions; again, we have the faculties by nature, but we are not made good or bad by nature; we have spoken of this before.

If, then, the virtues are neither passions nor faculties, all that remains is that they should be *states of character.*

Thus we have stated what virtue is in respect of its genus.

The differentia of moral virtue: it is a disposition to choose the mean

6. We must, however, not only describe virtue as a state of character, but also say what sort of state it is. We may remark, then, that every virtue or excellence both brings into good condition the thing of which it is the excellence and makes the work of that thing be done well; e.g. the excellence of the eye makes both the eye and its work good; for it is by the excellence of the eye that we see well. Similarly the excellence of the horse makes a horse both good in itself and good at running and at carrying its rider and at awaiting the attack of the enemy. Therefore, if this is true in every case, the virtue of man also will be the state of character which makes a man good and which makes him do his own work well.

How this is to happen we have stated already, but it will be made plain also by the following consideration of the specific nature of virtue. In everything that is continuous and divisible it is possible to take more, less, or an equal amount, and that either in terms of the thing itself or relatively to us; and the equal is an intermediate between excess and defect. By the intermediate in the object I mean that which is equidistant from each of the extremes, which is one and the same for all men; by the intermediate relatively to us that which is neither too much nor too little— and this is not one, nor the same for all. For instance, if ten is many and two is few, six is the intermediate, taken in terms of the object; for it exceeds and is exceeded by an equal amount; this is intermediate according to arithmetical proportion. But the intermediate relatively to us is not to be taken so; if ten pounds are too much for a particular person to eat and two too little, it does not follow that the trainer will order six pounds; for this also is perhaps too much for the person who is to take it, or too little—too little for Milo,* too much for the beginner in athletic exercises. The same is true of running and wrestling. Thus a master of any art avoids excess and defect, but seeks the intermediate and

*A famous athlete.

chooses this—the intermediate not in the object but relatively to us.

If it is thus, then, that every art does its work well—by looking to the intermediate and judging its works by this standard (so that we often say of good works of art that it is not possible either to take away or to add anything, implying that excess and defect destroy the goodness of works of art, as we say, look to this in their work), and if, further, virtue is more exact and better than any art, as nature also is, then virtue must have the quality of aiming at the intermediate. I mean moral virtue; for it is this that is concerned with passions and actions, and in these there is excess, defect, and the intermediate. For instance, both fear and confidence and appetite and anger and pity and in general pleasure and pain may be felt both too much and too little, and in both cases not well; but to feel them at the right times, with reference to the right objects, towards the right people, with the right motive, and in the right way, is what is both intermediate and best, and this is characteristic of virtue. Similarly with regard to actions also there is excess, defect, and the intermediate. Now virtue is concerned with passions and actions, in which excess is a form of failure, and so is defect, while the intermediate is praised and is a form of success; and being praised and being successful are both characteristics of virtue. Therefore virtue is a kind of mean, since, as we have seen, it aims at what is intermediate.

Again, it is possible to fail in many ways (for evil belongs to the class of the unlimited, as the Pythagoreans conjectured, and good to that of the limited), while to succeed is possible only in one way (for which reason also one is easy and the other difficult—to miss the mark easy, to hit it difficult); for these reasons also, then, excess and defect are characteristic of vice, and the mean of virtue;

For men are good in but one way, but bad in many.

Virtue, then, is a state of character concerned with choice, lying in a mean, i.e., the mean relative to us, this being determined by a rational principle, and by that principle by which the man of practical wisdom would determine it. Now it is a mean between two vices, that which depends on excess and that which depends on defect; and again it is a mean because the vices respectively fall short of or exceed what is right in both passions and actions, while virtue both finds and chooses that which is intermediate. Hence in respect of its substance and the definition which states its essence virtue is a mean, with regard to what is best and right an extreme.

But not every action nor every passion admits of a mean; for some have names that already imply badness, e.g. spite, shamelessness, envy, and in the case of actions adultery, theft, murder; for all of these and suchlike things imply by their names that they are themselves bad, and not the excesses or deficiencies of them. It is not possible, then, ever to be right with regard to them; one must always be wrong. Nor does goodness or badness with regard to such things depend on committing adultery with the right woman, at the right time, and in the right way, but simply to do any of them is to go wrong. It would be equally absurd, then, to expect that in unjust, cowardly, and voluptuous action there should be a mean, an excess, and a deficiency; for at that rate there would be a mean of excess and of deficiency, an excess of excess, and a deficiency of deficiency. But as there is no excess and deficiency of temperance and courage because what is intermediate is in a sense an extreme, so too of the actions we have mentioned there is no mean nor any excess and deficiency, but however they are done they are wrong; for in general there is neither a mean of excess and deficiency, nor excess and deficiency of a mean. . . .

Book X • Happiness
Happiness is good activity, not amusement

6. Now that we have spoken of the virtues, the forms of friendship, and the varieties of pleasure, what remains is to discuss in outline the nature

of happiness, since this is what we state the end of human nature to be. Our discussion will be the more concise if we first sum up what we have said already. We said, then, that it is not a disposition; for if it were it might belong to someone who was asleep throughout his life, living the life of a plant, or, again, to someone who was suffering the greatest misfortunes. If these implications are unacceptable, and we must rather class happiness as an activity, as we have said before, and if some activities are necessary, and desirable for the sake of something else, while others are so in themselves, evidently happiness must be placed among those desirable in themselves, not among those desirable for the sake of something else; for happiness does not lack anything, but is self-sufficient. Now those activities are desirable in themselves from which nothing is sought beyond the activity. And of this nature virtuous actions are thought to be; for to do noble and good deeds is a thing desirable for its own sake.

Pleasant amusements also are thought to be of this nature: we choose them not for the sake of other things; for we are injured rather than benefited by them, since we are led to neglect our bodies and our property. But most of the people who are deemed happy take refuge in such pastimes, which is the reason why those who are ready-witted at them are highly esteemed at the courts of tyrants; they make themselves pleasant companions in the tyrants' favourite pursuits, and that is the sort of man they want. Now these things are thought to be of the nature of happiness because people in despotic positions spend their leisure in them, but perhaps such people prove nothing; for virtue and reason, from which good activities flow, do not depend on despotic position; nor, if these people, who have never tasted pure and generous pleasure, take refuge in the bodily pleasures, should these for that reason be thought more desirable; for boys, too, think the things that are valued among themselves are the best. It is to be expected, then, that, as different things seem valuable to boys and to men, so they should be bad men and to good. Now, as we have often

maintained, those things are both valuable and pleasant which are such to the good man; and to each man the activity in accordance with his own disposition is most desirable, and therefore to the good man that which is in accordance with virtue. Happiness, therefore, does not lie in amusement; it would, indeed, be strange if the end were amusement, and one were to take trouble and suffer hardships all one's life in order to amuse oneself. For, in a word, everything that we choose we choose for the sake of something else—except happiness, which is an end. Now to exert oneself and work for the sake of amusement seems silly and utterly childish. But to amuse oneself in order that one may exert oneself, as Anacharsis* puts it, seems right; for amusement is a sort of relaxation, and we need relaxation because we cannot work continuously. Relaxation, then, is not an end; for it is taken for the sake of activity.

The happy life is thought to be virtuous; now a virtuous life requires exertion, and does not consist in amusement. And we say that serious things are better than laughable things and those connected with amusement, and that the activity of the better of any two things—whether it be two elements of our being or two men—is the more serious; but the activity of the better is *ipso facto* superior and more of the nature of happiness. And any chance person—even a slave—can enjoy the bodily pleasures no less than the best man; but no one assigns to a slave a share in happiness—unless he assigns to him also a share in human life. For happiness does not lie in such occupations, but, as we have said before, in virtuous activities.

Happiness in the highest sense is the contemplative life

7. If happiness is activity in accordance with virtue, it is reasonable that it should be in accordance with the highest virtue; and this will be

---

*A Scythian prince who was believed to have travelled in Greece, and to have been the author of many aphorisms.

that of the best thing in us. Whether it be reason or something else that is this element which is thought to be our natural ruler and guide and to take thought of things noble and divine, whether it be itself also divine or only the most divine element in us, the activity of this in accordance with its proper virtue will be perfect happiness. That this activity is contemplative we have already said.

Now this would seem to be in agreement both with what we said before and with the truth. For, firstly, this activity is the best (since not only is reason the best thing in us, but the objects of reason are the best of knowable objects); and, secondly, it is the most continuous, since we can contemplate truth more continuously than we can *do* anything. And we think happiness ought to have pleasure mingled with it, but the activity of philosophic wisdom is admittedly the pleasantest of virtuous activities; at all events the pursuit of it is thought to offer pleasures marvellous for their purity and their enduringness, and it is to be expected that those who know will pass their time more pleasantly than those who inquire. And the self-sufficiency that is spoken of must belong most to the contemplative activity. For while a philosopher, as well as a just man or one possessing any other virtue, needs the necessaries of life, when they are sufficiently equipped with things of that sort the just man needs people towards whom and with whom he shall act justly, and the temperate man, the brave man, and each of the others is in the same case, but the philosopher, even when by himself, can contemplate truth, and the better the wiser he is; he can perhaps do so better if he has fellow workers, but still he is the most self-sufficient. And this activity alone would seem to be loved for its own sake; for nothing arises from it apart from the contemplating, while from practical activities we gain more or less apart from the action. And happiness is thought to depend on leisure; for we are busy that we may have leisure, and make war that we may live in peace. Now the activity of the practical virtues is exhibited in political or military affairs, but the

actions concerned with these seem to be unleisurely. Warlike actions are completely so (for no one chooses to be at war, or provokes war, for the sake of being at war; anyone would seem absolutely murderous if he were to make enemies of his friends in order to bring about battle and slaughter); but the action of the statesman also is unleisurely, and aims—beyond the political action itself—at despotic power and honours, or at all events happiness, for him and his fellow citizens—a happiness different from political action, and evidently sought as being different. So if among virtuous actions political and military actions are distinguished by nobility and greatness, and these are unleisurely and aim at an end and are not desirable for their own sake, but the activity of reason, which is contemplative, seems both to be superior in serious worth and to aim at no end beyond itself, and to have its pleasure proper to itself (and this augments the activity), and the self-sufficiency, leisureliness, unweariedness (so far as this is possible for man), and all the other attributes ascribed to the supremely happy man are evidently those connected with this activity it follows that this will be the complete happiness of man, if it be allowed a complete term of life (for none of the attributes of happiness is *in*complete).

But such a life would be too high for man; for it is not in so far as he is man that he will live so, but in so far as something divine is present in him; and by so much as this is superior to our composite nature is its activity superior to that which is the exercise of the other kind of virtue. If reason is divine, then, in comparison with man, the life according to it is divine in comparison with human life. But we must not follow those who advise us, being men, to think of human things, and, being mortal, of mortal things, but must, so far as we can, make ourselves immortal, and strain every nerve to live in accordance with the best thing in us; for even if it be small in bulk, much more does it in power and worth surpass everything. This would seem, too, to be each man himself, since it is the authoritative and better part of him. It would be strange, then, if he were to choose not the life of his self but that of something else. And what we said before will apply now: that which is proper to each thing is by nature best and most pleasant for each thing; for man, therefore, the life according to reason is best and pleasantest, since reason more than anything else *is* man. This life therefore is also the happiest.

Study Questions

1. In what sense or senses is Aristotle's moral philosophy teleological?
2. What is Aristotle's defense of the claim that there must be a highest good? What is his argument for identifying it with happiness?
3. How is Aristotle's ethics connected to his theory of human nature regarding the good, happiness, and virtue?
4. What specifically are moral and intellectual virtues, and how can we achieve them? How are these virtues related? How do they differ? Does moral excellence involve intellectual traits? Does intellectual excellence involve moral traits?
5. What is the doctrine of the golden mean? How is the golden mean determined? Who determines what are moral virtues and vices? What moral guidance does Aristotle offer with this doctrine?
6. Is Aristotle's virtue ethics elitist?

Suggestions for Further Reading

Ackrill, J. L. *Aristotle the Philosopher* (Oxford: Oxford University Press, 1981). See Chapter 10 for a development of Aristotle's ethics.

Broadie, S. *Ethics with Aristotle* (Oxford: Oxford University Press, 1991). An exposition of Aristotle's ethical theory in seven chapters.

Joachim, H. H. *Aristotle: The Nicomachean Ethics* (Oxford, Clarendon Press, 1951). An analytical commentary of the arguments presented in the *Nicomachean Ethics* with ample reference to the Greek text.

Rorty, A., ed. *Essays on Aristotle's Ethics* (Berkeley: University of California Press, 1980). See essays 3,7, and 18 for different views of the *Nicomachean Ethics.*

Ross, W. D. *Aristotle,* 2d rev. ed. (London: Methuen, 1930). See Chapter VII for an account of the main features of Aristotle's ethics.

Sparshott, F. *Taking Life Seriously: A Study of the Argument of the Nicomachean Ethics* (Toronto: University of Toronto Press, 1994). A section-by-section analysis of the *Nicomachean Ethics.*

Urmson, J. O. *Aristotle's Ethics* (Oxford: Blackwell, 1988). A ten-chapter introduction designed to be read in conjunction with the *Nicomachean Ethics.*

Epicurus (341/42–270 B.C.E.)

Epicurus was born on the island of Samos, located in the Aegean Sea off the coast of Asia Minor. He eventually settled in Athens and established his famous school, the Garden of Epicurus, which served as a philosophical refuge from the prevailing social unrest and religious anxieties of the times. He was apparently a very charismatic figure in Greece and had a large following of devout students of both sexes and from different social classes. His philosophy was later a source of influence for the ancient Roman philosopher, Lucretius, and for Jeremy Bentham and John Stuart Mill, the modern British philosophers of utilitarianism.

The selected text, a letter Epicurus wrote to Meneoceus, a follower, is one of the few remaining fragments of the more than three hundred philosophical works he is reported to have written. Epicurus' philosophy is labeled "hedonism," from *hedone*—the Greek word for pleasure. The terms *hedonism* and *epicurean* today are associated with a life of indulgence in sensuous pleasures. However, Epicurus' philosophy upholds a life of simplicity, prudence, and good measure. Like Aristippus of Cyrene (his predecessor from the mid-fifth century B.C.E.) and his followers (the Cyrenaics), Epicurus believed that pleasure is both the end of life and the supreme good. However, Epicurus disagreed with them on the nature and importance of pleasure: Whereas the Cyrenaics conceived pleasure as the satisfaction of mainly physical desires, Epicurus viewed it as a negative, or absence—as freedom from bodily pain and mental suffering. He also stressed the importance of the duration of such pleasure over the momentary intensity of enjoyment. Epicurus defined pleasure as a state of tranquillity or unperturbedness (*ataraxia*) of the soul, and he considered virtues such as moderation and temperance conditions for such a state. Because physical pleasures soon fade, trouble the soul, and easily lead to pain, Epicurus gave preeminence to intellectual pleasures and attached value to philosophy as a means for knowing the true pleasures.

In his philosophical quest for the soul's peace, Epicurus developed a cosmology that could dispel the fears troubling his contemporaries concerning death and the gods' arbitrary dispensations of blessings and punishments. In his cosmology, Epicurus borrowed from the fifth-century B.C.E. atomist philosophy of Democritus, who believed that the cosmos is composed of an infinite number of indivisible units (atoms) moving in an infinite void. Like Democritus, Epicurus believed that the soul is itself composed of a special kind of atoms. Death is simply the dissolution of these atoms and—with this—the cessation of our perceptions. Thus, as Epicurus saw it, there is no reason to fear death which "is nothing to us, since so long as we exist, death is not with us; but when death comes, then we do not exist." Epicurus believed that this idea would also put an end to our painful craving for immortality. Moreover, whereas Democritus held that the motion of the atoms was absolutely mechanical (and thus completely determined), Epicurus' cosmology allowed for spontaneous deviations from and irregularities in the mechanical patterns. In Epicurus' view, humans are free in that they are not completely determined by these patterns and are able to make choices concerning the proper pleasures. He argued that since the gods neither create nor oversee the workings of the cosmos, our fears of fate, chance, or divine interventions are thus entirely unfounded.

EPICURUS TO MENEOCEUS

LET NO ONE WHEN YOUNG delay to study philosophy, nor when he is old grow weary of his study. For no one can come too early or too late to secure the health of his soul. And the man who says that the age for philosophy has either not yet come or has gone by is like the man who says that the age for happiness is not yet come to him, or has passed away. Wherefore both when young and old a man must study philosophy, that as he grows old he may be young in blessings through the grateful recollection of what has been, and that in youth he may be old as well, since he will know no fear of what is to come. We must then meditate on the things that make our happiness, seeing that when that is with us we have all, but when it is absent we do all to win it.

The things which I used unceasingly to commend to you, these do and practice, considering them to be the first principles of the good life. First of all believe that god is a being immortal and blessed, even as the common idea of a god is engraved on men's minds, and do not assign to him anything alien to his immortality or ill-suited to his blessedness: but believe about him everything that can uphold his blessedness and immortality. For gods there are, since the knowledge of them is by clear vision. But they are not such as the many believe them to be: for indeed they do not consistently represent them as they believe them to be. And the impious man is not he who denies the gods of the many, but he who attaches to the gods the beliefs of the many. For the statements of the many about the gods are not conceptions derived from sensation, but false suppositions, according to which the greatest misfortunes befall the wicked and the greatest blessings ⟨the good⟩ by the gift of the gods. For men being accustomed always to their own virtues welcome those like themselves, but regard all that is not of their nature as alien.

Become accustomed to the belief that death is nothing to us. For all good and evil consists in sensation, but death is deprivation of sensation. And therefore a right understanding that death is nothing to us makes the mortality of life enjoyable, not because it adds to it an infinite span of time, but because it takes away the craving for immortality. For there is nothing terrible in life for the man who has truly comprehended that there is nothing terrible in not living. So that the man speaks but idly who says that he fears death not because it will be painful when it comes, but because it is painful in anticipation. For that which gives no trouble when it comes, is but an empty pain in anticipation. So death, the most terrifying of ills, is nothing to us, since so long as we exist, death is not with us; but when death comes, then we do not exist. It does not then concern either the living or the dead, since for the former it is not, and the latter are no more.

But the many at one moment shun death as the greatest of evils, at another ⟨yearn for it⟩ as a respite from the ⟨evils⟩ in life. ⟨But the wise man neither seeks to escape life⟩ nor fears the cessation of life, for neither does life offend him nor does the absence of life seem to be any evil. And just as with food he does not seek simply the larger share and nothing else, but rather the most pleasant, so he seeks to enjoy not the longest period of time, but the most pleasant.

And he who counsels the young man to live well, but the old man to make a good end, is foolish, not merely because of the desirability of life, but also because it is the same training which teaches to live well and to die well. Yet much worse still is the man who says it is good not to be born, but

'once born make haste to pass the gates of Death'.

Epicurus, "Epicurus to Meneoceus," trans. C. Bailey. In The Extant Remains. *Oxford: Clarendon Press, 1926.*

For if he says this from conviction why does he not pass away out of life? For it is open to him to do so, if he had firmly made up his mind to this. But if he speaks in jest, his words are idle among men who cannot receive them.

We must then bear in mind that the future is neither ours, nor yet wholly not ours, so that we may not altogether expect it as sure to come, nor abandon hope of it, as if it will certainly not come.

We must consider that of desires some are natural, others vain, and of the natural some are necessary and others merely natural; and of the necessary some are necessary for happiness, others for the repose of the body, and others for very life. The right understanding of these facts enables us to refer all choice and avoidance to the health of the body and ⟨the soul's⟩ freedom from disturbance since this is the aim of the life of blessedness. For it is to obtain this end that we always act, namely, to avoid pain and fear. And when this is once secured for us, all the tempest of the soul is dispersed, since the living creature has not to wander as though in search of something that is missing, and to look for some other thing by which he can fulfil the good of the soul and the good of the body. For it is then that we have need of pleasure, when we feel pain owing to the absence of pleasure; ⟨but when we do not feel pain⟩, we no longer need pleasure. And for this cause we call pleasure the beginning and end of the blessed life. For we recognize pleasure as the first good innate in us, and from pleasure we begin every act of choice and avoidance, and to pleasure we return again, using the feeling as the standard by which we judge every good.

And since pleasure is the first good and natural to us, for this very reason we do not choose every pleasure, but sometimes we pass over many pleasures, when greater discomfort accrues to us as the result of them: and similarly we think many pains better than pleasures, since a greater pleasure comes to us when we have endured pains for a long time. Every pleasure then because of its natural kinship to us is good, yet not every pleasure is to be chosen: even as every pain

also is an evil, yet not all are always of a nature to be avoided. Yet by a scale of comparison and by the consideration of advantages and disadvantages we must form our judgement on all these matters. For the good on certain occasions we treat as bad, and conversely the bad as good.

And again independence of desire we think a great good—not that we may at all times enjoy but a few things, but that, if we do not possess many, we may enjoy the few in the genuine persuasion that those have the sweetest pleasure in luxury who least need it, and that all that is natural is easy to be obtained, but that which is superfluous is hard. And so plain savours bring us a pleasure equal to a luxurious diet, when all the pain due to want is removed; and bread and water produce the highest pleasure, when one who needs them puts them to his lips. To grow accustomed therefore to simple and not luxurious diet gives us health to the full, and makes a man alert for the needful employments of life, and when after long intervals we approach luxuries disposes us better towards them, and fits us to be fearless of fortune.

When, therefore, we maintain that pleasure is the end, we do not mean the pleasures of profligates and those that consist in sensuality, as is supposed by some who are either ignorant or disagree with us or do not understand, but freedom from pain in the body and from trouble in the mind. For it is not continuous drinkings and revellings, nor the satisfaction of lusts, nor the enjoyment of fish and other luxuries of the wealthy table, which produce a pleasant life, but sober reasoning, searching out the motives for all choice and avoidance, and banishing mere opinions, to which are due the greatest disturbance of the spirit.

Of all this the beginning and the greatest good is prudence. Wherefore prudence is a more precious thing even than philosophy: for from prudence are sprung all the other virtues, and it teaches us that it is not possible to live pleasantly without living prudently and honourably and justly, ⟨nor, again, to live a life of prudence, honour, and justice⟩ without living pleasantly. For the virtues are by nature bound up with the pleasant life, and the pleasant life is inseparable from them. For indeed who, think you, is a better man than he who holds reverent opinions concerning the gods, and is at all times free from fear of death, and has reasoned out the end ordained by nature? He understands that the limit of good things is easy to fulfil and easy to attain, whereas the course of ills is either short in time or slight in pain: he laughs at ⟨destiny⟩, whom some have introduced as the mistress of all things. ⟨He thinks that with us lies the chief power in determining events, some of which happen by necessity⟩ and some by chance, and some are within our control; for while necessity cannot be called to account, he sees that chance is inconstant, but that which is in our control is subject to no master, and to it are naturally attached praise and blame. For, indeed, it were better to follow the myths about the gods than to become a slave to the destiny of the natural philosophers: for the former suggests a hope of placating the gods by worship, whereas the latter involves a necessity which knows no placation. As to chance, he does not regard it as a god as most men do (for in a god's acts there is no disorder), nor as an uncertain cause ⟨of all things⟩: for he does not believe that good and evil are given by chance to man for the framing of a blessed life, but that opportunities for great good and a great evil are afforded by it. He therefore thinks it better to be unfortunate in reasonable action than to prosper in unreason. For it is better in a man's actions that what is well chosen ⟨should fail, rather than that what is ill chosen⟩ should be successful owing to chance.

Meditate therefore on these things and things akin to them night and day by yourself, and with a companion like to yourself, and never shall you be disturbed waking or asleep, but you shall live like a god among men. For a man who lives among immortal blessings is not like to a mortal being.

Study Questions

1. What is the overall importance of philosophy in Epicurus' hedonism? Why does he consider prudence the greatest good, even greater than philosophy?
2. What are the appropriate conceptions regarding the gods, death, the future, and the pleasures? Why does Epicurus postulate these as the first principles of the good life?
3. What specifically is *ataraxia* and how can we attain it?
4. What does Epicurus mean when he characterizes pleasure as the first natural good? What is the significance of calling pleasure "the end"?
5. How does Epicurus defend the superiority of the intellectual pleasures?
6. Is Epicurus' hedonist philosophy necessarily based on selfishness?

Suggestions for Further Reading

Bailey, C. *The Greek Atomists and Epicurus* (Oxford: Clarendon Press, 1928). A comparative study. See Part 2, Chapter 10, for a discussion of Epicurus' ethical theory.

Mitsis, P. *Epicurus' Ethical Theory: The Pleasures of Invulnerability* (Ithaca, NY: Cornell University Press, 1988). A ten-chapter analysis of Epicurus' ethics.

Rist, J. M. *Epicurus: An Introduction* (Cambridge: Cambridge University Press, 1972). A basic exposition of Epicurus' philosophy. See Chapter 6 for a discussion of his ethics.

Zeller, E. *Stoics, Epicureans and Sceptics,* trans. O. J. Reichel, rev. ed. (New York: Russell & Russell, 1962). See Chapters XIX and XX for an introduction to Epicurus' ethics.

Epictetus (c. 50–c. 138)

Born in Asia Minor, Epictetus was a slave to one of Nero's soldiers, but he was freed after his master died. While he was a slave, Epictetus received an education because he displayed a remarkable intelligence. Learning the doctrines of Stoic philosophy, he eventually became one of its leading teachers and representatives, like the Greek philosophers before him (Zeno, Chrysippus, and Cleanthes) and distinguished figures of the Roman empire (Cicero, Seneca, and the emperor Marcus Aurelius).

Stoic philosophy has its beginnings in the third century B.C.E., when Zeno founded a school in Athens known for its painted portico or porch (*stoa*). The common term *stoic* is usually applied to the person who remains composed and impervious to the pains and pleasures of life. This approximates the general maxim of Stoicism: Live according to nature. Believing in the oneness and inherent order of the cosmos, the Stoics understood nature as a manifestation of divine reason. As a part of the cosmic whole, human nature shares in this reason. To live according to nature thus means to live according to rational principles. In ethical terms, this involves an emphasis on character and self-mastery. Our freedom lies in our ability to control our inner attitudes while recognizing there are externals beyond our control. The Stoic moral virtues—prudence, courage, temperance, justice—are a matter of the whole person in her community with others. Reason is the unifying principle that links all humans and all societies into one community, under one law. The Stoic ideal of cosmopolitanism is based on this idea that we are citizens of one world, members of one cosmos. The Stoic ethics and ideal of cosmopolitanism were later a source of influence for the early Christian writers and remain alive today in various theories of politics and law.

The *Enchiridion,* or manual, was not actually written by Epictetus—whose writings (if any) have not been preserved—but contains one of his disciple's edited notes. It is a guide for moral conduct based on the principles and precepts of Stoicism. The guiding principle of reason offered by Epictetus is to distinguish between what is and what is not in our control. For this, we must determine what depends entirely and solely upon ourselves, and what is contingent upon other things, events, or persons. The things under our control (conception, choice, desire, aversion) are our internal states, attitudes, and dispositions, whereas those beyond our control are external to us. Our moral responsibility lies in the things we can control. By circumscribing ourselves within that sphere, we can attain true freedom and happiness. The terms *good* and *evil* are themselves properly applied only to this sphere. The Stoic attitude of apathy or lack of passion (*apathes*) is properly directed toward the things beyond one's control as being "nothing to me," including one's own death and those of others. Since we have no control over what happens externally, all we can and ought to control in this regard are our judgments about these occurrences.

Like other Stoic philosophies, Epictetus' ethics seeks to apply the ancient Socratic maxim, "Know thyself," in recognizing our limits and where our freedom and responsibilities lie. This recognition involves seeing our place and playing out our roles within the larger context of society and of the cosmos as a whole. Thus, for Epictetus, ethical wisdom can be attained by keeping our "moral purpose in harmony with nature."

THE ENCHIRIDION

I.

There are things which are within our power, and there are things which are beyond our power. Within our power are opinion, aim, desire, aversion, and, in one word, whatever affairs are our own. Beyond our power are body, property, reputation, office, and, in one word, whatever are not properly our own affairs.

Now, the things within our power are by nature free, unrestricted, unhindered; but those beyond our power are weak, dependent, restricted, alien. Remember, then, that if you attribute freedom to things by nature dependent, and take what belongs to others for your own, you will be hindered, you will lament, you will be disturbed, you will find fault both with gods and men. But if you take for your own only that which is your own, and view what belongs to others just as it really is, then no one will ever compel you, no one will restrict you, you will find fault with no one, you will accuse no one, you will do nothing against your will; no one will hurt you, you will not have an enemy, nor will you suffer any harm.

Aiming therefore at such great things, remember that you must not allow yourself any inclination, however slight, towards the attainment of the others; but that you must entirely quit some of them, and for the present postpone the rest. But if you would have these, and possess power and wealth likewise, you may miss the latter in seeking the former; and you will certainly fail of that by which alone happiness and freedom are procured.

Seek at once, therefore, to be able to say to every unpleasing semblance, "You are but a semblance and by no means the real thing." And then examine it by those rules which you have; and first and chiefly, by this: whether it concerns the things which are within our own power, or those which are not; and if it concerns anything beyond our power, be prepared to say that it is nothing to you.

II.

Remember that desire demands the attainment of that of which you are desirous; and aversion demands the avoidance of that to which you are averse; that he who fails of the object of his desires is disappointed; and he who incurs the object of his aversion is wretched. If, then, you shun only those undesirable things which you can control, you will never incur anything which you shun; but if you shun sickness, or death, or poverty, you will run the risk of wretchedness. Remove [the habit of] aversion, then, from all things that are not within our power, and apply it to things undesirable, which are within our power. But for the present altogether restrain desire; for if you desire any of the things not within our own power, you must necessarily be disappointed; and you are not yet secure of those which are within our power, and so are legiti-

The Enchiridion, *trans. T. W. Higginson. In* The Works of Epictetus. *Boston: Little, Brown, 1866.*

mate objects of desire. Where it is practically necessary for you to pursue or avoid anything, do even this with discretion, and gentleness, and moderation.

III.

With regard to whatever objects either delight the mind, or contribute to use, or are tenderly beloved, remind yourself of what nature they are, beginning with the merest trifles: if you have a favorite cup, that it is but a cup of which you are fond,—for thus, if it is broken, you can bear it; if you embrace your child, or your wife, that you embrace a mortal,—and thus, if either of them dies, you can bear it.

IV.

When you set about any action, remind yourself of what nature the action is. If you are going to bathe, represent to yourself the incidents usual in the bath,—some persons pouring out, others pushing in, others scolding, others pilfering. And thus you will more safely go about this action, if you say to yourself, "I will now go to bathe, and keep my own will in harmony with nature." And so with regard to every other action. For thus, if any impediment arises in bathing, you will be able to say, "It was not only to bathe that I desired, but to keep my will in harmony with nature; and I shall not keep it thus, if I am out of humor at things that happen."

V.

Men are disturbed not by things, but by the views which they take of things. Thus death is nothing terrible, else it would have appeared so to Socrates. But the terror consists in our notion of death, that it is terrible. When, therefore, we are hindered, or disturbed, or grieved, let us never impute it to others, but to ourselves; that is, to our own views. It is the action of an unin-

structed person to reproach others for his own misfortunes; of one entering upon instruction, to reproach himself; and of one perfectly instructed, to reproach neither others nor himself.

VII.

As in a voyage, when the ship is at anchor, if you go on shore to get water, you may amuse yourself with picking up a shell-fish or a truffle in your way, but your thoughts ought to be bent towards the ship, and perpetually attentive, lest the captain should call, and then you must leave all these things, that you may not have to be carried on board the vessel, bound like a sheep; thus likewise in life, if, instead of a truffle or shell-fish, such a thing as a wife or a child be granted you, there is no objection; but if the captain calls, run to the ship, leave all these things, and never look behind. But if you are old, never go far from the ship, lest you should be missing when called for.

VIII.

Demand not that events should happen as you wish; but wish them to happen as they do happen, and you will go on well. . . .

XV.

Remember that you must behave as at a banquet. Is anything brought round to you? Put out your hand, and take a moderate share. Does it pass by you? Do not stop it. Is it not yet come? Do not yearn in desire towards it, but wait till it reaches you. So with regard to children, wife, office, riches; and you will some time or other be worthy to feast with the gods. And if you do not so much as take the things which are set before you, but are able even to forego them, then you will not only be worthy to feast with the gods, but to rule with them also. For, by thus doing, Diogenes and Heraclitus, and others like them, deservedly became divine, and were so recognized.

XVII.

Remember that you are an actor in a drama of such sort as the author chooses,—if short, then in a short one; if long, then in a long one. If it be his pleasure that you should enact a poor man, see that you act it well; or a cripple, or a ruler, or a private citizen. For this is your business, to act well the given part; but to choose it, belongs to another.

XVIII.

When a raven happens to croak unluckily, be not overcome by appearances, but discriminate, and say, "Nothing is portended to *me;* but either to my paltry body, or property, or reputation, or children, or wife. But to *me* all portents are lucky, if I will. For whatsoever happens, it belongs to me to derive advantage therefrom."

XIX.

You can be unconquerable, if you enter into no combat in which it is not in your own power to conquer. When, therefore, you see any one eminent in honors or power, or in high esteem on any other account, take heed not to be bewildered by appearances and to pronounce him happy; for if the essence of good consists in things within our own power, there will be no room for envy or emulation. But, for your part, do not desire to be a general, or a senator, or a consul, but to be free; and the only way to this is a disregard of things which lie not within our own power.

XX.

Remember that it is not he who gives abuse or blows who affronts; but the view we take of these things as insulting. When, therefore, any one provokes you, be assured that it is your own opinion which provokes you. Try, therefore, in the first place, not to be bewildered by appearances. For if you once gain time and respite, you will more easily command yourself.

XXI.

Let death and exile, and all other things which appear terrible, be daily before your eyes, but death chiefly; and you will never entertain any abject thought, nor too eagerly covet anything.

XXX.

Duties are universally measured by relations. Is a certain man your father? In this are implied, taking care of him; submitting to him in all things; patiently receiving his reproaches, his correction. But he is a bad father. Is your natural tie, then, to a *good* father? No, but to a father. Is a brother unjust? Well, preserve your own just relation towards him. Consider not what *he* does, but what *you* are to do, to keep your own will in a state conformable to nature. For another cannot hurt you, unless you please. You will then be hurt when you consent to be hurt. In this manner, therefore, if you accustom yourself to contemplate the relations of neighbor, citizen, commander, you can deduce from each the corresponding duties.

XXXI.

Be assured that the essence of piety towards the gods lies in this, to form right opinions concerning them, as existing, and as governing the universe justly and well. And fix yourself in this resolution, to obey them, and yield to them, and willingly follow them amidst all events, as being ruled by the most perfect wisdom. For thus you will never find fault with the gods, nor accuse them of neglecting you. And it is not possible for this to be effected in any other way than by withdrawing yourself from things which are not within our own power, and by making good or evil to consist only in those which are. For if you suppose any other things to be either good or evil, it is inevitable that, when you are disappointed of what you wish, or incur what you would avoid, you should reproach and blame their authors. . . .

Study Questions

1. What conceptions of human nature and of the cosmos transpire in the distinction between what we can and cannot control? Are they pessimist or optimist views?
2. In what way does the distinction between what lies within our control and what lies beyond it serve as a basis for Epictetus' ethics? How specifically is it related to the Socratic maxim "Know thyself"?
3. Are the examples of things within and beyond our control convincing? Can we clearly distinguish between what is our own doing and what is not? Why is the body included in the latter category?
4. What does Epictetus mean by "moral purpose in harmony with nature"? How can it lead to freedom and happiness?
5. Is Epictetus' moral philosophy based on selfish principles? How are the self and others conceived? How is this conception translated into his conception of our duties toward others? Are these duties compatible with our apathy toward things beyond our control?

Suggestions for Further Reading

Annas, J. *Morality of Happiness* (Oxford: Oxford University Press, 1993). An historical study of ancient ethical theory (including Stoicism) from a systematic and thematic perspective.

Blanshard, B. *Reason and Goodness* (London: Allen & Unwin, 1961). Chapter II provides a critique of the Stoic ideal of reason and morality.

Hicks, R. D. *Stoic and Epicurean* (New York: Russell & Russell, 1962). Chapters 3 and 4 provide an interpretation and comparison of Epictetus' moral philosophy with that of other Stoics.

Rist, J. M., ed. *The Stoics* (Berkeley: University of California Press, 1978). Essay 11 analyzes the Stoic idea of moral action. Essay 12 offers a critique of the Stoic concept of detachment.

Zeller, E. *Stoics, Epicureans and Sceptics,* trans. O. J. Reichel, rev. ed. (New York: Russell & Russell, 1962). See Chapter X for a general introduction to Stoic ethics and Chapters XI and XII for a discussion of its applications to practice.

Augustine (354–430)

Augustinus Aurelius, known as Saint Augustine and called a Father of the Church, is one of Christianity's greatest theologians. He was the son of a Christian mother and a pagan father who lived in Tagaste, a small town in the Roman province of Numidia, in North Africa. Augustine was exposed to the many different cultures and religions coexisting in the crumbling Roman Empire after the emperor Constantine's edict of religious tolerance in 313. Inspired as a young man after reading Cicero's exhortation to "love wisdom," Augustine pursued truth by exploring the different doctrines of his time. One of the most pressing problems for him was how to explain the existence of evil and suffering in a world created by a good God. Finding the Bible lacking in intellectual rigor, Augustine rejected Christianity, to his mother's chagrin, and with the hope of finding a reasonable answer to the question of the existence of evil, embraced Manicheanism. The Manichean doctrine (based on the teachings of the prophet Mani from the third century B.C.E.) was dualist, proposing that two eternal and opposing principles constitute the universe—the good and the evil, light and darkness, soul and matter. Leading a life of sensuous pleasures, Augustine lived with a mistress and their son, far removed from the Christian moral ideals of his mother. However, he later found the Manichean doctrines intellectually unsatisfactory and was drawn to Neoplatonic philosophy as a more rigorous system of thought. Particularly compelling intellectually was the Neoplatonic explanation of evil offered by Plotinus. Drawing from Plato's theory of an eternal, immutable, and supreme good that is the source of all being, Plotinus proposed that "the Good" (or "the One") is the highest reality beyond the physical realm from which all else, including the material world, emanates. Evil is merely the lack, absence, or privation of good, rather than a positive or real thing. This conception would be later appropriated by Augustine in his own formulation of the Christian doctrine of evil.

Still later, living in Milan as a public orator and teacher of rhetoric, Augustine came into contact with Bishop Ambrose, whose sermons he admired initially only for their rhetorical power. Yet, Augustine soon converted back to Christianity after having a religious experience that revealed to him the truth of the Christian life. Baptized by Bishop Ambrose, Augustine later became a priest and was eventually appointed Bishop of Hippo, in North Africa.

Augustine's incorporation of ancient Greek philosophy into Christian theology illustrates his conviction that matters of the intellect and matters of faith are compatible, and must be connected in the Christian life of salvation. In its pursuit of the eternal incorruptible truth, wisdom is an intellectual path toward God, the eternal and perfect creator, himself "the Truth." Finding this Truth is accomplished by inward reflection, for God dwells within each person and illuminates our understanding. However, it is not a matter of intellectual discovery but of divine revelation. Faith must precede the intellect, though the intellect may assist faith in grasping the Truth. Salvation is not—as other theologians (known as the Pelagians and the Donatists) proposed—something we can achieve solely through our individual efforts; rather it is something we can receive only as a gift of God's grace.

Augustine offers a religious ethics whereby the highest good for humans, happiness, is found only in our personal union of love with God. It is an ethics of love by which we are commanded to love God, our creator, and to love our neighbor as we love ourselves. We are free to turn our souls toward or away from God, so that through our wills we can become either morally virtuous or morally evil. Because God, the creator of our wills, is himself perfect goodness, he is not the cause of moral evil. Nor is the will itself the cause, for as one of God's creations it too is good. Moral evil is the turning away of the will from God and from his divine purpose in creating us. It is a privation of good. Thus, the evil will is not an effect, but a defect; its cause is a "deficient" rather than an "efficient" one.

In the *City of God*, Augustine develops a conception of history as a linear sequence of events that begins with the moment of creation and culminates with God's final judgment. In the course of this history, people divide into two kinds: those who turn their soul toward God and those who turn it away from him. The first are citizens of the city of God who, by following the Christian ethics of love, can attain eternal peace. The second are citizens of the earthly city who, in their narcissistic and materialistic loves, can attain only temporal peace. It is not a matter of coincidence that Augustine wrote his treatise (consisting of twenty-two books) over a course of thirteen years (from 413 to 426) during the fall of the Roman Empire. In fact, the *City of God* is a defense of Christianity against the prevailing anti-Christian attitudes that arose from the belief that Rome was being punished by its abandoned pagan gods. Moreover, it offers the first philosophy of history in the European tradition, completed with a religious and moral conception of the universe as God's creation.

CITY OF GOD

3. *That the enemies of God are so, not by nature but by will, which, as it injures them, injures a good nature; for if vice does not injure, it is not vice.*

In Scripture they are called God's enemies who oppose His rule, not by nature, but by vice; having no power to hurt Him, but only themselves. For they are His enemies, not through their power to hurt, but by their will to oppose Him. For God is unchangeable, and wholly proof against injury. Therefore the vice which makes those who are called His enemies resist Him, is an evil not to God, but to themselves. And to them it is an evil, solely because it corrupts the good of their nature. It is not nature, therefore, but vice, which is contrary to God. For that which is evil is contrary to the good. And who will deny that God is the supreme good? Vice, therefore, is contrary to God, as evil to good. Further, the nature it vitiates is a good, and therefore to this good also it is contrary. But while it is contrary to God only as evil to good, it is contrary to the nature it vitiates, both as evil and as hurtful. For to God no evils are hurtful;

but only to natures mutable and corruptible, though, by the testimony of the vices themselves, originally good. For were they not good, vices could not hurt them. For how do they hurt them but by depriving them of integrity, beauty, welfare, virtue, and, in short, whatever natural good vice is wont to diminish or destroy? But if there be no good to take away, then no injury can be done, and consequently there can be no vice. For it is impossible that there should be a harmless vice. Whence we gather, that though vice cannot injure the unchangeable good, it can injure nothing but good; because it does not exist where it does not injure. This, then, may be thus formulated: Vice cannot be in the highest good, and cannot be but in some good. Things solely good, therefore, can in some circumstances exist; things solely evil, never; for even those natures which are vitiated by an evil will, so far indeed as they are vitiated, are evil, but in so far as they are natures they are good. And when a vitiated nature is punished, besides the good it has in being a nature, it has this also, that it is not unpunished. For this is just, and certainly

Augustine. City of God, Vols. I and II, trans. Rev. M. Dods. Edinburgh: T & T Clark, 1881, Books XII and XIX.

everything just is a good. For no one is punished for natural, but for voluntary vices. For even the vice which by the force of habit and long continuance has become a second nature, had its origin in the will. For at present we are speaking of the vices of the nature, which has a mental capacity for that enlightenment which discriminates between what is just and what is unjust.

4. *Of the nature of irrational and lifeless creatures, which in their own kind and order do not mar the beauty of the universe.*

But it is ridiculous to condemn the faults of beasts and trees, and other such mortal and mutable things as are void of intelligence, sensation, or life, even though these faults should destroy their corruptible nature; for these creatures received, at their Creator's will, an existence fitting them, by passing away and giving place to others, to secure that lowest form of beauty, the beauty of seasons, which in its own place is a requisite part of this world. For things earthly were neither to be made equal to things heavenly, nor were they, though inferior, to be quite omitted from the universe. Since, then, in those situations where such things are appropriate, some perish to make way for others that are born in their room, and the less succumb to the greater, and the things that are overcome are transformed into the quality of those that have the mastery, this is the appointed order of things transitory. Of this order the beauty does not strike us, because by our mortal frailty we are so involved in a part of it, that we cannot perceive the whole, in which these fragments that offend us are harmonized with the most accurate fitness and beauty. And therefore, where we are not so well able to perceive the wisdom of the Creator, we are very properly enjoined to believe it, lest in the vanity of human rashness we presume to find any fault with the work of so great an Artificer. At the same time, if we attentively consider even these faults of earthly things, which are neither voluntary nor penal, they seem to illustrate the excellence of the natures themselves, which are all originated and created by God; for it is that

which pleases us in this nature which we are displeased to see removed by the fault,—unless even the natures themselves displease men, as often happens when they become hurtful to them, and then men estimate them not by their nature, but by their utility; as in the case of those animals whose swarms scourged the pride of the Egyptians. But in this way of estimating, they may find fault with the sun itself; for certain criminals or debtors are sentenced by the judges to be set in the sun. Therefore it is not with respect to our convenience or discomfort, but with respect to their own nature, that the creatures are glorifying to their Artificer. Thus even the nature of the eternal fire, penal though it be to the condemned sinners, is most assuredly worthy of praise. For what is more beautiful than fire flaming, blazing, and shining? What more useful than fire for warming, restoring, cooking, though nothing is more destructive than fire burning and consuming? The same thing, then, when applied in one way, is destructive, but when applied suitably, is most beneficial. . . .

5. *That in all natures, of every kind and rank, God is glorified.*

All natures, then, inasmuch as they are, and have therefore a rank and species of their own, and a kind of internal harmony, are certainly good. And when they are in the places assigned to them by the order of their nature, they preserve such being as they have received. And those things which have not received everlasting being, are altered for better or for worse, so as to suit the wants and motions of those things to which the Creator's law has made them subservient; and thus they tend in the divine providence to that end which is embraced in the general scheme of the government of the universe. So that, though the corruption of transitory and perishable things brings them to utter destruction, it does not prevent their producing that which was designed to be their result. And this being so, God, who supremely is, and who therefore created every being which has not supreme existence (for that which was made of nothing could not be equal to Him, and indeed could not be at all had He not made it), is not to be found fault with on account of the creature's faults, but is to be praised in view of the natures He has made.

7. *That we ought not to expect to find any efficient cause of the evil will.*

Let no one, therefore, look for an efficient cause of the evil will; for it is not efficient, but deficient, as the will itself is not an effecting of something, but a defect. For defection from that which supremely is, to that which has less of being,—this is to begin to have an evil will. Now, to seek to discover the causes of these defections,—causes, as I have said, not efficient, but deficient,—is as if some one sought to see darkness, or hear silence. Yet both of these are known by us, and the former by means only of the eye, the latter only by the ear; but not by their positive actuality, but by their want of it. Let no one, then, seek to know from me what I know that I do not know; unless he perhaps wishes to learn to be ignorant of that of which all we know is, that it cannot be known. For those things which are known not by their actuality, but by their want of it, are known, if our expression may be allowed and understood, by not knowing them, that by knowing them they may be not known. For when the eyesight surveys objects that strike the sense, it nowhere sees darkness but where it begins not to see. And so no other sense but the ear can perceive silence, and yet it is only perceived by not hearing. Thus, too, our mind perceives intelligible forms by understanding them; but when they are deficient, it knows them by not knowing them; for "who can understand defects?"[1]

8. *Of the misdirected love whereby the will fell away from the immutable to the mutable good.*

This I do know, that the nature of God can never, nowhere, nowise be defective, and that natures made of nothing can. These latter, how-

ever, the more being they have, and the more good they do (for then they do something positive), the more they have efficient causes; but in so far as they are defective in being, and consequently do evil (for then what is their work but vanity?), they have deficient causes. And I know likewise, that the will could not become evil, were it unwilling to become so; and therefore its failings are justly punished, being not necessary, but voluntary. For its defections are not to evil things, but are themselves evil; that is to say, are not towards things that are naturally and in themselves evil, but the defection of the will is evil, because it is contrary to the order of nature, and an abandonment of that which has supreme being for that which has less. For avarice is not a fault inherent in gold, but in the man who inordinately loves gold, to the detriment of justice, which ought to be held in incomparably higher regard than gold. Neither is luxury the fault of lovely and charming objects, but of the heart that inordinately loves sensual pleasures, to the neglect of temperance, which attaches us to objects more lovely in their spirituality, and more delectable by their incorruptibility. Nor yet is boasting the fault of human praise, but of the soul that is inordinately fond of the applause of men, and that makes light of the voice of conscience. Pride, too, is not the fault of him who delegates power, nor of power itself, but of the soul that is inordinately enamoured of its own power, and despises the more just dominion of a higher authority. Consequently he who inordinately loves the good which any nature possesses, even though he obtain it, himself becomes evil in the good, and wretched because deprived of a greater good.

14. *Of the order and law which obtain in heaven and earth, whereby it comes to pass that human society is served by those who rule it.*

The whole use, then, of things temporal has a reference to this result of earthly peace in the earthly community, while in the city of God it is connected with eternal peace. And therefore, if we were irrational animals, we should desire

[1] Ps. xix. 12.

nothing beyond the proper arrangement of the parts of the body and the satisfaction of the appetites,—nothing, therefore, but bodily comfort and abundance of pleasures, that the peace of the body might contribute to the peace of the soul. For if bodily peace be awanting, a bar is put to the peace even of the irrational soul, since it cannot obtain the gratification of its appetites. And these two together help out the mutual peace of soul and body, the peace of harmonious life and health. For as animals, by shunning pain, show that they love bodily peace, and, by pursuing pleasure to gratify their appetites, show that they love peace of soul, so their shrinking from death is a sufficient indication of their intense love of that peace which binds soul and body in close alliance. But, as man has a rational soul, he subordinates all this which he has in common with the beasts to the peace of his rational soul, that his intellect may have free play and may regulate his actions, and that he may thus enjoy the well-ordered harmony of knowledge and action which constitutes, as we have said, the peace of the rational soul. And for this purpose he must desire to be neither molested by pain, nor disturbed by desire, nor extinguished by death, that he may arrive at some useful knowledge by which he may regulate his life and manners. But, owing to the liability of the human mind to fall into mistakes, this very pursuit of knowledge may be a snare to him unless he has a divine Master, whom he may obey without misgiving, and who may at the same time give him such help as to preserve his own freedom. And because, so long as he is in this mortal body, he is a stranger to God, he walks by faith, not by sight; and he therefore refers all peace, bodily or spiritual or both, to that peace which mortal man has with the immortal God, so that he exhibits the well-ordered obedience of faith to eternal law. But as this divine Master inculcates two precepts,—the love of God and the love of our neighbour,—and as in these precepts a man finds three things he has to love,—God, himself, and his neighbour,—and that he who loves God loves himself thereby, it follows that he must endeavour to get

his neighbour to love God, since he is ordered to love his neighbour as himself. He ought to make this endeavour in behalf of his wife, his children, his household, all within his reach, even as he would wish his neighbour to do the same for him if he needed it; and consequently he will be at peace, or in well-ordered concord, with all men, as far as in him lies. And this is the order of this concord, that a man, in the first place, injure no one, and, in the second, do good to every one he can reach. Primarily, therefore, his own household are his care, for the law of nature and of society gives him readier access to them and greater opportunity of serving them. And hence the apostle says, "Now, if any provide not for his own, and specially for those of his own house, he hath denied the faith, and is worse than an infidel."[2] This is the origin of domestic peace, or the well-ordered concord of those in the family who rule and those who obey. For they who care for the rest rule,—the husband the wife, the parents the children, the masters the servants; and they who are cared for obey,—the women their husbands, the children their parents, the servants their masters. But in the family of the just man who lives by faith and is as yet a pilgrim journeying on to the celestial city, even those who rule serve those whom they seem to command; for they rule not from a love of power, but from a sense of the duty they owe to others—not because they are proud of authority, but because they love mercy.

17. *What produces peace, and what discord, between the heavenly and earthly cities.*

But the families which do not live by faith seek their peace in the earthly advantages of this life; while the families which live by faith look for those eternal blessings which are promised, and use as pilgrims such advantages of time and of earth as do not fascinate and divert them from God, but rather aid them to endure with greater ease, and to keep down the number of those bur-

[2] 1 Tim. v. 8.

dens of the corruptible body which weigh upon the soul. Thus the things necessary for this mortal life are used by both kinds of men and families alike, but each has its own peculiar and widely different aim in using them. The earthly city, which does not live by faith, seeks an earthly peace, and the end it proposes, in the well-ordered concord of civic obedience and rule, is the combination of men's wills to attain the things which are helpful to this life. The heavenly city, or rather the part of it which sojourns on earth and lives by faith, makes use of this peace only because it must, until this mortal condition which necessitates it shall pass away. Consequently, so long as it lives like a captive and a stranger in the earthly city, though it has already received the promise of redemption, and the gift of the Spirit as the earnest of it, it makes no scruple to obey the laws of the earthly city, whereby the things necessary for the maintenance of this mortal life are administered; and thus, as this life is common to both cities, so there is a harmony between them in regard to what belongs to it. But, as the earthly city has had some philosophers whose doctrine is condemned by the divine teaching, and who, being deceived either by their own conjectures or by demons, supposed that many gods must be invited to take an interest in human affairs, and assigned to each a separate function and a separate department . . . and as the celestial city, on the other hand, knew that one God only was to be worshipped . . . it has come to pass that the two cities could not have common laws of religion, and that the heavenly city has been compelled in this matter to dissent, and to become obnoxious to those who think differently, and to stand the brunt of their anger and hatred and persecutions, except in so far as

the minds of their enemies have been alarmed by the multitude of the Christians and quelled by the manifest protection of God accorded to them. This heavenly city, then, while it sojourns on earth, calls citizens out of all nations, and gathers together a society of pilgrims of all languages, not scrupling about diversities in the manners, laws, and institutions whereby earthly peace is secured and maintained, but recognising that, however various these are, they all tend to one and the same end of earthly peace. It therefore is so far from rescinding and abolishing these diversities, that it even preserves and adopts them, so long only as no hindrance to the worship of the one supreme and true God is thus introduced. Even the heavenly city, therefore, while in its state of pilgrimage, avails itself of the peace of earth, and, so far as it can without injuring faith and godliness, desires and maintains a common agreement among men regarding the acquisition of the necessaries of life, and makes this earthly peace bear upon the peace of heaven; for this alone can be truly called and esteemed the peace of the reasonable creatures, consisting as it does in the perfectly ordered and harmonious enjoyment of God and of one another in God. When we shall have reached that peace, this mortal life shall give place to one that is eternal, and our body shall be no more this animal body which by its corruption weighs down the soul, but a spiritual body feeling no want, and in all its members subjected to the will. In its pilgrim state the heavenly city possesses this peace by faith; and by this faith it lives righteously when it refers to the attainment of that peace every good action towards God and man; for the life of the city is a social life.

Study Questions

1. What is Augustine's argument for identifying our highest good with our love of God? What makes this an ethical claim?
2. How does Augustine defend the claim that the universe is good? How does he explain the existence of evil in the universe?

3. What does Augustine mean when he claims that the evil will has a deficient cause? Is he suggesting that we are not morally responsible for our choices?
4. How are reason and faith related in Augustine's ethics?
5. What are the important features distinguishing the heavenly and earthly cities? In what way is this distinction based on a moral and religious understanding of history?

Suggestions for Further Reading

Evans, G. R. *Augustine on Evil* (New York: Cambridge University Press, 1982). A study of the development of Augustine's conception of evil.

Gilson, E. *The Christian Philosophy of Saint Augustine* (New York: Random House, 1960). See the Introduction for a general view of Augustine's philosophy and Part 2 for an exposition of his ethics.

Markus, R. A. *Augustine* (New York: Doubleday Anchor, 1972). A collection of essays. See the Introduction for an analysis of Augustine's competing roles as a philosopher and theologian.

Portalié, E. *A Guide to the Thought of Saint Augustine* (Chicago: Regnery, 1960). Chapter XV provides an introduction to Augustine's moral theology.

Preston, R. "Christian Ethics," in *A Companion to Ethics*, ed. P. Singer (Oxford; Cambridge, MA: Blackwell, 1991). A general introduction to the Christian tradition in ethics.

Moses Maimonides (1135–1204)

Maimonides, whose Hebrew name is "Rabbam" (for "Our Rabbi Moses son of Maimon"), was born in Córdoba, Spain. After a period of peaceful coexistence between the Jewish and Islamic communities living in Córdoba, the religious intolerance of the Mohammedans forced the Jews to flee Spain. Maimonides and his family eventually settled in Cairo, Egypt, where Maimonides became a court physician to the ruler Saladin and combined this task with his spiritual duties as head of the Jewish Community in Egypt. At the same time, Maimonides managed to write scholarly works on Judaic theology and philosophy.

Through his exposure to Islamic philosophy, Maimonides developed an appreciation for ancient Greek philosophy, especially for the Neoplatonists and, later, for Aristotle. Maimonides sought to reconcile the apparent metaphysical and ethical differences between the principles of Jewish faith and the principle of reason in natural science and philosophy. His major works reflect his attempt to develop a cogent understanding of the Jewish law and faith. In his *Misneh Torah,* or *Review of [Talmudic] Law,* for example, Maimonides codified the Jewish law while he developed a notion of God that agrees in part with Neoplatonic and Aristotelian conceptions.

Although Maimonides believed that prophecy and philosophy can be united in the search for truth, he insisted that the visions of the prophets far exceeded the demonstrative proofs of the philosophers. For him, the truth of God's existence can be reached through philosophical reasoning such as that of Aristotle—who argued that God is the final cause of the universe. Yet, unlike Aristotle, Maimonides proposed that God is the creator of all things. He also argued against various philosophical and religious notions, such as that God is a plurality of persons, that God has corporeal features, or that God's supreme will is absolutely arbitrary or unbound to anything higher. In contrast, Maimonides proposed God as an absolute unity or one who is incorporeal, and whose will is in harmony with his divine intellect and its supreme wisdom. Like the Neoplatonists—who believed that God's divine intellect emanates or overflows from its supreme perfection onto the human being—Maimonides emphasized further that it is because of "the divine intellect conjoined with man" that we are in God's image and likeness.

Insisting that God's divine nature as the absolute being cannot be known positively, Maimonides developed a "negative theology"; that is, if we cannot say what God is without limiting his perfection, we can properly say only what God is not. Thus, when we ascribe or affirm positive attributes to God, we should interpret these attributes negatively. For Maimonides, these negative attributes bring us "nearer . . . to the cognition and apprehension of God." Because Maimonides emphasized the importance of knowing God and used many positive attributes to characterize God in his own philosophy, there is considerable debate over how to interpret his seemingly paradoxical position.

Written in 1190, *The Guide of the Perplexed* is Maimonides' best-known work. Dedicating this treatise to a favorite disciple, Rabbi Joseph, Maimonides states that he composed it for him and others like him to guide them out of their perplexity and to truth concerning divine matters. Maimonides explicitly intended readers are those who have believed and followed the Jewish law in their hearts but have become perplexed over its meanings after learning how to use their reason in natural science and philosophy. Because they are confused about whether to follow their faith or their reason when interpreting the Jewish law, Maimonides' stated purpose is to explain the meanings of certain terms and parables that appear in the sacred books of the prophets—in the "Account of the Beginning" (concerning creation) and the "Account of the Chariot" (concerning Ezekiel's prophecies).

In writing *The Guide of the Perplexed*, Maimonides had to find a way to avoid violating the Jewish law's prohibition against explaining its doctrines in public. This prohibition has the purpose of ensuring that only those who are intellectually and spiritually fit may gain access to its sacred secrets. Maimonides managed to uphold this sacred principle of secrecy by writing his treatise in a sort of secret code—by scattering the chapter headings, giving indirect clues to important points, and deliberately contradicting himself on others. Maimonides is thus purposely obscure, letting "truths be glimpsed and concealed again." However, he provides the key for his intended readers by urging them to connect the chapters and grasp every word that appears throughout the text, stating that "the diction . . . has not been chosen at haphazard, but with great exactness and exceeding precision." Although Maimonides believed that beginners could derive partial benefit from reading the treatise, he was hopeful that apostates and pedantics would find it unbearable to read.

Maimonides' main principle of guidance of the perplexed is exegetical; that is, he guides them by showing them how to interpret certain terms and parables. Crucial to this enterprise is the awareness that some terms and parables can have various meanings, which may differ or oppose one another and may even remain concealed to the unobservant reader. Aware of the multiplicity of meanings, the careful reader can begin to weed out incorrect interpretations of the divine words. This process of discernment requires those who are perplexed to apply the same intellect they developed through the study of natural science and philosophy to their interpretation of the sacred scriptures. By applying reason to matters of faith in this way they will be able to arrive at the true and proper meanings, which are often lost in their ordinary and literal interpretations.

The following selection is the second chapter of the First Part of the *Guide.* Maimonides maintains here that morality is not a matter of intellect but of passions and preferences. The intellect is exclusively concerned with truth and falsehood; that is, with the realm of knowledge. The moral distinction between "the fine and bad," however, is not a matter of knowledge but "of things generally accepted as known," or opinion. Against the view that morality is our "noblest" trait, Maimonides argues that our highest dignity resides in our intellect, which "God made overflow unto" us. He interprets the Garden of Eden episode as an account of human deterioration, from a life of intellectual contemplation and purity to a life consumed with moral judgments of "the bad or fine." Given the freedom to choose, Adam chose to disobey God's first commandment and to follow his own "pleasures and imaginings," rather than his intellect. His punishment was to be banished from the life of intellectual peace to one of physical hardships and moral uncertainty. Because our morality depends on something other than the intellect, human laws are arbitrary and conventional. Yet, through the prophets, God provides us with his divine and absolute law.

THE GUIDE OF THE PERPLEXED

YEARS AGO A LEARNED MAN propounded as a challenge to me a curious objection. It behooves us now to consider this objection and our reply invalidating it. However, before mentioning this objection and its invalidation, I shall make the following statement. Every Hebrew knew that the term *Elohim* is equivocal, designating the deity, the angels, and the rulers governing the cities. *Ongelos the Proselyte,* peace be on him, has made it clear, and I his clarification is correct, that in the dictum of Scripture, *And ye shall be as Elohim,* *knowing good and evil,*[1] the last sense is intended. For he has translated: *And ye shall be as rulers.*

After thus having set forth the equivocality of this term, we shall begin to expound the objection. This is what the objector said: It is manifest from the clear sense of the biblical text that the primary purpose with regard to man was that he should be, as the other animals are, devoid of intellect, of thought, and of the capacity to distin-

[1] Gen. 3:5.

Moses Maimonides. The Guide of the Perplexed, *trans. S. Pines. Chicago and London: University of Chicago Press, 1963, Part I, Chapter 2. Copyright © The University of Chicago Press.*

guish between good and evil. However, when he disobeyed, his disobedience procured him as its necessary consequence the great perfection peculiar to man, namely, his being endowed with the capacity that exists in us to make this distinction. Now this capacity is the noblest of the characteristics[2] existing in us; it is in virtue of it that we are constituted as substances. Now it is a thing to be wondered at that man's punishment for his disobedience should consist in his being granted a perfection that he did not possess before, namely, the intellect. This is like the story told by somebody that a certain man from among the people disobeyed and committed great crimes, and in consequence was made to undergo a metamorphosis,[3] becoming a star in heaven. This was the intent and the meaning of the objection, though it was not textually as we have put it.

Hear now the intent of our reply. We said: O you who engage in theoretical speculation using the first notions that may occur to you and come to your mind and who consider withal that you understand a book that is the guide of the first and the last men while glancing through it as you would glance through a historical work or a piece of poetry—when, in some of your hours of leisure, you leave off drinking and copulating: collect yourself and reflect, for things are not as you thought following the first notion that occurred to you, but rather as is made clear through reflection upon the following speech.[4] For the intellect that God made overflow unto man and that is the latter's ultimate perfection, was that which *Adam* had been provided with before he disobeyed. It was because of this that it was said of him that he was created *in the image of God and in His likeness*. It was likewise on account of it that he was addressed by God and given commandments, as it says: *And the Lord | God commanded, and so on.*[5] For commandments are not given to beasts and beings devoid of intellect. Through the intellect one distinguishes between truth and falsehood, and that was found in [Adam] in its perfection and integrity. Fine and bad,[6] on the other hand, belong to the things generally accepted as known,[7] not to those cognized by the intellect. For one does not say: it is fine that heaven is spherical, and it is bad that the earth if flat; rather one says true and false with regard to these assertions. Similarly one expresses in our language the notions of truth and falsehood by means of the terms *emeth* and *sheqer,* and those of fine and bad by means of the terms *tov* and *ra'.*[8] Now man in virtue of his intellect knows *truth* from *falsehood;* and this holds good for all intelligible things. Accordingly when man was in his most perfect and excellent state, in accordance with his inborn disposition and possessed of his intellectual cognitions—because of which it is said of him: *Thou hast made him but little lower than Elohim*[9]—he had no faculty that was engaged in any way in the consideration of generally accepted things, and he did not apprehend them. So among these generally accepted things even that which is most manifestly bad, namely, uncovering the genitals, was not bad according to him, and he did not apprehend that it was bad. However, when he disobeyed and inclined toward his desires of the imagination and the pleasures of his corporeal senses—inasmuch as it is said: *that the tree was good for food and that it was a delight to the eyes*[10]—he was punished by being deprived of that intellectual apprehension. He

---

[2] *ma'ānī.* The term has many meanings and often, as in this passage, cannot be satisfactorily translated.

[3] The Arabic verb sometimes designates a particular kind of transmigration.

[4] The word may also refer to the scriptural story, but the translation given in the text is somewhat more probable.

[5] Gen. 2:16.

[6] These two terms, rather than good and evil, have been chosen because the Arabic text does not use here the two most common terms (*al-khayr wa'l-sharr* employed earlier in this chapter) denoting the two notions in question, but rather has *al-ḥasan* and *al-qabīḥ.*

[7] The expression, "the words (the things) generally accepted as known," renders the Arabic term *al-mashhūrāt,* which is used as a translation of the Greek *endoza.*

[8] In Hebrew.

[9] Ps. 8:6.

[10] Gen. 3:6.

therefore disobeyed the commandment that was imposed upon him on account of his intellect and, becoming endowed with the faculty of apprehending generally accepted things, he became absorbed in judging things to be bad or fine. Then he knew how great his loss was, what he had been deprived of, and upon what a state he had entered. Hence it is said: *And ye shall be like Elohim knowing good and evil;*[11] and not: *knowing the false and the true,* or *apprehending the false and the true.* With regard to what is of necessity, there is no *good* and *evil* at all, but only the *false* and the *true.* Reflect on the dictum: *And the eyes of them both were opened, and they knew that they were naked.*[12] It is not said: *And the eyes of them both were opened, | and they saw.* For what was seen previously was exactly that which was seen afterwards. There had been no membrane over the eye that was now removed, but rather he entered upon another state in which he considered as bad things that he had not seen in that light before. Know moreover that this expression, I mean, *to open,*[13] refers only to uncovering mental vision and in no respect is applied to the circumstance that the sense of sight has been newly acquired. Thus: *And God opened her eyes;*[14] *Then the eyes of the blind shall be opened;*[15] *Opening the ears, he heareth not*[16]—a verse that is analogous to its dictum, *That have eyes to see and see not.*[17] Now concerning its dictum with regard to *Adam*—*He changes his face and Thou sendest him forth*[18]—the interpretation and explanation

of the verse are as follows: when the direction toward which man tended[19] changed, he was driven forth. For *panim*[20] is a term deriving from the verb *panoh* [*to turn*], since man turns his face toward the thing he wishes to take as his objective. The verse states accordingly that when man changed the direction toward which he tended and took as his objective the very thing a previous commandment had bidden him not to aim at, he was driven out of the *Garden of Eden.* This was the punishment corresponding to his disobedience; it was *measure for measure.* He had been given license to eat good things and to enjoy ease and tranquillity. When, however, as we have said, he became greedy, followed his pleasures and his imaginings, and ate what he had been forbidden to eat, he was deprived of everything and had to eat the meanest kinds of foods, which he had not used as aliment before—and this only after toil and labor. As it says: *Thorns also and thistles shall it bring forth to thee, and so on; In the sweat of thy brow, and so on.*[21] And it explains and says: *And the Lord God sent him forth from the Garden of Eden, to till the ground.*[22] And God reduced him, with respect to his food and most of his circumstances, to the level of the beast. It says accordingly: *And thou shalt eat the grass of the field.*[23] And it also says in explanation of this story: *Adam,*[24] *unable to dwell in dignity, is like the beasts that speak not.*[25]

Praise be to the Master of the will whose aims and wisdom cannot be apprehended!

---

[11] Gen. 3:5.
[12] Gen. 3:7.
[13] Used in the verse.
[14] Gen. 21:19.
[15] Isa. 35:5.
[16] Isa. 42:20.
[17] Ezek. 12:2.
[18] Job 14:20.

[19] The Arabic word derives from a root from which the usual word for "face" is likewise derived.
[20] The Hebrew word for "face."
[21] Gen. 3:18–19.
[22] Gen. 3:23.
[23] Gen. 3:18.
[24] Or: man.
[25] Ps. 49:13.

Study Questions

1. What is the objector's conception of human nature and morality? What characterizes his manner of arguing for these points? Why do you think Maimonides presents him in this style?
2. What points does Maimonides make (directly and indirectly) in response to the objector? What is Maimonides' conception of human nature and morality? What consequences can we draw from this about the value and validity of human laws and ethics?
3. Why do you think Maimonides uses different terms such as *good* or *fine* and *evil* or *bad* in different places? What is his purpose in explaining what the name Elohim stands for? How is this connected to the phrase "like Elohim knowing good and evil"?
4. Is Maimonides' moral theory elitist? In what way or ways?
5. Eve is not explicitly mentioned in the selection. What is the significance of this fact? Are there implicit references to her and her role in the Garden of Eden episode? What does all this imply about the conception of woman in relation to man?

Suggestions for Further Reading

Buijes, J. A., ed. *Maimonides: A Collection of Critical Essays* (Notre Dame, IN: University of Notre Dame Press, 1988). Contains three essays directly pertaining to ethics and divine law.

Fox, M. *Interpreting Maimonides: Studies in Methodology, Metaphysics, and Moral Philosophy* (Chicago and London: University of Chicago Press, 1990). See Part II, Chapters 7 and 8, for aspects of Maimonides' ethical theory.

Klein, C. *The Credo of Maimonides: A Synthesis* (New York: Philosophical Library, 1958). See Chapters 4 and 5 for a view of Maimonides' moral philosophy.

Singer, P. *A Companion to Ethics* (Oxford; Cambridge, MA: Blackwell Reference, 1991). For an introduction to the general principles of Jewish ethics, see M. Kellner's "Jewish Ethics."

Weiss, R. L. *Maimonides' Ethics* (Chicago: University of Chicago Press, 1991). An analysis of Maimonides' ethics and its Aristotelian influences.

Thomas Aquinas (c. 1225–1274)

Thomas Aquinas was born in the Castle of Roccasecca in Aquino, near Naples. His father was the Count of Aquino and his uncle was the Abbott of Monte Casino—the abbey where Thomas Aquinas was educated in his early years by Benedictine monks. While studying at the University of Naples, Aquinas decided to join the Dominicans, an order of friars who uphold a life of religious devotion, poverty, and chastity. His parents preferred the then more prestigious and politically influential order of the Benedictines. So, they had him locked in their castle for a year hoping to change his mind. Remaining steadfast in his choice, Aquinas left his home and became a Dominican friar.

Aquinas studied under Albert the Great, a renowned scholar who supported the study of Aristotle's works—particularly those that had been preserved by Arab philosophers but had remained unknown in Europe until its contact with the Islamic world during the High Middle Ages. Aquinas later surpassed his teacher with his incorporation of Aristotelian philosophy into Christian theology. While his fellow students called him the "dumb ox" (because of his large build and slow, methodical manners), Albert defended Aquinas by predicting he "will bellow so loud his bellowing will fill the world." Aquinas became a highly respected teacher and lecturer in theology, wrote prolifically, served as a consultant in important Church councils and as a mediator in ecclesiastical controversies between different clerical orders. Prone to intense states of absorption, Aquinas reported, a year before his death, that he had had experiences of mystical union and ecstasy. As he confided to a friend, these experiences led him to declare "all I have written seems like straw to me." After he died, some of his works were condemned by Church authorities, though only briefly. He was later canonized as Saint Thomas Aquinas.

Aquinas' contribution to the European philosophical tradition lies in his synthesis of ancient Greek philosophy with Christian theology, for he combines principles of reason and faith into a grand systematic account of God and the universe. Like Aristotle, Aquinas held a teleological conception of the universe, believing that all things act for an end (*telos*) or have a final cause (their "what for"). Unlike Aristotle, however, Aquinas believed that God is the perfect creator of the universe and that the world can be understood in terms of God's divine plan and supernatural order. Aristotle had defined humans as rational beings, and he argued that we achieve our excellence and greatest happiness by exercising our highest faculty—reason—in intellectual contemplation. In Aquinas' view, however, we possess more than the natural faculty of reason, for we are endowed with a supernatural soul that has an afterlife and finds its highest good in the vision of God. Though natural reason can aid in establishing some religious truths, the human soul can progress to other truths only through divine revelation. Thus, while believing in the harmony of reason and faith, and of the natural with the divine, Aquinas conceived of philosophy as a handmaiden to theology.

Like Aristotle's ethics, Aquinas' moral theory is teleological—conceiving human action in terms of ends or goods—and eudaimonistic—pointing to happiness or well-being (*eudaimonia*) as the human being's highest good. Aquinas also agreed with Aristotle's conception of excellence or virtue as being a matter of character, of developing good traits through habit (moral virtue) or through intellectual discipline (intellectual virtue). However, because for Aquinas the greatest happiness or good for humans consists in the sublime vision of God, the highest excellence in the human soul is neither intellectual (as Aristotle believed) nor moral, but theological or divine.

Aquinas proposed that God's divine plan is inscribed in the form of an eternal law that determines and governs the universe according to his perfect reason. Thus, all things are designed by God to tend toward their end, which is their proper good. As rational beings, humans are special because they can understand and voluntarily conduct themselves in accordance with the eternal law. By virtue of our natural faculty of reason, we share in God's eternal reason and participate in his eternal law. This participation is what Aquinas calls "natural law," which he argues is the same in all humans. By this he means that, as rational beings, all of us have a natural or innate sense of good and evil. When applied to action, our (practical) reason naturally aims toward our good and away from evil. The good that is proper to us as rational beings resides in our reason, which seeks to know God and to live among other rational beings. However, our highest good as beings who are supernaturally endowed lies beyond our natural reason, in the beatific vision of God.

The *Summa Theologica* (Theological Summary) has the purpose of giving beginners a systematic understanding of Christian theology. This complex and imposing masterpiece is divided into four parts and covers 512 topics or "Questions," each with its own subtopics or "Articles" phrased as questions. Aquinas follows an elaborate structure of discussion, but our selections simply contain some of his questions and the core arguments with which he answers these questions by discussing what constitutes human happiness, characterizing the theological virtues, and defining and relating the eternal and natural laws.

SUMMA THEOLOGICA

Question 2, Article 8. Whether Any Created Good Constitutes Man's Happiness?

We proceed thus to the Eighth Article: It seems that some created good constitutes man's happiness.

Objection 1. For Dionysius says (*Div. Nom.* vii) that "Divine wisdom unites the ends of first things to the beginnings of second things," from which we may gather that the summit of a lower nature touches the base of the higher nature. But man's highest good is happiness. Since then the angel is above man in the order of nature, as stated in the First Part (Q.CXI, A. I; Q. CVIII, AA. 2, 8; Q. CXI, A. I), it seems that man's happiness consists in man somehow reaching to the angel.

Obj. 2. Further, the last end of each thing is that which, in relation to it, is perfect; hence the part is for the whole, as for its end. But the universe of creatures which is called the macrocosm, is compared to man who is called the microcosm, as perfect to imperfect. Therefore man's happiness consists in the whole universe of creatures.

Obj. 3. Further, man is made happy by that in which his natural desire takes its rest. But man's desire does not reach out to a good surpassing his capacity. Since then man's capacity does not include that good which surpasses the limits of all creation, it seems that man can be made happy by some created good. Consequently some created good constitutes man's happiness.

On the contrary, Augustine says, "As the soul is the life of the body, so God is man's life of happiness; of Whom it is written": *Happy is that people whose God is the Lord* (Ps. 143 15).

I answer that, It is impossible for any created good to constitute man's happiness. For happiness is the perfect good, which, quiets the appetite altogether since it would not be the last end if something yet remained to be desired. Now the object of the will, that is, of man's appetite, is the universal good, just as the object of the intellect is the universal true. Hence it is evident that nothing can quiet man's will except the

Saint Thomas Aquinas, Summa Theologica, *Vols. 1 and 2, trans. the English Dominican Fathers. New York: Benzinger, 1947, Vol. 2, Part I of the Second Part, Question 2, Art. 8; Question 3, Art. 8; Question 5, Art. 5; Question 62, Art. 1; Question 91, Art. 1 & 2; Question 94, Art. 2 & 4.*

universal good. This is to be found not in any creature, but in God alone, because every creature has goodness by participation. Therefore God alone can satisfy the will of man, according to the words of Ps. 102.5: *Who satisfieth thy desire with good things.* Therefore God alone constitutes man's happiness.

Reply Obj. 1. The summit of man does indeed touch the base of the angelic nature, by a kind of likeness; but man does not rest there as in his last end, but reaches out to the universal fount itself of good, which is the common object of happiness of all the blessed, as being the infinite and perfect good.

Reply Obj. 2. If a whole be not the last end, but ordered to a further end, then the last end of its part is not the whole itself, but something else. Now the universe of creatures, to which man is related as part to whole, is not the last end, but is ordered to God, as to its last end. Therefore the last end of man is not the good of the universe, but God Himself.

Reply Obj. 3. Created good is not less than that good of which man is capable, as of something intrinsic and inherent to him, but it is less than the good of which he is capable as of an object, and which is infinite. And the participated good which is in the angel, and in the whole universe, is a finite and restricted good.

Question 3, Article 8. Whether Man's Happiness Consists in the Vision of the Divine Essence?

We proceed thus to the Eighth Article:—

Objection 1. It would seem that man's happiness does not consist in the vision of the Divine Essence. For Dionysius says (*Myst. Theol.* i) that by that which is highest in his intellect, man is united to God as to something altogether unknown. But that which is seen in its essence is not altogether unknown. Therefore the final perfection of the intellect, namely, happiness, does not consist in God being seen in His Essence.

Obj. 2. Further, the higher perfection belongs to the higher nature. But to see His own Essence is the perfection proper to the Divine intellect.

Therefore the final perfection of the human intellect does not reach to this, but consists in something less.

On the contrary, It is written (1 Jo. iii. 2): *When He shall appear, we shall be like to Him; and* (Vulg., *because*) *we shall see Him as He is.*

I answer that, Final and perfect happiness can consist in nothing else than the vision of the Divine Essence. To make this clear, two points must be observed. First, that man is not perfectly happy, so long as something remains for him to desire and seek: secondly, that the perfection of any power is determined by the nature of its object. Now the object of the intellect is *what a thing is, i.e.,* the essence of a thing, according to *De Anima* iii. 6. Wherefore the intellect attains perfection, in so far as it knows the essence of a thing. If therefore an intellect know the essence of some effect, whereby it is not possible to know the essence of the cause, *i.e.* to know of the cause *what it is;* that intellect cannot be said to reach that cause simply, although it may be able to gather from the effect the knowledge that the cause is. Consequently, when man knows an effect, and knows that it has a cause, there naturally remains in man the desire to know about that cause, *what it is.* And this desire is one of wonder, and causes inquiry, as is stated in the beginning of the *Metaphysics* (i. 2). For instance, if a man, knowing the eclipse of the sun, consider that it must be due to some cause, and know not what that cause is, he wonders about it, and from wondering proceeds to inquire. Nor does this inquiry cease until he arrive at a knowledge of the essence of the cause.

If therefore the human intellect, knowing the essence of some created effect, knows no more of God than *that He is;* the perfection of that intellect does not yet reach simply the First Cause, but there remains in it the natural desire to seek the cause. Wherefore it is not yet perfectly happy. Consequently, for perfect happiness the intellect needs to reach the very Essence of the First Cause. And thus it will have its perfection through union with God as with that object, in which alone man's happiness consists, as stated above (AA. 1, 7; Q. 2, A. 8).

Reply Obj. 1. Dionysius speaks of the knowledge of wayfarers journeying towards happiness.

Reply Obj. 2. As stated above (Q. 1, A. 8), the end has a twofold acceptation. First, as to the thing itself which is desired: and in this way, the same thing is the end of the higher and of the lower nature, and indeed of all things, as stated above (*ibid.*). Secondly, as to the attainment of this thing; and thus the end of the higher nature is different from that of the lower, according to their respective habitudes to that thing. So then the happiness of God, Who, in understanding his Essence, comprehends It, is higher than that of a man or angel who sees It indeed, but comprehends It not.

Question 5, Article 5. Whether Man Can Attain Happiness by His Natural Powers?

We proceed thus to the Fifth Article: It seems that man can attain Happiness by his natural powers.

Objection 1. For nature does not fail in necessary things. But nothing is so natural to man as that by which he attains the last end. Therefore this is not lacking to human nature. Therefore man can attain Happiness by his natural powers.

Obj. 2. Further, since man is more noble than irrational creatures, it seems that he must be more self-sufficient. But irrational creatures can attain their end by their natural powers. Much more therefore can man attain Happiness by his natural powers.

Obj. 3. Further, "Happiness is a perfect operation," according to the Philosopher. Now the beginning of a thing and its perfecting pertain to the same principle. Since, therefore, the imperfect operation, which is as it were the beginning in human operations, is subject to man's natural power, by which he is master of his own actions, it seems that he can attain to perfect operation, that is, Happiness, by his natural powers.

On the contrary, Man is naturally the principle of his action by his intellect and will. But final Happiness prepared for the saints surpasses the intellect and will of man; for the Apostle says (I Cor. 2. 9): *Eye hath not seen, nor ear heard, neither hath it entered into the heart of man, what things God hath prepared for them that love Him.* Therefore man cannot attain Happiness by his natural powers.

I answer that, Imperfect happiness that can be had in this life can be acquired by man by his natural powers, in the same way as virtue, in whose operation it consists; on this point we shall speak further on (Q. LXIII). But man's perfect Happiness, as stated above (Q. III. A.8), consists in the vision of the Divine Essence. Now the vision of God's Essence surpasses the nature not only of man, but also of every creature, as was shown in the First Part (Q. XII. A. 4). For the natural knowledge of every creature is in keeping with the mode of its substance; thus it is said of the intelligence (*De Causis*) that it knows things that are above it, and things that are below it, according to the mode of its substance. But every knowledge that is according to the mode of created substance falls short of the vision of the Divine Essence, which infinitely surpasses all created substance. Consequently neither man, nor any creature, can attain final Happiness by his natural powers.

Reply Obj. 1. Just as nature does not fail man in necessaries, although it has not provided him with weapons and clothing as it provided other animals, because it gave him reason and hands, with which he is able to get these things for himself, so neither did it fail man in things necessary, by not giving him the means to attain Happiness, since this was impossible. But it did give him free choice, with which he can turn to God, that He may make him happy. "For what we do by means of our friends, is done, in a sense, by ourselves."

Reply Obj. 2. The nature that can attain perfect good, although it needs help from without in order to attain it, is of more noble condition than a nature which cannot attain perfect good but attains some imperfect good, although it need no help from without in order to attain it, as the Philosopher says. Thus he is better disposed to health who can attain perfect health, even though by means of medicine, than he who can attain but imperfect health without the help of medicine. And therefore the rational creature, which can attain the perfect good of Happiness, but needs the Divine assistance for the purpose, is more perfect than the irrational creature, which is not capable of attaining this good, but attains some imperfect good by its natural powers.

Reply Obj. 3. When imperfect and perfect are of the same species, they can be caused by the same power. But this does not follow of necessity, if they be of different species, for not everything that can cause the disposition of matter can confer the final perfection. Now the imperfect operation, which is subject to man's natural power, is not of the same species as that perfect operation which is man's happiness, since operation takes its species from its object. Consequently the argument does not prove.

Question 62, Article 1. Whether There Are Any Theological Virtues?

We proceed thus to the First Article: It would seem that there are not any theological virtues.

Objection 1. For according to the *Physics*, "virtue is the disposition of a perfect thing to that which is best; and by perfect, I mean that which is disposed according to nature." But that which is Divine is above man's nature. Therefore the theological virtues are not virtues of a man.

Obj. 2. Further, theological virtues are quasi-Divine virtues. But the Divine virtues are exemplars, as stated above (Q. LXI, A. 5), which are not in us but in God. Therefore the theological virtues are not virtues of man.

Obj. 3. Further, the theological virtues are so called because they direct us to God, Who is the first beginning and last end. But by the very nature of his reason and will man is directed to his first beginning and last end. Therefore there is no need for any habits of theological virtue, to direct the reason and will to God.

On the contrary, The precepts of the Law are about acts of virtue. Now the Divine Law contains precepts about the acts of faith, hope, and charity, for it is written (*Ecclus.* 2. 8, *sqq.*): *Ye that fear the Lord believe Him,* and again, *hope in Him,* and again, *love Him.* Therefore faith,

hope, and charity are virtues directing us to God. Therefore they are theological virtues.

I answer that, Man is perfected by virtue for those actions by which he is directed to happiness, as was explained above (Q. V, A. 7). Now man's happiness is twofold, as was also stated above (*ibid.,* A. 5). One is proportionate to human nature, a happiness, namely, which man can obtain by means of the principles of his nature. The other is a happiness surpassing man's nature, and which man can obtain by the power of God alone, by a kind of participation of the Godhead, about which it is written (II Pet. 1.4) that by Christ we are made *partakers of the Divine nature.* And because such happiness surpasses the proportion of human nature, man's natural principles which enable him to act well according to his capacity do not suffice to direct man to this same happiness. Hence it is necessary for man to receive from God some additional principles, by means of which he may be directed to supernatural happiness, even as he is directed to his connatural end by means of his natural principles, although not without the Divine assistance. Such principles are called theological virtues: first, because their object is God, because they direct us rightly to God; secondly, because they are infused in us by God alone; thirdly, because these virtues are not made known to us except by Divine revelation, contained in Holy Writ.

Reply Obj. 1. A certain nature may be ascribed to a certain thing in two ways. First, essentially: and thus these theological virtues surpass the nature of man. Secondly, by participation, as kindled wood partakes of the nature of fire, and thus, after a fashion, man becomes a partaker of the Divine Nature, as stated above. And so these virtues belong to man in respect of the Nature of which he is made a partaker.

Reply Obj. 2. These virtues are called Divine not as though God were virtuous by reason of them, but because by them God makes us virtuous, and directs us to Himself. Hence they are not exemplar virtues but virtues resulting from the exemplar.

Reply Obj. 3. The reason and will are naturally directed to God, according as He is the beginning and end of nature, but in proportion to nature. But the reason and will, according to their nature, are not sufficiently directed to Him in so far as He is the object of supernatural happiness.

Question 91, Article 1. Whether There Is an Eternal Law?

We proceed thus to the First Article: It would seem that there is no eternal law.

Objection 1. Because every law is imposed on someone. But there was not someone from eternity on whom a law could be imposed, since God alone was from eternity. Therefore no law is eternal.

Obj. 2. Further, promulgation is essential to law. But promulgation could not be from eternity because there was no one to whom it could be promulgated from eternity. Therefore no law can be eternal.

Obj. 3. Further, a law implies order to an end. But nothing ordered to an end is eternal, for the last end alone is eternal. Therefore no law is eternal.

On the contrary, Augustine says (*De Lib. Arb.* i, 6): "That Law which is the Supreme Reason cannot be understood to be otherwise than unchangeable and eternal."

I answer that, As stated above (Q. XC, A. 1, Reply 2; AA. 3, 4), a law is nothing else but a dictate of practical reason emanating from the ruler who governs a perfect community. Now it is evident, granted that the world is ruled by Divine Providence, as was stated in the First Part (Q. XXII, AA. 1, 2), that the whole community of the universe if governed by Divine Reason. Therefore the very Idea of the government of things in God, the Ruler of the universe, has the nature of a law. And since the Divine Reason's conception of things is not subject to time but is eternal, according to Prov. 8. 23, hence it is that this kind of law must be called eternal.

Reply Obj. 1. Those things that are not in themselves exist with God, since they are foreknown and preordained by Him, according to Rom. 4. 17: *Who calls those things that are not, as those that are.* Accordingly the eternal concept of the Divine law bears the character of an eternal law, in so far as it is ordained by God to the government of things foreknown by Him.

Reply Obj. 2. Promulgation is made by word of mouth or in writing, and in both ways the eternal law is promulgated, because both the Divine Word and the writing of the Book of Life are eternal. But the promulgation cannot be from eternity on the part of the creature that hears or reads.

Reply Obj. 3. The law implies order to the end actively, in so far, that is, as it directs certain things to the end; but not passively—that is to say, the law itself is not ordered to the end—except accidentally, in a governor whose end is extrinsic to him, and to which end his law must be ordered. But the end of the Divine government is God Himself, and His law is not distinct from Himself. Therefore the eternal law is not ordained to another end.

Question 91, Article 2. Whether There Is in Us a Natural Law?

We proceed thus to the Second Article: It would seem that there is no natural law in us.

Objection 1. Because man is governed sufficiently by the eternal law, for Augustine says (*De Lib. Arb.* i, 6) that "the eternal law is that by which it is right that all things should be most orderly." But nature does not abound in superfluities as neither does she fail in necessaries. Therefore no law is natural to man.

Obj. 2. Further, by the law man is ordered in his acts to the end, as states above (Q. XC, A. 2). But the ordering of human acts to their end is not a function of nature, as is the case in irrational creatures, which act for an end solely by their natural appetite; but man acts for an end by his reason and will. Therefore no law is natural to man.

Obj. 3. Further, the more a man is free, the less is he under law. But man is freer than all the animals, on account of free choice, with which he is endowed above all other animals. Since therefore other animals are not subject to a natural law, neither is man subject to a natural law.

On the contrary, A gloss on Rom. 2. 14: *When the Gentiles, who have not the law, do by nature those things that are of the law,* comments *as follows:* "Although they have no written law, yet they have the natural law, whereby each one knows, and is conscious of, what is good and what is evil."

I answer that, As stated above (Q. XC, A. 1, Reply 1), law, being a rule and measure, can be in a person in two ways: in one way as in him that rules and measures; in another way, as in that which is ruled and measured, since a thing is ruled and measured in so far as it partakes of the rule or measure. Therefore, since all things subject to Divine providence are ruled and measured by the eternal law, as was stated above (A. 1), it is evident that all things partake somewhat of the eternal law, in so far as, namely, from its being imprinted on them, they derive their respective inclinations to their proper acts and ends. Now among all others, the rational creature is subject to Divine providence in the most excellent way, in so far as it partakes of a share of providence, by being provident both for itself and for others. Therefore it has a share of the Eternal Reason, by which it has a natural inclination to its due act and end; and this participation of the eternal law in the rational creature is called the natural law. Hence the Psalmist after saying (Ps. 4. 6): *Offer up the sacrifice of justice,* as though someone asked what the works of justice are, adds: *Many say, Who showeth us good things?* in answer to which question he says: *The light of Thy countenance, O Lord, is signed upon us,* thus implying that the light of natural reason, by which we discern what is good and what is evil, which is the function of the natural law, is nothing else than an imprint on us of the Divine light. It is therefore evident that the natural law is nothing else than the rational creature's participation of the eternal law.

Reply Obj. 1. This argument would hold if the natural law were something different from the eternal law. But it is nothing other than a participation of the eternal law, as stated above.

Reply Obj. 2. Every operation of reason and will in us is based on that which is according to nature, as stated above (Q. X, A. 1.), for every act of reasoning is based on principles that are known naturally, and every act of appetite in respect of the means is derived from the natural appetite in respect of the last end. And so also the first direction of our acts to their end must be in virtue of the natural law.

Reply Obj. 3. Even irrational animals partake in their own way of the Eternal Reason, just as the rational creature does. But because the rational creature partakes of it in an intellectual and rational manner, therefore the participation of the eternal law in the rational creature is properly called a law, since a law is something pertaining to reason, as stated above (Q. XC, A. 1). Irrational creatures, however, do not partake of it in a rational manner, and so there is no participation of the eternal law in them, except by way of likeness.

Question 94, Article 2. Whether the Natural Law Contains Several Precepts, or One Only?

We proceed thus to the Second Article: It would seem that the natural law contains not several precepts, but one only.

Objection 1. For law is a kind of precept, as stated above (Q. XCII, A. 2). If therefore there were many precepts of the natural law, it would follow that there are also many natural laws.

Obj. 2. Further, the natural law is consequent to human nature. But human nature, as a whole, is one, though as to its parts it is manifold. Therefore, either there is but one precept of the law of nature, on account of the unity of nature as a whole, or there are many by reason of the number of parts of human nature. The result would be that even things relating to the inclination of the concupiscible faculty belong to the natural law.

Obj. 3. Further, law is something pertaining to reason, as stated above (Q. XC, A. 1). Now reason is but one in man. Therefore there is only one precept of the natural law.

On the contrary, The precepts of the natural law in man stand in relation to practical matters as the first principles to matters of demonstration. But there are several first indemonstrable principles. Therefore there are also several precepts of the natural law.

I answer that, As stated above (Q. XCI, A. 3), the precepts of the natural law are to the practical reason what the first principles of demonstrations are to the speculative reason; because both are self-evident principles. Now a thing is said to be self-evident in two ways: first, in itself; secondly, in relation to us. Any proposition is said to be self-evident in itself if its predicate is contained in the notion of the subject, although to one who does not know the definition of the subject it happens that such a proposition is not self-evident. For instance, this proposition, Man is a rational being, is, in its very nature, self-evident, since who says man, says a rational being; and yet to one who does not know what a man is this proposition is not self-evident. Hence it is that, as Boëthius says (*De Hebdom.*), certain axioms or propositions are universally self-evident to all; and such are those propositions whose terms are known to all, as, Every whole is greater than its part, and, Things equal to one and the same are equal to one another. But some propositions are self-evident only to the wise, who understand the meaning of the terms of such propositions: thus to one who understands that an angel is not a body, it is self-evident that an angel is not circumscriptively in a place; but this is not evident to the unlearned, for they cannot grasp it.

Now a certain order is to be found in those things that are apprehended by man. For that which, before anything else falls under apprehension, is being, the understanding of which is included in all things whatsoever a man apprehends. Therefore the first indemonstrable principle is that the same thing cannot be affirmed and denied at the same time, which is based on the notion of being and not-being; and on this principle all others are based, as is stated in the *Metaphysics.* Now as being is the first thing that falls under the apprehension absolutely, so good is the first thing that falls under the apprehension of the practical reason, which is directed to action; for every agent acts for an end, which has the aspect of good. Consequently the first principle in the practical reason is one founded on the notion of good, namely, that the good is what all desire. Hence this is the first precept of

law, that good is to be pursued and done, and evil is to be avoided. All other precepts of the natural law are based upon this, so that whatever the practical reason naturally apprehends as man's good belongs to the precepts of the natural law as something to be done or avoided.

Since, however, good has the nature of an end, and evil, the nature of a contrary, hence it is that all those things to which man has a natural inclination are naturally apprehended by reason as being good, and consequently as objects of pursuit, and their contraries as evil, and objects of avoidance. Therefore the order of the precepts of the natural law is according to the order of natural inclinations. Because in man there is first of all an inclination to good in accordance with the nature which he has in common with all substances; that is, every substance seeks the preservation of its own being, according to its nature. And by reason of this inclination, whatever is a means of preserving human life and of warding off its obstacles belongs to the natural law. Secondly, there is in man an inclination to things that pertain to him more specially, according to that nature which he has in common with other animals. And in virtue of this inclination, those things are said to belong to the natural law "which nature has taught to all animals," such as sexual intercourse, education of offspring and so forth. Thirdly, there is in man an inclination to good, according to the nature of his reason, which nature is proper to him; thus man has a natural inclination to know the truth about God, and to live in society. And in this respect, whatever pertains to this inclination belongs to the natural law; for instance, to shun ignorance, to avoid offending those among whom one has to live, and other such things regarding the above inclination.

Question 94, Article 4. Whether the Natural Law Is the Same in All Men?

We proceed thus to the Fourth Article: It would seem that the natural law is not the same in all.

Objection 1. For it is stated in the Decretals (*Dist.* i) that "the natural law is that which is contained in the Law and the Gospel." But this is not common to all men, because, as it is written (Rom. 10. 16), *all do not obey the gospel.* Therefore the natural law is not the same in all men.

Obj. 2. Further, "Things which are according to the law are said to be just," as stated in the *Ethics.* But it is stated in the same book that nothing is so just for everybody as not to be subject to change in regard to some men. Therefore even the natural law is not the same in all men.

Obj. 3. Further, as stated above (AA. 2, 3), to the natural law pertains everything to which a man is inclined according to his nature. Now different men are naturally inclined to different things; some to the desire of pleasures, others to the desire of honours, and other men to other things. Therefore there is not one natural law for all.

On the contrary, Isidore says (*Etym.* v. 4): *The natural law is common to all nations.*

I answer that, As stated above (AA. 2, 3), to the natural law belongs those things to which a man is inclined naturally: and among these it is proper to man to be inclined to act according to reason. Now the process of reason is from the common to the proper, as stated in *Phys.* i. The speculative reason, however, is differently situated in this matter, from the practical reason. For, since the speculative reason is busied chiefly with necessary things, which cannot be otherwise than they are, its proper conclusions, like the universal principles, contain the truth without fail. The practical reason, on the other hand, is busied with contingent matters, about which human actions are concerned: and consequently, although there is necessity in the general principles, the more we descend to matters of detail, the more frequently we encounter defects. Accordingly then in speculative matters truth is the same in all men, both as to principles and as to conclusions: although the truth is not known to all as regards the conclusions, but only as regards the principles which are called common notions. But in matters of action, truth or practical rectitude is not the same for all, as to matters of detail, but only as to the general principles: and

where there is the same rectitude in matters of detail, it is not equally known to all.

It is therefore evident that, as regards the general principles whether of speculative or of practical reason, truth or rectitude is the same for all, and is equally known by all. As to the proper conclusions of the speculative reason, the truth is the same for all, but is not equally known to all: thus it is true for all that the three angles of a triangle are together equal to two right angles, although it is not known to all. But as to the proper conclusions of the practical reason, neither is the truth or rectitude the same for all, nor, where it is the same, is it equally known by all. Thus it is right and true for all to act according to reason: and from this principle it follows as a proper conclusion, that goods entrusted to another should be restored to their owner. Now this is true for the majority of cases: but it may happen in a particular case that it would be injurious, and therefore unreasonable, to restore goods held in trust; for instance if they are claimed for the purpose of fighting against one's country. And this principle will be found to fail the more, according as we descend further into detail, *e.g.,* if one were to say that goods held in trust should be restored with such and such a guarantee, or in such and such a way; because the greater the number of conditions added, the greater the number of ways in which the principle may fail, so that it be not right to restore or not to restore.

Consequently we must say that the natural law, as to general principles, is the same for all, both as to rectitude and as to knowledge. But as to certain matters of detail, which are conclusions, as it were, of those general principles, it is the same for all in the majority of cases, both as to rectitude and as to knowledge; and yet in some few cases it may fail, both as to rectitude, by reason of certain obstacles (just as natures subject to generation and corruption fail in some few cases on account of some obstacle), and as to knowledge, since in some the reason is perverted by passion, or evil habit, or an evil disposition of nature; thus formerly, theft, although it is expressly contrary to the natural law, was not considered wrong among the Germans, as Julius Caesar relates (*De Bello Gall.* vi).

Reply Obj. 1. The meaning of the sentence quoted is not that whatever is contained in the Law and Gospel belongs to the natural law, since they contain many things that are above nature; but that whatever belongs to the natural law is fully contained in them. Wherefore Gratian, after saying that *the natural law is what is contained in the Law and the Gospel,* adds at once, by way of example, *by which everyone is commanded to do to others as he would be done by.*

Reply Obj. 2. The saying of the Philosopher is to be understood of things that are naturally just, not as general principles, but as conclusions drawn from them, having rectitude in the majority of cases, but failing in a few.

Reply Obj. 3. As, in man, reason rules and commands the other powers, so all the natural inclinations belonging to the other powers must needs be directed according to reason. Wherefore it is universally right for all men, that all their inclinations should be directed according to reason.

Study Questions

1. How does Aquinas defend the claim that we find happiness neither in natural things nor through their natural powers? How is this claim related to his conception of God as our creator?

2. How does Aquinas support the claim that our highest happiness resides in the vision of God? How is his argument based on his particular conception of the human being? How and when can we reach this kind of happiness?

3. What is a theological virtue? On what is it based? How can we attain it? How is it related to our highest happiness?

4. What are the eternal and natural laws? How are they related? How do they differ? What is Aquinas' argument supporting his statement that the natural law is the same in all humans? What does this assume about human beings? about God? What follows when we accept that there is the same natural law in all of us?

5. What role does reason play in morality? How is it related to faith? What makes divine revelation superior to reason?

Suggestions for Further Reading

Copleston, F. C. *Aquinas* (Baltimore, MD: Penguin Books, 1955). Chapter 5 provides an analysis of Aquinas' views on morality with emphasis on the different ethical roles of church and state.

Gilson, E. *The Christian Philosophy of Saint Thomas Aquinas* (New York: Random House, 1956). Part 3 offers an exposition of Aquinas' ethics.

McInery, R. *Ethica Thomistica: The Moral Philosophy of Thomas Aquinas* (Washington, D.C.: Catholic University American Press, 1982). A basic overview of Aquinas' ethics.

O'Connor, D. J. *Aquinas and the Natural Law* (London: Macmillan, 1968). See Chapters 5 and 6 for a critical analysis of Aquinas' ethics.

Redpath, P. *The Moral Wisdom of Saint Thomas* (Lanham, MD: University Press of America, 1983). A seven-chapter exposition of Aquinas' moral doctrine.

David Hume (1711–1776)

David Hume was born in Edinburgh into an aristocratic family of moderate means. Having to support himself for a living, Hume held a number of different jobs throughout his lifetime. Though his family wanted him to become a lawyer like his father, he preferred the pursuit of scholarly activities in literature, history, and philosophy. Hume published his *Treatise on Human Nature* when he was twenty-six years old. Although this book would form the basis of many of his later writings in philosophy, it was initially so unsuccessful that he characterized it as "dead-born from the press." He began to gain recognition with the later publication of his *Essays, Moral and Political,* and felt encouraged to apply for a chair position in moral philosophy at the University of Edinburgh. However, perhaps because of his reputation as a skeptic and an atheist, he did not attain the position.

Hume rewrote his *Treatise* and published a final revised version of the first part in 1751 under the title *An Enquiry Concerning Human Understanding.* That same year, he published a revised version of the third part of his *Treatise* as *An Enquiry Concerning the Principles of Morals,* which he would later call his best work. A year later, he published his well-received *Political Discourses* and became a librarian of the Faculty of Advocates in Edinburgh. Hume's growing reputation as a scholar was further enhanced with the publication of his *History of England.* However, he later lost his job because he was accused of stocking the library with "obscene" books. Hume left to Paris, where he served as secretary to the British embassy and became a popular member of the social elite and the intellectual circles of the time (especially the Encyclopedists). Eventually, Hume returned to Edinburgh, where he died after ensuring the posthumous publication of his *Dialogues Concerning Natural Religion.*

Hume takes the methodology of Newtonian science as the basis for his empiricist philosophy. Newton's famous statement, "I don't feign hypotheses," underscored the importance of sense observations as the basis of science and the crucial role of inductive reasoning from experience to the gradual formulation of universal laws. Hume sought to apply these principles of natural science to the study of human nature, calling his method a "science" based on "the experimental method." His basic premise is that all knowledge has its origin in sense experience (*empeiria*). He divided our mental perceptions into two kinds, impressions (internal feelings and external sensations) and ideas, which he argued were mere copies of impressions. Compared with ideas, impressions are those perceptions that have a higher degree of "force and vivacity."

From his basic premise, Hume argued against the speculative powers of reason regarding matters of knowledge, morality, and religion. He developed a formidable skepticism over reason's ability to determine the truth about matters of fact with absolute certainty. His attacks were directed against fundamental principles of philosophy, most notably, toward the notion of causality in metaphysics. Claiming that the idea of cause and effect is derived from our impressions, Hume argued that causality is not real or objective, but psychological or subjective. The idea of cause and effect arises as a mere feeling of connection after we become accustomed to experiencing two kinds of events that repeatedly and constantly occur together.

Hume applied the empirical and inductive method in his moral philosophy, and kept a skeptical eye on the place of reason in morality. He claimed that the true source of our morality comes from our sentiments, while reason plays the role of aiding in moral education and argumentation. Moral sentiments are a matter of feelings of approval or disapproval that humans share universally. Morality—like causality—is not objective but subjective. Moral ideas, distinctions, and judgments all stem from our psychological makeup. When we pronounce a person virtuous, it is that we approve of her character and actions. The social virtues of benevolence and justice derive their merits from their public utility; that is, from the happiness or pleasure they bring to society. Utility, Hume argued, is not exclusively an issue of self-interest, for we naturally feel empathy toward others. Thus, Hume insisted that virtues ought to be pursued because they bring benefits to oneself and others.

AN ENQUIRY CONCERNING THE PRINCIPLES OF MORALS

Section I.— *Of the General Principles of Morals*

. . . There has been a controversy started of late . . . concerning the general foundation of MORALS: whether they be derived from REASON, or from SENTIMENT; whether we attain the knowledge of them by a chain of argument and induction, or by an immediate feeling and finer internal sense; whether, like all sound judgment of truth and falsehood, they should be the same to every rational intelligent being; or whether, like the perception of beauty and deformity, they be founded entirely on the particular fabric and constitution of the human species.

The ancient philosophers, though they often affirm, that virtue is nothing but conformity to reason, yet, in general, seem to consider morals as deriving their existence from taste and sentiment. On the other hand, our modern enquirers, though they also talk much of the beauty of virtue, and deformity of vice, yet have commonly endeavoured to account for these distinctions by metaphysical reasonings, and by deductions from the most abstract principles of the understanding. Such confusion reigned in these subjects, that an opposition of the greatest consequence could prevail between one system and another, and even in the parts of almost each individual system; and yet no body, till very lately, was ever sensible of it. The elegant LORD SHAFTESBURY, who first gave occasion to remark this distinction, and who, in general, adhered to the principles of the ancients, is not, himself, entirely free from the same confusion.

It must be acknowledged, that both sides of the question are susceptible of specious arguments. Moral distinctions, it may be said, are discernible by pure *reason:* Else, whence the many disputes that reign in common life, as well as in philosophy, with regard to this subject: The long chain of proofs often produced on both sides; the examples cited, the authorities appealed to, the analogies employed, the fallacies detected,

David Hume. An Enquiry Concerning the Principles of Morals, *ed. J. B. Schneewind. Indianapolis, IN: Hackett, 1983, Sections I, II, III, and V. Copyright © 1983. Reprinted by permission of Hackett Publishing Company. All right reserved.*

the inferences drawn, and the several conclusions adjusted to their proper principles. Truth is disputable; not taste: What exists in the nature of things is the standard of our judgment; what each man feels within himself is the standard of sentiment. Propositions in geometry may be proved, systems in physics may be controverted; but the harmony of verse, the tenderness of passion, the brilliancy of wit, must give immediate pleasure. No man reasons concerning another's beauty; but frequently concerning the justice or injustice of his actions. In every criminal trial the first object of the prisoner is to disprove the facts alleged, and deny the actions imputed to him: The second to prove, that, even if these actions were real, they might be justified, as innocent and lawful. It is confessedly by deductions of the understanding, that the first point is ascertained: How can we suppose that a different faculty of the mind is employed in fixing the other?

On the other hand, those who would resolve all moral determinations into *sentiment,* may endeavour to show, that it is impossible for reason ever to draw conclusions of this nature. To virtue, say they, it belongs to be *amiable,* and vice *odious.* This forms their very nature or essence. But can reason or argumentation distribute these different epithets to any subjects, and pronounce before-hand, that this must produce love, and that hatred? Or what other reason can we ever assign for these affections, but the original fabric and formation of the human mind, which is naturally adapted to receive them?

The end of all moral speculations is to teach us our duty; and, by proper representations of the deformity of vice and beauty of virtue, beget correspondent habits, and engage us to avoid the one, and embrace the other. But is this ever to be expected from inferences and conclusions of the understanding, which of themselves have no hold of the affections or set in motion the active powers of men? They discover truths: But where the truths which they discover are indifferent, and beget no desire or aversion, they can have no influence on conduct and behaviour. What is honourable, what is fair, what is becom-

ing, what is noble, what is generous, takes possession of the heart, and animates us to embrace and maintain it. What is intelligible, what is evident, what is probable, what is true, procures only the cool assent of the understanding; and gratifying a speculative curiosity, puts an end to our researches.

Extinguish all the warm feelings and prepossessions in favour of virtue, and all disgust or aversion to vice: Render men totally indifferent towards these distinctions; and morality is no longer a practical study, nor has any tendency to regulate our lives and actions.

These arguments on each side (and many more might be produced) are so plausible, that I am apt to suspect, they may, the one as well as the other, be solid and satisfactory, and that *reason* and *sentiment* concur in almost all moral determinations and conclusions. The final sentence, it is probable, which pronounces characters and actions amiable or odious, praise-worthy or blameable; that which stamps on them the mark of honour or infamy, approbation or censure; that which renders morality an active principle, and constitutes virtue our happiness, and vice our misery: It is probable, I say, that this final sentence depends on some internal sense or feeling, which nature has made universal in the whole species. For what else can have an influence of this nature? But in order to pave the way for such a sentiment, and give a proper discernment of its object, it is often necessary, we find, that much reasoning should precede, that nice distinctions be made, just conclusions drawn, distant comparisons formed, complicated relations examined, and general facts fixed and ascertained. Some species of beauty, especially the natural kinds, on their first appearance, command our affection and approbation; and where they fail of this effect, it is impossible for any reasoning to redress their influence, or adapt them better to our taste and sentiment. But in many orders of beauty, particularly those of the finer arts, it is requisite to employ much reasoning, in order to feel the proper sentiment; and a false relish may frequently be corrected by argument and reflection. There are just grounds to conclude, that moral beauty partakes much of this latter species, and demands the assistance of our intellectual faculties, in order to give it a suitable influence on the human mind.

But though this question, concerning the general principles of morals, be curious and important, it is needless for us, at present, to employ farther care in our researches concerning it. For if we can be so happy, in the course of this enquiry, as to discover the true origin of morals, it will then easily appear how far either sentiment or reason enters into all determinations of this nature. In order to attain this purpose, we shall endeavour to follow a very simple method: We shall analyse that complication of mental qualities, which form what, in common life, we call PERSONAL MERIT: We shall consider every attribute of the mind, which renders a man an object either of esteem and affection, or of hatred and contempt; every habit or sentiment or faculty, which, if ascribed to any person, implies either praise or blame, and may enter into any panegyric or satire of his character and manners. The quick sensibility, which, on this head, is so universal among mankind, gives a philosopher sufficient assurance, that he can never be considerably mistaken in framing the catalogue, or incur any danger of misplacing the objects of his contemplation: He needs only enter into his own breast for a moment, and consider whether or not he should desire to have this or that quality ascribed to him, and whether such or such an imputation would proceed from a friend or an enemy. The very nature of language guides us almost infallibly in forming a judgment of this nature; and as every tongue possesses one set of words which are taken in a good sense, and another in the opposite, the least acquaintance with the idiom suffices, without any reasoning, to direct us in collecting and arranging the estimable or blameable qualities of men. The only object of reasoning is to discover the circumstances on both sides, which are common to these qualities; to observe that particular in which the estimable qualities agree on the one

hand, and the blameable on the other; and thence to reach the foundation of ethics, and find those universal principles, from which all censure or approbation is ultimately derived. As this is a question of fact, not of abstract science, we can only expect success, by following the experimental method, and deducing general maxims from a comparison of particular instances. The other scientifical method, where a general abstract principle is first established, and is afterwards branched out into a variety of inferences and conclusions, may be more perfect in itself, but suits less the imperfection of human nature, and is a common source of illusion and mistake in this as well as in other subjects. Men are now cured of their passion for hypotheses and systems in natural philosophy, and will hearken to no arguments but those which are derived from experience. It is full time they should attempt a like reformation in all moral disquisitions; and reject every system of ethics, however subtile or ingenious, which is not founded on fact and observation.

We shall begin our enquiry on this head by the consideration of social virtues, benevolence and justice. The explication of them will probably give us an opening by which others may be accounted for.

Section II.— *Of Benevolence*

PART II

. . . We may observe, that, in displaying the praises of any humane, beneficent man, there is one circumstance which never fails to be amply insisted on, namely, the happiness and satisfaction, derived to society from his intercourse and good offices. To his parents, we are apt to say, he endears himself by his pious attachment and duteous care, still more than by the connexions of nature. His children never feel his authority, but when employed for their advantage. With him, the ties of love are consolidated by beneficence and friendship. The ties of friendship approach, in a fond observance of each obliging office, to those of love and inclination. His domestics and dependants have in him a sure resource; and no longer dread the power of fortune, but so far as she exercises it over him. From him the hungry receive food, the naked cloathing, the ignorant and slothful skill and industry. Like the sun, an inferior minister of providence, he cheers, invigorates, and sustains the surrounding world.

If confined to private life, the sphere of his activity is narrower; but his influence is all benign and gentle. If exalted into a higher station, mankind and posterity reap the fruit of his labours.

As these topics of praise never fail to be employed, and with success, where we would inspire esteem for any one; may it not thence be concluded, that the UTILITY, resulting from the social virtues, forms, at least, a *part* of their merit, and is one source of that approbation and regard so universally paid to them? . . .

In all determinations of morality, this circumstance of public utility is ever principally in view; and wherever disputes arise, either in philosophy or common life, concerning the bounds of duty, the question cannot, by any means, be decided with greater certainty, than by ascertaining, on any side, the true interests of mankind. If any false opinion, embraced from appearances, has been found to prevail; as soon as farther experience and sounder reasoning have given us juster notions of human affairs; we retract our first sentiment, and adjust anew the boundaries of moral good and evil. . . .

Upon the whole, then, it seems undeniable, *that* nothing can bestow more merit on any human creature than the sentiment of benevolence in an eminent degree; and *that* a *part,* at least, of its merit arises from its tendency to promote the interests of our species, and bestow happiness on human society. We carry our view into the salutary consequences of such a character and disposition: and whatever has so benign an influence, and forwards so desirable an end, is beheld with complacency and pleasure. The social virtues are never regarded without their beneficial tendencies, nor viewed as barren and

unfruitful. The happiness of mankind, the order of society, the harmony of families, the mutual support of friends, are always considered as the result of their gentle dominion over the breasts of men. . . .

Section III.—*Of Justice*

PART I

That Justice is useful to society, and consequently that *part* of its merit, at least, must arise from that consideration, it would be a superfluous undertaking to prove. That public utility is the *sole* origin of justice, and that reflections on the beneficial consequences of this virtue are the *sole* foundation of its merit; this proposition, being more curious and important, will better deserve our examination and enquiry.

Let us suppose, that nature has bestowed on the human race such profuse *abundance* of all *external* conveniences, that, without any uncertainty in the event, without any care or industry on our part, every individual finds himself fully provided with whatever his most voracious appetites can want, or luxurious imagination wish or desire. His natural beauty, we shall suppose, surpasses all acquired ornaments: The perpetual clemency of the seasons render useless all cloaths or covering: The raw herbage affords him the most delicious fare; the clear fountain, the richest beverage. No laborious occupation required: No tillage: No navigation. Music, poetry, and contemplation, form his sole business: Conversation, mirth, and friendship his sole amusement.

It seems evident, that, in such a happy state, every other social virtue would flourish, and receive tenfold encrease; but the cautious, jealous virtue of justice would never once have been dreamed of. For what purpose make a partition of goods, where every one has already more than enough? Why give rise to property, where there cannot possibly be any injury? Why call this object *mine,* when, upon the seizing of it by another, I need but stretch out my hand to possess myself of what is equally valuable? Justice, in that case, being totally USELESS, would be an idle ceremonial, and could never possibly have place in the catalogue of virtues.

We see, even in the present necessitous condition of mankind, that, wherever any benefit is bestowed by nature in an unlimited abundance, we leave it always in common among the whole human race, and make no subdivisions of right and property. Water and air, though the most necessary of all objects, are not challenged as the property of individuals; nor can any man commit injustice by the most lavish use and enjoyment of these blessings. In fertile extensive countries, with few inhabitants, land is regarded on the same footing. And no topic is so much insisted on by those, who defend the liberty of the seas, as the unexhausted use of them in navigation. Were the advantages, procured by navigation, as inexhaustible, these reasoners had never had any adversaries to refute; nor had any claims ever been advanced of a separate, exclusive dominion over the ocean.

It may happen, in some countries, at some periods, that there be established a property in water, none in land;[1] if the latter be in greater abundance than can be used by the inhabitants, and the former be found, with difficulty, and in very small quantities.

Again; suppose, that, though the necessities of human race continue the same as at present, yet the mind is so enlarged, and so replete with friendship and generosity, that every man has the utmost tenderness for every man, and feels no more concern for his own interest than for that of his fellows: It seems evident, that the USE of justice would, in this case, be suspended by such an extensive benevolence, nor would the divisions and barriers of property and obligation have ever been thought of. Why should I bind another, by a deed or promise, to do me any good office, when I know that he is already prompted, by the strongest inclination, to seek my happiness, and would, of himself, perform

the desired service; except the hurt, he thereby receives, be greater than the benefit accruing to me? in which case, he knows, that, from my innate humanity and friendship, I should be the first to oppose myself to his imprudent generosity. Why raise land-marks between my neighbour's field and mine, when my heart has made no division between our interests; but shares all his joys and sorrows with the same force and vivacity as if originally my own? Every man, upon this supposition, being a second self to another, would trust all his interests to the discretion of every man; without jealousy, without partition, without distinction. And the whole human race would form only one family; where all would lie in common, and be used freely, without regard to property; but cautiously too, with as entire regard to the necessities of each individual, as if our own interests were most intimately concerned.

In the present disposition of the human heart, it would, perhaps, be difficult to find compleat instances of such enlarged affections; but still we may observe, that the case of families approaches towards it; and the stronger the mutual benevolence is among the individuals, the nearer it approaches; till all distinction of property be, in a great measure, lost and confounded among them. Between married persons, the cement of friendship is by the laws supposed so strong as to abolish all division of possessions: and has often, in reality, the force ascribed to it. And it is observable, that, during the ardour of new enthusiasms, when every principle is inflamed into extravagance, the community of goods has frequently been attempted: and nothing but experience of its inconveniencies, from the returning or disguised selfishness of men, could make the imprudent fanatics adopt anew the ideas of justice and of separate property. So true is it, that this virtue derives its existence entirely from its necessary *use* to the intercourse and social state of mankind.

To make this truth more evident, let us reverse the foregoing suppositions; and carrying every thing to do the opposite extreme, consider

---

[1] Genesis, chap. xiii. and xxi.

what would be the effect of these new situations. Suppose a society to fall into such want of all common necessaries, that the utmost frugality and industry cannot preserve the greater number from perishing, and the whole from extreme misery: It will readily, I believe, be admitted, that the strict laws of justice are suspended, in such a pressing emergence, and give place to the stronger motives of necessity and self-preservation. Is it any crime, after a shipwreck, to seize whatever means or instrument of safety one can lay hold of, without regard to former limitations of property? Or if a city besieged were perishing with hunger; can we imagine, that men will see any means of preservation before them, and lose their lives, from a scrupulous regard to what, in other situations, would be the rules of equity and justice? The USE and TENDENCY of that virtue is to procure happiness and security, by preserving order in society: But where the society is ready to perish from extreme necessity, no greater evil can be dreaded from violence and injustice; and every man may now provide for himself by all the means, which prudence can dictate, or humanity permit. The public, even in less urgent necessities, opens granaries, without the consent of proprietors; as justly supposing, that the authority of magistracy may, consistent with equity, extend so far: But were any number of men to assemble, without the tye of laws or civil jurisdiction; would an equal partition of bread in a famine, though effected by power and even violence, be regarded as criminal or injurious?

Suppose likewise, that it should be a virtuous man's fate to fall into the society of ruffians, remote from the protection of laws and government; what conduct must he embrace in that melancholy situation? He sees such a desperate rapaciousness prevail; such a disregard to equity, such contempt of order, such stupid blindness to future consequences, as must immediately have the most tragical conclusion, and must terminate in destruction to the greater number, and in a total dissolution of society to the rest. He, mean while, can have no other expedient than to arm himself, to whomever the sword he seizes, or the buckler, may belong: To make provision of all means of defence and security: And his particular regard to justice being no longer of USE to his own safety or that of others, he must consult the dictates of self-preservation alone, without concern for those who no longer merit his care and attention.

When any man, even in political society, renders himself, by his crimes, obnoxious to the public, he is punished by the laws in his goods and person; that is, the ordinary rules of justice are, with regard to him, suspended for a moment, and it becomes equitable to inflict on him, for the *benefit* of society, what, otherwise, he could not suffer without wrong or injury.

The rage and violence of public war; what is it but a suspension of justice among the warring parties, who perceive, that this virtue is now no longer of any *use* or advantage to them? The laws of war, which then succeed to those of equity and justice, are rules calculated for the *advantage* and *utility* of that particular state, in which men are now placed. And were a civilized nation engaged with barbarians, who observed no rules even of war; the former must also suspend their observance of them, where they no longer serve to any purpose; and must render every action or rencounter as bloody and pernicious as possible to the first aggressors.

Thus, the rules of equity or justice depend entirely on the particular state and condition, in which men are placed, and owe their origin and existence to that UTILITY, which results to the public from their strict and regular observance. Reverse, in any considerable circumstance, the condition of men: Produce extreme abundance or extreme necessity: Implant in the human breast perfect moderation and humanity, or perfect rapaciousness and malice: By rendering justice totally *useless,* you thereby totally destroy its essence, and suspend its obligation upon mankind.

The common situation of society is a medium amidst all these extremes. We are naturally partial to ourselves, and to our friends; but are capable of learning the advantage resulting from a more equitable conduct. Few enjoyments are given us from the open and liberal hand of nature; but by art, labour, and industry, we can extract them in great abundance. Hence the ideas of property become necessary in all civil society: Hence justice derives its usefulness to the public: And hence alone arises its merit and moral obligation. . . .

Section V.—*Why Utility Pleases*

PART I

IT seems so natural a thought to ascribe to their utility the praise, which we bestow on the social virtues, that one would expect to meet with this principle every where in moral writers, as the chief foundation of their reasoning and enquiry. In common life, we may observe, that the circumstance of utility is always appealed to; nor is it supposed, that a greater eulogy can be given to any man, than to display his usefulness to the public, and enumerate the services, which he has performed to mankind and society. . . .

From the apparent usefulness of the social virtues, it has readily been inferred by sceptics, both ancient and modern, that all moral distinctions arise from education, and were, at first, invented, and afterwards encouraged, by the art of politicians, in order to render men tractable, and subdue their natural ferocity and selfishness, which incapacitated them for society. This principle, indeed, of precept and education, must so far be owned to have a powerful influence, that it may frequently encrease or diminish, beyond their natural standard, the sentiments of approbation or dislike; and may even, in particular instances, create, without any natural principle, a new sentiment of this kind; as is evident in all superstitious practices and observances: But that *all* moral affection or dislike arises from this origin, will never surely be allowed by any judicious enquirer. Had nature made no such distinction, founded on the original constitution of the mind, the words, *honourable* and *shameful, lovely*

and *odious, noble* and *despicable,* had never had place in any language; nor could politicians, had they invented these terms, ever have been able to render them intelligible, or make them convey any idea to the audience. So that nothing can be more superficial than this paradox of the sceptics; and it were well, if, in the abstruser studies of logic and metaphysics, we could as easily obviate the cavils of that sect, as in the practical and more intelligible sciences of politics and morals.

The social virtues must, therefore, be allowed to have a natural beauty and amiableness, which, at first, antecedent to all precept or education, recommends them to the esteem of uninstructed mankind, and engages their affections. And as the public utility of these virtues is the chief circumstance, whence they derive their merit, it follows, that the end, which they have a tendency to promote, must be some way agreeable to us, and take hold of some natural affection. It must please, either from considerations of self-interest, or from more generous motives and regards.

It has often been asserted, that, as every man has a strong connexion with society, and perceives the impossibility of his solitary subsistence, he becomes, on that account, favourable to all those habits or principles, which promote order in society, and insure to him the quiet possession of so inestimable a blessing. As much as we value our own happiness and welfare, as much must we applaud the practice of justice and humanity, by which alone the social confederacy can be maintained, and every man reap the fruits of mutual protection and assistance. . . .

A generous, a brave, a noble deed, performed by an adversary, commands our approbation; while in its consequences it may be acknowledged prejudicial to our particular interest.

Where private advantage concurs with general affection for virtue, we readily perceive and avow the mixture of these distinct sentiments, which have a very different feeling and influence on the mind. We praise, perhaps, with more alacrity, where the generous, humane action contributes to our particular interest: But the topics of praise, which we insist on, are very wide of this circumstance. And we may attempt to bring over others to our sentiments, without endeavouring to convince them, that they reap any advantage from the actions which we recommend to their approbation and applause. . . .

Usefulness is agreeable, and engages our approbation. This is a matter of fact, confirmed by daily observation. But, *useful?* For what?

For some body's interest, surely. Whose interest them? Not our own only: For our approbation frequently extends farther. It must, therefore, be the interest of those, who are served by the character or action approved of; and these we may conclude, however remote, are not totally indifferent to us. By opening up this principle, we shall discover one great source of moral distinctions.

Study Questions

1. How does Hume support the view that sentiments are the true origin of morals? How does he argue for his notion of reason as an instrument of the moral sentiments?

2. Given his distinction between the sentiments and reason, what assumptions is Hume making in his conception of each? Does our morality indeed stand or fall with feelings of approval and disapproval? Is reason merely a morally neutral aid?

3. What is Hume's defense of the claim that the social virtues of benevolence and justice derive their merits from their public utility? Why is benevolence only partly (and justice entirely) based on public utility?

4. What conception of human nature unfolds in Hume's discussion of morality?

5. Hume claims that moral sentiments are subjective, but universal. Is this a plausible claim? How would he construe actual differences in moral feelings? Is he convincing? Does he manage to escape moral relativism while arguing that there are no objective moral distinctions?

Suggestions for Further Reading

Broad, C. D. *Five Types of Ethical Theory* (London: Routledge, 1930). See Chapter 4 for a critical view of Hume's ethical theory.

Flew, A. *David Hume: Philosopher of Moral Science* (Oxford; New York: Blackwell, 1986). A basic analysis of Hume's moral theory.

Kemp Smith, N. *The Philosophy of David Hume* (London: Macmillan, 1941). A concise analysis of Hume's philosophical doctrines and their origins.

Mackie, J. L. *Hume's Moral Theory* (London: Routledge & Kegan Paul, 1980). An exposition of Hume's moral doctrines with a critique (in Part III).

Stroud, B. *Hume* (London: Routledge & Kegan Paul, 1977). Chapters 7–9 provide an analysis of Hume's views of morality.

Immanuel Kant (1724–1804)

Immanuel Kant was born in Königsberg, then a small provincial Prussian city on the southern coast of the Baltic Sea, and now known as Kaliningrad. He came from a working-class family of strong religious beliefs in puritanical pietism. Though he received a religious education in his early years, as a university student Kant turned toward Newtonian physics, mathematics, and philosophy. He made a modest living as a private tutor and (later) as professor of philosophy at the University of Königsberg. He taught a great number of courses in varied topics and was considered a very gifted lecturer. However, his writings are notoriously difficult and complex. His first published book, *The Critique of Pure Reason* (1781), was considered incomprehensible even by his colleagues. (Later, in 1783, he wrote a briefer and simplified version under the title *Prolegomena for Any Future Metaphysics* and, in 1787, he published a revised edition of his *Critique of Pure Reason.*) Kant also had a most idiosyncratic lifestyle. Unlike other philosophers of his time, he published late in his career and never traveled more than thirty miles from his home city. Preferring an orderly and calm life, he adhered to a strict daily routine, so precise that neighbors set their clocks by his customary stroll at 3:30 P.M. His route is still known today as "The Philosopher's Walk."

Kant's philosophy has made a profound impression upon the course of European thought, a mark that has endured from the eighteenth century to the present. Challenging the basic assumptions of his time concerning what we can know and how we can know it, his philosophy has influenced all subsequent systems and philosophies of knowledge. Kant himself described his contribution as a "Copernican Revolution" in knowledge. Like Copernicus, who changed the center of reference in the universe from the earth to the sun, Kant changed the center of reference in knowledge from the known object to the knowing subject. Breaking with the traditional notion of the mind as a passive receptor of knowledge about the world, Kant revolutionized our conception of the mind and its activities. Kant reversed the prevailing assumption that the mind conforms to its objects and proposed that objects conform to the mind. Instead of passively taking in objects and adopting their given order and structure, the mind is thus actively involved, imparting its order and structure to its objects.

Arguing that sense experience provides the material for knowledge, Kant insisted that the mind automatically receives, orders, and organizes this material according to its own principles. Things as they appear to us (phenomena) are thus already structured by our mind. In this sense, our knowledge of the things in the world reflects the structure of our own mind. For example, the universal and necessary laws of physics are products of the mind's way of structuring nature. However, Kant argued that it is impossible for us to know things in themselves because our mind provides our only access to things, and it invariably grasps them as phenomena.

Kant's revolutionary conception of knowledge is said to provide a synthesis between empiricism and rationalism. Empiricism proposes that all of our knowledge has its origin in sense experience and is thus dependent upon experience (*a posteriori*). Rationalism claims that the mind has ideas that are independent of sense experience (*a priori*) and that reason can operate without having its origin in experience. Kant partially agrees and partially disagrees with both positions. Our manner of knowing is in a certain way *a posteriori* because the mind must initially receive the material of sense experience to begin its knowledge. However, our manner of knowing is in a certain sense also *a priori* because the mind adds something of its own to sense experience through its structuring principles. Through his synthesis, Kant sought to rescue metaphysical and moral philosophy from the speculative excesses of rationalists and the devastating skepticism of empiricists. While one extreme pushed reason beyond its limits, the other doubted its ability to gain certainty in some fields of knowledge. Kant proposed that reason must reflect on itself and engage in a critique to discern its own powers and limits. Thus, he undertook the task of critiquing reason in its theoretical, practical or moral, and aesthetic dimensions.

Kant maintains that in order to find the ultimate basis for morality we should not look at how humans actually behave but how they ought to behave. Human conduct occurs in specific circumstances, depends on particularities, and often violates moral commands. Moral principles, however, are universal and necessary; that is, they invariably prescribe the same courses of action to all human beings. Thus, an anthropological investigation of human nature alone cannot render a satisfactory account of morality. Because our reason thinks in terms of necessity and universality, moral principles find their basis in our rationality. Hence, Kant proposes to investigate the role of reason in morality in his search for a supreme principle, the ultimate and universal moral standard.

The role of reason in morality is to guide our actions. Morality demands that we act rationally. Thus, it rules the human will in order to make it a good will. The good will is then the one that follows the dictates of reason. Moreover, it is the only thing that is absolutely or unqualifiedly good. The goodness of other human features, such as intelligence, depend upon the goodness of the will. In contrast, its worth lies in itself—in its willing—and not in its effects, results, or consequences. However, the human will is not perfect, as we often have desires and inclinations that go against what we ought to do. Our reason commands the will and dictates the right course of action. Hence, the supreme moral principle in Kant's philosophy is a (deontological) principle of duty (from the Greek word *deon*) or obligation.

Kant claims that the moral worth of an action depends exclusively on whether it is done from duty, regardless of our particular desires and inclinations. The only thing that matters morally regarding our actions is whether we act out of a sense of duty, that is, whether the will follows the dictates of reason. We may be particularly disinclined to act in accordance with our duty, but the important point is whether reason compels the will to comply with duty. Even in those instances when we are predisposed to perform our duty, because it suits our desires or inclinations, the crucial factor sits squarely on whether we act out of a sense of duty. Hence, Kant insists that actions that merely conform or coincide with duty but are not done from duty have no moral worth whatsoever.

By focusing on our rationality, Kant draws further conclusions that lead him to the supreme principle of morality. A law as such is an objective, universal principle that abstracts from particulars and holds necessarily and invariably. As rational beings, we are unique in our ability to be aware of and reflect on the law and to act according to reason's conception of the law. When we perform our duty, reason commands the will to follow the moral law out of respect or reverence for the law in its supreme ruling. Its command is thus formulated as an imperative in which it tells the will what it ought to do. A moral imperative does not depend upon our subjective and particular desires or inclinations; it is unconditional or categorical. An imperative that does depend upon our individual desires and inclinations is merely conditional or hypothetical, so it is not properly a moral imperative. Only a categorical imperative, then, can be the supreme principle of morality.

Kant argues that the absolute character of the moral law in its universality and necessity means that there is only one categorical imperative. Though he gives it different formulations, its character remains the same. One such formulation is: "Act only according to that maxim by which you can at the same time will that it should become a universal law." A maxim is an imperative of action, a subjective principle whereby each individual determines his or her particular course of action, as an "I ought to do x." Only the maxim that can be "universalized" or applied to all as a law, as an "everyone ought to do x," follows the categorical imperative. However, this "universalization" must occur without contradictions; otherwise it would not be rational. If universalizing my maxim yields a logically contradictory system or if it brings my will into contradiction with itself, then I cannot at the same time will that everyone ought to do what I ought to do.

Another formulation of the categorical imperative states: "Act so that you treat humanity whether in your person or in that of another, always as an end and never as a means only." Since we are rational beings, our reason conceives of ends and guides us toward achieving these ends through various means. As rational beings, we exist as ends in ourselves, not as a means for others. In this sense, we are "persons," not "things." Our worth is absolute and unconditional, not relative to or dependent upon the desires or needs of others. The categorical imperative thus commands us to respect the dignity of persons and their absolute worth by treating all persons, including ourselves, always as ends in themselves and never as mere means.

Kant envisions a kingdom or realm of ends where all rational beings live in accordance with the supreme practical law. Rational beings are capable not only of deliberately following universal laws but also of legislating universal laws. Our will is thus autonomous or capable of ruling itself. In the kingdom of ends, each rational being thus legislates the supreme practical law of respecting persons. Morality consists in each rational individual legislating this universal law. Because only those beings who are capable of legislating themselves are free, freedom is thus the possibility of morality. As Kant succinctly put it elsewhere: "Every 'ought' implies a 'can'."

FUNDAMENTAL PRINCIPLES OF THE METAPHYSIC OF MORALS

First Section

TRANSITION FROM THE COMMON RATIONAL KNOWLEDGE OF MORALITY TO THE PHILOSOPHICAL

Nothing can possibly be conceived in the world, or even out of it, which can be called good without qualification, except a Good Will. Intelligence, wit, judgment, and the other *talents* of the mind, however they may be named, or courage, resolution, perseverance, as qualities of temperament, are undoubtedly good and desirable in many respects; but these gifts of nature may also become extremely bad and mischievous if the will which is to make use of them, and which, therefore, constitutes what is called *character,* is not good. It is the same with the *gifts of fortune.* Power, riches, honour, even health, and the general well-being and contentment with one's condition which is called *happiness,* inspire pride, and often presumption, if there is not a good will to correct the influence of these on the mind, and with this also to rectify the whole principle of acting and adapt it to its end. The sight of a being who is not adorned with a single feature of a pure and good will, enjoying unbroken prosperity, can never give pleasure to an impartial rational spectator. Thus a good will appears to constitute the indispensable condition even of being worthy of happiness.

There are even some qualities which are of service to this good will itself, and may facilitate its action, yet which have no intrinsic unconditional value, but always presuppose a good will, and this qualifies the esteem that we justly have for them, and does not permit us to regard them as absolutely good. Moderation in the affections and passions, self-control and calm deliberation are not only good in many respects, but even seem to constitute part of the intrinsic worth of the person; but they are far from deserving to be called good without qualification, although they have been so unconditionally praised by the ancients. For without the principles of a good will, they may become extremely bad, and the coolness of a villain not only makes him far more dangerous, but also immediately makes him more abominable in our eyes than he would have been without it.

A good will is good not because of what it performs or effects, not by its aptness for the attainment of some proposed end, but simply by virtue of the volition, that is, it is good in itself, and considered by itself is to be esteemed much higher than all that can be brought about by it in favour of any inclination, nay even of the sum total of all inclinations. Even if it should happen that, owing to special disfavour of fortune, or the niggardly provision of a step-motherly nature, this will should wholly lack power to accomplish its purpose, if with its greatest efforts it should yet achieve nothing, and there should remain only the good will (not, to be sure, a mere wish, but the summoning of all means in our power), then, like a jewel, it would still shine by its own light, as a thing which has its whole value in itself. Its usefulness or fruitlessness can neither add nor take away anything from this value. It would be, as it were, only the setting to enable us to handle it the more conveniently in common commerce, or to attract to it the attention of

Immanuel Kant. Fundamental Principles of the Metaphysic of Morals, *Sections 1 and 2, trans. T. K. Abbott.*
In Kant's *Critique of Practical Reason and Other Works on the Theory of Ethics. London: Longmans,*
Green, 1898.

those who are not yet connoisseurs, but not to recommend it to true connoisseurs, or to determine its value. . . .

In the physical constitution of an organized being we assume it as a fundamental principle that no organ for any purpose will be found in it but what is also the fittest and best adapted for that purpose. Now in a being which has reason and a will, if the proper object of nature were its *conservation,* its *welfare,* in a word, its *happiness,* then nature would have hit upon a very bad arrangement in selecting the reason of the creature to carry out this purpose. For all the actions which the creature has to perform with a view to this purpose, and the whole rule of its conduct, would be far more surely prescribed to it by instinct, and that end would have been attained thereby much more certainly than it ever can be by reason. . . .

For as reason is not competent to guide the will with certainty in regard to its objects and the satisfaction of all our wants (which it to some extent even multiplies), this being an end to which an implanted instinct would have led with much greater certainty; and since, nevertheless, reason is imparted to us as a practical faculty, *i.e.,* as one which is to have influence on the *will,* therefore, admitting that nature generally in the distribution of her capacities has adapted the means to the end, its true destination must be to produce a *will,* not merely good as a *means* to something else, but *good in itself,* for which reason was absolutely necessary. This will then, though not indeed the sole and complete good, must be the supreme good and the condition of every other, even of the desire of happiness. . . .

We have then to develop the notion of a will which deserves to be highly esteemed for itself, and is good without a view to anything further, a notion which exists already in the sound natural understanding, requiring rather to be cleared up than to be taught, and which in estimating the value of our actions always takes the first place, and constitutes the condition of all the rest. In order to do this we will take the notion of duty, which includes that of a good will, al-

though implying certain subjective restrictions and hindrances. These, however, far from concealing it, or rendering it unrecognisable, rather bring it out by contrast, and make it shine forth so much the brighter.

I omit here all actions which are already recognised as inconsistent with duty, although they may be useful for this or that purpose, for with these the question whether they are done *from duty* cannot arise at all, since they even conflict with it. I also set aside those actions which really conform to duty, but to which men have *no* direct *inclination,* performing them because they are impelled thereto by some other inclination. For in this case we can readily distinguish whether the action which agrees with duty is done *from duty,* or from a selfish view. It is much harder to make this distinction when the action accords with duty, and the subject has besides a *direct* inclination to it. For example, it is always a matter of duty that a dealer should not overcharge an inexperienced purchaser, and wherever there is much commerce the prudent tradesman does not overcharge, but keeps a fixed price for every one, so that a child buys of him as well as any other. Men are thus *honestly* served; but this is not enough to make us believe that the tradesman has so acted from duty and from principles of honesty: his own advantage required it; it is out of the question in this case to suppose that he might besides have a direct inclination in favour of the buyers, so that, as it were, from love he should give no advantage to one over another. Accordingly the action was done neither from duty nor from direct inclination, but merely with a selfish view. On the other hand, it is a duty to maintain one's life; and, in addition, every one has also a direct inclination to do so. But on this account the often anxious care which most men take for it has no intrinsic worth, and their maxim has no moral import. They preserve their life *as duty requires,* no doubt, but not *because duty requires.* On the other hand, if adversity and hopeless sorrow have completely taken away the relish for life; if the unfortunate one, strong in mind, indignant at his fate rather than desponding or dejected, wishes for death, and yet preserves his life without loving it—not from inclination or fear, but from duty—then his maxim has a moral worth.

To be beneficent when we can is a duty; and besides this, there are many minds so sympathetically constituted that without any other motive of vanity or self-interest, they find a pleasure in spreading joy around them, and can take delight in the satisfaction of others so far as it is their own work. But I maintain that in such a case an action of this kind, however proper, however amiable it may be, has nevertheless no true moral worth, but is on a level with other inclinations, *e.g.,* the inclination to honour, which, if it is happily directed to that which is in fact of public utility and accordant with duty, and consequently honourable, deserves praise and encouragement, but not esteem. For the maxim wants the moral import, namely, that such actions be done *from duty,* not from inclination. Put the case that the mind of that philanthropist were clouded by sorrow of his own, extinguishing all sympathy with the lot of others, and that while he still has the power to benefit others in distress he is not touched by their trouble because he is absorbed with his own; and now suppose that he tears himself out of this dead insensibility, and performs the action without any inclination to it, but simply from duty, then first has his action its genuine moral worth. Further still; if nature has put little sympathy in the heart of this or that man; if he, supposed to be an upright man, is by temperament cold and indifferent to the sufferings of others, perhaps because in respect of his own he is provided with the special gift of patience and fortitude, and supposes, or even requires, that others should have the same—and such a man would certainly not be the meanest product of nature—but if nature had not specially framed him for a philanthropist, would he not still find in himself a source from whence to give himself a far higher worth than that of a good-natured temperament could be? Unquestionably. It is just in this that the moral worth of the character is broughtout which is incompar-

ably the highest of all, namely, that he is beneficent, not from inclination, but from duty. . . .

The second proposition is: That an action done from duty derives its moral worth, *not from the purpose* which is to be attained by it, but from the maxim by which it is determined, and therefore does not depend on the realization of the object of the action, but merely on the *principle of volition* by which the action has taken place, without regard to any object of desire. It is clear from what precedes that the purposes which we may have in view in our actions, or their effects regarded as ends and springs of the will, cannot give to actions any unconditional or moral worth. In what then can their worth lie, if it is not to consist in the will and in reference to its expected effect? It cannot lie anywhere but in the *principle of the will* without regard to the ends which can be attained by the action. For the will stands between its *à priori* principle which is formal, and its *à posteriori* spring which is material, as between two roads, and as it must be determined by something, it follows that it must be determined by the formal principle of volition when an action is done from duty, in which case every material principle has been withdrawn from it.

The third proposition, which is a consequence of the two preceding, I would express thus: *Duty is the necessity of acting from respect for the law.* I may have *inclination* for an object as the effect of my proposed action, but I cannot have *respect* for it, just for this reason, that it is an effect and not an energy of will. Similarly, I cannot have respect for inclination, whether my own or another's; I can at most if my own, approve it; if another's, sometimes even love it; *i.e.,* look on it as favourable to my own interest. It is only what is connected with my will as a principle, by no means as an effect—what does not subserve my inclination, but overpowers it, or at least in case of choice excludes it from its calculation—in other words, simply the law of itself, which can be an object of respect, and hence a command. Now an action done from duty must wholly exclude the influence of inclination, and with it every object of the will, so that nothing remains which can determine the will except objectively the *law,* and subjectively *pure respect* for this practical law, and consequently the maxim[1] to follow this law even to the thwarting of all my inclinations.

Thus the moral worth of an action does not lie in the effect expected from it, nor in any principle of action which requires to borrow its motive from this expected effect. For all these effects—agreeableness of one's condition, and even the promotion of the happiness of others—could have been also brought about by other causes, so that for this there would have been no need of the will of a rational being; it is in this, however, alone that the supreme and unconditional good can be found. The pre-eminent good which we call moral can therefore consist in nothing else than *the conception of law* in itself, *which certainly is only possible in a rational being.* . . .

Second Section

TRANSITION FROM POPULAR MORAL PHILOSOPHY TO THE METAPHYSICS OF MORALS

Everything in nature works according to laws. Rational beings alone have the faculty of acting according *to the conception* of laws, that is according to principles, *i.e.,* have a *will.* Since the deduction of actions from principles requires *reason,* the will is nothing but practical reason. If reason infallibly determines the will, then the actions of such a being which are recognised as objectively necessary are subjectively necessary also; *i.e.,* the will is a faculty to choose *that only* which reason independent on inclination recognises as practically necessary, *i.e.,* as good. But if reason of itself does not sufficiently determine the will, if the latter is subject also to subjective condi-

---

[1] A *maxim* is the subjective principle of volition. The objective principle (*i.e.,* that which would also serve subjectively as a practical principle to all rational beings if reason had full power over the faculty of desire) is the practical *law.*

tions (particular impulses) which do not always coincide with the objective conditions; in a word, if the will does not *in itself* completely accord with reason (which is actually the case with men), then the actions which objectively are recognised as necessary are subjectively contingent, and the determination of such a will according to objective laws is *obligation,* that is to say, the relation of the objective laws to a will that is not thoroughly good, is conceived as the determination of the will of a rational being by principles of reason, but which the will from its nature does not of necessity follow.

The conception of an objective principle, in so far as it is obligatory for a will, is called a command (of reason), and the formula of the command is called an Imperative.

All imperatives are expressed by the word *ought* [or *shall*], and thereby indicate the relation of an objective law of reason to a will, which from its subjective constitution is not necessarily determined by it (an obligation). They say that something would be good to do or to forbear, but they say it to a will which does not always do a thing because it is conceived to be good to do it. That is practically *good,* however, which determines the will by means of the conceptions of reason, and consequently not from subjective causes, but objectively, that is, on principles which are valid for every rational being as such. It is distinguished from the *pleasant,* as that which influences the will only by means of sensation from merely subjective causes, valid only for the sense of this or that one, and not as a principle of reason, which holds for every one.

A perfectly good will would therefore be equally subject to objective laws (viz., of good), but could not be conceived as *obliged* thereby to act lawfully, because of itself from its subjective constitution it can only be determined by the conception of good. Therefore no imperatives hold for the Divine will, or in general for a *holy* will; *ought* is here out of place, because the volition is already of itself necessarily in unison with the law. Therefore imperatives are only formulae to express the relation of objective laws of all volition to the subjective imperfection of the will of this or that rational being, *e.g.*, the human will.

Now all *imperatives* command either *hypothetically* or *categorically*. The former represent the practical necessity of a possible action as means to something else that is willed (or at least which one might possibly will). The categorical imperative would be that which represented an action as necessary of itself without reference to another end, *i.e.*, as objectively necessary.

Since every practical law represents a possible action as good, and on this account, for a subject who is practically determinable by reason, necessary, all imperatives are formulæ determining an action which is necessary according to the principle of a will good in some respects. If now the action is good only as a means *to something else*, then the imperative is *hypothetical;* if it is conceived as good *in itself* and consequently as being necessarily the principle of a will which of itself conforms to reason, then it is *categorical*. . . .

When I conceive a hypothetical imperative in general, I do not know beforehand what it will contain, until I am given the condition. But when I conceive a categorical imperative I know at once what it contains. For as the imperative contains, besides the law, only the necessity of the maxim[2] conforming to this law, while the law contains no condition restricting it, there remains nothing but the general statement that the maxim of the action should conform to a universal law, and it is this conformity alone that the imperative properly represents as necessary.

There is therefore but one categorical imperative, namely this: *Act only on that maxim whereby thou canst at the same time will that it should become a universal law.*

Now if all imperatives of duty can be deduced from this one imperative as from their prin-

[2] A maxim is a subjective principle of action and must be distinguished from the *objective principle*, namely practical law. The former contains the practical rule set by reason according to the conditions of the subject (often its ignorance or its inclinations), so that it is the principle on which the subject *acts;* but the law is the objective principle valid for every rational being, and is the principle on which it *ought to act* that is an imperative.

ciple, then although it should remain undecided whether what is called duty is not merely a vain notion, yet at least we shall be able to show what we understand by it and what this notion means.

Since the universality of the law according to which effects are produced constitutes what is properly called *nature* in the most general sense (as to form), that is the existence of things so far as it is determined by general laws, the imperative of duty may be expressed thus: *Act as if the maxim of thy action were to become by thy will a Universal Law of Nature*. . . .

We will now enumerate a few duties[:] . . .

1. A man reduced to despair by a series of misfortunes feels wearied of life, but is still so far in possession of his reason that he can ask himself whether it would not be contrary to his duty to himself to take his own life. Now he inquires whether the maxim of his action could become a universal law of nature. His maxim is: From self-love I adopt it as a principle to shorten my life when its longer duration is likely to bring more evil than satisfaction. It is asked then simply whether this principle of self-love can become a universal law of nature? Now we see at once that a system of nature of which it should be a law to destroy life by the very feeling which is designed to impel to the maintenance of life would contradict itself, and therefore could not exist as a system of nature; hence that maxim cannot possibly exist as a universal law of nature and consequently would be wholly inconsistent with the supreme principle of all duty.

2. Another finds himself forced by necessity to borrow money. He knows that he will not be able to repay it, but sees also that nothing will be lent to him, unless he promises stoutly to repay it in a definite time. He desires to make this promise, but he has still so much conscience as to ask himself: Is it not unlawful and inconsistent with duty to get out of a difficulty in this way? Suppose however that he resolves to do so: then the maxim of his action would be expressed thus: When I think myself in want of money, I will borrow money and promise to repay it, although I know that I never can do so. Now this principle of self-love or of one's own advantage may per-

haps be consistent with my whole future welfare; but the question now is, Is it right? I change then the suggestion of self-love into a universal law, and state the question thus: How would it be if my maxim were a universal law? Then I see at once that it could never hold as a universal law of nature, but would necessarily contradict itself. For supposing it to be a universal law that every one when he thinks himself in a difficulty should be able to promise whatever he pleases, with the purpose of not keeping his promise, the promise itself would become impossible, as well as the end that one might have in view in it, since no one would consider that anything was promised to him, but would ridicule all such statements as vain pretences.

3. A third finds in himself a talent which with the help of some culture might make him a useful man in many respects. But he finds himself in comfortable circumstances, and prefers to indulge in pleasure rather than to take pains in enlarging and improving his happy natural capacities. He asks, however, whether his maxim of neglect of his natural gifts, besides agreeing with his inclination to indulgence, agrees also with what is called duty? He sees then that a system of nature could indeed subsist with such a universal law, though men (like the South Sea islanders) should let their talents rust, and resolve to devote their lives merely to idleness, amusement, and propagation of their species, in a word to enjoyment; but he cannot possibly *will* that this should be a universal law of nature, or be implanted in us as such by a natural instinct. For, as a rational being, he necessarily wills that his faculties be developed, since they serve him for all sorts of possible purposes, and have been given him for this.

4. A fourth, who is in prosperity, while he sees that others have to contend with great wretchedness and that he could help them, thinks: What concern is it of mine? Let every one be as happy as heaven pleases or as he can make himself; I will take nothing from him nor even envy him, only I do not wish to contribute anything either to his welfare or to his assistance in distress! Now no doubt if such a mode of thinking were a univer-

sal law, the human race might very well subsist, and doubtless even better than in a state in which every one talks of sympathy and good will, or even takes care occasionally to put it into practice, but on the other side, also cheats when he can, betrays the rights of men or otherwise violates them. But although it is possible that a universal law of nature might exist in accordance with that maxim, it is impossible to *will* that such a principle should have the universal validity of a law of nature. For a will which resolved this would contradict itself, inasmuch as many cases might occur in which one would have need of the love and sympathy of others, and in which by such a law of nature, sprung from his own will, he would deprive himself of all hope of the aid he desires.

Supposing . . . that there were something *whose existence* has *in itself* an absolute worth, something which being *an end in itself*, could be a source of definite laws, then in this and this alone would lie the source of a possible categorical imperative, *i.e.*, a practical law. Now I say: man and generally any rational being *exists* as an end in himself, *not merely as a means* to be arbitrarily used by this or that will, but in all his actions, whether they concern himself or other rational beings, must always be regarded at the same time as an end. All objects of the inclinations have only a conditional worth, for if the inclinations and the wants founded on them did not exist, then their object would be without value. But the inclinations themselves being sources of want, are so far from having an absolute worth for which they should be desired, that on the contrary it must be the universal wish of every rational being to be wholly free from them. Thus the worth of any object which is *to be acquired* by our action is always conditional. Beings whose existence depends not on our will but on nature's, have nevertheless, if they are irrational beings, only a relative value as means, and are therefore called *things;* rational beings on the contrary, are called *persons,* because their very nature points them out as ends in themselves, that is as something which must not be used merely as means, and so far therefore restricts freedom of action (and is an object of respect). These, therefore, are not merely subjective ends whose existence has a worth *for us* as an effect of our action, but *objective ends,* that is things whose existence is an end in itself; an end moreover for which no other can be substituted, which they should subserve *merely* as means, for otherwise nothing whatever would possess *absolute worth;* but if all worth were conditioned and therefore contingent, then there would be no supreme practical principle of reason whatever.

If then there is a supreme practical principle or, in respect of the human will, a categorical imperative, it must be one which, drawn from the conception of that which is necessarily an end for every one because it is *an end in itself,* constitutes an *objective* principle of will, and can therefore serve as a universal practical law. The foundation of this principle is: *rational nature exists as an end in itself.* Man necessarily conceives his own existence as being so; so far then, this is a *subjective* principle of human actions. But every other rational being regards its existence similarly, just on the same rational principle that holds for me. So that it is at the same time an objective principle, from which as a supreme practical law all laws of the will must be capable of being deduced. Accordingly the practical imperative will be as follows: *So act as to treat humanity, whether in thine own person or in that of any other, in every case as an end withal, never as a means only.* . . .

Looking back now on all previous attempts to discover the principle of morality, we need not wonder why they all failed. It was seen that man was bound to laws by duty, but it was not observed that the laws to which he is subject are *only those of his own giving,* though at the same time they are *universal,* and that he is only bound to act in conformity with his own will; a will, however, which is designed by nature to give universal laws. For when he has conceived him only as subject to a law (no matter what), then this law required some interest, either by way of attraction or constraint, since it did not originate as a law from *his own* will, but this will was according to a law obliged by *something else* to act in a certain manner. Now by this necessary consequence all the labour spent in finding a supreme principle of *duty* was irrevocably lost. For men never could extract duty, but only a necessity of acting from a certain interest. Whether this interest was private or otherwise, in any case the imperative must be conditional, and could not by any means be capable of being a moral command. I will then call this the principle of *Autonomy* of the will, in contrast with every other which I therefore reckon as *Heteronomy.*

The conception of the will of every rational being as one which must consider itself as giving in all the maxims of its will universal laws, so as to judge itself and its actions from this point of view—this conception leads to another which depends on it and is very fruitful, namely that of *a kingdom of ends.*

By a *kingdom* I understand the union of different rational beings in a system by common laws. Now since it is by laws that ends are determined as regards their universal validity, hence, if we abstract from the personal differences of rational beings and likewise from all the content of their private ends, we shall be able to conceive all ends combined in a systematic whole (including both rational beings as ends in themselves, and also the special ends which each may propose to himself), that is to say, we can conceive a kingdom of ends, which on the preceding principles is possible.

For all rational beings come under the *law* that each of them must treat itself and all others *never merely as means,* but in every case *at the same time as ends in themselves.* Hence results a systematic union of rational beings by common objective laws, *i.e.,* a kingdom which may be called a kingdom of ends, since what these laws have in view is just the relation of these beings to one another as ends and means. It is certainly only an ideal.

Study Questions

1. Why does Kant begin his search for a universal principle of morality by examining the notion of a good will? How does he support his claim that the good will is the only thing

that is absolutely good? Why does he claim that its goodness does not lie in its effects but in its willing?

2. What purpose does reason have in morality? How does it accomplish its purpose? Why is it inadequate for pursuing happiness? What is Kant suggesting about the place of happiness in the moral life? What is he assuming with regard to reason?

3. What is the relation between the good will and duty? What role does reason play in this relation?

4. What is the moral significance of our motives? What is the difference between actions done from duty and actions that merely accord with duty? What is the moral worth of our feelings? Are we usually indifferent to what another person feels when he or she performs his or her duty?

5. What is a categorical imperative? What features does it have and why? How does it differ from the hypothetical imperative?

6. What is the supreme practical principle? What is its place in the kingdom of ends? Where does morality lie? Where does freedom lie? Where do nonrational beings, such as animals, stand in this kingdom? Do they have "dignity"?

Suggestions for Further Reading

Aune, B. *Kant's Theory of Morals* (Princeton, NJ: Princeton University Press, 1979). A seven-chapter basic introduction to Kant's moral philosophy that focuses mainly on his *Fundamental Principles of the Metaphysic of Morals.*

Nell, O. *Acting on Principle: An Essay on Kantian Ethics* (New York: Columbia University Press, 1975). An exposition supporting Kant's ethical theory.

O'Neill, O. "Kantian Ethics." In *A Companion to Ethics,* ed. P. Singer (Oxford; Cambridge, MA: Blackwell, 1991). Explains Kant's notion of the categorical imperative and considers common charges against it.

Paton, H. J. *The Categorical Imperative* (Chicago: University of Chicago Press, 1948). An analysis of Kant's notion of the categorical imperative.

Ross, W. D. *Kant's Ethical Theory* (Oxford: Clarendon Press, 1954). An analysis of Kant's incursion into the metaphysics of morals.

Sullivan, R. *An Introduction to Kant's Ethics* (Cambridge: Cambridge University Press, 1994). A ten-chapter introduction to Kant's ethics through the perspective of his political philosophy. Includes a detailed commentary of Kant's *Fundamental Principles of the Metaphysic of Morals.*

John Stuart Mill (1806–1873)

John Stuart Mill was born in London as the oldest of nine children. His father, James Mill, was a respected intellectual who followed and supported Jeremy Bentham's utilitarian philosophy. Educated at home by his father, Mill was subjected to a rigorous program of study. Learning Greek by the age of three and Latin by the age of seven, he had read several of Plato's dialogues in the original Greek by the time he was ten years old. His father's pedagogical experiments included morning lectures, questions about extensive reading assignments, and summaries of their discussions. Reflecting back on his childhood, Mill once said "I was never a boy."

When he was twenty years old, Mill realized that he had not attained personal happiness, and suffered a mental collapse. This was followed by a severe depression that lasted several months. Though James Mill had studied to be a minister and believed in a humanistic religion, he never taught his son matters of religion and failed to show him any "signs of feeling." Searching for a more fulfilling understanding of his own humanity, Mill began to read the works of great poets, where he gained a sense of the emotions he was denied as a child. He later met Mrs. Harriet Taylor, whom he described as the second greatest influence in his life after his father. At first his friend and collaborator, she later married Mill after her first husband died.

In his philosophy, Mill examines social, political, and economic issues through an empirical and practical lens. As a utilitarian, he shared Bentham's definition of the supreme moral principle as "the greatest happiness for the greatest number of people." Bentham's main interest was to apply the principle of utility in social legislation and reform. Mill had the similar but broader objective of improving the overall human condition. With this purpose in mind, he reflected not only on society, politics, and economics but also on logic, metaphysics, and ethics. In his later years, Mill was elected to Parliament, where he worked as a social reformer supporting the women's suffrage movement, the enfranchisement of the English working class, Irish land reform, and the rights of blacks in Jamaica.

Mill's collaborative works with Harriet Taylor (*Principles of Political Economy, On Liberty,* and *The Subjection of Women*) reveal his fervent belief in individual freedom and equality. His *System of Logic* reflects his methodological approach to the problem of knowledge through detailed analyses of inductive patterns and their application in the human or moral sciences. His book *Three Essays on Religion* (published posthumously according to his will) indicates the extent of his application of utilitarian principles to the problem of the belief in God and his practical concern for a natural, rather than supernatural, "religion of humanity."

Published in 1863, *Utilitarianism* is Mill's only work on moral philosophy. While explaining and defending the principles that were first formulated by Bentham, Mill presents his own version of utilitarianism. Bentham had founded his philosophy on hedonism, or the claim that pleasure (*hedone* in Greek) is the supreme good. Like the ancient Greek hedonist philosopher Epicurus, Bentham believed that we naturally seek pleasure and avoid pain (psychological hedonism). Our morality itself lies on these grounds, so that we also ought to seek pleasure (ethical hedonism). In his hedonist theory, Bentham developed an ethics that assigned moral import to the consequences or the effects of actions. From this consequentialist perspective, the agent of that action, his character, and his motives for acting are morally irrelevant. Equating happiness with pleasure and goodness with utility, Bentham developed his "hedonistic calculus," a method for determining the sum total of pleasure brought about through political laws. Stressing the importance and equality of the interests of individuals forming a society, Bentham's hedonistic calculus assumed that the only significant difference between individual experiences of pleasure resides in the amount or quantity of pleasure experienced. According to his famous formulation, "Quantity of pleasure being equal, pushpin [a child's game of the time] is as good as poetry." This turned out to be a rather unfortunate phrase, and Bentham's philosophy was portrayed as one "for swines."

In defense of Bentham, Mill upheld the "greatest happiness" principle. He claimed that it was practical, concrete, and well grounded in its focus on the ends of human actions and was effective in its applicability. Like Bentham, Mill defined utility as the criterion for distinguishing right from wrong. Following his predecessor, Mill also equated happiness with pleasure and inferred ethical hedonism from psychological hedonism. However, Mill's reformulation of utilitarian principles departs from Bentham's focus on the mere quantity of pleasure. Unlike Bentham, Mill explicitly attaches importance to the kind or quality of pleasure being measured according to the "greatest happiness principle," for he insists that he is searching for a distinctively human happiness. Humans have faculties more elevated than animal appetites. The uniquely human pleasures are pleasures of the mind, and they comprise our intellect, feelings, and imagination. As Mill puts it in his oft-quoted phrase, "It is better to be a human being dissatisfied than a pig satisfied; better to be Socrates dissatisfied than a fool satisfied." Those individuals who have experienced different kinds of pleasures—animal and mental (especially intellectual)—are the best judges for determining which is the higher kind. However, their judgments must still be directed toward producing the greatest amount of happiness for the greatest number of people. This happiness is attainable if it is conceived realistically as a life with moments of many varied pleasures and a few temporary pains.

WHAT UTILITARIANISM IS

A PASSING REMARK is all that needs be given to the ignorant blunder of supposing that those who stand up for utility as the test of right and wrong, use the term in that restricted and merely colloquial sense in which utility is opposed to pleasure. An apology is due to the philosophical opponents of utilitarianism, for even the momentary appearance of confounding them with any one capable of so absurd a misconception; which is the more extraordinary, inasmuch as the contrary accusation, of referring everything to pleasure, and that too in its grossest form, is another of the common charges against utilitarianism: and, as has been pointedly remarked by an able writer, the same sort of persons, and often the very same persons, denounce the theory "as impracticably dry when the word utility precedes the word pleasure, and as too practically voluptuous when the word pleasure precedes the word utility." Those who know anything about the matter are aware that every writer, from Epicurus to Bentham, who maintained the theory of utility, meant by it, not something to be contradistinguished from pleasure, but pleasure itself, together with exemption from pain; and instead of opposing the useful to the agreeable or the ornamental, have always declared that the useful means these, among other things. Yet the common herd, including the herd of writers, not only in newspapers and periodicals, but in books of weight and pretension, are perpetually falling into this shallow mistake. Having caught up the word utilitarian, while knowing nothing whatever about it but its sound, they habitually

John Stuart Mill. "*What Utilitarianism Is.*" *In* Utilitarianism. *London: Longmans, Green, 1897, Chapter 2.*

express by it the rejection, or the neglect, of pleasure in some of its forms; of beauty, of ornament, or of amusement. Nor is the term thus ignorantly misapplied solely in disparagement, but occasionally in compliment; as though it implied superiority to frivolity and the mere pleasures of the moment. And this perverted use is the only one in which the word is popularly known, and the one from which the new generation are acquiring their sole notion of its meaning. Those who introduced the word, but who had for many years discontinued it as a distinctive appellation, may well feel themselves called upon to resume it, if by doing so they can hope to contribute anything towards rescuing it from this utter degradation.

The creed which accepts as the foundation of morals, Utility, or the Greatest Happiness Principle, holds that actions are right in proportion as they tend to promote happiness, wrong as they tend to produce the reverse of happiness. By happiness is intended pleasure, and the absence of pain; by unhappiness, pain, and the privation of pleasure. To give a clear view of the moral standard set up by the theory, much more requires to be said; in particular, what things it includes in the ideas of pain and pleasure; and to what extent this is left an open question. But these supplementary explanations do not affect the theory of life on which this theory of morality is grounded—namely, that pleasure, and freedom from pain, are the only things desirable as ends; and that all desirable things (which are as numerous in the utilitarian as in any other scheme) are desirable either for the pleasure inherent in themselves, or as means to the promotion of pleasure and the prevention of pain.

Now, such a theory of life excites in many minds, and among them in some of the most estimable in feeling and purpose, inveterate dislike. To suppose that life has (as they express it) no higher end than pleasure—no better and nobler object of desire and pursuit—they designate as utterly mean and grovelling; as a doctrine worthy only of swine, to whom the followers of Epicurus were, at a very early period, contemptuously likened; and modern holders of the doctrine are occasionally made the subject of equally polite comparisons by its German, French, and English assailants.

When thus attacked, the Epicureans have always answered, that it is not they, but their accusers, who represent human nature in a degrading light; since the accusation supposes human beings to be capable of no pleasures except those of which swine are capable. If this supposition were true, the charge could not be gainsaid, but would then be no longer an imputation: for if the sources of pleasure were precisely the same to human beings and to swine, the rule of life which is good enough for the one would be good enough for the other. The comparison of the Epicurean life to that of beasts is felt as degrading, precisely because a beast's pleasures do not satisfy a human being's conceptions of happiness. Human beings have faculties more elevated than the animal appetites, and when once made conscious of them, do not regard anything as happiness which does not include their gratification. I do not, indeed, consider the Epicureans to have been by any means faultless in drawing out their scheme of consequences from the utilitarian principle. To do this in any sufficient manner, many Stoic, as well as Christian elements require to be included. But there is no known Epicurean theory of life which does not assign to the pleasures of the intellect, of the feelings and imagination, and of the moral sentiments, a much higher value as pleasures than to those of mere sensation. It must be admitted, however, that utilitarian writers in general have placed the superiority of mental over bodily pleasures chiefly in the greater permanency, safety, uncostliness, &c., of the former—that is, in their circumstantial advantages rather than in their intrinsic nature. And on all these points utilitarians have fully proved their case; but they might have taken the other, and as it may be called, higher ground, with entire consistency. It is quite compatible with the principle of utility to recognise the fact, that some *kinds* of pleasure are more desirable and more valuable than others. It would be absurd that while, in estimating all other things, quality is considered as well as quantity, the estimation of pleasures should be supposed to depend on quantity alone.

If I am asked, what I mean by difference of quality in pleasures, or what makes one pleasure more valuable than another, merely as a pleasure, except its being greater in amount, there is but one possible answer. Of two pleasures, if there be one to which all or almost all who have experience of both give a decided preference, irrespective of any feeling of moral obligation to prefer it, that is the more desirable pleasure. If one of the two is, by those who are competently acquainted with both, placed so far above the other that they prefer it, even though knowing it to be attended with a greater amount of discontent, and would not resign it for any quantity of the other pleasure which their nature is capable of, we are justified in ascribing to the preferred enjoyment a superiority in quality, so far outweighing quantity as to render it, in comparison, of small account.

Now it is an unquestionable fact that those who are equally acquainted with, and equally capable of appreciating and enjoying both, do give a most marked preference to the manner of existence which employs their higher faculties. Few human creatures would consent to be changed into any of the lower animals, for a promise of the fullest allowance of a beast's pleasures, no intelligent human being would consent to be a fool, no instructed person would be an ignoramus, no person of feeling and conscience would be selfish and base, even though they should be persuaded that the fool, the dunce, or the rascal is better satisfied with his lot than they are with theirs. They would not resign what they possess more than he, for the most complete satisfaction of all the desires which they have in common with him. If they ever fancy they would, it is only in cases of unhappiness so extreme, that to escape from it they would exchange their lot for almost any other, however undesirable in their own eyes. A being of higher faculties requires more to make him happy, is capable probably of more acute suffering, and is certainly accessible to it at more points, than one of an inferior type; but in spite of these liabilities, he can never really wish to sink into what he feels to be a lower grade of existence. . . . It is indisputable that the being whose capacities of enjoyment are low, has the greatest chance of having them fully satisfied; and a highly-endowed being will always feel that any happiness which he can look for, as the world is constituted, is imperfect. But he can learn to bear its imperfections, if they are at all bearable; and they will not make him envy the being who is indeed unconscious of the imperfections, but only because he feels not at all the good which those imperfections qualify. It is better to be a human being dissatisfied than a pig satisfied; better to be Socrates dissatisfied than a fool satisfied. And if the fool, or the pig, is of a different opinion, it is because they only know their own side of the question. The other party to the comparison knows both sides.

It may be objected, that many who are capable of the higher pleasures, occasionally, under the influence of temptation, postpone them to the lower. But this is quite compatible with a full appreciation of the intrinsic superiority of the higher. Men often, from infirmity of character, make their election for the nearer good, though they know it to be the less valuable; and this no less when the choice is between two bodily pleasures, than when it is between bodily and mental. They pursue sensual indulgences to the injury of health, though perfectly aware that health is the greater good. It may be further objected, that many who begin with youthful enthusiasm for everything noble, as they advance in years sink into indolence and selfishness. But I do not believe that those who undergo this very common change, voluntarily choose the lower description of pleasures in preference to the higher. I believe that before they devote themselves exclusively to the one, they have already become incapable of the other. Capacity for the nobler feelings is in most natures a very tender plant, easily killed, not only by hostile influences, but by mere want of sustenance; and in the majority of young persons it speedily dies away if the occupations to which their position in life has devoted them, and the society into which it has thrown them, are not favourable to keeping that higher capacity in exercise. Men lose their high aspirations as they lose their intellectual tastes, because they have not time or opportunity for indulging them; and they addict themselves to inferior pleasures, not because they deliberately prefer them, but because they are either the only ones to which they have access, or the only ones which they are any longer capable of enjoying. It may be questioned whether any one who has remained equally susceptible to both classes of pleasures, ever knowingly and calmly preferred the lower; though many, in all ages, have broken down in an ineffectual attempt to combine both.

From this verdict of the only competent judges, I apprehend there can be no appeal. On a question which is the best worth having of two pleasures, or which of two modes of existence is the most grateful to the feelings, apart from its moral attributes and from its consequences, the judgment of those who are qualified by knowledge of both, or, if they differ, that of the majority among them, must be admitted as final. And there needs be the less hesitation to accept this judgment respecting the quality of pleasures, since there is no other tribunal to be referred to even on the question of quantity. What means are there of determining which is the acutest of two pains, or the intensest of two pleasurable sensations, except the general suffrage of those who are familiar with both? Neither pains nor pleasure are homogeneous, and pain is always heterogeneous with pleasure. What is there to decide whether a particular pleasure is worth purchasing at the cost of a particular pain, except the feelings and judgment of the experienced? When, therefore, those feelings and judgment declare the pleasures derived from the higher faculties to be preferable *in kind,* apart from the question of intensity, to those of which the animal nature, disjoined from the higher faculties, is susceptible, they are entitled on this subject to the same regard.

I have dwelt on this point, as being a necessary part of a perfectly just conception of Utility or Happiness, considered as the directive rule of human conduct. But it is by no means an indispensable condition to the acceptance of the utilitarian standard; for that standard is not the agent's own greatest happiness, but the greatest amount of happiness altogether; and if it may possibly be doubted whether a noble character is always the happier for its nobleness, there can be no doubt that it makes other people happier, and that the world in general is immensely a gainer by it. Utilitarianism, therefore, could only attain its end by the general cultivation of nobleness of character, even if each individual were only benefited by the nobleness of others, and his own, so far as happiness is concerned, were a sheer deduction from the benefit. But the bare enunciation of such an absurdity as this last, renders refutation superfluous.

According to the Greatest Happiness Principle, as above explained, the ultimate end, with reference to and for the sake of which all other things are desirable (whether we are considering our own good or that of other people), is an existence exempt as far as possible from pain, and as rich as possible in enjoyments, both in point of quantity and quality; the test of quality, and the rule for measuring it against quantity, being the preference felt by those who, in their opportunities of experience, to which must be added their habits of self-consciousness and self-observation, are best furnished with the means of comparison. This, being, according to the utilitarian opinion, the end of human action, is necessarily also the standard of morality; which may accordingly be defined, the rules and precepts for human conduct, by the observance of which an existence such as has been described might be, to the greatest extent possible, secured to all mankind; and not to them only, but so far as the nature of things admits, to the whole sentient creation.

Study Questions

1. What concepts does Mill rely on in his definition of the principle of utility? What consequences follow this principle?
2. How does Mill support his equation of pleasure with happiness? Is pleasure happiness? Is happiness the end or purpose of all our actions? What place can other values like truth, justice, and human dignity have in Mill's philosophy?
3. What are Mill's arguments for distinguishing between different kinds of pleasures? What assumptions does he make about human nature?
4. How does Mill determine who should judge the value of pleasure? What assumptions does he make concerning the judges and their decisions?
5. Is Mill's utilitarian principle elitist or democratic? Where does psychological hedonism end and ethical hedonism begin in his theory?

Suggestions for Further Reading

Berger, F. *Happiness, Justice and Freedom: The Moral and Political Philosophy of John Stuart Mill* (Berkeley: University of California Press, 1984). Part I examines Mill's moral doctrine.

Moore, G. E. *Principia Ethica* (London: Cambridge University Press, 1903). Chapter 3 provides a critique of Mill's moral theory.

Plamenatz, J. *The English Utilitarian* (Oxford: Blackwell, 1966). A general exposition. Chapter 8 focuses on Mill and Chapter 10 offers a general critique of utilitarianism.

Semmel, B. *John Stuart Mill and the Pursuit of Virtue* (New Haven, CT: Yale University Press, 1984). Examines the development of Mill's theories and their correlation with events in his life.

Singer, P., ed. *A Companion to Ethics* (Oxford; Cambridge, MA: Blackwell, 1991). See P. Petit's "Consequentialism" and R. E. Goodin's "Utility and the Good" for two contrasting accounts of utiliarianism.

Strasser, M. *The Moral Philosophy of John Stuart Mill: Toward Modifications of Contemporary Utilitarianism* (Wakefield, NH: Longwood Academic, 1991). A ten-chapter defense of Mill against the charge that his moral theories are inconsistent with one another.

Søren Kierkegaard (1813–1855)

Søren Kierkegaard, the "melancholy Dane" whose philosophy would be the wellspring for twentieth-century existentialism, was born in Copenhagen as the last of seven children. Kierkegaard's father had been a laborer who had worked his way up to becoming a wealthy merchant and had married his first wife's former servant. A devout Lutheran, he had a stern and moody disposition—prone to brooding and melancholic fits—that left a deep imprint on Kierkegaard's life and thought. Born with a hunched back and uneven legs, the young Kierkegaard's keen mind and sharp wit compensated for the frailty of his body and earned him the family nickname of "the fork." Educated at home by his father, he was taught religion, literature, philosophy, logic, and history through a rigorous disciplining of his reason and imagination.

On bad weather days, rather than their usual excursions in the city, father and son would take "fantasy trips" living out scenes from history, literature, and imagination that helped to develop the young Kierkegaard's knowledge and psychological insight.

Though his father wanted him to become a Lutheran minister, Kierkegaard developed a preference for philosophy and literature while he was a student of theology at the University of Copenhagen. During his student years, he led an active social life, frequenting cafés and often playing the life of the party for his elite circle of friends. However, his outward carefree lifestyle was often accompanied by inner torment and desperation. Kierkegaard's dissatisfaction with the life he was leading came to a turning point when, shortly before his father's death, he learned the reasons for his father's sense of guilt and melancholy. His dying father revealed that he had once blasphemed and sinned against God, and thus believed that his family was cursed by divine retribution for this. Now reconciled with his father, Kierkegaard experienced a religious conversion that was marked by a feeling of "indescribable joy" and gave him deep insight into the personal and psychological dimension of faith. He perceived this experience as a calling to a radically spiritual life and broke off his engagement with his former sweetheart, Regine Olsen, believing that the responsibilities of married life were incompatible with his temperament and mission.

Kierkegaard's philosophy gave primacy to the existing individual and asserted that our highest fulfillment and freedom are found in a direct, unmediated relationship with God. Lutheranism postulated the necessity of such relationship, but it emphasized the perpetual gap between God and ourselves in our sinfulness. Kierkegaard insisted, however, that we can attain our fullest individuality only in a "leap of faith" toward God. He rejected anything that threatened individuality and the individual's relationship to God, and launched his attacks against institutionalized religion, abstract systems of thought, and the social anonymity of the "crowd" mentality.

Kierkegaard was especially critical of G. W. F. Hegel's system of absolute idealism, which placed an abstract universal spirit or mind above the finite individual. According to Hegel, the absolute spirit manifests itself in and through history, but the acts of individuals have meaning only in the process of unfolding of the absolute spirit. Hegel also saw history as a (dialectical) development where internal contradictions eventually culminate into higher syntheses or harmonies of opposites. The highest synthesis is achieved when the absolute mind develops into reason and comes to recognize that reality is its own reflection. At this point in history, where "the rational is real and the real is rational," reason is able to grasp religion, among other things, as a manifestation of itself.

In contrast with Hegel, Kierkegaard affirmed the independent reality of the concrete existing individual. He proposed that the highest level of the individual's existence is attained when she reaches beyond what is abstract and universal. Our very existence is an unfolding whereby each individual is defined by the choices made in her life. Such existential choices take the form of an "either-or." In all this, Kierkegaard insisted on the utter incapacity of reason to grasp the truths of God's existence and our own. Such truths are not open to rational, objective proofs and explanations; they are reached only through the lived reality of the individual's inwardness or interior life. Faith is the only avenue to God, and only through the intensity and depth of my passion for God can I reach my authenticity or my genuine self. Thus, Kierke-gaard claims that truth in its most important sense is "subjectivity." As he noted in a famous entry to his journal: "The thing is to understand myself, to see what God re-ally wishes *me* to do; the thing is to find a truth which is true *for me,* to find *the idea for which I can live and die.*"

According to Kierkegaard, our lives are a process of self-actualization through differ-ent stages of development. He identified three ascending stages on the way toward reaching our fullest individuality and authenticity: the aesthetic, the ethical, and the religious stages. The aesthetic stage is characterized by a life in the pursuit of sensu-ous or intellectual pleasures. The aesthetic person believes he is living a life of free-dom as he follows his desires without binding himself to anything. However, he is really a slave to his impulses. His life is marked by the boredom of fleeting moments of satisfaction and a feeling of emptiness that can lead to despair. The first crucial choice, the real "either-or," lies between a bottomless life of temporary gratifications and the rational life grounded in duty and responsibility according to the moral stan-dard of good and evil. Don Juan, the great seducer, typifies for Kierkegaard the per-son who remains at the aesthetic stage and thus never achieves a unified and grounded self-hood.

The ethical stage, as the life of duty and responsibility, provides universal moral commands that rule over all individuals regardless of their particular impulses. Sub-jecting the self to the universal moral law thus anchors the individual in something eternal and constant beyond the self. There is no higher *telos* (end or purpose) to the universal moral law, so the individual's *telos* is itself only found in complying with ethical duties. Because our duties may sometimes conflict with one another, our lives may be marked by the tragedy of facing moral dilemmas. The exceptionally ethical person who surrenders himself completely to the universal law while choosing the higher of two conflicting duties is, in Kierkegaard's view, a "tragic hero" or "knight of infinite resignation." They are typified in historical or literary figures as Socrates (who chose to die rather than to abandon reason and universal truth) and Agamemnon (who sacrificed his own daughter Iphigenia to appease the angry gods).

Though the ethical life represents a higher stage in the individual's develop-ment, it cannot offer the fullest self-actualization. As finite, temporal beings with con-stant desires, we are unable to comply absolutely with the infinite and eternal uni-versal law. Our guilt, our awareness of our sinfulness in the face of God, moves us toward the religious stage. Here, our choice is an act of faith by which we take a "leap" toward what lies beyond our comprehension, toward the absurd. Faith is the paradox whereby what is subjective and individual is higher than what is objective and universal. It is thus above the reach of our reason and cannot be made intelligi-ble. Through faith, the individual enters into a direct and absolute relation to God that can be neither relative to nor mediated by anything else. Abraham is the "knight of faith" or the exceptional individual who was called upon by God himself to transgress the ethical by sacrificing his son Isaac. From the perspective of the ethical, this rep-resents a violation of Abraham's duty as a father toward his son. The paradoxical character of Abraham's dilemma is that his temptation was to follow his ethical duty. Thus, he experienced the unavoidable dread in violating the universal moral law.

Hence, Abraham's supreme act of faith involves a "teleological suspension of the ethical" by which the individual is higher than the universal moral law for the sake of a higher end (*telos*).

In the first selection Kierkegaard works out his conception of existential choice and its ethical character. In the second selection he discusses the teleological suspension of the ethical through the leap of faith.

EITHER/OR

My Friend,

What I have so often said to you I say now once again, or rather I shout it: Either/or, *aut/aut*. For a single *aut* adjoined as a rectification does not make the situation clear, since the question here at issue is so important that one cannot rest satisfied with a part of it, and in itself it is too coherent to be possessed partially. There are situations in life where it would be ridiculous or a species of madness to apply an either/or; but also, there are men whose souls are too dissolute (in the etymological sense of the word) to grasp what is implied in such a dilemma, whose personalities lack the energy to say with pathos, Either/or. . . .

Now in case a man were able to maintain himself upon the pinnacle of the instant of choice, in case he could cease to be a man, in case he were in his inmost nature only an airy thought, in case personality meant nothing more than to be a kobold, which takes part, indeed, in the movements but nevertheless remains unchanged; in case such were the situation, it would be foolish to say that it might ever be too late for a man to choose, for in a deeper sense there could be no question of a choice. The choice itself is decisive for the content of the personality, through the choice the personality immerses itself in the thing chosen, and when it does not choose it withers away in consumption. For an instant it is so, for an instant it may seem as if the things between which a choice is to be made lie outside of the chooser, that he stands in no relationship to it, that he can preserve a state of indifference over against it. This is the instant of deliberation, but this, like the Platonic instant, has no existence, least of all in the abstract sense in which you would hold it fast, and the longer one stares at it the less it exists. That which has to be chosen stands in the deepest relationship to the chooser, and when it is a question of a choice involving a life problem the individual must naturally be living in the meantime, and hence, it comes about that the longer he postpones the choice the easier it is for him to alter its character, notwithstanding that he is constantly deliberating and deliberating and believes that thereby he is holding the alternatives distinctly apart. When life's either/or is regarded in this way one is not easily tempted to jest with it. One sees, then, that the inner drift of the personality leaves no time for thought experiments, that it constantly hastens onward and in one way or another posits this alternative or that, making the choice more difficult the next instant because what has thus been posited must be revoked. Think of the captain on his ship at the instant when it has to come about. He will perhaps be able to say, "I can either do this or that"; but in case he is not a pretty poor navigator, he will be aware at the same time that the ship is all the while making its usual headway, and that therefore it is only an instant when it is indifferent whether he does this or that. So it is with a man. If he forgets to take account of the headway, there comes at last an instant when there no longer is any question of an either/or, not because he has chosen but because he has neglected to choose, which is equivalent to saying, because others have chosen for him, because he has lost his self. . . .

The act of choosing is essentially a proper and stringent expression of the ethical. Whenever in a stricter sense there is question of an either/or, one can always be sure that the ethical is involved. The only absolute either/or is the choice between good and evil, but that is also absolutely ethical. The aesthetic choice is either entirely immediate and to that extent no choice, or it loses itself in the multifarious. Thus, when a young girl follows the choice of her heart, this choice, however beautiful it may be, is in the strictest sense no choice, since it is entirely immediate. When a man deliberates aesthetically upon a multitude of life's problems, as you did in the foregoing, he does not easily get one either/or, but a whole multiplicity, because the self-determining factor in the choice is not ethically accentuated, and because when one does not choose absolutely one chooses only for the moment, and therefore can choose something different the next moment. The ethical choice is therefore in a certain sense much easier, much simpler, but in another sense it is infinitely harder. He who would define his life task ethically has ordinarily not so considerable a selection to choose from; on the other hand, the act of choice has far more importance for him. If you will understand me aright, I should like to say that in making a choice it is not so much a question of choosing the right as of the energy, the earnestness, the pathos with which one chooses. Thereby the personality announces its inner infinity, and thereby, in turn, the personality is consolidated. Therefore, even if a man were to choose the wrong, he will nevertheless discover, precisely by reason of the energy with which he chose, that he had chosen the wrong. For the

choice being made with the whole inwardness of his personality, his nature is purified and he himself brought into immediate relation to the eternal Power whose omnipresence interpenetrates the whole of existence. This transfiguration, this higher consecration, is never attained by that man who chooses merely aesthetically. The rhythm in that man's soul, in spite of all its passion, is only a *spiritus lenis*. . . .

What is it, then, that I distinguish in my either/or? Is it good and evil? No, I would only bring you up to the point where the choice between the evil and the good acquires significance for you. Everything hinges upon this. As soon as one can get a man to stand at the crossways in such a position that there is no recourse but to choose, he will choose the right. Hence, if it should chance that, while you are in the course of reading this somewhat lengthy dissertation, which again I send you in the form of a letter, you were to feel that the instant for choice had come, then throw the rest of this away, never concern yourself about it, you have lost nothing—but choose, and you shall see what validity there is in this act, yea, no young girl can be so happy with the choice of her heart as is a man who knows how to choose. So then, one either has to live aesthetically or one has to live ethically. In this alternative, as I have said, there is not yet in the strictest sense any question of a choice; for he who lives aesthetically does not choose, and he who after the ethical has manifested itself to him chooses the aesthetical is not living aesthetically, for he is sinning and is subject to ethical determinants even though his life may be described as unethical. Lo, this is, as it were, a *character indelebilis* impressed upon the ethical, that though it modestly places itself on a level with the aesthetical, it is nevertheless that which makes the choice a choice. And this is the pitiful thing to one who contemplates human life, that so many live on in a quiet state of perdition; they outlive themselves, not in the sense that the content of life is successively unfolding and now is possessed in this expanded state, but they live their lives as it were, outside of themselves, they vanish like shadows, their immortal soul is blown away, and they are not alarmed by the problem of its immortality, for they are already in a state of dissolution before they die. They do not live aesthetically, but neither has the ethical manifested itself in its entirety, so they have not exactly rejected it either, they therefore are not sinning, except in so far as it is sin not to be either one thing or the other; neither are they ever in doubt about their immortality, for he who deeply and sincerely is in doubt of it on his own behalf will surely find the right. *On his own behalf,* I say, and surely it is high time to utter a warning against the great-hearted, heroic objectivity with which many thinkers think on behalf of others and not on their own behalf. If one would call this which I here require selfishness, I would reply that this comes from the fact that people have no conception of what this "self" is, and that it would be of very little use to a man if he were to gain the whole world and lose himself, and that it must necessarily be a poor proof which does not first of all convince the man who presents it.

My either/or does not in the first instance denote the choice between good and evil; it denotes the choice whereby one chooses good *and* evil/or excludes them. Here the question is under what determinants one would contemplate the whole of existence and would himself live. That the man who chooses good and evil chooses the good is indeed true, but this becomes evident only afterwards; for the aesthetical is not the evil but neutrality, and that is the reason why I affirmed that it is the ethical which constitutes the choice. It is, therefore, not so much a question of choosing between willing the good *or* the evil, as of choosing to will, but by this in turn the good and the evil are posited. He who chooses the ethical chooses the good, but here the good is entirely abstract, only its being is posited, and hence it does not follow by any means that the chooser cannot in turn choose the evil, in spite of the fact that he chose the good. Here you see again how important it is that a choice be made, and that the crucial thing is not deliberation but the baptism of the will which lifts up the choice into the ethical.

FEAR AND TREMBLING

Problem I. Is there such a thing as a teleological suspension of the ethical?

The ethical as such is the universal, and as the universal it applies to everyone, which may be expressed from another point of view by saying that it applies every instant. It reposes immanently in itself, it has nothing without itself which is its *telos,* but is itself *telos* for everything outside it, and when this has been incorporated by the ethical it can go no further. Conceived immediately as physical and psychical, the particular individual is the individual who has his *telos* in the universal, and his ethical task is to express himself constantly in it, to abolish his particularity in order to become the universal. As soon as the individual would assert himself in his particularity over against the universal he sins, and only by recognizing this can he again reconcile himself with the universal. Whenever the individual after he has entered the universal feels an impulse to assert himself as the particular, he is in temptation (*Anfechtung*), and he can labor himself out of this only by penitently abandoning himself as the particular in the universal. If this be the highest thing that can be said of man and of his existence, then the ethical has the same character as man's eternal blessedness, which to all eternity and at every instant is his *telos,* since it would be a contradiction to say that this might be abandoned (i.e. teleologically suspended), inasmuch as this is no sooner suspended than it is forfeited, whereas in other cases what is suspended is not forfeited but is preserved precisely in that higher thing which is its *telos.*

If such be the case, then Hegel is right when in his chapter on "The Good and the Conscience," he characterizes man merely as the particular and regards this character as "a moral form of evil" which is to be annulled in the teleology of the moral, so that the individual who remains in this stage is either sinning or subjected to temptation (*Anfechtung*). On the other hand, Hegel is wrong in talking of faith, wrong in not protesting loudly and clearly against the fact that Abraham enjoys honor and glory as the father of faith, whereas he ought to be prosecuted and convicted of murder.

For faith is this paradox, that the particular is higher than the universal—yet in such a way, be it observed, that the movement repeats itself, and that consequently the individual, after having been in the universal, now as the particular isolates himself as higher than the universal. If this be not faith, then Abraham is lost, then faith has never existed in the world . . . because it has always existed. For if the ethical (i.e. the moral) is the highest thing, and if nothing incommensurable remains in man in any other way but as the evil (i.e. the particular which has to be expressed in the universal), then one needs no other categories besides those which the Greeks possessed or which by consistent thinking can be derived from them. This fact Hegel ought not to have concealed, for after all he was acquainted with Greek thought. . . .

Faith is precisely this paradox, that the individual as the particular is higher than the universal, is justified over against it, is not subordinate but superior—yet in such a way, be it observed, that it is the particular individual who, after he has been subordinated as the particular to the universal, now through the universal becomes the individual who as the particular is superior to the universal, for the fact that the individual as the particular stands in an absolute relation to the absolute. This position cannot be mediated, for all mediation comes about precisely by virtue of the universal; it is and remains to all eternity a paradox, inaccessible to thought. And yet faith is this paradox—or else (these are the logical deductions which I would beg the reader to have *in mente* at every point, though it would be too prolix for me to reiterate them on every occasion)—or else there never has been faith . . . precisely because it always has been. In other words, Abraham is lost.

That for the particular individual this paradox may easily be mistaken for a temptation (*Anfechtung*) is indeed true, but one ought not for this reason to conceal it. That the whole constitution of many persons may be such that this paradox repels them is indeed true, but one ought not for this reason to make faith something different in order to be able to possess it, but ought rather to admit that one does not possess it, whereas those who possess faith should take care to set up certain criteria so that one might distinguish the paradox from a temptation (*Anfechtung*).

Now the story of Abraham contains such a teleological suspension of the ethical. There have not been lacking clever pates and profound investigators who have found analogies to it. Their wisdom is derived from the pretty proposition that at bottom everything is the same. If one will look a little more closely, I have not much doubt that in the whole world one will not find a single analogy (except a later instance which proves nothing), if it stands fast that Abraham is the representative of faith, and that faith is normally expressed in him whose life is not merely the most paradoxical that can be thought but so paradoxical that it cannot be thought at all. He acts by virtue of the absurd, for it is precisely absurd that he as the particular is higher than the universal. This paradox cannot be mediated; for as soon as he begins to do this he has to admit that he was in temptation (*Antechtung*), and if such was the case, he never gets to the point of sacrificing Isaac, or, if he has sacrificed Isaac, he must turn back repentantly to the universal. By virtue of the absurd he gets Isaac again. Abraham is therefore at no instant a tragic hero but something quite different, either a murderer or a believer. The middle term which saves the tragic hero, Abraham has not. Hence it is that I can understand the tragic hero but cannot understand Abraham, though in a certain crazy sense I admire him more than all other men.

Abraham's relation to Isaac, ethically speaking, is quite simply expressed by saying that a father shall love his son more dearly than himself. Yet within its own compass the ethical has various gradations. Let us see whether in this story there is to be found any higher expression for the ethical such as would ethically explain his conduct, ethically justify him in suspending the ethical obligation toward his son, without in this search going beyond the teleology of the ethical.

When an undertaking in which a whole nation is concerned is hindered, when such an enterprise is brought to a standstill by the disfavor of heaven, when the angry deity sends a calm which mocks all efforts, when the seer performs his heavy task and proclaims that the deity demands a young maiden as a sacrifice—then will the father heroically make the sacrifice. He will magnanimously conceal his pain, even though he might wish that he were "the lowly man who dares to weep," not the king who must act royally. And though solitary pain forces its way into his breast, he has only three confidants among the people, yet soon the whole nation will be cognizant of his pain, but also cognizant of his exploit, that for the welfare of the whole he was willing to sacrifice her, his daughter, the lovely young maiden. O charming bosom! O beautiful cheeks! O bright golden hair! (v.687). And the daughter will affect him by her tears, and the father will turn his face away, but the hero will raise the knife.—When the report of this reaches the ancestral home, then will the beautiful maidens of Greece blush with enthusiasm, and if the daughter was betrothed, her true love will not be

angry but be proud of sharing in the father's deed, because the maiden belonged to him more feelingly than to the father.

When the intrepid judge who saved Israel in the hour of need in one breath binds himself and God by the same vow, then heroically the young maiden's jubilation, the beloved daughter's joy, he will turn to sorrow, and with her all Israel will lament her maiden youth; but every free-born man will understand, and every stout-hearted woman will admire Jephtha, and every maiden in Israel will wish to act as did his daughter. For what good would it do if Jephtha were victorious by reason of his vow if he did not keep it? Would not the victory again be taken from the nation?

When a son is forgetful of his duty, when the state entrusts the father with the sword of justice, when the laws require punishment at the hand of the father, then will the father heroically forget that the guilty one is his son, he will magnanimously conceal his pain, but there will not be a single one among the people, not even the son, who will not admire the father, and whenever the law of Rome is interpreted, it will be remembered that many interpreted it more learnedly, but none so gloriously as Brutus.

If, on the other hand, while a favorable wind bore the fleet on with swelling sails to its goal, Agamemnon had sent that messenger who fetched Iphigenia in order to be sacrificed; if Jephtha, without being bound by any vow which decided the fate of the nation, had said to his daughter, "Bewail now thy virginity for the space of two months, for I will sacrifice thee"; if Brutus had had a righteous son and yet would have ordered the lictors to execute him—who would have understood them? If these three men had replied to the query why they did it by saying, "It is a trial in which we are tested," would people have understood them better?

When Agamemnon, Jephtha, Brutus at the decisive moment heroically overcome their pain, have heroically lost the beloved and have merely to accomplish the outward sacrifice, then there never will be a noble soul in the world who will not shed tears of compassion for their pain and of admiration for their exploit. If, on the other hand, these three men at the decisive moment were to adjoin to their heroic conduct this little word, "But for all that it will not come to pass," who then would understand them? If as an explanation they added, "This we believe by virtue of the absurd," who would understand them better? For who would not easily understand that it was absurd, but who would understand that one could then believe it?

The difference between the tragic hero and Abraham is clearly evident. The tragic hero still remains within the ethical. He lets one expression of the ethical find its *telos* in a higher expression of the ethical; the ethical relation between father and son, or daughter and father, he reduces to a sentiment which has its dialectic in its relation to the idea of morality. Here there can be no question of a teleological suspension of the ethical itself.

With Abraham the situation was different. By his act he overstepped the ethical entirely and possessed a higher *telos* outside of it, in relation to which he suspended the former. For I should very much like to know how one would bring Abraham's act into relation with the universal, and whether it is possible to discover any connection whatever between what Abraham did and the universal . . . except the fact that he transgressed it. It was not for the sake of saving a people, not to maintain the idea of the state, that Abraham did this, and not in order to reconcile angry deities. If there could be a question of the deity being angry, he was angry only with Abraham, and Abraham's whole action stands in no relation to the universal, is a purely private undertaking. Therefore, whereas the tragic hero is great by reason of his moral virtue, Abraham is great by reason of a purely personal virtue. In Abraham's life there is no higher expression for the ethical than this, that the father shall love his son. Of the ethical in the sense of morality there can be no question in this instance. In so far as the universal was present, it was indeed cryptically present in Isaac, hidden as it were in Isaac's loins, and must therefore cry out with Isaac's mouth, "Do it not! Thou art bringing everything to naught."

Why then did Abraham do it? For God's sake, and (in complete identity with this) for his own sake. He did it for God's sake because God required this proof of his faith; for his own sake he did it in order that he might furnish the proof. The unity of these two points of view is perfectly expressed by the word which has always been used to characterize this situation: it is a trial, a temptation (*Fristelse*). A temptation—but what does that mean? What ordinarily tempts a man is that which would keep him from doing his duty, but in this case the temptation is itself the ethical . . . which would keep him from doing God's will. But what then is duty? Duty is precisely the expression for God's will.

Here is evident the necessity of a new category if one would understand Abraham. Such a relationship to the deity paganism did not know. The tragic hero does not enter into any private relationship with the deity, but for him the ethical is the divine, hence the paradox implied in his situation can be mediated in the universal.

Abraham cannot be mediated, and the same thing can be expressed also by saying that he cannot talk. So soon as I talk I express the universal, and if I do not do so, no one can understand me. Therefore if Abraham would express himself in terms of the universal, he must say that his situation is a temptation (*Anfechtung*), for he has no higher expression for that universal which stands above the universal which he transgresses.

Therefore, though Abraham arouses my admiration, he at the same time appalls me. He who denies himself and sacrifices himself for duty gives up the finite in order to grasp the infinite, and that man is secure enough. The tragic hero gives up the certain for the still more certain, and the eye of the beholder rests upon him confidently. But he who gives up the universal in order to grasp something still higher which is not the universal—what is he doing? Is it possible that this can be anything else but a temptation (*Anfechtung*)? And if it be possible . . . but the individual was mistaken—what can save him? He suffers all the pain of the tragic hero, he brings to naught his joy in the world, he renounces everything . . . and perhaps at the same instant debars himself from the sublime joy which to him was so precious that he would purchase it at any price. Him the beholder cannot understand nor let his eye rest confidently upon him. Perhaps it is not possible to do what the believer proposes, since it is indeed unthinkable. Or if it could be done, but if the individual had misunderstood the deity—what can save him? The tragic hero has need of tears and claims them, and where is the envious eye which would be so barren that it could not weep with Agamemnon; but where is the man with a soul so bewildered that he would have the presumption to weep for Abraham? The tragic hero accomplishes his act at a definite instant in time, but in the course of time he does something not less significant, he visits the man whose soul is beset with sorrow, whose breast for stifled sobs cannot draw breath, whose thoughts pregnant with tears weigh heavily upon him, to him he makes his appearance, dissolves the sorcery of sorrow, loosens his corslet, coaxes forth his tears by the fact that in his sufferings the sufferer forgets his own. One cannot weep over Abraham. One approaches him with a *horror religiosus,* as Israel approached Mount Sinai.—If then the solitary man who ascends Mount Moriah, which with its peak rises heaven-high above the plain of Aulis, if he be not a somnambulist who walks securely above the abyss while he who is stationed at the foot of the mountain and is looking on trembles with fear and out of reverence and dread dare not even call to him—if this man is disordered in his mind, if he had made a mistake! Thanks and thanks again to him who proffers to the man whom the sorrows of life have assaulted and left naked—proffers to him the fig-leaf of the word with which he can cover his wretchedness. Thanks be to thee, great Shakespeare, who art able to express everything, absolutely everything, precisely as it is—and yet why didst thou never pronounce this pang? Didst thou perhaps reserve it to thyself—like the loved one whose name one cannot endure that the world should mention? For the poet purchases the power of words, the power of uttering all the dread secrets of others, at the price of a little secret he is unable to utter . . . and a poet is not an apostle, he casts out devils only by the power of the devil.

But now when the ethical is thus teleologically suspended, how does the individual exist in

whom it is suspended? He exists as the particular in opposition to the universal. Does he then sin? For this is the form of sin, as seen in the idea. Just as the infant, though it does not sin, because it is not as such yet conscious of its existence, yet its existence is sin, as seen in the idea, and the ethical makes its demands upon it every instant. If one denies that this form can be repeated [in the adult] in such a way that it is not sin, then the sentence of condemnation is pronounced upon Abraham. How then did Abraham exist? He believed. This is the paradox which keeps him upon the sheer edge and which he cannot make clear to any other man, for the paradox is that he as the individual puts himself in an absolute relation to the absolute. Is he justified in doing this? His justification is once more the paradox; for if he is justified, it is not by virtue of anything universal, but by virtue of being the particular individual. . . .

Who was ever so great as that blessed woman, the Mother of God, the Virgin Mary? And yet how do we speak of her? We say that she was highly favored among women. And if it did not happen strangely that those who hear are able to think as inhumanly as those who talk, every young girl might well ask, "Why was not I too the highly favored?" And if I had nothing else to say, I would not dismiss such a question as stupid, for when it is a matter of favor, abstractly considered, everyone is equally entitled to it. What they leave out is the distress, the dread, the paradox. My thought is as pure as that of anyone, and the thought of the man who is able to think such things will surely become pure—and if this be not so, he may expect the dreadful; for he who once has evoked these images cannot be rid of them again, and if he sins against them, they avenge themselves with quiet wrath, more terrible than the vociferousness of ten ferocious reviewers. To be sure, Mary bore the child miraculously, but it came to pass with her after the manner of women, and that season is one of dread, distress and paradox. To be sure, the angel was a ministering spirit, but it was not a servile spirit which obliged her by saying to the other young maidens of Israel, "Despise not Mary. What befalls her is the extraordinary." But the Angel came only to Mary, and no one could understand her. After all, what woman was so mortified as Mary? And is it not true in this instance also that one whom God blesses He curses in the same breath? This is the spirit's interpretation of Mary, and she is not (as it shocks me to say, but shocks me still more to think that they have thoughtlessly and coquettishly interpreted her thus)—she is not a fine lady who sits in state and plays with an infant god. Nevertheless, when she says, "Behold the handmaid of the Lord"—then she is great, and I think it will not be found difficult to explain why she became the Mother of God. She has no need of worldly admiration, any more than Abraham has need of tears, for she was not a heroine, and he was not a hero, but both of them became greater than such, not at all because they were exempted from distress and torment and paradox, but they became great through these. . . .

I return, however, to Abraham. Before the result, either Abraham was every minute a murderer, or we are confronted by a paradox which is higher than all mediation.

The story of Abraham contains therefore a teleological suspension of the ethical. As the individual he became higher than the universal. This is the paradox which does not permit of mediation. It is just as inexplicable how he got into it as it is inexplicable how he remained in it. If such is not the position of Abraham, then he is not even a tragic hero but a murderer. To want to continue to call him the father of faith, to talk of this to people who do not concern themselves with anything but words is thoughtless. A man can become a tragic hero by his own powers— but not a knight of faith. When a man enters upon the way, in a certain sense the hard way of the tragic hero, many will be able to give him counsel; to him who follows the narrow way of faith no one can give counsel, him no one can understand. Faith is a miracle, and yet no man is excluded from it; for that in which all human life is unified is passion, and faith is a passion.

Study Questions

1. What is the existential significance of choice? In what way does aesthetic choice differ from ethical choice? Is Kierkegaard suggesting that we actually choose to be moral? Is he suggesting that the aesthetic person is amoral or immoral?

2. What does Kierkegaard mean in his characterization of the ethical as the universal, immanent *telos*? What is the nature of the relation of the individual to the ethical? In what way is the ethical inadequate for the individual's highest *telos*?

3. What characterizes faith for Kierkegaard? Why does it involve a "teleological suspension of the ethical"? Why is it a "paradox"?

4. What is the significance of dread in the teleological suspension of the ethical? Is Kierkegaard suggesting that faith is amoral? How would Kierkegaard distinguish between Abraham and a deranged murderer who claims to be following God's command?

5. Why is our highest individuality and authenticity attained only in an unmediated relationship with God? What significance do others have in our lives?

Suggestions for Further Reading

Collins, J. *The Mind of Kierkegaard* (Chicago: Regnery, 1953). A general exposition of Kierkegaard's life and philosophy.

Gardner, P. *Kierkegaard* (Oxford: Oxford University Press, 1988). An analysis of the historical and philosophical background to Kierkegaard's thought.

Preston, R. "Christian Ethics." In *A Companion to Ethics,* ed. P. Singer (Oxford; Cambridge, MA: Blackwell, 1991). A general introduction to the Christian tradition in ethics.

Rudd, A. *Kierkegaard and the Limits of the Ethical* (Oxford: Clarendon Press, 1993). An analysis of Kiekegaard's views on the individual's development.

Stack, G. J. *Kierkegaard's Existential Ethics* (Tuscaloosa: University of Alabama Press, 1977). A four-chapter interpretation of Kiekegaard's ethics from the perspective of the problem of nihilem.

Valone, J. J. *The Ethics and Existentialism of Kierkegaard* (Lanham, MD: University Press of America, 1983). A basic exposition of Kiekegaard's theory of the three stages of development.

Karl Marx (1811–1883)

Karl Marx, the revolutionary communist thinker, was born in Trier, in the German Rhineland. His parents were of Jewish ancestry but converted to Protestantism, apparently for nonreligious reasons. The son of a government lawyer, Marx began his studies in law at the University of Bonn, but eventually went to the University of Berlin, where he turned to philosophy. In Berlin, he came under the influence of G. W. F. Hegel's philosophy of absolute idealism. Hegel had proposed that reality is a spirit or an infinite mind that transcends all finite human minds. History, in Hegel's view, was a process of development of the absolute mind where reality and rationality become one. The "right-wing" or "older" Hegelians believed that the Prussian state and the Christian religion embodied the absolute mind in its historical moment of culmination. Marx became one of the "left-wing" or "young" Hegelians who claimed that such a moment had not yet arrived. From this perspective, the present state and religion were examined critically to see whether rationality had become actualized in them.

Marx completed his doctorate in philosophy at the University of Jena with a dissertation on the ancient Greek philosophers Democritus and Epicurus. However, his involvement in leftist politics prevented Marx from obtaining a position teaching philosophy. Some time after receiving his doctorate, he began to draw on Ludwig Feuerbach's *Essence of Christianity* (1841), which developed a critical perspective of religion and Hegelian philosophy. Feuerbach proposed a materialist conception that defined reality solely in terms of matter and saw God as the human being's self-alienation (loss of identity by objectifying or viewing one's self in another being). Feuerbach concluded that the essence of religion lies in human self-alienation and that Hegel's absolute idealism is nothing but a rationalized version of religion. Marx agreed with Feuerbach's conception of religion as alienation. However, he noted that, as "the opium of the people," religion is both a hallucinogenic and a palliative that mitigates the suffering of the oppressed. Marx also embraced Feuerbach's materialism, but he retained Hegel's conception of reality or history as a (dialectical) process whereby the contradictions between two things develop and produce higher unities. In Marx's view, history is the development of the material or physical forces between economic classes in contradiction with one another. He believed such development would culminate in a classless society without internal conflicts. Thus, Marx's philosophy has been labeled dialectical materialism (though he never used this term himself).

While he developed his philosophy of dialectical materialism, Marx sought to put his philosophy into practice by becoming further involved in leftist politics. He worked mainly as editor for various leftist journals, but constantly lost these jobs and was expelled from several states because of his political work. While working as coeditor of the *Deutsch-Französische Jahrbücher* in Paris (after his expulsion from Berlin, where he had been editor of the *Rheinische Zeitung*), Marx met Friedrich Engels, with whom he established a lifelong friendship and collaboration. Throughout the years, Engels—who came from a wealthy family of textile industrialists—provided financial support to Marx and his family. Marx and Engels coauthored a number of writings, including the famous *Communist Manifesto* (1848), which they had been commissioned to write by the 1847 Congress of the Communist League, held in London.

Marx spent his later years living in London in political exile with his family. Barely able to support his family, he had to rely on Engels' generosity and on his own meager earnings as contributor to the *New York Tribune.* Marx became a regular visitor of the reading room at the British Museum, where he spent long hours collecting data for his writings on political economy. His magnum opus, *Capital* (1867, vol. 1) was one of the writings he began during that period. Marx continued his political activities as leader of the International Working Men's Association until 1872, when he disassembled the organization because of internal conflicts. In a family life tragically marked by fatal illnesses, he lost two of his children and his wife. Marx himself once suffered a disease that covered his body with boils, and he later died of bronchitis.

The spirit of Marx's philosophy is captured in his famous remark that "philosophers have only *interpreted* the world in various ways; the point is to *change* it." Taking his own philosophy as an instrument for change, he proposed a radical transformation of the economic, social, and political structures of capitalism. His unique contribution to European thought was to define our humanity in terms of our labor. In his conception of humans as laboring beings, Marx viewed our consciousness as the starting point for a freedom that is realized only in and through labor. Through our laboring, we are able to produce things in the objective world and endow them with the value of our crystallized work. Our very humanity is thus actualized through such production.

Marx placed particular importance on the material world where the human being exists and labors, for he defined reality in material terms. Unlike Hegel, who construed labor solely in the idealist terms of the mind's activity in relation to its objects, Marx emphasized the physical character of humans as concrete, embodied subjects existing in the realm of nature and acting upon nature in their production of material things. Although he agreed with Hegel on the fundamentally social character of human beings, Marx insisted that the mode of production determines the nature of social relations. Thus, the economic "infrastructure" is that basis upon which society develops. Historically, the relations of production have been marked by the contradiction between two main classes and by the domination and oppression of one by the other. All other social structures—political, legal, religious, cultural, and moral—are "superstructures" that develop on the basis of the economic infrastructure. Our material activities and relations of production determine our ideas, beliefs, and norms—in short, human consciousness. The social web of ideas, beliefs, and norms—the "ideology" of a given society—reflects those of the dominant class and thus tends to conserve and perpetuate its interests.

Though Marx did not develop a systematic moral theory, his philosophy carried deep moral implications. As a witness to the capitalist world of the industrial revolution, he was horrified by the inhumanity of a system that submitted workers to brutal exploitation. He identified the two main classes in contradiction in the capitalist mode of production as the "proletariat," those who must sell their labor in order to make a living, and the "bourgeoisie," those who own the social means of production. Because he saw labor as the process by which our humanity can be actualized and developed to its fullest potential, Marx conceived the capitalist mode of production as an unprecedented dehumanization that imposed on the proletariat a multifold alienation. The proletarian is alienated or estranged from the product of her labor because she receives only a portion of the value she creates, while the bourgeois reaps in the remaining (surplus) value for himself. The proletarian is also alienated in the very process of production that is designed solely to serve the capitalist's interests, in her very humanity as a laboring being whose labor has become something alien to her, and in her relation to other human beings. However, according to Marx, rather than being a result of private property, alienated labor is the condition for private property. Without the proletariat, there could not be a class of capitalists, for their capital comes from the surplus value created by proletarians. Therefore, the radical solution to the problem of human alienation in capitalism is the abolition of private property. For Marx, only a communist mode of production, in which laborers control the means of production and enjoy the crystallized value of their labor, can bring humans to their fullest realization.

ECONOMIC AND PHILOSOPHICAL MANUSCRIPTS

POLITICAL ECONOMY BEGINS with the fact of private property; it does not explain it. It conceives the *material* process of private property, as this occurs in reality, in general and abstract formulas which then serve it as laws. It does not *comprehend* these laws; that is, it does not show how they arise out of the nature of private property. Political economy provides no explanation of the basis for the distinction of labour from capital, of capital from land. When, for example, the relation of wages to profits is defined, this is explained in terms of the interests of capitalists; in other words, what should be explained is assumed. Similarly, competition is referred to at every point and is explained in terms of external conditions. Political economy tells us nothing about the extent to which these external and apparently accidental conditions are simply the expression of a necessary development. We have seen how exchange itself seems an accidental fact. The only motive forces which political economy recognizes are *avarice* and the *war between the avaricious, competition.* . . .

Let us not begin our explanation, as does the economist, from a legendary primordial condition. Such a primordial condition does not explain anything; it merely removes the question into a grey and nebulous distance. It asserts as a fact or event what it should deduce, namely, the necessary relation between two things; for example, between the division of labour and exchange. In the same way theology explains the origin of evil by the fall of man; that is, it asserts as a historical fact what it should explain.

We shall begin from a *contemporary* economic fact. The worker becomes poorer the more wealth he produces and the more his production increases in power and extent. The worker becomes an ever cheaper commodity the more goods he creates. The *devaluation* of the human world increases in direct relation with the *increases in value* of the world of things. Labour does not only create goods; it also produces itself and the worker as a *commodity,* and indeed in the same proportion as it produces goods.

This fact simply implies that the object produced by labour, its product, now stands opposed to it as an *alien being,* as a *power independent* of the producer. The product of labour is labour which has been embodied in an object and turned into a physical thing; this product is an *objectification* of labour. The performance of work is at the same time its objectification. The performance of work appears in the sphere of political economy as a *vitiation* of the worker, objectification as a *loss* and as *servitude to the object,* and appropriation as *alienation.*

So much does the performance of work appear as vitiation that the worker is vitiated to the point of starvation. So much does objectification appear as loss of the object that the worker is deprived of the most essential things not only of life but also of work. Labour itself becomes an object which he can acquire only by the greatest effort and with unpredictable interruptions. So much does the appropriation of the object appear as alienation that the more objects the worker produces the fewer he can possess and the more he falls under the domination of his product, of capital.

All these consequences follow from the fact that the worker is related to the *product of his labour* as to an *alien* object. For it is clear on this presupposition that the more the worker expends himself in work the more powerful becomes the world of objects which he creates in face of himself, the poorer he becomes in his inner life, and the less he belongs to himself. It is just the same as in religion. The more of himself man attributes to God the less he has left in himself. The worker puts his life into the object, and his life then belongs no longer to himself but to the object. The greater his activity, therefore, the less he possesses. What is embodied in the product of his labour is no longer his own. The greater this product is, therefore, the more he is diminished. The *alienation* of the worker in his product means not only that his labour becomes an object, assumes an *external* existence, but that it exists independently, *outside himself,* and alien to him, and that it stands opposed to him as an autonomous power. The life which he has given to the object sets itself against him as an alien and hostile force. . . .

(The alienation of the worker in his object is expressed as follows in the laws of political economy: the more the worker produces the less he has to consume; the more value he creates the more worthless he becomes; the more refined his product the more crude and misshapen the worker; the more civilized the product the more barbarous the worker; the more powerful the work the more feeble the worker; the more the work manifests intelligence the more the worker declines in intelligence and becomes a slave of nature.)

Political economy conceals the alienation in the nature of labour in so far as it does not examine the direct relationship between the worker (work) and production. Labour certainly produces marvels for the rich but it produces privation for the worker. It produces palaces, but hovels for the worker. It produces beauty, but deformity for the worker. It replaces labour by machinery, but it casts some of the workers back into a barbarous kind of work and turns the others into machines. It produces intelligence, but also stupidity and cretinism for the workers. . . .

So far we have considered the alienation of the worker only from one aspect; namely, *his relationship with the products of his labour.* However, alienation appears not merely in the result but also in the *process* of *production,* within *productive activity* itself. How could the worker stand in an alien relationship to the product of his activity if he did not alienate himself in the act of production itself? The product is indeed only the *résumé* of activity, of production. Consequently, if the product of labour is alienation, production itself must be active alienation—the alienation of activity and the activity of alienation. The alienation of the object of labour merely summarizes the alienation in the work activity itself.

What constitutes the alienation of labour? First, that the work is *external* to the worker, that it is not part of his nature; and that, consequently, he does not fulfil himself in his work but denies himself, has a feeling of misery rather than well-being, does not develop freely his mental and physical energies but is physically exhausted and mentally debased. The worker, therefore, feels himself at home only during his leisure time, whereas at work he feels homeless. His work is not voluntary but imposed, *forced labour.* It is not the satisfaction of a need, but only a *means* for satisfying other needs. Its alien character is clearly shown by the fact that as soon as there is no physical or other compulsion it is avoided like the plague. External labour, labour in which man alienates himself, is a labour of self-sacrifice, of mortification. Finally, the external character of work for the worker is shown by the fact that it is not his own work but work for someone else, that in work he does not belong to himself but to another person.

Just as in religion the spontaneous activity of human fantasy, of the human brain and heart, reacts independently as an alien activity of gods or devils upon the individual, so the activity of the worker is not his own spontaneous activity. It is another's activity and a loss of his own spontaneity.

We arrive at the result that man (the worker) feels himself to be freely active only in his animal functions—eating, drinking and procreating, or at most also in his dwelling and in personal adornment—while in his human functions he is reduced to an animal. The animal becomes human and the human becomes animal.

Eating, drinking and procreating are of course also genuine human functions. But abstractly considered, apart from the environment of human activities, and turned into final and sole ends, they are animal functions. . . .

[XXIV] We have now to infer a third characteristic of *alienated labour* from the two we have considered.

Man is a species-being not only in the sense that he makes the community (his own as well as those of other things) his object both practically and theoretically, but also (and this is simply another expression for the same thing) in the sense that he treats himself as the present, living species, as a *universal* and consequently free being.

Species-life, for man as for animals, has its physical basis in the fact that man (like animals) lives from inorganic nature, and since man is more universal than an animal so the range of inorganic nature from which he lives is more universal. Plants, animals, minerals, air, light, etc. constitute, from the theoretical aspect, a part of human consciousness as objects of natural science and art; they are man's spiritual inorganic nature, his intellectual means of life, which he must first prepare for enjoyment and perpetuation. So also, from the practical aspect, they form a part of human life and activity. In practice man lives only from these natural products, whether in the form of food, heating, clothing, housing, etc. The universality of man appears in practice in the universality which makes the whole of nature into his inorganic body: (1) as a direct means of life; and equally (2) as the material object and instrument of his life activity. Nature is the inorganic body of man; that is to say nature, excluding the human body itself. To say that man *lives* from nature means that nature is his *body* with which he must remain in a continuous interchange in order not to die. The statement that the physical and mental life of man, and nature, are interdependent means simply that nature is interdependent with itself, for man is a part of nature.

Since alienated labour: (1) alienates nature from man; and (2) alienates man from himself, from his own active function, his life activity; so it alienates him from the species. It makes *species-life* into a means of individual life. In the first place it alienates species-life and individual life, and secondly, it turns the latter, as an abstraction, into the purpose of the former, also in its abstract and alienated form.

For labour, *life activity, productive life,* now appear to man only as *means* for the satisfaction of a need, the need to maintain his physical existence. Productive life is, however, species-life. It is life creating life. In the type of life activity resides the whole character of a species, its species-character; and free, conscious activity is the species-character of human beings. Life itself appears only as a *means of life.*

The animal is one with its life activity. It does not distinguish the activity from itself. It is *its activity.* But man makes his life activity itself an object of his will and consciousness. He has a conscious life activity. It is not a determination with which he is completely identified. Conscious life activity distinguishes man from the life activity of animals. Only for this reason is he a species-being. Or rather, he is only a self-conscious being, i.e. his own life is an object for him, because he is a species-being. Only for this reason is his activity free activity. Alienated labour reverses the relationship, in that man because he is a self-conscious being makes his life activity, his *being,* only a means for his *existence.*

The practical construction of an *objective world,* the *manipulation* of inorganic nature, is the confirmation of man as a conscious species-being, i.e. a being who treats the species as his own being or himself as a species-being. Of course, animals also produce. They construct nests, dwellings, as in the case of bees, beavers, ants, etc. But they only produce what is strictly necessary for themselves or their young. They produce only in a single direction, while man produces universally. They produce only under the compulsion of direct physical needs, while man produces when he is free from physical need and only truly produces in freedom from such need. Animals produce only themselves, while man reproduces the whole of nature. The products of animal production belong directly to their physical bodies, while man is free in face of his product. Animals construct only in accordance with the standards and needs of the species to which they belong, while man knows how to produce in accordance with the standards of every species and knows how to apply the appropriate standard to the object. Thus man constructs also in accordance with the laws of beauty.

It is just in his work upon the objective world that man really proves himself as a *species-being.* This production is his active species-life. By means of it nature appears as *his* work and his reality. The object of labour is, therefore, the *objectification of man's species-life;* for he no longer reproduces himself merely intellectually, as in consciousness, but actively and in a real sense, and he sees his own reflection in a world which he has constructed. While, therefore, alienated labour takes away the object of production from man, it also takes away his *species-life,* his real objectivity as a species-being, and changes his advantage over animals into a disadvantage in so far as his inorganic body, nature, is taken from him.

Just as alienated labour transforms free and self-directed activity into a means, so it transforms the species-life of man into a means of physical existence.

Consciousness, which man has from his species, is transformed through alienation so that species-life becomes only a means for him. (3) Thus alienated labour turns the *species-life of man,* and also nature as his mental species-property, into an *alien* being and into a *means* for his *individual existence*. It alienates from man his own body, external nature, his mental life and his *human* life. (4) A direct consequence of the alienation of man from the product of his labour, from his life activity and from his species-life, is that *man* is *alienated* from other *men*. When man confronts himself he also confronts *other* men. What is true of man's relationship to his work, to the product of his work and to himself, is also true of his relationship to other men, to their labour and to the objects of their labour.

The *alien* being to whom labour and the product of labour belong, to whose service labour is devoted, and to whose enjoyment the product of labour goes, can only be *man* himself. If the product of labour does not belong to the worker, but confronts him as an alien power, this can only be because it belongs to *a man other than the worker*. If his activity is a torment to him it must be a source of *enjoyment* and pleasure to another. Not the gods, nor nature, but only man himself can be this alien power over men.

Thus, through alienated labour the worker creates the relation of another man, who does not work and is outside the work process, to this labour. The relation of the worker to work also produces the relation of the capitalist (or whatever one likes to call the lord of labour) to work. *Private property* is, therefore, the product, the necessary result, of *alienated labour,* of the external relation of the worker to nature and to himself.

3. *Communism* is the *positive* abolition of *private property,* of *human self-alienation,* and thus the real *appropriation* of *human* nature through and for man. It is, therefore, the return of man himself as a *social,* i.e. really human, being, a complete and conscious return which assimilates all the wealth of previous development. Communism as a fully developed naturalism is humanism and as a fully developed humanism is naturalism. It is the *definitive* resolution of the antagonism between man and nature, and between man and man. It is the true solution of the conflict between existence and essence, between objectification and self-affirmation, between freedom and necessity, between individual and species. It is the solution of the riddle of history and knows itself to be this solution.

It is easy to understand the necessity which leads the whole revolutionary movement to find its empirical, as well its as theoretical, basis in the development of *private property,* and more precisely of the economic system.

This material, directly *perceptible* private property is the material and sensuous expression of *alienated human* life. Its movement—production and consumption—is the *sensuous* manifestation of the movement of all previous production, i.e. the realization or reality of man. Religion, the family, the state, law, morality, science, art, etc. are only *particular* forms of production and come under its general law. The positive supersession of *private property,* as the appropriation of *human* life, is, therefore, the positive supersession of all alienation, and the return of man from religion, the family, the state, etc. to his *human,* i.e. social life. Religious alienation as such occurs only in the sphere of *consciousness,* in the inner life of man, but economic alienation is that of *real life* and its supersession, therefore, affects both aspects. Of course, the development in different nations has a different beginning according to whether the actual and *established* life of the people is more in the realm of mind or more in the external world, is a real or ideal life. Communism begins where atheism begins (Owen), but atheism is at the outset still far from being *communism;* indeed it is still for the most part an abstraction. . . .

[VI] Social activity and social mind by no means exist *only* in the form of activity or mind which is directly communal. Nevertheless, communal activity and mind, i.e. activity and mind which express and confirm themselves directly in a *real association* with other men, occur everywhere where this direct expression of sociability arises from the content of the activity or corresponds to the nature of mind.

Even when I carry out *scientific* work, etc., an activity which I can seldom conduct in direct association with other men, I perform a *social,* because *human,* act. It is not only the material of my activity—such as the language itself which the thinker uses—which is given to me as a social product. My *own existence* is a social activity. For this reason, what I myself produce I produce for society, and with the consciousness of acting as a social being.

My universal consciousness is only the *theoretical* form of that whose *living* form is the real community, the social entity, although at the present day this universal consciousness is an abstraction from real life and is opposed to it as an enemy. That is why the *activity* of my universal consciousness as such is my *theoretical* existence as a social being.

It is above all necessary to avoid postulating "society" once again as an abstraction confronting the individual. The individual *is* the *social being.* The manifestation of his life—even when it does not appear directly in the form of a communal manifestation, accomplished in association with other men—is, therefore, a manifestation and affirmation of *social life.* Individual human life and species-life are not different things, even though the mode of existence of individual life is necessarily either a more *specific* or a more *general* mode of species-life, or that of species-life a *specific* or more *general* mode of individual life.

In his *species-consciousness* man confirms his real *social life,* and reproduces his real existence in thought; while conversely, species-life confirms itself in species-consciousness and exists for itself in its universality as a thinking being. Though man is a unique individual—and it is just his particularity which makes him an individual, a really *individual* communal being—he is equally the *whole,* the ideal whole, the subjective existence of society as thought and experienced. He exists in reality as the representation and the real mind of social existence, and as the sum of human manifestations of life. . . .

Private property has made us so stupid and partial that an object is only *ours* when we have it, when it exists for us as capital or when it is directly eaten, drunk, worn, inhabited, etc., in short, *utilized* in some way. But private property itself only conceives these various forms of possession as *means of life,* and the life for which they serve as means is the *life* of *private property*—labour and creation of capital.

Thus *all* the physical and intellectual senses have been replaced by the simple alienation of *all* these senses; the sense of *having.* The human being had to be reduced to this absolute poverty in order to be able to give birth to all his inner wealth. . . .

The supersession of private property is, therefore, the complete *emancipation* of all the human qualities and senses. It is such an emancipation because these qualities and senses have become *human,* from the subjective as well as the objective point of view. The eye has become a *human* eye when its *object* has become a *human,* social object, created by man and destined for him. The senses have, therefore, become directly theoreticians in practice. They relate themselves to the thing for the sake of the thing, but the thing itself is an *objective human* relation to itself and to man, and vice versa. Need and enjoyment have thus lost their *egoistic* character and nature has lost its mere *utility* by the fact that its utilization has become *human* utilization.

Study Questions

1. What does Marx mean by "alienation"? What forms does it take in the capitalist system? How are they related? How do they differ? Is the proletarian the only victim of alienation?

2. How is Marx's notion of alienation related to his conception of human nature? What assumptions does he make about humans in general? What assumptions does he make about the proletarian? about the bourgeois?

3. Is Marx suggesting that capitalism is an immoral system? that communism is a moral system?

4. What is the significance of assuming private property as a given? What is the significance of seeing private property as the result of alienated labor?

5. Do you agree with Marx on the negative effects that private property has on humans? Do you consider the abolition of private property a desirable and realistic goal for human beings?

6. How do you interpret the historical applications of Marxism in socialist countries such as Russia, China, and Cuba? Do you think history has proved Marx wrong?

Suggestions for Further Reading

Berlin, I. *Karl Marx: His Life and Environment,* 4th ed. (New York: Oxford University Press, 1978). An intellectual biography of Marx in eleven chapters.

Churchich, N. *Marxism and Morality: A Critical Examination of Marxist Ethics* (Cambridge, MA: James Clarke & Co., 1994). Provides an exposition and critique of Marx and Marxist views on morality and ethical theory.

Fromm, E. *Marx's Concept of Man* (New York: Ungar, 1966). Contains an eight-chapter analysis of Marx's philosophy.

Nielsen, K., and S. C. Patten, eds. *Marx and Morality* (Guelph, Ontario: Canadian Association for Publishing in Philosophy, 1981). Contains thirteen essays on various issues concerning Marx, Marxism, and morality.

Ollman, B. *Alienation: Marx's Conception of Man in Capitalist Society,* 2nd. ed. (Cambridge, MA: Cambridge University Press, 1976). See Chapter 4 for a critical view of the possibility of a Marxist ethics.

Wood, A. "Marx Against Morality." In *A Companion to Ethics,* ed. P. Singer (Oxford; Cambridge, MA: Blackwell, 1991). Considers the question of whether Marx's critique of capitalism was inconsistent with his views of morality.

Friedrich Nietzsche (1844–1900)

Friedrich Nietzsche, one of the most incisive and provocative critics of European culture, was born in Röcken, Germany, into a family with two Lutheran ministers—his father and his maternal grandfather. Nietzsche's father died, leaving him at an early age as the only male in a household with five females—his mother, sister, a grandmother, and two maiden aunts. Nietzsche began his studies in theology and philology at the University of Bonn, but he soon lost his religious faith and resumed his studies in philology at the University of Leipzig. At the extraordinary age of twenty-four, he received his doctorate (without having to complete the formal requirements) and was named associate professor of philology at the University of Basel. He was appointed full professor a year later, and a few years afterwards published his first book, *The Birth of Tragedy* (1872). After eleven years of teaching, Nietzsche left his position at the university, alleging ill health. In the years following his resignation, he traveled throughout Switzerland and Italy and wrote some of his most brilliant works, which include *Thus Spoke Zarathustra* (1883–1885), *Beyond Good and Evil* (1886), *Toward a Genealogy of Morals* (1887), *Twilight of the Idols* (1889), and *The Anti-Christ* (1895).

Beginning with *The Birth of Tragedy,* a number of Nietzsche's writings assess the cultural significance of the music of Richard Wagner, whom he had befriended and admired until the relation ended in a hostility that became evident in writings such as *Nietzsche Contra Wagner* (1895). Nietzsche's conviction that German culture had reached a state of dissolution led him to investigate the causes for such decline and to search for alternative cultural paradigms. The art of the ancient Greek world offered him an explanation for the cultural decay of his times and a model for a new cultural beginning. In his view, two forces operated in ancient Greek art, the Apollonian (after Apollo, the god of the sun) representing harmony and order, and the Dionysian (after Dionysius, the god of wine) representing passion and intoxication. After these two forces achieved their highest synthesis with Greek tragedy, Socrates' philosophical pursuit of eternal essences grasped by reason initiated an imbalance of these forces and brought about the decay of culture. Nietzsche heard in Wagner's music the promise of a new synthesis that would restore the lost balance between the Apollonian and the Dionysian. However, he was later disillusioned with Wagner's style and came to find his anti-Semitism and German nationalism intolerable.

Nietzsche's health was rarely stable; he suffered from various ailments, including blinding migraine headaches and severe stomach cramps. Toward the beginning of 1889, he suffered a major episode of madness and collapsed in Turin while hugging a horse's neck. His mother and (later) his sister took him under their care until he died eleven years later, without ever recovering his sanity. His insanity has been attributed to various causes: two of them being a"softening of the brain" inherited from his father and as the result of syphilis contracted during an uncustomary visit to a prostitute. After his death, Nietzsche's sister proceeded to alter his image and writings to make him appear as an anti-Semite. She published and "edited" a number of his works written in 1888—including an unfinished manuscript under the title *Will to Power* —to portray him as a proto-Nazi. Sadly, some of his ideas were appropriated by the Nazis to suit their propaganda of the Aryan race and the extermination of the Jews.

Nietzsche presented his thought in an unusual form for his time by expressing them in a nonsystematic fashion through aphorisms, poems, stories, parables, and essays. Despite the variety of form, certain themes prevail and interlock with one another. One predominant notion is that the will is the blind and unceasing force of all life in its drive to power. The "will to power" is life in its unending impulse to surpass itself. It underlies all human activities as the constant impetus to surmount oneself. The ultimate point of this impelling force is not directly to overpower others but to increase the power over oneself and to gain command over one's own strength.

Nietzsche envisioned the unfolding of the will to power in the course of humanity as one in which "man is something that should be overcome." The "overman" (*Übermensch*) is thus "man overcome," a higher expression of the will to power, a more elevated stage of life in its unending drive to self-elevation. Until now, we have expressed this will to power in a distorted fashion by denying life as it is, in its ultimately purposeless becoming, and by embracing beliefs in an "other" permanent and eternal world beyond and above ours. Philosophy, religion, science, culture, and morality have all tended toward "nihilism" in their negation of this world as real or true, in their creation of life-denying values, and in their cultivation of absolutes.

In his famous proclamation that "God is dead," Nietzsche pointed to the invalidity of the "other" world and to the demise of the eternal and objective values that have served as standards for our lives. The death of God is not the mere passing into nonexistence of the deity who created the universe; rather, it is the ending of our enslavement to idols of the absolute. The significance of God's death is for us as horrifying as it is exhilarating, for it represents—at one and the same time—the loss of our illusions and the freedom to create new values. According to Nietzsche, we need a "transvaluation of all values," a radical transformation of the order and standards of our lives according to a life-affirming perspective whereby we "remain faithful to the earth." The overman is "the meaning of the earth" as the one who says "Yes" to life and fulfills his freedom through self-mastery.

Nietzsche developed a scathing critique of traditional morality by tracing its origin in life-denying forces. Modern European morality upholds the values of Platonist metaphysics, Judeo-Christian religion, and liberal democracy. Each of these traditions expresses a nihilist attitude toward life as the will to power. Platonism alleges that there is a higher reality, an eternal and permanent world of being beyond this world of becoming. Judeo-Christian religion upholds the "holy lie" of the heavenly afterlife as the ultimate goal and purpose of our life on earth while it judges our actions according to the standards of "piety." Modern democracy affirms the basic equality of all humans, regardless of their individual strengths and weaknesses. In forming our traditional morality, these perspectives give expression to the "slave" or "herd" mentality of those individuals who have remained weak in their will. Sensing their own weakness, those of slave mentality develop a morality based on their resentment for all that is life-affirming. Slave morality says "Nay" to life by denying our basic instincts and condemning our vital strengths. Still striving in their will to power, the weak create a system of values in which the moral standard is that of "good and evil." While "good" is defined in terms of what is beneficial, all that is harmful to the herd or the masses is called "evil." Thus, the slave mentality develops an ethics that extols altruistic or selfless acts and commends the meekness of spirit.

The mentality of those few individuals who have mastered their own will gives expression to a "master" morality that affirms life as the will to power. Their morality refers to the worth of individuals, according to their levels of self-overcoming. Those who are "noble" or have attained excellence are judged "good," while those who are "despicable" or have remained inferior are deemed "bad." As those who constantly strive toward their self-elevation, masters develop an ethics of egoism that is centered on the self and its glorification. What is "good" from the perspective of master morality is, as Nietzsche once put it, "everything that heightens the feeling of power in man, the will to power, power itself." However, this is precisely what has been construed as "evil" in the herd mentality of traditional morality. Hence, Nietzsche insisted on the need for a transvaluation of moral values by stepping beyond "good and evil." At the same time, he seemed to urge us to move toward the "good and bad" of the morality of the overman.

WHAT IS NOBLE?

Ninth Chapter. What Is Noble?

257

Every elevation of the type "man," has hitherto been the work of an aristocratic society—and so will it always be—a society believing in a long scale of gradations of rank and differences of worth among human beings, and requiring slavery in some form or other. Without the *pathos of distance,* such as grows out of the incarnated difference of classes, out of the constant outlooking and down-looking of the ruling caste on subordinates and instruments, and out of their equally constant practice of obeying and commanding, of keeping down and keeping at a distance—that other more mysterious pathos could never have arisen, the longing for an ever new widening of distance within the soul itself, the formation of ever higher, rarer, further, more extended, more comprehensive states, in short, just the elevation of the type "man," the continued "self-surmounting of man," to use a moral formula in a supermoral sense. To be sure, one must not resign oneself to any humanitarian illusions about the history of the origin of an aristocratic society (that is to say, of the preliminary condition for the elevation of the type "man"): the truth is hard. Let us acknowledge unprejudicedly how every higher civilisation hitherto has *originated!* Men with a still natural nature, barbarians in every terrible sense of the word, men of prey, still in possession of unbroken strength of will and desire for power, threw themselves upon weaker, more moral, more peaceful races (perhaps trading or cattle-rearing communities), or upon old mellow civilisations in which the final vital force was flickering out in brilliant fireworks of wit and depravity. At the commencement, the noble caste was always the barbarian caste: their superiority did not consist first of all in their physical, but in their psychical power—they were more *complete* men (which at every point also implies the same as "more complete beasts"). . . .

259

To refrain mutually from injury, from violence, from exploitation, and put one's will on a par with that of others: this may result in a certain rough sense in good conduct among individuals when the necessary conditions are given (namely, the actual similarity of the individuals in amount of force and degree of worth, and their co-relation within one organisation). As soon, however, as one wished to take this principle more generally, and if possible even as *the fundamental principle of society,* it would immediately disclose what it really is—namely, a Will to the *denial* of life, a principle of dissolution and decay. Here one must think profoundly to the very basis and resist all sentimental weakness: life itself is *essentially* appropriation, injury, conquest of the strange and weak, suppression, severity, obtrusion of peculiar forms, incorporation, and at the least, putting it mildest, exploitation;—but why should one for ever use precisely these words on which for ages a disparaging purpose has been stamped? Even the organisation within which, as was previously supposed, the individuals treat each other as equal—it takes place in every healthy aristocracy—must itself, if it be a living and not a dying organisation, do all that towards other bodies, which the individuals within it refrain from doing to each other: it will have to be the incarnated Will to Power, it will endeavour to grow, to gain ground, attract to itself and acquire ascendency—not owing to any morality or immorality, but because it *lives,* and because life *is* precisely Will to Power. On no

Friedrich Nietzsche. "What Is Noble?" in Beyond Good and Evil, *trans. H. Zimmern. In* The Complete Works of Friedrich Nietzsche, *Vol. 12, ed. O. Levy. New York: Russell & Russell, 1964. Reprinted by permission of Dover Publications, Inc.*

point, however, is the ordinary consciousness of Europeans more unwilling to be corrected than on this matter; people now rave everywhere, even under the guise of science, about coming conditions of society in which "the exploiting character" is to be absent:—that sounds to my ears as if they promised to invent a mode of life which should refrain from all organic functions. "Exploitation" does not belong to a depraved, or imperfect and primitive society: it belongs to the *nature* of the living being as a primary organic function; it is a consequence of the intrinsic Will to Power, which is precisely the Will to Life.—Granting that as a theory this is a novelty—as a reality it is the *fundamental fact* of all history: let us be so far honest towards ourselves!

260

In a tour through the many finer and coarser moralities which have hitherto prevailed or still prevail on the earth, I found certain traits recurring regularly together, and connected with one another, until finally two primary types revealed themselves to me, and a radical distinction was brought to light. There is *master-morality* and *slave-morality;*—I would at once add, however, that in all higher and mixed civilisations, there are also attempts at the reconciliation of the two moralities; but one finds still oftener the confusion and mutual misunderstanding of them, indeed, sometimes their close juxtaposition—even in the same man, within one soul. The distinctions of moral values have either originated in a ruling caste, pleasantly conscious of being different from the ruled—or among the ruled class, the slaves and dependents of all sorts. In the first case, when it is the rulers who determine the conception "good," it is the exalted, proud disposition which is regarded as the distinguishing feature, and that which determines the order of rank. The noble type of man separates from himself the beings in whom the opposite of this exalted, proud disposition displays itself: he despises them. Let it at once be noted that in this first kind of morality the antithesis "good" and "bad" means practically the same as "noble" and

"despicable";—the antithesis "good" and "*evil*" is of a different origin. The cowardly, the timid, the insignificant, and those thinking merely of narrow utility are despised; moreover, also, the distrustful, with their constrained glances, the self-abasing, the dog-like kind of men who let themselves be abused, the mendicant flatterers, and above all the liars:—it is a fundamental belief of all aristocrats that the common people are untruthful. "We truthful ones"—the nobility in ancient Greece called themselves. It is obvious that everywhere the designations of moral value were at first applied to *men,* and were only derivatively and at a later period applied to *actions;* it is a gross mistake, therefore, when historians of morals start with questions like, "Why have sympathetic actions been praised?" The noble type of man regards *himself* as a determiner of values; he does not require to be approved of; he passes the judgment: "What is injurious to me is injurious in itself"; he knows that it is he himself only who confers honour on things; he is a *creator of values.* He honours whatever he recognises in himself: such morality is self-glorification. In the foreground there is the feeling of plenitude, of power, which seeks to overflow, the happiness of high tension, the consciousness of a wealth which would fain give and bestow:—the noble man also helps the unfortunate, but not—or scarcely—out of pity, but rather from an impulse generated by the super-abundance of power. The noble man honours in himself the powerful one, him also who has power over himself, who knows how to speak and how to keep silence, who takes pleasure in subjecting himself to severity and hardness, and has reverence for all that is severe and hard. "Wotan placed a hard heart in my breast," says an old Scandinavian Saga: it is thus rightly expressed from the soul of a proud Viking. Such a type of man is even proud of *not* being made for sympathy; the hero of the Saga therefore adds warningly: "He who has not a hard heart when young, will never have one." The noble and brave who think thus are the furthest removed from the morality which sees precisely in sympathy, or in acting for the good of others, or in *désintéressement,* the characteristic of the moral; faith in oneself, pride in oneself, a radical enmity and irony towards "selflessness," belong as definitely to noble morality, as do a careless scorn and precaution in presence of sympathy and the "warm heart."—It is the powerful who *know* how to honour, it is their art, their domain for invention. The profound reverence for age and for tradition—all law rests on this double reverence,—the belief and prejudice in favour of ancestors and unfavourable to newcomers, is typical in the morality of the powerful; and if, reversely, men of "modern ideas" believe almost instinctively in "progress" and the "future," and are more and more lacking in respect for old age, the ignoble origin of these "ideas" has complacently betrayed itself thereby. A morality of the ruling class, however, is more especially foreign and irritating to present-day taste in the sternness of its principle that one has duties only to one's equals; that one may act towards beings of a lower rank, towards all that is foreign, just as seems good to one, or "as the heart desires," and in any case "beyond good and evil": it is here that sympathy and similar sentiments can have a place. The ability and obligation to exercise prolonged gratitude and prolonged revenge—both only within the circle of equals,—artfulness in retaliation, *raffinement* of the idea in friendship, a certain necessity to have enemies (as outlets for the emotions of envy, quarrelsomeness, arrogance—in fact, in order to be a good *friend*): all these are typical characteristics of the noble morality, which, as has been pointed out, is not the morality of "modern ideas," and is therefore at present difficult to realise, and also to unearth and disclose.—It is otherwise with the second type of morality, *slave-morality.* Supposing that the abused, the oppressed, the suffering, the unemancipated, the weary, and those uncertain of themselves, should moralise, what will be the common element in their moral estimates? Probably a pessimistic suspicion with regard to the entire situation of man will find expression, perhaps a condemnation of man, together with his situation. The slave has an unfavourable eye for the virtues of the powerful; he has a scepticism and distrust, a *refinement* of distrust of every-

thing "good" that is there honoured—he would fain persuade himself that the very happiness there is not genuine. On the other hand, *those* qualities which serve to alleviate the existence of sufferers are brought into prominence and flooded with light; it is here that sympathy, the kind, helping hand, the warm heart, patience, diligence, humility, and friendliness attain to honour; for here these are the most useful qualities, and almost the only means of supporting the burden of existence. Slave-morality is essentially the morality of utility. Here is the seat of the origin of the famous antithesis "good" and "*evil*":—power and dangerousness are assumed to reside in the evil, a certain dreadfulness, subtlety, and strength, which do not admit of being despised. According to slave-morality, therefore, the "evil" man arouses fear; according to master-morality, it is precisely the "good" man who arouses fear and seeks to arouse it, while the bad man is regarded as the despicable being. The contrast attains its maximum when, in accordance with the logical consequences of slave-morality, a shade of depreciation—it may be slight and well-intentioned—at last attaches itself even to the "good" man of this morality; because, according to the servile mode of thought, the good man must in any case be the *safe* man: he is good-natured, easily deceived, perhaps a little stupid, *unbonhomme.* Everywhere that slave-morality gains the ascendency, language shows a tendency to approximate the significations of the words "good" and "stupid."—A last fundamental difference: the desire for *freedom,* the instinct for happiness and the refinements of the feeling of liberty belong as necessarily to slave-morals and morality, as artifice and enthusiasm in reverence and devotion are the regular symptoms of an aristocratic mode of thinking and estimating.—Hence we can understand without further detail why love *as a passion*—it is our European speciality— must absolutely be of noble origin; as is well known, its invention is due to the Provençal poet-cavaliers, those brilliant ingenious men of the "*gai saber,*" to whom Europe owes so much, and almost owes itself. . . .

263

There is an *instinct for rank,* which more than anything else is already the sign of a *high* rank; there is a *delight* in the *nuances* of reverence which leads one to infer noble origin and habits. The refinement, goodness, and loftiness of a soul are put to a perilous test when something passes by that is of the highest rank, but is not yet protected by the awe of authority from obtrusive touches and incivilities: something that goes its way like a living touchstone, undistinguished, undiscovered, and tentative, perhaps voluntarily veiled and disguised. He whose task and practice it is to investigate souls, will avail himself of many varieties of this very art to determine the ultimate value of a soul, the unalterable, innate order of rank to which it belongs: he will test it by its *instinct for reverence. Différence engendre haine:* the vulgarity of many a nature spurts up suddenly like dirty water, when any holy vessel, any jewel from closed shrines, any book bearing the marks of great destiny, is brought before it; while on the other hand, there is an involuntary silence, a hesitation of the eye, a cessation of all gestures, by which it is indicated that a soul *feels* the nearness of what is worthiest of respect. The way in which, on the whole, the reverence for the *Bible* has hitherto been maintained in Europe, is perhaps the best example of discipline and refinement of manners which Europe owes to Christianity: books of such profoundness and supreme significance require for their protection an external tyranny of authority, in order to acquire the *period* of thousands of years which is necessary to exhaust and unriddle them. Much has been achieved when the sentiment has been at last instilled into the masses (the shallow-pates and the boobies of every kind) that they are not allowed to touch everything, that there are holy experiences before which they must take off their shoes and keep away the unclean hand—it is almost their highest advance towards humanity. On the contrary, in the so-called cultured classes, the believers in "modern ideas," nothing is perhaps so repulsive as their lack of shame, the easy insolence of eye and hand with which they touch, taste, and finger everything; and it is possible that even yet there is more *relative* nobility of taste, and more tact for reverence among the people, among the lower classes of the people, especially among peasants, than among the newspaper-reading *demimonde* of intellect, the cultured class.

264

It cannot be effaced from a man's soul what his ancestors have preferably and most constantly done: whether they were perhaps diligent economisers attached to a desk and a cash-box, modest and citizen-like in their desires, modest also in their virtues; or whether they were accustomed to commanding from morning till night, fond of rude pleasures and probably of still ruder duties and responsibilities; or whether, finally, at one time or another, they have sacrificed old privileges of birth and possession, in order to live wholly for their faith—for their "God,"—as men of an inexorable and sensitive conscience, which blushes at every compromise. It is quite impossible for a man *not* to have the qualities and predilections of his parents and ancestors in his constitution, whatever appearances may suggest to the contrary. This is the problem of race. Granted that one knows something of the parents, it is admissible to draw a conclusion about the child: any kind of offensive incontinence, any kind of sordid envy, or of clumsy self-vaunting—the three things which together have constituted the genuine plebeian type in all times—such must pass over to the child, as surely as bad blood; and with the help of the best education and culture one will only succeed in *deceiving* with regard to such heredity.—And what else does education and culture try to do nowadays! In our very democratic, or rather, very plebeian age, "education" and "culture" *must* be essentially the art of deceiving—deceiving with regard to origin, with regard to the inherited plebeianism in body and soul. An educator who nowadays preached truthfulness above everything else, and called out constantly to his pupils: "Be true! Be natural! Show yourselves as you are!"—even such a virtuous and sincere ass would learn in a short time to have recourse to the *furca* of Horace, *naturam expellere:* with what results? "Plebeianism" *usque recurret.*[1]

265

At the risk of displeasing innocent ears, I submit that egoism belongs to the essence of a noble soul, I mean the unalterable belief that to a being such as "we," other beings must naturally be in subjection, and have to sacrifice themselves. The noble soul accepts the fact of his egoism without question, and also without consciousness of harshness, constraint, or arbitrariness therein, but rather as something that may have its basis in the primary law of things:—if he sought a designation for it he would say: "It is justice itself." He acknowledges under certain circumstances, which made him hesitate at first, that there are other equally privileged ones; as soon as he has settled this question of rank, he moves among those equals and equally privileged ones with the same assurance, as regards

[1] Horace's "Epistles," I. x. 24.

modesty and delicate respect, which he enjoys in intercourse with himself—in accordance with an innate heavenly mechanism which all the stars understand. It is an *additional* instance of his egoism, this artfulness and self-limitation in intercourse with his equals—every star is a similar egoist; he honours *himself* in them, and in the rights which he concedes to them, he has no doubt that the exchange of honours and rights, as the *essence* of all intercourse, belongs also to the natural condition of things. The noble soul gives as he takes, prompted by the passionate and sensitive instinct of requital, which is at the root of his nature. The notion of "favour" has, *inter pares,* neither significance nor good repute; there may be a sublime way of letting gifts as it were light upon one from above, and of drinking them thirstily like dew-drops; but for those arts and displays the noble soul has no aptitude. His egoism hinders him here: in general, he looks "aloft" unwillingly—he looks either *forward,* horizontally and deliberately, or downwards—*he knows that he is on a height.*

Study Questions

1. What are the slave and master moralities? How do they originate? What are their standards and values? How do they differ? How does Nietzsche assess each?

2. In what way is slave morality still an expression of the will to power? What accounts for its prevalence in tradition? How does it take form in religious and democratic ideals?

3. How is master morality related to the transvaluation of all values? In what sense does it go beyond good and evil? In what sense could it be the morality of the overman?

4. What is Nietzsche's doctrine of ethical egoism? In what sense is it elitist? Would a society based on this ethics necessarily end in chaos?

Suggestions for Further Reading

Berkowitz, P. *Nietzsche: The Ethics of an Immoralist* (Cambridge, MA: Harvard University Press, 1995). See Chapter 9 for an interpretation of *Beyond Good and Evil.*

Danto, A. *Nietzsche as Philosopher* (New York: Macmillan, 1965). Chapter 5 provides a general view of Nietzsche's theory of morality.

Kaufmann, W. A. *Nietzsche: Philosopher, Psychologist, Antichrist* (Princeton, NJ: Princeton University Press, 1968). A general exposition of Nietzsche's thought. See Chapters 7–10 for aspects of his ethical theory.

Solomon, R. C., ed. *Nietzsche: A Collection of Critical Essays* (New York: Anchor Press, 1973). Contains twenty-one essays on a wide range of aspects of Nietzsche's thought. The essays by Kaufmann, Foot, Pyne Parsons, and Solomon pertain specifically to Nietzsche's moral philosophy.

G. E. Moore (1873–1958)

George Edward Moore was born in London. He studied classics and philosophy at Trinity College, Cambridge University, where his thesis on Immanuel Kant's philosophy gained him a fellowship. He published his first book, *Principia Ethica* (1903), while he was a fellow there. In 1911, after a seven-year absence, Moore became a lecturer at the university, from which he retired as emeritus professor of philosophy in 1939. During his time at Cambridge University, Moore published two other books, *Ethics* (1912) and *Philosophical Studies* (1922), and wrote numerous articles. Between 1921 and 1947, Moore also served as editor of the distinguished philosophical journal *Mind.* Upon his retirement from the university, Moore spent a few years in the United States lecturing and teaching at various institutions, including Smith College and Princeton and Columbia Universities. He later returned to England, where, for a highly successful academic career, the British government awarded him the Order of Merit in 1951.

G. E. Moore's *Principia Ethica* had a great impact on British moral theory and was influential in the development of analytic philosophy—a branch of twentieth-century philosophy that defines its task primarily in terms of the analysis of language and logic. His book proposes a new approach to ethics that focuses on clarifying fundamental concepts and their meaning before engaging in the elaboration of systems of thought. In Moore's view of the situation of moral philosophy, "the difficulties and disagreements . . . are mainly due to a very simple cause: namely the attempt to answer questions, without first discovering *what* the question it is which you desire to answer." In response to this problem, Moore places emphasis on the language and logic of ethics—on the precise meaning of fundamental ethical terms, their classification, and their proper usage in moral reasoning and argumentation. His task as a moral philosopher is one of "analysis and distinction" to dispel confusions and to assure clarity and rigor. Thus, the main objective of his book is to outline the necessary features for a "scientific ethics" by discovering the "fundamental principles of ethical reasoning."

The following selection is taken from Chapter I, "The Subject-Matter of Ethics," of Moore's *Principia Ethica*. With the objective of defining the field of ethics by identifying and describing its fundamental features, Moore focuses on the kinds of questions that are posed in ethics and the judgments or statements that are issued in response. In his view, questions and judgments that pertain to what is good or bad in human conduct fail to point to what defines ethics in its simplest or most basic and universal aspects. The term *good conduct* is itself not a simple term, for it denotes a complex notion or object; namely, a conduct that has the property of being good. Moreover, it does not refer to what is good in general. Moore proposes instead to define ethics as the general inquiry into what is good. Its main question is "What is good?" Such a question, he insists, does not ask what thing or things are good, but how the word *good* or *goodness* is defined. It does not ask for its meaning in common usage; rather, it seeks the object or idea that it generally represents.

Moore's response to the question "What is good?" is known as the thesis of the indefinability of good. As he phrases it: "My answer is that good is good, and that is the end of the matter." Good, Moore insists, "cannot be defined" because the word *good* is not a complex notion but a simple one. It cannot be defined by reducing it to simpler terms or by stating what are the parts that invariably compose the whole. As an adjective, the word *good* refers to a simple object, a unique property or quality that is irreducible to any other. Rather than affirming that the word *good* is meaningless, Moore contends that it denotes a real thing, a unique object or distinctive property of things. We intuit or are aware of it whenever we think of a thing as having an intrinsic value or worth, or as something that ought to exist.

Moore argues that the failure to grasp the indefinability of good has led moral philosophers to make mistakes in their reasoning and to form invalid arguments. The attempt to define good in terms of other properties is a "naturalistic fallacy." This means that philosophers who seek to define goodness in terms of the nature, existence, or reality of other things, properties, or qualities commit an error in logic. However, Moore is not suggesting that the term *the good* is also indefinable. As a noun, *the good* refers to that which is good, to a thing that always has the property of goodness. As Moore sees it, the objective of ethics is to define the good while adhering to the fundamental principle of the indefinability of goodness.

THE SUBJECT-MATTER OF ETHICS

1. IT IS VERY EASY to point out some among our every-day judgments, with the truth of which Ethics is undoubtedly concerned. Whenever we say, 'So and so is a good man,' or 'That fellow is a villain'; whenever we ask, 'What ought I to do?' or 'Is it wrong for me to do like this?'; whenever we hazard such remarks as 'Temperance is a virtue and drunkenness a vice'—it is undoubtedly the business of Ethics to discuss such questions and such statements; to argue what is the true answer when we ask what it is right to do, and to give reasons for thinking that our statements about the character of persons or the morality of actions are true or false. In the vast majority of cases, where we make statements involving any of the terms 'virtue,' 'vice,' 'duty,' 'right,' 'ought,' 'good,' 'bad,' we are making ethical judgments; and if we wish to discuss their truth, we shall be discussing a point of Ethics.

So much as this is not disputed; but it falls very far short of defining the province of Ethics. That province may indeed be defined as the whole truth about that which is at the same time common to all such judgments and peculiar to them. But we have still to ask the question: What is it that is thus common and peculiar? And this is a question to which very different answers have been given by ethical philosophers of acknowledged reputation, and none of them, perhaps, completely satisfactory.

2. If we take such examples as those given above, we shall not be far wrong in saying that they are all of them concerned with the question of 'conduct'—with the question, what, in the conduct of us, human beings, is good, and what is bad, what is right, and what is wrong. For when we say that a man is good, we commonly mean that he acts rightly; when we say that

G. E. Moore. *"The Subject-Matter of Ethics."* In Principia Ethica. *Cambridge: Cambridge University Press, 1971, Chapter I. Reprinted with the permission of Cambridge University Press.*

drunkenness is a vice, we commonly mean that to get drunk is a wrong or wicked action. And this discussion of human conduct is, in fact, that with which the name 'Ethics' is most intimately associated. It is so associated by derivation; and conduct is undoubtedly by far the commonest and most generally interesting object of ethical judgments.

Accordingly, we find that many ethical philosophers are disposed to accept as an adequate definition of 'Ethics' the statement that it deals with the question what is good or bad in human conduct. They hold that its enquiries are properly confined to 'conduct' or to 'practice'; they hold that the name 'practical philosophy' covers all the matter with which it has to do. Now, without discussing the proper meaning of the word (for verbal questions are properly left to the writers of dictionaries and other persons interested in literature; philosophy, as we shall see, has no concern with them), I may say that I intend to use 'Ethics' to cover more than this—a usage, for which there is, I think, quite sufficient authority. I am using it to cover an enquiry for which, at all events, there is no other word: the general enquiry into what is good.

Ethics is undoubtedly concerned with the question what good conduct is; but, being concerned with this, it obviously does not start at the beginning, unless it is prepared to tell us what is good as well as what is conduct. For 'good conduct' is a complex notion: all conduct is not good; for some is certainly bad and some may be indifferent. And on the other hand, other things, beside conduct, may be good; and if they are so, then, 'good' denotes some property, that is common to them and conduct; and if we examine good conduct alone of all good things, then we shall be in danger of mistaking for this property, some property which is not shared by those other things: and thus we shall have made a mistake about Ethics even in this limited sense; for we shall not know what good conduct really is. This is a mistake which many writers have actually made, from limiting their enquiry to conduct. And hence I shall try to avoid it by considering first what is good in general; hoping, that

if we can arrive at any certainty about this, it will be much easier to settle the question of good conduct: for we all know pretty well what 'conduct' is. This, then, is our first question: What is good? and What is bad? and to the discussion of this question (or these questions) I give the name of Ethics, since that science must, at all events, include it.

3. But this is a question which may have many meanings. If, for example, each of us were to say 'I am doing good now' or 'I had a good dinner yesterday,' these statements would each of them be some sort of answer to our question, although perhaps a false one. So, too, when A asks B what school he ought to send his son to, B's answer will certainly be an ethical judgment. And similarly all distribution of praise or blame to any personage or thing that has existed, now exists, or will exist, does give some answer to the question 'What is good?' In all such cases some particular thing is judged to be good or bad: the question 'What?' is answered by 'This.' But this is not the sense in which a scientific Ethics asks the question. Not one, of all the many million answers of this kind, which must be true, can form a part of an ethical system; although that science must contain reasons and principles sufficient for deciding on the truth of all of them. There are far too many persons, things and events in the world, past, present, or to come, for a discussion of their individual merits to be embraced in any science. Ethics, therefore, does not deal at all with facts of this nature, facts that are unique, individual, absolutely particular; facts with which such studies as history, geography, astronomy, are compelled, in part at least, to deal. And, for this reason, it is not the business of the ethical philosopher to give personal advice or exhortation.

4. But there is another meaning which may be given to the question 'What is good?' 'Books are good' would be an answer to it, though an answer obviously false; for some books are very bad indeed. And ethical judgments of this kind do indeed belong to Ethics; though I shall not deal with many of them. Such is the judgment 'Pleasure is good'—a judgment, of which

Ethics should discuss the truth, although it is not nearly as important as that other judgment, with which we shall be much occupied presently—'Pleasure *alone* is good.' It is judgments of this sort, which are made in such books on Ethics as contain a list of 'virtues'—in Aristotle's 'Ethics' for example. . . .

5. But our question 'What is good?' may have still another meaning. We may, in the third place, mean to ask, not what thing or things are good, but how 'good' is to be defined. This is an enquiry which belongs only to Ethics, [. . .] and this is the enquiry which will occupy us first.

It is an enquiry to which most special attention should be directed; since this question, how 'good' is to be defined, is the most fundamental question in all Ethics. That which is meant by 'good' is, in fact, except its converse 'bad,' the *only* simple object of thought which is peculiar to Ethics. Its definition is, therefore, the most essential point in the definition of Ethics; and moreover a mistake with regard to it entails a far larger number of erroneous ethical judgments than any other. Unless this first question be fully understood, and its true answer clearly recognised, the rest of Ethics is as good as useless from the point of view of systematic knowledge. . . .

6. What, then, is good? How is good to be defined? Now, it may be thought that this is a verbal question. A definition does indeed often mean the expressing of one word's meaning in other words. But this is not the sort of definition I am asking for. Such a definition can never be of ultimate importance in any study except lexicography. If I wanted that kind of definition I should have to consider in the first place how people generally used the word 'good'; but my business is not with its proper usage, as established by custom. I should, indeed, be foolish, if I tried to use it for something which it did not usually denote: if, for instance, I were to announce that, whenever I used the word 'good,' I must be understood to be thinking of that object which is usually denoted by the word 'table.' I shall, therefore, use the word in the sense in which I think it is ordinarily used; but at the same time I am not anxious to discuss whether I am right in thinking that it is so used. My business is solely with that object or idea, which I hold, rightly or wrongly, that the word is generally used to stand for. What I want to discover is the nature of that object or idea, and about this I am extremely anxious to arrive at an agreement.

But, if we understand the question in this sense, my answer to it may seem a very disappointing one. If I am asked 'What is good?' my answer is that good is good, and that is the end of the matter. Or if I am asked 'How is good to be defined?' my answer is that it cannot be defined, and that is all I have to say about it. But disappointing as these answers may appear, they are of the very last importance. To readers who are familiar with philosophic terminology, I can express their importance by saying that they amount to this: That propositions about the good are all of them synthetic and never analytic; and that is plainly no trivial matter. And the same thing may be expressed more popularly, by saying that, if I am right, then nobody can foist upon us such an axiom as that 'Pleasure is the only good' or that 'The good is the desired' on the pretence that this is 'the very meaning of the word.'

7. Let us, then, consider this position. My point is that 'good' is a simple notion, just as 'yellow' is a simple notion; that, just as you cannot, by any manner of means, explain to any one who does not already know it, what yellow is, so you cannot explain what good is. Definitions of the kind that I was asking for, definitions which describe the real nature of the object or notion denoted by a word, and which do not merely tell us what the word is used to mean, are only possible when the object or notion in question is something complex. You can give a definition of a horse, because a horse has many different properties and qualities, all of which you can enumerate. But when you have enumerated them all, when you have reduced a horse to his simplest terms, then you can no longer define those terms. They are simply something which you think of or perceive, and to any one who cannot think of or perceive them, you can never, by

any definition, make their nature known. It may perhaps be objected to this that we are able to describe to others, objects which they have never seen or thought of. We can, for instance, make a man understand what a chimaera is, although he has never heard of one or seen one. You can tell him that it is an animal with a lioness's head and body, with a goat's head growing from the middle of its back, and with a snake in place of a tail. But here the object which you are describing is a complex object; it is entirely composed of parts, with which we are all perfectly familiar—a snake, a goat, a lioness; and we know, too, the manner in which those parts are to be put together, because we know what is meant by the middle of a lioness's back, and where her tail is wont to grow. And so it is with all objects, not previously known, which we are able to define: they are all complex; all composed of parts, which may themselves, in the first instance, be capable of similar definition, but which must in the end be reducible to simplest parts, which can no longer be defined. But yellow and good, we say, are not complex: they are notions of that simple kind, out of which definitions are composed and with which the power of further defining ceases. . . .

9. But I am afraid I have still not removed the chief difficulty which may prevent acceptance of the proposition that good is indefinable. I do not mean to say that *the* good, that which is good, is thus indefinable; if I did think so, I should not be writing on Ethics, for my main object is to help towards discovering that definition. It is just because I think there will be less risk of error in our search for a definition of 'the good,' that I am now insisting that *good* is indefinable. I must try to explain the difference between these two. I suppose it may be granted that 'good' is an adjective. Well the good, 'that which is good,' must therefore be the substantive to which the adjective 'good' will apply: it must be the whole of that to which the adjective will apply, and the adjective must *always* truly apply to it. But if it is that to which the adjective will apply, it must be something different from that adjective itself;

and the whole of that something different, whatever it is, will be our definition of *the* good. Now it may be that this something will have other adjectives, beside 'good,' that will apply to it. It may be full of pleasure, for example; it may be intelligent: and if these two adjectives are really part of its definition, then it will certainly be true, that pleasure and intelligence are good. And many people appear to think that, if we say 'Pleasure and intelligence are good,' or if we say 'Only pleasure and intelligence are good,' we are defining 'good.' Well, I cannot deny that propositions of this nature may sometimes be called definitions; I do not know well enough how the word is generally used to decide upon this point. I only wish it to be understood that that is not what I mean when I say there is no possible definition of good, and that I shall not mean this if I use the word again. I do most fully believe that some true proposition of the form 'Intelligence is good and intelligence alone is good' can be found; if none could be found, our definition of *the* good would be impossible. As it is, I believe *the* good to be definable; and yet I still say that good itself is indefinable.

10. 'Good,' then, if we mean by it that quality which we assert to belong to a thing, when we say that the thing is good, is incapable of any definition, in the most important sense of that word. The most important sense of 'definition' is that in which a definition states what are the parts which invariably compose a certain whole; and in this sense 'good' has no definition because it is simple and has no parts. It is one of those innumerable objects of thought which are themselves incapable of definition, because they are the ultimate terms by reference to which whatever *is* capable of definition must be defined. That there must be an indefinite number of such terms is obvious, on reflection; since we cannot define anything except by an analysis, which, when carried as far as it will go, refers us to something, which is simply different from anything else, and which by that ultimate difference explains the peculiarity of the whole which we are defining: for every whole contains some

parts which are common to other wholes also. There is, therefore, no intrinsic difficulty in the contention that 'good' denotes a simple and indefinable quality. There are many other instances of such qualities.

Consider yellow, for example. We may try to define it, by describing its physical equivalent; we may state what kind of light-vibrations must stimulate the normal eye, in order that we may perceive it. But a moment's reflection is sufficient to shew that those light-vibrations are not themselves what we mean by yellow. *They* are not what we perceive. Indeed we should never have been able to discover their existence, unless we had first been struck by the patent difference of quality between the different colours. The most we can be entitled to say of those vibrations is that they are what corresponds in space to the yellow which we actually perceive.

Yet a mistake of this simple kind has commonly been made about 'good.' It may be true that all things which are good are *also* something else, just as it is true that all things which are yellow produce a certain kind of vibration in the light. And it is a fact, that Ethics aims at discovering what are those other properties belonging to all things which are good. But far too many philosophers have thought that when they named those other properties they were actually defining good; that these properties, in fact, were simply not 'other,' but absolutely and entirely the same with goodness. This view I propose to call the 'naturalistic fallacy'. . . .

11. Let us consider what it is such philosophers say. And first it is to be noticed that they do not agree among themselves. They not only say that they are right as to what good is, but they endeavour to prove that other people who say that it is something else, are wrong. One, for instance, will affirm that good is pleasure, another, perhaps, that good is that which is desired; and each of these will argue eagerly to prove that the other is wrong. But how is that possible? One of them says that good is nothing but the object of desire, and at the same time tries to prove that it is not pleasure. But from his first assertion, that good just means the object of desire, one of two things must follow as regards his proof:

(1) He may be trying to prove that the object of desire is not pleasure. But, if this be all, where is his Ethics? The position he is maintaining is merely a psychological one. Desire is something which occurs in our minds, and pleasure is something else which so occurs; and our would-be ethical philosopher is merely holding that the latter is not the object of the former. But what has that to do with the question in dispute? His opponent held the ethical proposition that pleasure was the good, and although he should prove a million times over the psychological proposition that pleasure is not the object of desire, he is no nearer proving his opponent to be wrong. The position is like this. One man says a triangle is a circle: another replies 'A triangle is a straight line, and I will prove to you that I am right: *for*' (this is the only argument) 'a straight line is not a circle.' 'That is quite true,' the other may reply; 'but nevertheless a triangle is a circle, and you have said nothing whatever to prove the contrary. What is proved is that one of us is wrong, for we agree that a triangle cannot be both a straight line and a circle: but which is wrong, there can be no earthly means of proving, since you define triangle as straight line and I define it as circle.'—Well, that is one alternative which any naturalistic Ethics has to face; if good is *defined* as something else, it is then impossible either to prove that any other definition is wrong or even to deny such definition.

(2) The other alternative will scarcely be more welcome. It is that the discussion is after all a verbal one. When A says 'Good means pleasant' and B says 'Good means desired,' they may merely wish to assert that most people have used the word for what is pleasant and for what is desired respectively. And this is quite an interesting subject for discussion: only it is not a whit more an ethical discussion than the last was. Nor do I think that any exponent of naturalistic Ethics would be willing to allow that this was all he meant. They are all so anxious to persuade us

that what they call the good is what we really ought to do. 'Do, pray, act so, because the word "good" is generally used to denote actions of this nature': such, on this view, would be the substance of their teaching. And in so far as they tell us how we ought to act, their teaching is truly ethical, as they mean it to be. But how perfectly absurd is the reason they would give for it! 'You are to do this, because most people use a certain word to denote conduct such as this.' 'You are to say the thing which is not, because most people call it lying.' That is an argument just as good!—My dear sirs, what we want to know from you as ethical teachers, is not how people use a word; it is not even, what kind of ac-

tions they approve, which the use of this word 'good' may certainly imply: what we want to know is simply what *is* good. We may indeed agree that what most people do think good, is actually so; we shall at all events be glad to know their opinions: but when we say their opinions about what *is* good, we do mean what we say; we do not care whether they call that thing which they mean 'horse' or 'table' or 'chair,' 'gut' or 'bon' or 'ἀγαθός'; we want to know what it is that they so call. When they say 'Pleasure is good,' we cannot believe that they merely mean 'Pleasure is pleasure' and nothing more than that.

Study Questions

1. In what ways does Moore's discussion of the subject matter of ethics illustrate his new approach? What assumptions are involved in adopting this approach to ethics? Could this approach yield entirely different conclusions from Moore's?
2. How does Moore support the claim that ethics is not the inquiry into what is good or bad in human conduct but into what is good in general? How is this claim related to his understanding of definitions and simple and complex notions?
3. What is Moore's thesis of the indefinability of good? How does "good" differ from "the good"? What significance do this distinction and his thesis have for his definition of the field and tasks of ethics?
4. What does Moore label a "naturalistic fallacy"? What specific mistakes are involved according to him in defining good?
5. How does Moore characterize good? Given these features, how would Moore respond to relativist theories? Do you think any of Moore's characterizations are themselves definitions?

Suggestions for Further Reading

Baldwin, T. *G. E. Moore* (London: Routledge, 1990). See Chapters III and IV for an advanced analysis of Moore's ethics.

Frankena, W. K. "The Naturalistic Fallacy," *Mind* 48 (October 1939): 464–467. A classical critique of Moore's notion of the naturalistic fallacy.

Schilpp, P. A., ed. *The Philosophy of G. E. Moore* (LaSalle, IL: Open Court, 1942). Essays 1–6 provide critical discussions of Moore's ethics. See also his replies, Part I, "Ethics."

Sarker, S. *The Epistemology and Ethics of G. E. Moore: A Critical Evaluation* (New York: Humanities Press, 1981). See Part Two, "Ethics," for an introductory overview.

Sylvester, R. P. *The Moral Philosophy of G. E. Moore* (Evanston, IL: Northwestern University Press, 1982). Provides a detailed exposition of Moore's ethics.

White, A. R. *G. E. Moore: A Critical Exposition* (New York: Humanities Press, 1969). See Chapter VII, "Ethics," for an advanced, critical analysis.

Martin Buber (1878–1965)

Martin Buber was born in Vienna into a Jewish family. He studied philosophy and art history in Vienna, Zurich, and Berlin. He was professor of the philosophy of Jewish religion and ethics at Frankfurt-am-Main University and (later) professor of the sociology of religion at the Hebrew University of Jerusalem. An active member of the Zionist movement, Buber worked as editor of a Zionist journal, participated in the founding of a Jewish publishing house and an institute for adult Jewish education, and founded a German Jewish journal. He also helped to lead the Yihud movement, which advocated for a better understanding between Arabs and Jews and for the creation of a binational state. His work started a revival of the Jewish mystical tradition of Hasidism and had a great influence on many intellectual currents, particularly after World War II.

Buber's best-known work, *I and Thou* (1923), had an enormous impact on philosophy and theology because of its author's unique understanding of human existence as a twofold dialogue phrased in terms of an I-It and an I-Thou. These phrases designate different modes of human existence or attitudes toward the world. Those holding the I-It attitude experience and use other beings as objects or things; they encounter them merely in their particular properties or uses. By contrast, those holding the I-Thou attitude relate to other beings as a You; they respond to the whole being of the other in the fullness of the other's presence. These two attitudes can be applied to any being, whether it is a plant, an animal, another human, or a divine being. The crucial difference is that the I-It addresses them merely as things, whereas the I-Thou responds to them by addressing them as a You. In the I-It attitude, there is no relation as such and thus no reciprocity.

For Buber, the I-Thou is the more primal or basic of the two attitudes because it opens up the world as an interrelated whole to which I belong as a "person." The I-It attitude, however, divides the world into particulars and comes with the detachment of the I from the world as an "ego" that sets itself apart from other beings. In this sense, the I-Thou attitude is the genuine mode of human existence because it reaches toward the wholeness of the world. Significantly, the Thou of particular beings is "a glimpse" of the eternal Thou; in every Thou, we address that eternal Thou (who is named "God" in religion and theology). The relation to the eternal Thou is the "perfect relationship" because the eternal Thou is the basis of every Thou in the universe. Thus, in the eternal Thou we comprehend the world in its wholeness.

In *I and Thou*, Buber does not develop an ethics proper or a moral philosophy in the strict sense. However, his notions of the eternal Thou and of the "perfect relationship" between the I and the eternal Thou provide a ground for ethics of the "perfect relationship." The crucial moral distinction lies in the contrast of the I-Thou attitude with the I-It attitude. In my relation to the eternal Thou, the world is validated as a Thou to which I relate as the whole in which I belong. In this sense, moral responsibility has its roots in our intimacy with the eternal Thou, not in our detached experiences of duty and obligation toward the world. Thus, Buber challenges traditional conceptions of ethics and religion, as well as the view that God and the world pertain to separate dimensions of our existence.

I AND THOU

First Part

The world is twofold for man in accordance with his twofold attitude.

The attitude of man is twofold in accordance with the two basic words he can speak.

The basic words are not single words but word pairs.

One basic word is the word pair I-You.

The other basic word is the word pair I-It; but this basic word is not changed when He or She takes the place of It.

Thus the I of man is also twofold.

For the I of the basic word I-You is different from that in the basic word I-It.

. . .

Basic words do not state something that might exist outside them; by being spoken they establish a mode of existence.

Basic words are spoken with one's being.

When one says You, the I of the word pair I-You is said, too.

When one says It, the I of the word pair I-It is said, too.

The basic word I-You can only be spoken with one's whole being.

The basic word I-It can never be spoken with one's whole being.

. . .

There is no I as such but only the I of the basic word I-You and the I of the basic word I-It.

When a man says I, he means one or the other. The I he means is present when he says I.

And when he says You or It, the I of one or the other basic word is also present.

Being I and saying I are the same. Saying I and saying one of the two basic words are the same.

Whoever speaks one of the basic words enters into the word and stands in it.

. . .

The life of a human being does not exist merely in the sphere of goal-directed verbs. It does not consist merely of activities that have something for their object.

I perceive something. I feel something. I imagine something. I want something. I sense something. I think something. The life of a human being does not consist merely of all this and its like.

All this and its like is the basis of the realm of It.

But the realm of You has another basis.

Whoever says You does not have something for his object. For wherever there is something there is also another something; every It borders on other Its; It is only by virtue of bordering on others. But where You is said there is no something. You has no borders.

Whoever says You does not have something; he has nothing. But he stands in relation. . . .

Egos appear by setting themselves apart from other egos.

Persons appear by entering into relation to other persons.

One is the spiritual form of natural differentiation, the other that of natural association.

The purpose of setting oneself apart is to experience and use, and the purpose of that is "living"—which means dying one human life long.

The purpose of relation is the relation itself—touching the You. For as soon as we touch a You, we are touched by a breath of eternal life.

Whoever stands in relation, participates in an actuality; that is, in a being that is neither merely a part of him nor merely outside him. All actuality is an activity in which I participate without being able to appropriate it. Where there is no participation, there is no actuality. Where there is self-appropriation, there is no actuality. The more directly the You is touched, the more perfect is the participation.

The I is actual through its participation in actuality. The more perfect the participation is, the more actual the I becomes.

But the I that steps out of the event of the relation into detachment and the self-consciousness accompanying that, does not lose its actuality. Participation remains in it as a living potentiality. To use words that originally refer to the highest relation but may also be applied to all others: the seed remains in him. This is the realm of subjectivity in which the I apprehends simultaneously its association and its detachment. Genuine subjectivity can be understood only dynamically, as the vibration of the I in its lonely truth. This is also the place where the desire for ever higher and more unconditional relation and for perfect participation in being arises and keeps rising. In subjectivity the spiritual substance of the person matures.

The person becomes conscious of himself as participating in being, as being-with, and thus as a being. The ego becomes conscious of himself as being this way and not that. The person says, "I am"; the ego says, "That is how I am." "Know thyself" means to the person: know yourself as being. To the ego it means: know your being-that-way. By setting himself apart from others, the ego moves away from being.

This does not mean that the person "gives up" his being-that-way, his being different; only, this is not the decisive perspective but merely the necessary and meaningful form of being. The ego, on the other hand, wallows in his being-that-way—or rather for the most part in the fiction of his being-that-way—a fiction that he has devised for himself. For at bottom self-knowledge usually means to him the fabrication of an effective apparition of the self that has the power to deceive him ever more thoroughly; and through the contemplation and veneration of this apparition one seeks the semblance of knowledge of one's own being-that-way, while actual knowledge of it would lead one to self-destruction—or rebirth.

The person beholds his self; the ego occupies himself with his My: my manner, my race, my works, my genius.

The ego does not participate in any actuality nor does he gain any. He sets himself apart from everything else and tries to possess as much as possible by means of experience and use. That is *his* dynamics: setting himself apart and taking possession—and the object is always It, that which is not actual. He knows himself as a subject, but this subject can appropriate as much as it wants to, it will never gain any substance: it remains like a point, functional, that which experiences, that which uses, nothing more. All of its extensive and multifarious being-that-way, all of its eager "individuality" cannot help it to gain any substance.

There are not two kinds of human beings, but there are two poles of humanity.

No human being is pure person, and none is pure ego, none is entirely actual, none entirely lacking in actuality. Each lives in a twofold I. But some men are so person-oriented that one may call them persons, while others are so ego-oriented that one may call them egos. Between these and those true history takes place.

The more a human being, the more humanity is dominated by the ego, the more does the I fall prey to inactuality. In such ages the person in the human being and in humanity comes to lead a subterranean, hidden, as it were invalid existence—until it is summoned.

· · ·

How much of a person a man is depends on how strong the I of the basic word I-You is in the human duality of his I.

The way he says I—what he means when he says I—decides where a man belongs and where he goes. The word "I" is the true shibboleth of humanity.

Listen to it! . . .

Third Part

Extended, the lines of relationships intersect in the eternal You.

Every single You is a glimpse of that. Through every single You the basic word addresses the eternal You. The mediatorship of the You of all beings accounts for the fullness of our relationships to them—and for the lack of fulfillment. The innate You is actualized each time without ever being perfected. It attains perfection solely in the immediate relationship to the You that in accordance with its nature cannot become an It.

Men have addressed their eternal You by many names. When they sang of what they had thus named, they still meant You: the first myths were hymns of praise. Then the names entered into the It-language; men felt impelled more and more to think of and to talk about their eternal You as an It. But all names of God remain hallowed—because they have been used not only to speak *of* God but also to speak *to* him.

Some would deny any legitimate use of the word God because it has been misused so much. Certainly it is the most burdened of all human words. Precisely for that reason it is the most imperishable and unavoidable. And how much weight has all erroneous talk about God's nature and works (although there never has been nor can be any such talk that is not erroneous) compared with the one truth that all men who have addressed God really meant him? For whoever pronounces the word God and really means You, addresses, no matter what his delusion, the true You of his life that cannot be restricted by any other and to whom he stands in a relationship that includes all others.

But whoever abhors the name and fancies that he is godless—when he addresses with his whole devoted being the You of his life that cannot be restricted by any other, he addresses God. . . .

Every actual relationship to another being in the world is exclusive. Its You is freed and steps forth to confront us in its uniqueness. It fills the firmament—not as if there were nothing else, but everything else lives in *its* light. As long as the presence of the relationship endures, this world-wideness cannot be infringed. But as soon as a You becomes an It, the world-wideness of the relationship appears as an injustice against the world, and its exclusiveness as an exclusion of the universe.

In the relation to God, unconditional exclusiveness and unconditional inclusiveness are one. For those who enter into the absolute relationship, nothing particular retains any importance—neither things nor beings, neither earth nor heaven—but everything is included in the relationship. For entering into the pure relationship does not involve ignoring everything but seeing everything in the You, not renouncing the world but placing it upon its proper ground. Looking away from the world is no help toward God; staring at the world is no help either; but whoever beholds the world in him stands in his presence. "World here, God there"—that is It-talk; and "God in the world"—that, too, is It-talk; but leaving out nothing, leaving nothing behind, to comprehend all—all the world—in comprehending the You, giving the world its due and truth, to have nothing besides God but to grasp everything in him, that is the perfect relationship.

One does not find God if one remains in the world; one does not find God if one leaves the world. Whoever goes forth to his You with his whole being and carries to it all the being of the world, finds him whom one cannot seek.

Of course, God is "the wholly other"; but he is also the wholly same: the wholly present. Of course, he is the *mysterium tremendum* that appears and overwhelms; but he is also the mystery of the obvious that is closer to me than my own I.

When you fathom the life of things and of conditionality, you reach the indissoluble; when you dispute the life of things and of conditionality, you wind up before the nothing; when you consecrate life you encounter the living God. . . .

. . .

People speak of the "religious man" as one who can dispense with all relationships to the world and to beings because the social stage that is allegedly determined from outside is supposed to have been transcended here by a force that works entirely from within. But two basically different notions are confused when people use the concept of the social: the community built of relation and the amassing of human units that have no relation to one another—the palpable manifestation of modern man's lack of relation. The bright edifice of community, however, for which one can be liberated even from the dungeon of "sociability," is the work of the same force that is alive in the relation between man and God. But this is not one relation among others; it is the universal relation into which all rivers pour without drying up for that reason. Sea and rivers—who would make bold to separate here and define limits? There is only the one flood from I to You, ever more infinite, the one boundless flood of actual life. One cannot divide one's life between an actual relationship to God and an inactual I-It relationship to the world—praying to God in truth and utilizing the world. Whoever knows the world as something to be utilized knows God the same way. His prayers are a way of unburdening himself—and fall into the ears of the void. He—and not the "atheist" who from the night and longing of his garret window addresses the nameless—is godless.

It is said further that the "religious" man steps before God as one who is single, solitary, and detached insofar as he has also transcended the stage of the "ethical" man who still dwells in duty and obligation to the world. The latter is said to be still burdened with responsibility for the actions of agents because he is wholly determined by the tension between is and ought,

and into the unbridgeable gap between both he throws, full of grotesquely hopeless sacrificial courage, piece upon piece of his heart. The "religious" man is supposed to have transcended this tension between world and God; the commandment for him is to leave behind the restlessness of responsibility and of making demands on himself; for him there is no longer any room for a will of one's own, he accepts his place in the Plan; any ought is dissolved in unconditional being, and the world, while still persisting, has lost its validity; one still has to do one's share in it but, as it were, without obligation, in the perspective of the nullity of all activity. Thus men fancy that God has created his world to be an illusion and his man to reel. Of course, whoever steps before the countenance has soared way beyond duty and obligation—but not because he has moved away from the world; rather because he has come truly close to it. Duties and obligations one has only toward the stranger: toward one's intimates one is kind and loving. When a man steps before the countenance, the world becomes wholly present to him for the first time in the fullness of the presence, illuminated by eternity, and he can say You in one word to the being of all beings. There is no longer any tension between world and God but only the one actuality. He is not rid of responsibility: for the pains of the finite version that explores effects he has exchanged the momentum of the infinite kind, the power of loving responsibility for the whole unexplorable course of the world, the deep inclusion in the world before the countenance of God. Ethical judgments, to be sure, he has left behind forever: "evil" men are for him merely those commended to him for a deeper responsibility, those more in need of love; but decisions he must continue to make in the depths of spontaneity unto death—calmly deciding ever again in favor of right action. Thus action is not null: it is intended, it is commanded, it is needed, it belongs to the creation; but this action no longer imposes itself upon the world, it grows upon it as if it were non-action.

Study Questions

1. How does Buber define the I-It and I-Thou modes? How are they similar? How do they differ?
2. What is the difference between the I that appears as an "ego" and the I that appears as a "person"? What attitude prevails in each? Why is the I that is more person-oriented than ego-oriented more actualized in its humanity?
3. What does Buber understand by the eternal Thou? How does our relation to the eternal Thou affect our relation to all beings?
4. What conceptions of the "religious" man and of the "ethical" man does Buber criticize? What relation between religion and ethics does he reject? What is the nature of the "deeper responsibility" according to his conception?

Suggestions for Further Reading

Diamond, M. L. *Martin Buber, Jewish Existentialist* (New York: Harper & Row, 1968, Oxford University Press). A general exposition of Buber's philosophy of religion.

Friedman, M. S. *Martin Buber: The Life of Dialogue* (New York: Harper & Row, 1960, University of Chicago Press). A basic introduction to Buber's thought. See Chapter 22 on his ethics.

Schilpp, P. A., and M. Friedman, eds. *The Philosophy of Martin Buber. The Library of Living Philosophers, Volume XII.* (La Salle, IL: Open Court, 1967). See Essays 6 and 7 for critical views of Buber's ethics. See also Buber's "Replies to My Critics," in the same volume.

Ruth Benedict (1887–1948)

Ruth Benedict, a notable American anthropologist, was born Ruth Fulton in New York City. She studied English literature at Vassar College and received her Ph.D. in anthropology from Columbia University. Her book *Patterns of Culture* (1934) proved to be influential in its argument against the leading social Darwinist theories of the time. Social Darwinism proposed that there is a universal standard of cultural progress that finds its height in Western civilization and morality. Along with other prominent anthropologists and sociologists, such as Franz Boas and Emile Durkheim, Benedict attacked social Darwinism by upholding the claim that social standards and norms are relative to each culture. The cultural relativists questioned the social Darwinist assumption that there are transcultural or universal standards. They also criticized the social Darwinist claim that the degree of progress shown by certain societies manifested the cultural and moral supremacy of those societies over others.

In her article "Anthropology and the Abnormal," Benedict develops her cultural relativist position through a discussion of the psychological and sociological categories of normality and abnormality. Drawing from anthropological observations of various "primitive" cultures, she details how different social orders define these categories differently. Noting the wide variety of these social definitions, Benedict claims that one culture cannot represent all possible ways in which mores are embodied in social institutions. Social standards of behavior are "culturally defined." That is, such standards are necessarily internal to each culture insofar as they are formed through the "nonrational and subconscious" process of adaptations of human behavior with its environment. Hence, particular conceptions of what is moral or good are not a matter of human nature but of socially conditioned habits. In this sense, morality is completely determined by culture. For Benedict, this implies that there are no universal, absolute principles in social and moral categories. Denying the existence of universal social and moral standards, Benedict questions the validity of judging one culture or morality from the perspective of another and of claiming the superiority of one culture or morality over others.

ANTHROPOLOGY AND THE ABNORMAL

MODERN SOCIAL ANTHROPOLOGY has become more and more a study of the varieties and common elements of cultural environment and the consequences of these in human behavior. For such a study of diverse social orders primitive peoples fortunately provide a laboratory not yet entirely vitiated by the spread of a standardized worldwide civilization. Dyaks and Hopis, Fijians and Yakuts are significant for psychological and sociological study because only among these simpler peoples has there been sufficient isolation to give opportunity for the development of localized social forms. In the higher cultures the standardization of custom and belief over a couple of continents has given a false sense of the inevitability of the particular forms that have gained currency, and we need to turn to a wider survey in order to check the conclusions we hastily base upon this near-universality of familiar customs. Most of the simpler cultures did not gain the wide currency of the one which, out of our experience, we identify with human nature, but this was for various historical reasons, and

certainly not for any that gives us as its carriers a monopoly of social good or of social sanity. Modern civilization, from this point of view, becomes not a necessary pinnacle of human achievement but one entry in a long series of possible adjustments.

These adjustments, whether they are in mannerisms like the ways of showing anger, or joy, or grief in any society, or in major human drives like those of sex, prove to be far more variable than experience in any one culture would suggest. In certain fields, such as that of religion or of formal marriage arrangements, these wide limits of variability are well known and can be fairly described. In others it is not yet possible to give a generalized account, but that does not absolve us of the task of indicating the significance of the work that has been done and of the problems that have arisen.

One of these problems relates to the customary modern normal-abnormal categories and our conclusions regarding them. In how far are such categories culturally determined, or in how far

"Anthropology and the Abnormal," by Ruth Benedict (1934). The Journal of General Psychology *10 (1934): 59–82. Reprinted with permission of the Helen Dwight Reid Foundation. Published by Heldref Publications, 1319 Eighteenth St., NW, Washington, DC 20036-1802. Copyright © 1934.*

can we with assurance regard them as absolute? In how far can we regard inability to function socially as diagnostic of abnormality, or in how far is it necessary to regard this as a function of the culture?

As a matter of fact, one of the most striking facts that emerge from a study of widely varying cultures is the ease with which our abnormals function in other cultures. It does not matter what kind of "abnormality" we choose for illustration, those which indicate extreme instability, or those which are more in the nature of character traits like sadism or delusions of grandeur or of persecution, there are well-described cultures in which these abnormals function at ease and with honor, and apparently without danger or difficulty to the society. . . .

No one civilization can possibly utilize in its mores the whole potential range of human behavior. Just as there are great numbers of possible phonetic articulations, and the possibility of language depends on a selection and standardization of a few of these in order that speech communication may be possible at all, so the possibility of organized behavior of every sort, from the fashions of local dress and houses to the dicta of a people's ethics and religion, depends upon a similar selection among the possible behavior traits. In the field of recognized economic obligations or sex tabus this selection is as non-rational and subconscious a process as it is in the field of phonetics. It is a process which goes on in the group for long periods of time and is historically conditioned by innumerable accidents of isolation or of contact of peoples. In any comprehensive study of psychology, the selection that different cultures have made in the course of history within the great circumference of potential behavior is of great significance.

Every society,[1] beginning with some slight inclination in one direction or another, carries its preference farther and farther, integrating itself

more and more completely upon its chosen basis, and discarding those types of behavior that are uncongenial. Most of those organizations of personality that seem to us most incontrovertibly abnormal have been used by different civilizations in the very foundations of their institutional life. Conversely the most valued traits of our normal individuals have been looked on in differently organized cultures as aberrant. Normality, in short, within a very wide range, is culturally defined. It is primarily a term for the socially elaborated segment of human behavior in any culture; and abnormality, a term for the segment that that particular civilization does not use. The very eyes with which we see the problem are conditioned by the long traditional habits of our own society.

It is a point that has been made more often in relation to ethics than in relation to psychiatry. We do not any longer make the mistake of deriving the morality of our own locality and decade directly from the inevitable constitution of human nature. We do not elevate it to the dignity of a first principle. We recognize that morality differs in every society, and is a convenient term for socially approved habits. Mankind has always preferred to say, "It is a morally good," rather than "It is habitual," and the fact of this preference is matter enough for a critical science of ethics. But historically the two phrases are synonymous.

The concept of the normal is properly a variant of the concept of the good. It is that which society has approved. A normal action is one which falls well within the limits of expected behavior for a particular society. Its variability among different peoples is essentially a function of the variability of the behavior patterns that different societies have created for themselves, and can never be wholly divorced from a consideration of culturally institutionalized types of behavior.

Each culture is a more or less elaborate working-out of the potentialities of the segment it has chosen. In so far as a civilization is well integrated and consistent within itself, it will tend to carry farther and farther, according to its nature,

---

[1] This phrasing of the process is deliberately animistic. It is used with no reference to a group mind or a superorganic, but in the same sense in which it is customary to say, "Every art has its own canons."

its initial impulse toward a particular type of action, and from the point of view of any other culture those elaborations will include more and more extreme and aberrant traits.

Each of these traits, in proportion as it reinforces the chosen behavior patterns of that culture, is for that culture normal. Those individuals to whom it is congenial either congenitally, or as the result of childhood sets, are accorded prestige in that culture, and are not visited with the social contempt or disapproval which their traits would call down upon them in a society that was differently organized. On the other hand, those individuals whose characteristics are not congenial to the selected type of human behavior in that community are the deviants, no matter how valued their personality traits may be in a contrasted civilization. . . .

It is clear that statistical methods of defining normality, so long as they are based on studies in a selected civilization, only involve us, unless they are checked against the cultural configuration, in deeper and deeper provincialism. The recent tendency in abnormal psychology to take the laboratory mode as normal and to define abnormalities as they depart from this average has value in so far as it indicates that the aberrants in any culture are those individuals who are liable to serious disturbances because their habits are culturally unsupported. On the other hand, it overlooks the fact that every culture besides its abnormals of conflict has presumably its abnormals of extreme fulfillment of the cultural type. From the point of view of a universally valid abnormal psychology the extreme types of abnormality would probably be found in this very group—a group which in every study based upon one culture goes undescribed except in its end institutionalized forms.

The relativity of normality is important in what may some day come to be a true social engineering. Our picture of our own civilization is no longer in this generation in terms of a changeless and divinely derived set of categorical imperatives. We must face the problems our changed perspective has put upon us. In this matter of mental ailments, we must face the fact that even our normality is man-made, and is of our own seeking. Just as we have been handicapped in dealing with ethical problems so long as we held to an absolute definition of morality, so too in dealing with the problems of abnormality we are handicapped so long as we identify our local normalities with the universal sanities. I have taken illustrations from different cultures, because the conclusions are most inescapable from the contrasts as they are presented in unlike social groups. But the major problem is not a consequence of the variability of the normal from culture to culture, but its variability from era to era. This variability in time we cannot escape if we would, and it is not beyond the bounds of possibility that we may be able to face this inevitable change with full understanding and deal with it rationally. No society has yet achieved self-conscious and critical analysis of its own normalities and attempted rationally to deal with its own social process of creating new normalities within its next generation. But the fact that it is unachieved is not therefore proof of its impossibility. It is a faint indication of how momentous it could be in human society. . . .

The problem of understanding abnormal human behavior in any absolute sense independent of cultural factors is still far in the future. The categories of borderline behavior which we derive from the study of the neuroses and psychoses of our civilization are categories of prevailing local types of instability. They give much information about the stresses and strains of Western civilization, but no final picture of inevitable human behavior. Any conclusions about such behavior must await the collection by trained observers of psychiatric data from other cultures. Since no adequate work of the kind has been done at the present time, it is impossible to say what core of definition of abnormality may be found valid from the comparative material. It is as it is in ethics: all our local conventions of moral behavior and of immoral are without absolute validity, and yet it is quite possible that a modicum of what is considered right and what wrong could be disentangled that is shared by the whole human race. When data are available in psychiatry, this minimum definition of abnormal human tendencies will be probably quite unlike our culturally conditioned, highly elaborated psychoses such as those that are described, for instance, under the terms of schizophrenia and manic-depressive.

Study Questions

1. On what basis does Benedict argue against the existence of universal standards of morality? Does the claim that there are cultural differences in morality necessarily mean that commonalities and universals are impossible?
2. What assumptions does Benedict make regarding human behavior and social order? How can her theory account for individual variances and social changes?
3. Does Benedict's cultural relativist theory allow for the possibility of criticizing a given culture for its moral standards? Does it allow for individuals to criticize the standards of their own culture?
4. Is Benedict's cultural relativist position consistent? Is she making ethical claims? Is she making culturally relative or universal claims?

Suggestions for Further Reading

Ladd, J. *Ethical Relativism* (Belmont, CA: Wadsworth, 1973). Contains essays on various aspects of ethical relativism.

Kraus M., and J. W. Meiland, eds. *Relativism: Cognitive and Moral* (Notre Dame, IN: University of Notre Dame Press, 1982). A collection of essays by leading contemporary ethicists.

Wong, D. "Relativism." In *A Companion to Ethics* , ed. P. Singer (Oxford; Cambridge, MA: Blackwell Reference, 1991). A discussion of various kinds of relativism and a defense of (metaethical) relativism.

Stace, W. T. *The Concept of Morals* (New York: Macmillan, 1962). See Chapters 1 and 2 for a discussion of the issues and problems of moral relativism.

A. J. Ayer (1910–1989)

Alfred Jules Ayer was an English philosopher who taught at two colleges of Oxford University and was Grote Professor of Philosophy of Mind and Logic at University College, London, later returning to Oxford, where he remained until his retirement in 1978. He was one of the later exponents of the early-twentieth-century movement in philosophy known as logical positivism or logical empiricism. His best-known book, *Language, Truth and Logic* (published in 1936 and revised in 1946), developed the principles of logical positivism in their clearest and most accessible forms.

The logical positivist movement had its beginnings in the 1920s with the "Vienna Circle," a group of philosophers, scientists, and mathematicians who redefined the task of philosophy in terms of its service to science. Claiming that science is the only genuine source of factual knowledge, they proposed that the proper function of philosophy is merely to analyze and clarify the language and logical structure of scientific statements. Armed with their new definition of philosophy, the logical positivists rejected the traditional view of philosophy as providing metaphysical knowledge about a transcendent reality. Traditional philosophical statements, such as "The soul is immortal," failed to meet their criterion for meaningful statements or propositions. Meaningful statements are declarative sentences that are, in principle, capable of being determined true or false. Most logical positivists argued that there were only two kinds of meaningful statements: synthetic (empirical or factual), such as "Water boils at 100 degrees Celsius," and analytic (nonempirical or nonfactual), such as "A triangle is a figure with three angles." Both kinds of statements are verifiable sentences. The truth or falsity of synthetic statements can be verified objectively through sense experience. The truth or falsity of analytic statements is self-evident by definition of the terms used in it. According to this classification, traditional philosophical statements are neither self-evident nor empirically verifiable. So, they are judged to be cognitively meaningless or nonsensical. They are classified as "pseudostatements" because, though they appear to state something about reality, they have no cognitive value and are incapable of being determined true or false. On these grounds, logical positivists generally labeled most of traditional philosophy "nonsense" and argued for the elimination of metaphysics.

From the general perspective of logical positivism, statements of aesthetic and moral value were classified as "noncognitive" and were considered subjective expressions of emotions or feelings. Most logical positivists discarded the possibility not only of a science but also of a philosophy of ethics because of the normative or prescriptive character of ethical statements. Although Ayer agreed with the basic "emotive" theory of morality, he also allowed for the possibility of scientific and philosophical inquiries into ethics. By drawing attention to the different kinds of statements in ethics, he insisted that some kinds of statements belonged in the field either of science or of philosophy. Statements that describe the phenomena of moral experiences in individuals or societies are genuine empirical statements of psychology or sociology, and those that define ethical terms or evaluate certain definitions belong properly within the sphere of ethical philosophy. However, moral exhortations, such as "You ought to do x," and moral judgments, such as "x action is wrong," are excluded from the spheres of science and philosophy. They are not properly statements or propositions; that is, sentences with a cognitive meaning capable of being proved true or false. Moral exhortations are not descriptive statements, but normative commands. Moral judgments, on the other hand, play a sheerly "emotive" function.

Calling his position "radical subjectivism," Ayer argues that moral judgments are not statements or propositions that describe subjective facts or feelings. Rather, they are the venting of our feelings or our attempts to induce such feelings in others. Ethical symbols or terms, such as "good" and "wrong," which occur in normative sentences that express moral judgments, have no factual meaning whatsoever, either objective or subjective. Thus, Ayer calls normative ethical concepts "pseudoconcepts" because they seem to have factual content but really have none at all. With this pronouncement, Ayer deems the task of ethics or moral philosophy completed, leaving the task of providing empirical knowledge about morality to the fields of psychology and sociology.

CRITIQUE OF ETHICS AND THEOLOGY

THERE IS STILL one objection to be met before we can claim to have justified our view that all synthetic propositions are empirical hypotheses. This objection is based on the common supposition that our speculative knowledge is of two distinct kinds—that which relates to questions of empirical fact, and that which relates to questions of value. It will be said that "statements of value" are genuine synthetic propositions, but that they cannot with any show of justice be represented as hypotheses, which are used to predict the course of our sensations; and, accordingly, that the existence of ethics and æsthetics as branches of speculative knowledge presents an insuperable objection to our radical empiricist thesis.

In face of this objection, it is our business to give an account of "judgements of value" which is both satisfactory in itself and consistent with our general empiricist principles. We shall set ourselves to show that in so far as statements of value are significant, they are ordinary "scientific" statements; and that in so far as they are not scientific, they are not in the literal sense significant, but are simply expressions of emotion which can be neither true nor false. In maintaining this view, we may confine ourselves for the present to the case of ethical statements. What is said about them will be found to apply, *mutatis mutandis,* to the case of æsthetic statements also.

The ordinary system of ethics, as elaborated in the works of ethical philosophers, is very far from being a homogeneous whole. Not only is it apt to contain pieces of metaphysics, and analyses of non-ethical concepts: its actual ethical contents are themselves of very different kinds. We may divide them, indeed, into four main classes. There are, first of all, propositions which express definitions of ethical terms, or judgements about the legitimacy or possibility of certain definitions.

Secondly, there are propositions describing the phenomena of moral experience, and their causes. Thirdly, there are exhortations to moral virtue. And, lastly, there are actual ethical judgements. It is unfortunately the case that the distinction between these four classes, plain as it is, is commonly ignored by ethical philosophers; with the result that it is often very difficult to tell from their works what it is that they are seeking to discover or prove.

In fact, it is easy to see that only the first of our four classes, namely that which comprises the propositions relating to the definitions of ethical terms, can be said to constitute ethical philosophy. The propositions which describe the phenomena of moral experience, and their causes, must be assigned to the science of psychology, or sociology. The exhortations to moral virtue are not propositions at all, but ejaculations or commands which are designed to provoke the reader to action of a certain sort. Accordingly, they do not belong to any branch of philosophy or science. As for the expressions of ethical judgements, we have not yet determined how they should be classified. But inasmuch as they are certainly neither definitions nor comments upon definitions, nor quotations, we may say decisively that they do not belong to ethical philosophy. A strictly philosophical treatise on ethics should therefore make no ethical pronouncements. But it should, by giving an analysis of ethical terms, show what is the category to which all such pronouncements belong. And this is what we are now about to do. . . .

It is advisable here to make it plain that it is only normative ethical symbols, and not descriptive ethical symbols, that are held by us to be indefinable in factual terms. There is a danger of confusing these two types of symbols, because they are commonly constituted by signs of the same sensible form. Thus a complex sign of the

A. J. Ayer. "Critique of Ethics and Theology." In Language, Truth and Logic. *New York: Dover, 1935; 2d rev. ed., 1946, Chapter VI.*

form "*x* is wrong" may constitute a sentence which expresses a moral judgement concerning a certain type of conduct, or it may constitute a sentence which states that a certain type of conduct is repugnant to the moral sense of a particular society. In the latter case, the symbol "wrong" is a descriptive ethical symbol, and the sentence in which it occurs expresses an ordinary sociological proposition; in the former case, the symbol "wrong" is a normative ethical symbol, and the sentence in which it occurs does not, we maintain, expresses an empirical proposition at all. It is only with normative ethics that we are at present concerned; so that whenever ethical symbols are used in the course of this argument without qualification, they are always to be interpreted as symbols of the normative type. . . .

We begin by admitting that the fundamental ethical concepts are unanalysable, inasmuch as there is no criterion by which one can test the validity of the judgements in which they occur. So far we are in agreement with the absolutists. But, unlike the absolutists, we are able to give an explanation of this fact about ethical concepts. We say that the reason why they are unanalysable is that they are mere pseudo-concepts.

The presence of an ethical symbol in a proposition adds nothing to its factual content. Thus if I say to someone, "You acted wrongly in stealing that money," I am not stating anything more than if I had simply said, "You stole that money." In adding that this action is wrong I am not making any further statement about it. I am simply evincing my moral disapproval of it. It is as if I had said, "You stole that money," in a peculiar tone of horror, or written it with the addition of some special exclamation marks. The tone, or the exclamation marks, adds nothing to the literal meaning of the sentence. It merely serves to show that the expression of it is attended by certain feelings in the speaker.

If now I generalise my previous statement and say, "Stealing money is wrong," I produce a sentence which has no factual meaning—that is, expresses no proposition which can be either true or false. It is as if I had written "Stealing money!!"—where the shape and thickness of the

exclamation marks show, by a suitable convention, that a special sort of moral disapproval is the feeling which is being expressed. It is clear that there is nothing said here which can be true or false. Another man may disagree with me about the wrongness of stealing, in the sense that he may not have the same feelings about stealing as I have, and he may quarrel with me on account of my moral sentiments. But he cannot, strictly speaking, contradict me. For in saying that a certain type of action is right or wrong, I am not making any factual statement, not even a statement about my own state of mind. I am merely expressing certain moral sentiments. And the man who is ostensibly contradicting me is merely expressing his moral sentiments. So that there is plainly no sense in asking which of us is in the right. For neither of us is asserting a genuine proposition.

What we have just been saying about the symbol "wrong" applies to all normative ethical symbols. Sometimes they occur in sentences which record ordinary empirical facts besides expressing ethical feeling about those facts: sometimes they occur in sentences which simply express ethical feeling about a certain type of action, or situation, without making any statement of fact. But in every case in which one would commonly be said to be making an ethical judgement, the function of the relevant ethical word is purely "emotive." It is used to express feeling about certain objects, but not to make any assertion about them.

It is worth mentioning that ethical terms do not serve only to express feeling. They are calculated also to arouse feeling, and so to stimulate action. Indeed some of them are used in such a way as to give the sentences in which they occur the effect of commands. Thus the sentence "It is your duty to tell the truth" may be regarded both as the expression of a certain sort of ethical feeling about truthfulness and as the expression of the command "Tell the truth." The sentence "You ought to tell the truth" also involves the command "Tell the truth," but here the tone of the command is less emphatic. In the sentence "It is good to tell the truth" the command has become little more than a suggestion. And thus the "meaning" of the word "good," in its ethical usage, is differentiated from that of the word "duty" or the word "ought." In fact we may define the meaning of the various ethical words in terms both of the different feelings they are ordinarily taken to express, and also the different responses which they are calculated to provoke.

We can now see why it is impossible to find a criterion for determining the validity of ethical judgements. It is not because they have an "absolute" validity which is mysteriously independent of ordinary sense-experience, but because they have no objective validity whatsoever. If a sentence makes no statement at all, there is obviously no sense in asking whether what it says is true or false. And we have seen that sentences which simply express moral judgements do not say anything. They are pure expressions of feeling and as such do not come under the category of truth and falsehood. They are unverifiable for the same reason as a cry of pain or a word of command is unverifiable—because they do not express genuine propositions.

Thus, although our theory of ethics might fairly be said to be radically subjectivist, it differs in a very important respect from the orthodox subjectivist theory. For the orthodox subjectivist does not deny, as we do, that the sentences of a moralizer express genuine propositions. All he denies is that they express propositions of a unique non-empirical character. His own view is that they express propositions about the speaker's feelings. If this were so, ethical judgements clearly would be capable of being true or false. They would be true if the speaker had the relevant feelings, and false if he had not. And this is a matter which is, in principle, empirically verifiable. Furthermore they could be significantly contradicted. For if I say, "Tolerance is a virtue," and someone answers, "You don't approve of it," he would, on the ordinary subjectivist theory, be contradicting me. On our theory, he would not be contradicting me, because, in saying that tolerance was a virtue, I should not be making any statement about my own feelings or about anything else. I should simply be evinc-

ing my feelings, which is not at all the same thing as saying that I have them. . . .

We have already remarked that the main objection to the ordinary subjectivist theory is that the validity of ethical judgements is not determined by the nature of their author's feelings. And this is an objection which our theory escapes. For it does not imply that the existence of any feelings is a necessary and sufficient condition of the validity of an ethical judgement. It implies, on the contrary, that ethical judgements have no validity.

There is, however, a celebrated argument against subjectivist theories which our theory does not escape. It has been pointed out by Moore that if ethical statements were simply statements about the speaker's feelings, it would be impossible to argue about questions of value. To take a typical example: if a man said that thrift was a virtue, and another replied that it was a vice, they would not, on this theory, be disputing with one another. One would be saying that he approved of thrift, and the other that *he* didn't; and there is no reason why both these statements should not be true. Now Moore held it to be obvious that we do dispute about questions of value, and accordingly concluded that the particular form of subjectivism which he was discussing was false.

It is plain that the conclusion that it is impossible to dispute about questions of value follows from our theory also. For as we hold that such sentences as "Thrift is a virtue" and "Thrift is a vice" do not express propositions at all, we clearly cannot hold that they express incompatible propositions. We must therefore admit that if Moore's argument really refutes the ordinary subjectivist theory, it also refutes ours. But, in fact, we deny that it does refute even the ordinary subjectivist theory. For we hold that one really never does dispute about questions of value. . . .

In short, we find that argument is possible on moral questions only if some system of values is presupposed. If our opponent concurs with us in expressing moral disapproval of all actions of a given type *t,* then we may get him to condemn a particular action A, by bringing forward arguments to show that A is of type *t*. For the question whether A does or does not belong to that type is a plain question of fact. Given that a man has certain moral principles, we argue that he must, in order to be consistent, react morally to certain things in a certain way. . . .

Having upheld our theory against the only criticism which appeared to threaten it, we may now use it to define the nature of all ethical enquiries. We find that ethical philosophy consists simply in saying that ethical concepts are pseudo-concepts and therefore unanalysable. The further task of describing the different feelings that the different ethical terms are used to express, and the different reactions that they customarily provoke, is a task for the psychologist. There cannot be such a thing as ethical science, if by ethical science one means the elaboration of a "true" system of morals. For we have seen that, as ethical judgements are mere expressions of feeling, there can be no way of determining the validity of any ethical system, and, indeed, no sense in asking whether any such system is true. All that one may legitimately enquire in this connection is, What are the moral habits of a given person or group of people, and what causes them to have precisely those habits and feelings? And this enquiry falls wholly within the scope of the existing social sciences.

It appears, then, that ethics, as a branch of knowledge, is nothing more than a department of psychology and sociology. And in case anyone thinks that we are overlooking the existence of casuistry, we may remark that casuistry is not a science, but is a purely analytical investigation of the structure of a given moral system. In other words, it is an exercise in formal logic.

Study Questions

1. What are the central claims of Ayer's emotive theory of ethics? Why does he label his subjectivist position "radical"?
2. What does Ayer criticize about traditional ethics or moral philosophy? Why does he label ethical concepts "pseudo-concepts"? Why is it impossible to determine the validity of an ethical judgment?
3. How does Ayer define the proper role of ethics? How does he support this definition? How does it apply to his own position?
4. What assumptions does Ayer make regarding the distinction between facts and values? between the cognitive and the emotive?
5. Why does Ayer argue that it is impossible to dispute over matters of moral and aesthetic value? What do we argue over in moral disputes? Why must we share the same system of values? Is he suggesting that morality is relative and conventional?

Suggestions for Further Reading

Foster, J., and T. Honderich, eds. *A. J. Ayer* (London: Routledge and Kegan Paul, 1985). See Part 1, Section 8, for a critical view of Ayer's approach to ethics.

Kupperman, J. J. *Ethical Knowledge* (London: Allen & Unwin, 1970). See Chapter 4 for a critique of Ayer's view of ethical knowledge.

Stevenson, C. L. *Ethics and Language* (New Haven, CT: Yale University Press, 1944). See Part 2 of Chapter 12 for a general comparison between Ayer and other philosophers on the problem of ethics and language.

Urmson, J. O. *The Emotive Theory of Ethics* (London: Hutchinson, 1968). Chapters 1–3 provide a general introduction to the theory of emotivism.

Jean-Paul Sartre (1905–1980)

Jean-Paul Sartre, the famous literary and philosophical figure of the French existentialist movement, was born in Paris. Talking about his early years, Sartre said that he found his "religion" in books and by his early teens had already reached the conclusion that God does not exist. He studied literature and philosophy at the prestigious *École Normale Supérieure* in Paris and German philosophy in Berlin and Freiburg. Though he taught philosophy at various *lycée,* Sartre eventually abandoned teaching to focus on his writing. He developed his existentialist themes in different literary forms, including novels (*Nausea*), plays (*No Exit*), and short stories (*The Wall*). During World War II, he wrote one of his major philosophical works, *Being and Nothingness,* in which he elaborates the principles of existentialism in a highly systematic form. While serving as an army private during World War II, Sartre was held prisoner by the Germans. After his release, he became a leader of the French Resistance and gained a reputation as a leftist political activist and commentator. When the war ended, he co-founded *Les Temps Modernes*—the leading existentialist journal among French intellectuals—with two other famous French philosophers, Simone de Beauvoir (his lifelong companion) and Maurice Merleau-Ponty. During the 1960s, Sartre served on an international committee that criticized the U.S. military involvement in Vietnam. In 1964, he was awarded the Nobel Prize in literature, but he declined the award, believing that institutional structures would thwart his freedom as a writer.

Sartre was one of the main exponents of existentialist philosophy in the twentieth century, along with others such as Albert Camus, Gabriel Marcel, Karl Jaspers, and José Ortega y Gasset. With its roots in the nineteenth-century philosophies of Søren Kierkegaard and Friedrich Nietzsche, existentialism centered on the lived reality of the individual in confronting the uniquely human condition of freedom. Like their predecessors, the twentieth-century existentialists were critical of traditional philosophical approaches that defined the human being abstractly in terms of a fixed nature or essence. Such essence was believed to determine each individual's identity in isolation from the concrete context of his or her existence with other human beings. Traditional philosophers believed that abstract universal principles provide eternal, objective frameworks of value and meaning for humanity. Against this view, existentialists argued that human subjects give value and meaning to their lives through the concrete structuring of their existence. They insisted that human existence has a distinctive character as the life of conscious beings who find themselves thrown into a given world with other human beings and who are aware of the range of alternatives open to their particular lives in their concrete context of existence. Thus, the existentialists emphasized that individuals are "radically" free in that they must become who they are, with no choice but to shape their selves through the choices made throughout their lives. In this sense, human existence is a process of self-creation whereby individuals face the possibilities of freedom and the burden of responsibility for their lives. Only those who boldly confront their reality, take hold of their freedom, and assume the burden of responsibility are "authentic," whereas those who let their fear rule by trying to surrender their possibilities and evade their burdens are "inauthentic."

The existentialists differed from one another in their ways of approaching and responding to the problem of human existence, but (as Sartre himself noted) they agreed that "existence precedes essence." This means that there is no fixed human nature that determines the terms of our existence; rather, it is through our existence that we determine who we are. Sartre explicitly distinguished himself from Christian existentialists, like Marcel and Jaspers, by calling himself an atheistic existentialist. Thus, Sartre's understanding that existence precedes essence and his view of the human predicament of freedom and responsibility begin with the assumption that God does not exist.

According to Sartre, if God does not exist, then ultimately we are "condemned to be free," for there is no given human essence and there are no absolutes—fixed values and eternal meanings—determining our existence. The individual confronts a life that is not preordained by a higher being, an existence where we are "alone, without excuses." We are utterly free in a universe where no single value has a greater or lesser intrinsic worth than any other. At the same time, we are utterly responsible for the values we create through our choices. Hence, our authenticity lies in our ability to confront this radical freedom and assume this inescapable responsibility. Sartre emphasizes, however, that individuals are responsible not only for themselves or for their particular existence but for all human beings. When we choose, we affirm the value of one alternative over another. So, in each of our choices, we create the ideal of what human beings ought to be. Because there is no given absolute ideal of humans, the choices we make in our individual lives have the universal weight of humanity. And because in creating ourselves we create humanity, the tremendous burden of responsibility produces an anguish from which many of us try to escape by living inauthentically.

Like other existentialists, Sartre offers the basis for an ethics that is centered on the notion of the authentic versus the inauthentic existence. Because there are no moral givens or absolute values, Sartre does not chart the course of the authentic existence by offering an ethical code of determinate actions that are called "right" or "wrong." It is entirely up to individuals in their radical freedom to determine their moral paths and thus to create their own morality.

EXISTENTIALISM AND HUMAN EMOTIONS

. . . [T]HERE ARE TWO KINDS of existentialist; first, those who are Christian, among whom I would include Jaspers and Gabriel Marcel, both Catholic; and on the other hand the atheistic existentialists, among whom I class Heidegger, and then the French existentialists and myself. What they have in common is that they think that existence precedes essence, or, if you prefer, that subjectivity must be the starting point.

Just what does that mean? Let us consider some object that is manufactured, for example, a book or a paper-cutter: here is an object which

Jean-Paul Sartre. Existentialism and Human Emotions, *trans. B. Frechtman. New York: The Philosophical Library, 1957. Reprinted by permission.*

has been made by an artisan whose inspiration came from a concept. He referred to the concept of what a paper-cutter is and likewise to a known method of production, which is part of the concept, something which is, by and large, a routine. Thus, the paper-cutter is at once an object produced in a certain way and, on the other hand, one having a specific use; and one can not postulate a man who produces a paper-cutter but does not know what it is used for. Therefore, let us say that, for the paper-cutter, essence—that is, the ensemble of both the production routines and the properties which enable it to be both produced and defined—precedes existence. Thus, the presence of the paper-cutter or book in front of me is determined. Therefore, we have here a technical view of the world whereby it can be said that production precedes existence.

When we conceive God as the Creator, He is generally thought of as a superior sort of artisan. Whatever doctrine we may be considering, whether one like that of Descartes or that of Leibnitz, we always grant that will more or less follows understanding or, at the very least, accompanies it, and that when God creates He knows exactly what He is creating. Thus, the concept of man in the mind of God is comparable to the concept of paper-cutter in the mind of the manufacturer, and, following certain techniques and a conception, God produces man, just as the artisan, following a definition and a technique, makes a paper-cutter. Thus, the individual man is the realization of a certain concept in the divine intelligence.

In the eighteenth century, the atheism of the *philosophes* discarded the idea of God, but not so much for the notion that essence precedes existence. To a certain extent, this idea is found everywhere; we find it in Diderot, in Voltaire, and even in Kant. Man has a human nature; this human nature, which is the concept of the human, is found in all men, which means that each man is a particular example of a universal concept, man. In Kant, the result of this universality is that the wild-man, the natural man, as well as the bourgeois, are circumscribed by the same definition and have the same basic qualities.

Thus, here too the essence of man precedes the historical existence that we find in nature.

Atheistic existentialism, which I represent, is more coherent. It states that if God does not exist, there is at least one being in whom existence precedes essence, a being who exists before he can be defined by any concept, and that this being is man, or, as Heidegger says, human reality. What is meant here by saying that existence precedes essence? It means that, first of all, man exists, turns up, appears on the scene, and, only afterwards, defines himself. If man, as the existentialist conceives him, is indefinable, it is because at first he is nothing. Only afterward will he be something, and he himself will have made what he will be. Thus, there is no human nature, since there is no God to conceive it. Not only is man what he conceives himself to be, but he is also only what he wills himself to be after this thrust toward existence.

Man is nothing else but what he makes of himself. Such is the first principle of existentialism. It is also what is called subjectivity, the name we are labeled with when charges are brought against us. But what do we mean by this, if not that man has a greater dignity than a stone or table? For we mean that man first exists, that is, that man first of all is the being who hurls himself toward a future and who is conscious of imagining himself as being in the future. Man is at the start a plan which is aware of itself, rather than a patch of moss, a piece of garbage, or a cauliflower; nothing exists prior to this plan; there is nothing in heaven; man will be what he will have planned to be. Not what he will want to be. Because by the word "will" we generally mean a conscious decision, which is subsequent to what we have already made of ourselves. I may want to belong to a political party, write a book, get married; but all that is only a manifestation of an earlier, more spontaneous choice that is called "will." But if existence really does precede essence, man is responsible for what he is. Thus, existentialism's first move is to make every man aware of what he is and to make the full responsibility of his existence rest on him. And when we say that a man is responsible for himself, we do not only mean that he is responsible for his own individuality, but that he is responsible for all men.

The word subjectivism has two meanings, and our opponents play on the two. Subjectivism means, on the one hand, that an individual chooses and makes himself; and, on the other, that it is impossible for man to transcend human subjectivity. The second of these is the essential meaning of existentialism. When we say that man chooses his own self, we mean that every one of us does likewise; but we also mean by that that in making this choice he also chooses all men. In fact, in creating the man that we want to be, there is not a single one of our acts which does not at the same time create an image of man as we think he ought to be. To choose to be this or that is to affirm at the same time the value of what we choose, because we can never choose evil. We always choose the good, and nothing can be good for us without being good for all.

If, on the other hand, existence precedes essence, and if we grant that we exist and fashion our image at one and the same time, the image is valid for everybody and for our whole age. Thus, our responsibility is much greater than we might have supposed, because it involves all mankind. If I am a workingman and choose to join a Christian trade-union rather than be a communist, and if by being a member I want to show that the best thing for man is resignation, that the kingdom of man is not of this world, I am not only involving my own case—I want to be resigned for everyone. As a result, my action has involved all humanity. To take a more individual matter, if I want to marry, to have children; even if this marriage depends solely on my own circumstances or passion or wish, I am involving all humanity in monogamy and not merely myself. Therefore, I am responsible for myself and for everyone else. I am creating a certain image of man of my own choosing. In choosing myself, I choose man.

This helps us understand what the actual content is of such rather grandiloquent words as anguish, forlornness, despair. As you will see, it's all quite simple.

First, what is meant by anguish? The existentialists say at once that man is anguish. What that means is this: the man who involves himself and who realizes that he is not only the person he chooses to be, but also a lawmaker who is, at the same time, choosing all mankind as well as himself, can not help escape the feeling of his total and deep responsibility. Of course, there are many people who are not anxious; but we claim that they are hiding their anxiety, that they are fleeing from it. Certainly, many people believe that when they do something, they themselves are the only ones involved, and when someone says to them, "What if everyone acted that way?" they shrug their shoulders and answer, "Everyone doesn't act that way." But really, one should always ask himself, "What would happen if everybody looked at things that way?" There is no escaping this disturbing thought except by a kind of double-dealing. A man who lies and makes excuses for himself by saying "not everybody does that," is someone with an uneasy conscience, because the act of lying implies that a universal value is conferred upon the lie.

Anguish is evident even when it conceals itself. This is the anguish that Kierkegaard called the anguish of Abraham. You know the story: an angel has ordered Abraham to sacrifice his son; if it really were an angel who has come and said, "You are Abraham, you shall sacrifice your son," everything would be all right. But everyone might first wonder, "Is it really an angel, and am I really Abraham? What proof do I have?"

There was a madwoman who had hallucinations; someone used to speak to her on the telephone and give her orders. Her doctor asked her, "Who is it who talks to you?" She answered, "He says it's God." What proof did she really have that it was God? If an angel comes to me, what proof is there that it's an angel? And if I hear voices, what proof is there that they come from heaven and not from hell, or from the subconscious, or a pathological condition? What proves that they are addressed to me? What proof is there that I have been appointed to impose my choice and my conception of man on humanity? I'll never find any proof or sign to convince me of that. If a voice addresses me, it is always for me to decide that this is the angel's voice; if I consider that such an act is a good one, it is I who will choose to say that it is good rather than bad.

Now, I'm not being singled out as an Abraham, and yet at every moment I'm obliged to perform exemplary acts. For every man, everything happens as if all mankind had its eyes fixed on him and were guiding itself by what he does. And every man ought to say to himself, "Am I really the kind of man who has the right to act in such a way that humanity might guide itself by my actions?" And if he does not say that to himself, he is masking his anguish.

There is no question here of the kind of anguish which would lead to quietism, to inaction. It is a matter of a simple sort of anguish that anybody who has had responsibilities is familiar with. For example, when a military officer takes the responsibility for an attack and sends a certain number of men to death, he chooses to do so, and in the main he alone makes the choice. Doubtless, orders come from above, but they are too broad; he interprets them, and on this interpretation depend the lives of ten or fourteen or twenty men. In making a decision he can not help having a certain anguish. All leaders know this anguish. That doesn't keep them from acting; on the contrary, it is the very condition of their action. For it implies that they envisage a number of possibilities, and when they choose one, they realize that it has value only because it is chosen. We shall see that this kind of anguish, which is the kind that existentialism describes, is explained, in addition, by a direct responsibility to the other men whom it involves. It is not a curtain separating us from action, but is part of action itself.

When we speak of forlornness, a term Heidegger was fond of, we mean only that God does not exist and that we have to face all the consequences of this. The existentialist is strongly opposed to a certain kind of secular ethics which would like to abolish God with the least possible expense. About 1880, some French teachers tried to set up a secular ethics which went some-

thing like this: God is a useless and costly hypothesis; we are discarding it; but, meanwhile, in order for there to be an ethics, a society, a civilization, it is essential that certain values be taken seriously and that they be considered as having an *a priori* existence. It must be obligatory, *a priori*, to be honest, not to lie, not to beat your wife, to have children, etc., etc. So we're going to try a little device which will make it possible to show that values exist all the same, inscribed in a heaven of ideas, though otherwise God does not exist. In other words—and this, I believe, is the tendency of everything called reformism in France—nothing will be changed if God does not exist. We shall find ourselves with the same norms of honesty, progress, and humanism, and we shall have made of God an outdated hypothesis which will peacefully die off by itself.

The existentialist, on the contrary, thinks it very distressing that God does not exist, because all possibility of finding values in a heaven of ideas disappears along with Him; there can no longer be an *a priori* Good, since there is no infinite and perfect consciousness to think it. Nowhere is it written that the Good exists, that we must be honest, that we must not lie; because the fact is we are on a plane where there are only men. Dostoievsky said, "If God didn't exist, everything would be possible." That is the very starting point of existentialism. Indeed, everything is permissible if God does not exist, and as a result man is forlorn, because neither within him nor without does he find anything to cling to. He can't start making excuses for himself.

If existence really does precede essence, there is no explaining things away by reference to a fixed and given human nature. In other words, there is no determinism, man is free, man is freedom. On the other hand, if God does not exist, we find no values or commands to turn to which legitimize our conduct. So, in the bright realm of values, we have no excuse behind us, nor justification before us. We are alone, with no excuses.

That is the idea I shall try to convey when I say that man is condemned to be free. Condemned, because he did not create himself, yet, in other respects is free; because, once thrown into the world, he is responsible for everything he does. The existentialist does not believe in the power of passion. He will never agree that a sweeping passion is a ravaging torrent which fatally leads a man to certain acts and is therefore an excuse. He thinks that man is responsible for his passion.

The existentialist does not think that man is going to help himself by finding in the world some omen by which to orient himself. Because he thinks that man will interpret the omen to suit himself. Therefore, he thinks that man, with no support and no aid, is condemned every moment to invent man. Ponge, in a very fine article, has said, "Man is the future of man." That's exactly it. But if it is taken to mean that this future is recorded in heaven, that God sees it, then it is false, because it would really no longer be a future. If it is taken to mean that, whatever a man may be, there is a future to be forged, a virgin future before him, then this remark is sound. But then we are forlorn.

Study Questions

1. What does it mean that "existence precedes essence"? Why does Sartre consider this synonymous with the claim that "subjectivity is the starting point"?
2. In what sense are humans radically free? What does it mean that we are "condemned to be free"?
3. Why are individuals entirely responsible for themselves? What does this suggest about the individual's given world and social circumstances?
4. How does Sartre support the claim that we are responsible for all of humanity in our individual choices? What does it mean that "we always choose the good"? In what sense is the individual a "lawmaker" for humanity?
5. What does Sartre suggest about the nature of moral values and ethics? How does he deal with the fact that society provides given value systems and ethical codes for individuals?

Suggestions for Further Reading

Anderson, T. C. *The Foundation and Structure of Sartrean Ethics* (Lawrence: The Regents Press of Kansas, 1979). A six-chapter study of the development of Sartre's ethical theory with critiques of standard interpretations.

Bell, L. *Sartre's Ethics of Authenticity* (Tuscaloosa: University of Alabama Press, 1989). Examines the question of whether a coherent viable Sartrean ethics is possible.

Danto, A. *Jean-Paul Sartre* (New York: Viking Press, 1975). Chapter V provides a brief analysis of Sartre's concept of anguish in terms of the problem of morality and freedom.

Greene, M. N. *Jean-Paul Sartre: The Existentialist Ethic* (Ann Arbor: University of Michigan Press, 1960). An analysis of the ethical implications of Sartre's view of the human being.

Stack, J. G. *Sartre's Philosophy of Social Existence* (Saint Louis, MO: Warren H. Green, 1977). An advanced study of the development of Sartre's thought on social relations.

John Rawls (1921–)

John Rawls was born in Baltimore, Maryland, and received his Ph.D. in philosophy from Princeton University in 1950. He was a Fulbright scholar at Oxford from 1952 to 1953. He is emeritus professor of philosophy at Harvard University and has also taught at Princeton, Cornell, and the Massachusetts Institute of Technology. His work has had a considerable impact on moral, social, and political theories, particularly since 1957, when he delivered his paper "Justice and Fairness" to the American Philosophical Association.

In his major book, *A Theory of Justice* (1971), Rawls develops his conception of justice from social contract theory: the idea that society is based on implicit agreements between its members. These agreements take form in the social structure and political institutions. The social contract approach gained much popularity among such seventeenth- and eighteenth-century philosophers as Thomas Hobbes, John Locke, and Jean-Jacques Rousseau. Though these modern philosophers proposed very different versions of the social contract, all started from a similar hypothesis of a "natural" state or condition of human beings before they enter into a social contract to form a political state. The common philosophical purpose of social contract theories was to search for the fundamental principles operating in the inner rationality and basic structure of an ideal society.

Social contract theories lost general approval during the nineteenth century, when Jeremy Bentham and John Stuart Mill proposed their utilitarian principle of the greatest happiness of the greatest number as the ideal basis for society. The main rival of utilitarianism during that time had its roots in the eighteenth-century philosophy of Immanuel Kant. Kant's moral theory placed emphasis on the concept of duty or moral obligation, and he insisted that the basis for our morality is our rationality. By focusing on humans as agents who are capable of making choices on the basis of reason, Kant underscored our autonomy or freedom to rule ourselves according to rational principles with universal validity. Human dignity is founded in our rationality and autonomy. Consequently, our worth resides in the fact that we are ends in ourselves, never only means or instruments for other ends. For Kant, the model society is thus the "kingdom of ends," a system in which rational beings treat themselves and others as ends.

Rawls' contribution to twentieth-century philosophy resides in his effort to revitalize social contract theory and defend it against utilitarianism while developing his particular paradigm of a just society. The Kantian idea of morality—as the duty of rational and autonomous agents who respect one another as ends—serves as Rawls' starting point in these endeavors.

In *A Theory of Justice*, Rawls elaborates his conception of justice as fairness in the assignment of rights and duties and in the distribution of social and economic resources. Like his seventeenth- and eighteenth-century predecessors, Rawls begins with a hypothetical state, which he calls the "original position" and characterizes as an initial situation in which all parties to the contract stand on an equal level. His central claim is that a social contract between free and rational persons who are initially equal would give origin to a social structure based on principles of justice that are fair. In such position, no one knows her particular social role and individual assets, so that each person stands behind what Rawls calls the "veil of ignorance." Since everyone is equally ignorant of the personal advantages or disadvantages they would reap from their agreement, the principles of justice to which they would agree would be fair.

In Rawls' view of the initial condition of equality, free and rational persons would choose two basic principles of justice that have no connection with the utilitarian principle of the greatest happiness for the greatest number. The first principle would govern the assignment of rights and duties by requiring equality for all. In other words, it would affirm that each person has an equal right to the maximum basic liberty compatible with the same liberty for everyone else. The second principle would govern the distribution of social and economic resources by requiring that any inequality must be to everyone's advantage and positions of authority must be equally accessible to all. This principle thus allows for social and economic inequalities, but only as long as everyone gains some benefit from these and everyone has the same opportunity to be in the chain of command. However, the first principle is prior to the second principle, for equal liberty is the higher social good and must never be violated in the application of the second principle. Thus, a social structure ruled by these two principles of justice would, according to Rawls, provide for a fair governance of society.

A THEORY OF JUSTICE

3. *The Main Idea of the Theory of Justice*

My aim is to present a conception of justice which generalizes and carries to a higher level of abstraction the familiar theory of the social contract as found, say, in Locke, Rousseau, and Kant. In order to do this we are not to think of the original contract as one to enter a particular society or to set up a particular form of government. Rather, the guiding idea is that the principles of justice for the basic structure of society are the object of the original agreement. They are the principles that free and rational persons concerned to further their own interests would accept in an initial position of equality as defining the fundamental terms of their association. These principles are to regulate all further agreements; they specify the kinds of social cooperation that can be entered into and the forms of government that can be established. This way of regarding the principles of justice I shall call justice as fairness.

Thus we are to imagine that those who engage in social cooperation choose together, in one joint act, the principles which are to assign basic rights and duties and to determine the division of social benefits. Men are to decide in ad-

Reprinted by permission of the publisher from in A Theory of Justice *by John Rawls, 11–15, 17–19, 60–63, Cambridge, Mass.: The Belknap Press of Harvard University Press, Copyright © 1971 by the President and Fellows of Harvard College.*

vance how they are to regulate their claims against one another and what is to be the foundation charter of their society. Just as each person must decide by rational reflection what constitutes his good, that is, the system of ends which it is rational for him to pursue, so a group of persons must decide once and for all what is to count among them as just and unjust. The choice which rational men would make in this hypothetical situation of equal liberty, assuming for the present that this choice problem has a solution, determines the principles of justice.

In justice as fairness the original position of equality corresponds to the state of nature in the traditional theory of the social contract. This original position is not, of course, thought of as an actual historical state of affairs, much less as a primitive condition of culture. It is understood as a purely hypothetical situation characterized so as to lead to a certain conception of justice. Among the essential features of this situation is that no one knows his place in society, his class position or social status, nor does any one know his fortune in the distribution of natural assets and abilities, his intelligence, strength, and the like. I shall even assume that the parties do not know their conceptions of the good or their special psychological propensities. The principles of justice are chosen behind a veil of ignorance. This ensures that no one is advantaged or disadvantaged in the choice of principles by the outcome of natural chance or the contingency of social circumstances. Since all are similarly situated and no one is able to design principles to favor his particular condition, the principles of justice are the result of a fair agreement or bargain. For given the circumstances of the original position, the symmetry of everyone's relations to each other, this initial situation is fair between individuals as moral persons, that is, as rational beings with their own ends and capable, I shall assume, of a sense of justice. The original position is, one might say, the appropriate initial status quo, and thus the fundamental agreements reached in it are fair. This explains the propriety of the name "justice as fairness": it conveys the idea that the principles of justice are agreed to in an initial situation that is fair. The name does not mean that the concepts of justice and fairness are the same, any more than the phrase "poetry as metaphor" means that the concepts of poetry and metaphor are the same.

Justice as fairness begins, as I have said, with one of the most general of all choices which persons might make together, namely, with the choice of the first principles of a conception of justice which is to regulate all subsequent criticism and reform of institutions. Then, having chosen a conception of justice, we can suppose that they are to choose a constitution and a legislature to enact laws, and so on, all in accordance with the principles of justice initially agreed upon. Our social situation is just if it is such that by this sequence of hypothetical agreements we would have contracted into the general system of rules which defines it. Moreover, assuming that the original position does determine a set of principles (that is, that a particular conception of justice would be chosen), it will then be true that whenever social institutions satisfy these principles those engaged in them can say to one another that they are cooperating on terms to which they would agree if they were free and equal persons whose relations with respect to one another were fair. They could all view their arrangements as meeting the stipulations which they would acknowledge in an initial situation that embodies widely accepted and reasonable constraints on the choice of principles. The general recognition of this fact would provide the basis for a public acceptance of the corresponding principles of justice. No society can, of course, be a scheme of cooperation which men enter voluntarily in a literal sense; each person finds himself placed at birth in some particular position in some particular society, and the nature of this position materially affects his life prospects. Yet a society satisfying the principles of justice as fairness comes as close as a society can to being a voluntary scheme, for it meets the principles which free and equal persons would assent to under circumstances that are fair. In this sense its members are autonomous and the obligations they recognize self-imposed.

One feature of justice as fairness is to think of the parties in the initial situation as rational and mutually disinterested. This does not mean that the parties are egoists, that is, individuals with only certain kinds of interests, say in wealth, prestige, and domination. But they are conceived as not taking an interest in one another's interests. They are to presume that even their spiritual aims may be opposed, in the way that the aims of those of different religions may be opposed. Moreover, the concept of rationality must be interpreted as far as possible in the narrow sense, standard in economic theory, of taking the most effective means to given ends. I shall modify this concept to some extent, as explained later (§ 25), but one must try to avoid introducing into it any controversial ethical elements. The initial situation must be characterized by stipulations that are widely accepted.

In working out the conception of justice as fairness one main task clearly is to determine which principles of justice would be chosen in the original position. To do this we must describe this situation in some detail and formulate with care the problem of choice which it presents. These matters I shall take up in the immediately succeeding chapters. It may be observed, however, that once the principles of justice are thought of as arising from an original agreement in a situation of equality, it is an open question whether the principle of utility would be acknowledged. Offhand it hardly seems likely that persons who view themselves as equals, entitled to press their claims upon one another, would agree to a principle which may require lesser life prospects for some simply for the sake of a greater sum of advantages enjoyed by others. Since each desires to protect his interests, his capacity to advance his conception of the good, no one has a reason to acquiesce in an enduring loss for himself in order to bring about a greater net balance of satisfaction. In the absence of strong and lasting benevolent impulses, a rational man would not accept a basic structure merely because it maximized the algebraic sum of advantages irrespective of its permanent effects on his own basic rights and interests. Thus it seems that the principle of utility is incompatible with the conception of social cooperation among equals for mutual advantage. It appears to be inconsistent with the idea of reciprocity implicit in the notion of a well-ordered society. Or, at any rate, so I shall argue.

I shall maintain instead that the persons in the initial situation would choose two rather different principles: the first requires equality in the assignment of basic rights and duties, while the second holds that social and economic inequalities, for example inequalities of wealth and authority, are just only if they result in compensating benefits for everyone, and in particular for the least advantaged members of society. These principles rule out justifying institutions on the grounds that the hardships of some are offset by a greater good in the aggregate. It may be expedient but it is not just that some should have less in order that others may prosper. But there is no injustice in the greater benefits earned by a few provided that the situation of persons not so fortunate is thereby improved. The intuitive idea is that since everyone's well-being depends upon a scheme of cooperation without which no one could have a satisfactory life, the division of advantages should be such as to draw forth the willing cooperation of everyone taking part in it, including those less well situated. Yet this can be expected only if reasonable terms are proposed. The two principles mentioned seem to be a fair agreement on the basis of which those better endowed, or more fortunate in their social position, neither of which we can be said to deserve, could expect the willing cooperation of others when some workable scheme is a necessary condition of the welfare of all. Once we decide to look for a conception of justice that nullifies the accidents of natural endowment and the contingencies of social circumstance as counters in quest for political and economic advantage, we are led to these principles. They express the result of leaving aside those aspects of the social world that seem arbitrary from a moral point of view.

4. *The Original Position and Justification*

I have said that the original position is the appropriate initial status quo which insures that the fundamental agreements reached in it are fair. This fact yields the name "justice as fairness." It is clear, then, that I want to say that one conception of justice is more reasonable than another, or justifiable with respect to it, if rational persons in the initial situation would choose its principles over those of the other for the role of justice. Conceptions of justice are to be ranked by their acceptability to persons so circumstanced. Understood in this way the question of justification is settled by working out a problem of deliberation: we have to ascertain which principles it would be rational to adopt given the contractual situation. This connects the theory of justice with the theory of rational choice.

If this view of the problem of justification is to succeed, we must, of course, describe in some detail the nature of this choice problem. A problem of rational decision has a definite answer only if we know the beliefs and interests of the parties, their relations with respect to one another, the alternatives between which they are to choose, the procedure whereby they make up their minds, and so on. As the circumstances are presented in different ways, correspondingly different principles are accepted. The concept of the original position, as I shall refer to it, is that of the most philosophically favored interpretation of this initial choice situation for the purposes of a theory of justice.

But how are we to decide what is the most favored interpretation? I assume, for one thing, that there is a broad measure of agreement that principles of justice should be chosen under certain conditions. To justify a particular description of the initial situation one shows that it incorporates these commonly shared presumptions. One argues from widely accepted but weak premises to more specific conclusions. Each of the presumptions should by itself be natural and plausible; some of them may seem innocuous or even trivial. The aim of the contract approach is to establish that taken together they impose significant bounds on acceptable principles of justice. The ideal outcome would be that these conditions determine a unique set of principles; but I shall be satisfied if they suffice to rank the main traditional conceptions of social justice.

One should not be misled, then, by the somewhat unusual conditions which characterize the original position. The idea here is simply to make vivid to ourselves the restrictions that it seems reasonable to impose on arguments for principles of justice, and therefore on these principles themselves. Thus it seems reasonable and generally acceptable that no one should be advantaged or disadvantaged by natural fortune or social circumstances in the choice of principles. It also seems widely agreed that it should be impossible to tailor principles to the circumstances of one's own case. We should insure further that particular inclinations and aspirations, and persons' conceptions of their good do not affect the principles adopted. The aim is to rule out those principles that it would be rational to propose for acceptance, however little the chance of success, only if one knew certain things that are irrelevant from the standpoint of justice. For example, if a man knew that he was wealthy, he might find it rational to advance the principle that various taxes for welfare measures be counted unjust; if he knew that he was poor, he would most likely propose the contrary principle. To represent the desired restrictions one imagines a situation in which everyone is deprived of this sort of information. One excludes the knowledge of those contingencies which sets men at odds and allows them to be guided by their prejudices. In this manner the veil of ignorance is arrived at in a natural way. This concept should cause no difficulty if we keep in mind the constraints on arguments that it is meant to express. At any time we can enter the original position, so to speak, simply by following a certain procedure, namely, by arguing for principles of justice in accordance with these restrictions.

It seems reasonable to suppose that the parties in the original position are equal. That is, all have the same rights in the procedure for choosing principles; each can make proposals, submit reasons for their acceptance, and so on. Obviously the purpose of these conditions is to represent equality between human beings as moral persons, as creatures having a conception of their good and capable of a sense of justice. The basis of equality is taken to be similarity in these two respects. Systems of ends are not ranked in value; and each man is presumed to have the requisite ability to understand and to act upon whatever principles are adopted. Together with the veil of ignorance, these conditions define the principles of justice as those which rational persons concerned to advance their interests would consent to as equals when none are known to be advantaged or disadvantaged by social and natural contingencies.

11. Two Principles of Justice

I shall now state in a provisional form the two principles of justice that I believe would be chosen in the original position. In this section I wish to make only the most general comments, and therefore the first formulation of these principles is tentative. As we go on I shall run through several formulations and approximate step by step the final statement to be given much later. I believe that doing this allows the exposition to proceed in a natural way.

The first statement of the two principles reads as follows.

First: each person is to have an equal right to the most extensive basic liberty compatible with a similar liberty for others.

Second: social and economic inequalities are to be arranged so that they are both (a) reasonably expected to be to everyone's advantage, and (b) attached to positions and offices open to all. There are two ambiguous phrases in the

second principle, namely "everyone's advantage" and "open to all." . . .

By way of general comment, these principles primarily apply, as I have said, to the basic structure of society. They are to govern the assignment of rights and duties and to regulate the distribution of social and economic advantages. As their formulation suggests, these principles presuppose that the social structure can be divided into two more or less distinct parts, the first principle applying to the one, the second to the other. They distinguish between those aspects of the social system that define and secure the equal liberties of citizenship and those that specify and establish social and economic inequalities. The basic liberties of citizens are, roughly speaking, political liberty (the right to vote and to be eligible for public office) together with freedom of speech and assembly; liberty of conscience and freedom of thought; freedom of the person along with the right to hold (personal) property; and freedom from arbitrary arrest and seizure as defined by the concept of the rule of law. These liberties are all required to be equal by the first principle, since citizens of a just society are to have the same basic rights.

The second principle applies, in the first approximation, to the distribution of income and wealth and to the design of organizations that make use of differences in authority and responsibility, or chains of command. While the distribution of wealth and income need not be equal, it must be to everyone's advantage, and at the same time, positions of authority and offices of command must be accessible to all. One applies the second principle by holding positions open, and then, subject to this constraint, arranges social and economic inequalities so that everyone benefits.

These principles are to be arranged in a serial order with the first principle prior to the second. This ordering means that a departure from the institutions of equal liberty required by the first principle cannot be justified by, or compensated for, by greater social and economic advantages.

The distribution of wealth and income, and the hierarchies of authority, must be consistent with both the liberties of equal citizenship and equality of opportunity.

It is clear that these principles are rather specific in their content, and their acceptance rests on certain assumptions that I must eventually try to explain and justify. A theory of justice depends upon a theory of society in ways that will become evident as we proceed. For the present, it should be observed that the two principles (and this holds for all formulations) are a special case of a more general conception of justice that can be expressed as follows.

> All social values—liberty and opportunity, income and wealth, and the bases of self-respect—are to be distributed equally unless an unequal distribution of any, or all, of these values is to everyone's advantage.

Injustice, then, is simply inequalities that are not to the benefit of all. Of course, this conception is extremely vague and requires interpretation.

As a first step, suppose that the basic structure of society distributes certain primary goods, that is, things that every rational man is presumed to want. These goods normally have a use whatever a person's rational plan of life. For simplicity, assume that the chief primary goods at the disposition of society are rights and liberties, powers and opportunities, income and wealth. (Later on in Part Three the primary good of self-respect has a central place.) These are the social primary goods. Other primary goods such as health and vigor, intelligence and imagination, are natural goods; although their possession is influenced by the basic structure, they are not so directly under its control. Imagine, then, a hypothetical initial arrangement in which all the social primary goods are equally distributed: everyone has similar rights and duties, and income and wealth are evenly shared. This state of affairs provides a benchmark for judging improvements. If certain inequalities of wealth and organizational powers would make everyone better off than in this hypothetical starting situation, then they accord with the general conception.

Now it is possible, at least theoretically, that by giving up some of their fundamental liberties men are sufficiently compensated by the resulting social and economic gains. The general conception of justice imposes no restrictions on what sort of inequalities are permissible; it only requires that everyone's position be improved. We need not suppose anything so drastic as consenting to a condition of slavery. Imagine instead that men forego certain political rights when the economic returns are significant and their capacity to influence the course of policy by the exercise of these rights would be marginal in any case. It is this kind of exchange which the two principles as stated rule out; being arranged in serial order they do not permit exchanges between basic liberties and economic and social gains. The serial ordering of principles expresses an underlying preference among primary social goods. When this preference is rational so likewise is the choice of these principles in this order.

Study Questions

1. What does justice as fairness mean for Rawls? How are justice and fairness related? How do they differ?

2. What does Rawls mean by the "original position"? What is the significance of this position for his conception of justice? Why does he characterize it in terms of the "veil of ignorance"? What assumptions does Rawls make about human nature in his description of the original position?

3. What are the two basic principles of justice according to Rawls' theory? What are the central concepts in each principle? Why would persons in the original position choose these principles?

4. Why does the principle of equal liberty have priority over the principle of social and economic inequality? How does Rawls support the claim that fairness does not necessarily exclude social and economic inequalities?

5. Is there an actual society that comes close in its principles to Rawls' model of a social structure? Why would this matter when considering his position?

Suggestions for Further Reading

Barry, B. M. *The Liberal Theory of Justice* (Oxford: Clarendon Press, 1973). A sixteen-chapter critical commentary of Rawls' *A Theory of Justice*.

Blocker, H. G., and E. H. Smith, eds. *John Rawls' Theory of Social Justice* (Athens: Ohio University Press, 1980). A compilation of sixteen essays on fundamentals of Rawls' theory, problems in applying his theory, and his place in the history of philosophy.

Daniels, N., ed. *Reading Rawls* (New York: Basic Books, 1975). Contains critical essays on Rawls' theory.

Martin, R. *Rawls and Rights* (Lawrence: University of Kansas Press, 1985). A systematic study that charts the place of rights in Rawls' theory through nine chapters.

Social Theory and Practice, Vol. III, No. 1 (Spring 1974). A volume of essays on Rawls' theory.

Wolff, R. P. *Understanding Rawls* (Princeton, NJ: Princeton University Press, 1976). A critical analysis of Rawls' theory.

Emmanuel Levinas (1906–1995)

Emmanuel Levinas, one of the major ethical thinkers in contemporary continental philosophy, was born in Kaunas, Lithuania, into a Jewish family. He was raised mainly in the Russian Ukraine, but when he was seventeen years old he left for France to study philosophy at the University of Strasburg. He continued his studies in Germany at the University of Freiburg with the leading phenomenologists of the time, Edmund Husserl and Martin Heidegger. When Levinas was twenty-four years old, he became a French citizen. That same year, he published his first book, *The Theory of Intuition in Husserl's Phenomenology*, which was acclaimed by philosophers such as Simone de Beauvoir and Jean-Paul Sartre as a significant contribution to the development of phenomenology. Levinas became director of the *École Normale Israélite Orientale* in Paris after World War II and lectured on philosophy in various French universities, including Poitiers, Paris-Nanterre, and Sorbonne.

Much of Levinas' thought reflects his Judaic heritage and his constant dialogue with the philosophies of Husserl and Heidegger. Husserl was the main founder of the phenomenological movement in twentieth-century philosophy. He proposed phenomenology as a new method of investigation that begins, not with theories or interpretations, but with the things themselves as they appear (phenomena) to consciousness; that is, with reality as experienced. Therefore, for Husserl, to study reality is to study consciousness, for reality as he defined it always includes an experiencing subject. Consciousness is characterized by "intentionality," which means that consciousness is always consciousness of something that it intends as its object. Husserl's phenomenological projects aimed to discover the essential patterns and objects of such consciousness.

Heidegger rejected traditional metaphysics in favor of a study of being (ontology) that placed the human being at its center. However, he also rejected Husserl's approach because it failed to consider the most fundamental question, "What does being in general mean?" Heidegger proposed his "project of fundamental ontology" as an attempt to pose this question. Since to be human is to exist in an awareness of being, Heidegger placed the human being as the starting point for investigating the meaning of being in general. Thus, he developed an "existential phenomenology" that focused on the structure of human existence as such. Critical of metaphysical definitions of humans as mere subjects that represent objects of knowledge, Heidegger argued that we exist in a pretheoretical understanding of being in general. "Being-in-the-world" is the basic structure of our existence as beings who always act and think in terms of an interrelated meaningful whole of life. In his analyses of our "being-in-the-world," Heidegger pointed to the anxiety over our own death as one of the fundamental features of human existence. He also characterized "authentic existence" in terms of our readiness to face our "being-towards-death" and assume responsibility for our finite existence.

Unlike Husserl and Heidegger, Levinas' central claim is that ethics, not metaphysics or ontology, is first philosophy. As he puts it, "to be or not to be" is not the fundamental question on which all other questions depend. Being does not have its justification in itself, nor is my individual existence based on an absolute right to exist. Rather, my right to be can only come with my responsibility for "the Other," in the general sense of all others. To be human is to be in relation and in response to the Other. More specifically, we are only human in our "sociality," in our infinite responsibility of being for the other person. Responsibility for the Other constitutes our very subjectivity or identity. This moral force is primal in the sense that it precedes knowledge, reflection, or theory and grounds all our relations to others. By placing ethics beyond being, essence, knowledge, and identity, Levinas thus moves away from both of his predecessors. However, Husserl's conception of consciousness as intentionality and Heidegger's insights into the existential character of anxiety and responsibility serve as important counterpoints for Levinas' own reflections.

The following selections are from *Ethics and Infinity*, the published transcription of an interview of Levinas by the French philosopher, Philippe Nemo. The interview was broadcast by Radio France-Culture during February and March of 1981. Levinas discusses his notion of the Other as "the face" that calls us to responsibility. My consciousness of the Other in his radical otherness is a nontheoretical or nonreflective encounter with "the face," not as this or that character's face with these or those particular features, but as a human being in all its vulnerability. The face of the Other thus issues the first ethical command, "Thou shalt not kill." Unlike Heidegger, Levinas attaches primacy to the death of the Other and he emphasizes our responsibility for the Other's existence in our response to that command. Elaborating on his notion of responsibility for the Other as what constitutes our subjectivity, Levinas explains how we become "subjects" only by "subjecting" ourselves to the Other and for his sake. However, Levinas underscores the fact that our lives in a community with a multiplicity of Others create the need for justice as a means for regulating our interpersonal relations. On the other hand, he is quick to suggest that the political institutions that are created for the purpose of justice must themselves be evaluated according to how they preserve the basic ethical relation of responsibility for the Other.

THE FACE AND RESPONSIBILITY FOR THE OTHER

[*Phillippe Nemo*]: In *Totality and Infinity* you speak at great length of the face. It is one of your frequent themes. What does this phenomenology of the face, that is, this analysis of what happens when I look at the Other face to face, consist in and what is its purpose?

[*Emannuel Levinas*]: I do not know if one can speak of a "phenomenology" of the face, since phenomenology describes what appears. So, too, I wonder if one can speak of a look turned toward the face, for the look is knowledge, perception. I think rather that access to the face is straightaway ethical. You turn yourself toward the Other as toward an object when you see a nose, eyes, a forehead, a chin, and you can describe them. The best way of encountering the Other is not even to notice the color of his eyes! When one observes the color of the eyes one is not in social relationship with the Other. The relation with the face can surely be dominated by perception, but what is specifically the face is what cannot be reduced to that.

There is first the very uprightness of the face, its upright exposure, without defense. The skin of the face is that which stays most naked, most destitute. It is the most naked, though with a decent nudity. It is the most destitute also: there is an essential poverty in the face; the proof of this is that one tries to mask this poverty by putting on poses, by taking on a countenance. The face

is exposed, menaced, as if inviting us to an act of violence. At the same time, the face is what forbids us to kill.

Ph. N.: War stories tell us in fact that it is difficult to kill someone who looks straight at you.

E.L.: The face is signification, and signification without context. I mean that the Other, in the rectitude of his face, is not a character within a context. Ordinarily one is a "character": a professor at the Sorbonne, a Supreme Court justice, son of so-and-so, everything that is in one's passport, the manner of dressing, of presenting oneself. And all signification in the usual sense of the term is relative to such a context: the meaning of something is in its relation to another thing. Here, to the contrary, the face is meaning all by itself. You are you. In this sense one can say that the face is not "seen". It is what cannot become a content, which your thought would embrace; it is uncontainable, it leads you beyond. It is in this that the signification of the face makes it escape from being, as a correlate of a knowing. Vision, to the contrary, is a search for adequation; it is what par excellence absorbs being. But the relation to the face is straightaway ethical. The face is what one cannot kill, or at least it is that whose *meaning* consists in saying: "thou shalt not kill." Murder, it is true, is a banal fact: one can kill the Other; the ethical exigency is not an ontological necessity. The prohibition

Emmanuel Levinas. "The Face" and "Responsibility for the Other." In Ethics and Infinity: Conversations with Philippe Nemo, *trans. R. A. Cohen. Pittsburgh: Duquesne University Press, 1985.*

against killing does not render murder impossible, even if the authority of the prohibition is maintained in the bad conscience about the accomplished evil—malignancy of evil. It also appears in the Scriptures, to which the humanity of man is exposed inasmuch as it is engaged in the world. But to speak truly, the appearance in being of these "ethical peculiarities"—the humanity of man—is a rupture of being. It is significant, even if being resumes and recovers itself.

Ph.N.: The Other is face; but the Other, equally, speaks to me and I speak to him. Is not human discourse another way of breaking what you call "totality"?

E.L.: Certainly. Face and discourse are tied. The face speaks. It speaks, it is in this that it renders possible and begins all discourse. I have just refused the notion of vision to describe the authentic relationship with the Other; it is discourse and, more exactly, response or responsibility which is this authentic relationship.

Ph.N.: But since the ethical relationship is beyond knowledge, and, on the other hand, it is authentically assumed through discourse, it is thus that discourse itself is not something of the order of knowledge?

E.L.: In discourse I have always distinguished, in fact, between the *saying* and the *said*. That the *saying* must bear a *said* is a necessity of the same order as that which imposes a society with laws, institutions and social relations. But the *saying* is the fact that before the face I do not simply remain there contemplating it, I respond to it. The saying is a way of greeting the Other, but to greet the Other is already to answer for him. It is difficult to be silent in someone's presence; this difficulty has its ultimate foundation in this signification proper to the saying, whatever is the said. It is necessary to speak of something, of the rain and fine weather, no matter what, but to speak, to respond to him and already to answer for him.

Ph.N.: In the face of the Other you say there is an "elevation," a "height." The Other is higher than I am. What do you mean by that?

E.L.: The first word of the face is the "Thou shalt not kill." It is an order. There is a commandment in the appearance of the face, as if a master spoke to me. However, at the same time, the face of the Other is destitute; it is the poor for whom I can do all and to whom I owe all. And me, whoever I may be, but as a "first person," I am he who finds the resources to respond to the call.

Ph.N.: One is tempted to say to you: yes, in certain cases. But in other cases, to the contrary, the encounter with the Other occurs in the mode of violence, hate and disdain.

E.L.: To be sure. But I think that whatever the motivation which explains this inversion, the analysis of the face such as I have just made, with the mastery of the Other and his poverty, with my submission and my wealth, is primary. It is the presupposed in all human relationships. If it were not that, we would not even say, before an open door, "After you, sir!" It is an original "After you, sir!" that I have tried to describe.

You have spoken of the passion of hate. I feared a much graver objection: How is it that one can punish and repress? How is it that there is justice? I answer that it is the fact of the multiplicity of men and the presence of someone else next to the Other, which condition the laws and establish justice. If I am alone with the Other, I owe him everything; but there is someone else. Do I know what my neighbor is in relation to someone else? Do I know if someone else has an understanding with him or his victim? Who is my neighbor? It is consequently necessary to weigh, to think, to judge, in comparing the incomparable. The interpersonal relation I establish with the Other, I must also establish with other men; there is thus a necessity to moderate this privilege of the Other; from whence comes justice. Justice, exercised through institutions, which are inevitable, must always be held in check by the initial interpersonal relation. . . .

Ph.N.: In your last great book published, *Otherwise than Being or Beyond Essence,* you speak of moral responsibility. Husserl had already spoken of responsibility, but of a responsibility for the truth; Heidegger had spoken of authenticity; as for yourself, what do you understand by responsibility?

E.L.: In this book I speak of responsibility as the essential, primary and fundamental structure of subjectivity. For I describe subjectivity in ethical terms. Ethics, here, does not supplement a preceding existential base; the very node of the subjective is knotted in ethics understood as responsibility.

I understand responsibility as responsibility for the Other, thus as responsibility for what is not my deed, or for what does not even matter to me; or which precisely does matter to me, is met by me as face.

Ph.N.: How, having discovered the Other in his face, does one discover him as he to whom one is responsible?

E.L.: In describing the face positively, and not merely negatively. You recall what we said: meeting the face is not of the order of pure and simple perception, of the intentionality which goes toward adequation. Positively, we will say that since the Other looks at me, I am responsible for him, without even having *taken* on responsibilities in his regard; his responsibility *is incumbent on me.* It is responsibility that goes beyond what I do. Usually, one is responsible for what one does oneself. I say, in *Otherwise than Being,* that responsibility is initially a *for the Other.* This means that I am responsible for his very responsibility.

Ph.N.: What in this responsibility for the Other defines the structure of subjectivity?

E.L.: Responsibility in fact is not a simple attribute of subjectivity, as if the latter already existed in itself, before the ethical relationship. Subjectivity is not for itself; it is, once again, initially for another. In the book, the proximity of the Other is presented as the fact that the Other is not simply close to me in space, or close like a parent, but he approaches me essentially insofar as I feel myself—insofar as I am—responsible for him. It is a structure that in nowise resembles the intentional relation which in knowledge at-

taches us to the object—to no matter what object, be it a human object. Proximity does not revert to this intentionality; in particular it does not revert to the fact that the Other is known to me.

Ph.N.: I can know someone to perfection, but this knowledge will never by itself be a proximity?

E.L.: No. The tie with the Other is knotted only as responsibility, this moreover, whether accepted or refused, whether knowing or not knowing how to assume it, whether able or unable to do something concrete for the Other. To say: here I am [*me voici*].[1] To do something for the Other. To give. To be human spirit, that's it. The incarnation of human subjectivity guarantees its spirituality (I do not see what angels could give one another or how they could help one another). Dia-chrony before all dialogue: I analyze the inter-human relationship as if, in proximity with the Other—beyond the image I myself make of the other man—his face, the expressive in the Other (and the whole human body is in this sense more or less face), were what *ordains* me to serve him. I employ this extreme formulation. The face orders and ordains me. Its signification is an order signified. To be precise, if the face signifies an order in my regard, this is not in the manner in which an ordinary sign signifies its signified; this order is the very signifyingness of the face.

Ph.N.: You say at once "it orders me" and "it ordains me." Is this not a contradiction?

E.L.: It orders me as one orders someone one commands, as when one says: "Someone's asking for you."

Ph.N.: But is not the Other also responsible in my regard?

E.L.: Perhaps, but that is *his* affair. One of the fundamental themes of *Totality and Infinity* about which we have not yet spoken is that the

---

[1] Cf., *Genesis* 22, lines 1, 7 and 11, and *Isaiah* 6, line 8, for *Hineni.* Also, cf., Emmanuel Levinas, "God and Philosophy," in *Philosophy Today,* Vol. XXII, no. 2, Summer 1978, pp. 127–145. [Tr. note]

intersubjective relation is a non-symmetrical relation. In this sense, I am responsible for the Other without waiting for reciprocity, were I to die for it. Reciprocity is *his* affair. It is precisely insofar as the relationship between the Other and me is not reciprocal that I am subjection to the Other; and I am "subject" essentially in this sense. It is I who support all. You know that sentence in Dostoyevsky: "*We are all guilty of all and for all men before all, and I more than the others.*" [2] This is not owing to such or such a guilt which is really mine, or to offenses that I would have committed; but because I am responsible for a total responsibility which answers for all the others and for all in the others, even for their responsibility. The I always has one responsibility *more* than all the others.

[2] Cf., Fyodor Dostoyevsky, *The Brothers Karamazou*, transl. by Constance Garnett (New York: New American Library, 1957), p. 264.

Study Questions

1. What does Levinas mean when he says that "access to the face is straightaway ethical"? What does he mean by "the face"? What sort of access is he considering? In what sense is this "the ethical"?

2. What role does death play in ethics for Levinas? Why is it the death of the Other and not my own death? Why is the first ethical command "Thou shalt not kill"?

3. In what sense is ethics a "response" to the Other? In what sense is it a "subjection" to the Other?

4. Why must I subject myself to the Other? Why is there no room for me to demand the same from the Other? Why do I owe all to the Other?

5. Is Levinas proposing a morality of self-denial? of self-sacrifice? Is there room in his view of ethics for a self-actualization and self-fulfillment apart from others?

6. What would a society based on Levinas' conception of responsibility and justice be like?

Suggestions for Further Reading

Bergo, B. *Levinas Between Ethics and Politics: For the Beauty that Adorns the Earth* (Dordrecht; Boston: Kluwer Academic, 1999). For a comprehensive introduction to Levinas' thought, see Part One "Presentation and Analysis of the Philosophy of Emmanuel Levinas."

Bernasconi, R., and D. Wood, eds. *The Provocation of Levinas: Rethinking the Other* (London; New York: Routledge, 1988). A collection of essays on various aspects of Levinas' conception of the Other.

Bernasconi, R., and S. Critchley, eds. *Re-reading Levinas* (Bloomington: Indiana University Press, 1991). A collection of advanced essays on Levinas' conception of ethical responsibility. Includes "The Paradox of Morality: An Interview with Emmanuel Levinas."

Cohen, R., ed. *Face to Face with Levinas* (Albany: State University of New York Press, 1986). A collection of critical essays and an interview of Levinas by R. Kearney.

Davis, C. *Levinas: An Introduction* (Notre Dame, IN: University of Notre Dame Press, 1996). A five-chapter basic introduction to Levinas' thought that discusses concepts such as the Other.

Milchman, A., and A. Rosenberg, eds. *Postmodernism and the Holocaust* (Amsterdam: Rodopi, 1998). Includes various essays that examine Levinas' thought on issues concerning the Holocaust.

Alasdair MacIntyre (1929–)

Alasdair MacIntyre, the leading contemporary proponent of virtue ethics, was born in Glasgow, Scotland. He did graduate studies in England and, since 1969, has taught at various universities in the United States, including Boston University, the University of Notre Dame, and Duke University.

In his major work, *After Virtue: A Study in Moral Theory*, MacIntyre criticizes contemporary moral philosophies and attitudes and proposes a return to a classical conception of the human being that has its roots in Aristotle's ethics of virtue. Aristotle offered an understanding of humans as rational animals whose essence is to be directed toward an end (*telos*) that lies in their rationality. For Aristotle, the full actualization of our potential as rational beings consists in exercising our reason well, in becoming excellent or achieving virtue. MacIntyre emphasizes that ethics in the Aristotelian sense is a matter of a whole human life as it unfolds within the context of a given community. According to MacIntyre, this view sees the moral rules of a community as rules designed to guide individuals toward their ultimate end as humans. Thus, from an Aristotelian perspective, rules are defined in terms of the human good.

In MacIntyre's assessment, the modern rejection of the understanding of humans in terms of essence, *telos,* and virtue has had disastrous consequences for the individual and society. With its denial of an ultimate human end, the modern conception of the human being is that of an isolated self or individual who is detached from his social and historical context, and whose morality is not oriented by the sense of an ultimate human good. MacIntyre argues that the modern attempt to define morality in terms of rules that do not refer to a human end and good has led to a fragmented morality. Though modern philosophers have claimed to ground morality in rationality, their moral discourse is a language of disorder that lacks a true foundation. Thus, modern moral discourse is really rooted in something arbitrary and nonrational: emotions. MacIntyre argues that we should not abandon the idea of a rational morality. Instead, we should re-inscribe this idea within a teleological conception of humans and return to an ethics of virtue for individuals within the context of their communities.

The following selection is taken from the chapter of MacIntyre's *After Virtue* in which he develops his "narrative" conception of the self. The narrative view proposes that the individual's life is a story of which he is both the author and the actor. MacIntyre argues that this conception allows us to see each human life as a whole, as a unity that begins with birth and ends with death. Unlike the isolated and fragmented life of the self in the modern conception, the narrative view enables us to understand virtues as a matter of a person's character; that is, in terms of the unity of a life. It also allows us to see that the individual story unfolds within a larger historical and social context. The individual learns to play given historical and social roles in his relation to others, and these roles give form to his personal identity. Each individual is accountable for his life because he is the subject of his own story. Moreover, since individuals form parts of the interrelated wholes of their society, we are all account-able to one other in a correlative and interlocking fashion.

Whereas the unity of an individual life consists in asking "What is the good for me?" the unity of all human life resides in asking "What is good for man?" The story of humankind is that of a search for the good life for the human being. But any idea of a "good" life requires that we have some idea of what is "*the* good," of what is the ultimate good from which all other goods are understood and ordered. Thus, Mac-Intyre states that the unity of a human life is the unity of a "narrative quest" for a conception of the good. Virtues play a crucial role in enabling us to seek for the good human life and for the conception of the good. This quest is sustained in the historical and social contexts provided by living traditions that define and prescribe the good life for the individual. The life of a tradition depends in part on the kinds of virtues it upholds. Only those virtues that tend to preserve the tradition—such as justice, truthfulness, and courage—allow it to continue living.

THE VIRTUES, THE UNITY OF A HUMAN LIFE AND THE CONCEPT OF A TRADITION

ANY CONTEMPORARY ATTEMPT to envisage each human life as a whole, as a unity, whose character provides the virtues with an adequate *telos* encounters two different kinds of obstacle, one social and one philosophical. The social obstacles derive from the way in which modernity partitions each human life into a variety of segments, each with its own norms and modes of behavior. So work is divided from leisure, private life from public, the corporate from the personal. So both childhood and old age have been wrenched away from the rest of human life and made over into distinct realms. And all these separations have been achieved so that it is the distinctiveness of each and not the unity of the life of the individual who passes through those parts in terms of which we are taught to think and to feel. . . .

That particular actions derive their character as parts of larger wholes is a point of view alien to our dominant ways of thinking and yet one which it is necessary at least to consider if we are to begin to understand how a life may be more than a sequence of individual actions and episodes.

Equally the unity of a human life becomes invisible to us when a sharp separation is made either between the individual and the roles that he or she plays.

At the same time the liquidation of the self into a set of demarcated areas of role-playing allows no scope for the exercise of dispositions which could genuinely be accounted virtues in any sense remotely Aristotelian. For a virtue is not a disposition that makes for success only in some one particular type of situation. What are spoken of as the virtues of a good committee man or of a good administrator or of a gambler or a pool hustler are professional skills professionally deployed in those situations where they can be effective, not virtues. Someone who gen-

"*The Virtues, the Unity of a Human Life and the Concept of a Tradition,*" by Alasdair MacIntyre. From After Virtue: A Study of Moral Theory, *2nd edition, Chapter 15. Reprinted by permission of University of Notre Dame Press.*

uinely possesses a virtue can be expected to manifest it in very different types of situation, many
of them situations where the practice of a virtue
cannot be expected to be effective in the way that
we expect a professional skill to be. . . .

A central thesis then begins to emerge: man is
in his actions and practice, as well as in his
fictions, essentially a story-telling animal. He is
not essentially, but becomes through his history,
a teller of stories that aspire to truth. But the key
question for men is not about their own authorship; I can only answer the question 'What am I
to do?' if I can answer the prior question 'Of
what story or stories do I find myself a part?' We
enter human society, that is, with one or more
imputed characters—roles into which we have
been drafted—and we have to learn what they are
in order to be able to understand how others respond to us and how our responses to them are
apt to be construed. It is through hearing stories
about wicked stepmothers, lost children, good
but misguided kings, wolves that suckle twin
boys, youngest sons who receive no inheritance
but must make their own way in the world and
eldest sons who waste their inheritance on ri-
otous living and go into exile to live with the
swine, that children learn or mislearn both what
a child and what a parent is, what the cast of
characters may be in the drama into which they
have been born and what the ways of the world
are. Deprive children of stories and you leave
them unscripted, anxious stutterers in their actions as in their words. Hence there is no way to
give us an understanding of any society, including our own, except through the stock of stories
which constitute its initial dramatic resources.
Mythology, in its original sense, is at the heart of
things. Vico was right and so was Joyce. And so
too of course is that moral tradition from heroic
society to its medieval heirs according to which
the telling of stories has a key part in educating
us into the virtues.

What the narrative concept of selfhood requires is thus twofold. On the one hand, I am
what I may justifiably be taken by others to be in
the course of living out a story that runs from my
birth to my death; I am the *subject* of a history

that is my own and no one else's, that has its own
peculiar meaning. When someone complains—as
do some of those who attempt or commit sui-
cide—that his or her life is meaningless, he or she
is often and perhaps characteristically complaining that the narrative of their life has become un-
intelligible to them, that it lacks any point, any
movement towards a climax or a *telos*. Hence the
point of doing any one thing rather than another
at crucial junctures in their lives seems to such
person to have been lost.

To be the subject of a narrative that runs from
one's birth to one's death is, I remarked earlier,
to be accountable for the actions and experiences which compose a narratable life. It is, that
is, to be open to being asked to give a certain
kind of account of what one did or what happened to one or what one witnessed at any earlier point in one's life than the time at which the
question is posed. . . .

The other aspect of narrative selfhood is correlative: I am not only accountable, I am one
who can always ask others for an account, who
can put others to the question. I am part of their
story, as they are part of mine. The narrative of
any one life is part of an interlocking set of narratives. Moreover this asking for and giving of
accounts itself plays an important part in consti-
tuting narratives. Asking you what you did and
why, saying what I did and why, pondering the
differences between your account of what I did
and my account of what I did, and *vice versa*,
these are essential constituents of all but the very
simplest and barest of narratives. Thus without
the accountability of the self those trains of
events that constitute all but the simplest and
barest of narratives could not occur; and without
that same accountability narratives would lack
that continuity required to make both them and
the actions that constitute them intelligible. . . .

It is now possible to return to the question
from which this enquiry into the nature of human action and identity started: In what does the
unity of an individual life consist? The answer is
that its unity is the unity of narrative embodied
in a single life. To ask 'What is the good for me
to ask how best I might live out that unity and

bring it to completion.' To ask 'What is the good for man?' is to ask what all answers to the former question must have in common. But now it is important to emphasize that it is the systematic asking of these two questions and the attempt to answer them in deed as well as in word which provide the moral life with its unity. The unity of a human life is the unity of a narrative quest. Quests sometimes fail, are frustrated, abandoned or dissipated into distractions; and human lives may in all these ways also fail. But the only criteria for success or failure in a human life as a whole are the criteria of success or failure in a narrated or to-be-narrated quest. A quest for what?

Two key features of the medieval conception of a quest need to be recalled. The first is that without some at least partly determinate conception of the final *telos* there could not be any beginning to a quest. Some conception of the good for man is required. Whence is such a conception to be drawn? Precisely from those questions which led us to attempt to transcend that limited conception of the virtues which is available in and through practices. It is in looking for a conception of *the* good which will enable us to order other goods, for a conception of *the* good which will enable us to extend our understanding of the purpose and content of the virtues, for a conception of *the* good which will enable us to understand the place of integrity and constancy in life, that we initially define the kind of life which is a quest for the good. But secondly it is clear the medieval conception of a quest is not at all that of a search for something already adequately characterized, as miners search for gold or geologists for oil. It is in the course of the quest and only through encountering and coping with the various particular harms, dangers, temptations and distractions which provide any quest with its episodes and incidents that the goal of the quest is finally to be understood. A quest is always an education both as to the character of that which is sought and in self-knowledge.

The virtues therefore are to be understood as those dispositions which will not only sustain practices and enable us to achieve the goods internal to practices, but which will also sustain us in the relevant kind of quest for the good, by enabling us to overcome the harms, dangers, temptations and distractions which we encounter, and which will furnish us with increasing self-knowledge and increasing knowledge of the good. The catalogue of the virtues will therefore include the virtues required to sustain the kind of households and the kind of political communities in which men and women can seek for the good together and the virtues necessary for philosophical enquiry about the character of the good. We have then arrived at a provisional conclusion about the good life for man: the good life for man is the life spent in seeking for the good life for man, and the virtues necessary for the seeking are those which will enable us to understand what more and what else the good life for man is. . . .

I am never able to seek for the good or exercise the virtues only *qua* individual. This is partly because what it is to live the good life concretely varies from circumstance to circumstance even when it is one and the same conception of the good life and one and the same set of virtues which are being embodied in a human life. What the good life is for a fifth-century Athenian general will not be the same as what it was for a medieval nun or a seventeenth-century farmer. But it is not just that different individuals live in different social circumstances; it is also that we all approach our own circumstances as bearers of a particular social identity. I am someone's son or daughter, someone else's cousin or uncle; I am a citizen of this or that city, a member of this or that guild or profession; I belong to this clan, that tribe, this nation. Hence what is good for me has to be the good for one who inhabits these roles. As such, I inherit from the past of my family, my city, my tribe, my nation, a variety of debts, inheritances, rightful expectations and obligations. These constitute the given of my life, my moral starting point. This is in part what gives my life its own moral particularity.

This thought is likely to appear alien and even suprising from the standpoint of modern individualism. From the standpoint of individualism I am what I myself choose to be. I can always, if

I wish to, put in question what are taken to be the merely contingent social features of my existence. I may biologically be my father's son; but I cannot be held responsible for what he did unless I choose implicitly or explicitly to assume such responsibility. I may legally be a citizen of a certain country; but I cannot be held responsible for what my country does or has done unless I choose implicitly or explicitly to assume such responsibility. . . .

The contrast with the narrative view of the self is clear. For the story of my life is always embedded in the story of those communities from which I derive my identity. I am born with a past; and to try to cut myself off from that past, in the individualist mode, is to deform my present relationships. The possession of an historical identity and the possession of a social identity coincide. Notice that rebellion against my identity is always one possible mode of expressing it. . . .

What I am, therefore, is in key part what I inherit, a specific past that is present to some degree in my present. I find myself part of a history and that is generally to say, whether I like it or not, whether I recognize it or not, one of the bearers of a tradition. . . .

A living tradition then is an historically extended, socially embodied argument, and an argument precisely in part about the goods which constitute that tradition. Within a tradition the pursuit of goods extends through generations, sometimes through many generations. Hence the individual's search for his or her good is generally and characteristically conducted within a context defined by those traditions of which the individual's life is a part, and this is true both of those goods which are internal to practices and of the goods of a single life. Once again the narrative phenomenon of embedding is crucial: the history of a practice in our time is generally and characteristically embedded in and made intelligible in terms of the larger and longer history of the tradition through which the practice in its

present form was conveyed to us; the history of each of our own lives is generally and characteristically embedded in and made intelligible in terms of the larger and longer histories of a number of traditions. I have to say 'generally and characteristically' rather than 'always', for traditions decay, disintegrate and disappear. What then sustains and strengthens traditions? What weakens and destroys them?

The answer in key part is: the exercise or the lack of exercise of the relevant virtues. The virtues find their point and purpose not only in sustaining those relationships necessary if the variety of goods internal to practices are to be achieved and not only in sustaining the form of an individual life in which that individual may seek out his or her good as the good of his or her whole life, but also in sustaining those traditions which provide both practices and individual lives with their necessary historical context. Lack of justice, lack of truthfulness, lack of courage, lack of the relevant intellectual virtues—these corrupt traditions, just as they do those institutions and practices which derive their life from the traditions of which they are the contemporary embodiments. To recognize this is of course also to recognize the existence of an additional virtue, one whose importance is perhaps most obvious when it is least present, the virtue of having an adequate sense of the traditions to which one belongs or which confront one. This virtue is not to be confused with any form of conservative antiquarianism; I am not praising those who choose the conventional conservative role of *laudator temporis acti*. It is rather the case that an adequate sense of tradition manifests itself in a grasp of those future possibilities which the past has made available to the present. Living traditions, just because they continue a not-yet-completed narrative, confront a future whose determinate and determinable character, so far as it possesses any, derives from the past.

Study Questions

1. What does MacIntyre define as the "narrative conception of the self"? What does it assume about human nature? How does it differ from the modern or contemporary conception of the self?

2. How do virtues fit into MacIntyre's narrative conception of the self? What role do they play in the individual narrative? How is this related to their role in the larger narrative of living traditions?

3. What does MacIntyre mean by "unity of a human life"? In what way is the question "What is the good for me?" related to the question "What is the good for man?" Why is a teleological conception of the human being necessary for a proper understanding of the good?

4. Does MacIntyre's virtue ethics support the idea that morality is culturally relative? Does it present a conservative view of morality?

Suggestions for Further Reading

Frankena, W. K. "MacIntyre and Modern Morality." *Ethics* 93 (1982–1983): 579–587. A critique of *After Virtue.*

Geach, P. *The Virtues* (Cambridge, MA: Cambridge University Press, 1977). An introductory survey of virtue theories in religion and ethics.

Midwest Studies in Philosophy, Vol. XIII (1988). A volume devoted to virtue theory.

Pence, G. "Virtue Theory." In *A Companion to Ethics*, ed. P. Singer (Oxford; Cambridge, MA: Blackwell Reference, 1991). A critical examination of virtue theory as an alternative approach to ethics.

Philosophia, Vol. 20, Nos. 1, 2 (1990). A series of essays on virtue ethics.

The Asian Traditions

Lao Tzu (SIXTH CENTURY B.C.E.?)

The authorship of one of China's most influential classics, the *Tao Teh Ching* (Classic of the Way and Its Virtue or Power) has been attributed to Lao Tzu. Though he is counted among China's greatest sages, little is known with certainty about his life. The *Records of the Historian,* written in the first century B.C.E., identify him as a native of Ch'u (in today's Honan province) whose original name was Erh Li and posthumous honorary name was Tan. The *Records* state that he was the curator of the imperial archives in the capital of Ch'u and was once visited by Confucius seeking information on rituals. Though this statement places him in the sixth century B.C.E., the *Records* also mention the names of Lao Lai Tzu, from the sixth century, and of Tan, from the fourth century. In addition, it expresses uncertainty over whether these persons were the same Lao Tzu and notes that Lao Tzu's son was a general from the third century. Lao Tzu's name is itself ambiguous, for it can be translated as "Master Lao" or literally as "Old Master." There is also debate over when the *Tao Teh Ching* was written and whether it was written by one hand or compiled by various persons.

The *Tao Teh Ching* is one of the most translated books in the world, next to the Bible and the Bhagavad Gita, and has received more written commentaries than any other Chinese classic. Consisting of 5,250 words that were later divided into eighty-one sections or chapters, the book contains poetic, philosophical, and mystical thoughts with profound and subtle meanings. It gives expression to Taoism, one of the three major strands of thought in Chinese history, along with Confucianism and Buddhism. Though Confucianism is historically the dominant philosophy, Taoism stands on a par with it in its influence on the Chinese way of life and thought. Though all ancient Chinese philosophies, including Confucianism, taught the Way (*Tao* or *Dao*) of life, only Taoism is named "the Way." The other philosophies spoke of the Way mainly as a moral system or principle and focused on teaching the proper way humans ought to live in relation to others. However, Taoism speaks of the Way more broadly as the way of Nature or the way of the universe and it focuses on teaching the proper way to live in accordance with Nature.

For Lao Tzu, the Way is the One, the eternal source. It is the course of all things, yet it is not itself a thing. Thus, he refers to it as "the Nameless," as what is indefinable. It is utter simplicity, for it contains no distinctions in itself, though all distinctions originate from it. The universe stemming from it is a harmonious whole of opposites that complement and eventually transform into each other. In other words, the universe is a balance of *yin* (the passive and receptive, the feminine) and *yang* (the active and aggressive, the masculine). Lao Tzu says that the Way is "like an empty bowl, which in being used can never be filled up." Such emptiness is, then, not sheer nothingness, but the inexhaustible whole of all life energy. It is spontaneous, free, and unselfish in its giving. When the Way is manifest in individual things, it becomes their virtue or power (*teh*), so that things that follow their natural course achieve their proper excellence.

For Lao Tzu, the ideal life is the life that follows the Way. This means to live the natural way, by letting Nature take its course. Lao Tzu's emphasis on nonaction (*wu-wei*) indicates the path through which we can achieve virtue or power. Rather than being a doctrine of total inaction, the Way tells us not to take any action that is contrary to Nature; that is, in moral terms, to lead a life based on spontaneity, simplicity, tranquillity, unselfishness, and humility. To be virtuous is to be "weak" in the sense of being like water: pliant and ductile. It is only when we "go with the natural flow," so to speak, that we attain true power and strength. In political terms, Lao Tzu proposes that an ideal ruler is not even noticed by the people, for he is the sage-ruler who does not interfere with the natural course of the state. The ideal is thus laissez-faire government. Reacting against anything unnatural, Lao Tzu developed a nonconformist position that shunned the artificialities and formalities of social living while emphasizing the importance of inner peace in being true to one's nature.

TAO TEH CHING

2

When all the world recognizes beauty as
  beauty, this in itself is ugliness.
When all the world recognizes good as
  good, this in itself is evil.
Indeed, the hidden and the manifest give
  birth to each other.
Difficult and easy complement each other.
Long and short exhibit each other.
High and low set measure to each other.
Voice and sound harmonize each other.
Back and front follow each other.
Therefore, the Sage manages his affairs without ado,
And spreads his teaching without talking.
He denies nothing to the teeming things.
He rears them, but lays no claim to them.
He does his work, but sets no store by it.
He accomplishes his task, but does not dwell
  upon it.
And yet it is just because he does not dwell
  on it
That nobody can ever take it away from him.

8

The highest form of goodness is like water.
Water knows how to benefit all things without striving with them.
It stays in places loathed by all men.
Therefore, it comes near the Tao.
In choosing your dwelling, know how to keep to the ground.
In cultivating your mind, know how to dive in the hidden deeps.
In dealing with others, know how to be gentle and kind.
In speaking, know how to keep your words.
In governing, know how to maintain order.
In transacting business, know how to be efficient.
In making a move, know how to choose the right moment.
If you do not strive with others,
You will be free from blame.

From Lao Tzu: Tao Teh Ching, *trans. by John C. H. Wu,* © 1961 by St. John's University Press, NY. Reprinted *by arrangement with Shambhala Publications, Inc., Boston, www.shambhala.com.*

9

As for holding to fullness,
Far better were it to stop in time!
Keep on beating and sharpening a sword,
And the edge cannot be preserved for long.
Fill your house with gold and jade,
And it can no longer be guarded.
Set store by your riches and honour,
And you will only reap a crop of calamities.
Here is the Way of Heaven:
When you have done your work, retire!

10

In keeping the spirit and the vital soul
  together,
Are you able to maintain their perfect
  harmony?
In gathering your vital energy to attain
  suppleness,
Have you reached the state of a new-born
  babe?
In washing and clearing your inner vision,
Have you purified it of all dross?
In loving your people and governing your
  state,
Are you able to dispense with cleverness?
In the opening and shutting of heaven's
  gate,
Are you able to play the feminine part?
Enlightened and seeing far into all
  directions,
Can you at the same time remain detached
  and non-active?
Rear your people!
Feed your people!
Rear them without claiming them for
  your own!
Do your work without setting any store
  by it!
Be a leader, not a butcher!
This is called hidden Virtue.

16

Attain to utmost Emptiness.
Cling single-heartedly to interior peace.
While all things are stirring together,
I only contemplate the Return.
For flourishing as they do,
Each of them will return to its root.
To return to the root is to find peace.
To find peace is to fulfill one's destiny.
To fulfill one's destiny is to be constant.
To know the Constant is called Insight.
If one does not know the Constant,
One runs blindly into disasters.
If one knows the Constant,
One can understand and embrace all.
If one understands and embraces all,
One is capable of doing justice.
To be just is to be kingly;
To be kingly is to be heavenly;
To be heavenly is to be one with the Tao;
To be one with the Tao is to abide forever.
Such a one will be safe and whole
Even after the dissolution of his body.

21

It lies in the nature of Grand Virtue
To follow the Tao and the Tao alone.
Now what is the Tao?
It is Something elusive and evasive.
Evasive and elusive!
And yet It contains within Itself a Form.
Elusive and evasive!
And yet It contains within Itself a Substance.
Shadowy and dim!
And yet It contains within Itself a Core of
  Vitality.
The Core of Vitality is very real,
It contains within Itself an unfailing Sincerity.
Throughout the ages Its Name has been
  preserved
In order to recall the Beginning of all things.
How do I know the ways of all things at the
  Beginning?
By what is within me.

22

Bend and you will be whole.
Curl and you will be straight.
Keep empty and you will be filled.
Grow old and you will be renewed.
Have little and you will gain.
Have much and you will be confused.
Therefore, the Sage embraces the One,
And becomes a Pattern to all under Heaven.
He does not make a show of himself,
Hence he shines;
Does not justify himself,
Hence he becomes known;
Does not boast of his ability,
Hence he gets his credit;
Does not brandish his success,
Hence he endures;
Does not compete with anyone,
Hence no one can compete with him.
Indeed, the ancient saying: "Bend and you
    will remain whole" is no idle word.
Nay, if you have really attained wholeness,
    everything will flock to you.

23

Only simple and quiet words will ripen of
    themselves.
For a whirlwind does not last a whole
    morning,
Nor does a sudden shower last a whole day.
Who is their author? Heaven-and-Earth!
Even Heaven-and-Earth cannot make such
    violent things last long;
How much truer is it of the rash endeavours
    of men?
Hence, he who cultivates the Tao is one with
    the Tao;
He who practices Virtue is one with Virtue;
And he who courts after Loss is one with
    Loss.
To be one with the Tao is to be a welcome
    accession to the Tao;
To be one with Virtue is to be a welcome ac-
    cession to Virtue;
To be one with Loss is to be a welcome ac-
    cession to Loss.

Deficiency of faith on your part
Entails faithlessness on the part of others.

28

Know the masculine,
Keep to the feminine,
And be the Brook of the World.
To be the Brook of the World is
To move constantly in the path of Virtue
Without swerving from it,
And to return again to infancy.
Know the white,
Keep to the black,
And be the Pattern of the World.
To be the Pattern of the World is
To move constantly in the path of Virtue
Without erring a single step,
And to return again to the Infinite.
Know the glorious,
Keep to the lowly,
And be the Fountain of the World.
To be the Fountain of the World is
To live the abundant life of Virtue,
And to return again to Primal Simplicity.
When Primal Simplicity diversifies,
It becomes useful vessels,
Which, in the hands of the Sage, become
    officers.
Hence, "a great tailor does little cutting."

38

High Virtue is non-virtuous;
Therefore it has Virtue.
Low Virtue never frees itself from
    virtuousness;
Therefore it has no Virtue.
High Virtue makes no fuss and has no pri-
    vate ends to serve;
Low Virtue not only fusses but has private
    ends to serve.
High humanity fusses but has no private
    ends to serve:
High morality not only fusses but has private
    ends to serve.
High ceremony fusses but finds no response;

Then it tries to enforce itself with rolled-up
  sleeves.
Failing Tao, man resorts to Virtue.
Failing Virtue, man resorts to humanity.
Failing humanity, man resorts to morality.
Failing morality, man resorts to ceremony.
Now, ceremony is the merest husk of faith
  and loyalty;
It is the beginning of all confusion and
  disorder.
As to foreknowledge, it is only the flower
  of Tao,
And the beginning of folly.
Therefore, the full-grown man sets his heart
  upon the substance rather than the husk;
Upon the fruit rather than the flower.
Truly, he prefers what is within to what is
  without.

57

You govern a kingdom by normal rules;
You fight a war by exceptional moves;
But you win the world by letting alone.
How do I know that this is so?
By what is within me!
The more taboos and inhibitions there are in
  the world,
The poorer the people become.
The sharper the weapons the people possess,
The greater confusion reigns in the realm.
The more clever and crafty the men,
The oftener strange things happen.
The more articulate the laws and ordinances,
The more robbers and thieves arise.
Therefore, the Sage says:
I do not make any fuss, and the people trans-
  form themselves.
I love quietude, and the people settle down
  in their regular grooves.
I do not engage myself in anything, and the
  people grow rich.
I have no desires, and the people return to
  Simplicity.

Study Questions

1. What kind of life ought we to live, according to Lao Tzu? Why? What is involved in living
   the natural way?
2. How does Lao Tzu conceive virtue? What characterizes the virtuous person? Why is
   weakness a virtue?
3. What is the meaning of nonaction (*wu-wei*)? How is it related to the Way? How is nonaction practiced?
4. How is the Way most fully revealed to us? How can we determine what is the natural
   course?
5. What is the ideal form of government in Lao Tzu's view? Why?

Suggestions for Further Reading

Carr, B., and I. Mahalingam, eds. *Companion Encyclopedia of Asian Philosophy* (London;
New York: Routledge, 1997). See Part IV, "Chinese Philosophy," especially C. Wei-hsun Fu's
"Daoism in Chinese Philosophy."

Deutsch, E., and R. Bonteke, eds. *A Companion to World Philosophies* (Cambridge, MA;
Oxford: Blackwell, 1997). For a general overview of Chinese philosophy, see T. Weiming's
"Chinese Philosophy: A Synoptic View," S. Kwong-Loi's "Ideas of the Good in Chinese Phi-
losophy" and especially P. J. Ivanhoe's "Human Beings and Nature in Traditional Chinese
Thought."

Singer, P., ed. *A Companion to Ethics* (Oxford; Cambridge, MA: Blackwell, 1991). For a
general background, see C. Hansen's "Classical Chinese Ethics."

Waley, A., ed. and trans. *The Way and Its Power: A Study of the Tao Teh Ching and Its Place in Chinese Thought* (London: Allen and Unwin, 1942). Provides a comprehensive introductory essay, six appendices, and a translation of the text.

Yu-Lan, Fung. *A History of Chinese Philosophy*, Volume I, trans. D. Boddes (Princeton, NJ: Princeton University Press, 1952). See Chapter VIII, "Lao Tzu and His School of Taoism."

The Bhagavad Gita (SIXTH CENTURY B.C.E.?)

The Bhagavad Gita (Song of the Lord) is one of the world's religious classics. Written in the ancient language of Sanskrit, it forms part of one of India's great epic poems, the *Mahabharata* (the Great Bharata, descendant of the founder of an Indian dynasty of kings). The authorship of the *Mahabharata* has not been determined precisely, but it is believed to have been written some time between the sixth and second centuries B.C.E. Known as the world's longest poem, with more than one hundred thousand couplets divided into eighteen books, the *Mahabharata* tells the story of the rivalry between the relatives of two brothers in their fight to control a kingdom near what is now Delhi. Though the war may be based on historical facts, the *Mahabharata* is a tale of good and evil represented, respectively, in the Pandavas and the Kuravas.

In the Bhagavad Gita, the war between two clans or tribes, the Pandavas and the Kuravas, takes on a symbolic meaning to represent the spiritual struggle of the soul that begins, as its opening lines tell us, "on the field of Truth, on the battlefield of life." It is a religious-philosophical poem, consisting of seven hundred couplets divided into eighteen chapters and takes the form of a dialogue between the warrior Arjuna, of the Pandavas, and Krishna, a personal manifestation of the divine. Placed between the two armies that are about to begin battle, Arjuna realizes with horror that his relatives and friends are on both sides. At one and the same time, he has the duty to fight for his family and the duty to destroy his family. Facing this moral crisis, he decides it is better to let his opponents kill him and drops his bow and arrows as he sinks in his chariot overcome by grief and despair. The spirit of Krishna arises, instructing Arjuna to fulfill his duty as a warrior and offering him guidance to the path of supreme spiritual enlightenment and liberation. The dialogue that ensues contains some of the most important teachings of the Hindu tradition on the nature of the universe, the divine, the self, and morality.

In the traditional Hindu conception, the universe and God, or the divine (*Brahman*), are one. *Brahman* is the ultimate reality, the Absolute, the ground of all being, the God beyond all gods, the One from which all things proceed. However, as the cause of the universe, *Brahman* is not exhausted in the universe. Thus, the divine is understood as both immanent and transcendent, or as dwelling both in and beyond the universe.

As the universe and *Brahman* are one, so the eternal Self (*Atman*) and *Brahman* are one. This means that the world-soul or spirit of the universe is one and the same with the soul of our individual existing selves. Like a drop of water from the ocean, which is the same as the ocean itself, so is *Atman* the same as *Brahman*. However, awareness of our oneness with the divine is a matter of spiritual development. The ultimate aim of Hindu religion is thus to guide us toward realizing and attaining our true identity with the divine. This is the goal of *moksha,* the release or liberation of the soul from the bonds of the temporal self and its identification with its eternal Self. It requires the discipline of renunciation or nonattachment, a process of withdrawing from the temporal world and its illusions to embrace reality in its fullness and eternity.

The concept of *dharma,* which means "duty" or "law," is central to the Hindu doctrine in its understanding of moral and spiritual matters. *Dharma* is understood not only as duty in the social sense regarding one's place in society, but also in the spiritual sense regarding one's true, eternal nature. *Dharma* thus pertains to the levels of one's moral and spiritual development. Traditionally conceived, Hindu society is divided into four major classes or castes (*brahmins,* or priests and intellectuals; *kshatriya,* or warriors; *vaisyas,* or farmers and merchants; and *sudra,* or servants). Each caste has its particular social and religious obligations. Social order rests on the proper fulfillment of the *dharma* or social duty appointed to individuals according to their castes. In eternal terms, the very order of the universe is itself interconnected with the proper fulfillment of the *dharma* or spiritual duty of the individual.

Another important concept in the traditional moral and spiritual doctrines of Hinduism is *karma,* which means "deed," "action," or "work," and is understood as the law of cause and effect governing the universe. It is a both a natural and a moral law according to which every action or deed necessarily produces its accompanying results. Present dispositions are the effect of past deeds and are the cause of future effects. In this sense, we are morally accountable for all of our actions. Because *karma* holds throughout the cycle of reincarnations, from one lifetime to another, we are each morally responsible for the actions of our eternal souls.

Spiritual perfection or the realization of the eternal Self can be attained through *yoga.* The root meaning of the word *yoga* is "to yoke" and carries the connotation of "joining" or "uniting." In this sense, *yoga* involves various physical practices and meditation exercises designed to harmonize or balance the soul and the body together as one. *Yoga* also contains the ideas of detachment—by disciplining one's lower self—and of attachment to one's higher Self—by cultivating one's Self-knowledge. The word "*yoga*" is also used to refer to different "ways" of attaining supreme spiritual realization. Among the various forms of *yoga* mentioned in the Bhagavad Gita are *karma yoga* (path of action), *bhakti yoga* (path of devotion), and *jñana yoga* (path of knowledge).

In a sense, the Bhagavad Gita is a book about the paths of life, love, and light toward the divine because it focuses on the *yogas* of action, devotion, and knowledge. These ways are interconnected and interdependent. Together, they enable us to learn to love the divine intelligently. Arjuna's despair over his moral conflict of duties and Krishna's instruction to fulfill his duty as a warrior provide the context for understanding these ways and their interconnectedness.

It is significant that in the following selections, Krishna begins by reminding Arjuna that humans have an eternal nature, for Arjuna's duty as a warrior is not measured only by the finite but by the infinite as well; it is Arjuna's *dharma.* It is no less important that Krishna continues by commanding Arjuna to act in the fulfillment of his duty, thereby directing him toward the yoga of action or work, *karma yoga.* Work is life and all of life is action. The emphasis on action in *karma yoga* is not, however, on merely external religious rituals, but on the inner, spiritual life. Moreover, *kri,* the root of the word *karma,* means "to create," so that every action is a creation. In this sense, every finite action carries with it the weight of the infinite, for the eternal Self is at stake. When Krishna urges Arjuna to "work not for a reward" and "free from selfish desires," he is pointing to the need for detachment from the lower, temporal self and its illusions, so that one may find the eternal in oneself.

THE BHAGAVAD GITA

2

SANJAYA

1. Then arose the spirit of Krishna and spoke to Arjuna, his friend, who with eyes filled with tears, thus had sunk into despair and grief.

KRISHNA

2. Whence this lifeless dejection, Arjuna, in this hour, the hour of trial? Strong men know not despair, Arjuna, for this wins neither heaven nor earth.

3. Fall not into degrading weakness, for this becomes not a man who is a man. Throw off this ignoble discouragement, and arise like a fire that burns all before it.

ARJUNA

4. I owe veneration to Bhishma and Drona. Shall I kill with my arrows my grandfather's brother, great Bhishma? Shall my arrows in battle slay Drona, my teacher?

5. Shall I kill my own masters who, though greedy of my kingdom, are yet my sacred teachers? I would rather eat in this life the food of a beggar than eat royal food tasting of their blood.

6. And we know not whether their victory or ours be better for us. The sons of my uncle and king, Dhrita-rashtra, are here before us: after their death, should we wish to live?

7. In the dark night of my soul I feel desolation. In my self-pity I see not the way of righteousness. I am thy disciple, come to thee in supplication: be a light unto me on the path of my duty.

8. For neither the kingdom of the earth, nor the kingdom of the gods in heaven, could give me peace from the fire of sorrow which thus burns my life.

SANJAYA

9. When Arjuna the great warrior had thus unburdened his heart, 'I will not fight, Krishna,' he said, and then fell silent.

10. Krishna smiled and spoke to Arjuna—there between the two armies the voice of God spoke these words:

KRISHNA

11. Thy tears are for those beyond tears; and are thy words words of wisdom? The wise grieve

The Bhagavad Gita, *trans. Juan Mascaró (Penguin Classics, 1962). Copyright © Juan Mascaró, 1962, Chapters 2, 3, 4, 5, and 18.*

not for those who live; and they grieve not for those who die—for life and death shall pass away.

12. Because we all have been for all time: I, and thou, and those kings of men. And we all shall be for all time, we all for ever and ever.

13. As the Spirit of our mortal body wanders on in childhood and youth and old age, the Spirit wanders on to a new body: of this the sage has no doubts.

17. Interwoven in his creation, the Spirit is beyond destruction. No one can bring to an end the Spirit which is everlasting.

18. For beyond time he dwells in these bodies, though these bodies have an end in their time; but he remains immeasurable, immortal. Therefore, great warrior, carry on thy fight.

19. If any man thinks he slays, and if another thinks he is slain, neither knows the ways of truth. The Eternal in man cannot kill: the Eternal in man cannot die.

20. He is never born, and he never dies. He is in Eternity: he is for evermore. Never-born and eternal, beyond times gone or to come, he does not die when the body dies.

21. When a man knows him as never-born, everlasting, never-changing, beyond all destruction, how can that man kill a man, or cause another to kill?

30. The Spirit that is in all beings is immortal in them all: for the death of what cannot die, cease thou to sorrow.

31. Think thou also of thy duty and do not waver. There is no greater good for a warrior than to fight in a righteous war.

32. There is a war that opens the doors of heaven, Arjuna! Happy the warriors whose fate is to fight such war.

38. Prepare for war with peace in thy soul. Be in peace in pleasure and pain, in gain and in loss, in victory or in the loss of a battle. In this peace there is no sin.

47. Set thy heart upon thy work, but never on its reward. Work not for a reward; but never cease to do thy work.

48. Do thy work in the peace of Yoga and, free from selfish desires, be not moved in success or in failure. Yoga is evenness of mind—a peace that is ever the same.

49. Work done for a reward is much lower than work done in the Yoga of wisdom. Seek salvation in the wisdom of reason. How poor those who work for a reward!

50. In this wisdom a man goes beyond what is well done and what is not well done. Go thou therefore to wisdom: Yoga is wisdom in work.

3

ARJUNA

1. If thy thought is that vision is greater than action, why dost thou enjoin upon me the terrible action of war?

2. My mind is in confusion because in thy words I find contradictions. Tell me in truth therefore by what path may I attain the Supreme.

KRISHNA

3. In this world there are two roads of perfection, as I told three before, O prince without sin: Jñana Yoga, the path of wisdom of the Sankhyas, and Karma Yoga, the path of action of the Yogis.

4. Not by refraining from action does man attain freedom from action. Not by mere renunciation does he attain supreme perfection.

5. For not even for a moment can a man be without action. Helplessly are all driven to action by the forces born of Nature.

6. He who withdraws himself from actions, but ponders on their pleasures in his heart, he is under a delusion and is a false follower of the Path.

7. But great is the man who, free from attachments, and with a mind ruling its powers in harmony, works on the path of Karma Yoga, the path of consecrated action.

8. Action is greater than inaction: perform therefore thy task in life. Even the life of the body could not be if there were no action.

9. The world is in the bonds of action, unless the action is consecration. Let thy actions then be pure, free from the bonds of desire.

19. In liberty from the bonds of attachment, do thou therefore the work to be done: for the man whose work is pure attains indeed the Supreme.

21. In the actions of the best men others find their rule of action. The path that a great man follows becomes a guide to the world.

22. I have no work to do in all the worlds, Arjuna—for these are mine. I have nothing to obtain, because I have all. And yet I work.

23. If I was not bound to action, never-tiring, everlastingly, men that follow many paths would follow my path of inaction.

24. If ever my work had an end, these worlds would end in destruction, confusion would reign within all: this would be the death of all beings.

25. Even as the unwise work selfishly in the bondage of selfish works, let the wise man work unselfishly for the good of all the world.

26. Let not the wise disturb the mind of the unwise in their selfish work. Let him, working with devotion, show them the joy of good work.

27. All actions take place in time by the interweaving of the forces of Nature; but the man lost in selfish delusion thinks that he himself is the actor.

28. But the man who knows the relation between the forces of Nature and actions, sees how some forces of Nature work upon other forces of Nature, and becomes not their slave.

29. Those who are under the delusion of the forces of Nature bind themselves to the work of these forces. Let not the wise man who sees the All disturb the unwise who sees not the All.

30. Offer to me all thy works and rest thy mind on the Supreme. Be free from vain hopes and selfish thoughts, and with inner peace fight thou thy fight.

31. Those who ever follow my doctrine and who have faith, and have a good will, find through pure work their freedom.

32. But those who follow not my doctrine, and who have ill-will, are men blind to all wisdom, confused in mind: they are lost.

33. 'Even a wise man acts under the impulse of his nature: all beings follow nature. Of what use is restraint?'

34. Hate and lust for things of nature have their roots in man's lower nature. Let him not fall under their power: they are the two enemies in his path.

35. And do thy duty, even if it be humble, rather than another's, even if it be great. To die in one's duty is life: to live in another's is death.

4

KRISHNA

13. The four orders of men arose from me, in justice to their natures and their works. Know that this work was mine, though I am beyond work, in Eternity.

14. In the bonds of works I am free, because in them I am free from desires. The man who can see this truth, in his work he finds his freedom.

15. This was known by men of old times, and thus in their work they found liberation. Do thou therefore thy work in life in the spirit that their work was done.

16. What is work? What is beyond work? Even some seers see this not aright. I will teach thee the truth of pure work, and this truth shall make thee free.

17. Know therefore what is work, and also know what is wrong work. And also know of a work that is silence: mysterious is the path of work.

18. The man who in his work finds silence, and who sees that silence is work, this man in truth sees the Light and in all his works finds peace.

19. He whose undertakings are free from anxious desire and fanciful thought, whose work is made pure in the fire of wisdom: he is called wise by those who see.

20. In whatever work he does such a man in truth has peace: he expects nothing, he relies on nothing, and ever has fullness of joy.

21. He has no vain hopes, he is the master of his soul, he surrenders all he has, only his body works: he is free from sin.

22. He is glad with whatever God gives him, and he has risen beyond the two contraries here below; he is without jealousy, and in success or in failure he is one: his works bind him not.

23. He has attained liberation: he is free from all bonds, his mind has found peace in wisdom, and his work is a holy sacrifice. The work of such a man is pure.

24. Who in all his work sees God, he in truth goes unto God: God is his worship, God is his offering, offered by God in the fire of God.

41. He who makes pure his works by Yoga, who watches over his soul, and who by wisdom destroys his doubts, is free from the bondage of selfish work.

42. Kill therefore with the sword of wisdom the doubt born of ignorance that lies in thy heart. Be one in self-harmony, in Yoga, and arise, great warrior, arise.

5

ARJUNA

1. Renunciation is praised by thee, Krishna, and then the Yoga of holy work. Of these two, tell me in truth, which is the higher path?

KRISHNA

2. Both renunciation and holy work are a path to the Supreme; but better than surrender of work is the Yoga of holy work.

3. Know that a man of true renunciation is he who craves not nor hates; for he who is above the two contraries soon finds his freedom.

6. But renunciation, Arjuna, is difficult to attain without Yoga of work. When a sage is one in Yoga he soon is one in God.

7. No work stains a man who is pure, who is in harmony, who is master of his life, whose soul is one with the soul of all.

8–9. 'I am not doing any work', thinks the man who is in harmony, who sees the truth. For in seeing or hearing, smelling or touching, in eating or walking, or sleeping, or breathing, in talking or grasping or relaxing, and even in opening or closing his eyes, he remembers: 'It is the servants of my soul that are working.'

10. Offer all thy works to God, throw off selfish bonds, and do thy work. No sin can then stain thee, even as waters do not stain the leaf of the lotus.

18

ARJUNA

1. Speak to me, Krishna, of the essence of renunciation, and of the essence of surrender.

KRISHNA

2. The renunciation of selfish works is called renunciation; but the surrender of the reward of all work is called surrender.

3. Some say there should be renunciation of action—since action disturbs contemplation; but others say that works of sacrifice, gift and self-harmony should not be renounced.

4. Hear my truth about the surrender of works, Arjuna. Surrender, O best of men, is of three kinds.

5. Works of sacrifice, gift, and self-harmony should not be abandoned, but should indeed be performed; for these are works of purification.

6. But even these works, Arjuna, should be done in the freedom of a pure offering, and

without expectation of a final reward. This is my final word.

7. It is not right to leave undone the holy work which ought to be done. Such a surrender of action would be a delusion of darkness.

8. And he who abandons his duty because he has fear of pain, his surrender is of Rajas, impure, and in truth he has no reward.

9. But he who does holy work, Arjuna, because it ought to be done and surrenders selfishness and thought of reward, his work is pure, and is peace.

10. This man sees and has no doubts: he surrenders, he is pure and has peace. Work, pleasant or painful, is for him joy.

11. For there is no man on earth who can fully renounce living work, but he who renounces the reward of his work is in truth a man of renunciation.

12. When work is done for a reward, the work brings pleasure, or pain, or both, in its time; but when a man does work in Eternity, then Eternity is his reward.

23. When work is done as sacred work, unselfishly, with a peaceful mind, without lust or hate, with no desire for reward, then the work is pure.

24. But when work is done with selfish desire, or feeling it is an effort, or thinking it is a sacrifice, then the work is impure.

25. And that work which is done with a confused mind, without considering what may follow, or one's own powers, or the harm done to others, or one's own loss, is work of darkness.

30. There is a wisdom which knows when to go and when to return, what is to be done and what is not to be done, what is fear and what is courage, what is bondage and what is liberation—that is pure wisdom.

46. A man attains perfection when his work is worship of God, from whom all things come and who is in all.

47. Greater is thine own work, even if this be humble, than the work of another, even if this be great. When a man does the work God gives him, no sin can touch this man.

48. And a man should not abandon his work, even if he cannot achieve it in full perfection; because in all work there may be imperfection, even as in all fire there is smoke.

49. When a man has his reason in freedom from bondage, and his soul is in harmony, beyond desires, then renunciation leads him to a region supreme which is beyond earthly action.

50. Hear now how he then reaches Brahman, the highest vision of Light,

51 When the vision of reason is clear, and in steadiness the soul is in harmony; when the world of sound and other senses is gone, and the spirit has risen above passion and hate;

52. When a man dwells in the solitude of silence, and meditation and contemplation are ever with him; when too much food does not disturb his health, and his thoughts and words and body are in peace; when freedom from passion is his constant will;

53. And his selfishness and violence and pride are gone; when lust and anger and greediness are no more, and he is free from the thought 'this is mine'; then this man has risen on the mountain of the Highest: he is worthy to be one with Brahman, with God.

54. He is one with Brahman, with God, and beyond grief and desire his soul is in peace. His love is one for all creation, and he has supreme love for me.

63. I have given thee words of vision and wisdom more secret than hidden mysteries. Ponder them in the silence of thy soul, and then in freedom do thy will.

ARJUNA

73. By thy grace I remember my Light, and now gone is my delusion. My doubts are no more, my faith is firm; and now I can say 'Thy will be done'.

Study Questions

1. What is the moral predicament in which Arjuna finds himself? What duties are in conflict? Why does he decide not to act?
2. What is Krishna's command to Arjuna? What does this command suggest about the nature of the two duties in conflict? How is this command related to the Hindu conception of the eternal Self (*Atman*)? What does this command suggest about Arjuna's initial motives in deciding not to act?
3. What is Arjuna confused about? How does his confusion relate to his predicament and Krishna's command?
4. What is the relation between the path of action and the path of knowledge? What is the nature of holy work?
5. What is the nature of renunciation and surrender? How are renunciation and surrender related to the Hindu conception of the eternal Self (*Atman*)? How do renunciation and surrender lead to freedom?
6. In what sense is the command to follow one's *dharma* both a moral and a spiritual task? Does this command help to solve conflicts between our social and spiritual duties? How does one determine what is one's *dharma*?

Suggestions for Further Reading

Carr, B., and I. Mahalingam, eds. *Companion Encyclopedia of Asian Philosophy* (London; New York: Routledge, 1997). For a general background, see Part II, "Indian Philosophy."

Deutsch, E., trans. *The Bhagavad Gita* (New York: Holt, Rinehart & Winston, 1968). Provides an introduction and critical essays on the text.

Deutsch, E., and R. Bonteke, eds. *A Companion to World Philosophies* (Cambridge, MA; Oxford: Blackwell, 1997). See J. N. Mohanty's "A History of Indian Philosophy" and "The Idea of the Good in Indian Thought."

Herman, A. L. *An Introduction to Indian Thought* (Englewood Cliffs, NJ: Prentice-Hall, 1976). See Section F, "The *Bhagavad Gita* and Its Philosophy," especially Part IV, "The Ethics of the *Bhagavad Gita*."

Kaveeshwar, G. W. *The Ethics of the Gita* (Delhi: Motilal Banarsidass, 1971). A detailed sixteen-chapter analysis of the ethical problem as the central problem of the *Gita*.

Patel, R. N. *Philosophy of the Gita* (New York: Peter Lang, 1991). An advanced study of the Gita. See Section II, "War and Morality."

Singer, P., ed. *A Companion to Ethics* (Oxford; Cambridge, MA: Blackwell, 1991). For a general introduction, see P. Bilimoria's "Indian Ethics."

The Buddha (563–483 B.C.E.)

Buddhism is based on the teachings of Siddhartha Gautama, the historical Buddha, who was born in the Ganges River valley, at the foot of the Himalayas. Many myths and legends surround his life—ranging from the time he was conceived, through the stages of his spiritual awakening, to the moment of his death.

In his earlier years, Gautama seems to have led a privileged courtly life sheltered by his father from the harsh realities of human misery. However, as a young man he was jarred from his comfortable existence when—upon seeing an old man, a diseased man, and a corpse—he realized that old age, sickness, and death are the inevitable miseries of life. Leaving his family behind, he became a spiritual seeker in an attempt to understand the nature of pain or suffering. He studied under the great yogi masters of his time and, after years of arduous practice, became an extreme ascetic, following what is called the "Path of Great Renunciation." Having experienced both extremes in the course of his life—luxurious indulgence and severe self-mortification—he saw the necessity for a balanced approach or for moderation in human action. This is one of the reasons that his doctrine is known as the Middle Way.

Legend has it that Gautama sat under a sacred bodhi tree (the tree of spiritual awakening), resolving not to leave until he attained enlightenment. He was in deep meditation for a long time, during which he was tempted by Mara, a deceiving deity from the realm of desire and death. Yet, he remained unmoved, gained knowledge, and reached the state of spiritual awakening (*nirvana*). Thus, he is named the Buddha (the Awakened or Enlightened One).

The Buddha emerged from his meditation to teach others how to attain spiritual enlightenment. His basic insight is that all of existence is pain or suffering (*dukkha*). He taught how suffering originates in desires and how we can overcome it. The way toward ending the bondage of suffering altogether is called the path to liberation or truth (*dharma*). This is a path of release from the wheel of life, death, and rebirth (*samsara*). The goal is to get off this wheel because life, death, and rebirth bring repeated suffering. To attain this goal we have to develop an understanding of the interconnectedness of all actions, learning to see them in terms of cause and effect. This refers to the moral law of causality (*karma*)—where good actions bring good results and bad actions cause bad effects. Karma is not a judgment or an evaluation but a natural law—a law of things as they are. It does not entitle us to abandon moral accountability for our actions. Rather, it requires us to recognize and assume responsibility for the causes and effects we create in our daily lives. Knowledge of the law of causality enables us to work out our liberation for ourselves, in what is called "wisdom in action." The moral life is thus the path of the wise to absolute freedom.

The Buddha taught that existence has the characteristic of becoming, that life as such is constantly changing. Another characteristic of existence is that it is unsatisfactory in that we are insatiable in our desires and are thus constantly and endlessly craving. The final characteristic of existence is that it lacks an underlying reality or identity that we can call the self or ego. Contrary to the earlier (Hindu) belief in an eternal Self (*atman*) that reincarnates from one lifetime to another, the Buddha denied the existence of a permanent unchanging self. This is known as the doctrine of the nonself (*anatman*). Yet, the Buddha did not agree with those who believed all life was merely matter and denied the possibility of a reincarnating immaterial self. This is another reason why the Buddha's doctrine is called the Middle Way, as it goes between these two opposing beliefs (eternalism and materialism) and their corresponding moralities.

According to the Buddha, what goes through the wheel of life, death, and rebirth is not a permanent identical self, but a continuous flow of ever-changing experiences in a chain of causes and effects. As one candle lights another, and this one lights the next, so our past lives are the basis for our present life and so on, without there being one same self. This does not mean that the "I" that you call yourself doesn't exist. It is a bundle of experiences or five aggregates called *khandhas* (form or body, feelings, perceptions, dispositions, consciousness), which come together giving us a sense of individuality. Even within the span of one lifetime, we are constantly changing, but have the sense of being the same "I." However, becoming attached to this "I" only leads to suffering, mainly because we crave its continued existence.

The Buddha offers an ethics that is different from those of eternalism and materialism. The eternalist belief leads to an ethics bent on advancing the interests of a reincarnating permanent self. The materialist belief leads to an ethics based on the pursuit of material pleasures. Both kinds of desires keep us on the wheel of life, death, and rebirth. In criticizing these beliefs, the Buddha was challenging the established religious doctrines and philosophies, particularly those of the priestly caste (brahmins), who upheld eternalism and dictated the institutionalized morality. As the Middle Way, the Buddha's ethics thus offers a veritable reformation of the traditional morality of his times.

The doctrine of the Middle Way contains the Four Noble Truths and the Eightfold Path. The Four Noble Truths detail the nature of suffering based on an understanding of the law of causality. The first Noble Truth of suffering states that suffering is inherent to existence. The second Noble Truth is that suffering is caused by craving. The third Noble Truth states that suffering can cease through renunciation. The fourth Noble Truth is the path leading to the cessation of suffering. This is the Eightfold Path, which indicates how we must live to attain release. It encompasses the many facets of our existence, prescribing the right outlook, the right resolves, the right speech, the right acts, the right livelihood, the right endeavor, the right mindfulness, and the right concentration through meditation. What is right in general are those acts leading away from the attachment to the self. However, this statement cannot be made categorically because the rightness of specific acts depends on the contextual whole of causes and effects. In other words, a particular act in and of itself is neither right nor wrong; it depends on whether or not it leads to suffering for oneself and others. Since the chain of cause and effects can span many lifetimes, morality itself is not a matter of one lifetime. In fact, the goal of morality is freedom from rebirth. One who has attained this freedom is called "the one who has done what has to be done."

THE FIRST SERMON AND THE SYNOPSIS OF TRUTH

2. The First Sermon

These two extremes, O monks, are not to be practised by one who has gone forth from the world. What are the two? That conjoined with the passions, low, vulgar, common, ignoble, and useless, and that conjoined with self-torture, painful, ignoble, and useless. Avoiding these two extremes the Tathāgata[1] has gained the knowledge of the Middle Way, which gives sight and knowledge, and tends to calm, to insight, enlightenment, *nirvāṇa*.

What, O monks, is the Middle Way, which gives sight . . . ? It is the noble Eightfold Path, namely, right views, right intention, right speech, right action, right livelihood, right effort, right mindfulness, right concentration. This, O monks, is the Middle Way. . . .

(1) Now this, O monks, is the noble truth of pain: birth is painful, old age is painful, sickness is painful, death is painful, sorrow, lamentation, dejection, and despair are painful. Contact with unpleasant things is painful, not getting what one wishes is painful. In short the five *khandhas* of grasping are painful.[2]

(2) Now this, O monks, is the noble truth of the cause of pain: that craving which leads to rebirth, combined with pleasure and lust, finding pleasure here and there, namely, the craving for passion, the craving for existence, the craving for non-existence.

(3) Now this, O monks, is the noble truth of the cessation of pain: the cessation without a remainder of that craving, abandonment, forsaking, release, non-attachment.

[1] "Tathāgata" is a name for the Buddha. Literally it means one who has "thus come."
[2] The five *khandhas* (groups or aggregates) are form, feeling (or sensation), perception (volitional disposition), predispositions (or impressions), and consciousness. These will be described in detail later in this chapter.

(4) Now this, O monks, is the noble truth of the way that leads to the cessation of pain: this is the noble Eightfold Path, namely, right views, right intention, right speech, right action, right livelihood, right effort, right mindfulness, right concentration. . . .

As long as in these noble truths my threefold knowledge and insight duly with its twelve divisions was not well purified, even so long, O monks, in the world with its gods, Māra,[3] Brahmā,[4] with ascetics, *brāhmins*, gods, and men, I had not attained the highest complete enlightenment. Thus I knew.

But when in these noble truths my threefold knowledge and insight duly with its twelve divisions was well purified, then, O monks, in the world . . . I had attained the highest complete enlightenment. Thus I knew. Knowledge arose in me; insight arose that the release of my mind is unshakable; this is my last existence; now there is no rebirth.

3. The Synopsis of Truth

Thus have I heard. Once when the Lord was staying at Benares in the Isipatana deerpark, he addressed the almsmen as follows: It was here in this very deerpark at Benares that the Truth-finder, *Arahat* [*arhat*] all-enlightened, set a-rolling the supreme Wheel of the Doctrine—which shall not be turned back from its onward course by recluse or *brāhmin*, god or Māra or Brahmā or by anyone in the universe,—the announcement of the Four Noble Truths, the teaching, declaration, and establishment of those Four Truths, with their unfolding, exposition, and manifestation.

[3] The goddess of temptation.
[4] God in the role of creator.

"The First Sermon" and *"The Synopsis of Truth."* In A Sourcebook in Indian Philosophy, *eds. S. Radhakrishnan and C. A. Moore. Princeton, NJ: Princeton University Press, 1973.*

What are these four?—The announcement, teaching . . . and manifestation of the Noble Truth of suffering—of the origin of suffering—of the cessation of suffering—of the path that leads to the cessation of suffering.

Follow, almsmen, Sāriputta and Moggallāna and be guided by them; they are wise helpers unto their fellows in the higher life. . . .

Sāriputta is able to announce, teach . . . and manifest the Four Noble Truths in all their details.

Having thus spoken, the Blessed One arose and went into his own bed.

The Lord had not been gone long when the reverent Sāriputta proceeded to the exposition of the Truth-finder's Four Noble Truths, as follows:

What, reverend sirs, is the Noble Truth of suffering?—Birth is a suffering; decay is a suffering; death is a suffering; grief and lamentation, pain, misery and tribulation are sufferings; it is a suffering not to get what is desired;—in brief all the factors of the fivefold grip of existence are suffering.

Birth is, for living creatures of each several class, the being born are produced, the issue, the arising or the re-arising, the appearance of the impressions, the growth of faculties.

Decay, for living creatures of each several class, is the decay and decaying, loss of teeth, grey hair, wrinkles, a dwindling term of life, sere faculties.

Death, for living creatures of each several class, is the passage and blessing hence, the dissolution, disappearance, dying, death, decease, are dissolution of the impressions, the discarding of the dead body.

Grief is the grief, grieving, and grievousness, the inward grief and inward anguish of anyone who suffers under some misfortune or is in the grip of some type of suffering.

Lamentation is the lament and lamentation, the wailing and the lamenting of anyone who suffers under some misfortune or is in the grip of some type of suffering.

Pain is any bodily suffering or bodily evil, and suffering bred of bodily contact, any evil feeling.

Misery is mental suffering and evil, any evil feeling of the mind.

Tribulation is the tribulation of heart and mind, the state to which tribulation brings them, in anyone who suffers under some misfortune or is in the grip of some type of suffering.

There remains not to get what is desired. In creatures subject to birth—or decay—or death—or grief and lamentation, pain, misery, and tribulation—the desire arises not to be subject thereto but to escape them. But escape is not to be won merely by desiring it; and failure to win it is another suffering.

What are in brief all the factors of the fivefold grip on existence which are sufferings?—They are: the factors of form, feeling, perception, impressions, and consciousness.

The foregoing, sirs, constitutes the Noble Truth of suffering.

What now is the Noble Truth of the origin of suffering? It is any craving that makes for re-birth and is tied up with passion's delights and culls satisfaction now here now there—such as the craving for sensual pleasure, the craving for continuing existence, and the craving for annihilation.

Next, what is the Noble Truth of the cessation of suffering?—It is the utter and passionless cessation of this same craving,—the abandonment and rejection of craving, deliverance from craving, and aversion from craving.

Lastly, what is the Noble Truth of the Path that leads to the cessation of suffering?—It is just the Noble Eightfold Path, consisting of right outlook, right resolves, right speech, right acts, right livelihood, right endeavour, right mindfulness and right rapture of concentration.

Right outlook is to know suffering, the origin of suffering, the cessation of suffering, and the path that leads to the cessation of suffering.

Right resolves are the resolve to renounce the world and to do no hurt or harm.

Right speech is to abstain from lies and slander, from reviling, and from tattle.

Right acts are to abstain from taking life, from stealing, and from lechery.

Right livelihood is that by which the disciple of the Noble One supports himself, to the exclusion of wrong modes of livelihood.

Right endeavour is when an almsman brings his will to bear, puts forth endeavour and energy, struggles and strives with all his heart, to stop bad and wrong qualities which have not yet arisen from ever arising, to renounce those which have already arisen, to foster good qualities which have not yet arisen, and, finally, to establish, clarify, multiply, enlarge, develop, and perfect those good qualities which are there already.

Right mindfulness is when realizing what the body is—what feelings are—what the heart is—and what the mental states are—an almsman dwells ardent, alert, and mindful, in freedom from the wants and discontents attendant on any of these things.

Right rapture of concentration is when, divested of lusts and divested of wrong dispositions, an almsman develops, and dwells in, the first ecstasy with all its zest and satisfaction, a state bred of aloofness and not divorced from observation and reflection. By laying to rest observation and reflection, he develops and dwells in inward serenity, in [the] focussing of heart, in the zest and satisfaction of the second ecstasy, which is divorced from observation and reflection and is bred of concentration—passing thence to the third and fourth ecstasies.

This, sirs, constitutes the Noble Truth of the Path that leads to the cessation of suffering. . . .

Study Questions

1. What does it mean that any craving that makes for rebirth is the origin of suffering? Why does this include the craving for nonexistence or annihilation?
2. Why is the cessation of craving described as passionless? Why is the right rapture of concentration based on states of aloofness and inward serenity?
3. How does each of the ways of the Eightfold Path help to cease suffering?
4. How specifically can we attain what is called "wisdom in action"?
5. Is the Buddha's ethics pessimistic or liberating? In what ways?

Suggestions for Further Reading

Carr, B., and I. Mahalingam, eds. *Companion Encyclopedia of Asian Philosophy* (London; New York: Routledge, 1997). See Part III, "Buddhist Philosophy," especially N. Smart's "The Buddha."

Deutsch, E., and R. Bonteke, eds. *A Companion to World Philosophies* (Cambridge, MA; Oxford: Blackwell, 1997). See N. Smart's "Survey of Buddhist Thought" and P. D. Premasiri's "Ideas of the Good in Buddhist Philosophy."

Dharmasiri, G. *Fundamentals of Buddhist Ethics* (Antioch, CA: Golden Leaves, 1989). A detailed twelve-chapter introduction to the basic concepts of Buddhist ethics.

Kalupahana, D. *Ethics in Early Buddhism* (Honolulu: University of Hawaii Press, 1995). A three-part analysis of Buddhist ethics. Part Two examines the moral life as expounded in the Buddha's discourse.

Rahula, W. *What the Buddha Taught* (New York: Grove Press, 1954). Contains a detailed analysis of the Four Noble Truths besides other Buddhist doctrines.

Robinson, R. H., and W. L. Johnson. *The Buddhist Religion: A Historical Introduction,* 4th ed. (Belmont, CA: Wadsworth, 1997). A comprehensive introduction to Buddhism. Chapters 1 and 2 discuss the Buddha's life and teachings.

Confucius (551–479 B.C.E.)

Confucius, one of the most revered Chinese sages, was born in the small feudal state of Lu, in what is now the province of Shantung in northeastern China. His original name was K'ung Ch'iu, but he was later called K'ung Fu-tzu (K'ung the Master); the name "Confucius" is the Latinized version of the latter. It seems that he came from a noble family of modest means and that he held various positions as a public servant in the state of Lu. He lived during a time of social misery, political instability, and corruption. There were constant battles between the many states then dividing China, abusive state governments, and within the states internal strife among nobles for power. Deeply concerned about the chaos of his times, Confucius dedicated his life to the idea of social reform, with education as the key to improvement. His ideal was that of a harmonious and well-ordered society, formed by a community of good people who are governed by morally excellent rulers. These rulers would lead the people by virtue and example, rather than by coercion and punishment.

A self-educated man, Confucius became the first professional teacher in China. He changed the idea of education from a program in vocational training into a way of developing the whole human being by building up a person's character. Looking back to sage-kings from previous dynasties, Confucius developed his model of a ruler who would fulfill the ideal of a human being, the exemplary man who is genuinely sensitive to the needs of others and concerned for their welfare. Going against tradition, which limited education to the men of nobility, Confucius sought to make education open to all males according to their ability to learn, rather than their social rank and status. Hoping to influence the course of governance and public administration, he secured public offices for his students and tried to implement various social policies. Unsuccessful in getting his plans realized, Confucius left Lu with some of his pupils when he was fifty-six years old. He traveled to different Chinese states while he continued teaching and trying to persuade rulers to apply his principles. Thirteen years later, Confucius returned to Lu, without having attained his goals, and continued teaching until his death.

Confucius' philosophy stands out as the most elevated expression of the humanism that had been steadily emerging in China more than five hundred years before Confucius was born. Rather than attributing events to supernatural forces and establishing moral guidance according to the will of spiritual beings, Chinese philosophers began to focus on human actions and to give increasing importance to the human's abilities and moral virtue. Confucius captured this new humanist perspective when he stated: "It is man who can make the Way (*Tao* or *Dao*) great, and not the Way that can make man great." His philosophy stands as the first attempt in the history of Chinese thought to deal primarily with ethical matters for their own sake and not for reasons related to spiritual beings and the afterlife. His main concern was to cultivate the living humanity of the individual and society in harmony, according to the Way or the ideal course of moral conduct.

The main concept of Confucius' philosophy is *jen* or *ren,* which he understood as the general virtue that embraced all other virtues, our humaneness. Receiving various translations, such as humanity, goodness, benevolence, and kindheartedness, the Chinese graph consists of the word *human* with the word *two* to signify the moral ideal of our conduct toward others. For Confucius, it represents humanity at its best, in oneself and in one's relations to others, and it gives rise to moral principles of conscientiousness and altruism. The man of *jen* is the ideal or exemplary man, the *chun-tzu* or *junzi* (literally, son of a ruler), the gentleman whose moral superiority resides in his wisdom and kindness toward others. Confucius describes him as he who "wishing to establish his own character, . . . also establishes the character of others." In his humaneness, the exemplary man follows the Golden Rule of reciprocity or mutual consideration by not doing to others what he would not want done to himself.

Confucius understands the individual as a relational or social self whose moral development is intimately bound with society. The individual's virtues are social virtues insofar as they are defined by his relations to others. Another concept in Confucius' philosophy, the rectification of names, emphasized the importance of an order in which each name corresponds properly with each person's place in society and each person's words correspond with his action. Placing emphasis on the everydayness of moral conduct, Confucius attached much significance to family life and the duties involved in family relationships, particularly in the practice of what he called "filial piety" or devotion between family members. Society is itself like a large family, a single indivisible unit whose moral welfare depends upon its harmony as a whole. Expanding on the common meaning of *li,* which was understood as "religious reverence or ritual," Confucius used the term to denote reverence or ritual behavior in all human activities in which we conduct ourselves with propriety; that is, by following custom or looking back to tradition, the established and thus the right way to conduct oneself. When everybody conducts himself appropriately, there is order in the individual, the family, society, and the universe. For Confucius, proper behavior follows the Mandate of Heaven, the divine order or will of the cosmos, the Way according to which all things properly are.

The Analects consists of sayings that are attributed to Confucius and to some of his disciples. These sayings were probably compiled into different versions by Confucius' followers after his death. It contains almost five hundred "chapters" (short pieces, a few sentences long) that are collected into twenty books. The following selections come from various books of *The Analects* and contain his teachings on concepts such as humaneness, the gentleman, propriety, the Golden Rule, and the Way.

THE ANALECTS

Book 1

1. The Master said: 'To learn something and at times to practise it—surely that is a pleasure? To have friends coming from distant places—surely that is delightful? But not to be resentful at others' failure to appreciate one—surely that is to be a true gentleman?'

2. Master You said: 'Few indeed are those who are naturally filial towards their parents and dutiful towards their elder brothers but are fond of opposing their superiors; and it never happens that those who do not like opposing their superiors are fond of creating civil disorder. The gentleman concerns himself with the root; and if the root is firmly planted, the Way grows. Filial piety and fraternal duty—surely they are the roots of humaneness.'

3. The Master said: 'Clever words and a plausible appearance have seldom turned out to be humane.' . . .

14. The Master said: 'A gentleman avoids seeking to satisfy his appetite to the full when he eats and avoids seeking comfort when he is at home. He is diligent in deed and cautious in word, and he associates with possessors of the Way and is put right by them. He may simply be said to be fond of learning.' . . .

Book 2

1. The Master said: 'The practice of government by means of virtue may be compared with the pole-star, which the multitudinous stars pay homage to while it stays in its place.'

20. Ji Kang Zi asked how the people might be induced to be respectful and loyal so that they might be properly encouraged. The Master said: 'If you oversee them with dignity, they will be respectful. If you are dutiful towards your parents and kind to your children, then they will be loyal. If you promote the good and instruct the incompetent, then they will be encouraged.' . . .

Book 4

1. The Master said: 'It is humaneness which is the attraction of a neighbourhood. If from choice one does not dwell in humaneness, how does one obtain wisdom?'

2. The Master said: 'It is impossible for those who are not humane to dwell for a long time in adversity, and it is also impossible for them to dwell for long in pleasurable circumstances. Those who are humane rest content with humaneness and those who are wise derive advantage from humaneness.'

3. The Master said: 'Only one who is humane is able to like other people and able to dislike other people.'

4. The Master said: 'If one sets one's heart on humaneness, one will be without evil.'

5. The Master said: 'Riches and honours—these are what men desire, but if this is not achieved in accordance with the appropriate principles, one does not cling to them. Poverty and obscurity—these are what men hate, but if this is not achieved in accordance with the appropriate principles, one does not avoid them. If a gentleman abandons humaneness, how does he make a reputation? The gentleman never shuns humaneness even for the time it takes to finish a meal. If his progress is hasty, it is bound to arise from this; and if his progress is unsteady, it is bound to arise from this.'

6. The Master said: 'I have never come across anyone who loved humaneness and hated inhumaneness. As far as anyone who loved humaneness is concerned, there would be no way of surpassing him. As far as anyone who hated

inhumaneness is concerned, in his practice of humaneness he would not let the inhumane come near his person. Does there exist anyone who is capable of devoting his energies to humaneness for a single day? I have never come across anyone whose energies were inadequate. Surely such people exist, but I have never come across them.'

7. The Master said: 'People's mistakes all come in the same category in that, if one contemplates a mistake, then one gains an understanding of humaneness.'

8. The Master said: 'If one has heard the Way in the morning, it is all right to die in the evening.' . . .

11. The Master said: 'The gentleman cherishes virtue, but the small man cherishes the soil; the gentleman cherishes the rigours of the law, but the small man cherishes leniency.' . . .

15. The Master said: 'Can, by one single thread is my Way bound together.' Master Zeng said: 'Yes.' When the Master went out the disciples asked: 'What did he mean?' Master Zeng said: 'Our Master's Way simply consists of loyalty and reciprocity.' . . .

Book 7

6. The Master said: 'Set your heart on the Way, base yourself on virtue, rely on humaneness, and take your relaxation in the arts.' . . .

30. The Master said: 'Is humaneness really so far away? If we ourselves wanted humaneness, then humaneness would arrive.' . . .

Book 8

2. The Master said: 'If one is courteous but does without ritual, then one dissipates one's energies; if one is cautious but does without ritual, then one becomes timid; if one is bold but does without ritual, then one becomes reckless; if one is forthright but does without ritual, then one becomes rude. When gentlemen deal sincerely with their kinsfolk, then the people are stimulated towards humaneness. When old friends are not neglected, then the people will not behave irresponsibly.' . . .

13. The Master said: 'Be of sincere good faith and love learning. Be steadfast unto death in pursuit of the good Way. One does not enter a state which is in peril, nor reside in one which is rebellious. When the Way prevails in the world, then be seen. When it does not, then hide. When the Way prevails in your own state, to be made poor and obscure by it is a disgrace; but when the Way does not prevail in your own state, to be made rich and honourable by it is a disgrace.' . . .

Book 12

1. Yan Hui asked about humaneness. The Master said: 'To subdue oneself and return to ritual is to practise humaneness. If someone subdued himself and returned to ritual for a single day, then all under Heaven would ascribe humaneness to him. For the practice of humaneness does surely proceed from the man himself, or does it proceed from others?' Yan Hui said: 'I beg to ask for the details of this.' The Master said: 'Do not look at what is contrary to ritual, do not listen to what is contrary to ritual, do not speak what is contrary to ritual, and make no movement which is contrary to ritual.' Yan Hui said: 'Although I am not clever, I beg to put this advice into practice.'

2. Zhonggong asked about humaneness. The Master said: 'When you are away from home, behave as if receiving an important guest. Employ the people as if you were officiating at a great sacrifice. Do not impose on others what you would not like yourself. Then there will be no resentment against you, either in the state or in the family.' Zhonggong said: 'Although I am not clever, I beg to put this advice into practice.'

3. Sima Niu asked about humaneness. The Master said: 'The humane person is hesitant in his speech.' He said: 'Hesitant in his speech! Is that all that is meant by humaneness?' The Master said: 'To do it is difficult, so in speaking about it can one avoid being hesitant?' . . .

Book 14

28. The Master said: 'The ways of the gentleman are three but I have no ability in them: the

humane do not worry; the wise are not perplexed; and the courageous do not feel fear.' Zigong said: 'Our Master is talking about himself.' . . .

Book 15

24. Zigong asked: 'Is there a single word such that one could practise it throughout one's life?' The Master said: 'Reciprocity perhaps? Do not inflict on others what you yourself would not wish done to you.' . . .

33. The Master said: 'If knowledge attains something but humaneness cannot safeguard it, then one is bound to lose it even if one has got hold of it. If knowledge attains something and humaneness can safeguard it and if one does not govern them with dignity, then the people will not be respectful. If knowledge attains something and humaneness can safeguard it and if one governs them with dignity, but if in moving them into action one does not accord with the rites, one is not yet good.'

35. The Master said: 'The people's connection with humaneness is more important than water or fire. As for water and fire, I have come across people who have died through stepping on them, but I have never come across people who have died through stepping on humaneness.'

Book 20

2. Zizhang asked Master Kong: 'What sort of person must one be so that one may take part in government?' 'If one honours the five excellences and puts away the four abominations, one may take part in government', said the Master. 'What is meant by the five excellences?' said Zizhang. Master Kong said: 'When the gentleman is not wasteful although he is bounteous, when he is not resented although he gets people to work hard, when he is not greedy although he has desires, when he is not arrogant although he is dignified, when he is not fearsome although he is awe-inspiring.' 'What is meant by not being wasteful although one is bounteous?' said Zizhang. Master Kong said: 'If he benefits the people on the basis of what the people will really find beneficial, then surely he is not wasteful although he is bounteous. If he gets people to work hard by choosing tasks which may properly be worked hard at, then who will feel resentful? If through desiring humaneness, he gets humaneness, then how is he being greedy? No matter whether he is dealing with the multitude or with the few, with the small or with the great, if the gentleman never ventures to be rude, then surely he is not arrogant although he is dignified. When the gentleman adjusts his clothes and cap and makes the people gaze on him with honour, and men look upon him in dread because of his majestic appearance, surely he is not fearsome although he is awe-inspiring?' 'What is meant by the four abominations?' said Zizhang. The Master said: 'To impose the death penalty without people previously being given any instruction is called ruthlessness. To look to the completion of tasks without giving notice in advance is called harshness. To insist on a time limit although dilatory in giving orders is called oppressiveness. And generally speaking in dealing with people, niggardliness in giving is called officiousness.'

3. The Master said: 'If one does not understand fate, one has no means of becoming a gentleman; if one does not understand the rites, one has no means of taking one's stand; if one does not understand words, one has no means of understanding people.'

Study Questions

1. What does Confucius mean by "humaneness"? How does it translate into the individual's moral conduct? In what sense does the individual have the duty to be humane? What other duties are involved?

2. What characterizes the "gentleman" for Confucius? What role does the gentleman play in society? What virtues must he cultivate? Why is it especially important for him to cultivate these virtues?

3. What does Confucius' notion of "propriety" involve? Why is it essential for following the Way? In what sense does it uphold tradition? Does it necessarily result in radical conservatism?

4. How does Confucius conceive the individual, society, and the state? How are the values of the self and the community related?

5. What constitutes the proper order of society? In what sense does this definition of order have a universal or cosmological significance?

6. Is Confucius' ethics an ethics of duty (deontology)? Is it a virtue ethics?

Suggestions for Further Reading

Carr, B., and I. Mahalingam, eds. *Companion Encyclopedia of Asian Philosophy* (London; New York: Routledge, 1997). See Part IV, "Chinese Philosophy," especially H. Nansen's "Confucius and Confucianism" and R. Sheng Wang's "Morals and Society in Chinese Philosophy."

Deutsch, E., and R. Bonteke, eds. *A Companion to World Philosophies* (Cambridge, CA; Oxford: Blackwell, 1997). See T. Weiming's "Chinese Philosophy: A Synoptic View" and especially S. Kwong-Loi's "Ideas of the Good in Chinese Philosophy."

Chan, Wing-Tsit. *A Sourcebook in Chinese Philosophy* (Princeton, NJ: Princeton University Press, 1963). Chapter 2 provides a brief introduction with text selections and commentary.

Hall, D. L., and R. T. Ames. *Thinking Through Confucius* (New York: State University of New York Press, 1987). A six-part advanced analysis of Confucius' *Analects* with philological and critical philosophical commentaries.

Koller, J. *Oriental Philosophies*, 2d. ed. (New York: Charles Scribner's Sons, 1985). See Part Three, "Chinese Philosophies," especially Chapter 18, "Confucianism."

Singer, P., ed. *A Companion to Ethics* (Oxford; Cambridge, MA: Blackwell, 1991). For a general background, see C. Hansen's "Classical Chinese Ethics."

Mencius (371–289 B.C.E.?)

Mencius, the "second sage" of China after Confucius, was probably a contemporary of the Greek philosopher Plato. His original name was Meng K'o, but he was later called Meng-tzu (Master Meng). It appears he studied under a disciple of Confucius and led a life that was very similar to that of Confucius. Like Confucius, he was born in what is today's Shantung province, in northeastern China, worked as a public servant, spent some years as a traveling scholar, and later returned to his home province without having succeeded in persuading any rulers to follow his principles. However, circumstances might have been against him: the social and political disarray that gripped China during Confucius' lifetime had worsened with time, and Mencius was born during what is historically known as the Period of the Warring States (400 B.C.E.–221 B.C.E.).

Mencius embraced many of Confucius' teachings, but he developed his own philosophical position regarding certain aspects of Confucian thought. One crucial point of difference is the question of the quality of human nature. Although Confucius seemed to imply that human nature is good, he did not say so explicitly; he said only that "by nature men are alike, [but] . . . through practice they become far apart." By contrast, Mencius explicitly claimed that human nature is originally good. For this reason, his philosophy is called idealistic Confucianism.

Mencius believed that humans are born with an innate knowledge of the good and have a natural inclination to do good. He maintained that humans have inborn tendencies to be benevolent, dutiful, and wise (in the sense of distinguishing right from wrong) and to behave with propriety by observing rites. In his view, evil is not innate; rather, it is the result of negative environmental influences and the lack of a proper moral education. Thus, like Confucius, Mencius attached central importance to education for moral self-cultivation, but he also saw it as a way to recover the human being's "lost mind" or original nature.

Like Confucius, Mencius sought to identify the moral principles for a good, or humane, government. However, Mencius took this notion a step further than Confucius by insisting that the good of the people is what is most important, so that they have a moral right to revolt when the government fails to secure this. Mencius' understanding of the Confucian concept of humaneness (*jen* or *ren*) was also broader than that of his predecessor, for he always included the notion of righteousness (*li*) with it. In this sense, Mencius stressed the need for making distinctions in our humaneness or love toward others.

The Book of Mencius was probably compiled by his disciples after his death. It is divided into seven books, each consisting of two parts, and contains both Mencius' sayings and his conversations with various rulers, officials, friends, and students. In the first selection, Mencius argues against Kao Tzu—who claimed that humans are neither innately good nor bad—and defends his own position through various analogies. In the second selection, Mencius claims that all humans have an innate compassion for the suffering of others, along with other innate feelings.

THE BOOK OF MENCIUS

Book Six, Part I

6A:1. Kao Tzu said, "Human nature is like the willow tree, and righteousness is like a cup or a bowl. To turn human nature into humanity and righteousness is like turning the willow into cups and bowls." Mencius said, "Sir, can you follow the nature of the willow tree and make the cups and bowls, or must you violate the nature of the willow tree before you can make the cups and bowls? If you are going to violate the nature of the willow tree in order to make cups and bowls, then must you also violate human nature in order to make it into humanity and righteousness? Your words, alas! would lead all people in the world to consider humanity and righteousness as calamity [because they required the violation of human nature]!"

6A:2. Kao Tzu said, "Man's nature is like whirling water. If a breach in the pool is made to the east it will flow to the east. If a breach is made to the west it will flow to the west. Man's nature is indifferent to good and evil, just as water is indifferent to east and west." Mencius said, "Water, indeed, is indifferent to the east and west, but is it indifferent to high and low? Man's nature is naturally good just as water naturally flows downward. There is no man without this good nature; neither is there water that does not flow downward. Now you can strike water and cause it to splash upward over your forehead, and by damming and leading it, you can force it uphill. Is this the nature of water? It is the forced circumstance that makes it do so. Man can be made to do evil, for his nature can be treated in the same way."

6A:3. Kao Tzu said, "What is inborn is called nature." Mencius said, "When you say that what is inborn is called nature, is that like saying that white is white?" "Yes." "Then is the whiteness of the white feather the same as the whiteness of snow? Or, again, is the whiteness of snow the same as the whiteness of white jade?" "Yes." "Then is the nature of a dog the same as the nature of an ox, and is the nature of an ox the same as the nature of a man?" . . .

6A:6. Kung-tu Tzu said, "Kao Tzu said that man's nature is neither good nor evil. Some say that man's nature may be made good or evil, therefore when King Wen and King Wu were in power the people loved virtue, and when Kings Yu and Li were in power people loved violence. Some say that some men's nature is good and some men's nature is evil. Therefore even under (sage-emperor) Yao there was Hsiang [who daily plotted to kill his brother], and even with a bad father Ku-sou, there was [a most filial] Shun (Hsiang's brother who succeeded Yao), and even with (wicked king) Chou as nephew and ruler, there were Viscount Ch'i of Wei and Prince Pi-kan. Now you say that human nature is good. Then are those people wrong?"

Mencius said, "If you let people follow their feelings (original nature), they will be able to do good. This is what is meant by saying that human nature is good. If man does evil, it is not the fault of his natural endowment. The feeling of commiseration is found in all men; the feeling of shame and dislike is found in all men; the feeling of respect and reverence is found in all men; and the feeling of right and wrong is found in all men. The feeling of commiseration is what we call humanity; the feeling of shame and dislike is what we call righteousness; the feeling of respect and reverence is what we call propriety (*li*); and the feeling of right and wrong is what we call wisdom. Humanity, righteousness, propriety, and wisdom are not drilled into us from outside. We originally have them with us. Only we do not think [to find them]. Therefore it is said, 'Seek

"The Book of Mencius." In A Source Book in Chinese Philosophy, *trans., ed. Wing-Tsit Chan. Princeton, NJ: Princeton University Press, 1963, Chapter 3.*

and you will find it, neglect and you will lose it.' [Men differ in the development of their endowments], some twice as much as others, some five times, and some, to an incalculable degree, because no one can develop his original endowment to the fullest extent. The *Book of Odes* says, 'Heaven produces the teeming multitude. As there are things there are their specific principles. When the people keep their normal nature they will love excellent virtue.' Confucius said, 'The writer of this poem indeed knew the Way (Tao). Therefore as there are things, there must be their specific principles, and since people keep to their normal nature, therefore they love excellent virtue.'"

6A:7. Mencius said, "In good years most of the young people behave well. In bad years most of them abandon themselves to evil. This is not due to any difference in the natural capacity endowed by Heaven. The abandonment is due to the fact that the mind is allowed to fall into evil. Take for instance the growing of wheat. You sow the seeds and cover them with soil. The land is the same and the time of sowing is also the same. In time they all grow up luxuriantly. When the time of harvest comes, they are all ripe. Although there may be a difference between the different stalks of wheat, it is due to differences in the soil, as rich or poor, to the unequal nourishment obtained from the rain and the dew, and to differences in human effort. Therefore all things of the same kind are similar to one another. Why should there be any doubt about men? The sage and I are the same in kind. Therefore Lung Tzu said, 'If a man makes shoes without knowing the size of people's feet, I know that he will at least not make them to be like baskets.' Shoes are alike because people's feet are alike. There is a common taste for flavor in our mouths. I-ya was the first to know our common taste for food. Suppose one man's taste for flavor is different from that of others, as dogs and horses differ from us in belonging to different species, then why should the world follow I-ya in regard to flavor? Since in the matter of flavor the whole world regards I-ya as the standard, it shows that our tastes for flavor are alike. The same is true of

our ears. Since in the matter of sounds the whole world regards Shih-k'uang as the standard, it shows that our ears are alike. The same is true of our eyes. With regard to Tzu-tu, none in the world did not know that he was handsome. Any one who did not recognize his handsomeness must have no eyes. Therefore I say there is a common taste for flavor in our mouths, a common sense for sound in our ears, and a common sense for beauty in our eyes. Can it be that in our minds alone we are not alike? What is it that we have in common in our minds? It is the sense of principle and righteousness (*i-li*, moral principles). The sage is the first to possess what is common in our minds. Therefore moral principles please our minds as beef and mutton and pork please our mouths."

6A:8. Mencius said, "The trees of the Niu Mountain were once beautiful. But can the mountain be regarded any longer as beautiful since, being in the borders of a big state, the trees have been hewed down with axes and hatchets? Still with the rest given them by the days and nights and the nourishment provided them by the rains and the dew, they were not without buds and sprouts springing forth. But then the cattle and the sheep pastured upon them once and again. That is why the mountain looks so bald. When people see that it is so bald, they think that there was never any timber on the mountain. Is this the true nature of the mountain? Is there not [also] a heart of humanity and righteousness originally existing in man? The way in which he loses his originally good mind is like the way in which the trees are hewed down with axes and hatchets. As trees are cut down day after day, can a mountain retain its beauty? To be sure, the days and nights do the healing, and there is the nourishing air of the calm morning which keeps him normal in his likes and dislikes. But the effect is slight, and is disturbed and destroyed by what he does during the day. When there is repeated disturbance, the restorative influence of the night will not be sufficient to preserve (the proper goodness of the mind). When the influence of the night is not sufficient to preserve it, man becomes not much different from the beast. People see that he acts like an animal, and think that he never had the original endowment (for goodness).

But is that his true character? Therefore with proper nourishment and care, everything grows, whereas without proper nourishment and care, everything decays. Confucius said, "Hold it fast and you preserve it. Let it go and you lose it. It comes in and goes out at no definite time and without anyone's knowing its direction." He was talking about the human mind.

. . .

2A:6.   Mencius said, "All men have the mind which cannot bear [to see the suffering of] others. The ancient kings had this mind and therefore they had a government that could not bear to see the suffering of the people. When a government that cannot bear to see the suffering of the people is conducted from a mind that cannot bear to see the suffering of others, the government of the empire will be as easy as making something go round in the palm.

"When I say that all men have the mind which cannot bear to see the suffering of others, my meaning may be illustrated thus: Now, when men suddenly see a child about to fall into a well, they all have a feeling of alarm and distress, not to gain friendship with the child's parents, nor to seek the praise of their neighbors and friends, nor because they dislike the reputation [of lack of humanity if they did not rescue the child]. From such a case, we see that a man without the feeling of commiseration is not a man; a man without the feeling of shame and dislike is not a man; a man without the feeling of deference and compliance is not a man; and a man without the feeling of right and wrong is not a man. The feeling of commiseration is the beginning of humanity; the feeling of shame and dislike is the beginning of righteousness; the feeling of deference and compliance is the beginning of propriety; and the feeling of right and wrong is the beginning of wisdom. Men have these Four Beginnings just as they have their four limbs. Having these Four Beginnings, but saying that they cannot develop them is to destroy themselves. When they say that their ruler cannot develop them, they are destroying their ruler. If anyone with these Four Beginnings in him knows how to give them the fullest extension and development, the result will be like fire beginning to burn or a spring beginning to shoot forth. When they are fully developed, they will be sufficient to protect all people within the four seas (the world). If they are not developed, they will not be sufficient even to serve one's parents."

Study Questions

1. What does Mencius mean by the claim that "all men have a mind which cannot bear to see the suffering of others"? What other explanations of our feelings does he discard?

2. What are the four innate feelings in humans? On what principles are they based? How are they related to morality? What is the role of education regarding these feelings?

3. What are Mencius' and Kao Tzu's positions regarding human nature? How does each account for human goodness and badness?

4. How does Mencius account for the difference in morality among humans? What does he claim is common in all humans? How does he support this claim? What assumptions does he make?

5. How does Mencius account for the presence of evil? Is his explanation consistent with his claim that human nature is originally good?

Suggestions for Further Reading

Carr, B., and I. Mahalingam, eds. *Companion Encyclopedia of Asian Philosophy* (London; New York: Routledge, 1997). See Part IV, "Chinese Philosophy," especially H. Nansen's "Confucius and Confucianism" and R. Sheng Wang's "Morals and Society in Chinese Philosophy."

Deutsch, E., and R. Bonteke, eds. *A Companion to World Philosophies* (Cambridge, MA; Oxford: Blackwell, 1997). See T. Weiming's "Chinese Philosophy: A Synoptic View," S. Kwong-Loi's "Ideas of the Good in Chinese Philosophy," and especially P. J. Ivanhoe's "Human Beings and Nature in Traditional Chinese Thought."

Singer, P., ed. *A Companion to Ethics* (Oxford; Cambridge, MA; Oxford: Blackwell, 1997). See T. Weiming's "Chinese Philosophy: A Synoptic View" and C. Hansen's "Classical Chinese Ethics."

Chai, Ch'u, and Winberg Chai. *Confucianism* (Woodbury, NY: Barron's Educational Series, 1973). Chapter 3 offers an overview of Mencius' philosophy.

Ivanhoe, P. J. *Ethics in the Confucian Tradition: The Thought of Mencius and Wang Yang-Ming* (Atlanta: Scholar's Press, 1990). A five-chapter comparative study. See Chapter II, "Human Nature: Mencius."

Verwilghen, A. F. *Mencius: The Man and His Ideas* (New York: St. John's University Press, 1967). An eight-chapter general introduction to Mencius' character and thought.

Yu-Lan, Fung. *A History of Chinese Philosophy*, Volume I, trans. D. Boddes (Princeton, NJ: Princeton University Press, 1952). See Chapter VI, "Mencius and His School of Confucianism," especially Part 4, "The Goodness of Human Nature."

Hsün Tzu (c. 320– c. 238 B.C.E.)

Hsün Tzu was born in the state of Chao, in what is today the province of Shansi, in north central China. His original name was Hsün K'uang but he is better known as Hsün Tzu (Master Hsün). There is no certainty about his biographical dates, but it is known that he traveled to Ch'i, where he was a distinguished scholar and was thrice honored as officer for sacrificial ceremonies. He left Ch'i, after being the object of slander, and went to Ch'u, where he served as a magistrate. After losing this position, he continued teaching until his death.

Hsün Tzu is the third member of the triumvirate of ancient Chinese sages that includes Confucius and Mencius. The positions of these three Chinese philosophers has been compared to that of the Greek philosophers Socrates, Plato, and Aristotle. Hsün Tzu made significant philosophical contributions in dialectic, epistemology, law, logic, and psychology. His influence lasted until the ninth century C.E. and then resurged in the twelfth century and is still strong in contemporary Chinese philosophy.

Hsün Tzu's philosophy is labeled "naturalistic Confucianism"; he represents the opposite wing to Mencius' idealistic Confucianism. Whereas Confucius did not explicitly state his position on human nature, Mencius argued that humans are originally good. Hsün Tzu counterargued that the nature of humans is evil and that goodness is acquired only through training. In Hsün Tzu's view, humans in their natural state have instinctual drives that are selfish, anarchic, and antisocial. However, our intelligence distinguishes us from animals and allows us to realize that we cannot survive in our natural state. Thus, humans must undergo a civilizing process, thereby becoming socialized through education and law. Hsün Tzu insisted that goodness is the result of *wei,* which in its narrow sense means "artificial," but is more broadly understood as "man's activity." In this sense, he proposed that goodness is not a result of natural conditions but is created by humans, is a product of human activity.

According to Hsün Tzu, sages are the ones who strive to make "the crooked straight"; that is, to formulate rules of propriety (*li*) to control social conduct. For him, Confucian morality, with its emphasis on humaneness and righteousness, is the proper basis for society and for the socialization of the originally evil human nature. Though he disagreed with Mencius' basic tenet on our original goodness, like Mencius and Confucius, Hsün Tzu stressed the importance of education in the cultivation of morality. However, whereas Confucius and Mencius conceived of the Way of Heaven (*T'ien-tao* or *Tian-dao*) in terms of an all-embracing moral law, order or principle, Hsün Tzu saw it merely as a natural law ruling almost mechanically and without moral purpose over the universe.

Unlike the works of Confucius and Mencius, which were sayings and conversations compiled by disciples, *The Hsün Tzu* was written by Hsün Tzu himself. It comprises thirty-two chapters, with various headings under which he writes essays on different topics. In the following selection, from Chapter 23, he writes on his conception of our evil nature by taking Mencius as his main opponent. Hsün Tzu elaborates his position on evil by describing human nature and its negative consequences. Defending his conception that goodness is the result of *wei*, he also argues for the need for education and law in the moral cultivation of humans.

THE NATURE OF MAN IS EVIL

THE NATURE OF MAN is evil; his goodness is the result of his activity.[1] Now, man's inborn nature is to seek for gain. If this tendency is followed, strife and rapacity result and deference and compliance disappear. By inborn nature one is envious and hates others. If these tendencies are followed, injury and destruction result and loyalty and faithfulness disappear. By inborn nature one possesses the desires of ear and eye and likes sound and beauty. If these tendencies are followed, lewdness and licentiousness result, and the pattern and order of propriety and righteousness disappear. Therefore to follow man's nature and his feelings will inevitably result in strife and rapacity, combine with rebellion and disorder, and end in violence. Therefore there must be the civilizing influence of teachers and laws and the guidance of propriety and righteousness, and then it will result in deference and compliance, combine with pattern and order, and end in discipline. From this point of view, it is clear that the nature of man is evil and that his goodness is the result of activity.

---

[1]According to Yang Liang, *wei* (artificial) is "man's activity." It means what is created by man and not a result of natural conditions. This is accepted by most commentators, including Hao I-hsing, who has pointed out that in ancient times *wei* (ordinarily meaning false or artificial) and *wei* (activity) were interchangeable.

Hsün Tzu. "*The Nature of Man Is Evil.*" *In* A Source Book in Chinese Philosophy, *trans., ed. Wing-Tsit Chan. Princeton, NJ: Princeton University Press, 1963, Chapter 6.*

Crooked wood must be heated and bent before it becomes straight. Blunt metal must be ground and whetted before it becomes sharp. Now the nature of man is evil. It must depend on teachers and laws to become correct and achieve propriety and righteousness and then it becomes disciplined. Without teachers and laws, man is unbalanced, off the track, and incorrect. Without propriety and righteousness, there will be rebellion, disorder, and chaos. The sage-kings of antiquity, knowing that the nature of man is evil, and that it is unbalanced, off the track, incorrect, rebellious, disorderly, and undisciplined, created the rules of propriety and righteousness and instituted laws and systems in order to correct man's feelings, transform them, and direct them so that they all may become disciplined and conform with the Way (Tao). Now people who are influenced by teachers and laws, accumulate literature and knowledge, and follow propriety and righteousness are superior men, whereas those who give rein to their feelings, enjoy indulgence, and violate propriety and righteousness are inferior men. From this point of view, it is clear that the nature of man is evil and that his goodness is the result of his activity. . . .

Mencius said, "Man learns because his nature is good." This is not true. He did not know the nature of man and did not understand the distinction between man's nature and his effort. Man's nature is the product of Nature; it cannot be learned and cannot be worked for. Propriety and righteousness are produced by the sage. They can be learned by men and can be accomplished through work. What is in man but cannot be learned or worked for is his nature. What is in him and can be learned or accomplished through work is what can be achieved through activity. This is the difference between human nature and human activity. Now by nature man's eye can see and his ear can hear. But the clarity of vision is not outside his eye and the distinctness of hearing is not outside his ear. It is clear that clear vision and distinct hearing cannot be learned. Mencius said, "The nature of man is good; it [becomes evil] because man destroys his original nature." This is a mistake. By nature

man departs from his primitive character and capacity as soon as he is born, and he is bound to destroy it. From this point of view, it is clear that man's nature is evil.

By the original goodness of human nature is meant that man does not depart from his primitive character but makes it beautiful, and does not depart from his original capacity but utilizes it, so that beauty being [inherent] in his primitive character and goodness being [inherent] in his will are like clear vision being inherent in the eye and distinct hearing being inherent in the ear. Hence we say that the eye is clear and the ear is sharp. Now by nature man desires repletion when hungry, desires warmth when cold, and desires rest when tired. This is man's natural feeling. But now when a man is hungry and sees some elders before him, he does not eat ahead of them but yields to them. When he is tired, he dares not seek rest because he wants to take over the work [of elders]. The son yielding to or taking over the work of his father, and the younger brother yielding to or taking over the work of his older brother—these two lines of action are contrary to original nature and violate natural feeling. Nevertheless, the way of filial piety is the pattern and order of propriety and righteousness. If one follows his natural feeling, he will have no deference or compliance. Deference and compliance are opposed to his natural feelings. From this point of view, it is clear that man's nature is evil and that his goodness is the result of his activity.

Someone may ask, "If man's nature is evil, whence come propriety and righteousness?" I answer that all propriety and righteousness are results of the activity of sages and not originally produced from man's nature. The potter pounds the clay and makes the vessel. This being the case, the vessel is the product of the artisan's activity and not the original product of man's nature. The artisan hews a piece of wood and makes a vessel. This being the case, the vessel is the product of the artisan's activity and not the original product of man's nature. The sages gathered together their ideas and thoughts and became familiar with activity, facts, and principles, and thus produced propriety and righteousness and instituted laws and systems. This being the case, propriety and righteousness, and laws and systems are the products of the activity of the sages and not the original products of man's nature.

As to the eye desiring color, the ear desiring sound, the mouth desiring flavor, the heart desiring gain, and the body desiring pleasure and ease—all these are products of man's original nature and feelings. They are natural reactions to stimuli and do not require any work to be produced. But if the reaction is not naturally produced by the stimulus but requires work before it can be produced, then it is the result of activity. Here lies the evidence of the difference between what is produced by man's nature and what is produced by his effort. Therefore the sages transformed man's nature and aroused him to activity. As activity was aroused, propriety and righteousness were produced, and as propriety and righteousness were produced, laws and systems were instituted. This being the case, propriety, righteousness, laws, and systems are all products of the sages. In his nature, the sage is common with and not different from ordinary people. It is in his effort that he is different from and superior to them.

It is the original nature and feelings of man to love profit and seek gain. Suppose some brothers are to divide their property. If they follow their natural feelings, they will love profit and seek gain, and thus will do violence to each other and grab the property. But if they are transformed by the civilizing influence of the pattern and order of propriety and righteousness, they will even yield to outsiders. Therefore, brothers will quarrel if they follow their original nature and feeling but, if they are transformed by righteousness and propriety, they will yield to outsiders.

People desire to be good because their nature is evil. If one has little he wants abundance. If he is ugly, he wants good looks. If his circumstances are narrow, he wants them to be broad. If poor, he wants to be rich. And if he is in a low position, he wants a high position. If he does not have it himself, he will seek it outside. If he is rich, he does not desire more wealth, and if he is in a high position, he does not desire more power. If he has it himself, he will not seek it outside. From this point of view, [it is clear that] people desire to be good because their nature is evil.

Now by nature a man does not originally possess propriety and righteousness; hence he makes strong effort to learn and seeks to have them. By nature he does not know propriety and righteousness; hence he thinks and deliberates and seeks to know them. Therefore, by what is inborn alone, man will not have or know propriety and righteousness. There will be disorder if man is without propriety and righteousness. There will be violence if he does not know propriety and righteousness. Consequently by what is inborn alone, disorder and violence are within man himself. From this point of view, it is clear that the nature of man is evil and that his goodness is the result of his activity.

Mencius said, "The nature of man is good." I say that this is not true. By goodness at any time in any place is meant true principles and peaceful order, and by evil is meant imbalance, violence, and disorder. This is the distinction between good and evil. Now do we honestly regard man's nature as characterized by true principles and peaceful order? If so, why are sages necessary and why are propriety and righteousness necessary? What possible improvement can sages make on true principles and peaceful order?

Now this is not the case. Man's nature is evil. Therefore the sages of antiquity, knowing that man's nature is evil, that it is unbalanced and incorrect, and that it is violent, disorderly, and undisciplined, established the authority of rulers to govern the people, set forth clearly propriety and righteousness to transform them, instituted laws and governmental measures to rule them, and made punishment severe to restrain them, so that all will result in good order and be in accord with goodness. Such is the government of sage-kings and the transforming influence of propriety and righteousness.

But suppose we try to remove the authority of the ruler, do away with the transforming influence of propriety and righteousness, discard the use of laws and governmental measure, do away with the restraint and punishment, and stand and see how people of the world deal with one another. In this situation, the strong would injure the weak and rob them, and the many would do violence to the few and shout them down. The whole world would be in violence and disorder and all would perish in an instant. From this point of view, it is clear that man's nature is evil and that his goodness is the result of his activity.

The man versed in ancient matters will certainly support them with evidences from the present, and he who is versed in [the principles of] Nature will certainly support them with evidences from the world of men. In any discussion, the important things are discrimination[2] and evidence. One can then sit down and talk about things, propagate them, and put them into practice. But now Mencius said that man's nature is good. He had neither discrimination nor evidence. He sat down and talked about the matter but rose and could neither propagate it nor put it into practice. Is this not going too far? Therefore if man's nature is good, sage-kings can be done away with and propriety and righteousness can be stopped. But if his nature is evil, sage-kings are to be followed and propriety and righteousness are to be greatly valued. For bending came into existence because there was crooked wood, the carpenter's square and ruler came into existence because things are not straight, and the authority of rule is instituted and propriety and righteousness are made clear because man's nature is evil. From this point of view, it is clear that man's nature is evil and that his goodness is the result of his activity. Straight wood does not depend on bending to become straight; it is straight by nature. But crooked wood must be bent and heated before it becomes straight because by nature it is not straight. Now, the nature of man is evil. It has to depend on the gov-

ernment of sage-kings and the transforming influence of propriety and righteousness, and then all will result in good order and be in accord with goodness. From this point of view, it is clear that man's nature is evil and that his goodness is the result of his activity.

The questioner may say, "It is by the nature of man that propriety and righteousness [can be produced] through accumulated effort and hence the sages can produce them." I answer that this is not true. The potter pounds the clay and produces the piece of pottery. Is the pottery [inherent] in the nature of the potter? The artisan hews wood and produces a vessel. Is the vessel [inherent] in the nature of the artisan? What the sages have done to propriety and righteousness is analogous to the potter's pounding and producing the pottery. This being the case, is it by the original nature of man that propriety and righteousness are produced through accumulated effort? With reference to the nature of man, it is the same in (sage-emperors) Yao and Shun, (wicked king) Chieh, and (robber) Chih.[3] It is the same in the superior or inferior man. If propriety and righteousness are products of accumulated effort and to be regarded as [inherent] in man's nature, then why are Yao and (sage-king) Yü highly honored, and why is the superior man highly honored? Yao, Yü, and the superior man are highly honored because they can transform nature and arouse effort. As effort is aroused, propriety and righteousness are produced. Thus the relation between the sages and propriety and righteousness produced through accumulated effort, is like the potter pounding the clay to produce the pottery. From this point of view, is it by the nature of man that propriety and righteousness are produced through accumulated effort? Chieh, Chih, and the inferior man are despised because they give rein to their nature, follow their feelings, and enjoy indulgence, and lead to the greed for gain, to quarrels and rapacity. It is clear that man's nature is evil and that his goodness is the result of his activity.

[2]According to Yang Liang and Wang Hsien-ch'ien, *pien-ho* literally means bamboo split into two pieces and yet coming together perfectly. Hence, the idea of analysis and discrimination.

[3]Chih was a notorious robber of ancient times.

Heaven is not partial to Tseng, Ch'ien, and Hsiao-i[4] and negligent to the common multitude. Then why did Tseng, Ch'ien, and Hsiao-i alone abundantly demonstrate the actuality of filial piety and preserve its good name? It is because they observed propriety and righteousness to the fullest extent. Heaven is not partial to the people of Ch'i and Lu[5] and negligent to the people of Ch'in.[6] Then why is it that in the righteous relation between father and son and the distinction of function between husband and wife,

[4]Tseng Ts'an, Min Tzu-ch'ien (both of whom were pupils of Confucious), and Hsiao-i (crown prince of 14th century B.C.), were all distinguished by their filial deeds.

[5]The state of Ch'i produced virtuous rulers and Lu was the native state of Confucious.

[6]Ch'in was a barbarian state which eventually overthrew the Chou, united China, and set up a dictatorship in the third century B.C.

the people of Ch'in are inferior to those of Ch'i and Lu in filial piety and in the mutual respect between husband and wife? It is because the people of Ch'in give rein to their nature and feelings, enjoy indulgence, and neglect propriety and righteousness. Is it because their natures are different?

"Any man in the street can become (sage-king) Yü."[7] What does this ancient saying mean? I say that Yü became sage-king Yü because he practiced humanity, righteousness, laws, and correct principles. This shows that these can be known and practiced. Every man in the street possesses the faculty to know them and the capacity to practice them. This being the case, it is clear that every man can be Yü.

[7]Compare this ancient saying with *Mencius,* 6B:2, to the effect that all men would become Yaos and Shuns.

Study Questions

1. What are Hsün Tzu's arguments against Mencius? Where does he think Mencius goes astray?

2. How does Hsün Tzu defend his claim that the nature of man is evil? What characterizes our evil nature? What follows from our original nature and feelings?

3. What does Hsün Tzu mean when he states that goodness is the result of man's activities? What is the significance of education and law?

4. What does Hsün Tzu understand by "nature"? How does he define "good and evil"?

5. What is Hsün Tzu's view of morality? How does he defend the need for morality? Does he explain how it is possible for humans to be good and to judge things in moral terms?

Suggestions for Further Reading

Carr, B., and I. Mahalingam, eds. *Companion Encyclopedia of Asian Philosophy* (London; New York: Routledge, 1997). See Part IV, "Chinese Philosophy," especially H. Nansen's "Confucius and Confucianism" and R. Sheng Wang's "Morals and Society in Chinese Philosophy."

Deutsch, E., and R. Bonteke, eds. *A Companion to World Philosophies* (Cambridge, MA; Oxford: Blackwell, 1997). See T. Weiming's "Chinese Philosophy: A Synoptic View," S. Kwong-Loi's "Ideas of the Good in Chinese Philosophy," and especially P. J. Ivanhoe's "Human Beings and Nature in Traditional Chinese Thought."

Dubs, H. H. *Hsüntze, the Moulder of Ancient Confucianism* (London: Arthur Probsthain, 1927; New York: Paragon, 1966). A comprehensive introduction to Hsün Tzu's thought in sixteen chapters. See especially Chapter VI, "Human Nature."

Singer, P., ed. *A Companion to Ethics* (Oxford; Cambridge, MA: Blackwell, 1991). See C. Hansen's "Classical Chinese Ethics."

Yu-Lan, Fung. *A History of Chinese Philosophy, Volume I,* trans. D. Boddes (Princeton, NJ: Princeton University Press, 1952). See Chapter XII, "Hsün Tzu and His School of Confucianism," especially Part 4, "Heaven and Human Nature."

The Dhammapada (THIRD CENTURY B.C.E.)

The Dhammapada forms part of the Pali canon, a collection of sacred Buddhist scriptures from the Theravada school (school of the Elders), written in the ancient Pali language. After the Buddha's death in 483 B.C.E., his followers assembled in the "First Council," where they decided to have his disciple Ananda repeat the Buddha's teachings. *The Dhammapada* is one of the canonical texts issued from Ananda's reports as they were compiled in the "Minor Collection" belonging to the "Basket of Discourses." The Pali version is one of various renditions of *The Dhammapada*. It was introduced into Ceylon by Buddhists during the third century B.C.E. and was put in written form probably during the first century C.E. In its finished form, it contains 423 verses divided into twenty-six chapters. According to the tradition of Theravada Buddhism, each one of these verses was spoken by the Buddha in response to a specific event.

The Pali word *dhamma,* like the Sanskrit word *dharma,* has the root meaning of "righteousness, virtue, or truth," while the word *pada* means "foot," "step," or "path." Thus, the title *Dhammapada* literally means "path of righteousness, virtue, or truth." The text itself provides spiritual guidance for right living, for living one's life in accordance with the teachings of the Buddha. In this sense, it offers a moral code that directs the follower on the path of spiritual perfection. The end is to achieve what in Pali is called *nibbana* and in Sanskrit *nirvana.* Literally meaning "blowing out," *nirvana* signifies the attainment of enlightenment through the extinction of passions and selfish desires. Viewed in purely negative terms, it denotes the absence of craving, while in its positive characterization it refers to a spiritual awakening.

In accordance with the Buddha's doctrine of the Four Noble Truths, suffering is inherent in existence. It is caused by cravings, but can cease with the renunciation of all cravings. Release can be attained by following the Eightfold Path of right living. Conditioned by ignorance, we become attached to our selves and mistakenly believe that our freedom lies in the fulfillment of our desires. However, the Buddha taught that the path of liberation is found through the control of and detachment from the self, and the cessation of cravings. The Buddha's teachings contained in *The Dhammapada* offer practical guidelines for achieving wisdom by understanding the law of causality that conditions existence. In addition, it provides us with specific instructions on how to conduct ourselves to attain the ultimate liberation, *nirvana.*

In verse 183 of *The Dhammapada,* the Buddha issues a simple prescription summarizing his message to us: "Do not what is evil, do what is good. Keep your mind pure. This is the teaching of the Buddha." This is a simple but not easy task. As the Buddha notes in verse 163, "it is very difficult to do what is right, to do what is good for oneself." Doing what is right and good requires detachment from the self. On the other hand, evil deeds are marked by an attachment to the self and lead to more attachment. Actions take place during our existence and bear their fruits of suffering or joy from one lifetime to another. The path of spiritual perfection to *nirvana* directs us toward the final liberation, the ultimate release from *samsara*—the wheel of life, death, and rebirth. Crossing the stream of existence, those who achieve *nirvana* rise above the goodness and evil that characterize our actions. Thus, good deeds ultimately lead us beyond good and evil.

THE DHAMMAPADA

1

CONTRARY WAYS

1   What we are today comes from our thoughts of yesterday, and our present thoughts build our life of tomorrow: our life is the creation of our mind.

If a man speaks or acts with an impure mind, suffering follows him as the wheel of the cart follows the beast that draws the cart.

2   What we are today comes from our thoughts of yesterday, and our present thoughts build our life of tomorrow: our life is the creation of our mind.

If a man speaks or acts with a pure mind, joy follows him as his own shadow.

7   He who lives only for pleasures, and whose soul is not in harmony, who considers not the food he eats, is idle and has not the power of virtue—such a man is moved by MARA, is moved by selfish temptations, even as a weak tree is shaken by the wind.

8   But he who lives not for pleasures, and whose soul is in self-harmony, who eats or fasts with moderation, and has faith and the power of virtue—this man is not moved by temptations, as a great rock is not shaken by the wind.

11   Those who think the unreal is, and think the Real is not, they shall never reach the Truth, lost in the path of wrong thought.

12   But those who know the Real is, and know the unreal is not, they shall indeed reach the Truth, safe on the path of right thought.

20   Whereas if a man speaks but a few holy words and yet lives the life of those words, free from passion and hate and illusion—with right vision and a mind free, craving for nothing both now and hereafter—the life of this man is a life of holiness.

2

WATCHFULNESS

21   Watchfulness is the path of immortality: un-watchfulness is the path of death. Those who are watchful never die: those who do not watch are already as dead.

3

THE MIND

33   The mind is wavering and restless, difficult to guard and restrain: let the wise man straighten his mind as a maker of arrows makes his arrows straight.

39   But he whose mind in calm self-control is free from the lusts of desires, who has risen above good and evil, he is awake and has no fear.

4

THE FLOWERS OF LIFE

45   The wise student shall conquer this world, and the world of the gods, and also the world of Yama, of death and of pain. The wise student shall find the DHAMMAPADA, the clear Path of

Perfection, even as a man who seeks flowers finds the most beautiful flower:

54 The perfume of flowers goes not against the wind, not even the perfume of sandalwood, of rose-bay, or of jasmine; but the perfume of virtue travels against the wind and reaches unto the ends of the world.

55 There is the perfume of sandalwood, of rose-bay, of the blue lotus and jasmine; but far above the perfume of those flowers the perfume of virtue is supreme.

5

THE FOOL

60 How long is the night to the watchman; how long is the road to the weary; how long is the wandering of lives ending in death for the fool who cannot find the path!

62 'These are my sons. This is my wealth.' In this way the fool troubles himself. He is not even the owner of himself: how much less of his sons and of his wealth!

67 For that deed is not well done when being done one has to repent; and when one must reap with tears the bitter fruits of the wrong deed.

68 But the deed is indeed well done when being done one has not to repent; and when one can reap with joy the sweet fruits of the right deed.

6

THE WISE MAN

86 But those who when they know the law follow the path of the law, they shall reach the other shore and go beyond the realm of death.

7

INFINITE FREEDOM

90 The traveller has reached the end of the journey! In the freedom of the Infinite he is free from all sorrows, the fetters that bound him are thrown away, and the burning fever of life is no more.

93 Who can trace the invisible path of the man who soars in the sky of liberation, the infinite Void without beginning, whose passions are peace, and over whom pleasures have no power? His path is as difficult to trace as that of the birds in the air.

96 In the light of his vision he has found his freedom: his thoughts are peace, his words are peace and his work is peace.

8

BETTER THAN A THOUSAND

103–104–105 If a man should conquer in battle a thousand and a thousand more, and another man should conquer himself, his would be the greater victory, because the greatest of victories is the victory over oneself; amd neither the gods in heaven above nor the demons down below can turn into defeat the victory of such a man.

9

GOOD AND EVIL

116 Make haste and do what is good; keep your mind away from evil. If a man is slow in doing good, his mind finds pleasure in evil.

117 If a man does something wrong, let him not do it again and again. Let him not find pleasure in his sin. Painful is the accumulation of wrongdoings.

118 If a man does something good, let him do it again and again. Let him find joy in his good work. Joyful is the accumulation of good work.

121 Hold not a sin of little worth, thinking 'this is little to me'. The falling of drops of water will in time fill a water-jar. Even so the foolish man becomes full of evil, although he gather it little by little.

122 Hold not a deed of little worth, thinking 'this is little to me'. The falling of drops of water will in time fill a water-jar. Even so the wise man becomes full of good, although he gather it little by little.

10

LIFE

129   All beings tremble before danger, all fear death. When a man considers this, he does not kill or cause to kill.

130   All beings fear before danger, life is dear to all. When a man considers this, he does not kill or cause to kill.

131   He who for the sake of happiness hurts others who also want happiness, shall not hereafter find happiness.

132   He who for the sake of happiness does not hurt others who also want happiness, shall hereafter find happiness.

144   Have fire like a noble horse touched by the whip. By faith, by virtue and energy, by deep contemplation and vision, by wisdom and by right action, you shall overcome the sorrows of life.

11

BEYOND LIFE

153   I have gone round in vain the cycles of many lives ever striving to find the builder of the house of life and death. How great is the sorrow of life that must die! But now I have seen thee, housebuilder: never more.

12

SELF-POSSESSION

160   Only a man himself can be the master of himself: who else from outside could be his master? When the Master and servant are one, then there is true help and self-possession.

161   Any wrong or evil a man does, is born in himself and is caused by himself; and this crushes the foolish man as a hard stone grinds the weaker stone.

163   It is easy to do what is wrong, to do what is bad for oneself; but very difficult to do what is right, to do what is good for oneself.

165   By oneself the evil is done and it is oneself who suffers: by oneself the evil is not done, and by one's Self one becomes pure. The pure and the impure come from oneself: no man can purify another.

166   Let no man endanger his duty, the good of his soul, for the good of another, however great. When he has seen the good of his soul, let him follow it with earnestness.

13

ARISE! WATCH

169   Follow the right path: follow not the wrong path. He who follows the right path has joy in this world and in the world beyond.

170   When a man considers this world as a bubble of froth, and as the illusion of an appearance, then the king of death has no power over him.

171   Come and look at this world. It is like a royal painted chariot wherein fools sink. The wise are not imprisoned in the chariot.

173   He who oversomes the evil has done with the good he afterwards does, he sheds a light over the world like that of the moon when free from clouds.

14

THE BUDDHA

183   Do not what is evil. Do what is good. Keep your mind pure. This is the teaching of Buddha.

184   Forbearance is the highest sacrifice. NIRVANA is the highest good. This say the Buddhas who are awake. If a man hurts another, he is not a hermit; if he offends another, he is not an ascetic.

185   Not to hurt by deeds or words, self-control as taught in the Rules, moderation in food, the solitude of one's room and one's bed, and the practice of the highest consciousness: this is teaching of the Buddhas who are awake.

195–196   Who could measure the excellence of the man who pays reverence to those worthy of reverence, a Buddha or his disciples, who have left evil behind and have crossed the river of sorrow, who, free from all fear, are in the glory of NIRVANA?

15

JOY

202   There is no fire like lust. There is no evil like hate. There is no pain like disharmony. There is no joy like NIRVANA.

203   The hunger of passions is the greatest disease. Disharmony is the greatest sorrow. When you know this well, the[n] you know that NIRVANA is the greatest joy.

204   Health is the greatest possession. Contentment is the greatest treasure. Confidence is the greatest friend. NIRVANA is the greatest joy.

16

TRANSIENT PLEASURES

217   He who has virtue and vision, who follows DHAMMA, the Path of Perfection, whose words are truth, and does the work to be done—the world loves such a man.

17

FORSAKE ANGER

224   Speak the truth, yield not to anger, give what you can to him who asks: these three steps lead you to the gods.

248   Know this therefore, O man: that lack of self-control means wrongdoing. Watch that greediness and vice bring thee not unto long suffering.

251   There is no fire like lust, and no chains like those of hate. There is no net like illusion, and no rushing torrent like desire.

19

RIGHTEOUSNESS

256–257   A man is not on the path of righteousness if he settles matters in a violent haste. A wise man calmly considers what is right and what is wrong, and faces different opinions with truth, non-violence and peace. This man is guarded by truth and is a guardian of truth. He is righteous and he is wise.

267   But he who is above good and evil, who lives in chastity and goes through life in meditation, he in truth is called a Bhikkhu.

271–272   Not by mere morals or rituals, by much learning or high concentration, or by a bed of solitude, can I reach that joy of freedom which is not reached by those of the world. Mendicant! Have not self-satisfaction, the victory has not yet been won.

20

THE PATH

273   The best of the paths is the path of eight. The best of truths, the four sayings. The best of states, freedom from passions. The best of men, the one who sees.

285   Pluck out your self-love as you would pull off a faded lotus in autumn. Strive on the path of peace, the path of NIRVANA shown by Buddha.

21

WAKEFULNESS

292   By not doing what should be done, and by doing what should not be done, the sinful desires of proud and thoughtless men increase.

293   But those who are ever careful of their actions, who do not what should not be done, are those who are watchful and wise, and their sinful desires come to an end.

294   The followers of Buddha Gotama are awake and for ever watch; and ever by night and by day they remember the Truth of the Law.

22

IN DARKNESS

306   He who says what is not goes down the path of hell; and he who says he has not done what he knows well he has done. Both in the end have to suffer, because both sinned against truth.

314   Better to do nothing than do what is wrong, for wrongdoing brings burning sorrow. Do therefore what is right, for good deeds never bring pain.

316   Those who are ashamed when they should not be ashamed, and who are not ashamed when they should be, are men of very wrong views and they go the downward path.

317   Those who fear what they should not fear, and who do not fear what they should fear, are men of very wrong views and they go the downward path.

318   Those who think that right is wrong, and who think that wrong is right, they are the men of wrong views and they go the downward path.

319   But those who think that wrong is wrong, and think that right is right, they are the men of right views and they go on the upward path.

23

ENDURANCE

327   Find joy in watchfulness; guard well your mind. Uplift yourself from your lower self, even as an elephant draws himself out of a muddy swamp.

24

CRAVINGS

334   If a man watches not for NIRVANA, his cravings grow like a creeper and he jumps from death like a monkey in the forest from one tree without fruit to another.

335   And when his cravings overcome him, his sorrows increase more and more, like the entangling creeper called *birana*.

349   The man who is disturbed by wrong thoughts, whose selfish passions are strong and who only seeks sensuous pleasures, increases his craving desires and makes stronger the chains he forges for himself.

25

THE MONK

360   Good is the control of the eye, and good is the control of the ear; good is the control of smell, and good is the control of taste.

361   Good is the control of the body, and good is the control of words; good is the control of the mind, and good is the control of our whole inner life. When a monk has achieved perfect self-control, he leaves all sorrows behind.

362   The man whose hands are controlled, whose feet are controlled, whose words are controlled, who is self-controlled in all things, who finds the inner joy, whose mind is self-possessed, who is one and has found perfect peace—this man I call a monk.

364   Who abides in the truth of DHAMMA, whose joy is in the truth of DHAMMA, who ponders on DHAMMA, and remembers the truth of DHAMMA—this monk shall never fall from DHAMMA, from Truth.

367   Arise! Rouse thyself by thy Self; train thyself by thy Self. Under the shelter of thy Self, and ever watchful, thou shalt live in supreme joy.

26

THE BRAHMIN

412   He who in this world has gone beyond good and evil and both, who free from sorrows is free from passions and is pure—him I call a Brahmin.

417   He who is free from the bondage of men and also from the bondage of the gods: who is free from all things in creation—him I call a Brahmin.

423   He who knows the river of his past lives and is free from life that ends in death, who knows the joys of heaven and the sorrows of hell, for he is a seer whose vision is pure, who in perfection is one with the Supreme Perfection—him I call a Brahmin.

Study Questions

1. What criteria does *The Dhammapada* offer for distinguishing between good and evil actions? How are these criteria related?
2. What must one do to achieve self-control and detachment from the self? What is the moral and spiritual significance of these practices?
3. In what sense is moral conduct a spiritual matter? In what sense does it involve knowledge and wisdom? In what sense is it aimed toward joy and supreme bliss?
4. In what way is the path of perfection one of self-liberation? What responsibilities must we assume in following this path? Why?
5. Are good and evil portrayed as relative or absolute terms? What does it mean that the wise man rises above good and evil? What does it mean that *nirvana* is the highest good?

Suggestions for Further Reading

Carr, B., and I. Mahalingam, eds. *Companion Encyclopedia of Asian Philosophy* (London; New York: Routledge, 1997). See Part III, "Buddhist Philosophy."

Deutsch, E., and R. Bonteke, eds. *A Companion to World Philosophies* (Cambridge, MA; Oxford: Blackwell, 1997). See N. Smart's "Survey of Buddhist Thought" and P. D. Premasiri's "Ideas of the Good in Buddhist Philosophy."

Dharmasiri, G. *Fundamentals of Buddhist Ethics* (Antioch, CA: Golden Leaves, 1989). A detailed twelve-chapter introduction to the basic concepts of Buddhist ethics.

Kalupahana, D. J. *A Path of Righteousness—Dhammapada: An Introductory Essay, Together with the Pali Text, English Translation and Commentary* (Lanham, MD: University Press of America, 1986). Provides a scholarly and detailed analysis of the text.

Radhakrishnan, S. *The Dhammapada, with Introductory Essays, Pali Text, English Translation and Notes*, 2d ed. (London: Oxford University Press, 1958). Provides a long introduction and detailed comments to the text.

Rahula, W. *What the Buddha Taught* (New York: Grove Press, 1962). Contains a detailed analysis of the Four Noble Truths besides other Buddhist doctrines.

Santideva (685–763)

Santideva was an Indian Buddhist monk who was a scholar, philosopher, and Sanskrit poet. He learned the Buddhist teachings under the sage Manjusri and was ordained at the monastic university of Nalanda, in the state of Bihar in North India. Little is known with certainty about his life. According to legendary accounts, Santideva (like the Buddha) was a prince who renounced his royal status to adopt a religious lifestyle. While living at the monastery, he was challenged by his fellow monks to give a recitation before the assembly. They considered him lazy and wanted to teach him a lesson in discipline and humility. Asked to recite something new from a lecturing seat that was deliberately placed too high, Santideva magically lowered the seat and began to recite his *Bodhicaryavatara*. When he reached the ninth chapter, he ascended and disappeared into the sky, though his voice continued to be heard. After this experience, Santideva left the monastery, claiming he did not want to live in a place where appearances counted more than inner spiritual truth.

As a Buddhist monk, Santideva dedicated his life to practicing and reflecting on the teachings of the historical Buddha. The Buddha's doctrine of the impermanence of all things conveys the message that true spiritual liberation (*nirvana*) is attained through release from the illusion of a permanent self. Our belief in a self that is permanent and fixed lies at the root of our suffering. Our grasping after this illusory self and its desires leads us to a constant suffering through *samsara,* the cycle of repeated rebirths. We can attain release by following the path of "letting go" of our grasp and our search for a real self. The process of "letting go" involves understanding that there is no permanent self. It also requires us to discipline our minds and bodies to achieve the cessation of all desires.

There are different interpretations of the Buddha's doctrines and thus various versions of Buddhism. Santideva was a follower of Mahayana Buddhism, the version known as the "Great Way (or Vehicle) to Enlightenment." Mahayana Buddhism emerged in a contrast with what it identifies as the "Lesser Way (or Vehicle) to Enlightenment," Hinayana Buddhism. The Hinayana version assigns central importance to the attainment of *nirvana* and extols the saintly life of the *arhat* (the Worthy One) as its ideal. Living a reclusive life of renunciation and the cultivation of wisdom through meditation, the *arhat* represents the culmination of human life for Hinayana Buddhism. Claiming that the *arhat* is still focused on the salvation of the individual self, Mahayana Buddhists argue that there is a higher ideal, the *bodhisattva* (enlightenment being), whose life is dedicated to helping others achieve spiritual liberation. Mahayana Buddhism thus emphasizes that compassion for the suffering of others is a greater or higher way to enlightenment in relation to *nirvana.* Having realized the impermanence of all things and reached beyond the stream of life and death (*samsara*), the *bodhisattva* returns for the benefit of all others who suffer because they have not "let go" of the illusory self and its desires. Hence, a *bodhisattva* vows: "When we have crossed the stream may we ferry others across, when we are liberated may we liberate others."

The title *Bodhicaryavatara* means "Introduction (*vatara*) to the Conduct (*carya*) that Leads to Enlightenment (*bodhi*)." In this book, Santideva outlines the path of the *bodhisattva* for those who have generated the Awakening Mind (*bodhicitta*). This includes those whose minds are resolved to move toward enlightenment and those who have already started the journey. Santideva portrays the path of the *bodhisattva* in terms of wisdom and compassion while he details the six perfections (*paramita*) to be attained. The perfection of wisdom (*prajnaparamita*)—insight into things as they really are—is necessary to complete the other five perfections (giving, morality, patience, vigor, and meditation). By following this path, we come to see that our concerns for the self are the cause of unhappiness. Since there is no real self, no real distinction between self and others exists; rather, there is a fundamental identity and equality. We can begin "to exchange self and others" by abandoning our selfishness. In comparison to the suffering of the many others, one's own happiness is irrelevant. "Exchanging self and others" involves embracing a life of selflessness, dedicated to the service of others and for the benefit of all. Thus, the pure altruism of the *bodhisattva* is manifested in a life of compassion for the suffering of all sentient beings.

THE BODHICARYAVATARA

Praise of the Awakening Mind

21. Immeasurable merit took hold of the well-intentioned person who thought 'Let me dispel the headaches of beings'.

22. What then of the person who longs to remove the unequalled agony of every single being and make their virtue infinite?

27. Worship of the Buddha is surpassed merely by the desire for the welfare of others; how much more so by the persistent effort for the complete happiness of every being?

28. Hoping to escape suffering, it is to suffering that they run. In the desire for happiness, out of delusion, they destroy their own happiness, like an enemy.

29. It satisfies with every happiness those starved of happiness, and cuts away oppressions from those oppressed in many ways.

30. It also drives off delusion. How could there be a holy man its equal, how such a friend, or how such merit?

31. Even if someone returns a favour, he is praised. What, then, can be said of the Bodhisattva, who does good without obligation?

32. People honour someone who gives alms to a few people, saying, 'He does good', because he contemptuously supports their life for half a day with a moment's gift of mere food.

33. What then of the one who offers to a limitless number of beings, throughout limitless time, the fulfilment of all desires, unending until the end of the sky and those beings?

Adopting the Awakening Mind

11. Abandonment of all is Enlightenment and Enlightenment is my heart's goal. If I must give up everything, better it be given to sentient beings.

17. I am the protector of the unprotected and the caravan-leader for travellers. I have become the boat, the causeway, and the bridge for those who long to reach the further shore.

Perfection of Meditative Absorption

90. At first one should meditate intently on the equality of oneself and others as follows: 'All equally experience suffering and happiness. I should look after them as I do myself.'

91. Just as the body, with its many parts from division into hands and other limbs, should be protected as a single entity, so too should this entire world which is divided, but undivided in its nature to suffer and be happy.

92. Even though suffering in me does not cause distress in the bodies of others, I should nevertheless find their suffering intolerable because of the affection I have for myself.

93. In the same way that, though I cannot experience another's suffering in myself, his suffering is hard for him to bear because of his affection for himself.

94. I should dispel the suffering of others because it is suffering like my own suffering. I

should help others too because of their nature as beings, which is like my own being.

95. When happiness is liked by me and others equally, what is so special about me that I strive after happiness only for myself?

96. When fear and suffering are disliked by me and others equally, what is so special about me that I protect myself and not the other?

97. If I give them no protection because their suffering does not afflict me, why do I protect my body against future suffering when it does not afflict me?

102. Without exception, no sufferings belong to anyone. They must be warded off simply because they are suffering. Why is any limitation put on this?

103. If one asks why suffering should be prevented, no one disputes that! If it must be prevented, then all of it must be. If not, then this goes for oneself as for everyone.

104. You may argue: compassion causes us so much suffering, why force it to arise? Yet when one sees how much the world suffers, how can this suffering from compassion be considered great?

105. If the suffering of one ends the suffering of many, then one who has compassion for others and himself must cause that suffering to arise.

108. Those who become oceans of sympathetic joy when living beings are released, surely it is they who achieve fulfilment. What would be the point in a liberation without sweetness?

109. In fact, though acting for the good of others, there is neither intoxication nor dismay, nor desire for the resulting reward, with a thirst solely for the well-being of others.

114. In the same way that the hands and other limbs are loved because they form part of the body, why are embodied creatures not likewise loved because they form part of the universe?

115. In the same way that, with practice, the idea of a self arose towards this, one's own body, though it is without a self, with prac-tice will not the same idea of a self develop towards others too?

116. Though acting like this for the good of others, there is neither intoxication nor dismay. Even after giving oneself as food, there arises no hope for reward.

117. Therefore, in the same way that one desires to protect oneself from affliction, grief, and the like, so an attitude of protective-ness and of compassion should be prac-tised towards the world.

120. Whoever longs to rescue quickly both himself and others should practise the supreme mystery: exchange of self and other.

125. 'If I give, what shall I enjoy?' Such concern for one's own welfare is fiendish. 'If I en-joy, what shall I give?' Such concern for the welfare of others is divine.

126. By oppressing another for one's own sake, one is roasted in hells, but by oppressing oneself for the sake of another, one meets with success in everything.

127. A bad rebirth, inferiority, and stupidity re-sult from the mere desire for self-advance-ment. By transferring that same desire to others, one achieves a good rebirth, hon-our, and intelligence.

128. By commanding another to one's own end one attains positions of servitude, whereas by commanding oneself to the benefit of others one attains positions of power.

129. All those who suffer in the world do so be-cause of their desire for their own happi-ness. All those happy in the world are so because of their desire for the happiness of others.

130. Why say more? Observe this distinction: between the fool who longs for his own advantage and the sage who acts for the advantage of others.

134. The calamities which happen in the world, the sufferings and fears, many as they are, they all result from clinging onto the no-tion of self, so what good is this clinging of mine?

135. If one does not let go of self one cannot let
go of suffering, as one who does not let go
of fire cannot let go of burning.

136. Therefore, in order to allay my own suffering and to allay the suffering of others, I
devote myself to others and accept them as
myself.

Dedication

5. As long as space abides and as long as the
world abides, so long may I abide, destroying the sufferings of the world.

Study Questions

1. What is the goal of the *bodhisattva*? How is it related to the welfare of all beings?
2. What is the moral importance of realizing the illusory nature of the self? How can
altruism and compassion arise from this realization? Why is the practice of meditation
required?
3. In what sense do "all equally experience suffering and happiness"? Why is it that "no suffering belongs to anyone"? How is the principle of "exchanging self and other" involved?
4. Why is our love for family and friends an obstacle for true compassion? Would all self-
love also prove to be a hindrance?
5. Do you think pure altruism and absolute selflessness is attainable?

Suggestions for Further Reading

Carr, B., and I. Mahalingam, eds. *Companion Encyclopedia of Asian Philosophy* (London;
New York: Routledge, 1997). See Part III, "Buddhist Philosophy."

Deutsch, E., and R. Bonteke, eds. *A Companion to World Philosophies* (Cambridge, MA;
Oxford: Blackwell, 1997). See N. Smart's "Survey of Buddhist Thought" and P. D. Premasiri's
"Ideas of the Good in Buddhist Philosophy."

Smith, J., ed. *Radiant Mind. Essential Buddhist Teachings and Texts* (New York: Riverhead
Books, 1999). See Section X, "Bodhisattvas," and K. Gyatso's contribution in Section X, "Enlightenment."

The Dalai Lama (Tenzin Gyatso). *A Flash of Lightning in the Dark of Night: A Guide to the
Bodhisattva's Way of Life* (Boston: Shambhala, 1994). Provides a section-by-section commentary on the text.

Williams, P. *Mahayana Buddhism: The Doctrinal Foundations* (London; New York: Routledge, 1989). See Chapter 9, "The Path of the *Bodhisattva*," especially the section "Compassion and the *Bodhicitta*."

Al-Ghazali (1058–1111)

Mohammed Ibn Mohammed Abu Hamid al-Ghazali, one of the most respected Islamic theologians and philosophers, was born at Tabaran, near Tus, in Persia. In his
philosophical autobiography, *The Deliverance from Error,* al-Ghazali characterized his

intellectual and spiritual development as one driven by the quest for absolutely certain knowledge. As a young man, he studied theology, jurisprudence, and Islamic mysticism (Sufism, from the Arabic word *suf* meaning "wool" for the garments worn by the mystics) under prominent theologians and religious leaders of the time. Endowed with a remarkable intelligence, al-Ghazali was appointed professor of theology in Baghdad when he was only thirty years old. He quickly became a renowned scholar. However, al-Ghazali grew increasingly dissatisfied with the powers of reason to afford indubitable certainty, and he became skeptical of the ability of theology and philosophy to attain truth on the basis of reason alone. Four years after his appointment, he suffered a physical and mental collapse and decided to abandon his prestigious career and renounce his wealth. In the midst of his spiritual crisis, al-Ghazali turned to Sufi mysticism and found that it offered the best way to truth through a form of apprehension higher than that of reason: "the immediate experience [*dhawq*—literally "tasting"] of God, by ecstasy and by a moral change." He spent the next ten years of his life in pilgrimage—to places like Damascus, Jerusalem, Medina, and Mecca—while cultivating an ascetic life. Though he later resumed his teaching at Nishapur, al-Ghazali soon retired from his professorship and founded a school in Tus, where he taught theology and Sufi doctrines until he died.

Al-Ghazali has been called the greatest Moslem after the prophet Mohammed, and he is entitled the "proof of Islam" (*Hujjat-al-Islam*). Considered the reformer or renewer (*Mujjadid*) of the fifth century of the Islamic era, al-Ghazali served as a bridge between Islamic theology and (predominantly ancient Greek) philosophy, and between orthodox (Ash'arite) theology and Sufi mysticism. Taking a critical approach to what he classified as the four kinds of "seekers" of truth (theologians, philosophers, authoritarians and mystics), al-Ghazali sought to establish a harmony among elements of reason, tradition, and faith. Aiming toward balance, he pointed to the limitations and excesses of each class of seekers while trying to preserve what was compatible with the fundamental principles of Islam.

Assessing theology in this fashion, al-Ghazali concluded that, though it attained its particular aim of preserving the creed of orthodoxy and defending it against heretics, it did not attain his own aim and was inadequate for his search for truth because it relied naïvely on unquestioned assumptions. In his famous *Incoherence of the Philosophers,* al-Ghazali also launched an attack against the metaphysical positions of philosophers—such as Aristotle, Ibn Sina or Avicenna, and al-Farabi—that were incompatible with Islamic orthodoxy by using their own techniques of thinking and showing how they led to inconsistencies. To the authoritarians, who held that the instructions of the *Imam,* or religious leader, were infallible, al-Ghazali responded by pointing to the prophet Mohammed as the only infallible authority while emphasizing the importance of independent reasoning and judgment. Finally, though he "learned with certainty" that "it is above all the mystics who walk on the path of God" and who "live the best life," al-Ghazali followed the Sufi mystic way while he remained a theologian and practiced his orthodox religious duties.

With its basis in the principles of Sufism, al-Ghazali's general moral theory is fundamentally religious and mystical without denying the relative value or usefulness of the intellect in attaining spiritual goals. The central concern of his ethics is to determine the path to well-being in the afterlife. The highest human end, happiness, is achieved only in the soul's vision of God in the hereafter. So, life in this world must involve a purification of the soul in its advance toward God. The cultivation of virtues conducive to the soul's purification, and the emphasis on the effects of our actions upon our soul, are thus among the crucial features of al-Ghazali's ethics. Ascetic and mystical practices help to break the soul's attachment to worldly things and bring it closer in its aspired nearness to God. However, the soul's love of God, divine love, is the highest stage in the spiritual path of our life in this world.

Al-Ghazali developed his ethics explicitly and systematically in his monumental magnum opus, *The Revival of the Religious Sciences,* but he offered an autobiographical account of his conversion to the mystical way in his *Deliverance from Error.* The following selection is taken from the latter book, where he offers a more personal insight into the spiritual basis of his moral theory. In this narrative of his soul's quest for absolute truth, he details the stages of his "deliverance from error" by pointing out the faults in three kinds of seekers of truth—theologians, philosophers, and authoritarians. It is only with the fourth kind of seekers—Sufi mystics—that he is able to find peace for his soul. Al-Ghazali's description of the mystical way thus outlines the basic moral principles for the path to well-being in the afterlife.

THE WAYS OF MYSTICISM

. . . WHEN I HAD FINISHED with these sciences, I next turned with set purpose to the method of mysticism (or Sufism). I knew that the complete mystic 'way' includes both intellectual belief and practical activity; the latter consists in getting rid of the obstacles in the self and in stripping off its base characteristics and vicious morals, so that the heart may attain to freedom from what is not God and to constant recollection of Him.

The intellectual belief was easier to me than the practical activity. I began to acquaint myself with their belief by reading their books, such as *The Food of the Hearts* by Abū Ṭālib al-Makkī (God have mercy upon him), the works of al-Ḥārith al-Muḥāsibī, the various anecdotes about al-Junayd, ash-Shiblī and Abū Yazīd al-Bisṭāmī (may God sanctify their spirits), and other discourses of their leading men. I thus compre-

hended their fundamental teachings on the intellectual side, and progressed, as far as is possible by study and oral instruction, in the knowledge of mysticism. It became clear to me, however, that what is most distinctive of mysticism is something which cannot be apprehended by study, but only by immediate experience (*dhawq*—literally 'tasting'), by ecstasy and by a moral change. What a difference there is between *knowing* the definition of health and satiety, together with their causes and presuppositions, and *being* healthy and satisfied! What a difference between being acquainted with the definition of drunkenness—namely, that it designates a state arising from the domination of the seat of the intellect by vapours arising from the stomach—and being drunk! Indeed, the drunken man while in that condition does not

Al-Ghazali. "The Ways of Mysticism." In Deliverance from Error and Attachment to the Lord of Might and Majesty, *trans. W. M. Watt. In* The Faith and Practice of Al-Ghazali. *London: Allen and Unwin, 1953.*

know the definition of drunkenness nor the scientific account of it; he has not the very least scientific knowledge of it. The sober man, on the other hand, knows the definition of drunkenness and its basis, yet he is not drunk in the very least. Again the doctor, when he is himself ill, knows the definition and causes of health and the remedies which restore it, and yet is lacking in health. Similarly there is a difference between knowing the true nature and causes and conditions of the ascetic life and actually leading such a life and forsaking the world.

I apprehended clearly that the mystics were men who had real experiences, not men of words, and that I had already progressed as far as was possible by way of intellectual apprehension. What remained for me was not to be attained by oral instruction and study but only by immediate experience and by walking in the mystic way.

Now from the sciences I had laboured at and the paths I had traversed in my investigation of the revelational and rational sciences (that is, presumably, theology and philosophy), there had come to me a sure faith in God most high, in prophethood (or revelation), and in the Last Day. These three credal principles were firmly rooted in my being, not through any carefully argued proofs, but by reason of various causes, coincidences and experiences which are not capable of being stated in detail.

It had already become clear to me that I had no hope of the bliss of the world to come save through a God-fearing life and the withdrawal of myself from vain desire. It was clear to me too that the key to all this was to sever the attachment of the heart to worldly things by leaving the mansion of deception and returning to that of eternity, and to advance towards God most high with all earnestness. It was also clear that this was only to be achieved by turning away from wealth and position and fleeing from all time-consuming entanglements.

Next I considered the circumstances of my life, and realized that I was caught in a veritable thicket of attachments. I also considered my activities, of which the best was my teaching and lecturing, and realized that in them I was dealing with sciences that were unimportant and contributed nothing to the attainment of eternal life.

After that I examined my motive in my work of teaching, and realized that it was not a pure desire for the things of God, but that the impulse moving me was the desire for an influential position and public recognition. I saw for certain that I was on the brink of a crumbling bank of sand and in imminent danger of hell-fire unless I set about to mend my ways.

I reflected on this continuously for a time, while the choice still remained open to me. One day I would form the resolution to quit Baghdad and get rid of these adverse circumstances; the next day I would abandon my resolution. I put one foot forward and drew the other back. If in the morning I had a genuine longing to seek eternal life, by the evening the attack of a whole host of desires had reduced it to impotence. Worldly desires were striving to keep me by their chains just where I was, while the voice of faith was calling, 'To the road! to the road! What is left of life is but little and the journey before you is long. All that keeps you busy, both intellectually and practically, is but hypocrisy and delusion. If you do not prepare *now* for eternal life, when will you prepare? If you do not now sever these attachments, when will you sever them?' On hearing that, the impulse would be stirred and the resolution made to take to flight.

Soon, however, Satan would return. 'This is a passing mood', he would say; 'do not yield to it, for it will quickly disappear; if you comply with it and leave this influential position, these comfortable and dignified circumstances where you are free from troubles and disturbances, this state of safety and security where you are untouched by the contentions of your adversaries, then you will probably come to yourself again and will not find it easy to return to all this'.

For nearly six months beginning with Rajab 488 A.H. (=July 1095 A.D.), I was continuously tossed about between the attractions of worldly desires and the impulses towards eternal life. In that month the matter ceased to be one of choice and became one of compulsion. God caused my tongue to dry up so that I was prevented from lecturing. One particular day I would make an effort to lecture in order to gratify the hearts of my following, but my tongue would not utter a single word nor could I accomplish anything at all.

This impediment in my speech produced grief in my heart, and at the same time my power to digest and assimilate food and drink was impaired; I could hardly swallow or digest a single mouthful of food. My powers became so weakened that the doctors gave up all hope of successful treatment. 'This trouble arises from the heart', they said, 'and from there it has spread through the constitution; the only method of treatment is that the anxiety which has come over the heart should be allayed'.

Thereupon, perceiving my impotence and having altogether lost my power of choice, I sought refuge with God most high as one who is driven to Him, because he is without further resources of his own. He answered me, He who 'answers him who is driven (to Him by affliction) when he calls upon Him' (Qur'an 27, 63). He made it easy for my heart to turn away from position and wealth, from children and friends. I openly professed that I had resolved to set out for Mecca, while privately I made arrangements to travel to Syria. I took this precaution in case the Caliph and all my friends should oppose my resolve to make my residence in Syria. This stratagem for my departure from Baghdad I gracefully executed, and had it in my mind never to return there. There was much talk about me among all the religious leaders of 'Iraq, since none of them would allow that withdrawal from such a state of life as I was in could have a religious cause, for they looked upon that as the culmination of a religious career; that was the sum of their knowledge.

Much confusion now came into people's minds as they tried to account for my conduct. Those at a distance from 'Iraq supposed that it was due to some apprehension I had of action by the government. On the other hand those who were close to the governing circles and had witnessed how eagerly and assiduously they sought

me and how I withdrew from them and showed no great regard for what they said, would say, 'This is a supernatural affair; it must be an evil influence which has befallen the people of Islam and especially the circle of the learned'.

I left Baghdad, then. I distributed what wealth I had, retaining only as much as would suffice myself and provide sustenance for my children. This I could easily manage, as the wealth of 'Iraq was available for good works, since it constitutes a trust fund for the benefit of the Muslims. Nowhere in the world have I seen better financial arrangements to assist a scholar to provide for his children.

In due course I entered Damascus, and there I remained for nearly two years with no other occupation than the cultivation of retirement and solitude, together with religious and ascetic exercises, as I busied myself purifying my soul, improving my character and cleansing my heart for the constant recollection of God most high, as I had learnt from my study of mysticism. I used to go into retreat for a period in the mosque of Damascus, going up the minaret of the mosque for the whole day and shutting myself in so as to be alone.

At length I made my way from Damascus to the Holy House (that is, Jerusalem). There I used to enter into the precinct of the Rock every day and shut myself in.

Next there arose in me a prompting to fulfil the duty of the Pilgrimage, gain the blessings of Mecca and Medina, and perform the visitation of the Messenger of God most high (peace be upon him), after first performing the visitation of al-Khalīl, the Friend of God (God bless him).[1] I therefore made the journey to the Hijaz. Before long, however, various concerns, together with the entreaties of my children, drew me back to my home (country); and so I came to it again, though at one time no one had seemed less likely than myself to return to it. Here, too, I sought

[1] That is, Abraham, who is buried in the cave of Machpelah under the mosque at Hebron, which is called 'al-Khalīl' in Arabic; similarly the visitation of the Messenger is the formal visit to his tomb at Medina.

retirement, still longing for solitude and the purification of the heart for the recollection (of God). The events of the interval, the anxieties about my family, and the necessities of my livelihood altered the aspect of my purpose and impaired the quality of my solitude, for I experienced pure ecstasy only occasionally, although I did not cease to hope for that; obstacles would hold me back, yet I always returned to it.

I continued at this stage for the space of ten years, and during these periods of solitude there were revealed to me things innumerable and unfathomable. This much I shall say about that in order that others may be helped: I learnt with certainty that it is above all the mystics who walk on the road of God; their life is the best life, their method the soundest method, their character the purest character; indeed, were the intellect of the intellectuals and the learning of the learned and the scholarship of the scholars, who are versed in the profundities of revealed truth, brought together in the attempt to improve the life and character of the mystics, they would find no way of doing so; for to the mystics all movement and all rest, whether external or internal, brings illumination from the light of the lamp of prophetic revelation; and behind the light of prophetic revelation there is no other light on the face of the earth from which illumination may be received.

In general, then, how is a mystic 'way' (*tarīqah*) described? The purity which is the first condition of it (*sc.* as bodily purity is the prior condition of formal Worship for Muslims) is the purification of the heart completely from what is other than God most high; the key to it, which corresponds to the opening act of adoration in prayer,[2] is the sinking of the heart completely in the recollection of God; and the end of it is complete absorption (*fanā*) in God. At least this is its end relatively to those first steps which almost

come within the sphere of choice and personal responsibility; but in reality in the actual mystic 'way' it is the first step, what comes before it being, as it were, the antechamber for those who are journeying towards it.

With this first stage of the 'way' there begin the revelations and visions. The mystics in their waking state now behold angels and the spirits of the prophets; they hear these speaking to them and are instructed by them. Later, a higher state is reached; instead of beholding forms and figures, they come to stages in the 'way' which it is hard to describe in language; if a man attempts to express these, his words inevitably contain what is clearly erroneous.

In general what they manage to achieve is nearness to God; some, however, would conceive of this as 'inherence' (*hulūl*), some as 'union' (*ittiḥād*), and some as 'connection' (*wuṣūl*). All that is erroneous. In my book, *The Noblest Aim*, I have explained the nature of the error here. Yet he who has attained the mystic 'state' need do no more than say:

Of the things I do not remember, what was, was;

Think it good; do not ask an account of it.

(Ibn al-Mu'tazz).

In general the man to whom He has granted no immediate experience at all, apprehends no more of what prophetic revelation really is than the name. The miraculous graces given to the saints are in truth the beginnings of the prophets; and that was the first 'state' of the Messenger of God (peace be upon him) when he went out to Mount Ḥirā', and was given up entirely to his Lord, and worshipped, so that the bedouin said, 'Muhammad loves his Lord passionately'.

Now this is a mystical 'state' which is realized in immediate experience by those who walk in the way leading to it. Those to whom it is not granted to have immediate experience can become assured of it by trial (*sc.* contact with mystics or observation of them) and by hearsay, if they have sufficiently numerous opportunities of associating with mystics to understand that (*sc.* ecstasy) with certainty by means of what accompanies the 'states'. Whoever sits in their company

---

[2]Literally, the 'prohibition', *taḥrīm;* the opening words of the Muslim Worship, 'God is great', are known as *takbīrat al-taḥrīm*, the prohibitory adoration, 'because it forbids to the worshipper what was previously allowable'. Cp. Calverley, *Worship in Islam*, p. 8, *etc.*

derives from them this faith; and none who sits in their company is pained.

Those to whom it is not even granted to have contacts with mystics may know with certainty the possibility of ecstasy by the evidence of demonstration, as I have remarked in the section entitled *The Wonders of the Heart* of my *Revival of the Religious Sciences*.

Certainty reached by demonstration is *knowledge* (*'ilm*); actual acquaintance with that 'state' is *immediate experience* (*dhawq*); the acceptance of it as probable from hearsay and trial (or observation) is *faith* (*īmān*). These are three degrees. 'God will raise those of you who have faith and those who have been given knowledge in degrees (*sc.* of honour)' (Q. 58, 12).

Behind the mystics, however, there is a crowd of ignorant people. They deny this fundamentally, they are astonished at this line of thought, they listen and mock. 'Amazing', they say. 'What nonsense they talk'! About such people God most high has said: 'Some of them listen to you, until, upon going out from you, they say to those to whom knowledge has been given, 'What did he say just now'? These are the people on whose hearts God sets a seal and they follow their passions'. (Q. 47, 18) He makes them deaf, and blinds their sight.

Among the things that necessarily became clear to me from my practice of the mystic 'way' was the true nature and special characteristics of prophetic revelation. The basis of that must undoubtedly be indicated in view of the urgent need for it.

Study Questions

1. What characterizes the practical activity of Sufism, according to al-Ghazali? How is it related to the method of immediate experience? What is the significance of this relation for al-Ghazali?

2. What is involved in walking in the mystic way, according to al-Ghazali? What is its ultimate goal? How does this goal determine the mystic way?

3. What does al-Ghazali see as the connection between the spiritual path and the sphere of choice and personal responsibility? How does the ascetic life fit into this framework?

4. Why does al-Ghazali consider the mystic way the best? Where does this way lead? Does he suggest that other ways can lead to the same? Does he suggest that the mystic way is open to everyone?

5. What is the spiritual significance of al-Ghazali's autobiographical account? What is its moral value?

Suggestions for Further Reading

Carr, B., and I. Mahalingam, eds. *Companion Encyclopedia of Asian Philosophy* (London; New York: Routledge, 1997). Part VI, "Islamic Philosophy," provides an introductory overview to Islamic philosophy in general. See especially W. M. Watt's essay, "Sufi Mysticism."

Deutsch, E., and R. Bonteke, eds. *A Companion to World Philosophies* (Cambridge, MA; Oxford: Blackwell, 1997). See T. Albertini's "Islamic Philosophy: An Overview" and especially M. Wahba's "The Concept of the Good in Islamic Philosophy."

Smith, M. *Al-Ghazali: The Mystic* (Lahore, India: Hijra International Publishers, 1983). Provides a biographical analysis of al-Ghazali and offers an account of his mystical teachings.

Sherif, M. A. *Ghazali's Theory of Virtue* (Albany: State University of New York Press, 1975). A detailed analysis of the different kinds of virtues emphasized in al-Ghazali's ethics.

Quasem, M. A. *The Ethics of Al-Ghazali: A Composite Ethics in Islam* (Delmar, NY: Caravan Books, 1978). A comprehensive introduction to al-Ghazali's moral theory in seven chapters.

Watt, W. M. *Muslim Intellectual: A Study of Al-Ghazali* (Edinburgh: Edinburgh University Press, 1971). An analysis of al-Ghazali's thought in its historical context and its relations to theology and philosophy.

Mohandas Gandhi (1869–1948)

Mohandas Karamchand Gandhi, the great spiritual leader, politician, and social activist known as *Mahatma* (Great Soul), was born at Porbandar, in Western India, into a traditional Hindu family. He studied law in London from 1887 to 1891 and returned to India to work as a lawyer. In 1893 he went to South Africa to work in an Indian firm, but later became actively involved in the struggle for the political rights of the Indians in South Africa. Toward the beginning of World War I, he returned to India with the conviction that his country was ready for *swaraj* (self-rule). Gandhi remained at the forefront of the independence movement for more than thirty years.

Ghandi devoted his life to the overall liberation of the Indian people; he organized social movements, founded religious communities (*ashrams*), provided grassroots education to develop the self-reliance and well-being of villagers, protested against the political and social injustices suffered by India's outcastes, the *Harijans* (untouchables), and participated in politics—often serving as mediator between the Indians and the British government and between Hindus and Moslems. A firm believer in the basic truth of Hinduism that all life is one, Gandhi perceived the political and social liberation of India, and his own task as leader, in fundamentally spiritual terms. In his view, the task of liberation was a religious duty of universal dimensions, for he saw the liberation of India as a step toward the liberation of humankind. Driven by his sense of mission, Gandhi was engaged in many activities, for which he was imprisoned, and often undertook fasting to induce others to change their ways. Though he lived to see India attain its independence from British rule in 1947, he disapproved of its division into separate Hindu and Moslem states. Almost a year later, he was assassinated by a Hindu extremist.

Gandhi's thought drew from both the Indian and the European traditions. The ancient teachings of Hinduism (particularly those contained in the *Bhagavad Gita*) and traditional Hindu beliefs provided a rich wellspring from which he developed his own ideas for a new India. He also found inspiration in Leo Tolstoy's idea of a religious socialism, Henry David Thoreau's notion of civil disobedience, and the Christian ideals contained in the New Testament. Unsurprisingly, Gandhi's life and teachings themselves influenced people from across the world, including figures such as Martin Luther King Jr. in his leadership of the civil rights movement, and the Dalai Lama's struggle for the liberation of Tibet.

A fundamental principle of Gandhi's teachings is that "Truth is God." Drawing attention to the Sanskrit word for truth, *satya,* and its derivation from the word for being, *sat,* Gandhi points out that "nothing is or exists in reality except Truth." Thus, he claims, "Truth is the most important name of God." It is no accident then that Gandhi entitled his autobiography *The Story of My Experiments with Truth.* There he relates his lifelong efforts to realize truth through various spiritual experiences and practices that emphasized self-discipline (*brahmachrya*) and self-reliance. Such experiments ranged from daily prayers and meditations to dietary regimens and fasts to learning various manual arts such as farming and hand-spinning. The personal, political, and spiritual were all intertwined in his striving "to see God face to face."

Gandhi was convinced that "the only means for the realization of Truth is *Ahimsa,*" that is, nonviolence. Nonviolence is not what is commonly understood as "passive resistance," but rather an active refusal to do harm, so that the test of truth is action. Moreover, for Gandhi, nonviolence is "not merely a negative state of harmlessness but it is a positive state of love, of doing good even to the evil-doer." Such love involves identifying oneself with everything that lives, and this can be accomplished only through self-purification. Gandhi believed that nonviolence is the "basic law of our being" and that violence is a corruption of the natural human state. Self-purification thus involves ridding our heart of violent tendencies as a way of restoring our fundamentally nonviolent nature. In this sense, *ahimsa* is a transformative force that reunites us with all that is, changing our selves, our relationships with others, and our environing world.

The term *satyagraha* was coined by Gandhi to identify his teachings. It means literally "holding on to Truth" and has often been translated as "truth-force" or "soul-force." As Gandhi explains it, "Truth (*Satya*) implies love and firmness (*Agraha*) engenders and therefore serves as a synonym for force." Thus, *satyagraha* is for him, "the Force which is born of Truth and Love or non-violence." It is an ethical and spiritual principle that translates into social and political action as a means of liberating, not only the oppressed, but also the oppressor. As such, it involves various nonviolent strategies to morally persuade others: through reason, self-suffering and self-sacrifice, and noncooperation or civil disobedience. In all this, Gandhi insisted that true nonviolence was not a "weapon of the weak" or a last resort for cowardice and impotence. Training for nonviolence requires the *satyagrahi* (follower of *satyagraha*) to learn "the art of dying" in order to become brave and overcome fear. *Satyagraha* thus belongs to the strong and courageous. It must be a "creed or a passion" coming from the heart, for truthfulness is needed to hold on to truth.

Gandhi expressed the "conviction that morality is the basis of things and that truth is the substance of all morality." His teachings on *satyagraha* as the force born of truth and nonviolence or love reflect this conviction. In this sense, the principles of nonviolence that he enunciates in the following selection are distinctively spiritual and moral principles. Nonviolence is thus a sacred duty. The true fulfillment of this sacred duty requires that we develop our spiritual courage and moral character.

GANDHI ON NON-VIOLENCE

THERE IS NO HALF WAY between truth and non-violence on the one hand and untruth and violence on the other. We may never be strong enough to be entirely non-violent in thought, word and deed. But we must keep non-violence as our goal and make steady progress towards it. The attainment of freedom, whether for a man, a nation or the world, must be in exact proportion to the attainment of non-violence by each.   I–58[1]

Non-violence is not a garment to be put on and off at will. Its seat is in the heart, and it must be an inseparable part of our very being.   I–61

The acquisition of the spirit of non-resistance is a matter of long training in self-denial and appreciation of the hidden forces within ourselves. It changes one's outlook on life. . . . It is the greatest force because it is the highest expression of the soul.   I–63

If one is to combat the fetish of force, it will only be by means totally different from those in vogue among the pure worshippers of brute force.   I–65

Principles

Non-violence implies as complete self-purification as is humanly possible.

Man for man the strength of non-violence is in exact proportion to the ability, not the will, of the non-violent person to inflict violence.

The power at the disposal of a non-violent person is always greater than he would have if he were violent.

[1]References throughout are to the two-volume edition of *Non-Violence in Peace and War*, published by Navajivan Publishing House, Ahmedabad, 1948.

There is no such thing as defeat in non-violence.   I–111

Ahimsa (Non-Violence)

It is the only true force in life.   I–114

This is the only permanent thing in life, this is the only thing that counts; whatever effort you bestow on mastering it is well spent.   I–114

If love or non-violence be not the law of our being, the whole of my argument falls to pieces.   I–121

When the practice of *ahimsa* becomes universal, God will reign on earth as He does in heaven.   I–121

I know this cannot be proved by argument. It shall be proved by persons living it in their lives with utter disregard of consequences in themselves.   I–122

Given the proper training and proper generalship, non-violence can be practiced by the masses of mankind.   I–168

Non-violence is the supreme law. During my half a century of experience I have not yet come across a situation when I had to say that I was helpless, that I had no remedy in terms of non-violence.   I–172

Belief in non-violence is based on the assumption that human nature in its essence is one and therefore unfailingly responds to the advances of love. . . . The non-violent technique does not depend for its success on the goodwill of the dictators, for a non-violent resister depends on the unfailing assistance of God which sustains him throughout difficulties which would otherwise be considered insurmountable.   I–175

Merton, T., ed. Gandhi on Non-Violence: A Selection from the Writings of Mahatma Gandhi. *Canada: New Directions, 1964.*

Jesus lived and died in vain if He did not teach us to regulate the whole of life by the eternal law of love.   I–181

If one does not practice non-violence in one's personal relations with others and hopes to use it in bigger affairs, one is vastly mistaken. . . . Mutual forbearance is not non-violence. Immediately you get the conviction that non-violence is the law of life, you have to practice it towards those who act violently towards you; and the law must apply to nations as to individuals. If the conviction is there, the rest will follow.   I–187

My optimism rests on my belief in the infinite possibilities of the individual to develop non-violence. The more you develop it in your own being, the more infectious it becomes till it overwhelms your surroundings and by and by might oversweep the world.   I–190

I believe that a state can be administered on a non-violent basis if the vast majority of the people are non-violent. So far as I know, India is the only country which has a possibility of being such a state. I am conducting my experiment in that faith.   I–265

[In non-violence] the bravery consists in dying, not in killing.   I–265

For me non-violence is a creed. I must act up to it whether I am alone or have companions. Since propaganda of non-violence is the mission of my life, I must pursue it in all weathers.   I–275

Non-violence, which is a quality of the heart, cannot come by an appeal to the brain.   I–276

I claim to be a passionate seeker after truth, which is but another name for God. In the course of that search the discovery of non-violence came to me. Its spread is my life mission. I have no interest in living except for the prosecution of that mission.   I–282

There will never be an army of perfectly non-violent people. It will be formed of those who will honestly endeavor to observe non-violence.   I–300

Those who are attracted to non-violence should, according to their ability and opportunity, join the experiment.   I–307

Man as animal is violent but as spirit is non-violent. The moment he awakes to the spirit within he cannot remain violent. Either he progresses towards *ahimsa* or rushes to his doom.   I–311

In the empire of non-violence every true thought counts, every true voice has its full value.   I–399

The first principle of non-violent action is that of non-cooperation with everything humiliating.   II–53

One has to speak out and stand up for one's convictions. Inaction at a time of conflagration is inexcusable.   II–56

To lay down one's life for what one considers to be right is the very core of *satyagraha*.   II–59

The sword of the *satyagrahi* is love, and the unshakable firmness that comes from it.   II–59

Non-violence is not a cover for cowardice, but it is the supreme virtue of the brave. . . . Cowardice is wholly inconsistent with non-violence. . . . Non-violence presupposes ability to strike.   II–59

He who cannot protect himself or his nearest and dearest or their honor by non-violently facing death, may and ought to do so by violently dealing with the oppressor. He who can do neither of the two is a burden.   I–77

It is better to be violent, if there is violence in our hearts, than to put on the cloak of non-violence to cover impotence. Violence is any day preferable to impotence. There is hope for a violent man to become non-violent. There is no such hope for the impotent.   I–240

Ahimsa is an attribute of the brave. Cowardice and *ahimsa* do not go together any more than water and fire.   I–243

I want the non-violence of the weak [many] to become the non-violence of the brave. It may be a dream, but I have to strive for its realization.   I–245

War is an unmitigated evil. But it certainly does one good thing. It drives away fear and brings bravery to the surface.   I–270

The votary of non-violence has to cultivate his capacity for sacrifice of the highest type in order to be free from fear. . . . He who has not overcome all fear cannot practice *ahimsa* to perfection. The votary of *ahimsa* has only one fear, that is of God. He who seeks refuge in God ought to have a glimpse of the *Atman* [the transcendent self] that transcends the body; and the moment one has glimpsed the imperishable *Atman* one sheds the love of the perishable body. . . . Violence is needed for the protection of things external; non-violence is needed for the protection of the *Atman*, for the protection of one's honor.   I–335

[Injustice must be resisted.] No doubt the non-violent way is always the best, but where that does not come naturally the violent way is both necessary and honorable. Inaction here is rank cowardice and unmanly. It must be shunned at all cost.   I–402

If the people are not ready for the exercise of the non-violence of the brave, they must be ready for the use of force in self-defense. There should be no camouflage. . . . it must never be secret.   II–146

To take the name of non-violence when there is a sword in your heart is not only hypocritical and dishonest but cowardly.   II–153

There is nothing more demoralizing than fake non-violence of the weak and impotent.   II–153

Study Questions

1. What is the meaning of *satyagraha* for Gandhi? What does it require? Why?
2. What is the meaning of *ahimsa* for Gandhi? How is it related to *satyagraha*?
3. What does nonviolence require? Why? When is violence preferable over nonviolence? What is the difference between true and false nonviolence? What results can each form of nonviolence bring about?
4. How are Gandhi's principles of nonviolence related to his conception of human nature? How do they serve as a basis for his ideas of social and political liberation?
5. Is nonviolence an effective means of overcoming social, political, and personal oppression? Why?

Suggestions for Further Reading

Bondurant, J. V. *Conquest of Violence: The Gandhian Philosophy of Conflict,* rev. ed. (Princeton, NJ: Princeton University Press, 1988). See Chapters 1 and 2 for a general introductory view of Gandhi's philosophy.

Datta, D. M. *The Philosophy of Mahatma Gandhi* (Madison: University of Wisconsin Press, 1961). See Chapter 3, "Morals, Society, and Politics," and Chapter 4, "Moral Leadership of the World."

Maitra, S. K. *The Ethics of Hindus* (New Delhi: Asian Publication Services, 1978, c. 1925 University of Calcutta). An analytical exposition of Hindu ethics. See especially Part I, "The Objective and Social Ethics of the Hindus: Classification of the Duties."

Merton, T., ed. *Gandhi on Non-Violence: A Selection from the Writings of Mahatma Gandhi.* (New York: New Directions, 1965). See especially "Gandhi and the One-Eyed Giant."

Ray, B. G. *Gandhian Ethics* (Ahmedabad: Navajivan Publishing, 1950). A four-chapter basic systematic introduction to Gandi's ethics. (The text is hard to find.)

Richards, G. *The Philosophy of Gandhi: A Study of His Basic Ideas* (London and Dublin: Curzon Press; Totowa, NJ: Barnes and Noble Books, 1982). See Chapters I–III for various aspects of Gandhi's concept of truth. See Chapter IV for his conception of *satyagraha.*

Thich Nhat Hanh (1926–)

Thich Nhat Hanh, the renowned Buddhist Zen monk, poet, and peace activist, was born in Nguyen Xuan Bao, in South Vietnam. The word *Thich* is a title meaning "reverend," while the words *Nhat Hanh* mean "one action." When he was ordained in 1949 at the Bao Quoc Institute, Nhat Hanh chose his name to evoke a venerated monk named *Van Hanh* (meaning "ten thousand actions") to highlight his particular need to focus on one thing. He studied at Saigon University and Princeton, has taught at the Sorbonne and Columbia, and has lectured widely throughout the world.

A prolific writer, with over seventy-five published books, Nhat Hanh is also the founder of the Van Hanh University, along with a number of schools, orders, and temples. During the Vietnam War, he acquired international recognition as a socially active Buddhist committed to the struggle for peace and the ending of political oppression. He was nominated in 1967 for the Nobel Peace Prize by Martin Luther King Jr., who claimed that "Thich Nhat Hanh's ideas for peace, if applied, would build a momentum to ecumenism, to world brotherhood, to humanity." He has lived in exile since 1966 and is currently living in Plum Village, a Buddhist retreat center in southwestern France.

As a major representative of "engaged Buddhism," Thich Nhat Hanh has followed a path that applies spiritual principles to social action. The Buddha's First Noble Truth, that all existence is suffering, is the starting point for engaged Buddhists in their effort to put an end to suffering. In their view, the social and political context must be taken into account if we are to understand the specific causes of suffering and the ways to eradicate them. Moreover, the spiritual duties to practice and propagate the teachings of the Buddha are always performed within a world conditioned by social and political forces. Hence, these Buddhists claim that in order to accomplish their religious obligations, they have the duty to engage in nonviolent action to change these conditions. The main impulse to this sense of duty is compassion for all those involved, not only for the victims. This is because the opposing sides are but different aspects of one and the same reality. Their aim is thus to work for the liberation of all others by going to the root of their suffering and helping them attain a reconciliation.

In "The Sun in My Heart," Thich Nhat Hanh develops his ethics of deep ecology based on the principles of Buddhism. Following the Buddhist doctrine of nondualism, which denies the reality of distinctions between self and nonself, he underscores the true oneness of the universe. According to his principle of "interbeing," diverse individual appearances (phenomena) are all interconnected in the unity of existence. All beings—humans, animals, plants, and minerals—exist interdependently, "inter-are." Our interpenetration with our environment ought to instill in us respect, humility, mindfulness, unconditional love, and compassion toward all other beings. In this sense, Thich Nhat Hanh's environmental ethics proposes a deep and universal ecology. The Buddha taught that our attachment to the notion of a permanent, fixed, eternal self prevents us from attaining spiritual liberation. For Thich Nhat Hanh, this attachment illustrates the obstacles in the way of our caring for the Earth. In order to practice an environmentalist ethics, we must break our bonds to this illusory self and become one with our environment. Thus, Thich Nhat Hanh stresses the importance of meditating on the oneness of the universe and in conducting our lives mindful of our interbeing with all that exists.

THE SUN IN MY HEART

. . . WE HAVE TO remember that our body is not limited to what lies within the boundary of our skin. Our body is much more immense. We know that if our heart stops beating, the flow of our life will stop, but we do not take the time to notice the many things outside of our bodies that are equally essential for our survival. If the ozone layer around our Earth were to disappear for even an instant, we would die. If the sun were to stop shining, the flow of our life would stop. The sun is our second heart, our heart outside of our body. It gives all life on Earth the warmth necessary for existence. Plants live thanks to the sun. Their leaves absorb the sun's energy, along with carbon dioxide from the air, to produce food for the tree, the flower, the plankton. And thanks to plants, we and other animals can live. All of us—people, animals, plants, and minerals—"consume" the sun, directly and indirectly. We cannot begin to describe all the effects of the sun, that great heart outside of our body. . . .

There is no phenomenon in the universe that does not intimately concern us, from a pebble resting at the bottom of the ocean, to the movement of a galaxy millions of light years away. Walt Whitman said, "I believe a blade of grass is no less than the journey-work of the stars . . ." These words are not philosophy. They come from the depths of his soul. He also said, "I am large, I contain multitudes."

This might be called a meditation on "interbeing endlessly interwoven." All phenomena are interdependent. When we think of a speck of dust, a flower, or a human being, our thinking cannot break loose from the idea of unity, of one, of calculation. We see a line drawn between one and many, one and not one. But if we truly realize the interdependent nature of the dust, the flower, and the human being, we see that unity cannot exist without diversity. Unity and diversity interpenetrate each other freely. Unity is diversity, and diversity is unity. This is the principle of interbeing.

Reprinted from Love in Action: Writings on Nonviolent Social Change *(1993) by Thich Nhat Hanh, with permission of Parallax Press, Berkeley, California.*

If you are a mountain climber or someone who enjoys the countryside or the forest, you know that forests are our lungs outside of our bodies. Yet we have been acting in a way that has allowed millions of square miles of land to be deforested, and we have also destroyed the air, the rivers, and parts of the ozone layer. We are imprisoned in our small selves, thinking only of some comfortable conditions for this small self, while we destroy our large self. If we want to change the situation, we must begin by being our true selves. To be our true selves means we have to *be* the forest, the river, and the ozone layer. If we visualize ourselves as the forest, we will experience the hopes and fears of the trees. If we don't do this, the forests will die, and we will lose our chance for peace. When we understand that we inter-are with the trees, we will know that it is up to us to make an effort to keep the trees alive. In the last twenty years, our automobiles and factories have created acid rain that has destroyed so many trees. Because we inter-are with the trees, we know that if they do not live, we too will disappear very soon.

We humans think we are smart, but an orchid, for example, knows how to produce noble, symmetrical flowers, and a snail knows how to make a beautiful, well-proportioned shell. Compared with their knowledge, ours is not worth much at all. We should bow deeply before the orchid and the snail and join our palms reverently before the monarch butterfly and the magnolia tree. The feeling of respect for all species will help us recognize the noblest nature in ourselves.

An oak tree is an oak tree. That is all an oak tree needs to do. If an oak tree is less than an oak tree, we will all be in trouble. In our former lives, we were rocks, clouds, and trees. We have also been an oak tree. This is not just Buddhist; it is scientific. We humans are a young species. We were plants, we were trees, and now we have become humans. We have to remember our past existences and be humble. We can learn a lot from an oak tree.

All life is impermanent. We are all children of the Earth, and, at some time, she will take us back to herself again. We are continually arising from Mother Earth, being nurtured by her, and then returning to her. Like us, plants are born, live for a period of time, and then return to the Earth. When they decompose, they fertilize our gardens. Living vegetables and decomposing vegetables are part of the same reality. Without one, the other cannot be. After six months, compost becomes fresh vegetables again. Plants and the Earth rely on each other. Whether the Earth is fresh, beautiful, and green, or arid and parched depends on the plants.

It also depends on us. Our way of walking on the Earth has a great influence on animals and plants. We have killed so many animals and plants and destroyed their environments. Many are now extinct. In turn, our environment is now harming us. We are like sleepwalkers, not knowing what we are doing or where we are heading. Whether we can wake up or not depends on whether we can walk mindfully on our Mother Earth. The future of all life, including our own, depends on our mindful steps.

Birds' songs express joy, beauty, and purity, and evoke in us vitality and love. So many beings in the universe love us unconditionally. The trees, the water, and the air don't ask anything of us; they just love us. Even though we need this kind of love, we continue to destroy them. By destroying the animals, the air, and the trees, we are destroying ourselves. We must learn to practice unconditional love for all beings so that the animals, the air, the trees, and the minerals can continue to be themselves.

Our ecology should be a deep ecology—not only deep, but universal. There is pollution in our consciousness. Television, films, and newspapers are forms of pollution for us and our children. They sow seeds of violence and anxiety in us and pollute our consciousness, just as we destroy our environment by farming with chemicals, clear-cutting the trees, and polluting the water. We need to protect the ecology of the Earth and the ecology of the mind, or this kind of violence and recklessness will spill over into even more areas of life.

Our Earth, our green beautiful Earth is in danger, and all of us know it. Yet we act as if our daily lives have nothing to do with the situation of the world. If the Earth were your body, you would be able to feel many areas where she is suffering. Many people are aware of the world's suffering, and their hearts are filled with compassion. They know what needs to be done, and they engage in political, social, and environmental work to try to change things. But after a period of intense involvement, they become discouraged, because they lack the strength needed to sustain a life of action. Real strength is not in power, money, or weapons, but in deep, inner peace.

If we change our daily lives—the way we think, speak, and act—we change the world. The best way to take care of the environment is to take care of the environmentalist.

Many Buddhist teachings help us understand our interconnectedness with our Mother, the Earth. One of the deepest is the *Diamond Sutra,* which is written in the form of a dialogue between the Buddha and his senior disciple, Subhuti. It begins with this question by Subhuti: "If daughters and sons of good families wish to give rise to the highest, most fulfilled, awakened mind, what should they rely on and what should they do to master their thinking?" This is the same as asking, "If I want to use my whole being to protect life, what methods and principles should I use?"

The Buddha answers, "We have to do our best to help every living being cross the ocean of suffering. But after all beings have arrived at the shore of liberation, no being at all has been carried to the other shore. If you are still caught up in the idea of a self, a person, a living being, or a life span, you are not an authentic bodhisattva." Self, person, living being, and life span are four notions that prevent us from seeing reality.

Life is one. We do not need to slice it into pieces and call this or that piece a "self." What we call a self is made only of non-self elements. When we look at a flower, for example, we may think that it is different from "non-flower" things. But when we look more deeply, we see that everything in the cosmos is in that flower.

Without all of the non-flower elements—sunshine, clouds, earth, minerals, heat, rivers, and consciousness—a flower cannot be. That is why the Buddha teaches that the self does not exist. We have to discard all distinctions between self and non-self. How can anyone work to protect the environment without this insight?

The second notion that prevents us from seeing reality is the notion of a person, a human being. We usually discriminate between humans and non-humans, thinking that we are more important than other species. But since we humans are made of non-human elements, to protect ourselves we have to protect all of the non-human elements. There is no other way. If you think, "God created man in His own image and He created other things for man to use," you are already making the discrimination that man is more important than other things. When we see that humans have no self, we see that to take care of the environment (the non-human elements) is to take care of humanity. The best way to take good care of men and women so that they can be truly healthy and happy is to take care of the environment.

I know ecologists who are not happy in their families. They work hard to improve the environment, partly to escape family life. If someone is not happy within himself, how can he help the environment? That is why the Buddha teaches that to protect the non-human elements is to protect humans, and to protect humans is to protect non-human elements.

The third notion we have to break through is the notion of a living being. We think that we living beings are different from inanimate objects, but according to the principle of interbeing, living beings are comprised of non-living-being elements. When we look into ourselves, we see minerals and all other non-living-being elements. Why discriminate against what we call inanimate? To protect living beings, we must protect the stones, the soil, and the oceans. Before the atomic bomb was dropped on Hiroshima, there were many beautiful stone benches in the parks. As the Japanese were rebuilding their city, they discovered that these stones were dead, so they carried them away and buried them. Then they brought in live stones. Do not think these things are not alive. Atoms are always moving. Electrons move at nearly the speed of light. According to the teaching of Buddhism, these atoms and stones are consciousness itself. That is why discrimination by living beings against non-living beings should be discarded.

The last notion is that of a life span. We think that we have been alive since a certain point in time and that prior to that moment, our life did not exist. This distinction between life and non-life is not correct. Life is made of death, and death is made of life. We have to accept death; it makes life possible. The cells in our body are dying every day, but we never think to organize funerals for them. The death of one cell allows for the birth of another. Life and death are two aspects of the same reality. We must learn to die peacefully so that others may live. This deep meditation brings forth non-fear, non-anger, and non-despair, the strengths we need for our work. With non-fear, even when we see that a problem is huge, we will not burn out. We will know how to make small, steady steps. If those who work to protect the environment contemplate these four notions, they will know how to be and how to act.

Study Questions

1. What is the significance of the title "The Sun in My Heart"? What Buddhist principles underlie this idea? How is it related to the notion of an ecology that is both deep and universal?

2. How does the principle of interbeing serve as an account of phenomena? What theory of human nature does it propose? In what ways are humans connected to all other beings?

3. Why is it necessary to change our conceptions of our body and our selves? What changes must occur in our conduct and attitudes toward our environment? Why? What is the significance of meditation?

4. How has our attachment to the notions of self, person, living being, and life span brought us to the brink of ecological disaster? Given our attachment, do you think it is possible for us to identify with our environment?

5. From the Buddhist perspective, good/evil and right/wrong are not absolute but relative terms. We mistakenly apply these terms to phenomena that are conditioned through an infinite chain of causes and effects. Is Thich Nhat Hanh's environmental ethics consistent with this Buddhist principle?

Suggestions for Further Reading

Badiner, A. H., ed. *Dharma Gaia: A Harvest of Essays in Buddhism and Ecology* (Berkeley, CA: Parallax Press, 1990). Contains thirty-three essays on various aspects of Buddhist ecology.

Callicot, J. B., and R. T. Ames, eds. *Nature in Asian Traditions of Thought: Essays in Environmental Philosophy* (Albany: State University of New York Press, 1989). A collection of essays on Asian (Chinese, Japanese, Buddhist, and Indian) environmental philosophy.

Carr, B., and I. Mahalingam, eds. *Companion Encyclopedia of Asian Philosophy* (London; New York: Routledge, 1997). See S. MacFarlane's "Morals and Society in Buddhism," F. J. Hoffman's "Contemporary Buddhist Philosophy," and especially P. de Silva and T. Ling's "Buddhism in Sri Lanka and south-east Asia."

Deutsch, E., and R. Bonteke, eds. *A Companion to World Philosophies* (Cambridge, MA; Oxford: Blackwell, 1997). See M. Yusa's "Contemporary Buddhist Philosophy."

Eppsteiner, F., ed. *The Path of Compassion: Writings on Socially Engaged Buddhism,* 2d. rev. ed. (Berkeley, CA: Parallax Press, 1988). A collection of essays on various aspects of socially engaged Buddhism, including one by Thich Nhat Hanh.

King, S. B. "Thich Nhat Hanh and the Unified Buddhist Church of Vietnam: Nondualism in Action." In *Engaged Buddhism: Buddhist Liberation Movements in Asia* (Albany: State University of New York Press, 1996). See especially pp. 338–342.

Part 3

Contemporary Cultural Perspectives

Kwame Nkrumah (1909–1972)

Kwame Nkrumah, one of Africa's most influential political leaders, who came to be known as the "Gandhi of Africa," was born in Nakroful, in the Gold Coast. He was the first prime minister of the Gold Coast, in 1952. In 1957, he became the first president of Ghana, the newly independent state combining the Gold Coast with the British Togoland. A steadfast advocate of pan-Africanism, before and after independence, Nkrumah supported the idea of a unified Africa with newly liberated societies firmly grounded in the traditional principles of their precolonial heritage. His books, which include *Ghana: An Autobiography, Towards Colonial Freedom, I Speak of Freedom, Africa Must Unite,* and *Consciencism,* develop the moral, political, and economic ideals of African unification, liberation, and socialism.

Nkrumah received his formal education at Achimota College, the Universities of Lincoln and Pennsylvania, and the London School of Economics. He lived in the United States for almost ten years while he studied and taught. In the introduction to his book *Consciencism,* Nkrumah explains that he decided to live in the United States because it "came to appeal to me as a Western country which stood refreshingly untainted by territorial colonialism." Nkrumah saw this time as "a crucial period in the development of my philosophical conscience." This development entailed recognizing that a "colonial student," like himself, "does not by origin belong to the intellectual history" of the European tradition. However, the student can become "so seduced" by this tradition that he "surrenders his whole personality." This means that he "loses sight of the fundamental social fact that he is a colonial subject" and "omits to draw from his education . . . anything which he might relate to the very real problem of colonial domination." Thus, Nkrumah counts himself as one of those African students with a philosophical conscience who, "animated by a lively national consciousness, sought knowledge as an instrument of national emancipation and integrity."

In the selection below, Nkrumah develops some of the main points supporting his idea of "philosophical consciencism," which interconnects thought and practice in the effort to attain the social liberation of Africa. Nkrumah argues that philosophy must find its roots in the traditional African conscience, plant itself firmly in the realities of African society, and become actively involved in its revolutionary transformation. Claiming that traditional African conscience upholds the ideal of socialist egalitarianism, he contends that philosophical consciencism must aim toward its restitution of that ideal in present African society.

Nkrumah elaborates on the metaphysical, ethical, political, and socioeconomic principles that must underlie philosophical consciencism. He claims that traditional African thought espouses the metaphysical theory that reality is ultimately matter in a constantly evolving tension of opposing forces that are alive. In the social realm, this translates into the ethical and political principles of egalitarianism, for if reality (matter) is basically one and the same, then human beings are naturally equal. From the objective fact of human equality, the general ethical principle that follows is that all humans ought to be treated as ends in themselves and never as means only. The implementation of such principle into the socioeconomic and political structures would produce a socialist egalitarian African society. Thus, Nkrumah proposes that philosophical consciencism must follow this moral ideal in its struggle toward a just African society.

CONSCIENCISM

PRACTICE WITHOUT THOUGHT IS BLIND; thought without practice is empty. The three segments of African society which I specified in the last chapter, the traditional, the Western, and the Islamic, co-exist uneasily; the principles animating them are often in conflict with one another. I have in illustration tried to show how the principles which inform capitalism are in conflict with the socialist egalitarianism of the traditional African society.

What is to be done then? I have stressed that the two other segments, in order to be rightly seen, must be accommodated only as experiences of the traditional African society. If we fail to do this our society will be racked by the most malignant schizophrenia.

Our attitude to the Western and the Islamic experience must be purposeful. It must also be guided by thought, for practice without thought is blind. What is called for as a first step is a body of connected thought which will determine the general nature of our action in unifying the society which we have inherited, this unification to take account, at all times, of the elevated ideals underlying the traditional African society. Social revolution must therefore have, standing firmly behind it, an intellectual revolution, a revolution in which our thinking and philosophy are directed towards the redemption of our society. Our philosophy must find its weapons in the environment and living conditions of the African people. It is from those conditions that the intellectual content of our philosophy must be created. The emancipation of the African continent is the emancipation of man. This requires two aims: first, the restitution of the egalitarianism of human society, and, second, the logistic mobilization of all our resources towards the attainment of that restitution.

The philosophy that must stand behind this social revolution is that which I have once referred to as philosophical consciencism; consciencism is the map in intellectual terms of the disposition of forces which will enable African society to digest the Western and the Islamic and the Euro-Christian elements in Africa, and develop them in such a way that they fit into the African personality. The African personality is itself defined by the cluster of humanist principles which underlie the traditional African society. Philosophical consciencism is that philosophical standpoint which, taking its start from the present content of the African conscience, indicates the way in which progress is forged out of the conflict in that conscience.

Its basis is in materialism. The minimum assertion of materialism is the absolute and independent existence of matter. Matter, however, is also a plenum of forces which are in antithesis to one another. The philosophical point of saying this is that matter is thus endowed with powers of self-motion. . . .

It is evident at least that philosophical consciencism cannot issue in a closed set of ethical rules, a set of rules which must apply in any society and at any time. Philosophical consciencism is incapable of this because it is itself based upon a view of matter, as caught in the grip of an inexorable dialectical evolution.

To the extent that materialism issues in egalitarianism on the social plane, it issues in ethics. Egalitarianism is not only political but also ethical; for it implies a certain range of human conduct which is alone acceptable to it. At the same time, because it conceives matter as a plenum of tensions giving rise to dialectical change, it cannot freeze its ethical rules with changelessness. It would be wrong, however, to seek to infer from this that the ethical principles which philosophical consciencism sanctions are at any one time gratuitous and devoid of objective grounding; for even when rules change, they can still be informed, still be governed by the same basic principles in the light of changing social conditions. . . .

According to philosophical consciencism, ethical rules are not permanent but depend on the stage reached in the historical evolution of a society, so however that cardinal principles of egalitarianism are conserved.

A society does not change its ethics by merely changing its rules. To alter its ethics, its principles must be different. Thus, if a capitalist society can become a socialist society, then a capitalist society will have changed its ethics. Any change of ethics constitutes a revolutionary change. . . .

The cardinal ethical principle of philosophical consciencism is to treat each man as an end in himself and not merely as a means. This is fundamental to all socialist or humanist conceptions of man. It is true that Immanuel Kant also identified this as a cardinal principle of ethics, but whereas he regarded it as an immediate command of reason, we derive it from a materialist viewpoint.

This derivation can be made by way of that egalitarianism which, we have seen, is the social reflection of materialism. Egalitarianism is based on the monistic thesis of materialism. Matter is one even in its different manifestations. . . .

It is the basic unity of matter, despite its varying manifestations, which gives rise to egalitarianism. Basically, man is one, for all men have the same basis and arise from the same evolution according to materialism. This is the objective ground of egalitarianism.

David Hume raised the question that ethical philosophies begin with statements of fact and suddenly seek to base statements of appraisal thereon, without explaining the legitimacy of their inference. If man is basically one, then if action is objectively attentive to this fact, it must be guided by principles. The guiding principles can be stated with such generality that they become autonomous. That is to say, first, that if action is to conform to the objectivity of human unity, then it must be guided by general principles which always keep this objectivity in view, principles which would prevent action from proceeding as if men were basically different. Second, these principles, because they relate to fact, can be stated boldly, as though they were autonomous, like the principle that an individual should not be treated by another merely as a means but always as an end.

If ethical principles are founded on egalitarianism, they must be objective. If ethical principles arise from an egalitarian idea of the nature of man, they must be generalizable, for according to such an idea man is basically one in the sense defined. It is to this non-differential generalization that expression is given in the command to treat each man as an end in himself, and not merely as a means. That is, philosophical consciencism, though it has the same cardinal principle of ethics as Kant, differs from Kant in founding ethics on a philosophical idea of the nature of man. This is what Kant describes as ethics based on anthropology. By anthropology Kant means any study of the nature of man, and he forbids ethics to be based on such a study.

It is precisely this that philosophical consciencism does. It also agrees with the traditional African outlook on many points, and thus fulfils one of the conditions which it sets for itself. . . .

The traditional African standpoint, of course, accepts the absolute and independent idea of matter. If one takes the philosophy of the African, one finds that in it the absolute and independent existence of matter is accepted. Further, matter is not just dead weight, but alive with forces in tension. Indeed, for the African, everything that exists, exists as a complex of forces in tension. In holding force in tension to be essential to whatever exists, he is, like Thales and like philosophical consciencists, endowing matter with an original power of self-motion, they were endowing it with what matter would need to initiate qualitative and substantial changes.

When a plurality of men exist in society, and it is accepted that each man needs to be treated as an end in himself, not merely as a means, there transpires a transition from ethics to politics. Politics become actual, for institutions need to be created to regulate the behaviour and actions of the plurality of men in society in such a way as to conserve the fundamental ethical principle of the initial worthiness of each individual. Philosophical consciencism consequently adumbrates a political theory and a social-political practice which together seek to ensure that the cardinal principles of ethics are effective.

The social-political practice is directed at preventing the emergence or the solidifying of classes, for in the Marxist conception of class structure, there is exploitation and the subjection of class to class. Exploitation and class-subjection are alike contrary to consciencism. By reason of its egalitarian tenet, philosophical consciencism seeks to promote individual development, but in such a way that the conditions for the development of all become the conditions for the development of each; that is, in such a way that the individual development does not introduce such diversities as to destroy the egalitarian basis. The social-political practice also seeks to co-ordinate social forces in such a way as to mobilize them logistically for the maximum development of society along true egalitarian lines. For this, planned development is essential.

In its political aspect, philosophical consciencism is faced with the realities of colonialism, imperialism, disunity and lack of development. Singly and collectively these four militate against the realization of a social justice based on ideas of true equality.

Study Questions

1. What does Nkrumah define as "philosophical consciencism"? What conception of philosophy underlies this idea? Is this conception itself a moral ideal? Does Nkrumah provide moral grounds for these views?

2. What reasons does Nkrumah offer to support his claim that philosophical consciencism must refer itself to the African tradition and present? How does he apply this in his own philosophical standpoint?

3. Why must philosophical consciencism be based on the metaphysical theory of materialism? Why can't it issue in a "closed set of rules"? Why must it uphold the ideal of a socialist egalitarian society? Is a non-African philosophical consciencism possible?

4. How does Nkrumah derive the idea of egalitarianism from the metaphysical theory of dialectical materialism? How does he derive the cardinal ethical principle (treating each human as an end in itself and never as a means) from the idea of egalitarianism? Do you find these derivations convincing? Why or why not?

5. How does Nkrumah distinguish his moral theory from those of David Hume and Immanuel Kant? Is there an underlying significance to these references to traditional European ethics?

Suggestions for Further Reading

Bretton, H. *The Rise and Fall of Kwame Nkrumah: A Study of Personal Rule in Africa* (New York: Praeger, 1966). A critical examination of Nkrumah's government and ideology. See Chapter VI, especially pp. 157–169.

English, P., and K. M. Kalumba, eds. *African Philosophy: A Classical Approach* (Englewood Cliffs, NJ: Prentice-Hall, 1996). See L. Senghor's "On African Homelands and Nation-States, Negritude, Assimilation and African Socialism" and especially P. J. Hountondji's "The Idea of Philosophy in Nkrumah's Consciencism."

Nkrumah, K. *Consciencism: Philosophy and Ideology for Decolonization and Development with Particular Reference to the African Revolution* (New York: Monthly Review, 1964). A fuller development of his idea of consciencism in five chapters.

Léopold Sédar Senghor (1906–2001)

Léopold Sédar Senghor, president of Senegal from 1960 to 1980, was born in Joal, on the Atlantic coast of Senegal, south of Dakar. A renowned poet who continued publishing poems and essays during his years as president, Senghor became the first African member of the French Academy when he was invested in 1984.

Senghor is one of the main representatives of the theory of negritude, a cultural and political movement that emphasizes the uniqueness of the African identity. The term *negritude,* which can be translated literally as "blackness," was coined by Aimé Césaire. Like Senghor, Césaire confronted the problems of racism as a black student living in Paris during the 1930s. In this movement, they began to reclaim their identity in terms of their race. Though initially a search for personal identity based on the individual experiences of writers of African heritage, the negritude movement has also pursued questions of national and pan-African identity, and has taken various political and social forms.

In the following essay, Senghor offers his definition of negritude in an effort to show how it contributes to humanism in the twentieth century. Defending the idea of negritude against the charges that it is tantamount to racialism (or racism) and that it gives expression to an inferiority complex, he explains that it refers rather to the "African personality" or "the sum of cultural values of the black world." He suggests that as a unique way of being, of relating to the world and others, negritude is necessary for today's world because it offers a humanist perspective.

According to Senghor, the African outlook is radically different from the European view that prevailed from the Renaissance to the late nineteenth century, though it coincides with some of the modern philosophical and scientific conceptions that have emerged in the European world since then. The traditional European perspective placed value on discursive reason, logic, and facts. It conceived the world as a static, mechanical, and objective totality marked by the duality of spirit and matter. However, in the African ontology (or conception of being), the world is a whole composed of complementary life forces that are but different aspects of one and the same reality that begins and ends with God. Rather than approaching the world abstractly through discursive reason, logic, and objective facts, the African experiences things in his or her deeper reality and is able to develop a sort of "intuitive reason" that grasps the underlying unity of the world.

Senghor draws points of comparison between African ontology and the modern ontology that developed in the twentieth century, but he also indicates features that arise from the former and give a distinctive character to the morality (and aesthetics) of negritude. Claiming that the African attitude to the world is fundamentally ethical, Senghor explains that the divine moral law is to fulfill the sense of the universe as an interlocked whole that is linked with God. To follow the moral law of unifying the universe is to follow our nature, for humans are themselves webs of complementary life forces that form increasingly higher concentric circles of interrelation, from family to humanity. Hence, with its prizing of unity and harmony, negritude offers the promise of a dialogue that can benefit humanity.

NEGRITUDE: A HUMANISM OF THE TWENTIETH CENTURY

DURING THE LAST THIRTY OR SO YEARS that we have been proclaiming negritude, it has become customary, especially among English-speaking critics, to accuse us of *racialism*. This is probably because the word is not of English origin. But, in the language of Shakespeare, is it not in good company with the words humanism and socialism? Mphahleles[1] have been sent about the world saying: "Negritude is an inferiority complex"; but the same word cannot mean both "racialism" and "inferiority complex" without contradiction. The most recent attack comes from Ghana, where the government has commissioned a poem entitled "I Hate Negritude"—as if one could hate oneself, hate one's being, without ceasing to be.

No, negritude is none of these things. It is neither racialism nor self-negation. Yet it is not just affirmation; it is rooting oneself in oneself, and self-confirmation: confirmation of one's *being*. Negritude is nothing more or less than what

some English-speaking Africans have called the *African personality*. It is no different from the "black personality" discovered and proclaimed by the American New Negro movement. As the American Negro poet, Langston Hughes, wrote after the first world war: "We, the creators of the new generation, want to give expression to our *black personality* without shame or fear . . . We know we are handsome. Ugly as well. The drums weep and the drums laugh." Perhaps our only originality, since it was the West Indian poet, Aimé Césaire, who coined the word negritude, is to have attempted to define the concept a little more closely; to have developed it as a weapon, as an instrument of liberation and as a contribution to the humanism of the twentieth century.

But, once again, what is negritude? Ethnologists and sociologists today speak of "different civilizations." It is obvious that peoples differ in their ideas and their languages, in their philosophies and their religions, in their customs and their institutions, in their literature and their art. Who would deny that Africans, too, have a certain way of conceiving life and of living it? A cer-

[1] The South African writer, Ezekiel Mphahlele, author, among other books, of *The African Image*, strongly disagrees with the concept of negritude.

Léopold Sédar Senghor. "Negritude: A Humanism of the Twentieth Century" (1966). In The Africa Reader,
Vols. 1 and 2, eds. W. Cartey and M. Kilso. New York: Random House, 1970, Vol. 2.

tain way of speaking, singing, and dancing; of painting and sculpturing, and even of laughing and crying? Nobody, probably; for otherwise we would not have been talking about "Negro art" for the last sixty years and Africa would be the only continent today without its ethnologists and sociologists. What, then, is negritude? It is—as you can guess from what precedes—*the sum of the cultural values of the black world*; that is, a certain active presence in the world, or better, in the universe. It is, as John Reed and Clive Wake call it, a certain "way of relating oneself to the world and to others."[2] Yes, it is essentially relations with others, an opening out to the world, contact and participation with others. Because of what it is, negritude is necessary in the world today: it is a humanism of the twentieth century. . . .

The paradox is only apparent when I say that negritude, by its ontology (that is, its philosophy of being), its moral law and its aesthetic, is a response to the modern humanism that European philosophers and scientists have been preparing since the end of the nineteenth century, and as Teilhard de Chardin and the writers and artists of the mid-twentieth century present it.

Firstly, African ontology. Far back as one may go into his past, from the northern Sudanese to the southern Bantu, the African has always and everywhere presented a concept of the world which is diametrically opposed to the traditional philosophy of Europe. The latter is essentially *static, objective, dichotomic*; it is, in fact, dualis-tic, in that it makes an absolute distinction between body and soul, matter and spirit. It is founded on separation and opposition: on analysis and conflict. The African, on the other hand, conceives the world, beyond the diversity of its forms, as a fundamentally mobile, yet unique, reality that seeks synthesis. This needs development.

It is significant that in Wolof, the main language of Senegal, there are at least three words to translate the word "spirit": *xel, sago,* or *degal*,

whereas images have to be used for the word "matter": *lef* (thing) or *yaram* (body). The African is, of course, sensitive to the external world, to the material aspect of beings and things. It is precisely because he is more so than the white European, because he is sensitive to the tangible qualities of things—shape, color, smell, weight, etc.—that the African considers these things merely as signs that have to be interpreted and transcended in order to reach the reality of human beings. Like others, more than others, he distinguishes the pebble from the plant, the plant from the animal, the animal from Man; but, once again, the accidents and appearances that differentiate these kingdoms only illustrate different aspects of the same reality. This reality is *being* in the ontological sense of the word, and it is life force. For the African, matter in the sense the Europeans understand it, is only a system of signs which translates the single reality of the universe: being, which is spirit, which is life force. Thus, the whole universe appears as an infinitely small, and at the same time an infinitely large, network of life forces which emanate from God and end in God, who is the source of all life forces. It is He who vitalizes and devitalizes all other beings, all the other life forces.

I have not wandered as far as might be thought from modern ontology. European ethnologists, Africanists and artists use the same words and the same expressions to designate the ultimate reality of the universe they are trying to know and to express: "spider's web," "network of forces," "communicating vessels," "system of canals," etc. This is not very different, either, from what the scientists and chemists say. As far as African ontology is concerned, too, there is no such thing as dead matter: every being, every thing—be it only a grain of sand—radiates a life force, a sort of wave-particle; and sages, priests, kings, doctors, and artists all use it to help bring the universe to its fulfilment.

For the African, contrary to popular belief, is not passive in face of the order—or disorder—of the world. His attitude is fundamentally ethical. If the moral law of the African has remained unknown for so long, it is because it derives,

---

[2] *Léopold Sédar Senghor: Selected Poems*, introduced and translated by John Reed and Clive Wake. See also: *Léopold Sédar Senghor: Prose and Poetry*, by the same authors.

naturally, from his conception of the world: from his ontology—so naturally, that both have remained unknown, denied even, by Europeans, because they have not been brought to their attention by being re-examined by each new generation of Africans.

So God tired of all the possibilities that remained confined within Him, unexpressed, dormant, and as if dead. And God opened His mouth, and he spoke at length a word that was harmonious and rhythmical. All these possibilities expressed by the mouth of God *existed* and had the vocation *to live*: to express God in their turn, by establishing the link with God and all the forces deriving from Him.

In order to explain this *morality in action* of negritude, I must go back a little. Each of the identifiable life forces of the universe—from the grain of sand to the ancestor[3]—is, itself and in its turn, a network of life forces—as modern physical chemistry confirms: a network of elements that are contradictory in appearance but really *complementary*. Thus, for the African, Man is composed, of course, of matter and spirit, of body and soul; but at the same time he is also composed of a virile and a feminine element: indeed of several "souls." Man is therefore a composition of mobile life forces which interlock: a world of solidarities that seek to knit themselves together. Because he exists, he is at once end and beginning: end of the three orders of the mineral, the vegetable, and the animal, but beginning of the human order.

Let us ignore for the moment the first three orders and examine the human order. Above

Man and based on him, lies this fourth world of concentric circles, bigger and bigger, higher and higher, until they reach God along with the whole of the universe. Each circle—family, village, province, nation, humanity—is, in the image of Man and by vocation, a close-knit society.

So, for the African, living according to the moral law means living according to his nature, composed as it is of contradictory elements but complementary life forces. Thus he gives stuff to the stuff of the universe and tightens the threads of the tissue of life. Thus he transcends the contradictions of the elements and works toward making the life forces complementary to one another: in himself first of all, as Man, but also in the whole of human society. It is by bringing the complementary life forces together in this way that Man reinforces them in their movement towards God and, in reinforcing them, he reinforces himself; that is, he passes from *existing* to *being*. He cannot reach the highest form of being, for in fact only God has this quality: and He has it all the more fully as creation, and all that exists, fulfil themselves and express themselves in Him. . . .

Ethnologists have often praised the unity, the balance, and the harmony of African civilization, of black society, which was based both on the *community* and on the *person*, and in which, because it was founded on dialogue and reciprocity, the group had priority over the individual without crushing him, but allowing him to blossom as a person. I would like to emphasize at this point how much these characteristics of negritude enable it to find its place in contemporary humanism, thereby permitting black Africa to make its contribution to the "Civilization of the Universal" which is so necessary in our divided but interdependent world of the second half of the twentieth century.

---

[3]In African religion, the ancestors are the essential link between the living and God. This is why they are surrounded by a complex ritual so as to ensure the maintenance of this link.

Study Questions

1. What does Senghor mean by "negritude"? Does he suggest that negritude is an essential feature of African identity? Is he offering a description or a prescription? Does he manage to dissolve the charges of racism and inferiority complex?

2. How does Senghor relate the African ontology to the morality of negritude? In what sense is negritude a form of humanism? How does negritude offer an ethics that is different from European ethics?
3. What is the significance of Senghor's various comparisons and contrasts between the ideas of negritude and those of traditional and modern European philosophy and science?
4. What specific form would human actions and interactions take if they followed the moral law of negritude? Does Senghor envision the possibility of a global ethics that is based on the values of negritude? Is it possible for non-Africans to adopt the morality of negritude?

Suggestions for Further Reading

English, P. "On Senghor's Theory of Negritude" In *African Philosophy: A Classical Approach,* eds. P. English and K. M. Kalumba (Englewood Cliffs, NJ: Prentice-Hall, 1996). Discusses the development of Senghor's theory of negritude and considers five of its most prominent critiques.

Mphahlele, E. *The African Image* (London: Faber and Faber, 1962). A general critique of the African image portrayed by middle-class Africans and seen by Europeans. See Chapters 2 and 3.

Sartre, J.-P. *Black Orpheus,* trans. S. W. Allen (Paris: Présence Africaine, 1963). A philosophical reflection on the theory of negritude.

Spleth, J. *Léopold Sédar Senghor* (Boston: Twayne, 1985). See Chapter Two, "The Philosophy of Negritude."

Vaillant, J. G. *Black, French and African: A Life of Léopold Sédar Senghor* (Cambridge, MA: Harvard University Press, 1990). See Chapter 10, "Negritude and African Socialism."

Paul Mbuya Akoko (c. 1891–1981)

Paul Mbuya Akoko was born in Karachuonoyo, South Nyanza (in present-day Kenya). He was the *Ker*—the ultimate moral or spiritual leader of the Luo, a tribe from his native land. Mbuya believed in both Christianity and the Luo traditional religion. In his view, the arrival of the European missionaries to Africa "introduced the element of fragmentation into religion," but their concept of God and the Luo's concept of God (called *Nyasaye*) "is basically the same for there is only one God." When asked whether he was a wise man, he would respond, "No. I do not think I am wise for there are many people who are wiser than I am. It is only that I do not know them. . . ." However, many people sought his advice on how to follow the Luo customs, and he published a book in 1938 written in the language of his people under the title *Luo Kitgi Gi Tembegi* (Luo Customs and Habits). Mbuya also served as paramount chief and as member of the East African Legislative Assembly.

Henry Odera Oruka, an African philosopher from Earlham College, in Richmond, Indiana, interviewed Mbuya, asking him to explain and comment on a number of Luo concepts. The text below is an excerpt of that interview in which Mbuya develops his philosophy of a better way of life for humans. In his responses to Odera, Mbuya outlines a form of society based on the Luo idea of communalism, and develops his own views on how peoples of different races and tribes must learn to live together in peace.

INTERVIEW WITH PAUL MBUYA AKOKO

Q. WHAT DO YOU THINK of the old Luo idea of communalism?

A. Now the sense in which we may justly say that the Luo in the traditional setting practised communalism is not one in which people generously shared property or wealth. Their idea of communalism is, I think, of a co-operative nature. For example, where one person had cattle, everybody "ipso fact" had cattle. For the owner of the cattle would distribute his cattle among people who did not have cattle so that the less well-off people may take care of them. However, the cattle was never completely given away. The poor were only given temporary charge of these animals by their better-off neighbours. For example, the cattle owner may give one poor man four cows, another five cows and so on to look after. The result is that everybody had cows to look after and so milk to drink.

Where a person wants to get married but did not have such things as cows, etc., other people would "chip in". One person might contribute a calf whilst another a bull, and so forth. Thus, with the co-operative help of neighbours and relatives, a man who otherwise would have been in difficulty became able to cope with the expenses of getting married. And when this person who himself was helped became able, he too felt obliged to help others. Help is thus spread throughout the community and everybody felt a sense of belonging. This is different from the "political" communism we hear so much about these days.

In a famine situation, no one was allowed or left to starve. Here, the communal spirit comes into its own. A wealthy man would give to the poor. He may feel able to give a basket of grains to one man, two baskets to another according to the needs of these individuals. Thus, everyone had something to eat. It was considered anti-social if any one kept things to himself alone. But then, there was also the extended family system which made people generally feel that they all belonged to one family; it turned mere neighbours into relations of a sort.

A person who brews beer would be happier when there are others to share it with him. On the other hand, a person may prepare food and invite others to share it with him. That is what used to happen. No person was allowed to become destitute. Where in a village, and this was extremely rare, a person died of hunger, the people of the village were made a laughing stock by people of the neighbouring villages because it was considered shameful for a person to be left to starve to death.

Q. Do you think this spirit exists today?

A. This communal spirit is sadly being allowed to die out through the importation of foreign ideas and process of modernization. A means ought to be found whereby what is good in our past is accommodated in things new and modern.

"Paul Mbuya Akoko." From Sage Philosophy: Indigenous Thinkers and Modern Debate on African Philosophy. *Reprinted by permission of Brill Academic Publishers, Inc.*

Q. Given the nature of things today, do you think that communalism can go on?

A. As I have tried to explain, the introduction of modern way of life is gradually bringing to an end this communal spirit. It is much to be regretted that everybody is now so obsessed with his person that he does not show much interest in what else is going on around him. The order of the day is now one in which individuals say: "I want a car, a large house, and so forth: therefore, in order to be able to afford all these things, I must concentrate all my efforts only upon my own person". Thus, the very laudable *communal spirit* is gradually giving way to the modern aggressive *individualism*. But are we tending or at any rate likely to become like the Europeans? I do not know.

Q. Do you think that all peoples are born equal or are there some races born with less intelligence?

A. Now it must be understood that people are born with certain differences which must be acknowledged. Even in a communist society, there are still people who have more strength than others. There are those who may, for example, have enough strength to be capable of fighting an animal as strong as a lion. There are those who can have so much food by sheer hard work. Others still are good only at rearing animals, and so forth. Thus we see that people are not equal in every respect.

However, it is my opinion that because a person is born with superior powers is all the more reason why that person ought to place his extra or superior powers at the service of his less well off neighbours. Given his superior powers, he can produce more food to feed others so that all may live together in happiness otherwise the people may develop jealousy of, or even hatred for, the more fortunate.

Q. What is the nature of the equality which existed in the communal environment?

A. The fact that I have expressed the view that people ought to continue to live together helping one another as in the old days is not to be taken to entail the possible conclusion that there still will not be those who, for example, have more power and wealth. . . .

Q. Do you think the world would have been better if there were only one race?

A. There are different types of people in the world and so there are different races on the macro-level; and tribes on the micro-level. This is undoubtedly a fact. Any tribe or race which attempts to wipe out other tribes or races such that only one tribe or race remains is embarking upon an exercise in futility. The Luo used to think albeit wrongly, that they could wipe out other tribes or at any rate subjugate them because they believed in the supremacy of their tribe. Clearly, this is a recipe for trouble. The Luo should therefore learn to understand the other tribes so that all live together in harmony. For, it is not possible, I think, for the Luo, Kisii, Kikuyu, Kamba and other tribes each to do away with their traditions. The differences will remain and so must be accommodated.

Q. What do you think accounts for the fighting among people of different tribes and races?

A. There is fighting and bad feelings among people of different tribes and even the effects as is all too often the case at present. Wars are caused by the avarice and greed of men for both wealth and power.

Q. What do you think brings about this bad feeling?

A. Now a race or tribe might consider itself so strong such that other races or tribes cannot equal it. Such race or tribe would therefore not tolerate any act which it considers a disrespect from an "inferior" race of tribe. This is the germ of the dangerous idea that weaker races or tribes are ripe for plunder. My own view is that this idea has an affinity with the belief that might is right, i.e., the "right" is always subordinate to "might". Such are the germs which cause wars.

Q. It has been claimed that some races have superior intellectual powers. Do you think there is any justification for this claim?

A. When a race is wealthy, there is an almost invariable tendency for it to claim superiority. However, I do not think that any particular people or race or tribe was created by God to be superior. Wealth can be acquired by any people. Thus, all races have, inherently, equal power. This power is nevertheless put to use in different ways and hence manifest differences in development. The intelligence which the Europeans present is the intelligence God prophesied would come into the world in the present phase of world history. However, this intelligence is not the property of any one people. God said intelligence would come into the world. The Europeans themselves gained some of their knowledge or intelligence from other races as we are now gaining much knowledge from them. We are, in time, likely to equal the Europeans in achievement. We may even surpass them. They were not born with more intelligence than other people. Even today, there are people in Europe who lack the intelligence which we see in some Europeans. Let us therefore define an intelligent race as a race which has used its acquired intelligence wisely. In this sense, "knowledge" has an affinity with "intelligence".

Of course, the foregoing are my own views which are not representative of the general Luo belief system. Long ago, the Luo believed no other tribe was superior to it. They thought they were the greatest. They used to boast in this way. They claimed that the Luo were second only to the Europeans and therefore were the "*wazungu wa Kisumu*", i.e. the Europeans of Kisumu, the town which they affectionately described as their "London" and the Luoland they termed "U.K.". They were crazy.

In those days, the Luo were not only warriors and fighters, but also very learned and intelligent people. They were thus able to work on European farms and also serve as the servants of the Europeans. They were to be found everywhere. The Luo were in ascendancy mainly, I think, because the other tribes did not think of engaging in these multifarious activities. As a result, the Luo wrongly thought they were superior to others.

Study Questions

1. What specifically is the Luo concept of communalism? What is its basic ethical tenet?
2. In what important ways does communalism differ from what Mbuya calls "political" communism?
3. Is the communal spirit incompatible with individualism? Why or why not?
4. In what sense, if any, are people equal in a communal society?
5. Does Mbuya seem to believe that we can have communalism on a global level? Do you think he is claiming that we ought to?

Suggestions for Further Reading

English, P., and K. M. Kalumba, eds. *African Philosophy: A Classical Approach* (Englewood Cliffs, NJ: Prentice-Hall, 1996). Part II contains essays on the "sagacity philosophy" under which Oruka classifies Mbuya's thought.

Odera Oruka, H., ed. *Sage Philosophy. Indigenous Thinkers and Modern Debate on African Philosophy* (Leiden, NY: E. J. Brill, 1990). Contains the full interview of Mbuya. Also offers an exposition and various critiques of Odera's notion of sage philosophy.

Oruka Rang'inya (1900–1979)

Oruka Rang'inya was born in the Siaya district of the Ugenya Location (in present-day Kenya). A self-educated man, Rang'inya was once a famous wrestler, a locational councilor, and the chair of traditional courts on land and marriages. In his later years, he lived as a farmer and businessman. Rang'inya was acknowledged as sage of the Ugenya Location, and served as adviser to the chiefs and members of his Luo community. He married ten wives and raised thirty-six children.

Henry Odera Oruka, an African philosopher from Earlham College, in Richmond, Indiana, interviewed Rang'inya asking him to explain and comment on a number of Luo concepts. In the first excerpt of that interview, Rang'inya develops his concept of God and religion as morally useful ideas. In the second excerpt, Rang'inya develops his notion of freedom (*Fuyanga*) as based on an individual's industriousness and ability to help others. Distinguishing his notion from the traditional Luo concept of freedom, Rang'inya underscores the importance of hard work for true political independence. His emphasis on the virtue of industriousness also comes forth in the third excerpt, in which he takes a critical view of the Luo's conceptions of racial and tribal differences.

INTERVIEW WITH ORUKA RANG'INYA

Q. WHAT DO YOU THINK GOD IS? What is religion?

A. We have always heard things concerning God. He was thought to be with people fighting in a battle on both sides. Even long before the Europeans came to Africa, there was the idea of God. However, the idea of denomination, a gathering of people which takes a name unto itself, is a new phenomenon. Examples of these imported denominations are Catholic Church, Church Missionary Society, and so forth.

So then, my own thinking leads me to the conclusion that God resides both in this world as well as in "heaven". For He is in the wind which blows. He is the concept of "open-heartedness", i.e. a person who is not greedy but makes sacrifices in order to help others, such a person is "*God*". It must be noted, however, that God lives in the wind. Thus, He is everywhere. It is therefore quite wrong to personalize Him. He is an idea. The *idea* which represents goodness itself. God is thus a useful concept from the practical point of view.

Q. Before the Europeans came here, did the Luo have their own religion?

A. Now, before the Europeans came, the Luo people had their religion. They worshipped *wang chieng*, the face of the sun. They always looked in the direction of the sun whenever they prayed. Their God was known as *Were Hagawa* which supposedly had its base in the sun and the moon. They therefore regarded these places as

"Oruka Rang'inya." From Sage Philosophy: Indigenous Thinkers and Modern Debate on African Philosophy. *Reprinted by permission of Brill Academic Publishers, Inc.*

the abode of their God. I think, given the above arguments, that the Luo were quite wrong to think of God in physical terms.

Q. Do you think there are people who do not care about religion?

A. No doubt, there are such people as may be secular. But these are not right-thinking people. For surely, everyone ought to love religion for its practical utility. Even a person, who wished the death of another, would pray God to help him because that other person had done him some wrong. It is not unknown that a thief when setting out to rob his prospective victim may pray for God's assistance so that he is not caught in his act. But I think God is only an idea. An idea, albeit a useful one, in the minds of people. . . .

Q. What is the significance of freedom to the Luo?

A. Fuyanga: or *Thuolo* (Freedom) is as important to the Luo people as indeed it ought to be to all peoples. If a person had many such sons such that many shields (fighters) could come from his home at a time of war, then that person was considered a free man. Or if one had many granaries such that at times of need, one was able to provide food for people other than members of one's immediate family, then one had freedom. Those who were fed were not to be considered free because they had to depend upon other people to provide them with food.

Q. How can a person gain his freedom?

A. Thus, if one liked people and worked hard and was able to help feed others, then one was free. Showing respect for other people or just being well behaved were other ways of gaining one's freedom.

Q. Do the Luo understand the concept "freedom"?

A. These are generally my own ideas of "freedom" because some people in the Luo community do not seem to understand what freedom meant. They lacked understanding because they wrongly thought that after political independence, clothes, maize, cattle and other things would be given to them without the need of working for them. They thought that free education and non-taxation are fruits of independence whereas independence means only one thing: *hard work* and the right to be rewarded accordingly.[1]

Q. Who do you think is independent and who is not?

A. Those who hold good government jobs and can feed themselves are free. But some people are jobless and are hungry. These are entitled to ask the question: "Who says that we are independent?" Farmers who feed themselves are also free. But those people who sit idle all day and drink beer in the evening neither know nor understand what independence is. . . .

Q. What do you think about the differences between the races of the world?

A. The differences which we notice in people: Africans, Europeans, Asians or what have you are only apparent. They are not real. For people are all the same. The only distinction lies in the fact that some people are lazy while others are hard working. Those who work hard are in Luo understanding termed *Wazungu* (Europeans). Thus, where the black man shows signs of industry, he is promptly described as a "European" as if this label has some magic performing effect. No doubt, it is industry which gives a person great wealth and lots of good. The European worked hard, as a result of which he was able to supply people with food and for this, he was respected. And yet people are equal. They all have the same amount of intelligence since this is not related to skin pigment. None is superior to the other. It only happens that some people are lazy and others are able to utilize the opportunities which are available to them.

Q. Do you think that political independence will make black people work harder?

A. However, with the advent of *"Fuyanga"* (freedom) people, black people, will find that

---

[1]The sage is referring to a myth created during the British Colonial rule in Kenya that if you are a Muzungu (white man), i.e. a ruler, you do not have to exert your energy to earn your livelihood. There were servants (black people) to work for you and your role is to order them and enjoy the fruits of their sweat. As a result, some Africans thought that, with independence, the roles would be reversed, i.e. the Muzungu would be the servant and the African the master.

they have to work hard. For no one now supplies others with food. The Europeans who used to make food available have now left. Therefore, people will have to inculcate the habit of working hard. They may even surpass the Europeans. Necessity may force them into this position.

Q. Do you think that any tribe is superior to another?

A. Just as peoples of different races are equal, peoples of different tribes are also equal. Yet some tribes are very arrogant. Their arrogance leads them to assert, unjustly, that they are superior to other tribes. I think that in most cases, this pride is the result of laziness. The most arrogant people in Kenya are the Luo. They believed, quite wrongly, that they were next in importance to the Europeans. Thus, they concluded that they were superior to the other tribes. They said they were *"Wazunga wa Kisumu"* (The Europeans of Kisumu) and called their town, Kisumu, "London". At first, the Nubians from Sudan used to accompany the Europeans. After the war, the Nubians went home and the Luo took their places.

The Luo were made soldiers with powers of arrest and detention. Thus, they would threaten people with arrest "because we are like the Europeans". Pride entered and blocked their heads. On the face of it, they appear lazy, for they do seem to concentrate more on dressing well and less on working hard. Indeed, more attention was paid to showing off. They forgot the virtues of humility.

Q. If, as you say, the Luo are lazy, does it mean that they are inferior to other tribes?

A. In spite of the foregoing however, the Luo were not born lazy. It is the Europeans who made them lazy. The Europeans made them lazy by employing them as servants, soldiers and what nots. Before the Europeans came, the Luo were among the most hard working tribes. But the Europeans gave them a soft life and turned them into lazy people just as the Europeans made the Nubians lazy.

Q. If the Luo give up this "easy life", do you think this could make them strong again?

A. So then, if the Luo were to give up the "easy life", they would become hard working, industrious people once again; very strong and hard working. They are great warriors and hard-fighters. All the past leading soldiers in Nairobi were Luo. Only fanciful dressing has now made them lazy.

Study Questions

1. In what sense is "God" a useful idea in Rang'inya's view? What is the practical utility of religion for Rang'inya? What is the significance of his identification of goodness with "openheartedness"?

2. What moral obligations are contained in Rang'inya's conception of freedom? How are they related to freedom? How are they related to one another?

3. Why do you think Rang'inya places so much importance on hard work? What other virtues depend upon it?

4. What is the moral significance of racial and tribal conceptions and relations for Rang'inya?

Suggestions for Further Reading

English, P., and K. M. Kalumba, eds. *African Philosophy: A Classical Approach* (Englewood Cliffs, NJ: Prentice-Hall, 1996). Part II contains essays on the "sagacity philosophy" under which Oruka classifies Rang'inya's thought.

Odera Oruka, H., ed. *Sage Philosophy. Indigenous Thinkers and Modern Debate on African Philosophy* (Leiden, NY: E. J. Brill, 1990). Contains the full interview of Rang'inya. Also offers an exposition and various critiques of Oruka's notion of sage philosophy.

W. E. B. Du Bois (1868–1963)

William Edward Burghardt Du Bois was born in Great Barrington, Massachusetts. His mother descended from a West African who was brought to America as a slave. His father's ancestors were French Huguenots who had migrated to America from Flanders. Never having met his father, Du Bois was raised by his mother. According to Du Bois, she instilled in him the value of "ability and hard work" as a weapon against racism. Living in a predominantly white town where Irish immigrants were the main victims of oppression and prejudice, Du Bois spent his early years having "no sense of difference or separation." However, he soon developed an awareness of being "different from the others" who were white, and of being "shut out of their world by a vast veil." Determined to "live above" rather than "creep through" that veil, he concentrated his efforts on attaining excellence.

In 1896, Du Bois became the first African American to receive a Ph.D. (in sociology) from Harvard University. His doctoral thesis on the suppression of African slave trade in the United States was published as the first volume in the Harvard Historical Series. After graduating from Harvard, Du Bois taught at the University of Pennsylvania while he worked on *The Philadelphia Negro,* the first systematic study of blacks, for which he personally interviewed five thousand people of Philadelphia's seventh ward. Upon the completion of this work in 1897, he left to teach at Atlanta University. Besides carrying out further sociological studies and producing a significant number of writings, Du Bois became politically involved—as the secretary of the first Pan-African Conference in 1900; as cofounder of the Niagara Movement in 1905, which was the basis for the founding of the NAACP (National Association for the Advancement of Colored People) in 1910; and as organizer of the First Universal Races Congress in 1911.

Du Bois abandoned his teaching career to become the full-time editor of the NAACP's journal, *The Crisis.* Growing increasingly sympathetic to socialism as the path to liberation for African Americans, he eventually parted ways with the NAACP and returned to teaching in Atlanta until he retired in 1943. Du Bois remained politically active after his retirement; he returned to the NAACP as director of special research, was a consultant for the founding of the United Nations, co-chaired the Fifth Pan-African Congress, was vice-chair of the Council of African Affairs, and chaired the Peace Information Center. Becoming more and more embittered by life in the United States, particularly after his indictment as an "unregistered agent" of the Soviet Union, he left to travel through Eastern Europe and China. In 1961, he left the United States permanently and became a citizen of the African state of Ghana, where he died at the age of ninety-five.

In his most renowned book, *The Souls of Black Folk* (1903), Du Bois gave central importance to the experience of the Negro as "being a problem." In the nineteenth century, the German philosopher G. W. F. Hegel had presented a conception of history as the rationally necessary development of the World Spirit to consciousness of itself as free. For Hegel, this development occurs through six historical peoples: Chinese, Indian, Egyptian, Greek, Roman, and German. Du Bois expanded on this concept by adding the Negro as the "seventh son, born with a veil, and gifted with second-sight in this American world." Hegel's famous analysis of the master-slave dialectic proposed that such relation is inadequate for the full development of self-consciousness in both master and slave. According to Du Bois, the Negro, like the slave in Hegel's analysis, lives in "a world which yields him no true self-consciousness, but only lets him see himself through the revelation of the other world." Hence, the Negro experiences a "double-consciousness" as he sees himself through the contemptuous eyes of the other. He feels a "twoness" as an American and as a Negro, with "two warring ideals in one dark body." The goal, as Du Bois saw it, is the merging of this double self into a higher synthesis, a truer self that preserves both selves without denying the integrity of each.

Throughout his life, Du Bois emphasized the importance of developing the "black soul" through education and work as a means to attaining liberation and justice. Work, he insisted, must be "inspired by the right ideals and guided by intelligence," while education "must not simply teach work—it must teach Life." Believing that "the Negro race is going to be saved by its exceptional men," he urged "the Talented Tenth" of the African American community to be "leaders of thought and missionaries of culture among their people." In the following essay, "The Development of a People" (1904), Du Bois points to these leaders and missionaries as the hope for the development of the Negro race. Deprived of the usual sources of inspiration for progress of a people (the precepts of parents, the vision of seers, the opinion of the majority, and the traditions of the past), the Negro race must be guided by exemplary men who will embody its new moral ideals while setting the ethical standards for their community.

THE DEVELOPMENT OF A PEOPLE

LET ME TAKE YOU journeying across mountains and meadows, threading the hills of Maryland, gliding over the broad fields of Virginia, climbing the blue ridge of Carolina and seating ourselves in the cotton kingdom. I would not like you to spend a day or a month here in this little town; I should much rather you would spend ten years, if you are really studying the problem; for casual visitors get casual ideas, and the problems here are the growth of centuries.

From the depot and the cluster of doubtful houses that form the town, pale crimson fields with tell-tale gullies stretch desolately away. The whole horizon looks shabby, and there is a certain awful leisure in the air that makes a westerner wonder when work begins. A neglected and uncertain road wanders up from the depot, past several little stores and a post-office, and then stops hesitatingly and melts away into crooked paths across the washed-out cotton fields. But I do not want you to see so much of the physical as of the spiritual town, and first you must see the color line. It stands at the depot with "waiting room for white people" and

W. E. B. Du Bois. "The Development of a People" (1904). In Writings by W. E. B. Du Bois in Periodicals Edited by Others, *Vols. 1 and 2, ed. H. Aptheker. Milwood, NY: Kraus Thompson, 1982, Vol. 1: 1891–1909.*

"waiting room for colored people," and then the uninitiated might lose sight of it; but it is there, there and curiously wandering, but continuous and never ending. And in that little town, as in a thousand others, they have an eleventh commandment, and it reads "Thou shalt not Cross the Line." Men may at times break the sixth commandment and the seventh, and it makes but little stir. But when the eleventh is broken, *the world heaves.* And yet you must not think the town inhabited by anything inhuman. Simple, good hearted folks are there—generosity and hospitality, politeness and charity, dim strivings and hard efforts—a human world, aye, even lovable at times; and one cannot argue about that strange line—it is simply so.

Were you there in person I could not take you easily across the line into the world I want to study. But in spirit let me lead you across. In one part of the town are sure to be clustered the majority of the Negro cabins; there is no strict physical separation; on some streets whites and blacks are neighbors, and yet the general clustering by color is plain. I want to take you among the houses of the colored people, and I start not with the best, but with the worst: a little one-room box with a family of eight. The cabin is dirty, ill-smelling and cheerless; the furniture is scanty, old and worn. The man works when he has no whiskey to drink, which is comparatively seldom. The woman washes and squanders and squanders and washes. I am not sure that the couple were ever married formally, but still they'll stick together in all probability for life, despite their quarreling. There are five children, and the nameless child of the eldest daughter makes the last member of the family. Three of the children can spell and read a bit, but there's little need of it. The rest of the family are in ignorance, dark and dense. Here is a problem of home and family. One shudders at it almost hopelessly, or flares in anger and says: why do these people live like animals? Why don't they work and strive to do? If the stranger be from the North he looks suspiciously at the color line and shakes his head. If he be from the South he looks at it thankfully and stamps his foot. And these

two attitudes are in some respects typical. We look around for the forces keeping this family down, or with fatalistic resignation conclude that nothing better is to be expected of black people. Exactly the same attitude with which the man of a century or so ago fought disease: looked about for the witch, or wondered at the chastening of the Lord; but withal continued to live in the swamps. There are forces in the little town to keep Negroes down, but they do not wholly explain the condition of this family. There are differences in human capabilities, but that they are not based on color can be seen in a dozen Negro homes up the street. What we have in degraded homes like this is a plain survival from the past. . . .

As I study this family in the little southern town, in all its degradation and uncleanness, I cannot but see a plain case of cause and effect. If you degrade people the result is degradation, and you have no right to be surprised at it. Nor am I called upon to apologize for these people, or to make fun of their dumb misery. For their condition there is an apology due, witness High Heaven; but not from me.

Upon the town we have visited, upon the state, upon this section, the awful incubus of the past broods like a writhing sorrow, and when we turn our faces from that past, we turn it not to forget but to remember; viewing degradation with fear and not contempt, with awe and not criticism, bowing our head and straining willing ears to the iron voice

> . . . of Nature merciful and stern.
> I teach by killing, let others learn.

But the Negroes of the South are not all upon this low level. From this Nadir they stretch slowly, resolutely upward, by infinite gradation, helped now by the hand of a kindly master or a master's son, now by the sacrifice of friends; always by the ceaseless energy of a people who will never submit to burial alive.

Look across the street of your little southern town: here is a better house—a mother and father, two sons and a girl. They are hard-working people and good people. They read and write a

little and, though they are slow and good na-
tured, they are seldom idle. And yet they are unskilled, without foresight, always in debt and living from hand to mouth. Hard pressed they may
sink into crime; encouraged they may rise to
comfort, but never to wealth. Why? Because they
and their fathers have been trained this way.
What does a slave know of saving? What can he
know of forethought? What could he learn even
of skill, save in exceptional cases? In other words,
slavery must of necessity send into the world of
work a mass of unskilled laborers who have no
idea of what thrift means; who have been a part
of a great economic organization but had nothing to do with its organizing; and so when they
are suddenly called to take a place in a greater organization, in which free individual initiative is a
potent factor, they cannot, for they do not know
how; they lack skill and, more than that, they
lack ideals!

And so we might go on: past problems of
work and wages, of legal protection, of civil
rights and of education, up to this jaunty, little
yellow house on a cross street with a flower-bed
struggling sturdily with the clay, with vines and
creepers and a gleam of white curtains and a
decorous parlor. If you enter this house you may
not find it altogether up to your ideals. A Dutch
housekeeper would find undiscovered corners,
and a fastidious person might object to the general scheme of decoration. And yet, compared
with the homes in the town, white or black, the
house is among the best. It may be the home of
a Negro butcher who serves both sides the color
line, or of a small grocer, a carpenter, a school
teacher or a preacher. Whatever this man may be,
he is a leader in a peculiar sense—the ideal-
maker in his group of people. The white world is
there, but it is the other side of the color line; it
is seen distinctly and from afar. Of white and
black there is no mingling in church and school,
in general gatherings. The black world is isolated
and alone; it gets its ideals, its larger thoughts, its
notions of life, from these local leaders; they set
the tone to that all-powerful spiritual world that
surrounds and envelopes the souls of men; their
standards of living, their interpretation of sun-

shine and rain and human hearts, their thoughts
of love and labor, their aspirations and dim imaginings—all that makes life *life*.

Not only does this group leader guide a mass
of men isolated in space, but also isolated in
time. For we must remember that not only did
slavery overthrow the Negro family and teach
few lessons of thrift and foresight; it also totally
broke a nation from all its traditions of the past
in every realm of life. I fear I cannot impress
upon you the full meaning of such a revolution.
A nation that breaks suddenly with its past is almost fatally crippled. No matter how crude or
imperfect that past may be, with all its defects, it
is the foundation upon which generations to
come must build. Beauty and finish and ar-
chitectural detail are not required of it, but the
massive weight of centuries of customs and traditions it must have. The slave trade, a new climate, a new economic regime, a new language
and a new religion separated the American Negro as completely from his fatherland as it is possible for human agencies to do. The result is curious. There is a certain swaying in the air, a
tilting and a crumbling, a vast difficulty of ad-
justment—of making the new ideas of work and
wealth, of authority and right, fit in and hitch
themselves to something gone; to the authority
of the fathers, the customs of the past in a nation
without grandfathers. So, then, the Negro group
leader not only sets present standards, but he
supplies in a measure the lack of past standards,
and his leading is doubly difficult, since with
Emancipation there came a second partial breaking with the past. The leader of the masses must
discriminate between the good and bad in the
past; he must keep the lesson of work and reject
the lesson of concubinage; he must add more
lessons of moral rectitude to the old religious
fervor; he must, in fine, stand to this group in the
light of the interpreter of the civilization of the
twentieth century to the minds and hearts of
people who, from sheer necessity, can but dimly
comprehend it. And this man—I care not what
his vocation may be—preacher, teacher, physician, or artisan, this person is going to solve the
Negro problem; for that problem is at bottom

the clash of two different standards of culture, and this priest it is who interprets the one to the other.

Let me for a moment recapitulate. In the life of advancing peoples there must go on simultaneously a struggle for existence, accumulation of wealth, education of the young, and a development in culture and the higher things of life. The more backward the nation the larger sum of effort goes into the struggle for existence; the more forward the nation the larger and broader is the life of the spirit. For guidance, in taking these steps in civilization, the nation looks to four sources: the precepts of parents, the sight of seers, the opinion of the majority and the traditions of the past.

Here, then, is a group of people in which every one of these great sources of inspiration is partially crippled: the family group is struggling to recover from the debauchery of slavery; and the number of the enlightened leaders must necessarily be small; the surrounding and more civilized white majority is cut off from its natural influence by the color line; and the traditions of the past are either lost, or largely traditions of evil and wrong.

Any one looking the problem squarely in the face might conclude that it was unjust to expect progress, or the signs of progress, until many generations had gone by. Indeed, we must not forget that those people who claimed to know the Negro best, freely and confidently predicted during the abolition controversy—

1. That free Negroes would not, and could not, work effectively.
2. That the freedman who did work, would not save.
3. That it was impossible to educate Negroes.
4. That no members of the race gave signs of ability and leadership.
5. That the race was morally degenerate.

Not only was this said, it was sincerely and passionately believed, by honorable men who, with their forefathers, had lived with the Negro three hundred years. And yet to-day the Negro in one generation forms the chief laboring force of the most rapidly developing part of the land. He owns twelve million acres of land, two hundred and fifty million dollars worth of farm property, and controls as owner or renter five hundred millions. Nearly three-fifths of the Negroes have learned to read and write. An increasing number have given evidence of ability and thoughtfulness—not, to be sure, of transcendent genius, but of integrity, large knowledge and commonsense. And finally there can be to-day no reasonable dispute but that the number of efficient, law-abiding and morally upright black people in this land is far larger than it ever was before, and is daily growing. Now these obvious and patent facts do not by any means indicate the full solution of the problem. There are still hosts of idle and unreliable Negro laborers; the race still, as a whole, has not learned the lesson of thrift and saving; fully seventy-five per cent are still fairly designated as ignorant. The number of group leaders of ability and character is far behind the demand, and the development of a trustworthy upper class has, as is usually true, been accompanied by the differentiation of a dangerous class of criminals.

What the figures of Negro advancement mean is, that the development has been distinctly and markedly in the right direction, and that, given justice and help, no honest man can doubt the outcome. The giving of justice means the recognition of desert wherever it appears; the right to vote on exactly the same terms as other people vote; the right to the equal use of public conveniences and the educating of youth in the public schools. On these points, important as they are, I will not dwell. I am more interested here in asking how these struggling people may be actually helped. I conceive that such help may take any one of four forms:—

1. Among a people deprived of guiding traditions, they may be furnished trained guidance in matters of civilization and ideals of living.
2. A people whose family life is not strongly established must have put before them and brought home to them the morals of sane and sanitary living.

3. The mass of Negro children must have the keys of knowledge put into their hands by good elementary schools.
4. The Negro youth must have the opportunity to learn the technical skill of modern industry.

All these forms of help are important. No one of them can be neglected without danger of increasing complications as time flies, and each one of them are lines of endeavor in which the Negro cannot be reasonably expected to help himself without aid from others. For instance, it cannot be seriously expected that a race of freedmen would have the skill necessary for modern industry. They cannot teach themselves what they themselves do not know, and consequently a legitimate and crying need of the south is the establishment of industrial schools. The public school system is one of the foundation stones of free republican government. Negro children, as well as other children, have a right to ask of the nation knowledge of reading, writing and the rules of number, together with some conception of the world in time and space. Not one Negro child in three is to-day receiving any such training or has any chance to receive it, and a decent public school system in the South, aided by the national government, is something that must come in the near future, if you expect the race problem to be settled.

Here then are two great needs: public schools and industrial schools. How are schools of any sort established? By furnishing teachers. Given properly equipped teachers and your schools are a foregone success; without them, I care not how much you spend on buildings and equipment, the schools are a failure. It is here that Negro colleges, like Atlanta University, show their first usefulness.

But, in my list of ways in which the Negro may legitimately be helped to help himself, I named two other avenues of aid, and I named them first because to my mind they are even of more importance than popular education. I mean the moral uplift of a people. Now moral uplift comes not primarily from schools, but from strong home life and high social ideals. I have spoken of the Negroes' deficiency in these lines and the reason of that deficiency. Here, then, is a chance for help, but how? Not by direct teaching, because that is often ineffective and it is precluded in the South by the color line. It can be done, to my mind, only by group leadership; by planting in every community of Negroes black men with ideals of life and thrift and civilization, such as must in time filter through the masses and set examples of moral living and correct thinking to the great masses of Negroes who spend but little of their life in schools. After all the education of men comes but in small degree from schools; it comes mostly from the fireside, from companionships, from your social set, from the opinion of each individual's little world. This is even more true of the Negro. His world is smaller. He is shut in to himself by prejudice; he has, by reason of his poverty, little time for school. If he is to learn, he must learn from his group leaders, his daily companions, his social surroundings, his own dark world of striving, longing and dreaming. Here, then, you must plant the seed of civilization. Here you must place men educated, not merely in the technique of teaching or skill of hand, but above and beyond that into a thorough understanding of their age and the demands and meaning of modern culture. In so far as the college of to-day stands for the transmission from age to age of all that is best in the world's deeds, thoughts and traditions, in so far it is a crying necessity that a race, ruthlessly torn from its traditions and trained for centuries awry, should receive back through the higher culture of its gifted children some of the riches of the great system of culture into which it has been thrust. If the meaning of modern life cannot be taught at Negro hearthsides because the parents themselves are untaught, then its ideals can be forced into the centres of Negro life only by the teaching of higher institutions of learning and the agency of thoroughly educated men.

Study Questions

1. What is the significance of Du Bois' narrative journey through a little southern town? What do the various landmarks of this journey represent in his conception of the development of a people?

2. What important differences exist between the two homes Du Bois describes in his narrative journey? What class distinctions exist between the different Negro families living in these homes? How are their moral differences reflected?

3. On what basis does Du Bois appoint certain Negro men as leaders of the race? What tasks does he assign to them? How does he justify the need for such tasks? What values will the leaders espouse? How could the leaders' values be related to their economic status?

4. What is the moral significance of education and work for the development of the Negro race, according to Du Bois? What form must education and work take? How is this related to Du Bois' conception of development?

5. Does Du Bois question the concepts of development, progress, and modernity? How are these connected to his ideas of morality and moral leadership?

Suggestions for Further Reading

Allen, E., Jr. "On the Reading of Riddles: Rethinking Du Boisian 'Double Consciousness'." In *Existence in Black: An Anthology of Black Existential Philosophy,* ed. L. R. Gordon (New York: Routledge, 1997). A critical essay on Du Bois' notion of double consciousness as containing two sets of conflicting ideals.

Bell, B. W., E. R. Grosholz, and J. B. Stewart, eds. *W. E. B. Du Bois on Race and Culture: Philosophy, Politics and Poetics* (New York; London: Routledge, 1996). A collection of essays on Du Bois and the questions of race, women, and pan-Africanism.

Gates, H. L., Jr., and C. West. *The Future of the Race* (New York: Alfred A. Knopf, 1996). Contains three critical essays on Du Bois, particularly on his idea of the Talented Tenth.

Lester, J., ed. Introduction to *The Seventh Son. The Thought and Writings of W. E. B. Du Bois,* Vol.1 (New York: Random House, 1971). A chronological account of Du Bois' life and thought.

Pittman, J. P., ed. *African-American Perspectives and Philosophical Traditions* (New York; London: Routledge, 1997). See "The African American Traditions," especially T. L. Lott's "Du Bois on the Invention of Race."

Williams, R. C. "W. E. B. Du Bois: Afro-American Philosopher of Social Reality." In *Philosophy Born of Struggle: Anthology of Afro-American Philosophy from 1917,* ed. L. Harris (Dubuque, IA: Kendall/Hunt, 1983). A brief analysis of Du Bois' view of American social reality.

Martin Luther King Jr. (1929–1968)

Martin Luther King Jr., the famous African-American civil rights leader, was born in Atlanta, Georgia, into a middle-class family with a standing tradition of Baptist ministry. He grew up during the time of the "Jim Crow" laws of racial segregation and witnessed the racial prejudice, hatred, and injustice against blacks prevalent in the South. However, his father, who was the pastor of the Ebenezer Baptist Church, instilled in him a faith in Christian ideals and a sense of commitment to the black community. Convinced of the value of education as a means to self-development in a white, racist society, King entered Morehouse College in Atlanta at the young age of fifteen. He initially majored in sociology but then decided to enter the ministry, motivated by what he later described as "an inner urge calling me to serve humanity."

During his studies at Morehouse College, King was most impressed with Henry David Thoreau's essay *On Civil Disobedience,* finding that it stirred profound emotions in him. Later, at the Crozer Theological Seminary in Chester, Pennsylvania, he developed an admiration for Gandhi's philosophy of nonviolence. Gandhi's philosophy later "furnished the method" while Jesus' teachings "furnished the spirit and motivation" for King's own political strategies. King also embraced many of the principles of liberal Protestant theology, in particular, the "social gospel" ideals that emphasize the religious importance of addressing the social and economic problems of modern society. While pursuing a doctoral degree in philosophy at Boston University, King came under influence of Edgar S. Brightman's personalist philosophy, which held that only personality, whether it is finite or infinite, is ultimately real. King's exposure to G. W. F. Hegel's philosophy during this time also provided him with a sense of the importance of a synthesis in the conflict between opposites while impressing upon him the idea that "growth comes from struggle."

King's studies in systematic theology at Boston University led him to write his Ph.D. dissertation on "A Comparison of the Conceptions of God in the Thinking of Paul Tillich and Henry Nelson Wieman." Before completing his dissertation, which he defended successfully in 1955, King became the pastor of the Dexter Avenue Baptist Church in Montgomery, Alabama. Following a number of racial incidents over the segregated bus service in Montgomery, including the famous Rosa Parks event, King became increasingly involved in the political struggle against segregation. Eventually, he became the leader of the Montgomery bus boycott, which lasted from 1955 to 1956, when the Supreme Court issued an order ending segregation.

The success of the Montgomery boycott gained King national recognition and led to the founding of the Southern Christian Leadership Conference in 1957 (with King as president). His leadership in the civil rights movement during the 1960s inscribed many important moments in America's history, such as the March on Washington of 1963. Many of his famous addresses, such as the "I Have a Dream" speech delivered on August 28, 1963, remain engraved in its collective memory. King's steadfast commitment to a nonviolent and direct action against racist segregation in the United States earned him the Nobel Peace Prize in 1964. Four years later, he was assassinated while he was staying at the Lorraine Motel in Memphis, Tennessee.

King wrote his famous "Letter from a Birmingham Jail" in 1963, after he had been arrested for leading a march in Birmingham despite an injunction. His letter was a reaction to "An Appeal for Law and Order and Common Sense" issued by eight prominent white ministers from Birmingham who criticized his activities as "unwise and untimely." In the following excerpt, King's response to his critics reflects his belief that human law must be based on justice in order to be the true foundation of a society. Addressing the white ministers' concern over the conscious violation of laws during the civil rights demonstrations, he points to the distinction between just and unjust laws to explain what justifies such violation. The difference depends on whether a society's laws are based on universal and eternal moral principles that uphold the dignity of the human person. If those laws degrade the human personality, they are unjust. Thus, the violation of segregation laws is morally justified because they are unjust laws. In this sense, civil disobedience is a moral duty that involves nonviolent action directed against injustice. Turning the tables against his critics, King concludes by questioning their moral integrity for supporting the unjust system and laws of a racially segregated society and for remaining passive in the fight for justice.

LETTER FROM A BIRMINGHAM JAIL

My Dear Fellow Clergymen,

While confined here in the Birmingham city jail, I came across your recent statement calling our present activities "unwise and untimely." Seldom, if ever, do I pause to answer criticism of my work and ideas. If I sought to answer all of the criticisms that cross my desk, my secretaries would be engaged in little else in the course of the day, and I would have no time for constructive work. But since I feel that you are men of genuine good will and your criticisms are sincerely set forth, I would like to answer your statement in what I hope will be patient and reasonable terms. . . .

. . . I am in Birmingham because injustice is here. Just as the eighth-century prophets left their little villages and carried their "thus saith the Lord" far beyond the boundaries of their hometowns; and just as the Apostle Paul left his little village of Tarsus and carried the gospel of Jesus Christ to practically every hamlet and city of the Graeco-Roman world, I too am compelled to carry the gospel of freedom beyond my particular hometown. Like Paul, I must constantly respond to the Macedonian call for aid.

Moreover, I am cognizant of the interrelatedness of all communities and states. I cannot sit idly by in Atlanta and not be concerned about what happens in Birmingham. Injustice anywhere is a threat to justice everywhere. We are caught in an inescapable network of mutuality, tied in a single garment of destiny. Whatever affects one directly affects all indirectly. Never again can we afford to live with the narrow, provincial "outside agitator" idea. Anyone who lives in the United States can never be considered an outsider anywhere in this country.

You deplore the demonstrations that are presently taking place in Birmingham. But I am sorry that your statement did not express a similar concern for the conditions that brought the demonstrations into being. I am sure that each of you would want to go beyond the superficial social analyst who looks merely at effects, and does not grapple with underlying causes. I would not hesitate to say that it is unfortunate that so-called demonstrations are taking place in Birmingham at this time, but I would say in more emphatic terms that it is even more unfortunate that the white power structure of this city left the Negro community with no other alternative.

In any nonviolent campaign there are four basic steps: (1) collection of the facts to determine whether injustices are alive, (2) negotiation, (3) self-purification, and (4) direct action. We have gone through all of these steps in Birmingham. There can be no gainsaying of the fact that racial injustice engulfs this community. . . .

You express a great deal of anxiety over our willingness to break laws. This is certainly a legitimate concern. Since we so diligently urge people to obey the Supreme Court's decision of 1954 outlawing segregation in the public schools, it is rather strange and paradoxical to find us consciously breaking laws. One may well ask, "How can you advocate breaking some laws and obeying others?" The answer is found in the fact that there are two types of laws: there are *just* and there are *unjust* laws. I would agree with Saint Augustine that "An unjust law is no law at all."

Now what is the difference between the two? How does one determine when a law is just or unjust? A just law is a man-made code that squares with the moral law or the law of God. An unjust law is a code that is out of harmony with the moral law. To put it in the terms of Saint Thomas Aquinas, an unjust law is a human law that is not rooted in eternal and natural law. Any law that uplifts human personality is just. Any law that degrades human personality is unjust. All segregation statutes are unjust because segregation distorts the soul and damages the personality. It gives the segregator a false sense of superiority, and the segregated a false sense of inferiority. To use the words of Martin Buber, the great Jewish philosopher, segregation substitutes an "I-it" relationship for the "I-thou" relationship, and ends up relegating persons to the status of things. So segregation is not only politically, economically and sociologically unsound, but it is morally wrong and sinful. Paul Tillich has said that sin is separation. Isn't segregation an existential expression of man's tragic separation, an expression of his awful estrangement, his terrible sinfulness? So I can urge men to disobey segregation ordinances because they are morally wrong.

Let us turn to a more concrete example of just and unjust laws. An unjust law is a code that a majority inflicts on a minority that is not binding on itself. This is difference made legal. On the other hand a just law is a code that a majority compels a minority to follow that it is willing to follow itself. This is sameness made legal.

Let me give another explanation. An unjust law is a code inflicted upon a minority which that minority had no part in enacting or creating because they did not have the unhampered right to vote. Who can say that the legislature of Alabama which set up the segregation laws was democratically elected? Throughout the state of Alabama all types of conniving methods are used to prevent Negroes from becoming registered voters and there are some counties without a single Negro registered to vote despite the fact that the Negro constitutes a majority of the population. Can any law set up in such a state be considered democratically structured?

These are just a few examples of unjust and just laws. There are some instances when a law is just on its face and unjust in its application. For instance, I was arrested Friday on a charge of parading without a permit. Now there is nothing wrong with an ordinance which requires a permit for a parade, but when the ordinance is used to preserve segregation and to deny citizens the First Amendment privilege of peaceful assembly and peaceful protest, then it becomes unjust.

I hope you can see the distinction I am trying to point out. In no sense do I advocate evading or defying the law as the rabid segregationist would do. This would lead to anarchy. One who breaks an unjust law must do it *openly, lovingly* (not hatefully as the white mothers did in New Orleans when they were seen on television screaming, "nigger, nigger, nigger"), and with a willingness to accept the penalty. I submit that an individual who breaks a law that conscience tells him is unjust, and willingly accepts the penalty by staying in jail to arouse the conscience of the community over its injustice, is in reality expressing the very highest respect for law.

Of course, there is nothing new about this kind of civil disobedience. It was seen sublimely in the refusal of Shadrach, Meshach and Abednego to obey the laws of Nebuchadnezzar because a higher moral law was involved. It was practiced superbly by the early Christians who were willing to face hungry lions and the excruciating pain of chopping blocks, before submitting to certain unjust laws of the Roman Empire. To a degree academic freedom is a reality today because Socrates practiced civil disobedience.

We can never forget that everything Hitler did in Germany was "legal" and everything the Hungarian freedom fighters did in Hungary was "illegal." It was "illegal" to aid and comfort a Jew in Hitler's Germany. But I am sure that if I had lived in Germany during that time I would have aided and comforted my Jewish brothers even though it was illegal. If I lived in a Communist country today where certain principles dear to the Christian faith are suppressed, I believe I would openly advocate disobeying these anti-religious laws. I must make two honest confessions to you, my Christian and Jewish brothers. First, I must confess that over the last few years I have been gravely disappointed with the white moderate. I have almost reached the regrettable conclusion that the Negro's great stumbling block in the stride toward freedom is not the White Citizens Counciler or the Ku Klux Klanner, but the white moderate who is more devoted to "order" than to justice; who prefers a negative peace which is the absence of tension to a positive peace which is the presence of justice; who constantly says, "I agree with you in the goal you seek, but I can't agree with your methods of direct action"; who paternalistically feels that he can set the timetable for another man's

freedom; who lives by the myth of time and who constantly advised the Negro to wait until a "more convenient season." Shallow understanding from people of good will is more frustrating than absolute misunderstanding from people of ill will. Lukewarm acceptance is much more bewildering than outright rejection.

I had hoped that the white moderate would understand that law and order exist for the purpose of establishing justice, and that when they fail to do this they become dangerously structured dams that block the flow of social progress. I had hoped that the white moderate would understand that the present tension of the South is merely a necessary phase of the transition from an obnoxious negative peace, where the Negro passively accepted his unjust plight, to a substance-filled positive peace, where all men will respect the dignity and worth of human personality. Actually, we who engage in non-violent direct action are not the creators of tension. We merely bring to the surface the hidden tension that is already alive. We bring it out in the open where it can be seen and dealt with. Like a boil that can never be cured as long as it is covered up but must be opened with all its pus-flowing ugliness to the natural medicines of air and light, injustice must likewise be exposed, with all of the tension its exposing creates, to the light of human conscience and the air of national opinion before it can be cured.

In your statement you asserted that our actions, even though peaceful, must be condemned because they precipitate violence. But can this assertion be logically made? Isn't this like condemning the robbed man because his possession of money precipitated the evil act of robbery? Isn't this like condemning Socrates because his unswerving commitment to truth and his philosophical delvings precipitated the misguided popular mind to make him drink the hemlock? Isn't this like condemning Jesus because His unique God-consciousness and never-ceasing devotion to his will precipitated the evil act of crucifixion? We must come to see, as federal courts have consistently affirmed, that it is immoral to urge an individual to withdraw his efforts to gain his basic constitutional rights because the quest precipitates violence. Society must protect the robbed and punish the robber. . . .

There was a time when the church was very powerful. It was during that period when the early Christians rejoiced when they were deemed worthy to suffer for what they believed. In those days the church was not merely a thermometer that recorded the ideas and principles of popular opinion; it was a thermostat that transformed the mores of society. Wherever the early Christians entered a town the power structure got disturbed and immediately sought to convict them for being "disturbers of the peace" and "outside agitators." But they went on with the conviction that they were "a colony of heaven," and had to obey God rather than man. They were small in number but big in commitment. They were too God-intoxicated to be "astronomically intimated." They brought an end to such ancient evils as infanticide and gladiatorial contest.

Things are different now. The contemporary church is often a weak, ineffectual voice with an uncertain sound. It is so often the arch-supporter of the status quo. Far from being disturbed by the presence of the church, the power structure of the average community is consoled by the church's silent and often vocal sanction of things as they are.

But the judgment of God is upon the church as never before. If the church of today does not recapture the sacrificial spirit of the early church, it will lose its authentic ring, forfeit the loyalty of millions, and be dismissed as an irrelevant social club with no meaning for the twentieth century. I am meeting young people every day whose disappointment with the church has risen to outright disgust.

Maybe again, I have been too optimistic. Is organized religion too inextricably bound to the status quo to save our nation and the world? Maybe I must turn my faith to the inner spiritual church, the church within the church, as the true *ecclesia* and the hope of the world. But again I

am thankful to God that some noble souls from the ranks of organized religion have broken loose from the paralyzing chains of conformity and joined us as active partners in the struggle for freedom. They have left their secure congregations and walked the streets of Albany, Georgia, with us. They have gone through the highways of the South on tortuous rides for freedom. Yes, they have gone to jail with us. Some have been kicked out of their churches, and lost support of their bishops and fellow ministers. But they have gone with the faith that right defeated is stronger than evil triumphant. These men have been the leaven in the lump of the race. Their witness has been the spiritual salt that has preserved the true meaning of the gospel in these troubled times. They have carved a tunnel of hope through the dark mountain of disappointment.

I hope the church as a whole will meet the challenge of this decisive hour. But even if the church does not come to the aid of justice, I have no despair about the future. I have no fear about the outcome of our struggle in Birmingham, even if our motives are presently misunderstood. We will reach the goal of freedom in Birmingham and all over the nation, because the goal of America is freedom. Abused and scorned through we may be, our destiny is tied up with the destiny of America. Before the Pilgrims landed at Plymouth we were here. Before the pen of Jefferson etched across the pages of history the majestic words of the Declaration of Independence, we were here. For more than two centuries our foreparents labored in this country without wages; they made cotton king; and they built the homes of their masters in the midst of brutal injustice and shameful humiliation—and yet out of a bottomless vitality they continued to thrive and develop. If the inexpressible cruelties of slavery could not stop us, the opposition we now face will surely fail. We will win our freedom because the sacred heritage of our nation and the eternal will of God are embodied in our echoing demands.

Study Questions

1. What criteria does King use to distinguish between just and unjust laws? How does he use this distinction to justify the disobedience of certain laws? How is this justification compatible with the obedience of other laws?
2. How does King support his claim that segregation laws are unjust? What religious and political principles does he appeal to in his argument?
3. When is civil disobedience a moral imperative? How does King relate the notion of civil disobedience to the steps for a nonviolent campaign?
4. Does King suggest why the disobedience of unjust laws must be "civil"? Does he suggest why the campaign against segregation must be "nonviolent"? What principles would support the notions of civility and nonviolence in King's argument?
5. What critiques does King level against "the white moderate" and "the contemporary church"? What are the grounds for his criticism? What moral injunctions does he issue to them?
6. What implications do King's notions of justice, morality, and human personality have for cultural relativism?

Suggestions for Further Reading

Cone, J. H. *Martin & Malcolm & America: A Dream or a Nightmare* (New York: Orbis Books, 1991). A comparison of Martin Luther King Jr.'s. and Malcolm X's views in twelve chapters. Chapters 1, 3, and 5 examine the development of King's ideas.

King, M. L., Jr. *The Trumpet of Conscience* (New York: Harper & Row, 1967). Contains five talks King gave shortly before his death that summarize his moral creed.

Lewis, D. L. *King: A Critical Biography* (New York: Praeger, 1970). A twelve-chapter exposition and evaluation of King's life and thought.

Pittman, J. P., ed. *African-American Perspectives and Philosophical Traditions* (New York; London: Routledge, 1997). For a general background, see B. Boxill's "Two Traditions in African American Political Philosophy."

Walton, H., Jr. *The Political Philosophy of Martin Luther King, Jr* . (Westport, CT: Greenwood, 1971). Analyzes the social and political principles of King's thought and their application in the civil rights movement.

Malcolm X (1925–1965)

Malcolm X was born in Omaha, Nebraska, under the name Malcolm Little. His mother was a West Indian of Scottish and black descent who was committed to a mental asylum when Malcolm was thirteen years old. His father was a Baptist preacher from Georgia who became a follower of Marcus Garvey's black nationalist "back-to-Africa" movement and was murdered when Malcolm was six years old. When he was sixteen, Malcolm went to live with a relative in Roxbury, Massachusetts, where he joined the underground society of burglars, drug dealers, and prostitutes. He was arrested for burglary when he was twenty-one and spent the next six and a half years of his life serving his sentence in the Charlestown Prison of Massachusetts. While in prison, Malcolm converted to Islam and became a follower of Elijah Muhammad, the leader of the Black Muslim Nation of Islam. Paroled from prison for his good conduct, Malcolm took the name Malcolm X, to rid himself of his slave name Little, and became a minister of the Nation of Islam. His charismatic leadership and remarkable skills as a speaker placed him in the spotlight of the public stage and gained him the title of National Minister in 1963.

Because of personal and ideological differences with Elijah Muhammad and other Black Muslim leaders, Malcolm X left the Nation of Islam in 1964 and founded the Muslim Mosque, Inc. In a press conference on March 12, 1964, he stated that the aim of this organization was to give all blacks a "religious base, and the spiritual force necessary to rid our people of the vices that destroy the moral fiber of our community," while offering them a "political philosophy of black nationalism." In his view, the principle of nonviolence that characterized the civil rights struggle led by Martin Luther King Jr. was "criminal" because it taught blacks "not to defend" themselves when they are victims of brutality. While insisting that blacks should be "peaceful, law-abiding," he stressed the need "for the American Negro to fight back in self-defense whenever and wherever he is being unjustly and unlawfully attacked."

In one of his most famous speeches, "The Ballot or the Bullet," first delivered on April 3, 1964, Malcolm X claimed to be joining the civil rights movement by giving it a "new" and "broader interpretation" with his principle of self-defense. In his view, the civil rights struggle had to be based on the philosophy of "by any means necessary," rather than on the "turn-the-other-cheek stuff." Expressing his intention to work "nonviolently as long as the enemy is nonviolent," he emphasized that blacks must be "violent when the enemy gets violent." Critical of the civil rights move toward the integration and identity of blacks as Americans, he construed blacks as "victims of Americanism" who see an "American nightmare" rather than an "American dream." In his judgment, America's "moral conscience" was "bankrupt," so that no political appeal or attempt to change whites would work. "Unity and harmony" among blacks was thus for him the way to "solve the problem ourselves."

After making the *Hajj*—the Muslim religious pilgrimage to Mecca—and visiting various countries in Africa and the Middle East, Malcolm X returned to the United States in May of 1964 with a sense of "true brotherhood" that transcended racial divisions and international borders. This translated into further calls for unity among blacks in the United States and, particularly, with other oppressed peoples of the world. For Malcolm X, the crucial objective was the defense of their human rights, rather than just of their civil rights. Less than a year later, in February of 1965, a firebomb destroyed Malcolm X's home, but no one was killed. However, Malcolm X was assassinated a week later as he addressed an audience at the Audubon Ballroom in Harlem.

Malcolm X delivered his speech "The Black Revolution" on April 8, 1964, in a meeting at Palm Gardens, New York, sponsored by the Militant Labor Forum. The following excerpt reflects his efforts to broaden the horizons of the struggle against racism. Pointing to the oppression of nonwhites in the United States, Africa, Asia, and Latin America, Malcolm X develops the idea of a "world-wide black revolution." The revolt of blacks in the United States is thus inscribed within this international struggle for "rights that are even greater than civil rights and that is human rights." Rather than remaining within the context of the American political system to fight for civil rights,

Malcolm X proposes to "take Uncle Sam to the world court." This proposal is based on his moral condemnation of American society as a system that claims to uphold the values of freedom, justice, and democracy while depriving blacks of their civil and human rights. A "bloodless revolution" of blacks in the United States is possible because its political principles afford all its citizens the right to vote. However, as long as America is "not morally equipped" to live up to its own principles, the black revolution will turn from the denied "ballot" to the "bullet."

THE BLACK REVOLUTION

. . . THERE ARE 22 MILLION African-Americans who are ready to fight for independence right here. When I say fight for independence right here, I don't mean any non-violent fight, or turn-the-other-cheek fight. Those days are gone. Those days are over.

If George Washington didn't get independence for this country nonviolently, and if Patrick Henry didn't come up with a nonviolent statement, and you taught me to look upon them as patriots and heroes, then it's time for you to realize that I have studied your books well. . . .

1964 will see the Negro revolt evolve and merge into the world-wide black revolution that has been taking place on this earth since 1945. The so-called revolt will become a real black revolution. Now the black revolution has been taking place in Africa and Asia and Latin America; when I say black, I mean non-white—black, brown, red or yellow. Our brothers and sisters in Asia, who were colonized by the Europeans, our brothers and sisters in Africa, who were colonized by the Europeans, and in Latin America, the peasants, who were colonized by the Europeans, have been involved in a struggle since 1945 to get the colonialists, or the colonizing powers, the Europeans, off their land, out of their country.

This is a real revolution. Revolution is always based on land. Revolution is never based on beg-

ging somebody for an integrated cup of coffee. Revolutions are never fought by turning the other cheek. Revolutions are never based upon love-your-enemy and pray-for-those-who-spitefully-use-you. And revolutions are never waged singing "We Shall Overcome." Revolutions are based upon bloodshed. Revolutions are never compromising. Revolutions are never based upon negotiations. Revolutions are never based upon any kind of tokenism whatsoever. Revolutions are never even based upon that which is begging a corrupt society or a corrupt system to accept us into it. Revolutions overturn systems. And there is no system on this earth which has proven itself more corrupt, more criminal, than this system that in 1964 still colonizes 22 million African-Americans, still enslaves 22 million Afro-Americans.

There is no system more corrupt than a system that represents itself as the example of freedom, the example of democracy, and can go all over this earth telling other people how to straighten out their house, when you have citizens of this country who have to use bullets if they want to cast a ballot.

The greatest weapon the colonial powers have used in the past against our people has always been divide-and-conquer. America is a colonial power. She has colonized 22 million Afro-Americans by depriving us of first-class citizenship, by depriving us of civil rights, actually by depriving us of human rights. She has not only deprived us of the right to be a citizen, she has deprived us of the right to be human beings, the right to be recognized and respected as men and women. In this country the black can be fifty years old and he is still a "boy."

I grew up with white people. I was integrated before they even invented the word and I have never met white people yet—if you are around them long enough—who won't refer to you as a "boy" or a "gal," no matter how old you are or what school you came out of, no matter what your intellectual or professional level is. In this society we remain "boys."

So America's strategy is the same strategy as that which was used in the past by the colonial powers: divide and conquer. She plays one Negro leader against the other. She plays one Negro organization against the other. She makes us think we have different objectives, different goals. As soon as one Negro says something, she runs to this Negro and asks him, "What do you think about what he said?" Why, anybody can see through that today—except some of the Negro leaders.

All of our people have the same goals, the same objective. That objective is freedom, justice, equality. All of us want recognition and respect as human beings. We don't want to be integrationists. Nor do we want to be separationists. We want to be human beings. Integration is only a method that is used by some groups to obtain freedom, justice, equality and respect as human beings. Separation is only a method that is used by other groups to obtain freedom, justice, equality or human dignity.

Our people have made the mistake of confusing the methods with the objectives. As long as we agree on objectives, we should never fall out with each other just because we believe in different methods or tactics or strategy to reach a common objective.

We have to keep in mind at all times that we are not fighting for integration, nor are we fighting for separation. We are fighting for recognition as human beings. We are fighting for the right to live as free humans in this society. In fact, we are actually fighting for rights that are even greater than civil rights and that is human rights. . . .

Among the so-called Negroes in this country, as a rule the civil-rights groups, those who believe in civil rights, spend most of their time trying to prove they are Americans. Their thinking is usually domestic, confined to the boundaries of America, and they always look upon themselves as a minority. When they look upon themselves upon the American stage, the American stage is a white stage. So a black man standing on that stage in America automatically is in the minority. He is the underdog, and in his struggle he always uses an approach that is a begging, hat-in-hand, compromising approach.

Whereas the other segment or section in America, known as the black nationalists, are more interested in human rights than they are in civil rights. And they place more stress on human rights than they do on civil rights. The difference between the thinking and the scope of the Negroes who are involved in the human-rights struggle and those who are involved in the civil-rights struggle is that those so-called Negroes involved in the human-rights struggle don't look upon themselves as Americans.

They look upon themselves as a part of dark mankind. They see the whole struggle not within the confines of the American stage, but they look upon the struggle on the world stage. And, in the world context, they see that the dark man outnumbers the white man. On the world stage the white man is just a microscopic minority.

So in this country you find two different types of Afro-Americans—the type who looks upon himself as a minority and you as the majority, because his scope is limited to the American scene; and then you have the type who looks upon himself as part of the majority and you as part of a microscopic minority. And this one uses a different approach in trying to struggle for his rights. He doesn't beg. He doesn't thank you for what you give him, because you are only giving him what he should have had a hundred years ago. He doesn't think you are doing him any favors.

He doesn't see any progress that he has made since the Civil War. He sees not one iota of progress because, number one, if the Civil War had freed him, he wouldn't need civil-rights legislation today. If the Emancipation Proclamation, issued by that great shining liberal called Lincoln, had freed him, he wouldn't be singing "We Shall Overcome" today. . . .

You have whites in the community who express sincerity when they say they want to help. Well, how can they help? How can a white person help the black man solve his problem? Number one, you can't solve it for him. You can help him solve it, but you can't solve it for him today. One of the best ways that you can help him solve it is to let the so-called Negro, who has been involved in the civil-rights struggle, see that the civil-rights struggle must be expanded beyond the level of civil rights to human rights. Once it is expanded beyond the level of civil rights to the level of human rights, it opens the door for all of our brothers and sisters in Africa and Asia, who have their independence, to come to our rescue. . . .

The civil-rights struggle involves the black man taking his case to the white man's court. But when he fights it at the human-rights level, it is a different situation. It opens the door to take Uncle Sam to the world court. The black man doesn't have to go to court to be free. Uncle Sam should be taken to court and made to tell why the black man is not free in a so-called free society. Uncle Sam should be taken into the United Nations and charged with violating the UN charter of human rights. . . .

So, in my conclusion, in speaking about the black revolution, America today is at a time or in a day or at an hour where she is the first country on this earth that can actually have a bloodless revolution. In the past, revolutions have been bloody. Historically you just don't have a peaceful revolution. Revolutions are bloody, revolutions are violent, revolutions cause bloodshed and death follows in their paths. America is the only country in history in a position to bring about a revolution without violence and bloodshed. But America is not morally equipped to do so.

Why is America in a position to bring about a bloodless revolution? Because the Negro in this country holds the balance of power, and if the Negro in this country were given what the Constitution says he is supposed to have, the added power of the Negro in this country would sweep all of the racists and the segregationists out of office. It would change the entire political structure of the country. It would wipe out the Southern segregationism that now controls America's foreign policy, as well as America's domestic policy.

And the only way without bloodshed that this can be brought about is that the black man has to be given full use of the ballot in every one of the fifty states. But if the black man doesn't get the ballot, then you are going to be faced with another man who forgets the ballot and starts using the bullet.

Revolutions are fought to get control of land, to remove the absentee landlord and gain control of the land and the institutions that flow from that land. The black man has been in a very low condition because he has had no control whatsoever over any land. He has been a beggar economically, a beggar politically, a beggar socially, a beggar even when it comes to trying to get some education. The past type of mentality, that was developed in this colonial system among our people, today is being overcome. And as the young ones come up, they know what they want. And as they listen to your beautiful preaching about democracy and all those other flowery words, they know what they're supposed to have.

So you have a people today who not only know what they want, but also know what they are supposed to have. And they themselves are creating another generation that is coming up that not only will know what it wants and know what it should have, but also will be ready and willing to do whatever is necessary to see that what they should have materializes immediately. Thank you.

Study Questions

1. What is the moral basis of Malcolm X's critique of the United States and Europe? What are the moral principles in his notion of a "world-wide black revolution"?
2. On what grounds does Malcolm X criticize the civil rights movement? How is this connected to his critique of the U.S. system?
3. What solutions does Malcolm X offer to the problem of racist oppression in the United States? Are they exclusively of a political nature? Is he advocating violence?
4. Has history proved that Malcolm X was wrong about the black revolution? What is the moral significance of his role in this history?

Suggestions for Further Reading

Cone, J. H. *Martin & Malcolm & America: A Dream or a Nightmare* (New York: Orbis Books, 1991). A comparison of Martin Luther King Jr.'s and Malcolm X's views in twelve chapters. Chapters 2, 4, and 7 examine the development of Malcolm X's ideas.

Davis, A. Y. "Meditations on the Legacy of Malcolm X." In *The Angela Davis Reader,* ed. J. James (Boston: Blackwell, 1998). Examines the feminist implications of Malcolm X's legacy.

Epps, A., ed. *Malcolm X: Speeches at Harvard* (New York: Paragon, 1991). Part I, "The Paradoxes of Malcolm X," contains an exploration of the imagery and ideas in Malcolm X's speeches.

Pittman, J. P., ed. *African-American Perspectives and Philosophical Traditions* (New York; London: Routledge, 1997). For a general background, see B. Boxill's "Two Traditions in African American Political Philosophy."

West, C. "Malcolm X on Black Rage." In *Race Matters* (Boston: Beacon Press, 1993). Argues that Malcolm X's role as the prophet of black rage was based on his love for blacks and his notion of pyschic conversion.

Angela Y. Davis (1944–)

Angela Yvonne Davis was born in Birmingham, Alabama, into a middle-class family. Following the footsteps of her grandmother and mother, Davis has been a social and political activist all her life. A revolutionary figure, she has struggled against racism and capitalism in the civil rights movement, the Black Panthers, and the Communist party. In 1970, Davis' political radicalism placed her on the FBI's ten most-wanted list on false charges of kidnapping, conspiracy, and murder. She was incarcerated but was acquitted on all charges in 1972. Driven by her interest in Karl Marx's thought, Davis studied philosophy under the guidance of Herbert Marcuse and Theodor Adorno, both major representatives of critical theory—a philosophical movement that took Marx's critique of capitalism as a main point of departure for its critique of modern technological societies. Davis has incorporated many of the philosophical principles of critical theory into her own work on issues regarding women, class, race, culture, and politics.

Davis' essay, which is included in her book *Women, Culture and Politics,* was originally addressed in 1987 to the National Women's Studies Association. Speaking to a
mainly feminist audience, Davis voices her concerns about the prevalence of color
and class lines within and outside the feminist movement. Feminists have constantly
pursued ways to empower women. Yet, Davis reminds them that African-American
women have a long history of battling not only against sexism but racism and classism as well. She claims that while feminism in the past failed to address the issues
affecting minority and working-class women, today it should incorporate these problems into its agenda. For Davis, the spirit of the African-American women's struggle
has been and should remain one of "lifting as we climb"—helping the oppressed, regardless of their gender or race. She contends that the unifying force for this empowerment of African-American women, which strives for a multiracial and nonsex-
ist unity, is political. Davis argues that since capitalism lies at the root of the problems
of sexism and racism, such empowerment can be attained with a new economic order: socialism.

RADICAL PERSPECTIVES ON EMPOWERMENT FOR AFRO-AMERICAN WOMEN: LESSONS FOR THE 1980S

THE CONCEPT OF EMPOWERMENT is hardly
new to Afro-American women. For almost a century, we have been organized in bodies that have
sought collectively to develop strategies that illuminate the way to economic and political power
for ourselves and our communities. In the last
decade of the nineteenth century, after having
been repeatedly shunned by the racially homogeneous women's rights movement, Black women
organized their own club movement. In 1895—
five years after the founding of the General Fed-
eration of Women's Clubs, which consolidated a
club movement reflecting concerns of middle-
class White women—one hundred Black women
from ten states met in the city of Boston, under
the leadership of Josephine St. Pierre Ruffin, to
discuss the creation of a national organization of
Black women's clubs. As compared to their
White counterparts, the Afro-American women

issuing the call for this national club movement
articulated principles that were more openly political in nature. They defined the primary function of their clubs as an ideological as well as an
activist defense of Black women—and men—
from the ravages of racism. When the meeting
was convened, its participants emphatically declared that, unlike their White sisters, whose organizational policies were seriously tainted by
racism, they envisioned their movement as one
open to all women:

> Our woman's movement is woman's movement
> in that it is led and directed by women for the
> good of women and men, for the benefit of *all*
> humanity, which is more than any one branch
> or section of it. We want, we ask the active in-
> terest of our men, and, too, we are not drawing
> the color line; we are women, American
> women, as intensely interested in all that per-

Angela Y. Davis. "Radical Perspectives on Empowerment for Afro-American Women: Lessons for the 1980s,"
Harvard Educational Review 58, no. 3 (Fall 1988): 348–353. Copyright © 1988 by the President and Fellows
of Harvard College. All rights reserved.

tains to us as such as all other American women; we are not alienating or withdrawing, we are only coming to the front, willing to join any others in the same work and cordially inviting and welcoming any others to join us.[1]

The following year, the formation of the National Association of Colored Women's Clubs was announced. The motto chosen by the Association was "Lifting as We Climb."[2]

The nineteenth-century women's movement was also plagued by classism. Susan B. Anthony wondered why her outreach to working-class women on the issue of the ballot was so frequently met with indifference. She wondered why these women seemed to be much more concerned with improving their economic situation than with achieving the right to vote.[3] As essential as political equality may have been to the larger campaign for women's rights, in the eyes of Afro-American and White working-class women it was not synonymous with emancipation. That the conceptualization of strategies for struggle was based on the peculiar condition of White women of the privileged classes rendered those strategies discordant with working-class women's perceptions of empowerment. It is not surprising that many of them told Ms. Anthony, "Women want bread, not the Ballot."[4] Eventually, of course, working-class White women, and Afro-American women as well, reconceptualized this struggle, defining the vote not as an end in itself—not as the panacea that would cure all the ills related to gender-based discrimination—but rather as an important weapon in the continuing fight for higher wages, better working condi-

tions, and an end to the omnipresent menace of the lynch mob.

Today, as we reflect on the process of empowering Afro-American women, our most efficacious strategies remain those that are guided by the principle used by Black women in the club movement. We must strive to "lift as we climb." In other words, we must climb in such a way as to guarantee that all of our sisters, regardless of social class, and indeed all of our brothers, climb with us. This must be the essential dynamic of our quest for power—a principle that must not only determine our struggles as Afro-American women, but also govern all authentic struggles of dispossessed people. Indeed, the overall battle for equality can be profoundly enhanced by embracing this principle.

Afro-American women bring to the women's movement a strong tradition of struggle around issues that politically link women to the most crucial progressive causes. This is the meaning of the motto, "Lifting as We Climb." This approach reflects the often unspoken interests and aspirations of masses of women of all racial backgrounds. Millions of women today are concerned about jobs, working conditions, higher wages, and racist violence. They are concerned about plant closings, homelessness, and repressive immigration legislation. Women are concerned about homophobia, ageism, and discrimination against the physically challenged. We are concerned about Nicaragua and South Africa, and we share our children's dreams that tomorrow's world will be delivered from the threat of nuclear omnicide. These are some of the issues that should be made a part of the overall struggle for women's rights, if there is to be a serious commitment to the empowerment of women who, throughout history, have been rendered invisible. These are some of the issues we should consider if we wish to lift as we climb.

During this decade we have witnessed an exciting resurgence of the women's movement. If the first wave of the movement appeared in the 1840s, and the second wave in the 1960s, then we are approaching the crest of a third wave in the final days of the 1980s. When the feminist

---

[1] Gerda Lerner, *Black Women in White America* (New York: Pantheon Books, 1972), p. 443.

[2] These clubs proliferated in the progressive political scene during this era. By 1916—twenty years later—50,000 women in 28 federations and over 1,000 clubs were members of the National Association of Colored Women's Clubs. See Paula Giddings's discussion of the origins and evolution of the Black Women's Club Movement in *When and Where I Enter* (New York: Wm. Morrow, 1984), Chps. 4–6.

[3] Miriam Schneir, ed., *Feminism: The Essential Historical Writings* (New York: Vintage, 1972), pp. 138–142.

[4] Schneir, *Feminism.*

historians of the twenty-first century attempt to recapitulate the third wave, will they ignore the momentous contributions of Afro-American women, who have been leaders and activists in movements often confined to women of color, but whose accomplishments have invariably advanced the cause of White women as well? Will the exclusionary policies of the mainstream women's movement—from its inception to the present—which have often compelled Afro-American women to conduct their struggle for equality outside the ranks of that movement, continue to result in the systematic omission of our names from the roster of prominent leaders and activists of the women's movement? Will there continue to be two distinct continua of the women's movement, one visible and another invisible? One publicly acknowledged and another ignored except by the conscious progeny of the working-class women—Black, Latina, Native American, Asian, and White—who forged that hidden continuum? If this question is answered in the affirmative, it will mean that women's quest for equality will continue to be gravely deficient. The revolutionary potential of the women's movement still will not have been realized. The racist-inspired flaws of the first and second waves of the women's movement will have become the inherited flaws of the third wave.

How can we guarantee that this historical pattern is broken? As advocates of and activists for women's rights in the latter 1980s, we must begin to merge that double legacy and create a single continuum, one that solidly represents the aspirations of all women in our society. We must begin to create a revolutionary, multiracial women's movement that seriously addresses the main issues affecting poor and working-class women. In order to tap the potential for such a movement, we must further develop those sectors of the movement that are addressing seriously issues affecting poor and working-class women, such as jobs, pay equity, paid maternity leave, federally subsidized child care, protection from sterilization abuse, and subsidized abortions. Women of all racial and class backgrounds will benefit greatly from such an approach.

Creating a revolutionary women's movement will not be simple. For decades, White women activists have repeated the complaint that Women of Color frequently fail to respond to their appeals: "We invited them to our meetings, but they didn't come; We asked them to participate in our demonstration, but they didn't show; They just don't seem to be interested in women's studies." The process cannot be initiated merely by intensified efforts to attract Latina or Afro-American or Asian or Native American women into the existing organizations dominated by White women of the more privileged economic strata. The particular concerns of women of color must be included in the agenda. . . .

Black women have organized before to oppose racist violence. The birth of the Black Women's Club Movement at the end of the nineteenth century was in large part a response to the epidemic of lynching during that era. Leaders like Ida B. Wells and Mary Church Terrell recognized that Black women could not move toward empowerment if they did not radically challenge the reign of lynch law in the land. Today, in the late 1980s, Afro-American women must actively take the lead in the movement against racist violence, as did our sister-ancestors almost a century ago. We must lift as we climb. As our ancestors organized for the passage of a federal anti-lynch law—and indeed involved themselves in the women's suffrage movement for the purpose of securing that legislation—we must today become activists in the effort to secure legislation declaring racism and anti-Semitism crimes. As extensive as publicized instances of racist violence may be at this time, many more racist-inspired crimes go unnoticed as a consequence of the failure of law enforcement to classify them specifically as such. A person scrawling swastikas or "KKK" on an apartment building may simply be charged—if criminal charges are brought at all—with defacing property or malicious mischief. Recently, a Ku Klux Klansman who burned a cross in front of a Black family's home was charged with "burning without a permit." We need federal and local laws against acts of racist and anti-Semitic violence. We must organize, lobby, march, and demonstrate in order to guarantee their passage.

As we organize, lobby, march, and demonstrate against racist violence, we who are women of color must be willing to appeal for multiracial unity in the spirit of our sister-ancestors. Like them we must proclaim: We do not draw the color line. The only line we draw is one based on our political principles. We know that empowerment for the masses of women in our country will never be achieved as long as we do not succeed in pushing back the tide of racism. It is not a coincidence that sexist-inspired violence—and, in particular, terrorist attacks on abortion clinics—has reached a peak during the same period in which racist violence has proliferated dramatically. Violent attacks on women's reproductive rights are nourished by these explosions of racism. The vicious anti-lesbian and anti-gay attacks are a part of the same menacing process. The roots of sexism and homophobia are found in the same economic and political institutions that serve as the foundation of racism in this country, and, more often than not, the same extremist circles that inflict violence on people of color are responsible for the eruptions of violence inspired by sexist and homophobic biases.

Our political activism must clearly manifest our understanding of these connections. . . .

I want to suggest, as I conclude, that we link our grassroots organizing, our essential involvement in electoral politics, and our involvement as activists in mass struggles with the long-range aim of fundamentally transforming the socioeconomic conditions that generate and persistently nourish the various forms of oppression we suffer. Let us learn from the strategies of our sisters in South Africa and Nicaragua. As Afro-American women, as Women of Color in general, as progressive women of all racial backgrounds, let us join our sisters *and* brothers across the globe who are attempting to forge a new socialist order—an order which will reestablish socioeconomic priorities so that the quest for monetary profit will never be permitted to take precedence over the real interests of human beings. This is not to say that our problems will magically dissipate with the advent of socialism. Rather, such a social order should provide us with the real opportunity to extend further our struggles, with the assurance that one day we will be able to redefine the basic elements of our oppression as useless refuse of the past.

Study Questions

1. Is Davis outlining an ethics that is exclusively for Afro-American women? Does she suggest an ethics for white women? for others who are oppressed? for those who are oppressors?

2. What moral connotations does the concept of empowerment and its opposite have for Davis? Can one dispense with the social, political, and economic character of these notions?

3. According to Davis, in what ways is capitalism the root of other problems such as sexism and racism? Is Davis suggesting that socialism is the only effective way to end racist and sexist oppression?

4. Is Davis suggesting that capitalism is immoral and that socialism is an economic order that can overcome the problems she identifies?

Suggestions for Further Reading

Collins, P. H. *Black Feminist Thought: Knowledge, Consciousness and the Politics of Empowerment* (New York: Routledge, 1991). A general exploration of the perspectives and issues in black feminism. See especially Chapters 1, 2, and 7.

Jaggar, A. M., and I. M. Young, eds. *A Companion to Feminist Philosophy* (Cambridge, MA: Blackwell, 1998). See the essays on "Racism" and "Socialism" for a general feminist perspective of the issues addressed by Davis.

James, J., ed. *The Angela Y. Davis Reader* (Boston: Blackwell, 1998). See James' Introduction and Part IV, "Interviews."

Meyers, D. T., ed. *Feminist Social Thought: A Reader* (New York; London: Routledge, 1997). See especially Part 5, "Social Identity, Solidarity and Political Engagement."

Yang, G., ed., *African American Philosophers. 17 Conversations* (New York; London: Routledge, 1998). Yang interviews Davis on her life and intellectual development.

Cornel West (1953–)

In the preface to his first book, *Prophesy Deliverance!: An Afro-American Revolutionary Christianity* (1982), Cornel West offers his readers an autobiographical sketch of his intellectual, existential, and political trajectory:

> I was nurtured in the bosom of a loving black Christian family and church (Shiloh Baptist Church in Sacramento, California) and I remained committed to the prophetic Christian gospel. I am a product of an Ivy League education which reinforced my unfathomable interest and unquenchable curiosity about the Western philosophical tradition, American culture and Afro-American history —and I have an affinity to a philosophical version of American pragmatism. Lastly, I was politically awakened by the crypto-Marxism of the Black Panther Party and schooled in the Hegelian Marxism of Georg Lukács, the Frankfurt school . . . and I possess an abiding allegiance to progressive Marxist social analysis and political praxis.

West was professor of religion and directed the Department of African American Studies at Yale University. Currently, he teaches in the Department of African American Studies at Harvard University and at the Harvard Divinity School. His books include *The American Evasion of Philosophy: A Genealogy of Pragmatism* (1989), *Keeping Faith: Philosophy and Race in America* (1993), and *Race Matters* (1993). He is also the coauthor with Michael Lerner of *Jews and Blacks: Let the Healing Begin* (1995), with bell hooks of *Breaking Bread: Insurgent Black Intellectual Life* (1993), and with Henry Louis Gates Jr. of *The Future of the Race* (1996).

In an interview by bell hooks, included in *Breaking Bread,* West characterizes his development as that of "an intellectual freedom fighter in the Black Christian tradition" who "understood ideas not only as sources of pleasure but also sources of power." Focusing on the "instrumental value of ideas," he emphasizes that "ideas can be used" for "the enhancement and advancement of poor people in general, and Black people in particular." West's own philosophy has reflected his conviction in the double value of ideas, as well as his belief that ideas and theories must always connect the multiple dimensions of life—from the political, social, and cultural to the existential, spiritual, and intellectual aspects.

The essay excerpted below, "The Pitfalls of Reasoning," is from West's book *Race Matters*. Plato found fault with Athenian democracy as being based on the ignorance and passions of the masses, and Du Bois saw American democracy as being rooted in the racist conception of blacks as a "problem people." West used both these critiques as the backdrop for his own critical reflections on the problem of race in American society today. West argues that a "serious discussion" of this problem "must begin not with the problems of black people but with the flaws of American society," for "the presence and predicaments of black people are neither additions to nor defections from American life, but rather *constitutive elements of that life*." Thus, to be healthy, race relations require a "new framework" where everyone's "basic humanness and Americanness" is recognized.

In West's view, the main challenge that a new order must meet is to generate a new, "visionary" leadership that is attuned to the complex problems of contemporary American society along with its ideals of freedom, democracy, and equality. In the "Pitfalls of Racial Reasoning," he develops a critique of the reasoning followed by black leaders in their response to the issues of race and gender that were raised in the confrontation between the two African-American public figures, Clarence Thomas and Anita Hill. West contends that most black leaders were ensnared in a line of "racial reasoning" that bases its notions of black identity, solidarity, and culture on race, rather than morality. The idea of a black authenticity, the mentality of blacks closing ranks against whites, and culturally conservative positions that support the subordination of black women to black men illustrate how these notions have been grounded in matters of race. Critically questioning the assumptions and inferences of this racial reasoning, West proposes a "new framework for black thought and practice," a "*prophetic* one of moral reasoning" that grounds its fundamental notions in ethical principles, ideals, and standards. The morally based ideas of black identity, black coalition strategy, and black cultural democracy can thus replace the racially based notions of the old framework.

THE PITFALLS OF RACIAL REASONING

INSISTENCE ON PATRIARCHAL VALUES, on equating black liberation with black men gaining access to male privilege that would enable them to assert power over black women, was one of the most significant forces undermining radical struggle. Thorough critiques of gender would have compelled leaders of black liberation struggles to envision new strategies and to talk about black subjectivity in a visionary manner.

bell hooks, *Yearning: Race, Gender, and Cultural Politics* (1990)

The most depressing feature of the Clarence Thomas/Anita Hill hearings was neither the mean-spirited attacks of the Republicans nor the spineless silences of the Democrats—both reveal the predictable inability of most white politicians to talk candidly about race and gender. Rather what was most disturbing was the low level of political discussion in black America about these hearings—a crude discourse about race and gender that bespeaks a failure of nerve of black leadership.

Most black leaders got lost in this thicket of reasoning and hence got caught in a vulgar form of racial reasoning: black authenticity → black closing-ranks mentality → black male subordination of black women in the interests of the black community in a hostile white racist country. . . .

Unfortunately, the very framework of racial reasoning was not called into question. Yet as long as racial reasoning regulates black thought and action, Clarence Thomases will continue to haunt black America—as Bush and other conservatives sit back, watch, and prosper. How does one undermine the framework of racial reasoning? By dismantling each pillar slowly and systematically. The fundamental aim of this undermining and dismantling is to replace racial reasoning with moral reasoning, to understand the black freedom struggle not as an affair of skin pigmentation and racial phenotype but rather as a matter of ethical principles and wise politics, and to combat the black nationalist attempt to subordinate the issues and interests of black women by linking mature black self-love and self-respect to egalitarian relations within and outside black communities. The failure of nerve of black leadership is its refusal to undermine and dismantle the framework of racial reasoning.

. . . What is black authenticity? Who is really black? First, blackness has no meaning outside of a system of race-conscious people and practices. After centuries of racist degradation, exploitation, and oppression in America, being black means being minimally subject to white supremacist abuse and being part of a rich culture and community that has struggled against such abuse. All people with black skin and African phenotype are subject to potential white supremacist abuse. Hence, all black Americans

have some interest in resisting racism—even if their interest is confined solely to themselves as individuals rather than to larger black communities. Yet how this "interest" is defined and how individuals and communities are understood vary. Hence any claim to black authenticity—beyond that of being a potential object of racist abuse and an heir to a grand tradition of black struggle—is contingent on one's political definition of black interest and one's ethical understanding of how this interest relates to individuals and communities in and outside black America. In short, blackness is a political and ethical construct. Appeals to black authenticity ignore this fact; such appeals hide and conceal the political and ethical dimension of blackness. This is why claims to racial authenticity trump political and ethical argument—and why racial reasoning discourages moral reasoning. Every claim to racial authenticity presupposes elaborate conceptions of political and ethical relations of interests, individuals, and communities. Racial reasoning conceals these presuppositions behind a deceptive cloak of racial consensus—yet racial reasoning is seductive because it invokes an undeniable history of racial abuse and racial struggle. . . .

But if claims to black authenticity are political and ethical conceptions of the relation of black interests, individuals, and communities, then any attempt to confine black authenticity to black nationalist politics or black male interests warrants suspicion. . . .

The claims to black authenticity that feed on the closing-ranks mentality of black people are dangerous precisely because this closing of ranks is usually done at the expense of black women. It also tends to ignore the divisions of class and sexual orientation in black America—divisions that require attention if *all* black interests, individuals, and communities are to be taken into consideration. . . .

. . . In white America, cultural conservatism takes the form of a chronic racism, sexism, and homophobia. Hence, only certain kinds of black people deserve high positions, that is, those who accept the rules of the game played by white America. In black America, cultural conservatism takes the form of a inchoate xenophobia (e.g., against whites, Jews, and Asians), systemic sexism, and homophobia. Like all conservatisms rooted in a quest for order, the pervasive disorder in white and, especially, black America fans and fuels the channeling of rage toward the most vulnerable and degraded members of the community. For white America, this means primarily scapegoating black people, women, gay men, and lesbians. For black America, this means principally attacking black women and black gay men and lesbians. In this way, black nationalist and black male-centered claims to black authenticity reinforce black cultural conservatism. . . .

The undermining and dismantling of the framework of racial reasoning—especially the basic notions of black authenticity, closed-ranks mentality, and black cultural conservatism—lead toward a new framework for black thought and practice. This new framework should be a *prophetic* one of moral reasoning with its fundamental ideas of a mature black identity, coalition strategy, and black cultural democracy. Instead of cathartic appeals to black authenticity, a prophetic viewpoint bases mature black self-love and self-respect on the moral quality of black responses to undeniable racist degradation in the American past and present. These responses assume neither a black essence that all black people share nor one black perspective to which all black people should adhere. Rather, a prophetic framework encourages *moral* assessment of the variety of perspectives held by black people and selects those views based on black dignity and decency that eschew putting any group of people or culture on a pedestal or in the gutter. Instead, blackness is understood to be either the perennial possibility of white supremacist abuse or the distinct styles and dominant modes of expression found in black cultures and communities. These styles and modes are diverse—yet they do stand apart from those of other groups (even as they are shaped by and shape those of other groups). And all such styles and modes stand in need of ethical evaluation. Mature black identity results from an acknowledgment of the specific black responses to white supremacist abuses and a moral assessment of these responses such that the humanity of black people does not rest on deifying or demonizing others.

Instead of a closing-ranks mentality, a prophetic framework encourages a coalition strategy that solicits genuine solidarity with those deeply committed to antiracist struggle. This strategy is neither naive nor opportunistic; black suspicion of whites, Latinos, Jews, and Asians runs deep for historical reasons. Yet there are slight though significant antiracist traditions among whites, Asians, and especially Latinos, Jews, and indigenous people that must not be cast aside. Such coalitions are important precisely because they not only enhance the plight of black people but also because they enrich the quality of life in America.

Last, a prophetic framework replaces black cultural conservatism with black cultural democracy. Instead of authoritarian sensibilities that subordinate women or degrade gay men and lesbians, black cultural democracy promotes the equality of black women and men and the humanity of black gay men and lesbians. In short, black cultural democracy rejects the pervasive patriarchy and homophobia in black American life.

Unfortunately, most black leaders remained caught in a framework of racial reasoning—even when they opposed Thomas and/or supported Hill. Rarely did we have a black leader highlight the moral content of a mature black identity, accent the crucial role of coalition strategy in the struggle for justice, or promote the ideal of black cultural democracy. Instead, the debate evolved around glib formulations of a black "role model" based on mere pigmentation, an atavistic defense of blackness that mirrors the increasing xenophobia in American life, and circled around a silence about the ugly authoritarian practices in black America that range from sexual harassment to indescribable violence against women. Hence a grand opportunity for substantive discussion and struggle over race and gender was missed in black America and the larger society. And black leadership must share some of the blame. . . . Yet I hear a cloud of witnesses from afar—Sojourner Truth, Wendell Phillips, Emma Goldman, A.

Phillip Randolph, Ella Baker, Myles Horton, Fannie Lou Hamer, Michael Harrington, Abraham Joshua Heschel, Tom Hayden, Harvey Milk, Robert Moses, Barbara Ehrenreich, Martin Luther King, Jr., and many anonymous others who championed the struggle for freedom and justice in a prophetic framework of moral reasoning. They understood that the pitfalls of racial reasoning are too costly in mind, body, and soul—especially for a downtrodden and despised people like black Americans. The best of our leadership recognized this valuable truth—and more must do so in the future if America is to survive with any moral sense.

Study Questions

1. What are the pillars of racial reasoning according to West's assessment? How are they interconnected? What are the pitfalls of each?
2. What are the fundamental components of West's proposed framework of moral reasoning? How are they related to one another? How do they overcome the problems of racial reasoning?
3. Why does West call his proposed new framework "prophetic"? What role must black leaders play? What requirements must they meet in order to be leaders?
4. Is West suggesting that racial reasoning is amoral or immoral? What racial considerations must prophetic moral reasoning itself make? Do these racial considerations include other races? What role do other races play?
5. What assumptions does West make regarding morality in his proposed new framework?

Suggestions for Further Reading

hooks, b., and C. West. *Breaking Bread: Insurgent Black Intellectual Life* (Boston: South End Press, 1993). Contains intellectual interviews and dialogues between West and hooks.

Johnson, C .S. "Cornel West as Pragmatist and Existentialist." In *Existence in Black: An Anthology of Black Existential Philosophy,* ed. L. R. Gordon (New York; London: Routledge, 1997). A critical examination of West's concern with black nihilism and his prophetic pragmatism.

Pittman, J. P., ed. *African-American Perspectives and Philosophical Traditions* (New York; London: Routledge, 1997). For a general perspective of the issues addressed by West, see "The African-American Tradition" and "Racism, Identity and Social Life."

West, C. "Nihilism in Black America" and "The Crisis in Black Leadership." In *Race Matters* (Boston: Beacon Press, 1993). Contains related reflections and proposals to the problem of race.

Yang, G. ed., *African American Philosophers. 17 Conversations* (New York; London: Routledge, 1998). Yang interviews West on his life and intellectual development.

Aimé Césaire (1913–)

Aimé Césaire, the most acclaimed contemporary poet of the French Caribbean, was born in Basse Pointe, Martinique. His many writings, which include his best-known poem *Journal of a Homecoming* and his controversial essay *Discourse on Colonial-*

ism, give expression to his social critique of colonization and racism while embodying his affirmation of the Negro identity of peoples of the African race throughout the world. A leader of the "negritude movement," which was begun in the 1930s by a group of black students from different countries living in Paris, Césaire is credited with coining the term *negritude* (blackness). He has explained that it arose as a "defiant name" to manifest the "resistance to the politics of assimilation" and the "struggle against alienation" of those who "affirmed that we were Negroes and that we were proud of it."

Besides being the recipient of many literary prizes and honors, Césaire has gained an international reputation as a politician. He has served as deputy in the French parliament, was the major of Fort-de-France, Martinique, and was instrumental in establishing the departmental status of Guadeloupe and Martinique after the Second World War. His political thought has proved to be no less influential for the development of postcolonial and critical race theories.

Written in 1950 and published in 1955, Césaire's *Discourse on Colonialism* attacks the traditional European association of the historical enterprise of colonization with the effort to bring civilization to other parts of the world. In radical opposition to this received view, Césaire develops a morally charged critique that highlights the roots of racism and the dehumanizing effects of colonialism. In this sense, far from being linked with civilization, colonization is nothing less than savagery. It is itself the product of the moral decadence and irrationality of bourgeois imperialism. However, the morally unconscionable acts of what Césaire terms the "so-called Western civilization" have reaped their punishment with the culmination of the racism represented in Hitler. Applying the nineteenth-century German philosopher G. W. F. Hegel's famous analysis of the master-slave dialectic, Césaire argues further that the colonizer's relationship to the colonized as something less than human has the effect of dehumanizing and "decivilizing" the colonizer himself. Thus, in the following selection, Césaire concludes by claiming that the efforts of the colonized toward liberation are themselves indicative of where the true drive for civilization lies.

DISCOURSE ON COLONIALISM

A CIVILIZATION that proves incapable of solving the problems it creates is a decadent civilization.

A civilization that chooses to close its eyes to its most crucial problems is a stricken civilization.

A civilization that uses its principles for trickery and deceit is a dying civilization.

The fact is that the so-called European civilization—"Western" civilization—as it has been shaped by two centuries of bourgeois rule, is incapable of solving the two major problems to which its existence has given rise: the problem of the proletariat and the colonial problem; that

Aimé Césaire. "Discourse on Colonialism." In Discourse on Colonialism, *trans. J. Pinkham. New York: Monthly Review Press, 1972, pp. 9–12, 19–25. Copyright © 1972 by Monthly Review Press. Reprinted by permission of Monthly Review Foundation.*

Europe is unable to justify itself either before the bar of "reason" or before the bar of "conscience"; and that, increasingly, it takes refuge in a hypocrisy which is all the more odious because it is less and less likely to deceive.

Europe is indefensible.

Apparently that is what the American strategists are whispering to each other.

That in itself is not serious.

What is serious is that "Europe" is morally, spiritually indefensible.

And today the indictment is brought against it not by the European masses alone, but on a world scale, by tens and tens of millions of men who, from the depths of slavery, set themselves up as judges.

The colonialists may kill in Indochina, torture in Madagascar, imprison in Black Africa, crack down in the West Indies. Henceforth the colonized know that they have an advantage over them. They know that their temporary "masters" are lying.

Therefore that their masters are weak.

And since I have been asked to speak about colonization and civilization, let us go straight to the principal lie which is the source of all the others.

Colonization and civilization?

In dealing with this subject, the commonest curse is to be the dupe in good faith of a collective hypocrisy that cleverly misrepresents problems, the better to legitimize the hateful solutions provided for them.

In other words, the essential thing here is to see clearly, to think clearly—that is, dangerously—and to answer clearly the innocent first question: what, fundamentally, is colonization? To agree on what it is not: neither evangelization, nor a philanthropic enterprise, nor a desire to push back the frontiers of ignorance, disease, and tyranny, nor a project undertaken for the greater glory of God, nor an attempt to extend the rule of law. To admit once for all, without flinching at the consequences, that the decisive actors here are the adventurer and the pirate, the wholesale grocer and the ship owner, the gold digger and the merchant, appetite and force, and

behind them, the baleful projected shadow of a form of civilization which, at a certain point in its history, finds itself obliged, for internal reasons, to extend to a world scale the competition of its antagonistic economies.

Pursuing my analysis, I find that hypocrisy is of recent date; that neither Cortez discovering Mexico from the top of the great teocalli, nor Pizzaro before Cuzco (much less Marco Polo before Cambalue), claims that he is the harbinger of a superior order; that they kill; that they plunder; that they have helmets, lances, cupidities; that the slavering apologists came later; that the chief culprit in this domain is Christian pedantry, which laid down the dishonest equations *Christianity=civilization, paganism=savagery,* from which there could not but ensue abominable colonialist and racist consequences, whose victims were to be the Indians, the yellow peoples, and the Negroes.

That being settled, I admit that it is a good thing to place different civilizations in contact with each other; that it is an excellent thing to blend different worlds; that whatever its own particular genius may be, a civilization that withdraws into itself atrophies; that for civilizations, exchange is oxygen; that the great good fortune of Europe is to have been a crossroads, and that because it was the locus of all ideas, the receptacle of all philosophies, the meeting place of all sentiments, it was the best center for the redistribution of energy.

But then I ask the following question: has colonization really *placed civilizations in contact*? Or, if you prefer, of all the ways of *establishing contact,* was it the best?

I answer no.

And I say that between *colonization* and *civilization* there is an infinite distance; that out of all the colonial expeditions that have been undertaken, out of all the colonial statutes that have been drawn up, out of all the memoranda that have been despatched by all the ministries, there could not come a single human value. . . .

First we must study how colonization works to *decivilize* the colonizer, to *brutalize* him in the true sense of the word, to degrade him, to awaken him to buried instincts, to covetousness, violence, race hatred, and moral relativism; and we must show that each time a head is cut off or an eye put out in Vietnam and in France they accept the fact, each time a little girl is raped and in France they accept the fact, each time a Madagascan is tortured and in France they accept the fact, civilization acquires another dead weight, a universal regression takes place, a gangrene sets in, a center of infection begins to spread; and that at the end of all these treaties that have been violated, all these lies that have been propagated, all these punitive expeditions that have been tolerated, all these prisoners who have been tied up and "interrogated," all these patriots who have been tortured, at the end of all the racial pride that has been encouraged, all the boastfulness that has been displayed, a poison has been instilled into the veins of Europe and, slowly but surely, the continent proceeds toward *savagery.* . . .

What am I driving at? At this idea: that no one colonizes innocently, that no one colonizes with impunity either; that a nation which colonizes, that a civilization which justifies colonization—and therefore force—is already a sick civilization, a civilization that is morally diseased, that irresistibly, progressing from one consequence to another, one repudiation to another, calls for its Hitler, I mean its punishment.

Colonization: bridgehead in a campaign to civilize barbarism, from which there may emerge at any moment the negation of civilization, pure and simple. . . .

. . . Colonization, I repeat, dehumanizes even the most civilized man; that colonial activity, colonial enterprise, colonial conquest, which is based on contempt for the native and justified by that contempt, inevitably tends to change him who undertakes it; that the colonizer, who in order to ease his conscience gets into the habit of seeing the other man as *an animal,* accustoms himself to treating him like an animal, and tends objectively to transform *himself* into an animal. It is this result, this boomerang effect of colonization, that I wanted to point out. . . .

Between colonizer and colonized there is room only for forced labor, intimidation, pressure, the police, taxation, theft, rape, compulsory crops, contempt, mistrust, arrogance, self-complacency, swinishness, brainless élites, degraded masses.

No human contact, but relations of domination and submission which turn the colonizing man into a class-room monitor, an army sergeant, a prison guard, a slave driver, and the indigenous man into an instrument of production.

My turn to state an equation: colonization = "thingification."

I hear the storm. They talk to me about progress, about "achievements," diseases cured, improved standards of living.

I am talking about societies drained of their essence, cultures trampled underfoot, institutions undermined, lands confiscated, religions smashed, magnificent artistic creations destroyed, extraordinary *possibilities* wiped out. . . .

They talk to me about civilization, I talk about proletarianization and mystification.

For my part, I make a systematic defense of the non-European civilizations. . . .

Every day that passes, every denial of justice, every beating by the police, every demand of the workers that is drowned in blood, every scandal that is hushed up, every punitive expedition, every police van, every gendarme and every militiaman, brings home to us the value of our old societies.

They were communal societies, never societies of the many for the few.

They were societies that were not only ante-capitalist, as has been said, but also *anti-capitalist.*

They were democratic societies, always.

They were cooperative societies, fraternal societies.

I make a systematic defense of the societies destroyed by imperialism.

. . . I maintain that colonialist Europe is dishonest in trying to justify its colonizing activity *a posteriori* by the obvious material progress that has been achieved in certain fields under the colonial regime—since *sudden change* is always possible, in history as elsewhere; since no one knows at what stage of material development these same countries would have been if Europe had not intervened; since the technical outfitting of Africa and Asia, their administrative reorganization, in a word, their "Europeanization," was (as is proved by the example of Japan) in no way tied to the European *occupation;* since the Europeanization of the non-European continents could have been accomplished otherwise than under the heel of Europe; since this movement of Europeanization *was in progress;* since it was even slowed down; since in any case it was distorted by the European takeover.

The proof is that at present it is the indigenous peoples of Africa and Asia who are demanding schools, and colonialist Europe which refuses them; that it is the African who is asking for ports and roads, and colonialist Europe which is niggardly on this score; that it is the colonized man who wants to move forward, and the colonizer who holds things back.

Study Questions

1. What are the moral grounds of Césaire's critique of colonialism? How are they related to his critique of racism and capitalism?
2. How does Césaire understand the distinction between civilization and savagery? Does he manage to overcome the racist basis of this distinction?
3. In what ways is colonialism "decivilizing"? How does this occur?
4. Does Césaire suggest that colonized societies are morally superior to imperialist ones? Does he explain why and how the colonized are truly the ones that "look forward"?
5. Does Césaire retain traditional European notions in his critique? If so, is this problematic?

Suggestions for Further Reading

Césaire, A. "An Interview with Aimé Césaire." In *Discourse on Colonialism,* trans. J. Pinkham. (New York: Monthly Review Press, 1972). René Depeste's interview of Césaire in 1967 on his poetry and his idea of negritude.

Davis, G. *Aimé Césaire* (Cambridge, MA: Cambridge University Press, 1997). A biographical account and analysis of Césaire's dual career as a poet and statesman.

English, P., and K. M. Kalumba, eds. *African Philosophy: A Classical Approach* (Englewood Cliffs, NJ: Prentice-Hall, 1996). See Part IV, "Liberation Philosophy."

Hord, F. L. (Mzee Lasana Okpara) and J. S. Lee, eds. *I Am Because We Are: Readings in Black Philosophy* (Amherst: University of Massachusetts Press, 1995). See "The Caribbean" for a sample of other perspectives.

Sartre, J.-P. *Black Orpheus,* trans. S. W. Allen (Paris: Présence Africaine, 1963). A philosophical reflection on the theory of negritude with special reference to Césaire.

Frantz Fanon (1925–1961)

Frantz Fanon was born in Fort-de-France, Martinique. He studied medicine in France, specializing in psychiatry. Drawing from his own experiences as a black man from a French colony, Fanon published *Black Skin, White Masks,* which he introduced as a psychological analysis or "clinical study" of "the various attitudes that the Negro adopts in contact with white civilization." Breaking from the traditional Freudian focus on the individual, Fanon emphasized the significance of the social and economic character of the alienation of the black man, particularly as it unfolds in the black-white relation. Diagnosing this relation as one that "created a massive psychoexistential complex," Fanon expressed the hope of "analyzing it to destroy it." His proposal for "the liberation of the man of color from himself" saw this as a process of extricating the individual from the aberrational universe that creates "the black" and dehumanizes him. In this sense, Fanon saw the search for a "black identity" as an attitude that "renounces the present and the future in the name of a mystical past." His "painful" conclusion was "For the black man there is only one destiny. And it is white." In this sense, the search for a "black soul" is a quest for a "white man's artifact" and thus remains within the white man's universe.

Shortly after the publication of *Black Skin, White Masks,* Fanon was appointed head of psychiatry at the Blida-Joinville Hospital in Algeria. Bearing witness to the economic, social, and political causes and the psychological effects of colonialism and racism in Algeria, Fanon began to stress the need for psychiatry to see the larger context of society and to critically assess its own role within that whole. Increasingly sympathetic to the rebel's causes during the Franco-Algerian war and dissatisfied with the absence of a socially transformative role for psychiatry, Fanon eventually abandoned his medical practice to join the revolution. He became a spokesperson for the Algerian revolution as he took an editorial position on *El Moudjadid,* the newspaper of the National Liberation Front (FLN) located in Tunis. Fanon died one year before Algeria achieved independence.

Fanon expanded his critical analyses of racism and colonialism and his call for liberation beyond Martinique and Algeria. He saw a deep connection between the outcome of the Algerian revolution and the fate of the African continent as a whole. He also highlighted the universal features of the causes, effects, and solutions to the problems of colonialism in the Antilles, Africa, and other countries of the third world. Fanon acknowledged the significance of the search for black identity in the negritude movement initiated by black intellectuals from various colonies. However, he insisted that these pursuits should be merely transitionary stages toward liberation. In his last book, *The Wretched of the Earth,* he proposed that since the capitalist exploitation of the "third world" had been marked by violence, violence was also a necessary means for decolonization and the attainment of nationhood in third world countries. However, Fanon emphasized that the armed struggles for national liberation should not end in an imitation of Europe or a return to a mystical pre-European past. As he urged his readers in his last lines, "we must turn over a new leaf, we must work out new concepts, and try to set afoot a new man."

Delivered in Paris in 1956 as a speech before the First National Congress of Negro Writers and Artists, Fanon's "Racism and Culture" examines the interrelation between these two aspects of the social fabric of colonialism. Fanon argues that racism is not a determining feature of all cultures or of culture as such. Rather, it arises from the drive to dominate and oppress others, and thus forms part of the colonizing culture. The development from biological to cultural racism is determined by the changes in the economic exploitation and social domination—from the crude beginnings of colonization to its more sophisticated industrialized stages. As an important element in the systematic oppression of the colonized, racism affects the conduct of both oppressors and oppressed. Fanon outlines the universal features or constants of racism at the cultural level while emphasizing that it pervades the whole of society in its structure, institutions, and values. In this sense, racism is not a matter of individual perspectives and psychological attitudes but of a social and cultural dynamic that is based on economic domination and exploitation. Therefore, the struggle of the oppressed must have the goal of a total liberation from colonialism and, with this, the end of racism. Only then can both cultures mutually respect each other in their differences and recognize their "reciprocal relativism."

RACISM AND CULTURE

THE UNILATERALLY DECREED normative value of certain cultures deserves our careful attention. One of the paradoxes immediately encountered is the rebound of egocentric, sociocentric definitions.

There is first affirmed the existence of human groups having no culture; then of a hierarchy of cultures; and finally, the concept of cultural relativity.

We have here the whole range from overall negation to singular and specific recognition. It is precisely this fragmented and bloody history that we must sketch on the level of cultural anthropology.

There are, we may say, certain constellations of institutions, established by particular men, in the framework of precise geographical areas, which at a given moment have undergone a direct and sudden assault of different cultural patterns. The technical, generally advanced development of the social group that has thus appeared enables it to set up an organized domination. The enterprise of deculturation turns out to be the negative of a more gigantic work of economic, and even biological, enslavement.

The doctrine of cultural hierarchy is thus but one aspect of a systematized hierarchization implacably pursued.

The modern theory of the absence of cortical integration of colonial peoples is the anatomic-physiological counterpart of this doctrine. The apparition of racism is not fundamentally determining. Racism is not the whole but the most visible, the most day-to-day and, not to mince matters, the crudest element of a given structure.

To study the relations of racism and culture is to raise the question of their reciprocal action. If culture is the combination of motor and mental behavior patterns arising from the encounter of man with nature and with his fellow-man, it can be said that racism is indeed a cultural element. There are thus cultures with racism and cultures without racism.

This precise cultural element, however, has not become encysted. Racism has not managed to harden. It has had to renew itself, to adapt itself, to change its appearance. It has had to undergo the fate of the cultural whole that informed it.

Frantz Fanon. "Racism and Culture." In Toward the African Revolution (Political Essays), *trans. H. Chevalier. New York: Monthly Review Press, 1967, pp. 31–44. Copyright © 1967 by Monthly Review Press. Reprinted by permission of Monthly Review Foundation.*

The vulgar, primitive, over-simple racism purported to find in biology—the Scriptures having proved insufficient—the material basis of the doctrine. It would be tedious to recall the efforts then undertaken: the comparative form of the skulls, the quantity and the configuration of the folds of the brain, the characteristics of the cell layers of the cortex, the dimensions of the vertebrae, the microscopic appearance of the epiderm, etc. . . .

We must look for the consequences of this racism on the cultural level.

Racism, as we have seen, is only one element of a vaster whole: that of the systematized oppression of a people. How does an oppressing people behave? Here we rediscover constants.

We witness the destruction of cultural values, of ways of life. Language, dress, techniques, are devalorized. How can one account for this constant? Psychologists, who tend to explain everything by movements of the psyche, claim to discover this behavior on the level of contacts between individuals: the criticism of an original hat, of a way of speaking, of walking . . .

Such attempts deliberately leave out of account the special character of the colonial situation. In reality the nations that undertake a colonial war have no concern for the confrontation of cultures. War is a gigantic business and every approach must be governed by this datum. The enslavement, in the strictest sense, of the native population is the prime necessity.

For this its systems of reference have to be broken. Expropriation, spoliation, raids, objective murder, are matched by the sacking of cultural patterns, or at least condition such sacking. The social panorama is destructured; values are flaunted, crushed, emptied.

The lines of force, having crumbled, no longer give direction. In their stead a new system of values is imposed, not proposed but affirmed, by the heavy weight of cannons and sabers.

The setting up of the colonial system does not of itself bring about the death of the native culture. Historic observation reveals, on the contrary, that the aim sought is rather a continued agony than a total disappearance of the pre-existing culture. This culture, once living and open to the future, becomes closed, fixed in the colonial status, caught in the yoke of oppression. Both present and mummified, it testifies against its members. It defines them in fact without appeal. The cultural mummification leads to a mummification of individual thinking. The apathy so universally noted among colonial peoples is but the logical consequence of this operation. The reproach of inertia constantly directed at "the native" is utterly dishonest. As though it were possible for a man to evolve otherwise than within the framework of a culture that recognizes him and that he decides to assume. . . .

The constantly affirmed concern with "respecting the culture of the native populations" accordingly does not signify taking into consideration the values borne by the culture, incarnated by men. Rather, this behavior betrays a determination to objectify, to confine, to imprison, to harden. Phrases such as "I know them," "that's the way they are," show this maximum objectification successfully achieved. I can think of gestures and thoughts that define these men.

Exoticism is one of the forms of this simplification. It allows no cultural confrontation. There is on the one hand a culture in which qualities of dynamism, of growth, of depth can be recognized. As against this, we find characteristics, curiosities, things, never a structure.

Thus in an initial phase the occupant establishes his domination, massively affirms his superiority. The social group, militarily and economically subjugated, is dehumanized in accordance with a polydimensional method.

Exploitation, tortures, raids, racism, collective liquidations, rational oppression take turns at different levels in order literally to make of the native an object in the hands of the occupying nation.

This object man, without means of existing, without a *raison d'être*, is broken in the very depth of his substance. The desire to live, to continue, becomes more and more indecisive, more and more phantom-like. It is at this stage that the well-known guilt complex appears. In his first novels, Wright gives a very detailed description of it.

Progressively, however, the evolution of techniques of production, the industrialization, limited though it is, of the subjugated countries, the increasingly necessary existence of collaborators, impose a new attitude upon the occupant. The complexity of the means of production, the evolution of economic relations inevitably involving the evolution of ideologies, unbalance the system. Vulgar racism in its biological form corresponds to the period of crude exploitation of man's arms and legs. The perfecting of the means of production inevitably brings about the camouflage of the techniques by which man is exploited, hence of the forms of racism.

It is therefore not as a result of the evolution of people's minds that racism loses its virulence. No inner revolution can explain this necessity for racism to seek more subtle forms, to evolve. On all sides men become free, putting an end to the lethargy to which oppression and racism had condemned them.

In the very heart of the "civilized nations" the workers finally discover that the exploitation of man, at the root of a system, assumes different faces. At this stage racism no longer dares appear without disguise. It is unsure of itself. In an ever greater number of circumstances the racist takes to cover. He who claimed to "sense," to "see through" those others, finds himself to be a target, looked at, judged. The racist's purpose has become a purpose haunted by bad conscience. He can find salvation only in a passion-driven commitment such as is found in certain psychoses. . . .

Racism is never a super-added element discovered by chance in the course of the investigation of the cultural data of a group. The social constellation, the cultural whole, are deeply modified by the existence of racism.

Racism bloats and disfigures the face of the culture that practices it. Literature, the plastic arts, songs for shopgirls, proverbs, habits, patterns, whether they set out to attack it or to vulgarize it, restore racism. This means that a social group, a country, a civilization, cannot be unconsciously racist.

We say once again that racism is not an accidental discovery. It is not a hidden, dissimulated element. No superhuman efforts are needed to bring it out.

Racism stares one in the face for it so happens that it belongs in a characteristic whole: that of the shameless exploitation of one group of men by another which has reached a higher stage of technical development. This is why military and economic oppression generally precedes, makes possible, and legitimizes racism.

The habit of considering racism as a mental quirk, as a psychological flaw, must be abandoned. . . .

Race prejudice in fact obeys a flawless logic. A country that lives, draws its substance from the exploitation of other peoples, makes those peoples inferior. Race prejudice applied to those peoples is normal.

Racism is therefore not a constant of the human spirit.

It is, as we have seen, a disposition fitting into a well-defined system. And anti-Jewish prejudice is no different from anti-Negro prejudice. A society has race prejudice or it has not. There are no degrees of prejudice. One cannot say that a given country is racist but that lynchings or extermination camps are not to be found there. The truth is that all that and still other things exist on the horizon. These virtualities, these latencies circulate, carried by the life-stream of psycho-affective, economic relations . . .

Discovering the futility of his alienation, his progressive deprivation, the inferiorized individual, after this phase of deculturation, of extraneousness, comes back to his original positions.

This culture, abandoned, sloughed off, rejected, despised, becomes for the inferiorized an object of passionate attachment. There is a very marked kind of overvaluation that is psychologically closely linked to the craving for forgiveness.

But behind this simplifying analysis there is indeed the intuition experienced by the inferiorized of having discovered a spontaneous truth. This is a psychological datum that is part of the texture of History and of Truth. . . .

Rediscovering tradition, living it as a defense mechanism, as a symbol of purity, of salvation, the decultured individual leaves the impression that the mediation takes vengeance by substantializing itself. This falling back on archaic positions having no relation to technical development is paradoxical. The institutions thus valorized no longer correspond to the elaborate methods of action already mastered.

The culture put into capsules, which has vegetated since the foreign domination, is revalorized. It is not reconceived, grasped anew, dynamized from within. It is shouted. And this headlong, unstructured, verbal revalorization conceals paradoxical attitudes.

It is at this point that the incorrigible character of the inferiorized is brought out for mention. Arab doctors sleep on the ground, spit all over the place, etc. . . .

Negro intellectuals consult a sorcerer before making a decision, etc. . . .

"Collaborating" intellectuals try to justify their new attitude. The customs, traditions, beliefs, formerly denied and passed over in silence are violently valorized and affirmed.

Tradition is no longer scoffed at by the group. The group no longer runs away from itself. The sense of the past is rediscovered, the worship of ancestors resumed . . .

The past, becoming henceforth a constellation of values, becomes identified with the Truth.

This rediscovery, this absolute valorization almost in defiance of reality, objectively indefensible, assumes an incomparable and subjective importance. On emerging from these passionate espousals, the native will have decided, "with full knowledge of what is involved," to fight all forms of exploitation and of alienation of man. At this same time, the occupant, on the other hand, multiplies appeals to assimilation, then to integration, to community.

The native's hand-to-hand struggle with his culture is too solemn, too abrupt an operation to tolerate the slightest slip-up. No neologism can mask the new certainty: the plunge into the chasm of the past is the condition and the source of freedom.

The logical end of this will to struggle is the total liberation of the national territory. In order to achieve this liberation, the inferiorized man brings all his resources into play, all his acquisitions, the old and the new, his own and those of the occupant.

The struggle is at once total, absolute. But then race prejudice is hardly found to appear.

At the time of imposing his domination, in order to justify slavery, the oppressor had invoked scientific argument. There is nothing of the kind here.

A people that undertakes a struggle for liberation rarely legitimizes race prejudice. Even in the course of acute periods of insurrectional armed struggle one never witnesses the recourse to biological justifications.

The struggle of the inferiorized is situated on a markedly more human level. The perspectives are radically new. The opposition is the henceforth classical one of the struggles of conquest and of liberation.

In the course of struggle the dominating nation tries to revive racist arguments but the elaboration of racism proves more and more ineffective. There is talk of fanaticism, of primitive attitudes in the face of death, but once again the now crumbling mechanism no longer responds. Those who were once unbudgeable, the constitutional cowards, the timid, the eternally inferiorized, stiffen and emerge bristling.

The occupant is bewildered.

The end of race prejudice begins with a sudden incomprehension.

The occupant's spasmed and rigid culture, now liberated, opens at last to the culture of people who have really become brothers. The two cultures can affront each other, enrich each other.

In conclusion, universality resides in this decision to recognize and accept the reciprocal relativism of different cultures, once the colonial status is irreversibly excluded.

Study Questions

1. What is the nature of the relation between racism and culture in Fanon's view? What is the basis of racism? How does racism manifest itself culturally? What are the constants in the effects of racism on the oppressor and the oppressed?

2. How does Fanon support his claim that racism is not inherent in all cultures? Is he suggesting that colonialism is necessarily racist?

3. Is Fanon suggesting that the system of moral values of the colonizing culture is completely determined by its economic oppression of the colonized? Is he suggesting that this moral system is pervaded by racism?

4. Is Fanon issuing a moral condemnation of colonialism? If so, on what grounds? Is there a moral significance to his depictions of the oppressed in their struggle for total liberation? to his portrayal of the end of colonialism?

5. How does Fanon's idea of "reciprocal relativism" translate into ethical terms? Is this a moral ideal for Fanon? How does this idea apply to his own critique of colonialism?

Suggestions for Further Reading

Caute, D. *Frantz Fanon* (New York: Viking Press, 1970). For a view of the development of Fanon's thoughts on racism and colonialism, see Chapter III, "A Philosophy in Transition."

English, P., and K. M. Kalumba, eds. *African Philosophy: A Classical Approach* (Englewood Cliffs, NJ: Prentice-Hall, 1996). For a sample of similar perspectives, see Part IV, "Liberation Philosophy."

Gordon, L. R. *Fanon: A Critical Reader* (Boston: Blackwell, 1996). Contains twenty-one essays covering Fanon's views on various issues.

Hord, F. L. (Mzee Lasana Okpara), and J. S. Lee, eds. *I Am Because We Are: Readings in Black Philosophy* (Amherst: University of Massachusetts Press, 1995). For a sample of Caribbean philosophies, see "The Caribbean."

Sartre, J.-P. Preface to Frantz Fanon's *The Wretched of the Earth,* trans. C. Farrington (New York: Grove Press, 1963). Provides an introduction to Fanon's thought through a philosophical reflection on his views of colonialism and racism.

Paulo Freire (1921–1997)

Paulo Freire, the Brazilian educator and philosopher, revolutionized the theory and practice of education throughout the world. After studying law and philosophy, Freire became a teacher of adult illiterates in Brazil. He worked as director of the Department of Education of the Social Service in Pernambuco, taught the history and philosophy of education at the University of Recife, and was placed in charge of a national governmental literacy campaign until the military coup of 1965. After being jailed, stripped of his citizenship, and sentenced to exile by the new military government, Freire left to Chile, where he worked for UNESCO and published his first book, *Pedagogy of the Oppressed* (1970). Gaining an international reputation for his radical reconception of education as a process of liberation from oppression, Freire participated in many educational projects in different countries and published a number of influential books on pedagogy. After almost fifteen years of political exile, Freire was allowed to returned to Brazil, where he continued his national and international work in education until his death.

Freire captured the central concept of his theory of education in the Portuguese term *conscientização:* he conceived education as the development from a naïve to a critical consciousness of one's situation of oppression and to an active effort to transform this situation. In this sense, learning is itself a process of liberation from social injustice. Modeling his theory of education on G. W. F. Hegel's analysis of the master-slave dynamic and Karl Marx's critical theory of the capitalist-proletarian class conflict, Freire proposes that the relation between oppressor and oppressed demands its own dissolution because it dehumanizes both social groups. Depriving the oppressed of freedom and independence reduces them to mere objects for an other. Indoctrinated into submission and fear by an ideology that serves the interests of the oppressors, the oppressed require an education that assists them in their self-liberation and self-transformation. Borrowing from the existentialist notion of authenticity, Freire emphasizes that the oppressed must themselves learn to become free, independent subjects developing their potential as human beings. Like the Socratic ideal of philosophy as midwifery, Freire's program of education is a dialogue in which the oppressed, with the aid of the educator, mark their own course of self-discovery, critical reflections, and decisions to take action.

The following selection is taken from Chapter 1 of Freire's *Pedagogy of the Oppressed.* Elaborating on the idea that oppression is dehumanization, Freire first makes an effort to justify the need for a pedagogy of the oppressed. Dehumanization distorts our absolute vocation to develop our human potential to its fullest. It is necessary to put an end to oppression, for wherever and whenever it occurs it thwarts humanization. Because the oppressors are themselves the agents of power and domination, they are socially incapable of breaking the dehumanizing bonds of oppression. Only the oppressed can accomplish this historic and humanist task by liberating themselves and their oppressors. Only then can the vicious circle of oppression be broken. The task of the educator is to assist the oppressed through the painful and difficult process of *conscientização*. As the oppression is overcome, this task thus evolves from a pedagogy of the oppressed into a pedagogy of all human beings for their permanent liberation and fullest humanization.

PEDAGOGY OF THE OPPRESSED

WHILE THE PROBLEM of humanization has always, from an axiological point of view, been man's central problem, it now takes on the character of an inescapable concern. Concern for humanization leads at once to the recognition of dehumanization, not only as an ontological possibility but as an historical reality. And as man perceives the extent of dehumanization, he asks himself if humanization is a viable possibility. Within history, in concrete, objective contexts, both humanization and dehumanization are possibilities for man as an uncompleted being conscious of his incompletion.

But while both humanization and dehumanization are real alternatives, only the first is man's vocation. This vocation is constantly negated, yet it is affirmed by that very negation. It is thwarted by injustice, exploitation, oppression, and the violence of the oppressors; it is affirmed by the yearning of the oppressed for freedom and justice, and by their struggle to recover their lost humanity.

Dehumanization, which marks not only those whose humanity has been stolen, but also (though in a different way) those who have stolen it, is a *distortion* of the vocation of becoming more fully human. This distortion occurs within history; but it is not an historical vocation. Indeed, to admit of dehumanization as an historical vocation would lead either to cynicism or total despair. The struggle for humanization, for the emancipation of labor, for the overcoming of alienation, for the affirmation of men as persons would be meaningless. This struggle is possible only because dehumanization, although a concrete historical fact, is *not* a given destiny but the result of an unjust order that engenders violence in the oppressors, which in turn dehumanizes the oppressed.

Because it is a distortion of being more fully human, sooner or later being less human leads the oppressed to struggle against those who made them so. In order for this struggle to have meaning, the oppressed must not, in seeking to regain their humanity (which is a way to create it), become in turn oppressors of the oppressors, but rather restorers of the humanity of both.

This, then, is the great humanistic and historical task of the oppressed: to liberate themselves and their oppressors as well. The oppressors, who oppress, exploit, and rape by virtue of their power, cannot find in this power the strength to liberate either the oppressed or themselves. Only power that springs from the weakness of the oppressed will be sufficiently strong to free both. Any attempt to "soften" the power of the oppressor in deference to the weakness of the oppressed almost always manifests itself in the form of false generosity; indeed, the attempt never goes beyond this. In order to have the continued opportunity to express their "generosity," the oppressors must perpetuate injustice as well. An unjust social order is the permanent fount of this "generosity," which is nourished by death, despair, and poverty. That is why the dispensers of false generosity become desperate at the slightest threat to its source.

True generosity consists precisely in fighting to destroy the causes which nourish false charity. False charity constrains the fearful and subdued, the "rejects of life," to extend their trembling hands. True generosity lies in striving so that these hands—whether of individuals or entire peoples—need be extended less and less in supplication, so that more and more they become human hands which work and, working, transform the world. . . .

The "fear of freedom" which afflicts the oppressed,[1] a fear which may equally well lead them to desire the role of oppressor or bind them to the role of oppressed, should be examined. One of the basic elements of the relationship between oppressor and oppressed is *prescription*. Every prescription represents the imposition of one man's choice upon another, transforming the consciousness of the man prescribed to into one that conforms with the prescriber's consciousness. Thus, the behavior of the oppressed is a prescribed behavior, following as it does the guidelines of the oppressor.

The oppressed, having internalized the image of the oppressor and adopted his guidelines, are fearful of freedom. Freedom would require them to eject this image and replace it with autonomy and responsibility. Freedom is acquired by conquest, not by gift. It must be pursued constantly and responsibly. Freedom is not an ideal located outside of man; nor is it an idea which becomes myth. It is rather the indispensable condition for the quest for human completion.

To surmount the situation of oppression, men must first critically recognize its causes, so that through transforming action they can create a new situation, one which makes possible the pursuit of a fuller humanity. But the struggle to be more fully human has already begun in the authentic struggle to transform the situation. Although the situation of oppression is a dehumanized and dehumanizing totality affecting both the oppressors and those whom they oppress, it is the latter who must, from their stifled humanity, wage for both the struggle for a fuller humanity; the oppressor, who is himself dehumanized because he dehumanizes others, is unable to lead this struggle. . . .

The oppressed suffer from the duality which has established itself in their innermost being. They discover that without freedom they cannot exist authentically. Yet, although they desire authentic existence, they fear it. They are at one and the same time themselves and the oppressor whose consciousness they have internalized. The conflict lies in the choice between being wholly themselves or being divided; between ejecting the oppressor within or not ejecting him; between human solidarity or alienation; between following prescriptions or having choices; between being spectators or actors; between acting or having the illusion of acting through the action of the oppressors; between speaking out or being silent, castrated in their power to create and re-create, in their power to transform the world. This is the tragic dilemma of the oppressed which their education must take into account.

This book will present some aspects of what the writer has termed the pedagogy of the oppressed, a pedagogy which must be forged *with*, not *for*, the oppressed (whether individuals or peoples) in the incessant struggle to regain their humanity. This pedagogy makes oppression and its causes objects of reflection by the oppressed, and from that reflection will come their necessary engagement in the struggle for their liberation. And in the struggle this pedagogy will be made and remade.

The central problem is this: How can the oppressed, as divided, unauthentic beings, participate in developing the pedagogy of their liberation? Only as they discover themselves to be "hosts" of the oppressor can they contribute to the midwifery of their liberating pedagogy. As long as they live in the duality in which *to be* is *to be like*, and *to be like* is *to be like the oppressor*, this contribution is impossible. The pedagogy of the oppressed is an instrument for their critical discovery that both they and their oppressors are manifestations of dehumanization.

Liberation is thus a childbirth, and a painful one. The man who emerges is a new man, viable only as the oppressor-oppressed contradiction is superseded by the humanization of all men. Or to put it another way, the solution of this contradiction is born in the labor which brings into

---

[1]This fear of freedom is also to be found in the oppressors, though, obviously, in a different form. The oppressed are afraid to embrace freedom; the oppressors are afraid of losing the "freedom" to oppress.

the world this new man: no longer oppressor nor longer oppressed, but man in the process of achieving freedom.

This solution cannot be achieved in idealistic terms. In order for the oppressed to be able to wage the struggle for their liberation, they must perceive the reality of oppression not as a closed world from which there is no exit, but as a limiting situation which they can transform. This perception is a necessary but not a sufficient condition for liberation; it must become the motivating force for liberating action. Nor does the discovery by the oppressed that they exist in dialectical relationship to the oppressor, as his antithesis—that without them the oppressor could not exist—in itself constitute liberation. The oppresed can overcome the contradiction in which they are caught only when this perception enlists them in the struggle to free themselves.

The pedagogy of the oppressed, animated by authentic, humanist (not humanitarian) generosity, presents itself as a pedagogy of man. Pedagogy which begins with the egoistic interests of the oppressors (an egoism cloaked in the false generosity of paternalism) and makes of the oppressed the objects of its humanitarianism, itself maintains and embodies oppression. It is an instrument of dehumanization. This is why, as we affirmed earlier, the pedagogy of the oppressed cannot be developed or practiced by the oppressors. It would be a contradiction in terms if the oppressors not only defended but actually implemented a liberating education.

But if the implementation of a liberating education requires political power and the oppressed have none, how then is it possible to carry out the pedagogy of the oppressed prior to the revolution? . . .

One aspect of the reply is to be found in the distinction between *systematic education,* which can only be changed by political power, and *educational projects,* which should be carried out *with* the oppressed in the process of organizing them.

The pedagogy of the oppressed, as a humanist and libertarian pedagogy, has two distinct stages. In the first, the oppressed unveil the world of oppression and through the praxis commit themselves to its transformation. In the second stage, in which the reality of oppression has already been transformed, this pedagogy ceases to belong to the oppressed and becomes a pedagogy of all men in the process of permanent liberation. In both stages, it is always through action in depth that the culture of domination is culturally confronted. In the first stage this confrontation occurs through the change in the way the oppressed perceive the world of oppression; in the second stage, through the expulsion of the myths created and developed in the old order, which like specters haunt the new structure emerging from the revolutionary transformation.

Study Questions

1. In what sense is Freire's pedagogy of the oppressed a theory of moral education? What moral claims are involved in his ideas of humanization, dehumanization, and oppression? in his critique of systematic education?

2. Why do the oppressed have an historic and humanist task? Does Freire suggest that this is the moral responsibility of the oppressed? Does he suggest it is solely theirs? Does he assign any moral responsibilities to the oppressor?

3. Why must the oppressed also liberate the oppressor? What moral standards must this process follow? Why?

4. What forms must education take in the pedagogy of the oppressed? Why? What is the role of *conscientização*? What is the significance of what Freire calls praxis?

5. What moral imperatives are there in role of educator? What possible moral conflicts and dilemmas could the educator face in this role?

Suggestions for Further Reading

English, P., and K. M. Kalumba, eds. *African Philosophy: A Classical Approach* (Englewood Cliffs, NJ: Prentice-Hall, 1996). For a sample of similar perspectives, see Part IV, "Liberation Philosophy."

Mackie, R., ed. *Literacy and Revolution: The Pedagogy of Paulo Freire* (New York: Continuum, 1981). Contains critical essays by educators on Freire's work and ideas. Includes an interview of Freire.

McLaren, P., and P. Leonard, eds. *Paulo Freire: A Critical Encounter* (London; New York: Routledge, 1993). A collection of essays by international scholars and educators. Includes an interview of Freire.

Schutte, O. *Cultural Identity and Social Liberation in Latin American Thought* (New York: State University of New York Press, 1993). Chapter 6 offers a critical perspective of liberation philosophy, including Freire's.

Enrique Dussel (1921–)

Enrique Dussel is an Argentinean philosopher known for his contributions to the Latin American philosophy of liberation. He is the author of more than twenty books; several have been translated into English—among them *Ethics and Theology of Liberation, Philosophy of Liberation,* and *Ethics and Community.* Because of his social and political beliefs, Dussel was persecuted and forced to leave Argentina after the right-wing military coup of 1976. He lives and teaches in Mexico.

The philosophy of liberation has its historical roots in the liberation theology movement that began in Brazil and Peru during the late 1960s. In liberation theology, the central idea is that of an integral liberation of human beings, in the sociopolitical as well as the spiritual or religious dimensions of their lives. The Christian ideal of salvation from sin is thus closely intertwined with the goals of freedom and redemption from oppression, exploitation, and poverty. In the 1970s, a new conception emerged that saw sociopolitical liberation as a matter of philosophical analysis and engagement, rather than an exclusive question of religious faith and spiritual mission. Dussel belonged to the group of Argentinean intellectuals who first formed the self-denominated philosophy of liberation movement. Over the years, he has combined Christian religious principles with philosophical ideas (from G. W. F. Hegel, Karl Marx, Martin Heidegger, and Emmanuel Levinas) into a philosophy of liberation that takes the social problem of domination as its starting point.

In the following selection, from a chapter in *Ethics and Community,* Dussel proposes to develop a social ethics from the perspective of liberation theology. He establishes a critical distinction between "morality," the set of beliefs and practices belonging to the given socioeconomic and political system, and "ethics," the ideal order of future liberation and social justice. His notion of "prevailing social morality" refers to socioeconomic and political orders that are based on domination. Following the Hebrew-Christian theological principle that equates the name "Babylon" with orders of oppression ruled by the Devil, Dussel associates the prevailing system of moral practices with an order based on sin. "Prevailing social morality" is really an inversion of morality, for it is not grounded on the spiritual order ruled by God, but on the worldly order ruled by men. Such morality plays the role of justifying and perpetuating oppression by enforcing the values that serve the system of domination. In this sense, its function is "ideological." So, it disguises itself in order to accomplish its task. Moral conscience is itself an ideological means that stresses obedience by emphasizing the adherence to established social norms and the application of given moral principles. In this manner, the system as a whole remains unquestioned and unchallenged. Dussel's ethics of liberation aims to redeem those oppressed from these fetters of morality. In direct opposition to the order of domination, its ethical ideal is that of a spiritual community based on justice.

PREVAILING SOCIAL MORALITY: THE "BABYLON PRINCIPLE"

. . . WE READ in holy scripture:

> In her hand she held a gold cup that was filled with the abominable and sordid deeds of her lewdness. On her forehead was written a symbolic name, "*Babylon the great,* mother of harlots and all the world's abominations." I saw that the woman was drunk with the blood of God's holy ones and the blood of those martyred for their faith in Jesus.
>
> When I saw her I was greatly astonished. The angel said to me: "Why are you so taken aback? I will explain to you the symbolism of the woman and of the seven-headed and ten-horned beast carrying her" [Rev. 17:4–7].

Evil, sin—whether individual but subsumed in the social, or concretely and historically social—is organized or "institutionalized." The mystery revealed in the Book of Revelation is actually more current today than ever, and merits our close attention. The Dragon, the Beast, the kings and authorities at their disposal, their envoys or angels, their servants, their customs, laws, and powers, all constitute a full-fledged order, that of *this world*—as category—and its prevailing morality. . . .

I now propose to borrow a number of terms from ordinary speech and endow each of them with a narrower, more precise, meaning for purposes of our discourse.

First, for purposes of our discourse, the term "morality" (or "morals," and so on)—of Latin origin—will denote any "practical" (from "praxis") system of the prevailing, established order, the order now in place (see 3.3). By "ethics" ("ethical," and so on)—of Greek derivation—I denote the future order of liberation, the demands of justice with respect to the poor, the oppressed, and their project (historical—see 1.9; or eschatological—see 1.10) of salvation.

Enrique Dussel. "Prevailing Social Morality: The 'Babylon Principle'." In Ethics and Community, *trans. R. R. Barr. Maryknoll, NY: Orbis Books, 1988. Reprinted by permission of Orbis Books.*

Thus something might be "moral" without being "ethical," and vice versa. All of this will become clearer in the following pages.

Secondly, "prevailing social," "social," even "society," will have a restricted, negative meaning, and will denote the "worldly"—the condition of the individual (labor, toil, and so on) in the prevailing order of domination, of sin. "Community," on the other hand (along with "communal," and so on), will stand for the face-to-face relationship of persons standing in a relationship of justice. So "community" will denote a utopian order from whose perspective we shall be able to criticize the prevailing "social" element. This is why I have entitled this work "Ethics and Community," and not "Prevailing Social Morality," or even "Social Morality."

Thus a praxis can be "good" in the eyes of the prevailing *morality* and "evil" for an *ethics* of liberation. Jesus was a blasphemer, a disturber of the social order, one who deserved to die, and so on—in other words, "evil"—for the order of the dominant values of the "elders, priests, and scribes," for Herod (governor of the nation), and for Pilate (representative of the occupying imperial power). . . .

Original Hebreo-Christian theology possessed a category to express the structural *totality* of the practices of sin. This totality assumed a distinct concrete physiognomy at each historical moment, while retaining an analogous essence.

At the time of Moses, the world—the system according to the dictates of the flesh—was Egypt. And God said, "I have beheld the oppression of my people in Egypt. I have heard their cries against their oppressors. I have fixed on their sufferings" (Exod. 3:7). "*In* Egypt" is a category. The Monarchy, which was founded on idolatry, came to represent the same category. God addressed the prophet Samuel: "As they dealt with me from the day I led them forth from Egypt, abandoning me to serve other gods, thus they treat you" (1 Sam. 8:8). The new order, the system of the practices of the kings, will make of the people an oppressed mass. "You shall be slaves! Then will you cry out against the kings

they have chosen for themselves, but God will not answer you" (1 Sam. 8:18).

Later the people was to have yet another experience of suffering and oppression: the Babylonion captivity: "All this land will lie desolate, and the neighboring nations will be subject to the king of Babylon" (Jer. 25:11). "Babylon" signifies the order of oppression, that of the Devil. "All, great and small, rich and poor, slave and free, he made that they mark them on the right hand or the forehead" (Rev. 13:17).

This system is closed in upon itself. It has replaced the universal human project with its own particular historical project. Its laws become natural, its virtues perfect, and the blood of those who offer any resistance—the blood of the prophets and heroes—is spilled by the system as if it were the blood of the wicked, the totally subversive. . . .

Essential to an ethics of liberation is a clear understanding of the starting point of the praxis of liberation. This starting point is sin, the world as a system of sin, the flesh as idolatrous desire, and a system that nevertheless is "moral," having its own morality and a justified, tranquil conscience.

Any system of prevailing, dominant practices (from Egypt or Babylon to Rome, the several Christendoms, or capitalist society) determines its established practices to be good. Its project (its end, its *telos,* its *beatitudo,* as the Latin theologians termed it) is confused with the "perfect human good" as such. Thus the norms that demand the execution of this project are "natural law." The prohibition, "Thou shalt not steal the private property of thy neighbor," for example, has been part of capitalism's "natural law" since the eighteenth century. The virtues of the project are now obligatory as the highest virtues of all. Somehow the habit of amassing wealth fails to remind anyone of the usury or avarice of feudalism.

Thus arises a "prevailing" *moral system* (regardless of its origin, regardless of the fact that it owes its subsistence to an "original," institutional sin of domination at all levels. The persons who comply with this system, in its practices, its norms, its values, its "virtues," its laws, are good, just, and meritorious persons, and they win the praise of their peers.

Now a total inversion has been achieved. Domination and sin have been transformed into the very foundation of reality. Perverse praxis is now goodness and justice. Ideology, operating as a cloak over the reality of domination, now legitimates the praxis of the flesh and of the world as if it were the praxis of the very reign of God. . . .

The "practical" universe within the moral system of the prevailing order is inverted. Accordingly, it is this system itself that determines the good or evil of an act.

The classic definition of morality was expressed in terms of relationship to a norm or law. Kant demanded the moral law be loved. For Thomas Aquinas it was the relations of an act to the moral law that determined its morality. The problem, obviously, is that once the system of the world has asserted itself as the foundation or law, morality will depend precisely on the actualization of the system. An act will be *morally* good if it is "adequated to," if it complies with, the ends of the prevailing system. If I pay taxes, the minimum wage, and so on, as required by law, I shall be a "just" person, a "good" person. The law itself may be unjust. The taxes may be insufficient, the wages may be starvation wages. But all of that lies *outside* any possible moral consideration.

Correlatively, *immorality* will be constituted by the sheer non-realization of the prevailing norm. The thief whose thievery is a vice is now less wicked than the prophet who criticizes the system in its totality. Barabbas and Jesus are both "evil" for the Jewish and Roman morality of their time. Juan del Valle, bishop of Popayán, was regarded by the *encomenderos* of sixteenth-century Latin America as "the *worst* bishop in the Indies" because he defended the Indians.

And so it comes about that, in their respect and love for the law of the prevailing system—its norms, its ends, its values—dominators, though they are sinners, are nevertheless seen to be just and good. The "Prince of *this world*" is now the judge of good and evil. Morality itself has been inverted. The "wisdom of the world" has become norm and law. . . .

To complete the circle, the "world" forms or educates the "moral" conscience of its members according to criteria of the flesh.

Classically, "*moral* conscience" was that faculty of the practical intelligence that applies moral principles to concrete cases. A principle states: "You shall not steal." But in this concrete case I desire to appropriate goods regarded by the system of prevailing practical moral principles as belonging to someone else. In this case my conscience commands me: "Do not do so, for by doing so you would constitute yourself liable to the penalty determined for those who 'steal' something." Whereupon, if I "steal" nonetheless, my conscience will recriminate me, accuse me, give me subjective culpability, by reason of this *morally* evil act.

If my *moral* conscience has been formed within a framework of the principles of the system, it will recriminate me if I fail to comply with the laws of the system. But it will be unable to tell me that the system *as a totality* is perverse (for conscience *applies* principles, and does not establish them). Thus the theft of property that is the private possession of someone else is a moral offense, and conscience indicates it to me. But my own private property, which may well constitute, in its origin, the (objectified) *dispossession of others of their labor* (see 11.6)—although that dispossession may have occurred imperceptibly as far as my own consciousness, my own conscience, is concerned—presents itself as legitimate and good. All other persons, "Hands off!"

Here I am being *blind* to the fact that private property denied to the workers whose labor has produced it is unjustified accumulation, taking over the capital of the fruits of their labor, previously stolen from them *without* my being conscious of the theft.

In this fashion, "moral" conscience, formed in the moral principles of the dominant system, creates a peaceful, remorseless conscience vis-à-vis a practice that the system approves but that may originally have been perverse (a praxis of domination). . . .

We have taken a further step. The negation of the *community* by sin, wickedness, and the death of the poor, has become a *society,* in which relationships among individuals enjoy institutionalization due to a *principle* of wickedness, of injustice: the reign of *this world,* Babylon. Sin, the domination of one human being by another, not only is not exclusively individual—its "social-ness" has taken on historical, concrete form. Sin has a transcendent principle (the Evil One, the Dragon), a principle immanent in history (the Beast—at the time of the prophet of Revelation, the Roman empire), its kings at its disposal, and its angels to fulfill its commands. They are the "rich," all those who are sinners and dominators in their being subjects or agents of sin and of the praxis that instrumentalizes neighbors as "things."

Study Questions

1. What distinction does Dussel make between morality and ethics? between society and community? How are these distinctions related? What is their overall significance in Dussel's social ethics?
2. What is Dussel's understanding of the prevailing system of morality and moral conscience? How does he associate these with the "Babylon principle"? Why does he characterize them as ideological?
3. What does Dussel mean by "inversion of morality"? Is there an original morality? How do we determine whether morality is inverted or not?
4. Is Dussel suggesting that all prevailing systems are evil? Does evil reside in the worldly character of prevailing systems? Does it reside in the order of domination? Does the worldly character of the prevailing systems necessarily bring out domination and social injustice?
5. What would be the crucial difference between a theology of domination and a theology of liberation? How would the theology of liberation respond to the practical dimension of the oppressors' lives? to their spiritual situation of sin?

Suggestions for Further Reading

Barber, M. *Ethical Hermeneutics: Rationality in Enrique Dussel's Philosophy of Liberation* (New York: Fordham University Press, 1999). Provides a comprehensive introduction to Dussel that traces the development, influences, and major criticisms of his philosophy of liberation.

Novak, M. *Will It Liberate?: Questions about Liberation Theology* (New York: Paulist Press, 1986). A critique of liberation theology that focuses on the concepts used by Dussel.

Preston, R. "Christian Ethics." In *A Companion to Ethics,* ed. P. Singer (Oxford; Cambridge, MA: Blackwell, 1991). A general introduction to the Christian tradition in ethics.

Schutte, O. *Cultural Identity and Social Liberation in Latin American Thought* (New York: State University of New York Press, 1993). Chapter 6 offers a critical perspective of liberation philosophy, including Dussel's.

———. "Origins and Tendencies of the Philosophy of Liberation in Latin American Thought: A Critique of Dussel's Ethics." *The Philosophical Forum 22,* no. 3 (Spring 1991): 270–295. Argues against Dussel that philosophy of liberation and Marxism are incompatible while questioning the progressive character of the philosophy of liberation.

Valadez, J. "Pre-Columbian and Modern Philosophical Perspectives in Latin America." In *From Africa to Zen: An Invitation to World Philosophy,* eds. R. C. Solomon and K. M. Higgins (Lanham, MD: Rowman & Littlefield, 1993). An overview of Latin American philosophy.

Black Elk (1863–1950)

Black Elk was a Native American who belonged to the Oglala Lakota or Sioux tribe. The Lakota perceive the universe as sacred, whole, and one. The totality of life forces animating and connecting the universe is called *Wakan Tanka,* the Great Mysteriousness. It manifests itself in spirit forces from the Six Directions of the universe (west, north, east, south, above, below), which are represented by the Six Grandfathers or spiritual leaders. When he was nine years old, Black Elk received a vision from the Thunder-beings (*Wakinyan*), the spirit forces of the west. In this vision, he saw himself as the Sixth Grandfather, symbolizing the "below" direction of the universe, and thus as the spiritual representative of the earth and humanity. As a Thunder dreamer, Black Elk had a spiritual calling to use his gifts of prophecy and healing. Like his grandfather and father, he became a healer who was highly revered by the Oglala as a holy man (*wichasha wakon*).

Living on the Pine Ridge Reservation in South Dakota, Black Elk witnessed the decline of the traditional Lakota ways in the face of the white people's dominance. When he was twenty-three, he decided to learn more about the white man's culture and joined Buffalo Bill's Wild West show. After three years of performing in places such as New York, England, Germany, Italy, and France, Black Elk returned to the Pine Ridge Reservation. He continued serving his people as their shamanic healer until he became a Catholic in his late thirties. Eventually, he became a fervent catechist, actively inducing the Oglala and other Native American tribes people into the Catholic faith. Though suffering from tuberculosis, like many other Oglala living on the reservation, Black Elk lived until he was eighty-six years old.

Black Elk's teachings were first put into writing by John G. Neihardt, poet laureate of Nebraska, who met Black Elk in 1930 while completing the final volume of his epic poem, *Cycle of the West.* Entitled *The Song of the Messiah,* Neihardt's poem narrates the story of the Ghost Dance, a spiritual movement in the late 1880s based on a revelation that promised Native Americans a return to their traditional life. This promise inspired them to continue the struggles against the white people's encroachment on their land. The Ghost Dance had a tragic ending (at the battle at Wounded Knee creek, South Dakota on December 29, 1890). More than two hundred Native Americans were killed two weeks later by the cavalry. Because Black Elk had joined the Ghost Dance movement and had fought at Wounded Knee, Neihardt approached him to gain further insight into the spiritual significance of this event. Black Elk, with his son Ben as interpreter, told his life story to Neihardt, stating that his chief purpose was to "save his Great Vision for man."

Two books resulted from Neihardt's interviews of Black Elk: *Black Elk Speaks* (1932) and *When the Tree Flowered* (1951). Later, John Epes Brown's book, *The Sacred Pipe: Black Elk's Account of the Seven Rites of the Oglala Sioux* (1963), joined Neihardt's two books to form the basic canon of Black Elk's spiritual teachings. However, although these teachings have made an enormous impact on Native Americans and non-Native Americans, there is much controversy as to whether they are true reflections of Black Elk's words and the Lakota system of beliefs. In particular, the extent and weight of Neihardt's interpretative and editorial licenses in *Black Elk Speaks* has been a topic of considerable debate.

In "The Offering of the Pipe," the first chapter of *Black Elk Speaks,* Black Elk describes to Neihardt the spiritual significance of the life story he is about to relate. Black Elk's emphasis on the transcendent meaning of his narration as "the story of all life that is holy and is good to tell" resonates with the traditional Lakota belief in the sacredness, wholeness, and oneness of the universe. His mission as a holy man is thus to share with others his wisdom—based on his visions into the holiness of the world. His offering of the pipe is inscribed within the Lakota system of beliefs and rituals emphasizing the oneness of the universe and the interrelatedness of all life forms. The Lakota see the ceremonial smoking of the pipe as a way in which humans bind themselves in relationships with higher spiritual beings and among themselves. These relationships call for aid and pity from the higher spiritual beings and assign moral duties of peace, friendship, and cooperation among humans. Black Elk's explanation of the symbolism of the pipe and his story on how it was brought to the Lakota by the sacred woman (known as White Buffalo Woman) convey these spiritual perspectives and their moral import. The values upheld in this Native American world view have been contrasted with the dominant way of thinking about the earth and humanity by critics of contemporary Western cultures. Black Elk's teachings remain today a classic source for such critiques, particularly for those concerned with developing an environmental ethics.

THE OFFERING OF THE PIPE

BLACK ELK SPEAKS:

My friend, I am going to tell you the story of my life, as you wish; and if it were only the story of my life I think I would not tell it; for what is one man that he should make much of his winters, even when they bend him like a heavy snow? So many other men have lived and shall live that story, to be grass upon the hills.

It is the story of all life that is holy and is good to tell, and of us two-leggeds sharing in it with the four-leggeds and the wings of the air and all green things; for these are children of one mother and their father is one Spirit.

This, then, is not the tale of a great hunter or of a great warrior, or of a great traveler, although I have made much meat in my time and fought for my people both as boy and man, and have gone far and seen strange lands and men. So also have many others done, and better than I. These things I shall remember by the way, and often they may seem to be the very tale itself, as when I was living them in happiness and sorrow. But now that I can see it all as from a lonely hilltop,

I know it was the story of a mighty vision given to a man too weak to use it; of a holy tree that should have flourished in a people's heart with flowers and singing birds, and now is withered; and of a people's dream that died in bloody snow.

But if the vision was true and mighty, as I know, it is true and mighty yet; for such things are of the spirit, and it is in the darkness of their eyes that men get lost.

So I know that it is a good thing I am going to do; and because no good thing can be done by any man alone, I will first make an offering and send a voice to the Spirit of the World, that it may help me to be true. See, I fill this sacred pipe with the bark of the red willow; but before we smoke it, you must see how it is made and what it means. These four ribbons hanging here on the stem are the four quarters of the universe. The black one is for the west where the thunder beings live to send us rain; the white one for the north, whence comes the great white cleansing wind; the red one for the east, whence springs the light and where the morning star lives to give men wisdom; the yellow for the south, whence come the summer and the power to grow.

But these four spirits are only one Spirit after all, and this eagle feather here is for that One, which is like a father, and also it is for the thoughts of men that should rise high as eagles do. Is not the sky a father and the earth a mother, and are not all living things with feet or wings or roots their children? And this hide upon the mouthpiece here, which should be bison hide, is for the earth, from whence we came and at whose breast we suck as babies all our lives, along with all the animals and birds and trees and grasses. And because it means all this, and more than any man can understand, the pipe is holy.

There is a story about the way the pipe first came to us. A very long time ago, they say, two scouts were out looking for bison; and when they came to the top of a high hill and looked north, they saw something coming a long way off, and when it came closer they cried out, "It is

a woman!," and it was. Then one of the scouts, being foolish, had bad thoughts and spoke them; but the other said: "That is a sacred woman; throw all bad thoughts away." When she came still closer, they saw that she wore a fine white buckskin dress, that her hair was very long and that she was young and very beautiful. And she knew their thoughts and said in a voice that was like singing: "You do not know me, but if you want to do as you think, you may come." And the foolish one went; but just as he stood before her, there was a white cloud that came and covered them. And the beautiful young woman came out of the cloud, and when it blew away the foolish man was a skeleton covered with worms.

Then the woman spoke to the one who was not foolish: "You shall go home and tell your people that I am coming and that a big tepee shall be built for me in the center of the nation." And the man, who was very much afraid, went quickly and told the people, who did at once as they were told; and there around the big tepee they waited for the sacred woman. And after a while she came, very beautiful and singing, and as she went into the tepee this is what she sang:

> "With visible breath I am walking.
> A voice I am sending as I walk.
> In a sacred manner I am walking.
> With visible tracks I am walking.
> In a sacred manner I walk."

And as she sang, there came from her mouth a white cloud that was good to smell. Then she gave something to the chief, and it was a pipe with a bison calf carved on one side to mean the earth that bears and feeds us, and with twelve eagle feathers hanging from the stem to mean the sky and the twelve moons, and these were tied with a grass that never breaks. "Behold!" she said. "With this you shall multiply and be a good nation. Nothing but good shall come from it. Only the hands of the good shall take care of it and the bad shall not even see it." Then she sang again and went out of the tepee; and as the people watched her going, suddenly it was a white bison galloping away and snorting, and soon it was gone.

This they tell, and whether it happened so or not I do not know; but if you think about it, you can see that it is true.

Now I light the pipe, and after I have offered it to the powers that are one Power, and sent forth a voice to them, we shall smoke together. Offering the mouthpiece first of all to the One above—so—I send a voice:

Hey hey! hey hey! hey hey! hey hey!

Grandfather, Great Spirit, you have been always, and before you no one has been. There is no other one to pray to but you. You yourself, everything that you see, everything has been made by you. The star nations all over the universe you have finished. The four quarters of the earth you have finished. The day, and in that day, everything you have finished. Grandfather, Great Spirit, lean close to the earth that you may hear the voice I send. You towards where the sun goes down, behold me; Thunder Beings, behold me! You where the White Giant lives in power, behold me! You where the sun shines continually, whence come the day-break star and the day, behold me! You where the summer lives, behold me! You in the depths of the heavens, an eagle of power, behold! And you, Mother Earth, the only Mother, you who have shown mercy to your children!

Hear me, four quarters of the world—a relative I am! Give me the strength to walk the soft earth, a relative to all that is! Give me the eyes to see and the strength to understand, that I may be like you. With your power only can I face the winds.

Great Spirit, Great Spirit, my Grandfather, all over the earth the faces of living things are all alike. With tenderness have these come up out of the ground. Look upon these faces of children without number and with children in their arms, that they may face the winds and walk the good road to the day of quiet.

This is my prayer; hear me! The voice I have sent is weak, yet with earnestness I have sent it. Hear me!

It is finished. Hetchetu aloh!

Now, my friend, let us smoke together so that there may be only good between us.

Study Questions

1. How is the Lakota belief in the sacredness and oneness of the universe reflected in Black Elk's characterization of his life story as the story of all life?

2. What is the moral significance of the Lakota system of beliefs? What is the spiritual and moral significance of Black Elk's characterization of his life story?

3. What spiritual and moral messages are conveyed in Black Elk's explanation of the pipe's symbolism? in the story of how the pipe was given to the Lakota? in his offering of the pipe?

4. How do Black Elk's conceptions of the earth and humanity contrast with those dominating Western cultures today? How do they differ in terms of moral values and principles?

Suggestions for Further Reading

DeMallie, R. J., ed. Introduction to *The Sixth Grandfather: Black Elk's Teachings Given to John G. Neihardt* (Lincoln; London: University of Nebraska Press, 1984). A comprehensive view of Black Elk's life and thoughts, the issues concerning his relation to Neihardt, and the basic beliefs of the Lakota.

McGaa, E. (Eagle Man). "We Are All Related." In *Mother Earth Spirituality: Native American Paths to Healing Ourselves and the World* (San Francisco: Harper & Row,

1990). Develops an ethics of relations to the earth and ourselves from the Oglala Lakota perspective.

Tedlock, D., and B. Tedlock, eds. *Teachings from the American Earth: Indian Religion and Philosophy* (New York: Liveright, 1975). A collection of essays on Native American religion and philosophy. See especially "Hanblecheyapi: Crying for a Vision" and "Oglala Metaphysics."

Part 4

Contemporary Feminist Philosophers

SIMONE DE BEAUVOIR (1908–1986)
Selections from *The Second Sex*

CAROL GILLIGAN (1936–)
Selections from "In a Different Voice: Women's Conceptions of Self and of Morality"

MARY DALY (1928–)
Selections from "The Metapatriarchal Journey of Exorcism and Ecstasy"

LUCE IRIGARAY (1930–)
Selections from "An Ethics of Sexual Difference"

MARÍA LUGONES (1944–) AND ELIZABETH SPELMAN (1945–)
Selections from "Have We Got a Theory for You!: Feminist Theory, Cultural Imperialism, and the Demand for a 'Woman's Voice'"

NEL NODDINGS (1929–)
Selections from *Caring: A Feminine Approach to Ethics and Moral Education*

ANNETTE BAIER (1929–)
Selections from "What Do Women Want in a Moral Theory?"

BELL HOOKS (1952–)
Selections from "Feminism: A Transformational Politic"

ALISON JAGGAR (1942–)
Selections from "Feminist Ethics: Projects, Problems, Prospects"

SARAH LUCIA HOAGLAND (1945–)
Selections from "Why Lesbian Ethics?"

SARA RUDDICK (1935–)
Selections from "From Maternal Thinking to Peace Politics"

ROSEMARY RADFORD RUETHER (1936–)
Selections from "Ecofeminism: Symbolic and Social Connections of the Oppression of Women and the Domination of Nature"

Simone de Beauvoir (1908–1986)

Simone de Beauvoir was born in Paris into an upper-middle-class family. Her mother was a devout Catholic; her father an attorney who later suffered financial misfortunes. Though educated as a Catholic, de Beauvoir claims to have lost her faith at a young age. She first studied literature and mathematics, but later went to the Sorbonne to study philosophy and eventually taught philosophy at *lycées* in Marseilles, Rouen, and Paris. When at the Sorbonne, she met Jean-Paul Sartre, with whom she established a life-long relationship in which they were intimate, but not exclusive, companions. Along with Albert Camus, they were hailed as the intellectual leaders of French existentialism. De Beauvoir attained renown not only as a philosopher but also as literary writer (in various genres), political activist, and leading feminist.

The nineteenth-century German philosopher G. W. F. Hegel developed the notion of the human being as an embodied consciousness. Like other existentialists, de Beauvoir was influenced by this view, which emphasizes that, though our bodies are subject to the drives and forces of nature, we are also conscious, or aware of ourselves. This self-awareness enables us to rise above and beyond our limits. In its self-reflectiveness, human consciousness is differentiated within itself and characterized by a tension of opposites between subject and object, self and other. De Beauvoir gave importance to this tension and assigned much significance to Hegel's further insights into how it is translated in the conflict between individual self-consciousnesses in the master-servant relation.

De Beauvoir also followed the nineteenth-century Danish philosopher Søren Kierkegaard in his rejection of abstract rationalist conceptions of the human being, such as Hegel's. Kierkegaard insisted that human existence is lived concretely at the level of individual subjectivity with all of its personal desires and fears. He stressed that freedom lies at the very heart of the human condition, so that such existence is constituted in and through the choices we make. With Friedrich Nietzsche, the late-nineteenth-century German philosopher, de Beauvoir also repudiated the idea of absolute, unchanging, and eternal realities, natures, or essences. Among other things, this meant that the human condition was marked by an utter absence of ultimate moral standards. Thus, the individual existence of the human being is a process of self-creation through a radical freedom. This was translated into an existentialist ethics, whereby the individual is held responsible for her own existence and accountable for who she becomes.

Before publishing *The Second Sex* in 1949, de Beauvoir had already published two novels and two philosophical treatises. One of the latter, *The Ethics of Ambiguity* (1947), is an explicit attempt to develop an existentialist ethics based on the idea of the tension or ambiguity of human existence. Born into circumstances she does not choose—within a context of given laws, institutions, and moral codes—the individual must will to be free in her relation to her world and others. Though not a specifically feminist program, the existentialist ethics that unfolds does reflect briefly on the condition of the contemporary woman in the European tradition as one who fails to will her own freedom.

According to de Beauvoir's own recollection, *The Second Sex* arose "almost by chance" as she discovered that when she wanted to think and talk about herself, she first had to say "I am a woman" and reflect on what it meant to be a woman. She begins her introduction to the book with the question "What is a woman?"; she rejects traditional definitions and critically examines the existential condition of woman. De Beauvoir's answer to the question is that woman "is the Other." If woman is, as the title of the book already suggests, the second sex, then the first sex is man, that is, "man is the Subject—the Absolute." Woman is thus defined by man, relative to or in terms of man, and exists in man's world. De Beauvoir uncovers how this is existentially possible and what it implies for the existence of both sexes. She proposes a moral principle for evaluating society and outlines an existentialist ethics in which all individuals have the moral duty to fulfill their freedom as subjects. Her book is an attempt to elucidate what is specific to woman's conditions and experiences, so as to learn of the obstacles and the way toward woman's liberation and existential fulfillment.

THE SECOND SEX

FOR A LONG TIME I have hesitated to write a book on woman. The subject is irritating, especially to women; and it is not new. Enough ink has been spilled in the quarreling over feminism, now practically over, and perhaps we should say no more about it. It is still talked about, however, for the voluminous nonsense uttered during the last century seems to have done little to illuminate the problem. After all, is there a problem? And if so, what is it? Are there women, really? Most assuredly the theory of the eternal feminine still has its adherents. . . .

But first we must ask: what is a woman? "*Tota mulier in utero,*" says one, "woman is a womb." But in speaking of certain women, connoisseurs declare that they are not women, although they are equipped with a uterus like the rest. All agree in recognizing the fact that females exist in the human species; today as always they make up about one half of humanity. And yet we are told that femininity is in danger; we are exhorted to be women, remain women, become women. It would appear, then, that every female human being is not necessarily a woman; to be so considered she must share in that mysterious and threatened reality known as femininity. Is this attribute something secreted by the ovaries? Or is it a Platonic essence, a product of the philosophic imagination? Is a rustling petticoat enough to bring it down to earth? Although some women try zealously to incarnate this essence, it is hardly patentable. It is frequently described in vague and dazzling terms that seem to have been borrowed from the vocabulary of the seers, and indeed in the times of St. Thomas it was considered an essence as certainly defined as the somniferous virtue of the poppy.

But conceptualism has lost ground. The biological and social sciences no longer admit the existence of unchangeably fixed entities that determine given characteristics, such as those ascribed to woman, the Jew, or the Negro. Science regards any characteristic as a reaction dependent in part upon a *situation.* If today femininity no longer exists, then it never existed. But does the word *woman,* then, have no specific content? This is stoutly affirmed by those who hold to the philosophy of the enlightenment, of rationalism, of nominalism; women, to them, are merely the human beings arbitrarily designated by the word *woman.* . . .

But nominalism is a rather inadequate doctrine, and the antifemininists have had no trouble in showing that women simply *are not* men. Surely woman is, like man, a human being; but such a declaration is abstract. The fact is that every concrete human being is always a singular, separate individual. To decline to accept such notions as the eternal feminine, the black soul, the Jewish character, is not to deny that Jews, Negroes, women exist today—this denial does not represent a liberation for those concerned, but rather a flight from reality. . . .

If her functioning as a female is not enough to define woman, if we decline also to explain her through "the eternal feminine," and if nevertheless we admit, provisionally, that women do exist, then we must face the question: what is a woman?

To state the question is, to me, to suggest, at once, a preliminary answer. The fact that I ask it is in itself significant. A man would never get the notion of writing a book on the peculiar situation of the human male. But if I wish to define myself, I must first of all say: "I am a woman"; on this truth must be based all further discussion. A man never begins by presenting himself as an individual of a certain sex; it goes without saying that he is a man. The terms *masculine* and *feminine* are used symmetrically only as a matter of form, as on legal papers. In actuality the relation of the two sexes is not quite like that of two electrical poles, for man represents both the positive and the neutral, as is indicated by the common use of *man* to designate human beings in general; whereas woman represents only the negative, defined by limiting criteria, without reciprocity. In the midst of an abstract discussion it is vexing to hear a man say: "You think thus and so because you are a woman"; but I know that my only defense is to reply: "I think thus and so because it is true," thereby removing my subjective self from the argument. It would be out of the question to reply: "And you think the contrary because you are a man," for it is under-

stood that the fact of being a man is no peculiarity. A man is in the right in being a man; it is the woman who is in the wrong. It amounts to this: just as for the ancients there was an absolute vertical with reference to which the oblique was defined, so there is an absolute human type, the masculine. Woman has ovaries, a uterus; these peculiarities imprison her in her subjectivity, circumscribe her within the limits of her own nature. It is often said that she thinks with her glands. Man superbly ignores the fact that his anatomy also includes glands, such as the testicles, and that they secrete hormones. He thinks of his body as a direct and normal connection with the world, which he believes he apprehends objectively, whereas he regards the body of woman as a hindrance, a prison, weighed down by everything peculiar to it. "The female is a female by virtue of a certain *lack* of qualities," said Aristotle; "we should regard the female nature as afflicted with a natural defectiveness." And St. Thomas for his part pronounced woman to be an "imperfect man," an "incidental" being. This is symbolized in Genesis where Eve is depicted as made from what Bossuet called "a supernumerary bone" of Adam.

Thus humanity is male and man defines woman not in herself but as relative to him; she is not regarded as an autonomous being. Michelet writes: "Woman, the relative being. . . ." And Benda is most positive in his *Rapport d' Uriel:* "The body of man makes sense in itself quite apart from that of woman, whereas the latter seems wanting in significance by itself. . . . Man can think of himself without woman. She cannot think of herself without man." And she is simply what man decrees; thus she is called "the sex," by which is meant that she appears essentially to the male as a sexual being. For him she is sex—absolute sex, no less. She is defined and differentiated with reference to man and not he with reference to her; she is the incidental, the inessential as opposed to the essential. He is the Subject, he is the Absolute—she is the Other.

The category of the *Other* is as primordial as consciousness itself. In the most primitive societies, in the most ancient mythologies, one finds the expression of a duality—that of the Self and the Other. This duality was not originally attached to the division of the sexes; it was not dependent upon any empirical facts. It is revealed in such works as that of Granet on Chinese thought and those of Dumézil on the East Indies and Rome. The feminine element was at first no more involved in such pairs as Varuna-Mitra, Uranus-Zeus, Sun-Moon, and Day-Night than it was in the contrasts between Good and Evil, lucky and unlucky auspices, right and left, God and Lucifer. Otherness is a fundamental category of human thought.

Thus it is that no group ever sets itself up as the One without at once setting up the Other over against itself. If three travelers chance to occupy the same compartment, that is enough to make vaguely hostile "others" out of all the rest of the passengers on the train. In small-town eyes all persons not belonging to the village are "strangers" and suspect; to the native of a country all who inhabit other countries are "foreigners"; Jews are "different" for the anti-Semite, Negroes are "inferior" for American racists, aborigines are "natives" for colonists, proletarians are the "lower class" for the privileged.

. . . These phenomena would be incomprehensible if in fact human society were simply a *Mitsein* or fellowship based on solidarity and friendliness. Things become clear, on the contrary, if, following Hegel, we find in consciousness itself a fundamental hostility toward every other consciousness; the subject can be posed only in being opposed—he sets himself up as the essential, as opposed to the other, the inessential, the object.

But the other consciousness, the other ego, sets up a reciprocal claim. The native traveling abroad is shocked to find himself in turn regarded as a "stranger" by the natives of neighboring countries. As a matter of fact, wars, festivals, trading, treaties, and contests among tribes, nations, and classes tend to deprive the concept *Other* of its absolute sense and to make manifest its relativity; willy-nilly, individuals and groups are forced to realize the reciprocity of their relations. How is it, then, that this reciprocity has not been recognized between the sexes, that one of the contrasting terms is set up as the sole essential, denying any relativity in regard to its correlative and defining the latter as pure otherness? Why is it that women do not dispute male sovereignty? No subject will readily volunteer to become the object, the inessential; it is not the Other who, in defining himself as the Other, establishes the One. The Other is posed as such by the One in defining himself as the One. But if the Other is not to regain the status of being the One, he must be submissive enough to accept this alien point of view. Whence comes this submission in the case of woman?

There are, to be sure, other cases in which a certain category has been able to dominate another completely for a time. Very often this privilege depends upon inequality of numbers—the majority imposes its rule upon the minority or persecutes it. But women are not a minority, like the American Negroes or the Jews; there are as many women as men on earth. Again, the two groups concerned have often been originally independent; they may have been formerly unaware of each other's existence, or perhaps they recognized each other's autonomy. But a historical event has resulted in the subjugation of the weaker by the stronger. The scattering of the Jews, the introduction of slavery into America, the conquests of imperialism are examples in point. In these cases the oppressed retained at least the memory of former days; they possessed in common a past, a tradition, sometimes a religion or a culture.

The parallel drawn by Bebel between women and the proletariat is valid in that neither ever formed a minority or a separate collective unit of mankind. And instead of a single historical event it is in both cases a historical development that explains their status as a class and accounts for the membership of *particular individuals* in that class. But proletarians have not always existed, whereas there have always been women. They are women in virtue of their anatomy and physiology. Throughout history they have always been subordinated to men, and hence their dependency is not the result of a historical event or a social change—it was not something that *occurred*. The reason why otherness in this case seems to be an absolute is in part that it lacks the contingent or incidental nature of historical facts. A condition brought about at a certain time can be abolished at some other time, as the Negroes of Haiti and others have proved; but it might seem that a natural condition is beyond the possibility of change. In truth, however, the nature of things is no more immutably given, once for all, than is historical reality. If woman seems to be the inessential which never becomes the essential, it is because she herself fails to bring about this change. Proletarians say "We"; Negroes also. Regarding themselves as subjects, they transform the bourgeois, the whites, into "others." But women do not say "We," except at some congress of feminists or similar formal demonstration; men say "women," and women use the same word in referring to themselves. They do not authentically assume a subjective attitude. The proletarians have accomplished the revolution in Russia, the Negroes in Haiti, the Indo-Chinese are battling for it in Indo-China; but the women's effort has never been anything more than a symbolic agitation. They have gained only what men have been willing to grant; they have taken nothing, they have only received.

The reason for this is that women lack concrete means for organizing themselves into a unit which can stand face to face with the correlative unit. They have no past, no history, no religion of their own; and they have no such solidarity of work and interest as that of the proletariat. They are not even promiscuously herded together in the way that creates community feeling among the American Negroes, the ghetto Jews, the workers of Saint-Denis, or the factory hands of Renault. They live dispersed among the males, attached through residence, housework, economic condition, and social standing to certain men—fathers or husbands—more firmly than

they are to other women. If they belong to the bourgeoisie, they feel solidarity with men of that class, not with proletarian women; if they are white, their allegiance is to white men, not to Negro women. The proletariat can propose to massacre the ruling class, and a sufficiently fanatical Jew or Negro might dream of getting sole possession of the atomic bomb and making humanity wholly Jewish or black; but woman cannot even dream of exterminating the males. The bond that unites her to her oppressors is not comparable to any other. The division of the sexes is a biological fact, not an event in human history. Male and female stand opposed within a primordial *Mitsein,* and woman has not broken it. The couple is a fundamental unity with its two halves riveted together, and the cleavage of society along the line of sex is impossible. Here is to be found the basic trait of woman: she is the Other in a totality of which the two components are necessary to one another.

One could suppose that this reciprocity might have facilitated the liberation of woman. When Hercules sat at the feet of Omphale and helped with her spinning, his desire for her held him captive; but why did she fail to gain a lasting power? To revenge herself on Jason, Medea killed their children; and this grim legend would seem to suggest that she might have obtained a formidable influence over him through his love for his offspring. In *Lysistrata* Aristophanes gaily depicts a band of women who joined forces to gain social ends through the sexual needs of their men; but this is only a play. In the legend of the Sabine women, the latter soon abandoned their plan of remaining sterile to punish their ravishers. In truth woman has not been socially emancipated through man's need—sexual desire and the desire for offspring—which makes the male dependent for satisfaction upon the female.

Master and slave, also, are united by a reciprocal need, in this case economic, which does not liberate the slave. In the relation of master to slave the master does not make a point of the need that he has for the other; he has in his grasp the power of satisfying this need through his own action; whereas the slave, in his dependent condition, his hope and fear, is quite conscious of the need he has for his master. Even if the need is at bottom equally urgent for both, it always works in favor of the oppressor and against the oppressed. That is why the liberation of the working class, for example, has been slow.

Now, woman has always been man's dependent, if not his slave; the two sexes have never shared the world in equality. And even today woman is heavily handicapped, though her situation is beginning to change. Almost nowhere is her legal status the same as man's, and frequently it is much to her disadvantage. Even when her rights are legally recognized in the abstract, long-standing custom prevents their full expression in the mores. In the economic sphere men and women can almost be said to make up two castes; other things being equal, the former hold the better jobs, get higher wages, and have more opportunity for success than their new competitors. In industry and politics men have a great many more positions and they monopolize the most important posts. In addition to all this, they enjoy a traditional prestige that the education of children tends in every way to support, for the present enshrines the past—and in the past all history has been made by men. At the present time, when women are beginning to take part in the affairs of the world, it is still a world that belongs to men—they have no doubt of it at all and women have scarcely any. To decline to be the Other, to refuse to be a party to the deal—this would be for women to renounce all the advantages conferred upon them by their alliance with the superior caste. Man-the-sovereign will provide woman-the-liege with material protection and will undertake the moral justification of her existence; thus she can evade at once both economic risk and the metaphysical risk of a liberty in which ends and aims must be contrived without assistance. Indeed, along with the ethical urge of each individual to affirm his subjective existence, there is also the temptation to forgo liberty and become a thing. This is an inauspicious road, for he who takes it—passive,

lost, ruined—becomes henceforth the creature of another's will, frustrated in his transcendence and deprived of every value. But it is an easy road; on it one avoids the strain involved in undertaking an authentic existence. When man makes of woman the *Other*, he may, then, expect her to manifest deep-seated tendencies toward complicity. Thus, woman may fail to lay claim to the status of subject because she lacks definite resources, because she feels the necessary bond that ties her to man regardless of reciprocity, and because she is often very well pleased with her role as the *Other*.

But it will be asked at once: how did all this begin? It is easy to see that the duality of the sexes, like any duality, gives rise to conflict. And doubtless the winner will assume the status of absolute. But why should man have won from the start? It seems possible that women could have won the victory; or that the outcome of the conflict might never have been decided. How is it that this world has always belonged to the men and that things have begun to change only recently? Is this change a good thing? Will it bring about an equal sharing of the world between men and women?

These questions are not new, and they have often been answered. But the very fact that woman *is the Other* tends to cast suspicion upon all the justifications that men have ever been able to provide for it. These have all too evidently been dictated by men's interest. . . . But the males could not enjoy this privilege fully unless they believed it to be founded on the absolute and the eternal; they sought to make the fact of their supremacy into a right. . . .

In proving woman's inferiority, the antifeminists then began to draw not only upon religion, philosophy, and theology, as before, but also upon science—biology, experimental psychology, etc. At most they were willing to grant "equality in difference" to the *other* sex. That profitable formula is most significant; it is precisely like the "equal but separate" formula of the Jim Crow laws aimed at the North American Negroes. As is well known, this so-called equalitarian segregation has resulted only in the most extreme discrimination. The similarity just noted is in no way due to chance, for whether it is a race, a caste, a class, or a sex that is reduced to a position of inferiority, the methods of justification are the same. "The eternal feminine" corresponds to "the black soul" and to "the Jewish character." True, the Jewish problem is on the whole very different from the other two—to the anti-Semite the Jew is not so much an inferior as he is an enemy for whom there is to be granted no place on earth, for whom annihilation is the fate desired. But there are deep similarities between the situation of woman and that of the Negro. Both are being emancipated today from a like paternalism, and the former master class wishes to "keep them in their place"—that is, the place chosen for them. In both cases the former masters lavish more or less sincere eulogies, either on the virtues of "the good Negro" with his dormant, childish, merry soul—the submissive Negro—or on the merits of the woman who is "truly feminine"—that is, frivolous, infantile, irresponsible—the submissive woman. In both cases the dominant class bases its argument on a state of affairs that it has itself created. As George Bernard Shaw puts it, in substance, "The American white relegates the black to the rank of shoeshine boy; and he concludes from this that the black is good for nothing but shining shoes." This vicious circle is met with in all analogous circumstances; when an individual (or a group of individuals) is kept in a situation of inferiority, the fact is that he *is* inferior. But the significance of the verb *to be* must be rightly understood here; it is in bad faith to give it a static value when it really has the dynamic Hegelian sense of "to have become." Yes, women on the whole *are* today inferior to men; that is, their situation affords them fewer possibilities. The question is: should that state of affairs continue?

So it is that many men will affirm as if in good faith that women *are* the equals of man and that they have nothing to clamor for, while *at the same time* they will say that women can never be

the equals of man and that their demands are in vain. It is, in point of fact, a difficult matter for man to realize the extreme importance of social discriminations which seem outwardly insignificant but which produce in woman moral and intellectual effects so profound that they appear to spring from her original nature. The most sympathetic of men never fully comprehend woman's concrete situation. And there is no reason to put much trust in the men when they rush to the defense of privileges whose full extent they can hardly measure. We shall not, then, permit ourselves to be intimidated by the number and violence of the attacks launched against women, nor to be entrapped by the self-seeking eulogies bestowed on the "true woman," nor to profit by the enthusiasm for woman's destiny manifested by men who would not for the world have any part of it. . . .

But it is doubtless impossible to approach any human problem with a mind free from bias. The way in which questions are put, the points of view assumed, presuppose a relativity of interest; all characteristics imply values, and every objective description, so called, implies an ethical background. Rather than attempt to conceal principles more or less definitely implied, it is better to state them openly at the beginning. This will make it unnecessary to specify on every page in just what sense one uses such words as *superior, inferior, better, worse, progress, reaction,* and the like. If we survey some of the works on woman, we note that one of the points of view most frequently adopted is that of the public good, the general interest; and one always means by this the benefit of society as one wishes it to be maintained or established. For our part, we hold that the only public good is that which assures the private good of the citizens; we shall pass judgment on institutions according to their effectiveness in giving concrete opportunities to individuals. But we do not confuse the idea of private interest with that of happiness, although that is another common point of view. Are not women of the harem more happy than women voters? Is not the housekeeper happier than the workingwoman? It is not too clear just what the word *happy* really means and still less what true values it may mask. There is no possibility of measuring the happiness of others, and it is always easy to describe as happy the situation in which one wishes to place them.

In particular those who are condemned to stagnation are often pronounced happy on the pretext that happiness consists in being at rest. This notion we reject, for our perspective is that of existentialist ethics. Every subject plays his part as such specifically through exploits or projects that serve as a mode of transcendence; he achieves liberty only through a continual reaching out toward other liberties. There is no justification for present existence other than its expansion into an indefinitely open future. Every time transcendence falls back into immanence, stagnation, there is a degradation of existence into the "*en-soi*"—the brutish life of subjection to given conditions—and of liberty into constraint and contingence. This downfall represents a moral fault if the subject consents to it; if it is inflicted upon him, it spells frustration and oppression. In both cases it is an absolute evil. Every individual concerned to justify his existence feels that his existence involves an undefined need to transcend himself, to engage in freely chosen projects.

Now, what peculiarly signalizes the situation of woman is that she—a free and autonomous being like all human creatures—nevertheless finds herself living in a world where men compel her to assume the status of the Other. They propose to stabilize her as object and to doom her to immanence since her transcendence is to be overshadowed and forever transcended by another ego (*conscience*) which is essential and sovereign. The drama of woman lies in this conflict between the fundamental aspirations of every subject (ego)—who always regards the self as the essential—and the compulsions of a situation in which she is the inessential. How can a human being in woman's situation attain fulfillment? What roads are open to her? Which are blocked? How can independence be recovered in a state of dependency? What circumstances limit woman's liberty and how can they be overcome? These are the fundamental questions on which I would fain throw some light. This means that I am interested in the fortunes of the individual as defined not in terms of happiness but in terms of liberty.

Quite evidently this problem would be without significance if we were to believe that woman's destiny is inevitably determined by physiological, psychological, or economic forces. Hence I shall discuss first of all the light in which woman is viewed by biology, psychoanalysis, and historical materialism. Next I shall try to show exactly how the concept of the "truly feminine" has been fashioned—why woman has been defined as the Other—and what have been the consequences from man's point of view. Then from woman's point of view I shall describe the world in which women must live; and thus we shall be able to envisage the difficulties in their way as, endeavoring to make their escape from the sphere hitherto assigned them, they aspire to full membership in the human race.

Study Questions

1. What is the moral significance of asking What is a woman?
2. Are man and woman both morally accountable for woman's existence as the Other? Are they accountable in different ways?
3. What are the moral grounds for the duty de Beauvoir places on the more privileged woman?
4. Does de Beauvoir provide any justification for the principle that a public good is measured by the private good? How does it fit in with the existentialist ethics she outlines?
5. Is de Beauvoir proposing different ethical codes for the existential fulfillment of man and woman?

Suggestions for Further Reading

Al-Hibri, A. Y., and M. A. Simons, eds. *Hypatia Reborn: Essays in Feminist Philosophy* (Bloomington: Indiana University Press, 1990). See Part III, "Beauvoir and Feminist Philosophy," for various feminist perspectives on de Beauvoir.

Leighton, J. *Simone de Beauvoir on Woman* (Rutherford, NJ: Fairleigh Dickinson University Press, 1975). A comprehensive critical exploration of de Beauvoir's feminism.

Mahon, J. *Existentialism, Feminism, and Simone de Beauvoir* (London: Macmillan, 1997; New York: St. Martin's Press, 1997). Chapters 9–12 and 16–19 examine *The Second Sex* from various perspectives.

Okely, J. *Simone de Beauvoir* (NewYork: Prometheus Books, 1986; London: Virago Press, 1986). Chapters 3 and 4 provide insights into the impact and problems of *The Second Sex.*

Simmons, M. A., ed. *Feminist Interpretations of Simone de Beauvoir* (College Park: Pennsylvania State University Press, 1995). Contains fourteen essays that examine de Beauvoir's philosophy from different feminist perspectives.

Carol Gilligan (1936–)

Carol Gilligan is professor of education at Harvard University's Graduate School of Education. She works primarily in the field of developmental psychology and specializes in moral development. Her impact on contemporary intellectual currents, however, extends far beyond her academic discipline. In particular, her studies and theories have challenged traditional methods, models, and theories not only in psychology but also in moral philosophy or ethics. Drawing primarily from the psychological theory of moral development proposed by Lawrence Kohlberg (her teacher when she was a student at Harvard), Gilligan works out a position that criticizes the assumptions, methodologies, and conclusions adopted by psychologists (including Kohlberg) and philosophers regarding women's conceptions of selfhood and morality. Confronting established views of women as psychologically and morally undeveloped and inadequate, Gilligan proposes that the problem lies not in women's supposed inferiority but in how they have been studied, represented, and interpreted. Her contention is that such approaches have failed to record, listen to, and construe women's ways of describing themselves and talking about moral issues in a "different voice." Gilligan argues that because this voice has been systematically canceled out in theories informed and framed by men's conceptions, including it as equal will expand our understanding of the human development and set the groundwork for theories that integrate both voices. In this vein, she also criticizes social conventions and models of morality for males and females.

For Gilligan, Kohlberg's theory of moral development is a notable example of the systematic exclusion of women's voices and the interpretation of their difference as a mark of inferiority. He employed men as the primary subjects of studies that framed his theory. In these studies, he found that most women failed to reach what he defined as the highest level of moral development. Kohlberg interpreted these findings as a sign of the immaturity of women.

Gilligan's starting point, however, is studies of subjects from both genders and studies of exclusively female subjects on questions in which issues revolving around women are central, such as abortion. In her studies, Gilligan found that most female subjects had a conception of self that was relational or closely tied to others. They had a view of morality that gave primacy to responsibility and issued an ethics of care. Observing that these conceptions correspond with the social ideal of feminine goodness, Gilligan notes that this correspondence results in a paradox for women, for the qualities that characterize the morally good woman according to social conventions are the same that serve to classify her as morally and psychologically immature.

Gilligan found that male subjects, in contrast to females, tended to conceive selfhood in terms of separation and autonomy. They defined morality primarily in terms of justice and rights, and stressed the importance of logical thinking in the application and formulation of abstract universal principles. Yet, Gilligan critically notes that social, psychological, and philosophical theories traditionally have upheld these conceptions of self and morality as the model for both genders. In response, Gilligan's theory outlines a different sequence of stages of psychological and moral development in females. At their intermediate level of development, females discover that they have a responsibility toward others and that the social ideal of goodness prescribed to them is phrased in terms of their caring for others. Such social demands, however, create an imbalance in the female between herself and others, and are the potential source of inner conflicts when she is trying to make a moral decision. Her highest level of maturity is attained when she redresses this imbalance by seeing herself as an equal to others. At this stage, she begins to conceive of responsibility for others as also being a reciprocal demand placed on others toward herself. While she sees morality in terms of a universal principle, it is not abstract but concrete in its concern for nonviolence. Significantly, she sees it as a moral principle that also includes herself as a recipient in its universality.

IN A DIFFERENT VOICE: WOMEN'S CONCEPTIONS OF SELF AND MORALITY

THE ARC OF DEVELOPMENTAL THEORY leads from infantile dependence to adult autonomy, tracing a path characterized by an increasing differentiation of self from other and a progressive freeing of thought from contextual constraints. The vision of Luther, journeying from the rejection of a self defined by others to the assertive boldness of "Here I stand" and the image of

Carol Gilligan. "*In a Different Voice: Women's Conceptions of Self and Morality,*" Harvard Educational Review *47, no. 4 (November 1977): 481–517. Copyright © 1977 by the President and Fellows of Harvard College.*

Plato's allegorical man in the cave, separating at last the shadows from the sun, have taken powerful hold on the psychological understanding of what constitutes development. Thus, the individual, meeting fully the developmental challenges of adolescence as set for him by Piaget, Erikson, and Kohlberg, thinks formally, proceeding from theory to fact, and defines both the self and the moral autonomously, that is, apart from the identification and conventions that had comprised the particulars of his childhood world. So equipped, he is presumed ready to live as an adult, to love and work in a way that is both intimate and generative, to develop an ethical sense of caring and a genital mode of relating in which giving and taking fuse in the ultimate reconciliation of the tension between self and other.

Yet the men whose theories have largely informed this understanding of development have all been plagued by the same problem, the problem of women, whose sexuality remains more diffuse, whose perception of self is so much more tenaciously embedded in relationships with others and whose moral dilemmas hold them in a mode of judgment that is insistently contextual. The solution has been to consider women as either deviant or deficient in their development.

That there is a discrepancy between concepts of womanhood and adulthood is nowhere more clearly evident than in the series of studies on sex-role stereotypes reported by Broverman, Vogel, Broverman, Clarkson, and Rosenkrantz (1972). The repeated finding of these studies is that the qualities deemed necessary for adulthood—the capacity for autonomous thinking, clear decision making, and responsible action—are those associated with masculinity but considered undesirable as attributes of the feminine self. The stereotypes suggest a splitting of love and work that relegates the expressive capacities requisite for the former to women while the instrumental abilities necessary for the latter reside in the masculine domain. Yet, looked at from a different perspective, these stereotypes reflect a conception of adulthood that is itself out of balance, favoring the separateness of the individual self over its connection to others and leaning more toward an autonomous life of work than toward the interdependence of love and care.

This difference in point of view is the subject of this essay, which seeks to identify in the feminine experience and construction of social reality a distinctive voice, recognizable in the different perspective it brings to bear on the construction and resolution of moral problems. The first section begins with the repeated observation of difference in women's concepts of self and of morality. This difference is identified in previous psychological descriptions of women's moral judgments and described as it again appears in current research data. Examples drawn from interviews with women in and around a university community are used to illustrate the characteristics of the feminine voice. The relational bias in women's thinking that has, in the past, been seen to compromise their moral judgment and impede their development now begins to emerge in a new developmental light. Instead of being seen as a developmental deficiency, this bias appears to reflect a different social and moral understanding.

This alternative conception is enlarged in the second section through consideration of research interviews with women facing the moral dilemma of whether to continue or abort a pregnancy. Since the research design allowed women to define as well as resolve the moral problem, developmental distinctions could be derived directly from the categories of women's thought. The responses of women to structured interview questions regarding the pregnancy decision formed the basis for describing a developmental sequence that traces progressive differentiations in their understanding and judgment of conflicts between self and other. While the sequence of women's moral development follows the three-level progression of all social developmental theory, from an egocentric through a societal to a universal perspective, this progression takes place within a distinct moral conception. This conception differs from that derived by Kohlberg from his all-male longitudinal research data.

This difference then becomes the basis in the third section for challenging the current assessment of women's moral judgment at the same time that it brings to bear a new perspective on developmental assessment in general. The inclusion in the overall conception of development of those categories derived from the study of women's moral judgment enlarges developmental understanding, enabling it to encompass better the thinking of both sexes. This is particularly true with respect to the construction and resolution of the dilemmas of adult life. Since the conception of adulthood retrospectively shapes the theoretical understanding of the development that precedes it, the changes in that conception that follow from the more central inclusion of women's judgments recast developmental understanding and lead to a reconsideration of the substance of social and moral development.

Characteristics of the Feminine Voice

The revolutionary contribution of Piaget's work is the experimental confirmation and refinement of Kant's assertion that knowledge is actively constructed rather than passively received. Time, space, self, and other, as well as the categories of developmental theory, all arise out of the active interchange between the individual and the physical and social world in which he lives and of which he strives to make sense. The development of cognition is the process of reappropriating reality at progressively more complex levels of apprehension, as the structures of thinking expand to encompass the increasing richness and intricacy of experience.

Moral development, in the work of Piaget and Kohlberg, refers specifically to the expanding conception of the social world as it is reflected in the understanding and resolution of the inevitable conflicts that arise in the relations between self and others. The moral judgment is a statement of priority, an attempt at rational resolution in a situation where, from a different point of view, the choice itself seems to do violence to justice.

Kohlberg (1969), in his extension of the early work of Piaget, discovered six stages of moral judgment, which he claimed formed an invariant sequence, each successive stage representing a more adequate construction of the moral problem, which in turn provides the basis for its more just resolution. The stages divide into three levels, each of which denotes a significant expansion of the moral point of view from an egocentric through a societal to a universal ethical conception. With this expansion in perspective comes the capacity to free moral judgment from the individual needs and social conventions with which it had earlier been confused and anchor it instead in principles of justice that are universal in application. These principles provide criteria upon which both individual and societal claims can be impartially assessed. In Kohlberg's view, at the highest stages of development morality is freed from both psychological and historical constraints, and the individual can judge independently of his own particular needs and of the values of those around him.

That the moral sensibility of women differs from that of men was noted by Freud (1925/ 1961) in the following by now well-quoted statement:

> I cannot evade the notion (though I hesitate to give it expression) that for women the level of what is ethically normal is different from what it is in man. Their superego is never so inexorable, so impersonal, so independent of its emotional origins as we require it to be in men. Character-traits which critics of every epoch have brought up against women—that they show less sense of justice than men, that they are less ready to submit to the great exigencies of life, that they are more often influenced in their judgments by feelings of affection or hostility—all these would be amply accounted for by the modification in the formation of their super-ego which we have inferred above. (pp. 257–258)

While Freud's explanation lies in the deviation of female from male development around the construction and resolution of the Oedipal problem, the same observations about the nature of morality in women emerge from the work of Piaget and Kohlberg. Piaget (1932/1965), in his study of the rules of children's games, observed that, in the games they played, girls were "less explicit about agreement [than boys] and less concerned with legal elaboration" (p. 93). In contrast to the boys' interest in the codification of rules, the girls adopted a more pragmatic attitude, regarding "a rule as good so long as the game repays it" (p. 83). As a result, in comparison to boys, girls were found to be "more tolerant and more easily reconciled to innovations" (p. 52).

Kohlberg (1971) also identifies a strong interpersonal bias in the moral judgments of women, which leads them to be considered as typically at the third of his six-stage developmental sequence. At that stage, the good is identified with "what pleases or helps others and is approved of by them" (p. 164). This mode of judgment is conventional in its conformity to generally held notions of the good but also psychological in its concern with intention and consequence as the basis for judging the morality of action.

That women fall largely into this level of moral judgment is hardly surprising when we read from the Broverman et al. (1972) list that prominent among the twelve attributes considered to be desirable for women are tact, gentleness, awareness of the feelings of others, strong need for security, and easy expression of tender feelings. And yet, herein lies the paradox, for the very traits that have traditionally defined the "goodness" of women, their care for and sensitivity to the needs of others, are those that mark them as deficient in moral development. The infusion of feeling into their judgments keeps them from developing a more independent and abstract ethical conception in which concern for others derives from principles of justice rather than from compassion and care. Kohlberg, however, is less pessimistic than Freud in his assessment, for he sees the development of women as extending beyond the interpersonal level, following the same path toward independent, principled judgment that he discovered in the research on men from which his stages were derived. In Kohlberg's view, women's development will proceed beyond Stage Three when they are challenged to solve moral problems that require them to see beyond the relationships that

have in the past generally bound their moral experience. . . .

The availability of choice and with it the onus of responsibility has now invaded the most private sector of the woman's domain and threatens a similar explosion. For centuries, women's sexuality anchored them in passivity, in a receptive rather than active stance, where the events of conception and childbirth could be controlled only by a withholding in which their own sexual needs were either denied or sacrificed. That such a sacrifice entailed a cost to their intelligence as well was seen by Freud (1908/1959) when he tied the "undoubted intellectual inferiority of so many women" to "the inhibition of thought necessitated by sexual suppression" (p. 199). The strategies of withholding and denial that women have employed in the politics of sexual relations appear similar to their evasion or withholding of judgment in the moral realm. The hesitance . . . to impose even a belief in the value of human life on others, like the reluctance to claim one's sexuality, bespeaks a self uncertain of its strength, unwilling to deal with consequence, and thus avoiding confrontation.

Thus women have traditionally deferred to the judgment of men, although often while intimating a sensibility of their own which is at variance with that judgment. Maggie Tulliver, in *The Mill on the Floss* (Eliot, 1860/1965) responds to the accusations that ensue from the discovery of her secretly continued relationship with Phillip Wakeham by acceding to her brother's moral judgment while at the same time asserting a different set of standards by which she attests her own superiority:

> I don't want to defend myself. . . . I know I've been wrong—often continually. But yet, sometimes when I have done wrong, it has been because I have feelings that you would be the better for if you had them. If you were in fault ever, if you had done anything very wrong, I should be sorry for the pain it brought you; I should not want punishment to be heaped on you. (p. 188)

An eloquent defense, Kohlberg would argue, of a Stage Three moral position, an assertion of the age-old split between thinking and feeling, justice and mercy, that underlies many of the cliches and stereotypes concerning the difference between the sexes. But considered from another point of view, it is a moment of confrontation, replacing a former evasion, between two modes of judging, two differing constructions of the moral domain—one traditionally associated with masculinity and the public world of social power, the other with femininity and the privacy of domestic interchange. While the developmental ordering of these two points of view has been to consider the masculine as the more adequate and thus as replacing the feminine as the individual moves toward higher stages, their reconciliation remains unclear.

The Development of Women's Moral Judgment

Recent evidence for a divergence in moral development between men and women comes from the research of Haan (Note 1) and Holstein (1976) whose findings lead them to question the possibility of a "sex-related bias" in Kohlberg's scoring system. This system is based on Kohlberg's six-stage description of moral development. Kohlberg's stages divide into three levels, which he designates as preconventional, conventional, and postconventional, thus denoting the major shifts in moral perspective around a center of moral understanding that equates justice with the maintenance of existing social systems. While the preconventional conception of justice is based on the needs of the self, the conventional judgment derives from an understanding of society. This understanding is in turn superseded by a postconventional or principled conception of justice where the good is formulated in universal terms. The quarrel with Kohlberg's stage scoring does not pertain to the structural differentiation of his levels but rather to questions of stage and sequence. Kohlberg's stages begin with an obedience and punishment orientation (Stage One), and go from there in invariant order to instrumental hedonism (Stage

Two), interpersonal concordance (Stage Three), law and order (Stage Four), social contract (Stage Five), and universal ethical principles (Stage Six).

The bias that Haan and Holstein question in this scoring system has to do with the subordination of the interpersonal to the societal definition of the good in the transition from Stage Three to Stage Four. This is the transition that has repeatedly been found to be problematic for women. In 1969, Kohlberg and Kramer identified Stage Three as the characteristic mode of women's moral judgments, claiming that, since women's lives were interpersonally based, this stage was not only "functional" for them but also adequate for resolving the moral conflicts that they faced. Turiel (1973) reported that while girls reached Stage Three sooner than did boys, their judgments tended to remain at that stage while the boys' development continued further along Kohlberg's scale. Gilligan, Kohlberg, Lerner, and Belenky (1971) found a similar association between sex and moral-judgment stage in a study of high-school students, with the girls' responses being scored predominantly at Stage Three while the boys' responses were more often scored at Stage Four.

This repeated finding of developmental inferiority in women may, however, have more to do with the standard by which development has been measured than with the quality of women's thinking per se. Haan's data (Note 1) on the Berkeley Free Speech Movement and Holstein's (1976) three-year longitudinal study of adolescents and their parents indicate that the moral judgments of women differ from those of men in the greater extent to which women's judgments are tied to feelings of empathy and compassion and are concerned more with the resolution of "real-life" as opposed to hypothetical dilemmas (Note 1, p. 34). However, as long as the categories by which development is assessed are derived within a male perspective from male research data, divergence from the masculine standard can be seen only as a failure of development. As a result, the thinking of women is often classified with that of children. The systematic exclusion from consideration of alternative criteria that might better encompass the development of women indicates not only the limitations of a theory framed by men and validated by research samples disproportionately male and adolescent but also the effects of the diffidence prevalent among women, their reluctance to speak publicly in their own voice, given the constraints imposed on them by the politics of differential power between the sexes.

In order to go beyond the question, "How much like men do women think, how capable are they of engaging in the abstract and hypothetical construction of reality?" it is necessary to identify and define in formal terms developmental criteria that encompass the categories of women's thinking. Such criteria would include the progressive differentiations, comprehensiveness, and adequacy that characterize higher-stage resolution of the "more frequently occurring, real-life moral dilemmas of interpersonal, empathic, fellow-feeling concerns" (Haan, Note 1, p. 34), which have long been the center of women's moral judgments and experience. To ascertain whether the feminine construction of the moral domain relies on a language different from that of men, but one which deserves equal credence in the definition of what constitutes development, it is necessary first to find the places where women have the power to choose and thus are willing to speak in their own voice.

When birth control and abortion provide women with effective means for controlling their fertility, the dilemma of choice enters the center of women's lives. Then the relationships that have traditionally defined women's identities and framed their moral judgments no longer flow inevitably from their reproductive capacity but become matters of decision over which they have control. Released from the passivity and reticence of a sexuality that binds them in dependence, it becomes possible for women to question with Freud what it is that they want and to assert their own answers to that question. However, while society may affirm publicly the woman's right to choose for herself, the exercise of such choice brings her privately into conflict with the conventions of femininity, particularly the moral equation of goodness with self-sacrifice. While independent assertion in judgment and action is considered the hallmark of adulthood and constitutes as well the standard of masculine development, it is rather in their care and concern for others that women have both judged themselves and been judged.

The conflict between self and other thus constitutes the central moral problem for women, posing a dilemma whose resolution requires a reconciliation between femininity and adulthood. In the absence of such a reconciliation, the moral problem cannot be resolved. The "good woman" masks assertion in evasion, denying responsibility by claiming only to meet the needs of others, while the "bad woman" forgoes or renounces the commitments that bind her in self-deception and betrayal. It is precisely this dilemma—the conflict between compassion and autonomy, between virtue and power—which the feminine voice struggles to resolve in its effort to reclaim the self and to solve the moral problem in such a way that no one is hurt. . . .

While the structural progression from a preconventional through a conventional to a postconventional moral perspective can readily be discerned in the women's responses to both actual and hypothetical dilemmas, the conventions that shape women's moral judgments differ from those that apply to men. The construction of the abortion dilemma, in particular, reveals the existence of a distinct moral language whose evolution informs the sequence of women's development. This is the language of selfishness and responsibility, which defines the moral problem as one of obligation to exercise care and avoid hurt. The infliction of hurt is considered selfish and immoral in its reflection of unconcern, while the expression of care is seen as the fulfillment of moral responsibility. The reiterative use of the language of selfishness and responsibility and the underlying moral orientation it reflects sets the women apart from the men whom Kohlberg studied and may be seen as the critical reason for their failure to develop within the constraints of his system. . . .

In . . . developmental sequence . . . women's moral judgments proceed from an initial focus on the self at the *first level* to the discovery, in the transition to the *second level,* of the concept of responsibility as the basis for a new equilibrium between self and others. The elaboration of this concept of responsibility and its fusion with a maternal concept of morality, which seeks to ensure protection for the dependent and unequal, characterizes the *second level* of judgment. At this level the good is equated with caring for others. However, when the conventions of feminine goodness legitimize only others as the recipients of moral care, the logical inequality between self and other and the psychological violence that it engenders create the disequilibrium that initiates the *second* transition. The relationship between self and others is then reconsidered in an effort to sort out the confusion between conformity and care inherent in the conventional definition of feminine goodness and to establish a new equilibrium, which dissipates the tension between selfishness and responsibility. At the *third level,* the self becomes the arbiter of an independent judgment that now subsumes both conventions and individual needs under the moral principle of nonviolence. Judgment remains psychological in its concern with the intention and consequences of action, but it now becomes universal in its condemnation of exploitation and hurt.

Developmental Theory Reconsidered

The developmental conception delineated at the outset, which has so consistently found the development of women to be either aberrant or incomplete, has been limited insofar as it has been predominantly a male conception, giving lipservice, a place on the chart, to the interdependence of intimacy and care but constantly stressing, at their expense, the importance and value of autonomous judgment and action. To admit to this conception the truth of the feminine perspective is to recognize for both sexes the central importance in adult life of the connection between self and other, the universality of the need for compassion and care. The concept of the separate self and of the moral principle uncompromised by the constraints of reality is an adolescent ideal, the elaborately wrought philosophy of a Stephen Daedalus, whose flight we know to be in jeopardy. Erikson (1964), in contrasting the ideological morality of the adolescent with the ethics of adult care, attempts to grapple with this problem of integration, but is impeded by the limitations of his own previous developmental conception. When his developmental stages chart a path where the sole precursor to the intimacy of adult relationships is the trust established in infancy and all intervening experience is marked only as steps toward greater independence, then separation itself becomes the model and the measure of growth. The observation that for women, identity has as much to do with connection as with separation led Erikson into trouble largely because of his failure to integrate this insight into the mainstream of his developmental theory (Erikson, 1968).

The moral imperative that emerges repeatedly in the women's interviews is an injunction to care, a responsibility to discern and alleviate the "real and recognizable trouble" of this world. For the men Kohlberg studied the moral imperative appeared rather as an injunction to respect the rights of others and thus to protect from interference the right to life and self-fulfillment. Women's insistence on care is at first self-critical rather than self-protective, while men initially conceive obligation to others negatively in terms of noninterference. Development for both sexes then would seem to entail an integration of rights and responsibilities through the discovery of the complementarity of these disparate views. For the women I have studied, this integration between rights and responsibilities appears to take place through a principled understanding of equity and reciprocity. This understanding tempers the self-destructive potential of a self-critical morality by asserting the equal right of all persons to care. For the men in Kohlberg's sample as well as for those in a longitudinal study of Harvard undergraduates (Gilligan & Murphy, Note 5) it appears to be the recognition through experience of the need for a more active responsibility in taking care that corrects the potential indifference of a morality of noninterference and turns attention from the logic to the consequences of choice. In the development of a post-conventional ethic understanding, women come to see the violence generated by inequitable relationships, while men come to realize the limitations of a conception of justice blinded to the real inequities of human life. . . .

Gandhi, whom Kohlberg has mentioned as exemplifying Stage Six moral judgment and whom Erikson sought as a model of an adult ethical sensibility, instead is criticized by a judgment that refuses to look away from or condone the infliction of harm. In denying the validity of his wife's reluctance to open her home to strangers and in his blindness to the different reality of adolescent sexuality and temptation, Gandhi compromised in his everyday life the ethic of nonviolence to which in principle and in public he was so steadfastly committed.

The blind willingness to sacrifice people to truth, however, has always been the danger of an ethics abstracted from life. This willingness links Gandhi to the biblical Abraham, who prepared to sacrifice the life of his son in order to demonstrate the integrity and supremacy of his faith. Both men, in the limitations of their fatherhood, stand in implicit contrast to the woman who comes before Solomon and verifies her motherhood by relinquishing truth in order to save the life of her child. It is the ethics of an adulthood that has become principled at the expense of care that Erikson comes to criticize in his assessment of Gandhi's life. . . .

The research findings that have been reported in this essay suggest that women impose a distinctive construction on moral problems, seeing moral dilemmas in terms of conflicting responsibilities. This construction was found to develop through a sequence of three levels and two transitions, each level representing a more complex understanding of the relationship between self and other and each transition involving a critical reinterpretation of the moral conflict between selfishness and responsibility. The development of women's moral judgment appears to proceed from an initial concern with survival, to a focus on goodness, and finally to a principled understanding of nonviolence as the most adequate guide to the just resolution of moral conflicts.

In counterposing to Kohlberg's longitudinal research on the development of hypothetical moral judgment in men a cross-sectional study of women's responses to actual dilemmas of moral conflict and choice, this essay precludes the possibility of generalization in either direction and leaves to further research the task of sorting out the different variables of occasion and sex. Longitudinal studies of women's moral judgments are necessary in order to validate the claims of stage and sequence presented here. Similarly, the contrast drawn between the moral judgments of men and women awaits for its confirmation a more systematic comparison of the responses of both sexes. Kohlberg's research on moral development has confounded the variables of age, sex, type of decision, and type of dilemma by presenting a single configuration (the responses of adolescent males to hypothetical dilemmas of conflicting rights) as the basis for a universal stage sequence. This paper underscores the need for systematic treatment of these variables and points toward their study as a critical task for future moral development research.

For the present, my aim has been to demonstrate the centrality of the concepts of responsibility and care in women's constructions of the moral domain, to indicate the close tie in women's thinking between conceptions of the self and conceptions of morality, and, finally, to argue the need for an expanded developmental theory that would include, rather than rule out from developmental consideration, the difference in the feminine voice. Such an inclusion seems essential, not only for explaining the development of women but also for understanding in both sexes the characteristics and precursors of an adult moral conception.

Study Questions

1. What problems does Gilligan find in traditional conceptions of selfhood and morality? How does she propose to address them?
2. In what ways does Gilligan's theory move from being a description to being a prescription of social, psychological, and philosophical conceptions of morality?
3. Does Gilligan's theory liberate women from traditional male conceptions of morality, or does it perpetuate gender-based moral stereotypes?
4. Does Gilligan's theory imply or suggest that women's morality is superior to men's ?
5. Given that Gilligan sees morality in terms of development and reasoning, does her own theory still manage to overcome tradition? If so, how?

Suggestions for Further Reading

Cole, E. B., and S. Coultrap-McQuin, eds. *Explorations in Feminist Ethics: Theory and Practice* (Bloomington: Indiana University Press, 1992). See Part I, "The Care Debate," for various feminist perspectives on the issue of care.

Gilligan, Carol. *In a Different Voice: Psychological Theory and Women's Development* (Cambridge, MA; London: Harvard University Press, 1982). Chapter 3 contains a later version of Gilligan's article within a larger theoretical framework.

————. "Hearing the Difference: Theorizing Connection," *Hypatia* 10, no. 2 (Spring 1995): 120–127. Distinguishes between feminine and feminist ethics of care.

Hekman, S. J. *Moral Voices, Moral Selves: Carol Gilligan and Feminist Theory* (University Park: Pennsylvania State University Press, 1995). An examination of the tenets, problems, and significance of Gilligan's moral theories beginning with her book *In a Different Voice*.

Larabee, M. J., ed. *An Ethic of Care: Feminist and Interdisciplinary Perspectives* (New York: Routledge, 1993). Contains eighteen essays on the controversial issues raised by Gilligan's ethics of care in such fields as moral philosophy and psychology. Includes Gilligan's reply to critics.

Social Research 50, no. 3 (Autumn 1983). Contains eight articles that examine Gilligan's theory of women and morality from different perspectives.

Mary Daly (1928–)

Mary Daly is a feminist philosopher and theologian who holds doctorates in religion, sacred theology, and philosophy. She is the author of numerous books, including *The Church and the Second Sex* (1968), *Beyond God the Father: Toward a Philosophy of Women's Liberation* (1973), and *Quintessence—Realizing the Archaic Future: A Radical Elemental Feminist Manifest* (1998). For over three decades, she was associate professor of theology at Boston College where she taught feminist ethics amidst much controversy over her work and her policy of excluding males from her classes. In response to critiques of her teaching practices, she has insisted on the need for women to have feminist classes in an environment free of patriarchal intrusions and interactions. Calling herself a "Nag-Gnostic" philosopher, Daly denounces misogyny and patriarchy, in both their secular and nonsecular forms, while she urges women to reclaim their ravaged powers and stolen myths.

Daly characterizes her life and writings as a journey through four spiral galaxies where she weaves her feminist visions and launches her battles against patriarchy. She marks her book, *Gyn/Ecology: The Metaethics of Radical Feminism* (1978), as revolving in her third spiral galaxy. Daly characterizes herself here as "a Pirate" who "Righteously Plundered treasures of knowledge that have been stolen and hidden from women" and has "struggled to Smuggle these back." Her book unfolds in three passages. The first section breaks through patriarchal myths. The second portion exposes the "Indecent" atrocities against women in cultural rituals (such as African genital mutilation) and practices (such as American gynecology). The third part envisions new modes of empowerment for women.

The following selection is taken from Daly's introduction to *Gyn/Ecology.* Entitled "The Metapatriarchal Journey of Exorcism and Ecstasy," it lays out the book's general purpose of charting women's journey through the evils of the patriarchal world into an "Otherworld" that is "metapatriarchal." Daly's understanding of the word "metapatriarchal" embraces various meanings of the term *meta*—"post," "behind," "change," "transformation," "beyond," and "transcending." Thus, Daly articulates a "radical feminism" that goes past the "foreground" or superficial level to the "Background," the deeper, more primal, and concealed level of women's reality and consciousness.

The passage from the "foreground" to the "Background" involves breaking away from the use of the term *evil,* a term that is used to oppress women. It also entails "confronting the demonic manifestations of evil" of patriarchy itself. Daly claims that women "must expel the Father" from themselves and become their "own exorcists." Such a move is accompanied by an ecstasy, because women can return to the "Background" or "wild realm of Hags and Crones"—understood in their original and positive sense as wise and powerful women. Daly proposes a similar retrieval of the term *Spinster,* by associating the whirling movement of spinning with women's processes of creation and self-creation. Because language itself serves as the medium of patriarchal deception, it is the site where the exorcism and ecstasy can begin. Daly's particular coinage and usage of terms reflects this belief and is also manifest in her metapatriarchal understanding of the terms *gynecology, ecology,* and *metaethical.*

THE METAPATRIARCHAL JOURNEY OF EXORCISM AND ECSTASY

THE TITLE OF THIS BOOK, *Gyn/Ecology,* says exactly what I mean it to say. "Ecology" is about the complex web of interrelationships between organisms and their environment. In her book, *Le Féminisme ou la mort,* Françoise d'Eaubonne coins the expression "eco-féminisme." She maintains that the fate of the human species and of the planet is at stake, and that no male-led "revolution" will counteract the horrors of overpopulation and destruction of natural resources. I share this basic premise, but my approach and emphasis are different. Although I am concerned with all forms of pollution in phallotechnic society, this book is primarily concerned with the mind/spirit/body pollution inflicted through patriarchal myth and language on all levels. These levels range from styles of grammar to styles of glamour, from religious myth to dirty jokes, from theological hymns honoring the "Real Presence" of Christ to commercial cooing of Coca-Cola as "The Real Thing," from dogmatic doctrines about the "Divine Host" to doctored ingredient-labeling of Hostess Cupcakes, from subliminal ads to "sublime" art. Phallic myth and language generate, legitimate, and mask the material pollution that threatens to terminate all sentient life on this planet.

The title *Gyn/Ecology* is a way of wrenching back some wordpower. The fact that most gynecologists are males is in itself a colossal comment on "our" society. It is a symptom and example of male control over women and over language, and a clue to the extent of this control. Add to this the fact, noted by Adrienne Rich, of "a certain indifference and fatalism toward the diseases of women, which persists to this day in the male gynecological and surgical professions." And add to this the fact that the self-appointed soul doctors, mind doctors, and body doctors who "specialize" in women are perpetrators of *iatrogenic disease.*[1] That is, soul doctors (priests and gurus), mind doctors (psychiatrists, ad-men, and academics), and body doctors (physicians and fashion designers) are by professional code causes of disease in women and hostile to female well-being.[2] Gynecologists fixate upon what they do not have, upon what they themselves cannot do. For this reason they epitomize and symbolize the practitioners of other patriarchal -ologies, and they provide important clues to the demonic patterns common to the labor of all of these. In their frantic fixation upon what they lack (biophilic energy)[3] and in their fanatic indifference to the destruction they wreak upon the Other—women and "Mother Nature"—the phallic -ologists coalesce. Their corporate merger is the Mystical Body of knowledge which is gynocidal gynecology.

Note that the *Oxford English Dictionary* defines *gynecology* as "that department of medical science which treats of the functions and diseases peculiar to women; also *loosely,* the science

[1] The technical term *iatrogenic,* used to describe the epidemic of doctor-made disease, is composed of the Greek word for physician (*iatros*) and for origins (*genesis*).

[2] Clearly, some women sometimes are helped through emergency situations by priests, ministers, gynecologists, therapists—but this is largely in spite of the institutions/professions within which they work. A great deal of the work of such exceptional professionals consists in repairing damages caused by their colleagues and by the methods of their professions. One serious liability associated with their ministrations is the conditioning of women to depend upon them rather than upon our own natural resources. It should not be necessary to repeat this distinction throughout this book, which criticizes patriarchal institutions and those who conform to them.

[3] By *biophilic* I mean life-loving. This term is not in the dictionary, although the term *necrophilic* is there, and is commonly used.

of womankind." I am using the term *Gyn/Ecology* very loosely, that is, freely, to describe the science, that is the process of know-ing, of "loose" women who choose to be subjects and not mere objects of enquiry. Gyn/Ecology is by and about women a-mazing all the male-authored "sciences of womankind," and weaving world tapestries *of our own kind.* That is, it is about dis-covering, de-veloping the complex web of living/loving relationships *of our own kind.* It is about women living, loving, creating our Selves, our cosmos. It *is* dis-possessing our Selves, enspiriting our Selves, hearing the call of the wild, naming our wisdom, spinning and weaving world tapestries out of genesis and demise. In contrast to gynecology, which depends upon fixation and dismemberment, Gyn/Ecology affirms that everything is connected.

Since "o-logies" are generally static "bodies of knowledge," it might at first glance seem that the name *Gyn/Ecology* clashes with the theme of the Journey. However, a close analysis unveils the fact that this is not so. For women can recognize the powerful and multidimensional gyno-centric symbolism of the "O." It represents the power of our moving, encircling presence, which can make nonbeing sink back into itself. Our "O" is totally other than "nothing" (a fact demonically distorted and reversed in the pornographic novel, *The Story of O*). As Denise Connors has pointed out, it can be taken to represent our aura, our O-Zone. Within this anti-pollutant, purifying, moving O-Zone, the aura of gynocentric consciousness, life-loving feminists have the power to affirm the basic Gyn/Ecological principle that everything is connected with everything else. It is this holistic process of knowing that can make Gyn/Ecology the O-logy of all the -ologies, encircling them, spinning around and through them, unmasking their emptiness. As the O-logy of all the -ologies, Gyn/Ecology can reduce their pretentious façades to Zero. It can free the flow of their "courses" and overcome their necrophilic circles, their self-enclosed processions, through spiraling creative process. It is women's own Gyn/Ecology that can break the brokenness of the

"fields," deriding their borders and boundaries, changing the nouns of knowledge into verbs of know-ing. . . .

By the subtitle, *The Metaethics of Radical Feminism,* I intend to convey that this book is concerned with the Background, most specifically of language and myth, which is disguised by the fathers' foreground fixations. Merriam-Webster gives as one of the definitions of the prefix, *meta:* "of a higher logical type—in nouns formed from names of disciplines and designating new but related disciplines such as can deal critically with the nature, structure, or behavior of the original ones (*meta*language, *meta*theory, *meta*system)." Despite the dullness of dictionary diction, there are clues here. I would say that radical feminist metaethics is of a *deeper intuitive* type than "ethics." The latter, generally written from one of several (but basically the same) patriarchal perspectives, works out of hidden agendas concealed in the texture of language, buried in mythic reversals which control "logic" most powerfully because unacknowledged. Thus for theologians and philosophers, Eastern and Western, and particularly for ethicists, woman-identified women do not exist. The metaethics of radical feminism seeks to uncover the background of such logic, as women ourselves move into the Background of this background. In this sense, it can be called "of a higher [read: deeper] logical type." It is, of course, a new discipline that "deals critically" with the nature, structure, and behavior of ethics and ethicists. It is able to do this because our primary concern is *not* male ethics and/or ethicists, but our own Journeying.

This book has to do with the mysteries of good and evil. To name it a "feminist ethics" might be a clue, but it would also be misleading, pointing only to foreground problems. It would be something like arguing for "equal rights" in a society whose very existence depends upon inequality, that is, upon the possession of female energy by men. The spring into free space, which is woman-identified consciousness, involves a veritable mental/behavioral mutation. The phallocratic categorizations of "good" and "evil" no longer apply when women *honor* women, when we become honorable to ourselves. As Barbara Starrett wrote, we are developing something like a new organ of the mind. This development both causes and affects qualitative leaping through galaxies of mindspace. It involves a new faculty and process of valuation. None of the dreary ethical texts, from those of Aristotle down to Paul Ramsey and Joseph Fletcher, can speak to the infinitely expanding universe of what Emily Culpepper has named "gynergy." Indeed, the texts of phallocratic ethicists function in the same manner as pornography, legitimating the institutions which degrade women's be-ing. Gyn/Ecological metaethics, in contrast to all of this, functions to affirm the deep dynamics of female be-ing. It is gynography.

There are, of course, male-authored, male-identified works which purport to deal with "metaethics." In relation to these, gynography is meta-metaethical. For while male metaethics claims to be "the study of ethical theories, as distinguished from the study of moral and ethical conduct itself," it remains essentially male-authored and male-identified theory about theory. Moreover, it is only theory about "ethical theories"—an enterprise which promises boundless boringness. In contrast to this, Gyn/Ecology is hardly "metaethical" in the sense of masturbatory meditations by ethicists upon their own emissions. Rather, we recognize that the essential omission of these emissions is of our own life/freedom. In the name of our life/freedom, feminist metaethics O-mits seminal omissions.

In making this metapatriarchal leap into our own Background, feminists are hearing/naming the immortal Metis, Goddess of wisdom, who presided over all knowledge. In patriarchal myth she was swallowed by Zeus when she was pregnant with Athena. Zeus claimed that Metis counseled him from inside his belly. In any case, the Greeks began ascribing wisdom to this prototype of male cannibalism. We must remember that Metis was originally the parthenogenetic mother of Athena. After Athena was "reborn" from the head of Zeus, her single "parent," she became Zeus's obedient mouthpiece. She became totally male-identified, employing priests, not priestesses, urging men on in battle, siding against women consistently. Radical feminist metaethics means moving past this puppet of Papa, dis-covering the immortal Metis. It also means dis-covering the parthenogenetic Daughter, the original Athena, whose loyalty is to her own kind, whose science/wisdom is of womankind. In this dis-covering there can be what Catherine Nicholson named "the third birth of Athena." As this happens, Athena will shuck off her robothood, will re-turn to her real Source, to her Self, leaving the demented Male Mother to play impotently with his malfunctioning machine, his dutiful dim-witted "Daughter," his broken Baby Doll gone berserk, his failed fembot. The metaethics of radical feminism means simply that while Zeus, Yahweh, and all the other divine male "Mothers" are trying to retrieve their dolls from the ashcan of patriarchal creation, women on our own Journey are dis-covering Metis and the third-born Athena: our own new be-ing. That is, we are be-ing in the Triple Goddess, who is, and is not yet.

Study Questions

1. What is the meaning of Daly's term *gyn/ecology*? What is its moral significance? How is this related to Daly's critical examination of the meanings of the terms *gynecology* and *ecology*?

2. What meaning does Daly give to the terms *metaethics* and *metapatriarchal*? What is their moral significance? How is this significance related to Daly's critique of traditional ethics and metaethics?

3. Why does Daly characterize her position as radical feminism? What critical message is suggested in this characterization?

4. What moral import does Daly give to language and myth? How is this import reflected in her particular phrasings and terms? How is it reflected in her move to the "Background"? Is she retrieving original myths or creating new ones?

5. Does Daly suggest why women have lived in a patriarchal world? How does she justify her proposal for a metapatriarchal journey? Is she suggesting that males necessarily develop patriarchal languages, myths, and ethics?

Suggestions for Further Reading

Adams. C. J., ed. *Ecofeminism and the Sacred* (New York: Continuum, 1993). A collection of essays on ecofeminism and spirituality. See especially Part 2, "Envisioning Ecofeminism."

Diamond, I., and G. F. Orenstein, eds. *Reweaving the World: The Emergence of Ecofeminism* (San Francisco: Sierra Club Books, 1990). A collection of essays on various perspectives of ecofeminism. See especially Part 2, "Reweaving the World: Reconnecting Politics and Ethics."

Hoagland, S. L., and M. Frye, eds. *Feminist Interpretations of Mary Daly* (University Park: Pennsylvania State University Press, 2000). Contains fifteen essays in defense of Daly as located in the Western intellectual tradition. See especially A. L. Katherine's two essays on *Gyn/Ecology*.

Lorde, A. "An Open Letter to Mary Daly." In *This Bridge Called My Back: Writings by Radical Women of Color,* eds. C. Morraga and G. Anzaldúa (New York: Kitchen Table: Women of Color Press, 1983). A brief critique of Daly's *Gyn/Ecology* for its exclusion of women of color.

Plaskow, J., and C. P. Christ, eds. *Weaving the Visions: New Patterns in Feminist Spirituality* (New York: Harper & Row, 1989). A collection of essays on various perspectives of feminist spirituality. See especially Part 2, "Naming the Sacred."

Luce Irigaray (1930–)

Luce Irigaray was born in Blanton, Belgium. She studied at the University of Louvain, the University of Paris, and the Paris Institute of Psychology and holds two doctorates (in linguistics and philosophy). Irigaray was a member of the Freudian School of Paris and a lecturer at the University of Paris at Vincennes until the publication of her book *Speculum of the Other Woman* (1974) led to her expulsion. She is a practicing psychoanalyst and is Director of Research in Philosophy at the National Center for Scientific Research in Paris.

Counted among the most controversial feminists today, Irigaray has drawn on her multidisciplinary background in linguistics, psychoanalysis, and philosophy to level a radical, all-embracing critique of the exclusively masculine perspective that has commanded the European tradition. Her basic contention is that the feminine has been excluded from the dominant forms of language and thought that produce and reproduce a male-centered (phallocentric) world. Accordingly, patriarchal culture tries to eradicate female sexuality in its autonomy and difference by repressing, assimilating, and absorbing it into male sexuality. All prevailing cultural structures are thus forms of sameness that aim to define the feminine in terms of the masculine and serve to silence, distort, subject, and exploit women.

Irigaray has argued that the attempt to erase women as women occurs not only in cultural practices such as language, politics, and the economy, but also in theoretical discourses such as psychoanalysis, science, and philosophy. Moreover, the images conveyed through these cultural structures refer in suggestive, subtle ways to the male sexual anatomy and desires. Sigmund Freud's psychoanalytic theory of the development of female sexuality in terms of the Oedipal model and "penis envy" is, for Irigaray, an instance of phallocentrism. The scientific model of objective knowledge of the universe as represented by a neutral, universal subject is yet another articulation of the masculine. Philosophy, as the master discourse that tries to reign over all other discourses, is itself what Irigaray calls "phal-logo-centric" with its masculine (phallic) focus on reason (logos) and logic. Centered on notions such as identity and form, philosophy has privileged a logic of discourse that exalts the masculine while it obliviates the feminine. In her critical assessments of European tradition, Irigaray thus uncovers its phallocentrism as she explores the feminine that has been excluded and reflects on the female anatomy and desires in their difference.

Irigaray's "An Ethics of Sexual Difference" is the text of a public lecture she delivered on November 18, 1982, at Erasmus University in Rotterdam, where she had been awarded the Jan Tinbergen Chair as a visiting scholar. The text is contained in a book by the same title that collects her lecture series on "The Ethics of Passions" at Rotterdam. In her introduction to the book, Irigaray points to sexual difference as "one of the major philosophical issues, if not the issue, of our age." In spite of its devastating consequences for our world, we have yet to address this problem adequately in our theories and practices. Irigaray proposes that we need a "revolution in thought and ethics" that reinterprets everything concerning the relations between the human subject and the universe.

Irigaray claims that, in the European tradition, the human subject has been interpreted in the masculine form. With this, man has been the subject of all discourse, while God and the universe have taken on a neutral guise that conceals the masculine. The sexual difference between women and men has been erased by nullifying the feminine and absorbing it into a masculine sameness. Much as the nineteenth-century German philosopher G. W. F. Hegel had proposed in his analysis of the master-slave relation, Irigaray argues that this male-female relation is inadequate for both sexes. Without a mutual recognition between man and woman of one another as subjects, each sex remains incomplete in itself. Irigaray suggests that it is as if the electrical poles had divided themselves into the sexes, with the masculine as the positive pole and the feminine as the negative pole, instead of each sex having both poles in itself. With this, there is no possibility left for a "double desire," for a mutual exchange of attraction and support, of human passions, uniting the sexes in their differences without canceling these differences out.

Irigaray's call for a "transition to a new age" thus announces the need for an ethics of sexual difference that is based on reciprocal passions between the sexes in their difference, such as mutual wonder, joy, and love. Until now, however, human passions have been reserved for the allegedly neutral space dividing the sexes, a space inhabited by God as the divine beyond the human, the child as the sole fruit of sexual union, or art as the realm of beauty inspiring our wonder. Because science is now the highest expression of phallocentric discourse, Irigaray also points out that it is morally imperative that we critically examine its alleged objectivity, neutrality, and universality. In this examination, she uncovers the model of the scientist as the detached observer of the physical universe as man's way of dismissing his body in its relatedness to woman, as mother and as sexual companion. Her suggestive claim that we have forgotten "the air" follows this line of reflection on man's separation from the physical.

The late-nineteenth-century German philosopher Friedrich Nietszche's claim that "God is dead" denounced the life-denying forces of civilization and announced the end of a world based on absolutes. Irigaray reflects on the devastating effects of modern civilization on life, but she sees these as a result of phallocentrism. Hence, the decline of our age is the death of the masculine God. Following the twentieth-century German philosopher Martin Heidegger, who proposed that "only a god can save us now" from our disastrous course, Irigaray suggests that we prepare for a new god, for a renewed sense of the divine that retains the sexual difference between human beings in their unity. Unlike the phallocentric ethics that has prevailed until now, Irigaray's ethics for the new age is thus one based on the human togetherness, "an ethics that is ours."

AN ETHICS OF SEXUAL DIFFERENCE

To each period corresponds a certain way of thinking. And even though the issues relating to passion and its ethics which need careful consideration today are still clearly linked to Descartes's *wonder* and Spinoza's *joy,* the perspective is no longer the same. This change in perspective is, precisely, a matter of ethics. We are no longer in an era where the subject reconstitutes the world in solitude on the basis of one fixed point: Descartes's certainty that he is a man. This is no longer the era of Spinoza, who wrote: "It is easy to see that if men and women together assumed political authority, peace would suffer great harm from the permanent probability of conflict."

An ethical imperative would seem to require a practical and theoretical revision of the role historically allotted to woman. Whereas this role was still interpreted by Freud as anatomic destiny, we need to understand that it has been determined by the necessities of a traditional sociocultural organization—one admittedly in the process of evolving today.

Philosophy, thought, and discourse do not evolve swiftly enough in response to "popular" movements. One of the places in our time where we can locate a people is the "world of women." Nonetheless, if there is to be neither repression of this "people" nor ethical error on its part, an access to sexual difference becomes essential, and

Reprinted from Luce Irigaray: An Ethics of Sexual Difference. *Translated by Carolyn Burke and Gillian Gill. Translation copyright © 1993 by Cornell University. Used by permission of the publisher, Cornell University Press.*

society must abandon the murderous hierarchy as well as the division of labor which bars woman from accomplishing the task reserved for her by Hegel: the task of going from the deepest depths to the highest heavens. In other words, of being faithful to a process of the divine which passes through her, whose course she must needs sustain, without regressing or yielding up her singular desire or falling prisoner to some fetish or idol of the question of "God." Could it be that one of the qualities of this divine process is to leave woman open, her threshold free, with no closure, no dogmatism? Could this be one of its ethical deeds, in sexual exchange as well? . . .

In the end, every "war" machine turns against the one who made it. At least according to Hegel? At least according to a certain logic of conscience? Unless we can pass into another?

Unless, at every opportunity, we ourselves take the negative upon ourselves. Which would amount to allowing the other his/her liberty, and sex. Which would assume that we accept losing ourselves by giving ourselves. Which would leave the decision about time to us. By giving us control over the debts we lay *on the future.*

Do we still have the time to face those debts?

Ethically, we have to give ourselves the time. Without forgetting to plan. Giving ourselves time is to plan on abjuring our deadly polemics so that we have time for living, and living together. . . .

This ethical question can be approached from different perspectives, if I give myself, give us, time to think it through.

Given that *science* is one of the last figures, if not the last figure, used to represent absolute knowledge, it is—ethically—essential that we ask science to reconsider the nonneutrality of the supposedly universal subject that constitutes its scientific theory and practice.

In actual fact, the self-proclaimed universal is the equivalent of an idiolect of men, a masculine imaginary, a sexed world. With no neuter. This will come as a surprise only to an out-and-out defender of idealism. It has always been men who spoke and, above all, wrote: in science, philosophy, religion, politics. . . . But it is apparent in many ways that the subject in science is not neuter or neutral. Particularly in the way certain things are not discovered at a given period as well as in the research goals that science sets, or fails to set, for itself. . . .

. . . Given that the scientist, now, wants to be *in front of* the world: naming the world, making its laws, its axioms. Manipulating nature, exploiting it, but forgetting that he too is *in* nature. That he is still *physical,* and not only when faced with phenomena whose *physical* nature he tends to ignore. As he progresses according to an objective method designed to shelter him from any instability, any "mood," any feelings and affective fluctuations, from any intuition that has not been programmed in the name of science, from any influence of his desire, particularly his *sexual* desires, over his discoveries. Perhaps by installing himself within a system, within something that can be assimilated to what is already dead? Fearing, sterilizing the losses of equilibrium even though these are necessary to achieve a new horizon of discovery.

One of the ways most likely to occasion an interrogation of the scientific horizon is to question discourse about the subject of science, and the psychic and sexuate involvement of that subject in scientific discoveries and their formulation.

Such questions clamor to be answered, or at least raised, from somewhere outside, from a place in which the subject has not or has scarcely begun to be spoken. An outside placed on the other slope of sexual difference, the one which, while useful for reproducing the infrastructure of social order, has been condemned to imprisonment and silence within and by society. It remains true that the feminine, in and through her language, can, today, raise questions of untold richness. Still she must be allowed to speak; she must be heeded.

This may lead to the avoidance of two ethical mistakes, if I may return again to Hegel:

> Subordinating women to destiny without allowing them any access to mind, or consciousness of self and for self. Offering them only death and violence as their part.

Closing man away in a consciousness of self and for self that leaves no space for the gods and whose discourse, even today and for that same reason, goes in search of its meaning.

In other words, in this division between the two sides of sexual difference, one part of the world would be searching for a way to find and speak its meaning, its side of signification, while the other would be questioning whether meaning is still to be found in language, values, and life.

This desperately important question of our time is linked to an injustice, an ethical mistake, a debt still owing to "natural law" and to its gods.

If this question is apparent in the dereliction of the feminine, it is also raised on the male side, in quest for its meaning. Humanity and humanism have proved that their ethos is difficult to apply outside certain limits of tolerance. Given that the world is not undifferentiated, not neuter, particularly insofar as the sexes are concerned.

The meaning that can be found on the male side is perhaps that of a debt contracted toward the one who gave and still gives man life, in language as well.

Language, however formal it may be, feeds on blood, on flesh, on material elements. Who and what has nourished language? How is this debt to be repaid? Must we produce more and more formal mechanisms and techniques which redound on man, like the inverted outcome of that mother who gave him a living body? And whom he fears in direct ratio to the unpaid debt that lies between them.

To remember that we must go on living and creating worlds is our task. But it can be accomplished only through the combined efforts of the two halves of the world: the masculine and the feminine.

And I shall end with an example of something that can constitute or entail an unpaid debt to the maternal, the natural, the matrical, the nourishing.

As we move farther away from our condition as living beings, we tend to forget the most indispensable element in life: *air.* The air we breathe, in which we live, speak, appear; the air in which everything "enters into presence" and can come into being.

This air that we never think of has been borrowed from a birth, a growth, a *phusis* and a *phuein* that the philosopher forgets.

To forget being is to forget the air, this first fluid given us gratis and free of interest in the mother's blood, given us again when we are born, like a natural profusion that raises a cry of pain: the pain of a being who comes into the world and is abandoned, forced henceforth to live without the immediate assistance of another body. Unmitigated mourning for the intrauterine nest, elemental homesickness that man will seek to assuage through his work as builder of worlds, and notably of the dwelling which seems to form the essence of his maleness: language.

In all his creations, all his works, man always seems to neglect thinking of himself as flesh, as one who has received his body as that primary home (that *Gestell*, as Heidegger would say, when, in "Logos," the seminar on Heraclitus, he recognizes that what metaphysics has not begun to address is the issue of the body) which determines the possibility of his coming into the world and the potential opening of a horizon of thought, of poetry, of celebration, that also includes the god or gods.

The fundamental dereliction in our time may be interpreted as our failure to remember or prize the element that is indispensable to life in all its manifestations: from the lowliest plant and animal forms to the highest. Science and technology are reminding men of their careless neglect by forcing them to consider the most frightening question possible, the question of a radical polemic: the destruction of the universe and of the human race through the splitting of the atom and its exploitation to achieve goals that are beyond our capacities as mortals.

"Only a god can save us now," said Heidegger, who was also remembering the words of Hölderlin, the poet with whom his thought was indissolubly linked. Hölderlin says that the god comes to us on a certain *wind* that blows from the icy cold of the North to the place where every sun rises: the East. The god arrives on the arms of a wind that sweeps aside everything that blocks the light, everything that separates fire and air and covers all with imperceptible ice and shadow. The god would refer back to a time before our space-time was formed into a closed world by an economy of natural elements forced to bow to man's affect and will. Demiurge that could have closed up the universe into a circle, or an egg, according to Empedocles.

Man's technical prowess today allows him to blow up the world just as, at the dawn of our culture, he was able to establish a finite horizon to it.

Is a god what we need, then? A god who can upset the limits of the possible, melt the ancient glaciers, a god who can make a future for us. A god carried on the breath of the *cosmos,* the song of the poets, the respiration of lovers.

We still have to await the god, remain ready and open to prepare a way for his coming. And, with him, for ourselves, to prepare, not an implacable decline, but a new birth, a new era in history.

Beyond the circularity of discourse, of the nothing that is in and of being. When the copula no longer veils the abyssal burial of the other in a gift of language which is neuter only in that it forgets the difference from which it draws its strength and energy. With a neuter, abstract *there is* giving way to or making space for a "we are" or "we become," "we live here" together.

This creation would be our opportunity, from the humblest detail of everyday life to the "grandest," by means of the opening of a *sensible transcendental* that comes into being through us, of which *we would be* the mediators and bridges. Not only in mourning for the dead God of Nietzsche, not waiting passively for the god to come, but by conjuring him up among us, within us, as resurrection and transfiguration of blood, of flesh, through a language and an ethics that is ours.

Study Questions

1. What is the meaning of Irigaray's ethics of sexual difference? Why does she claim that a change in perspective for our age is a matter of ethics? Why does this require a practical and theoretical revision of women's historical role?

2. Why does Irigaray consider it ethically essential to critically examine the assumptions of science? How is phallocentrism manifested in science?

3. What ethical mistakes does Irigaray suggest have been made in the European tradition? How is this related to phallocentrism?

4. What does Irigaray mean when she claims we have "forgotten the air"? How is this related to the feminine? What is the moral importance of "remembering the air"? How is this connected to Irigaray's allusions to a dead God and a new god?

5. Is Irigaray claiming that men and women are "essentially" different? Is she suggesting we are "biologically determined"? How is this related to her focus on our bodies in their sexual anatomy and desires? How does her proposal for an ethics of sexual difference make sense in this light?

Suggestions for Further Reading

Burke, C., N. Schor, and M. Whitford, eds. *Engaging with Irigaray* (New York: Columbia University Press, 1994). A collection of eighteen essays on various aspects of Irigaray's thought. See especially E. Grosz's essay, "The Hetero and the Homo: The Sexual Ethics of Luce Irigaray."

Chanter, T. *Ethics of Eros: Irigaray's Rewriting of the Philosophers* (London; New York: Routeledge, 1995). Examines the issue of Irigaray's alleged essentialism and explores her relation to the thought of other philosophers. Chapter Five compares Irigaray's ethics with that of Emmanuel Levinas.

Ross, S. D. *Plenishment in the Earth: An Ethic of Inclusion* (Albany: State University of New York Press, 1995). Develops an ethics that takes as its starting point Irigaray's question of sexual difference. Chapters 2–4 undertake a reading of her ethics.

Whitford, M. *Luce Irigaray: Philosophy in the Feminine* (London; New York: Routledge, 1991). Examines the issue of Irigaray's combination of psychoanalysis and philosophy. See especially Chapter 7, "Ethics, Sexuality, and Embodiment."

María C. Lugones (1944–) and Elizabeth V. Spelman (1945–)

María C. Lugones is a feminist philosopher, activist, and popular educator who has taught at the State University of New York at Binghamton and at the Escuela Popular Norteña in New Mexico. Her writings have been mainly on pluralist feminism and lesbian ethics. Elizabeth V. Spelman is associate professor of philosophy at Smith College. She has published philosophical articles and books on feminism, epistemology, and ethics. Lugones and Spelman have criticized traditional feminist theory for excluding and neglecting the experiences and perspectives of women from diverse ethnic, racial, cultural, and class backgrounds. They have collaborated on various articles, including the one below and another one entitled "Competition, Compassion, and Community: Models for a Feminist Ethos."

The ideas expressed in the following article are reflected in its structure and in the fact that it is coauthored by an Hispanic woman, Lugones, and a white/Anglo woman, Spelman. It is significant that the piece begins with a prologue spoken in the deliberately untranslated Spanish of an Hispana's voice and that it ends with the voice of a woman of color speaking to white/Anglo women. The prologue itself reveals the raison d'être of the writing as a dialogue between two different voices. Each of its four sections announces the voice speaking, and each of the last three also notes the tone of the voice. Lugones and Spelman issue the complaint that an elite group of feminists (white, middle-class, heterosexual, Christian) has constructed theories that ignore, abstract from, and assimilate the diverse experiences of minority women (African-American, Hispanic, lower-class, lesbian, Jewish). Because they are not spoken by minority women, such theories speak neither to nor for them. Arguing against the idea that there is one universal nature or essence for the term *woman,* Lugones and Spelman insist on the need to recognize, acknowledge the validity of, and respond effectively to the differences between women. Accordingly, they outline the practical criteria for a genuinely pluralistic feminist theory. They also prescribe an ethics for white/Anglo feminists that is based on respect, consideration, and pure motives of friendship.

HAVE WE GOT A THEORY FOR YOU! FEMINIST THEORY, CULTURAL IMPERIALISM AND THE DEMAND FOR "THE WOMAN'S VOICE"

Prologue

(In an Hispana voice) A veces quisiera mezclar en una voz el sonido canyenge, tristón y urbano del porteñismo que llevo adentro con la cadencia apacible, serrana y llena de corage de la hispana nuevo mejicana. Contrastar y unir

> el piolín y la cuerda
> el traé y el pepéname
> el camión y la troca
> la lluvia y el llanto

Pero este querer se me va cuando veo que he confundido la solidaridad con la falta de diferencia. La solidaridad requiere el reconocer, comprender, respetar y amar lo que nos lleva a llorar en distintas cadencias. El imperialismo cultural desea lo contrario, por eso necesitamos muchas voces. Porque una sola voz nos mata a las dos.

No quiero hablar por ti sino contigo. Pero si no aprendo tus modos y tu los mios la conversación es sólo aparente. Y la apariencia se levanta como una barrera sin sentido entre las dos. Sin sentido y sin sentimiento. Por eso no me debes dejar que te dicte tu ser y no me dictes el mio. Porque entonces ya no dialogamos. El diálogo entre nosotras requiere dos voces yo no una.

Tal vez un día jugaremos juntas y nos hablaremos no en una lengua universal sino que vos me hablarás mi voz y yo la tuya.

Preface

This paper is the result of our dialogue, of our thinking together about differences among women and how these differences are silenced. (Think, for example, of all the silences there are connected with the fact that this paper is in English—for that is a borrowed tongue for one of us.) In the process of our talking and writing together, we saw that the differences between us did not permit our speaking in one voice. For example, when we agreed we expressed the thought differently; there were some things that both of us thought were true but could not express as true of each of us; sometimes we could not say 'we'; and sometimes one of us could not express the thought in the first person singular, and to express it in the third person would be to present an outsider's and not an insider's perspective. Thus the use of two voices is central both to the process of constructing this paper and to the substance of it. We are both the authors of this paper and not just sections of it but we write together without presupposing unity of expression or of experience. So when we speak in unison it means just that—there are two voices and not just one.

I. Introduction

(In the voice of a white/Anglo woman who has been teaching and writing about feminist theory) Feminism is, among other things, a response to the fact that women either have been left out of, or included in demeaning and disfiguring ways in what has been an almost exclusively male account of the world. And so while part of what feminists want and demand for women is the right to move and to act in accordance with our own wills and not against them, another part is the desire and insistence that we give our *own* accounts of these movements and actions. For it matters to us what is said about us, who says it,

María C. Lugones and Elizabeth V. Spelman. "Have We Got a Theory for You! Feminist Theory, Cultural Imperialism, and the Demand for a 'Woman's Voice'." Women Studies International Forum 6, no. 6 (1983): 573–581. Reprinted with the permission of Elsevier Science.

and to whom it is said: having the opportunity to talk about one's life, to give an account of it, to interpret it, is integral to leading that life rather than being led through it; hence our distrust of the male monopoly over accounts of women's lives. To put the same point slightly differently, part of human life, human living, is talking about it, and we can be sure that being silenced in one's own account of one's life is a kind of amputation that signals oppression. Another reason for not divorcing life from the telling of it or talking about it is that as humans our experiences are deeply influenced by what is said about them, by ourselves or powerful (as opposed to significant) others. Indeed, the phenomenon of internalized oppression is only possible because this is so: one experiences her life in terms of the impoverished and degrading concepts others have found it convenient to use to describe her. We can't separate lives from the accounts given of them; the articulation of our experience is part of our experience.

Sometimes feminists have made even stronger claims about the importance of speaking about our own lives and the destructiveness of others presuming to speak about us or for us. First of all, the claim has been made that on the whole men's accounts of women's lives have been at best false, a function of ignorance; and at worst malicious lies, a function of a knowledgeable desire to exploit and oppress. Since it matters to us that falsehood and lies not be told about us, we demand, of those who have been responsible for those falsehoods and lies, or those who continue to transmit them, not just that we speak but that they learn to be able to hear us. It has also been claimed that talking about one's life, telling one's story, in the company of those doing the same (as in consciousness-raising sessions), is constitutive of feminist method.

And so the demand that the woman's voice be heard and attended to has been made for a variety of reasons: not just so as to greatly increase the chances that true accounts of women's lives will be given, but also because the articulation of experience (in myriad ways) is among the hallmarks of a self-determining individual or community. There are not just epistemological, but moral and political reasons for demanding that the woman's voice be heard, after centuries of androcentric din.

But what more exactly is the feminist demand that the woman's voice be heard? There are several crucial notes to make about it. First of all, the demand grows out of a complaint, and in order to understand the scope and focus of the demand we have to look at the scope and focus of the complaint. The complaint does not specify *which* women have been silenced, and in one way this is appropriate to the conditions it is a complaint about: virtually no women have had a voice, whatever their race, class, ethnicity, religion, sexual alliance, whatever place and period in history they lived. And if it is as women that women have been silenced, then of course the demand must be that women as women have a voice. But in another way the complaint is very misleading, insofar as it suggests that it is women as women who have been silenced, and that whether a woman is rich or poor, Black, brown, or white, etc. is irrelevant to what it means for her to be a woman. For the demand thus simply made ignores at least two related points: (1) it is only possible for a woman who does not feel highly vulnerable with respect to other parts of her identity, e.g. race, class, ethnicity, religion, sexual alliance, etc., to conceive of her voice simply or essentially as a 'woman's voice'; (2) just because not all women are equally vulnerable with respect to race, class, etc., some women's voices are more likely to be heard than others by those who have heretofore been giving—or silencing—the accounts of women's lives. For all these reasons, the women's voices most likely to come forth and the women's voices most likely to be heard are, in the US anyway, those of white, middle-class, heterosexual Christian (or anyway not self-identified non-Christian) women. Indeed, many Hispanas, Black women, Jewish women—to name a few groups—have felt it an invitation to silence rather than speech to be requested—if they are requested at all—to speak about being 'women' (with the plain wrapper—as if there were one) in distinction from speaking about being Hispana, Black, Jewish, working-class, etc., women.

The demand that the 'woman's voice' be heard, and the search for the 'woman's voice' as central to feminist methodology, reflects nascent feminist theory. It reflects nascent empirical theory insofar as it presupposes that the silencing of women is systematic, shows up in regular, patterned ways, and that there are discoverable causes of this widespread observable phenomenon; the demand reflects nascent political theory insofar as it presupposes that the silencing of women reveals a systematic pattern of power and authority; and it reflects nascent moral theory insofar as it presupposes that the silencing is unjust and that there are particular ways of remedying this injustice. Indeed, whatever else we know feminism to include—e.g. concrete direct political action—theorizing is integral to it: theories about the nature of oppression, the causes of it, the relation of the oppression of women to other forms of oppression. And certainly the concept of the woman's voice is itself a theoretical concept, in the sense that it presupposes a theory according to which our identities as human beings are actually compound identities, a kind of fusion or confusion of our otherwise separate identities as women or men, as Black or brown or white, etc. That is no less a theoretical stance than Plato's division of the person into soul and body or Aristotle's parcelling of the soul into various functions.

The demand that the 'woman's voice' be heard also invites some further directions in the exploration of women's lives and discourages or excludes others. For reasons mentioned above, systematic, sustained reflection on being a woman—the kind of contemplation that 'doing theory' requires—is most likely to be done by women who vis-à-vis other women enjoy a certain amount of political, social and economic privilege because of their skin color, class membership, ethnic identity. There is a relationship between the content of our contemplation and the fact that we have the time to engage in it at some length—otherwise we shall have to say that it is a mere accident of history that white middle-class women in the United States have in the main developed 'feminist theory' (as opposed to 'Black feminist theory', 'Chicana feminist theory', etc.) and that so much of the theory has failed to be relevant to the lives of women who are not white or middle class. Feminist theory—of all kinds—is to be based on, or anyway touch base with, the variety of real life stories women provide about themselves. But in fact, because, among other things, of the structural political and social and economic inequalities among women, the tail has been wagging the dog: feminist theory has not for the most part arisen out of a medley or women's voices; instead, the theory has arisen out of the voices, the experiences, of a fairly small handful of women, and if other women's voices do not sing in harmony with the theory, they aren't counted as women's voices—rather, they are the voices of the woman as Hispana, Black, Jew, etc. There is another sense in which the tail is wagging the dog, too: it is presumed to be the case that those who do the theory know more about those who are theorized than vice versa: hence it ought to be the case that if it is white/Anglo women who write for and about all other women, then white/Anglo women must know more about all other women than other women know about them. But in fact just in order to survive, brown and Black women have to know a lot more about white/Anglo women—not through the sustained contemplation theory requires, but through the sharp observation stark exigency demands.

(In an Hispana voice) I think it necessary to explain why in so many cases when women of color appear in front of white/Anglo women to talk about feminism and women of color, we mainly raise a complaint: the complaint of exclusion, of silencing, of being included in a universe we have not chosen. We usually raise the complaint with a certain amount of disguised or undisguised anger. I can only attempt to explain this phenomenon from a Hispanic viewpoint and a fairly

narrow one at that: the viewpoint of an Argentinian woman who has lived in the US for 16 yr, who has attempted to come to terms with the devaluation of things Hispanic and Hispanic people in 'America' and who is most familiar with Hispano life in the Southwest of the US. . . .

We and you do not talk the same language. When we talk to you we use your language: the language of your experience and of your theories. We try to use it to communicate our world of experience. But since your language and your theories are inadequate in expressing our experiences, we only succeed in communicating our experience of exclusion. We cannot talk to you in our language because you do not understand it. So the brute facts that we understand your language and that the place where most theorizing about women is taking place is your place, both combine to require that we either use your language and distort our experience not just in the speaking about it, but in the living of it, or that we remain silent. Complaining about exclusion is a way of remaining silent.

You are ill at ease in our world. You are ill at ease in our world in a very different way that we are ill at ease in yours. Your are not of our world and again, you are not of our world in a very different way that we are not of yours. In the intimacy of a personal relationship we appear to you many times to be wholly there, to have broken through or to have dissipated the barriers that separate us because you are Anglo and we are raza. When we let go of the psychic state that I referred to above in the direction of sympathy, we appear to ourselves equally whole in your presence but our intimacy is thoroughly incomplete. When we are in your world many times you remake us in your own image, although sometimes you clearly and explicitly acknowledge that we are not wholly there in our being with you. When we are in your world we ourselves feel the discomfort of having our own being Hispanas disfigured or not understood. And yet, we have had to be in your world and learn its ways. We have to participate in it, make a living in it, live in it, be mistreated in it, be ignored in

it, and rarely, be appreciated in it. In learning to do these things or in learning to suffer them or in learning to enjoy what is to be enjoyed or in learning to understand your conception of us, we have had to learn your culture and thus your language and self-conceptions. But there is nothing that necessitates that you understand our world: understand, that is, not as an observer understands things, but as a participant, as someone who has a stake in them understands them. So your being ill at ease in our world lacks the features of our being ill at ease in yours precisely because you can leave and you can always tell yourselves that you will be soon out of there and because the wholeness of your selves is never touched by us, we have no tendency to remake you in our image. . . .

II. Some Questionable Assumptions about Feminist Theorizing

(Unproblematically in Vicky's & Maria's voice) Feminist theories aren't just about what happens to the female population in any given society or across all societies; they are about the meaning of those experiences in the lives of women. They are about beings who give their own accounts of what is happening to them or of what they are doing, who have culturally constructed ways of reflecting on their lives. But how can the theorizer get at the meaning of those experiences? What should the relation be between a woman's own account of her experiences and the theorizer's account of it? . . .

Our suggestion in this paper, and at this time it is no more than a suggestion, is that only when genuine and reciprocal dialogue takes place between 'outsiders' and 'insiders' can we trust the outsider's account. At first sight it may appear that the insider/outsider distinction disappears in the dialogue, but it is important to notice that all that happens is that we are now both outsider and insider with respect to each other. The dialogue puts us both in position to give a better account of each other's and our own experience. Here we should again note that white/Anglo women are much less prepared for this dialogue with women of color than women of color are for dialogue with them in that women of color have had to learn white/Anglo ways, self-conceptions, and conceptions of them. . . .

III. Ways of Talking or Being Talked about That Are Helpful, Illuminating, Empowering, Respectful

(Unproblematically in Maria's & Vicky's voice) Feminists have been quite diligent about pointing out the ways in which empirical, philosophical and moral theories have been androcentric. They have thought it crucial to ask, with respect to such theories: who makes them? for whom do they make them? about what or whom are the theories? why? how are theories tested? what are the criteria for such tests and where did the criteria come from? Without posing such questions and trying to answer them, we'd never have been able to begin to mount evidence for our claims that particular theories are androcentric, sexist, biased, paternalistic, etc. Certain philosophers have become fond of—indeed, have made their careers on—pointing out that characterizing a statement as true or false is only one of many ways possible of characterizing it; it might also be, oh, rude, funny, disarming, etc.; it may be intended to soothe or to hurt; or it may have the effect, intended or not, of soothing or hurting. Similarly, theories appear to be the kinds of things that are true or false; but they also are the kinds of things that can be, e.g. useless, arrogant, disrespectful, ignorant, ethnocentric, imperialistic. The immediate point is that feminist theory is no less immune to such characterizations than, say, Plato's political theory, or Freud's theory of female psychosexual development. Of course this is not to say that if feminist theory manages to be respectful or helpful it will follow that it must be true. But if, say, an empirical theory is purported to be about 'women' and in fact is only about certain women, it is certainly false, probably ethnocentric, and of dubious useful-

ness except to those whose position in the world it strengthens (and theories, as we know, don't have to be true in order to be used to strengthen people's positions in the world). . . .

IV. Some Suggestions about How to Do Theory That Is Not Imperialistic, Ethnocentric, Disrespectful

(Problematically in the voice of a woman of color) What are the things we need to know about others, and about ourselves, in order to speak intelligently, intelligibly, sensitively, and helpfully about their lives? We can show respect or lack of it, in writing theoretically about others no less than in talking directly with them. This is not to say that here we have a well-worked out concept of respect, but only to suggest that together all of us consider what it would mean to theorize in a respectful way.

When we speak, write, and publish our theories, to whom do we think we are accountable? Are the concerns we have in being accountable to 'the profession' at odds with the concerns we have in being accountable to those about whom we theorize? Do commitments to 'the profession', method, getting something published, getting tenure, lead us to talk and act in ways at odds with what we ourselves (let alone others) would regard as ordinary, decent behavior? To what extent do we presuppose that really understanding another person or culture requires our behaving in ways that are disrespectful, even violent? That is, to what extent do we presuppose that getting and/or publishing the requisite information requires or may require disregarding the wishes of others, lying to them, wresting information from them against their wills? Why and how do we think theorizing about others provides *understanding* of them? Is there any sense in which theorizing about others is a shortcut to understanding them?

Finally, if we think doing theory is an important activity, and we think that some conditions lead to better theorizing than others, what are we going to do about creating those conditions?

If we think it not just desirable but necessary for women of different racial and ethnic identities to create feminist theory jointly, how shall that be arranged for? It may be the case that at this particular point we ought not even try to do that— that feminist theory by and for Hispanas needs to be done separately from feminist theory by and for Black women, white women, etc. But it must be recognized that white/Anglo women have more power and privilege than Hispanas, Black women, etc., and at the very least they can use such advantage to provide space and time for other women to speak (with the above caveats about implicit restrictions on what counts as 'the woman's voice'). And once again it is important to remember that the power of white/Anglo women vis-à-vis Hispanas and Black women is in inverse proportion to their working knowledge of each other.

This asymmetry is a crucial fact about the background of possible relationships between white women and women of color, whether as political coworkers, professional colleagues, or friends.

If white/Anglo women and women of color are to do theory jointly, in helpful, respectful, illuminating and empowering ways, the task ahead of white/Anglo women because of this asymmetry, is a very hard task. The task is a very complex one. In part, to make an analogy, the task can be compared to learning a text without the aid of teachers. We all know the lack of contact felt when we want to discuss a particular issue that requires knowledge of a text with someone who does not know the text at all. Or the discomfort and impatience that arise in us when we are discussing an issue that presupposes a text and someone walks into the conversation who does not know the text. That person is either left out or will impose herself on us and either try to engage in the discussion or try to change the subject. Women of color are put in these situations by white/Anglo women and men constantly. Now imagine yourself simply left out but wanting to do theory with us. The first thing to recognize and accept is that you disturb our own dialogues by putting yourself in the left-out position and not leaving us in some meaningful sense to ourselves.

You must also recognize and accept that you must learn the text. But the text is an extraordinarily complex one: viz. our many different cultures. You are asking us to make ourselves more vulnerable to you than we already are before we have any reason to trust that you will not take advantage of this vulnerability. So you need to learn to become unintrusive, unimportant, patient to the point of tears, while at the same time open to learning any possible lessons. You will also have to come to terms with the sense of alienation, of not belonging, of having your world thoroughly disrupted, having it criticized and scrutinized from the point of view of those who have been harmed by it, having important concepts central to it dismissed, being viewed with mistrust, being seen as of no consequence except as an object of mistrust.

Why would any white/Anglo woman engage in this task? Out of self-interest? What in engaging in this task would be, not just in her interest, but perceived as such by her before the task is completed or well underway? Why should we want you to come into our world out of self-interest? Two points need to be made here. The task as described could be entered into with the intention of finding out as much as possible about us so as to better dominate us. The person engaged in this task would act as a spy. The motivation is not unfamiliar to us. We have heard it said that now that Third World countries are more powerful as a bloc, westerners need to learn more about them, that it is in their self-interest to do so. Obviously there is no reason why people of color should welcome white/Anglo women into their world for the carrying out of this intention. It is also obvious that white/Anglo feminists should not engage in this task under this description since the task under this description would not lead to joint theorizing of the desired sort: respectful, illuminating, helpful and empowering. It would be helpful and empowering only in a one-sided way.

Self-interest is also mentioned as a possible motive in another way. White/Anglo women sometimes say that the task of understanding women of color would entail self-growth or self-expansion. If the task is conceived as described here, then one should doubt that growth or expansion will be the result. The severe self-disruption that the task entails should place a doubt in anyone who takes the task seriously about her possibilities of coming out of the task whole, with a self that is not as fragile as the selves of those who have been the victims of racism. But also, why should women of color embrace white/Anglo women's self-betterment without reciprocity? At this time women of color cannot afford this generous affirmation of white/Anglo women.

Another possible motive for engaging in this task is the motive of duty, 'out of obligation', because white/Anglos have done people of color wrong. Here again two considerations: coming into Hispano, Black, Native American worlds out of obligation puts white/Anglos in a morally self-righteous position that is inappropriate. You are active, we are passive. We become the vehicles of your own redemption. Secondly, we couldn't want you to come into our worlds 'out of obligation'. That is like wanting someone to make love to you out of obligation. So, whether or not you have an obligation to do this (and we would deny that you do), or whether this task could even be done out of obligation, this is an inappropriate motive.

Out of obligation you should stay out of our way, respect us and our distance, and forego the use of whatever power you have over us—for example, the power to use your language in our meetings, the power to overwhelm us with your education, the power to intrude in our communities in order to research us and to record the supposed dying of our cultures, the power to engrain in us a sense that we are members of dying cultures and are doomed to assimilate, the power to keep us in a defensive posture with respect to our own cultures.

So the motive of friendship remains as both the only appropriate and understandable motive

for white/Anglo feminists engaging in the task as described above. If you enter the task out of friendship with us, then you will be moved to attain the appropriate reciprocity of care for your and our wellbeing as whole beings, you will have a stake in us and in our world, you will be moved to satisfy the need for reciprocity of understanding that will enable you to follow us in our experiences as we are able to follow you in yours.

We are not suggesting that if the learning of the text is to be done out of friendship, you must enter into a friendship with a whole community and for the purpose of making theory. In order to understand what it is that we are suggesting, it is important to remember that during the description of her experience of exclusion, the Hispana voice said that Hispanas experience the intimacy of friendship with white/Anglo women friends as thoroughly incomplete. It is not until this fact is acknowledged by our white/Anglo women friends and felt as a profound lack in our experience of each other that white/Anglo women can begin to see us. Seeing us in our communities will make clear and concrete to you how incomplete we really are in our relationships with you. It is this beginning that forms the proper background for the yearning to understand the text of our cultures that can lead to joint theory-making.

Thus, the suggestion made here is that if white/Anglo women are to understand our voices, they must understand our communities and us in them. Again, this is not to suggest that you set out to make friends with our communities, though you may become friends with some of the members, nor is it to suggest that you should try to befriend us for the purpose of making theory with us. The latter would be a perversion of friendship. Rather, from within friendship you may be moved by friendship to undergo the very difficult task of understanding the text of our cultures by understanding our lives in our communities. This learning calls for circumspection, for questioning of yourselves and your roles in your own culture. It necessitates a striving to understand while in the comfortable position of not having an official calling card (as 'scientific' observers of our communities have); it demands recognition that you do not have the authority of knowledge; it requires coming to the task without ready-made theories to frame our lives. This learning is then extremely hard because it requires openness (including openness to severe criticism of the white/Anglo world), sensitivity, concentration, self-questioning, circumspection. It should be clear that it does not consist in a passive immersion in our cultures, but in a striving to understand what it is that our voices are saying. Only then can we engage in a mutual dialogue that does not reduce each one of us to instances of the abstraction called 'woman'.

Study Questions

1. What is the moral significance of the whole structure (sections, voices, tones) of the article in relation to the claims it makes?
2. On what moral grounds do Lugones and Spelman criticize traditional feminist theory? How do the guidelines they provide for feminist theory address these problems? Does their own theory reflect these standards?
3. Why is friendship the only morally acceptable motive for white/Anglo women? Why doesn't the voice of the woman of color develop an ethics for women of color? Ought she? Can an ethics based on difference and diversity issue moral prescriptions for other women? for all women?

Suggestions for Further Reading

Anzaldúa, G. *Making Face, Making Soul—Haciendo Cara: Creative and Critical Perspectives of Women of Color* (San Francisco: Aunt Lute Foundation Books, 1990). Contains prose, poetry, personal narrative, and feminist critique by women of color.

Lugones, M. C. "On the Logic of Pluralist Feminism." In *Feminist Ethics,* ed. C. Card (Lawrence: University Press of Kansas, 1991). A critical view of white feminist theory from the perspective of women of color.

Meyers, D. T., ed. *Feminist Social Thought: A Reader* (New York; London: Routledge, 1997). See Part 2, "Theorizing Diversity—Gender, Race, Class and Sexual Orientation," and essays 13 and 26.

Morraga, C., and G. Anzaldúa. *This Bridge Called My Back: Writings by Radical Women of Color* (New York: Kitchen Table: Women of Color Press, 1983). Contains prose, poetry, personal narrative, and feminist critique by women of color. See especially "And When You Leave, Take Your Pictures with You: Racism in the Women's Movement."

Spelman, E. V. *Inessential Woman: Problems of Exclusion in Feminist Thought* (Boston: Beacon Press, 1988). A critical examination of traditional philosophical conceptions and dominant feminist conceptions of women.

———. "The Virtue of Feeling the Feeling of Virtue." In *Feminist Ethics,* ed. C. Card (Lawrence: University Press of Kansas, 1991). Discusses the problem of women's inhumanity to other women.

Nel Noddings (1929–)

Nel Noddings is a professor of education at Stanford University. She is best known for her feminine ethics of caring, in which the classical feminine view of morality in terms of relations and affects serves as the basis for a universal model of moral conduct. Noddings' moral theory is indebted in part to Carol Gilligan's psychological studies of the different voice in women's conceptions of self and morality. However, unlike Gilligan, Noddings explicitly prescribes a feminine approach to morality in direct contrast to the traditional masculine focus on moral principles and their logic. Noddings' feminine theory of morality focuses on our concrete lived experiences and personal interactions with others while offering a specific and detailed practical ethics. Her feminine ethics of caring is thus closely woven into her philosophy of education as a general project for moral education.

In her book *Caring: A Feminine Approach to Ethics and Moral Education,* Noddings works out the feminine perspective of morality by analyzing its central ideas and developing an ethics based on its tenets. The feminine view sees that a fundamental feature of human existence is our relatedness to and with one another. The basic ethical relation is that of caring, which involves receptivity, relatedness, and responsiveness. It also requires that these special attitudes and affective responses occur in the "one-caring" and the "cared-for." We have a natural inclination to be the one-caring in certain relations, as that of a mother toward her child, and commonly associate the natural caring relation with goodness. Our morality is based on the fact that we long for such goodness and strive for a personal ideal of being the one-caring. Thus, ethical caring, whereby we direct ourselves and make an effort to care, arises from natural caring, from our memories of being cared-for or being the one-caring, and is guided by the picture of our better selves as ones-caring.

CARING: A FEMININE APPROACH TO ETHICS AND MORAL EDUCATION

ETHICS, THE PHILOSOPHICAL STUDY of morality, has concentrated for the most part on moral reasoning. Much current work, for example, focuses on the status of moral predicates and, in education, the dominant model presents a hierarchical picture of moral reasoning. This emphasis gives ethics a contemporary, mathematical appearance, but it also moves discussion beyond the sphere of actual human activity and the feeling that pervades such activity. Even though careful philosophers have recognized the difference between "pure" or logical reason and "practical" or moral reason, ethical argumentation has frequently proceeded as if it were governed by the logical necessity characteristic of geometry. It has concentrated on the establishment of principles and that which can be logically derived from them. One might say that ethics has been discussed largely in the language of the father: in principles and propositions, in terms such as justification, fairness, justice. The mother's voice has been silent. Human caring and the memory of caring and being cared for, which I shall argue form the foundation of ethical response, have not received attention except as outcomes of ethical behavior. One is tempted to say that ethics has so far been guided by Logos, the masculine spirit, whereas the more natural and, perhaps, stronger approach would be through Eros, the feminine spirit. I hesitate to give way to this temptation, in part because the terms carry with them a Jungian baggage that I am unwilling to claim in its totality. In one sense, "Eros" does capture the flavor and spirit of what I am attempting here; the notion of psychic relatedness lies at the heart of the ethic I shall propose. In another sense, however, even "Eros" is masculine in its roots and fails to capture the receptive rationality of caring that is characteristic of the feminine approach.

When we look clear-eyed at the world today, we see it wracked with fighting, killing, vandalism, and psychic pain of all sorts. One of the saddest features of this picture of violence is that the deeds are so often done in the name of principle. When we establish a principle forbidding killing, we also establish principles describing the exceptions to the first principle. Supposing, then, that we are moral (we are principled, are we not?), we may tear into others whose beliefs or behaviors differ from ours with the promise of ultimate vindication.

This approach through law and principle is not, I suggest, the approach of the mother. It is the approach of the detached one, of the father. The view to be expressed here is a feminine view. This does not imply that all women will accept it or that men will reject it; indeed, there is no reason why men should not embrace it. It is feminine in the deep classical sense—rooted in receptivity, relatedness, and responsiveness. It does not imply either that logic is to be discarded or that logic is alien to women. It represents an alternative to present views, one that begins with the moral attitude or longing for goodness and not with moral reasoning. It may indeed be the case that such an approach is more typical of women than of men, but this is an empirical question I shall not attempt to answer.

It seems to me that the view I shall try to present would be badly distorted if it were presented in what I have referred to as the "language of the father." Several theorists in education—among them, William Pinar, Madeleine Grumet, Dwayne Huebner, Elliot Eisner—have suggested that our pictures of the world are unduly cramped and narrowed by reliance on a restricted domain of language. Pinar and Grumet, in particular, have looked at this problem in the context of gender studies. I agree with their assessment. But we must realize, also, that one writing on philosophical/educational problems may be handicapped and even rejected in the attempt to bring a new voice to an old domain, particularly when entrance to that domain is gained by uttering the appropriate passwords. Whatever language is chosen, it must not be used as a cloak for sloppy thinking; that much is certain. This part of what I am doing, then, is not without risk.

Women, in general, face a similar problem when they enter the practical domain of moral action. They enter the domain through a different door, so to speak. It is not the case, certainly, that women cannot arrange principles hierarchically and derive conclusions logically. It is more likely that we see this process as peripheral to, or even alien to, many problems of moral action. Faced with a hypothetical moral dilemma, women often ask for more information. We want to know more, I think, in order to form a picture more nearly resembling real moral situations. Ideally, we need to talk to the participants, to see their eyes and facial expressions, to receive what they are feeling. Moral decisions are, after all, made in real situations; they are qualitatively different from the solution of geometry problems. Women can and do give reasons for their acts, but the reasons often point to feelings, needs, impressions, and a sense of personal ideal rather than to universal principles and their application. We shall see that, as a result of this "odd" approach, women have often been judged inferior to men in the moral domain.

Because I am entering the domain through a linguistic back door of sorts, much of what I say cannot be labeled "empirical" or "logical." (Some of it, of course, can be so labeled.) Well, what is it then? It is language that attempts to capture what Wittgenstein advised we "must pass over in silence." But if our language is extended to the expressive—and, after all, it is beautifully capable of such extension—perhaps we can say something in the realm of ethical feeling, and that something may at least achieve the status of conceptual aid or tool if not that of conceptual truth. We may present a coherent and enlightening picture without *proving* anything and, indeed, without claiming to present or to seek moral *knowledge* or moral *truth*. The hand that steadied us as we learned to ride our first bicycle did not provide propositional knowledge, but it guided and supported us all the same, and we finished up "knowing how."

This is an essay in practical ethics from the feminine view. It is very different from the utilitarian practical ethics of, say, Peter Singer. While both of us would treat animals kindly and sensitively, for example, we give very different reasons for our consideration. I must resist his charge that we are guilty of "speciesism" in our failure to accord rights to animals, because I shall locate the very wellspring of ethical behavior in human affective response. Throughout our discussion of ethicality we shall remain in touch with the affect that gives rise to it. This does not mean that our discussion will bog down in sentiment, but it is necessary to give appropriate attention and credit to the affective foundation of existence. Indeed, one who attempts to ignore or to climb above the human affect at the heart of ethicality may well be guilty of romantic rationalism. What

is recommended in such a framework simply cannot be broadly applied in the actual world.

I shall begin with a discussion of caring. What does it mean to care and to be cared for? The analysis will occupy us at length, since relation will be taken as ontologically basic and the caring relation as ethically basic. For our purposes, "relation" may be thought of as a set of ordered pairs generated by some rule that describes the affect—or subjective experience—of the members.

In order to establish a firm conceptual foundation that will be free of equivocation, I have given names to the two parties of the relation: the first member is the "one-caring" and the second is the "cared-for." Regular readers of "existentialist" literature will recognize the need for such terminology—bothersome as it is. One may recall Sartre's use of for-itself and in-itself, Heidegger's being-in-the-world, and Buber's I-Thou and I-It. There are at least two good reasons for invoking this mechanism. First, it allows us to speak about our basic entities without explaining the entire conceptual apparatus repeatedly; second, it prevents us from smuggling in meanings through the use of synonyms. Hence, even though hyphenated entities offend the stylist, they represent in this case an attempt to achieve both economy and rigor. Another matter of style in connection with "one-caring" and "cared-for" should be mentioned here. In order to maintain balance and avoid confusion, I have consistently associated the generic "one-caring" with the universal feminine, "she," and "cared-for" with the masculine, "he." Clearly, however, when actual persons are substituted for "one-caring" and "cared-for" in the basic relation, they may be both male, both female, female-male, or male-female. Taking *relation* as ontologically basic simply means that we recognize human encounter and affective response as a basic fact of human existence. As we examine what it means to care and to be cared for, we shall see that both parties contribute to the relation; my caring must be somehow completed in the other if the relation is to be described as caring.

This suggests that the ethic to be developed is one of reciprocity, but our view of reciprocity will be different from that of "contract" theorists such as Plato and John Rawls. What the cared-for gives to the caring relation is not a promise to behave as the one-caring does, nor is it a form of "consideration." The problem of reciprocity will be, possibly, the most important problem we shall discuss, and facets of the problem will appear in a spiral design throughout the book. When we see what it is that the cared-for contributes to the relation, we shall find it possible to separate human infants from nonhuman animals (a great problem for those who insist on some form of rationality in those we should treat ethically), and we shall do this without recourse to notions of God or some other external source of "sanctity" in human life.

The focus of our attention will be upon how to meet the other morally. Ethical caring, the relation in which we do meet the other morally, will be described as arising out of natural caring—that relation in which we respond as one-caring out of love or natural inclination. The relation of natural caring will be identified as the human condition that we, consciously or unconsciously, perceive as "good." It is that condition toward which we long and strive, and it is our longing for caring—to be in that special relation—that provides the motivation for us to be moral. We want to be *moral* in order to remain in the caring relation and to enhance the ideal of ourselves as one-caring.

It is this ethical ideal, this realistic picture of ourselves as one-caring, that guides us as we strive to meet the other morally. Everything depends upon the nature and strength of this ideal, for we shall not have absolute principles to guide us. Indeed, I shall reject ethics of principle as ambiguous and unstable. Wherever there is a principle, there is implied its exception and, too often, principles function to separate us from each other. We may become dangerously self-righteous when we perceive ourselves as holding a precious principle not held by the other. The other may then be devalued and treated "differ-

ently." Our ethic of caring will not permit this to happen. We recognize that in fear, anger, or hatred we will treat the other differently, but this treatment is never conducted ethically. Hence, when we must use violence or strategies on the other, we are already diminished ethically. Our efforts must, then, be directed to the maintenance of conditions that will permit caring to flourish. Along with the rejection of principles and rules as the major guide to ethical behavior, I shall also reject the notion of universalizability. Many of those writing and thinking about ethics insist that any ethical judgment—by virtue of its *being* an ethical judgment—must be universalizable; that is, it must be the case that, if under conditions X you are required to do A, then under sufficiently similar conditions, I too am required to do A. I shall reject this emphatically. First, my attention is not on judgment and not on the particular acts we perform but on how we meet the other morally. Second, in recognition of the feminine approach to meeting the other morally—our insistence on caring for the other—I shall want to preserve the uniqueness of human encounters. Since so much depends on the subjective experience of those involved in ethical encounters, conditions are rarely "sufficiently similar" for me to declare that you must do what I must do. There is, however, a fundamental universality in our ethic, as there must be to escape relativism. The caring attitude, that attitude which expresses our earliest memories of being cared for and our growing store of memories of both caring and being cared for, is universally accessible. Since caring and the commitment to sustain it form the universal heart of the ethic, we must establish a convincing and comprehensive picture of caring at the outset.

Another outcome of our dependence on an ethical ideal is the emphasis upon moral education. Since we are dependent upon the strength and sensitivity of the ethical ideal—both our own and that of others—we must nurture that ideal in all of our educational encounters. I shall claim that we are dependent on each other even in the quest for personal goodness. How good *I* can be is partly a function of how *you*—the other—receive and respond to me. Whatever virtue I exercise is completed, fulfilled, in you. The primary aim of all education must be nurturance of the ethical ideal.

To accomplish the purposes set out above, I shall strike many contrasts between masculine and feminine approaches to ethics and education and, indeed, to living. These are not intended to divide men and women into opposing camps. They are meant, rather, to show how great the chasm is that already divides the masculine and feminine in each of us and to suggest that we enter a dialogue of genuine dialectical nature in order to achieve an ultimate transcendence of the masculine and feminine in moral matters. The reader must keep in mind, then, that I shall use the language of both father and mother; I shall have to argue for the positions I set out expressively.

An important difference between an ethic of caring and other ethics that give subjectivity its proper place is its foundation in relation. The philosopher who begins with a supremely free consciousness—an aloneness and emptiness at the heart of existence—identifies *anguish* as the basic human affect. But our view, rooted as it is in relation, identifies *joy* as a basic human affect. When I look at my child—even one of my grown children—and recognize the fundamental relation in which we are each defined, I often experience a deep and overwhelming joy. It is the recognition of and longing for relatedness that form the foundation of our ethic, and the joy that accompanies fulfillment of our caring enhances our commitment to the ethical ideal that sustains us as one-caring.

In the final chapter on moral education, we shall explore how all this may be brought to bear on recommendations for the reorganization of schooling. The specific suggestions made there are not intended as fully developed plans for action but, rather, as illustrations of an approach, of a mode of thinking and feeling about education. They are an invitation to dialogue and not a challenge to enter battle.

Study Questions

1. What is the difference between the terms *masculine/feminine* and *male/female*? What does Noddings' usage of the term *feminine* suggest about most females? about most males? Why doesn't she use the term *feminist* to characterize her ethics?
2. What faults does Noddings find in the masculine approach to ethics? What ethical notions does she reject and on what grounds? Is she suggesting that we completely abandon the masculine perspective?
3. Is the ethics of caring entirely altruistic?

Suggestions for Further Reading

Cole, E. B., and S. Coultrap-McQuin, eds. *Explorations in Feminist Ethics: Theory and Practice* (Bloomington: Indiana University Press, 1992). See Part I, "The Care Debate," for various feminist perspectives on the issue of care.

Grimshaw, J. "The Idea of a Female Ethic." In *A Companion to Ethics,* ed. P. Singer (Oxford; Cambridge, MA: Blackwell, 1991). Critically examines the issue of the relation between ethics and gender.

Hoagland, S. L. "Some Thoughts about 'Caring'." In *Feminist Ethics,* ed. C. Card (Lawrence: University Press of Kansas, 1991). A critique of Noddings' use of mothering as a model of female moral agency.

Hypatia 5, no. 1 (Spring 1990). A review symposium containing four articles on Noddings' book and her response.

Larabee, M. J., ed. *An Ethic of Care: Feminist and Interdisciplinary Perspectives* (New York: Routledge, 1993). Contains eighteen essays on the various issues raised by Gilligan's ethics of care. Essays 5, 16, and 17 explicitly examine issues involving Noddings' approach.

Meyers, D. T., ed. *Feminist Social Thought: A Reader* (New York; London: Routledge, 1997). Part 6, "Care and Its Critics," contains a sample of the main feminist positions on care.

Annette C. Baier (1929–)

Annette C. Baier recently retired as professor of philosophy at the University of Pittsburgh. Her numerous articles cover topics in ethics, the history of philosophy, modern philosophy, and the philosophy of mind. She is also the author of various books on moral theory, including *Postures of the Mind: Essays on Mind and Morals* (1985), *A Progress of Sentiments: Reflections on Hume's Treatise* (1991), and *Moral Prejudices: Essays on Ethics* (1994).

Baier's question, "What do women want in a moral theory?" presupposes that, in general, women expect something different from moral theory than men expect. Baier asserts that women's contributions to moral philosophy have generally articulated women's "different voice." This voice speaks of an ethics of love. However, Baier claims that women have yet to produce moral theories that are based on a central concept, offer a broad systematic account of morality, and strive for universal acceptance. The latter condition calls for a theory that will incorporate the moral insights and concerns of both genders and eliminate the shortcomings of both kinds of moral philosophy.

In the following selection, Baier points to "appropriate trust" as the unifying concept for moral theory. To trust is to have an attitude that is informed by our beliefs and influences our actions. The concept of trust mediates between reason and emotions, for it is neither a belief nor a feeling regarding what we trust. More significantly, the concept of trust connects women's ethics of love with men's ethics of obligation. With the ethics of obligation, there is a need to justify the power that people have to shape and impose moral duties upon others. Trust is what justifies or gives reason for this manipulation and coercion exercised by moral authorities. The ethics of love, for its part, demands supreme trust and trustworthiness from us. However, the concept of trust brings in problems of its own. As Baier notes, there are risks involved in trusting oneself and others and in determining what are "appropriate" or "proper" levels of trust, trustworthiness, distrust, and untrustworthiness.

WHAT DO WOMEN WANT IN A MORAL THEORY?

WHEN I FINISHED READING Carol Gilligan's "In Another Voice", I asked myself the obvious question for a philosopher reader, namely what differences one should expect in the moral philosophy done by women, supposing Gilligan's sample of women representative, and supposing her analysis of their moral attitudes and moral development to be correct. Should one expect them to want to produce moral theories, and if so, what sort of moral theories? How will any moral theories they produce differ from those produced by men?

Obviously one does not have to make this an entirely *a priori* and hypothetical question. One can look and see what sort of contributions women have made to moral philosophy. Such a look confirms, I think, Gilligan's findings. What one finds *is* a bit different in tone and approach from the standard sort of moral philosophy as done by men following in the footsteps of the great moral philosophers (all men). . . . I hear the voice Gilligan heard, made reflective and philosophical. What women want in moral philosophy is what they are providing. And what they are providing seems to me to confirm Gilligan's theses about women. One has to be careful here, of course, for not all important contributions to moral philosophy by women fall easily into the Gilligan stereotype, nor its philosophical extension. Nor has it been only women who recently have been proclaiming discontent with the standard approach in moral philosophy, and trying new approaches. . . .

. . . supposing for the sake of argument that women can, if they wish, systematize as well as the next man, and if need be systematize in a mathematical fashion as well as the next mathematically minded moral philosopher, then what key concept, or guiding *motif*, might hold together the structure of a moral theory hypothetically produced by a reflective woman, Gilligan-

style, who has taken up moral theorizing as a calling? What would be a suitable central question, principle, or concept, to structure a moral theory which might accommodate those moral insights women tend to have more readily than men, and to answer those moral questions which, it seems, worry women more than men? I hypothesized that the women's theory, expressive mainly of women's insights and concerns, would be an ethics of love, and this hypothesis seems to be Gilligan's too. . . . But presumably women theorists will be like enough to men to want their moral theory to be acceptable to all, so acceptable both to reflective women and to reflective men. Like any good theory, it will need not to ignore the partial truth of previous theories. So it must accommodate both the insights men have more easily than women, and those women have more easily than men. It should swallow up its predecessor theories. Women moral theorists, if any, will have this very great advantage over the men whose theories theirs supplant, that they can stand on the shoulders of men moral theorists, as no man has yet been able to stand on the shoulders of any woman moral theorist. There can be advantages, as well as handicaps, in being latecomers. So women theorists will need to connect their ethics of love with what has been the men theorists' preoccupation, namely obligation.

The great and influential moral theorists have in the modern era taken *obligation* as the key and the problematic concept, and have asked what justifies treating a person as morally bound or obliged to do a particular thing. Since to be bound is to be unfree, by making obligation central one at the same time makes central the question of the justification of coercion, of forcing or trying to force someone to act in a particular way. The concept of obligation as justified limitation of freedom does just what one wants a

Annette C. Baier, "What Do Women Want in a Moral Theory?" Nous 19, no. 1 (1985): 53–63. *Copyright Blackwell Publishers. Reprinted by permission.*

good theoretical concept to do—to divide up the field (as one looks as different ways one's freedom may be limited, freedom in different spheres, different sorts and versions and levels of justification) and at the same time hold the subfields together. There must in a theory be some generalization and some speciation or diversification, and a good rich key concept guides on both in recognizing the diversity and in recognizing the unity in it. The concept of obligation has served this function very well for the area of morality it covers, and so we have some fine theories about that area. But as Aristotelians and Christians, as well as women, know, there is a lot of morality *not* covered by that concept, a lot of very great importance even for the area where there are obligations. . . .

Granted that the men's theories of obligation need supplementation, to have much chance of integrity and coherence, and that the women's hypothetical theories will want to cover obligation as well as love, then what concept brings them together? My tentative answer is—the concept of appropriate trust, oddly neglected in moral theory. This concept also nicely mediates between reason and feeling, those tired old candidates for moral authority, since to trust is neither quite to believe something about the trusted, nor necessarily to feel any emotion towards them—but to have a belief-informed and action-influencing attitude. To make it plausible that the neglected concept of appropriate trust is a good one for the enlightened moral theorist to make central, I need to show, or begin to show, how it could include obligation, indeed shed light on obligations and their justification, as well as include love and the other moral concerns of Gilligan's women, and many of the topics women moral philosophers have chosen to address, mosaic fashion. I would also need to show that it could connect all of these in a way which holds out promise both of synthesis and of comprehensive moral coverage. A moral theory which looked at the conditions for proper trust of all the various sorts we show, and at what sorts of reasons justify inviting such trust, giving it, and meeting it, would, I believe, not have to

avoid turning its gaze on the conditions for the survival of the practices it endorses, so it could avoid that unpleasant choice many current liberal theories seem to have—between incoherence and bad faith. I do not pretend that we will easily agree once we raise the questions I think we should raise, but at least we may have a language adequate to the expression of both men's and women's moral viewpoints. . . .

. . . it is fairly obvious that love, the main moral phenomenon women want attended to, involves trust, so I anticipate little quarrel when I claim that, if we had a moral theory spelling out the conditions for appropriate trust and distrust, that would include a morality of love in all its variants—parental love, love of children for their parents, love of family members, love of friends, of lovers in the strict sense, of co-workers, of one's country, and its figureheads, of exemplary heroines and heros, of goddesses and gods.

Love and loyalty demand maximal trust of one sort, and maximal trustworthiness, and in investigating the conditions for maximal trust and maximal risk we must think about the ethics of love. More controversial may be my claim that the ethics of obligation will also be covered. I see it as covered since to recognize a set of obligations is to trust some group of persons to instill them, to demand that they be met, possibly to levy sanctions if they are not, and this is to trust persons with very significant coercive power over others. Less coercive but still significant power is possessed by those shaping our conception of the virtues, and expecting us to display them, approving when we do, disapproving and perhaps shunning us when we do not. Such coercive and manipulative power over others requires justification, and is justified only if we have reason to trust those who have it to use it properly, and to use the discretion which is always given when trust is given in a way which serves the purpose of the whole system of moral control, and not merely self serving or morally improper purposes. Since the question of the justification of coercion becomes, at least in part, the question of the wisdom of trusting the coercers to do their job properly, the morality of obligation, in as far as it reduces to the morality of coercion, is covered by the morality of proper trust. Other forms of trust may also be involved, but trusting enforcers with the use of force is the most problematic form of trust involved.

The coercers and manipulators are, to some extent, all of us, so to ask what our obligations are and what virtues we should exhibit is to ask what it is reasonable to trust us to demand, expect, and contrive to get, from one another. It becomes, in part, a question of what powers we can in reason trust ourselves to exercise properly. But self-trust is a dubious or limit case of trust, so I prefer to postpone the examination of the concept of proper self-trust at least until proper trust of others is more clearly understood. Nor do we distort matters too much if we concentrate on those cases where moral sanctions and moral pressure and moral manipulation is not self applied but applied to others, particularly by older persons to younger persons. Most moral pressuring that has any effects goes on in childhood and early youth. Moral sanctions may continue to be applied, formally and informally, to adults, but unless the criminal courts apply them it is easy enough for adults to ignore them, to brush them aside. It is not difficult to become a sensible knave, and to harden one's heart so that one is insensible to the moral condemnation of one's victims and those who sympathize with them. Only if the pressures applied in the morally formative stage have given one a heart that rebels against the thought of such ruthless independence of what others think will one see any reason *not* to ignore moral condemnation, not to treat it as mere powerless words and breath. Condemning sensible knaves is as much a waste of breath as arguing with them—all we can sensibly do is to try to protect their children against their influence, and ourselves against their knavery. Adding to the criminal law will not be the way to do the latter, since such moves will merely challenge sensible knaves to find new knavish exceptions and loopholes, not protect us from sensible knavery. Sensible knaves are precisely those who exploit us without breaking the law. So the whole question of when moral pressure of various sorts, formative, reformative, and punitive, ought to be brought to bear by whom is subsumed under the question of whom to trust when and with what, and for what good reasons.

In concentrating on obligations, rather than virtues, modern moral theorists have chosen to look at the cases where more trust is placed in enforcers of obligations than is placed in ordinary moral agents, the bearers of the obligations. In taking, as contractarians do, contractual obligations as the model of obligations, they concentrate on a case where the very minimal trust is put in the obligated person, and considerable punitive power entrusted to the one to whom the obligation is owed (I assume here that Hume is right in saying that when we promise or contract, we formally subject ourselves to the penalty, in case of failure, of never being trusted as a promisor again). This is an interesting case of the allocation of trust of various sorts, but it surely distorts our moral vision to suppose that *all* obligations, let alone all morally pressured expectations we impose on others, conform to that abnormally coercive model. It takes very special conditions for it to be safe to trust persons to inflict penalties on other persons, conditions in which either we can trust the penalizers to have the virtues necessary to penalize wisely and fairly, or else we can rely on effective threats to keep unvirtuous penalizers from abusing their power—that is to say, rely on others to coerce the first coercers into proper behaviour. But that reliance too will either be trust, or will have to rely on threats from coercers of the coercers of coercers, and so on. Morality on this model becomes a nasty, if intellectually intriguing, game of mutual mutually corrective threats. The central question of who should deprive whom of what freedom soon becomes the question of whose anger should be dreaded by whom (the theory of obligation) supplemented perhaps by an afterthought on whose favor should be courted by whom (the theory of the virtues).

Undoubtedly some important part of morality does depend in part on a system of threats and bribes, at least for its survival in difficult conditions when normal goodwill and normally virtuous dispositions may be insufficient to motivate the conduct required for the preservation and justice of the moral network of relationships. But equally undoubtedly life will be nasty, emotionally poor, and worse that brutish (even if longer), if that is all morality is, or even if that coercive structure of morality is regarded as the backbone, rather than as an available crutch, should the main support fail. For the main support has to come from those we entrust with the job of rearing and training persons so that they can be trusted in various ways, some trusted with extraordinary coercive powers, some with public decision-making powers, all trusted as parties to promise, most trusted by some who love them and by one or more willing to become co-parents with them, most trusted by dependent children, dependent elderly relatives, sick friends, and so on. A very complex network of a great variety of sorts of trust structures our moral relationships with our fellows, and if there is a *main* support to this network it is the trust we place in those who respond to the trust of new members of the moral community, namely to children, and prepare them for new forms of trust.

A theory which took as its central question "Who should trust whom with what, and why?" would not have to forego the intellectual fun and games previous theorists have had with the various paradoxes of morality—curbing freedom to increase freedom, curbing self interest the better to satisfy self interest, not aiming at happiness in order to become happier. For it is easy enough to get a paradox of trust, to accompany or, if I am right, to generalize the paradoxes of freedom, self interest and hedonism. To trust is to make oneself or let oneself be more vulnerable than one might have been to harm from others—to give them an opportunity to harm one, in the confidence that they will not take it, because they have no good reason to. Why would one take such a risk? For risk it always is, given the partial opaqueness to us of the reasoning and motivation of those we trust and with whom we cooperate. Our confidence may be, and quite often is, misplaced. That is what we risk when we

trust. If the best reason to take such a risk is the expected gain in security which comes from a climate of trust, then in trusting we are always giving up security to get greater security, exposing our throats so that others become accustomed to not biting. A moral theory which made proper trust its central concern could have its own categorical imperative, could replace obedience to self made laws and freely chosen restraint on freedom with security-increasing sacrifice of security, distrust in the promoters of a climate of distrust, and so on.

Such reflexive use of one's central concept, negative or affirmative, is an intellectually satisfying activity which is bound to have appeal to those system-lovers who want to construct moral theories, and it may help them design their theory in an intellectually pleasing manner. But we should beware of becoming hypnotized by our slogans, or of sacrificing truth to intellectual elegance. Any theory of proper trust should not *prejudge* the question of when distrust is proper. We might find more objects of proper distrust than just the contributors to a climate of reasonable distrust, just as freedom should be restricted not just to increase human freedom but to protect human life from poisoners and other killers. I suspect, however, that all the objects of reasonable distrust are more reasonably seen as falling into the category of ones who contribute to a decrease in the scope of proper trust, than can all who are reasonably coerced be seen as themselves guilty of wrongful coercion. Still, even if all proper trust turns out to be for such persons and on such matters as will increase the scope or stability of a climate of reasonable trust, and all proper distrust for such persons and on such matters as increase the scope of reasonable distrust, overreliance on such nice reflexive formulae can distract us from asking all the questions about trust which need to be asked, if an adequate moral theory is to be constructed around that concept. These questions should include when to *respond* to trust with *un*trustworthiness, when and when not to invite trust, as well as when to give and refuse trust. We should not assume that promiscuous trustworthiness is any more a virtue than is undiscriminating distrust. It is appropriate trustworthiness, appropriate trustingness, appropriate encouragement to trust, which will be virtues, as will be judicious untrustworthiness, selective refusal to trust, discriminating discouragement of trust.

Women are particularly well placed to appreciate these last virtues, since they have sometimes needed them to get into a position to even consider becoming moral theorizers. The long exploitation and domination of women by men depended on men's trust in women and women's trustworthiness to play their allotted role and so to perpetuate their own and their daughters' servitude. However keen women now are to end the lovelessness of modern moral philosophy, they are unlikely to lose sight of the cautious virtue of appropriate distrust, or of the tough virtue of principled betrayal of the exploiters' trust.

Gilligan's girls and women saw morality as a matter of preserving valued ties to others, of preserving the conditions for that care and mutual care without which human life becomes bleak, lonely, and after a while, as the mature men in her study found, not self affirming, however successful in achieving the egoistic goals which had been set. The boys and men saw morality as a matter of finding workable traffic rules for self assertors, so that they not needlessly frustrate one another, and so that they could, should they so choose, cooperate in more positive ways to mutual advantage. Both for the women's sometimes unchosen and valued ties with others, and for the men's mutual respect as sovereigns and subjects

of the same minimal moral traffic rules (and for their more voluntary and more selective associations of profiteers) trust is important. Both men and women are concerned with cooperation, and the dimensions of trust-distrust structure the different cooperative relations each emphasize. The various considerations which arise when we try to defend an answer to any question about the appropriateness of a particular form of cooperation with its distinctive form of trust or distrust, that is when we look into the terms of all sorts of cooperation, at the terms of trust in different cases of trust, at what are fair terms and what are trust-enhancing and trust-preserving terms, are suitably many and richly interconnected. A moral theory (or family of theories) that made trust its central problem could do better justice to men's and women's moral intuitions than do the going men's theories. Even if we don't easily agree on the answer to the question of who should trust whom with what, who should accept and who should meet various sorts of trust, and why, these questions might enable us better to morally reason together than we can when the central moral questions are reduced to those of whose favor one must court and whose anger one must dread. But such programmatic claims as I am making wil be tested only when women standing on the shoulders of men, or men on the shoulders of women, or some theorizing Tiresias, actually work out such a theory. I am no Tiresias, and have not foresuffered all the labor pains of such a theory. I aim here only to fertilize.

Study Questions

1. What is the significance of characterizing trust as an attitude? What assumptions does Baier make about reason and feelings? Why does she qualify trust and distrust as "appropriate" or "proper"?

2. What assumptions does Baier make about the ethics of obligation and the ethics of love? Could trust itself depend upon obligation? Does love always demand supreme trust and trustworthiness?

3. Why does Baier consider self-trust a "dubious or limit case"? What does the paradox of trust involve? Does the solution to this paradox depend upon a moral obligation?

Suggestions for Further Reading

Baier, A. "Trust and Antitrust." *Ethics* 96 (1986): 231–260. Elaborates further on the moral import and significance of trust.

————. "Whom Can Women Trust?" In *Feminist Ethics,* ed. C. Card (Lawrence: University Press of Kansas, 1991). Critically examines the question of whom women can trust in a patriarchal society.

Govier. T. "Trust, Distrust, and Feminist Theory." *Hypatia* 7, no. 1 (Winter 1992): 16–34. Explores various positions on trust and distrust, including Baier's.

Grimshaw, J. "The Idea of a Female Ethic." In *A Companion to Ethics,* ed. P. Singer (Oxford; Cambridge, MA: Blackwell, 1991). Critically examines the issue of the relation between ethics and gender.

Meyers, D. T., ed. *Feminist Social Thought: A Reader* (New York; London: Routledge, 1997). Part 6, "Care and Its Critics," contains a sample of the main feminist positions on care, including Baier's.

bell hooks (1952–)

bell hooks was born in Kentucky into a large working-class family. Originally named Gloria Jean Watkins, she adopted her pen name in honor of her great grandmother, who was known for her sharp tongue. Her choice of name is an acknowledgment to the spiritual heritage of African-American women whose words and actions forged the path away from racism and sexism. Her use of small letters is intended to deflect attention away from the author to the written work and its meaning. With her first book, *Ain't I a Woman: Black Women and Feminism* (1981), hooks' own "sharp tongue" began to take form in critical writings on gender, race, and social and cultural issues. Writing against the racism, classism, and sexism prevalent in society and its cultural expressions, hooks has also criticized feminist and African-American movements as being permeated by problems of white supremacy, capitalism, and patriarchy.

"Feminism: A Transformational Politic" is included in a collection of essays titled *Talking Back: Thinking Feminist, Thinking Black.*" In the southern African-American community where hooks was raised, "talking back" or "back talking" meant to speak as an equal to an authority figure, thus risking punishment. It involves daring to make oneself heard, to speak in what she terms a "liberatory voice" against exploitation, oppression, and domination. To "talk back" involves developing a critical consciousness with which one "thinks feminist" against sexism and "thinks Black" against racism, and particularly with which African-Americans end their silence and find their voice. Doing so requires that we all also think critically about the ways domination connects the public and private spheres of our lives. Because the personal is where exploitation and oppression are made concrete and real, we must also overcome the fear of speaking the truth, of exposing false reality, of "getting real." It is a demand for a reparation and a transformation that is, at the same time, personal and political.

The demand to "get real" is echoed in the essay below, where hooks challenges the contemporary feminist assumption that sexism is the root of all domination. For hooks, this is the product of uncritical thinking by Western white upper-class feminists who fail to recognize the significance of racist and classist forms of domination because of their own experiences as agents of domination. Thinking critically about domination involves a task of acquiring self-knowledge sufficient to realize that each of us has the potential oppressor and the potential victim within. Because sex, race, and class form interlocking systems of domination, the feminist agenda must recognize the complexity and diversity of women's experiences of domination while remaining sensitive to the interconnectedness between different forms of domination. Developing a critical consciousness is a process of discovering the relationship between the personal and the political that can begin the transformation of self and society. The transformational politic of feminism ultimately depends on our ability to use the mediating power of love to help us accept our differences and overcome domination.

FEMINISM: A TRANSFORMATIONAL POLITIC

WE LIVE IN A WORLD IN CRISIS—a world governed by politics of domination, one in which the belief in a notion of superior and inferior, and its concomitant ideology—that the superior should rule over the inferior—effects the lives of all people everywhere, whether poor or privileged, literate or illiterate. Systematic dehumanization, worldwide famine, ecological devastation, industrial contamination, and the possibility of nuclear destruction are realities which remind us daily that we are in crisis. Contemporary feminist thinkers often cite sexual politics as the origin of this crisis. They point to the insistence on difference as that factor which becomes the occasion for separation and domination and suggest that differentiation of status between females and males globally is an indication that patriarchal domination of the planet is the root of the problem. Such an assumption has fostered the notion that elimination of sexist oppression would necessarily lead to the eradication of all forms of domination. It is an argument that has led influential Western white women to feel that feminist movement should be *the* central political agenda for females globally. Ideologically, thinking in this direction enables Western women, especially privileged white women, to suggest that racism and class exploitation are merely the offspring of the parent system: patriarchy. Within feminist movement in the West, this has led to the assumption that resisting patriarchal domination is a more legitimate feminist action than resisting racism and other forms of domination. Such thinking prevails despite radical critiques made by black women and other women of color who question this proposition. To speculate that an oppositional division between men and women existed in early human

bell hooks. "Feminism: A Transformational Politic." In Talking Back: Thinking Feminist, Thinking Black, pp. 19–27. Boston: South End Press, 1989.

communities is to impose on the past, on these non-white groups, a world view that fits all too neatly within contemporary feminist paradigms that name man as the enemy and woman as the victim.

Clearly, differentiation between strong and weak, powerful and powerless, has been a central defining aspect of gender globally, carrying with it the assumption that men should have greater authority than women, and should rule over them. As significant and important as this fact is, it should not obscure the reality that women can and do participate in politics of domination, as perpetrators as well as victims—that we dominate, that we are dominated. If focus on patriarchal domination masks this reality or becomes the means by which women deflect attention from the real conditions and circumstances of our lives, then women cooperate in suppressing and promoting false consciousness, inhibiting our capacity to assume responsibility for transforming ourselves and society.

Thinking speculatively about early human social arrangement, about women and men struggling to survive in small communities, it is likely that the parent-child relationship with its very real imposed survival structure of dependency, of strong and weak, of powerful and powerless, was a site for the construction of a paradigm of domination. While this circumstance of dependency is not necessarily one that leads to domination, it lends itself to the enactment of a social drama wherein domination could easily occur as a means of exercising and maintaining control. This speculation does not place women outside the practice of domination, in the exclusive role of victim. It centrally names women as agents of domination, as potential theoreticians, and creators of a paradigm for social relationships wherein those groups of individuals designated as "strong" exercise power both benevolently and coercively over those designated as "weak."

Emphasizing paradigms of domination that call attention to woman's capacity to dominate is one way to deconstruct and challenge the simplistic notion that man is the enemy, woman the victim; the notion that men have always been the oppressors. Such thinking enables us to examine our role as women in the perpetuation and maintenance of systems of domination. To understand domination, we must understand that our capacity as women and men to be either dominated or dominating is a point of connection, of commonality. Even though I speak from the particular experience of living as a black woman in the United States, a white-supremacist, capitalist, patriarchal society, where small numbers of white men (and honorary "white men") constitute ruling groups, I understand that in many places in the world oppressed and oppressor share the same color. I understand that right here in this room, oppressed and oppressor share the same gender. Right now as I speak, a man who is himself victimized, wounded, hurt by racism and class exploitation is actively dominating a woman in his life—that even as I speak, women who are ourselves exploited, victimized, are dominating children. It is necessary for us to remember, as we think critically about domination, that we all have the capacity to act in ways that oppress, dominate, wound (whether or not that power is institutionalized). It is necessary to remember that it is first the potential oppressor within that we must resist—the potential victim within that we must rescue—otherwise we cannot hope for an end to domination, for liberation.

This knowledge seems especially important at this historical moment when black women and other women of color have worked to create awareness of the ways in which racism empowers white women to act as exploiters and oppressors. Increasingly this fact is considered a reason we should not support feminist struggle even though sexism and sexist oppression is a real issue in our lives as black women (see, for example, Vivian Gordon's *Black Women, Feminism, Black Liberation: Which Way?*). It becomes necessary for us to speak continually about the convictions that inform our continued advocacy of feminist struggle. By calling attention to interlocking systems of domination—sex, race, and class—black women and many other groups of women acknowledge the diversity and complexity of female experience, of our relationship to power and domination. The intent is not to dissuade people of color from becoming engaged in feminist movement. Feminist struggle to end patriarchal domination should be of primary importance to women and men globally not because it is the foundation of all other oppressive structures but because it is that form of domination we are most likely to encounter in an ongoing way in everyday life.

Unlike other forms of domination, sexism directly shapes and determines relations of power in our private lives, in familiar social spaces, in that most intimate context—home—and in that most intimate sphere of relations—family. Usually, it is within the family that we witness coercive domination and learn to accept it, whether it be domination of parent over child, or male over female. Even though family relations may be, and most often are, informed by acceptance of a politic of domination, they are simultaneously relations of care and connection. It is this convergence of two contradictory impulses—the urge to promote growth and the urge to inhibit growth—that provides a practical setting for feminist critique, resistance, and transformation.

Growing up in a black, working-class, father-dominated household, I experienced coercive adult male authority as more immediately threatening, as more likely to cause immediate pain than racist oppression or class exploitation. It was equally clear that experiencing exploitation and oppression in the home made one feel all the more powerless when encountering dominating forces outside the home. This is true for many people. If we are unable to resist and end domination in relations where there is care, it seems totally unimaginable that we can resist and end it in other institutionalized relations of power. If we cannot convince the mothers and/or fathers who care not to humiliate and degrade us, how can we imagine convincing or resisting an employer, a lover, a stranger who systematically humiliates and degrades?

Feminist effort to end patriarchal domination should be of primary concern precisely because it insists on the eradication of exploitation and op-

pression in the family context and in all other intimate relationships. It is that political movement which most radically addresses the person—the personal—citing the need for transformation of self, of relationships, so that we might be better able to act in a revolutionary manner, challenging and resisting domination, transforming the world outside the self. Strategically, feminist movement should be a central component of all other liberation struggles because it challenges each of us to alter our person, our personal engagement (either as victims or perpetrators or both) in a system of domination.

Feminism, as liberation struggle, must exist apart from and as a part of the larger struggle to eradicate domination in all its forms. We must understand that patriarchal domination shares an ideological foundation with racism and other forms of group oppression, that there is no hope that it can be eradicated while these systems remain intact. This knowledge should consistently inform the direction of feminist theory and practice. Unfortunately, racism and class elitism among women has frequently led to the suppression and distortion of this connection so that it is now necessary for feminist thinkers to critique and revise much feminist theory and the direction of feminist movement. This effort at revision is perhaps most evident in the current widespread acknowledgement that sexism, racism, and class exploitation constitute interlocking systems of domination—that sex, race, and class, and not sex alone, determine the nature of any female's identity, status, and circumstance, the degree to which she will or will not be dominated, the extent to which she will have the power to dominate.

While acknowledgement of the complex nature of woman's status (which has been most impressed upon everyone's consciousness by radical women of color) is a significant corrective, it is only a starting point. It provides a frame of reference which must serve as the basis for thoroughly altering and revising feminist theory and practice. It challenges and calls us to re-think popular assumptions about the nature of feminism that have had the deepest impact on a large majority of women, on mass consciousness. It radically calls into question the notion of a fundamentally common female experience which has been seen as the prerequisite for our coming together, for political unity. Recognition of the inter-connectedness of sex, race, and class highlights the diversity of experience, compelling redefinition of the terms for unity. If women do not share "common oppression," what then can serve as a basis for our coming together?

Unlike many feminist comrades, I believe women and men must share a common understanding—a basic knowledge of what feminism is—if it is ever to be a powerful mass-based political movement. In *Feminist Theory: from margin to center,* I suggest that defining feminism broadly as "a movement to end sexism and sexist oppression" would enable us to have a common political goal. We would then have a basis on which to build solidarity. Multiple and contradictory definitions of feminism create confusion and undermine the effort to construct feminist movement so that it addresses everyone. Sharing a common goal does not imply that women and men will not have radically divergent perspectives on how that goal might be reached. Because each individual starts the process of engagement in feminist struggle at a unique level of awareness, very real differences in experience, perspective, and knowledge make developing varied strategies for participation and transformation a necessary agenda.

Feminist thinkers engaged in radically revisioning central tenets of feminist thought must continually emphasize the importance of sex, race and class as factors which *together* determine the social construction of femaleness, as it has been so deeply ingrained in the consciousness of many women active in feminist movement that gender is the sole factor determining destiny. However, the work of education for critical consciousness (usually called consciousness-raising) cannot end there. Much feminist consciousness-raising has in the past focussed on identifying the particular ways men oppress and exploit women. Using the paradigm of sex, race, and class means that the focus does not begin with men and what they do to women, but rather with women working to identify both individually and collectively the specific character of our social identity.

Imagine a group of women from diverse backgrounds coming together to talk about feminism. First they concentrate on working out their status in terms of sex, race, and class using this as the standpoint from which they begin discussing patriarchy or their particular relations with individual men. Within the old frame of reference, a discussion might consist solely of talk about their experiences as victims in relationship to male oppressors. Two women—one poor, the other quite wealthy—might describe the process by which they have suffered physical abuse by male partners and find certain commonalities which might serve as a basis for bonding. Yet if these same two women engaged in a discussion of class, not only would the social construction and expression of femaleness differ, so too would their ideas about how to confront and change their circumstances. Broadening the discussion to include an analysis of race and class would expose many additional differences even as commonalities emerged.

Clearly the process of bonding would be more complex, yet this broader discussion might enable the sharing of perspectives and strategies for change that would enrich rather than diminish our understanding of gender. While feminists have increasingly given "lip service" to the idea of diversity, we have not developed strategies of communication and inclusion that allow for the successful enactment of this feminist vision.

Small groups are no longer the central place for feminist consciousness-raising. Much feminist education for critical consciousness takes place in Women's Studies classes or at conferences which focus on gender. Books are a primary source of education which means that already masses of people who do not read have no access. The separation of grassroots ways of sharing feminist thinking across kitchen tables from the spheres where much of that thinking is generated, the academy, undermines feminist movement. It would further feminist movement if new feminist thinking could be once again shared in small group contexts, integrating critical analysis with discussion of personal experience. It would be useful to promote anew the small group setting as an arena for education for critical consciousness, so that women and men might come together in neighborhoods and communities to discuss feminist concerns.

Small groups remain an important place for education for critical consciousness for several reasons. An especially important aspect of the small group setting is the emphasis on communicating feminist thinking, feminist theory, in a manner that can be easily understood. In small groups, individuals do not need to be equally literate or literate at all because the information is primarily shared through conversation, in dialogue which is necessarily a liberatory expression. (Literacy should be a goal for feminists even as we ensure that it not become a requirement for participation in feminist education.) Reforming small groups would subvert the appropriation of feminist thinking by a select group of academic women and men, usually white, usually from privileged class backgrounds.

Small groups of people coming together to engage in feminist discussion, in dialectical struggle make a space where the "personal is political" as a starting point for education for critical consciousness can be extended to include politicization of the self that focusses on creating understanding of the ways sex, race, and class together determine our individual lot and our collective experience. It would further feminist movement if many well known feminist thinkers would participate in small groups, critically re-examining ways their works might be changed by incorporating broader perspectives. All efforts at self-transformation challenge us to engage in ongoing, critical self-examination and reflection about feminist practice, about how we live in the world. This individual commitment, when coupled with engagement in collective discussion, provides a space for critical feedback which strengthens our efforts to change and make ourselves new. It is in this commitment to feminist principles in our words and deeds that the hope of feminist revolution lies.

Working collectively to confront difference, to expand our awareness of sex, race, and class as interlocking systems of domination, of the ways we reinforce and perpetuate these structures, is the context in which we learn the true meaning of solidarity. It is this work that must be the foundation of feminist movement. Without it, we cannot effectively resist patriarchal domination; without it, we remain estranged and alienated from one another. Fear of painful confrontation often leads women and men active in feminist movement to avoid rigorous critical encounter, yet if we cannot engage dialectically in a committed, rigorous, humanizing manner, we cannot hope to change the world. True politicization—coming to critical consciousness—is a difficult, "trying" process, one that demands that we give up set ways of thinking and being, that we shift our paradigms, that we open ourselves to the unknown, the unfamiliar. Undergoing this process, we learn what it means to struggle and in this effort we experience the dignity and integrity of being that comes with revolutionary change. If we do not change our consciousness, we cannot change our actions or demand change from others.

Our renewed commitment to a rigorous process of education for critical consciousness will determine the shape and direction of future feminist movement. Until new perspectives are created, we cannot be living symbols of the power of feminist thinking. Given the privileged lot of many leading feminist thinkers, both in terms of status, class, and race, it is harder these days to convince women of the primacy of this process of politicization. More and more, we seem to form select interest groups composed of individuals who share similar perspectives. This limits our capacity to engage in critical discussion. It is difficult to involve women in new processes of feminist politicization because so many of us think that identifying men as the enemy, resisting male domination, gaining equal access to power and privilege is the end of feminist movement. Not only is it not the end, it is not even the place we want revitalized feminist movement to begin. We want to begin as women seriously addressing ourselves, not solely in relation to men, but in relation to an entire structure of domination of which patriarchy is one part. While the struggle to eradicate sexism and sexist oppression is and should be the primary thrust of feminist movement, to prepare ourselves politically for this effort we must first learn how to be in solidarity, how to struggle with one another.

Only when we confront the realities of sex, race, and class, the ways they divide us, make us different, stand us in opposition, and work to reconcile and resolve these issues will we be able to participate in the making of feminist revolution, in the transformation of the world. Feminism, as Charlotte Bunch emphasizes again and again in *Passionate Politics,* is a transformational politics, a struggle against domination wherein the effort is to change ourselves as well as structures. Speaking about the struggle to confront difference, Bunch asserts:

> A crucial point of the process is understanding that reality does not look the same from different people's perspective. It is not surprising that one way feminists have come to understand about differences has been through the love of a person from another culture or race. It takes persistence and motivation—which love often engenders—to get beyond one's ethnocentric assumptions and really learn about other perspectives. In this process and while seeking to eliminate oppression, we also discover new possibilities and insights that come from the experience and survival of other peoples.

Embedded in the commitment to feminist revolution is the challenge to love. Love can be and is an important source of empowerment when we struggle to confront issues of sex, race, and class. Working together to identify and face our differences—to face the ways we dominate and are dominated—to change our actions, we need a mediating force that can sustain us so that we are not broken in this process, so that we do not despair.

Not enough feminist work has focussed on documenting and sharing ways individuals con-

front differences constructively and successfully. Women and men need to know what is on the other side of the pain experienced in politicization. We need detailed accounts of the ways our lives are fuller and richer as we change and grow politically, as we learn to live each moment as committed feminists, as comrades working to end domination. In reconceptualizing and reformulating strategies for future feminist movement, we need to concentrate on the politicization of love, not just in the context of talking about victimization in intimate relationships, but in a critical discussion where love can be understood as a powerful force that challenges and resists domination. As we work to be loving, to create a culture that celebrates life, that makes love possible, we move against dehumanization, against domination. In *Pedagogy of the Oppressed,* Paulo Freire evokes this power of love, declaring:

> I am more and more convinced that true revolutionaries must perceive the revolution, because of its creative and liberating nature, as an act of love. For me, the revolution, which is not possible without a theory of revolution—and therefore science—is not irreconcilable with love . . . The distortion imposed on the word "love" by the capitalist world cannot prevent the revolution from being essentially loving in character, nor can it prevent the revolutionaries from affirming their love of life.

That aspect of feminist revolution that calls women to love womanness, that calls men to resist dehumanizing concepts of masculinity, is an essential part of our struggle. It is the process by which we move from seeing ourselves as objects to acting as subjects. When women and men understand that working to eradicate patriarchal domination is a struggle rooted in the longing to make a world where everyone can live fully and freely, then we know our work to be a gesture of love. Let us draw upon that love to heighten our awareness, deepen our compassion, intensify our courage, and strengthen our commitment.

Study Questions

1. What does hooks suggest is morally wrong with domination? On what moral grounds should we resist it? Given that we are all potential oppressors and victims, what moral features would enable us to overcome domination?

2. What is the ethical relevance of the connection between the personal and the political? Is there a moral necessity to develop a critical consciousness? What are the ethical consequences of developing such consciousness?

3. What is the moral significance of the challenge to love? Is an ethics of love possible? Is it desirable?

Suggestions for Further Reading

Collins, P. H. *Black Feminist Thought: Knowledge, Consciousness and the Politics of Empowerment* (New York: Routledge, 1991). A general exploration of the perspectives and issues in black feminism. See especially Chapters 1, 2, and 7.

Florence, N. *Bell Hooks' Engaged Pedagogy: A Transgressive Education for Critical Consciousness* (Westport, CT: Bergin & Garvey, 1998). A three-part critical study of hooks' theory of pedagogy. See Part I, "bell hooks' Social Theory," for a detailed analysis of hooks' views of racism, sexism, and classism.

hooks, b., and C. West. *Breaking Bread: Insurgent Black Intellectual Life* (Boston: South End Press, 1991). Contains various interviews and dialogues between hooks and Cornel West.

————, with T. McKinnon. "Sisterhood: Beyond Public and Private." *Signs* 21, no. 4 (Summer 1996): 814–829. McKinnon interviews hooks on her views on feminism.

Martin, J. M. "The Notion of Difference for Emerging Womanist Ethics: The Writings of Audre Lorde and bell hooks." *Journal of Feminist Studies in Religion* 9, no. 12 (Spring-Fall 1993): 39–53. Explores how Lorde's and hooks' notions of difference can be useful for African-American feminist ethics.

Meyers, D. T., ed. *Feminist Social Thought: A Reader* (New York; London: Routledge, 1997). See especially D. K. King's "Multiple Jeopardy, Multiple Consciousness: The Context of Black Feminist Ideology," A. M. Jaggar's "Love and Knowledge: Emotion in Feminist Epistemology," and hooks' "Sisterhood: Political Solidarity between Women."

Alison M. Jaggar (1942–)

Alison M. Jaggar is professor of philosophy and women's studies at the University of Colorado, Boulder. She is a founding member of the Society for Women in Philosophy, was the Laurie New Jersey Chair in Women's Studies at Rutgers University, and has chaired the American Philosophical Association Committee on the Status of Women. Her writings include *Feminist Politics and Human Nature* (1983), *Living with Contradictions: Controversies in Feminist Social Ethics* (1994) and, with Diana Tietjens Meyers and Virginia Held, *Feminists Rethink the Self (Feminist Theory and Politics)* (1997).

In the following selection, Jaggar defines what constitutes an adequate feminist approach to ethics through an historical analysis and a proposed agenda for future feminist ethics. She highlights the problems that various projects of feminist ethics present in their theoretical assumptions, concepts, methods, and social-political implications. She identifies two common assumptions shared by all feminist approaches to ethics: the view that the subordination of women is morally wrong, and the insistence that women's moral experiences are worthy of respect. There are approaches that claim there are exclusively "women's issues"; others develop their critiques on the basis of "feminine/masculine" categories; still others uphold moral relativism above feminist concerns. Jaggar considers these approaches to be inadequate, as she also judges those that purport to be "gender-neutral" and embrace the idea of a universal morality while failing to acknowledge gender inequalities and differences. Because we live in a "prefeminist" world, feminist ethics must continue struggling against male bias in moral theory and practice. By contributing to social-political transformations, feminist ethics is a transitional stage toward a "humanist" ethics that realizes distinctively feminist goals.

FEMINIST ETHICS: PROBLEMS, PROJECTS, PROSPECTS

. . . ONE MAJOR CRITICISM feminists have made of traditional Western ethics is that it has either devalued or ignored issues or spheres of life that are associated with women, whether the association be empirical, normative, or symbolic. Feminists have argued convincingly that this devaluation or neglect has been deleterious to women's interests in a variety of ways: women's virtues have been seen as less significant than those associated with men; women's work has gone unrecognized or its creativity has been unappreciated; and the abuse of women and children, especially girls, has been ignored. For all these reasons, then, it is essential that feminist ethics should address certain hitherto neglected issues or areas of life.

In turning philosophical attention to these issues or areas, however, one must be cautious in identifying them as "women's" issues or in "women's" sphere. There are several reasons why this caution is necessary. One is that such language may be taken to imply that there is something natural or inevitable about women's concern for these issues. In order to counter such still-prevalent sexual determinism, it is important to be continually explicit that if women indeed show more concern than men for so-called personal relationships and less for international politics, this difference is less likely to be the consequence of some innate predisposition than to be the result of women's culturally assigned confinement to and/or responsibility for the one area of life and their relative exclusion from the other.

In addition to reinforcing stereotypes about men's and women's predispositions, the language of women's issues may also be taken to suggest that moral or public policy issues can be

Alison M. Jaggar, "Feminist Ethics: Projects, Problems, Prospects." In Feminist Ethics, *ed. C. Card. Lawrence: University Press of Kansas, 1991. Reprinted with the permission of Alison Jaggar.*

divided cleanly into those that are and those that are not of special concern to women. This is mistaken for several reasons. On the one hand, since men's and women's lives are inextricably intertwined, there are no women's issues that are not also men's issues; the availability or otherwise of child care and abortion, for instance, has significant consequences for the lives of men as well as women. Typically, both men and women are involved in all areas of life (though usually in different ways), even those areas that have come to be coded culturally as masculine or feminine. Men are involved on domestic, sexual, and "personal" relations, just as women are involved in the economy, science, and even the military, despite the symbolic casting of the former as feminine concerns and the latter as masculine enterprises.

On the other hand, since men and women typically are not what lawyers call "similarly situated" relative to each other, it is difficult to think of any moral or public policy ("human") issue in which women do not have a gender-specific interest. For instance, such issues as war, peace, and world starvation, though they are certainly human issues in the sense of affecting entire populations, nevertheless have special significance for women because the world's hungry are disproportionately women (and children), because women are primarily those in need of the social services neglected to fund military spending, and because women benefit relatively little from militarism and the weapons industries.

For these reasons, it would be a mistake to identify feminist ethics with attention to some explicitly gendered subset of ethical issues. On the contrary, rather than being limited to a restricted ethical domain, feminist ethics has *enlarged* the traditional concerns of ethics. Approaching social life with an explicitly feminist consciousness has enabled it both to identify previously unrecognized ethical issues and to introduce fresh perspectives on issues already acknowledged as having an ethical dimension. . . .

Feminist critiques of the philosophical canon are obviously an indispensable part of feminist ethics. The specific history of ethics in the West sets the intellectual context for Western ethics today. Thus any contemporary project in philosophical ethics must engage with our tradition—even if it is in reaction to it. . . .

Before dismissing Western ethics entirely, however, feminists should take into account some other considerations. It is undeniable that we have inherited specific ethical discourses and even if these are sometimes inadequate for feminist purposes, it would hardly be conceivable, let alone prudent, for feminists (or anyone else) to resolve to start from scratch and reinvent everything. And contrary to the stereotypes that prevail in some quarters, the preceding brief survey has demonstrated that contemporary feminist ethics, like contemporary ethics in general, is characterized by variety, experimentation, and disagreement. . . .

. . . Given this variety in feminist ethics, and the ongoing nature of feminist evaluations of the canon, it would be presumptuous and sectarian to attempt to specify which aspects of Western ethical tradition are or are not suitable for feminist appropriation.

At this point, I'd like to address feminist claims that the Western tradition, or some parts of it, are distinctively masculine. Though such claims are often made, (indeed, I have made them myself), and though they can sometimes be suggestive or illuminating (for example, Di Stefano's analysis of Hobbes [1983]), there are many conceptual and methodological difficulties in the way of establishing them. Among the most obvious of these difficulties is that the canonical texts of our tradition, like all texts, are open to competing interpretations. . . . A second obvious difficulty is that since Western ethical tradition is immensely rich and varied, almost any generalization that one might make about it is open to immediate challenge by counter examples. It may be possible to argue that certain themes, such as a preference for permanence over change or for reason over emotion, have historically been dominant, but the existence of counter themes must also be recognized.

More difficult problems are raised by the variety and multidimensionality of the meanings of "masculinity" and "femininity." These terms may refer to empirical characteristics of men and women (empirical association), to social ideals for men and women (normative association), or to things or attributes culturally associated with maleness and femaleness (symbolic association). Note that something may be masculine or feminine in one or more of these senses but not in the others. For instance, chastity may be a social ideal for women regardless of women's actual sexual practice and even when women are culturally associated with sexual license. Rationality may be both normatively and culturally associated with masculinity even when actual men are often quite irrational.

The meanings of masculinity and femininity may be unclear in other ways. Not only do the characteristics considered masculine and feminine vary widely across cultures and history, but in complex societies they are also typically associated with other, seemingly nongendered, attributes such as class or race. For example, rationality and property owning may have been viewed as distinctively masculine attributes or ideals during certain periods in Western history, but obviously they were attributes or ideals only for men of a certain class and, perhaps, race. . . .

Even when relatively precise meanings for masculinity and femininity have been stipulated, it is not easy to justify their attribution to philosophical themes. If claims that Western tradition is masculine mean no more than that it has been constructed primarily by men rather than women, this is neither entirely true (Waithe 1987) nor, in itself, very interesting philosophically. If it means that certain assumptions or themes can be identified as empirically characteristic of men's thinking, then feminists have to account for those men whose views have been historically anomalous—though of course they can always assert that some men may think like women, just as some women are supposed to think like men. But claims about masculine and feminine ways of thinking, understood as claims about how men and women actually do think, are not easy to establish empirically, as we shall see in the next section. Nor is it much easier,

given the symbolic complexity of our culture, to establish certain philosophical themes as symbolically masculine or feminine.

Finally, even if some philosophical assumptions or themes could be persuasively established as masculine or feminine in some relatively precise and well-established sense, it is not clear what the implications would be for feminist ethics. Whether the feminine is construed as empirical characteristic, social ideal, or symbolic association, it has been constructed inevitably in circumstances of male domination, and its value for feminism is likely, therefore, to be very questionable. In some cases, it is arguable that feminists would do better to appropriate what may have been constructed as the masculine aspects of Western ethics rather than the feminine ones.

For all these reasons, I believe that it is often more to the point for feminists to evaluate the philosophical canon in terms of whether or not it is male-biased rather than in terms of its supposed masculinity or femininity. Such bias can be demonstrated only through detailed arguments showing that specific claims or assumptions, evident in specific texts, function ideologically to delegitimate women's interests or subordinate them to men's. I believe that if feminist ethics focuses on male bias rather than on masculinity and femininity, it will be more likely to produce results that are not only textually defensible but also philosophically interesting and politically significant. . . .

From a feminist point of view, the call to reflect on women's moral experience is politically and methodologically indispensable. Certainly, there is a political point in revalorizing what has been conceptualized as the feminine. Moreover, a basic respect for women's moral experience is necessary to acknowledging women's capacities as moralists and to countering traditional stereotypes of women as less than full moral agents, as childlike or close to nature. . . .

Like feminist attention to so-called women's issues, however, feminist attention to women's moral experience may be misinterpreted. For instance, it may be taken as presuming that women's moral experience is indeed substantially different from men's rather than simply as investigating the question. In addition, the enterprise of discovering women's moral experience is fraught with methodological difficulties. An obvious one is that the term "moral experience" is extremely broad, often used to cover such items as intuitions about the resolution of specific moral problems, perceptions of what is or is not moral, moral priorities, methodological commitments, even emotional responses and actual behavior. Studying women's moral experience, then, requires a careful analysis of the precise object and method of our investigation.

There is also the question of which women we choose as the subjects of our investigation. Just as feminists have complained that traditional claims about "our" moral experience have excluded women, so certain groups of women, such as women of color, lesbians, or nonmothers, have complained that the claims made by feminists about "women's" moral experience have excluded them. . . . It may well be that women's moral sensibilities vary so much, not only from culture to culture but even within cultures, that it is impossible to identify a single distinctively feminine approach to ethics, even within a given culture.

Yet another methodological (and moral) problem in investigating women's moral experience is that it does not come prepackaged in familiar philosophical language. We have already encountered Gilligan's claims that the language of traditional ethical theory distorts the actual process of (some) women's moral thinking. Sara Ruddick has asserted that to articulate women's moral experience, we need a new language. But who is to develop this language and who is to confirm that it is appropriate? Who is authorized to speak for women? How can philosophers (or anyone) appropriate the experience of other women? Perhaps what is needed is the opportunity for women to speak for themselves. But even when women speak for themselves, there remains the potential for confusion, ideological manipulation, even self-deception.

These possibilities point to a final problem that confronts attempts to derive feminist ethics

from women's moral experience: the problem that the feminine is not the feminist. This is true both on the empirical level where actual women are often strongly opposed to feminism, on the normative level where feminine ideals are often subversive of feminist aspirations, and on the symbolic level where what has been constructed as feminine in circumstances of male domination is often associated with values that are conspicuously nonfeminist and may even tend to promote women's subordination (Lloyd 1984).

Thus even though the project of feminist ethics must include a reevaluation of what has been constructed as feminine, and possibly even a rehabilitation of some aspects of it, this cannot be done in an uncritical way. Although *feminist* ethics may begin with *feminine* ethics, it cannot end with it. . . .

Several philosophical and political factors have combined to discredit the idea of a universal morality. On the political side, they include concerns to avoid ethnocentrism and postcolonial domination. On the philosophical side, they include concerns about the indeterminacy of moral principles and doubts about the possibility of a universal or transcendent moral reason. . . . These considerations point not only toward a naturalistic as opposed to a rationalistic moral epistemology—that is, toward an ethics grounded in actual moral experience—but also toward an understanding of ethics as plural and local rather than singular and universal, grounded not in transcendent reason but rather in historically specific moral practices and traditions of ethics.

The specter that haunts this regional understanding of ethics is, of course, the specter of relativism. . . . Such a view would seem to preclude feminist moral criticism of the domination of women where this is an accepted social practice and even to entail that only feminists are bound by feminist ethics. . . .

Against the relativist tendency in feminist ethics should be set feminism's concern that its moral critique of the practices (and theory) of the larger society—and perhaps even the practices (and theory) of other societies—should be objectively justified. Feminist ethics recognizes that we inhabit a painfully prefeminist world and takes itself to be contributing to the transformation of this world into one in which the basic moral commitments of feminism have become universally accepted—and in which, consequently, feminism has become otiose. From a feminist perspective, therefore, feminist ethics is necessarily transitional. Because of feminism's essential interest in social transformation, it is hard to see how feminists could be content with the parochial conventionalism or conservatism often associated at least with the communitarian tradition of contemporary moral relativism. . . .

The feminist commitment is incompatible with any form of moral relativism that condones the subordination of women or the devaluation of their moral experience. It is neutral, however, between the plural and local understanding of ethics on the one hand and the ideal of a universal morality on the other. Feminists are committed to ethical theories that do not rationalize women's subordination or devalue their moral experience—but there may be many such theories. . . .

The idea that feminist ethics is only transitional, a temporary adaptation to a prefeminist world, lends credence to claims that the most advanced forms of feminist ethics today are gender-blind, addressing issues no longer identified as men's or women's issues in terms of categories that do not recognize distinctions of gender. . . .

Even though they should not be dismissed a priori, I contend that feminists should look on such claims with great suspicion. We should not forget that much of the achievement of feminist scholarship in a number of disciplines over the past twenty years has consisted precisely in identifying various forms of male bias concealed within apparently gender-blind assumptions or conceptual frameworks. Failing to recognize distinctions of gender at a time when gender operates as a set of socially instituted expectations that regulate every aspect of our lives, mostly to the advantage of men, is equivalent to refusing to acknowledge a pervasive system of domination. . . .

In our present social and intellectual circumstances, it is more than likely that ethics that is not done with an explicitly feminist consciousness will embody at best unintentional forms of male bias. For the time being, it is prudent to begin from the assumption that every ethical issue, practical or theoretical, is also a feminist issue. When our present situation is still so conspicuously prefeminist, it is premature to talk about a humanist rather than an explicitly feminist ethics. Silence about women's subordination may often mean witting or unwitting consent to it. Although feminist ethics does indeed look forward to a world in which explicit feminist commitments have become otiose, that world is still far in the future.

Study Questions

1. What problems, according to Jaggar, are involved in claiming there are exclusively "women's issues"? in tracing hard distinctions between the "feminine" and the "masculine"? Are any of these problems of a moral nature?

2. What does Jaggar mean when she claims that feminist ethics may begin with feminine ethics but cannot end with it? What is her moral argument for this claim?

3. Jaggar claims that feminist ethics can be either relativist or universalist, but it must condemn women's subordination and the devaluation of their moral experience. Is this claim itself relativist or universalist? Does Jaggar's claim allow feminists to interpret women's subordination and devaluation in different ways?

4. What does the ideal of a "humanist" ethics suggest about ethics in its traditional and feminist approaches? What would a humanist ethics be like?

Suggestions for Further Reading

Andolsen, B. H., C. E. Gudorf, and M. D. Pellauer, eds. *Women's Consciousness, Women's Conscience: A Reader in Feminist Ethics* (San Francisco: Harper & Row, 1985). See Part 3 for a sample of other perspectives on the enterprise of feminist ethics.

Frazer, E., J. Hornsby, and S. Lovibond, eds. *Ethics: A Feminist Reader* (Oxford; Cambridge, MA: Blackwell, 1992). See Section III for a sample of other perspectives on the move toward a feminist ethics.

Grimshaw, J. "The Idea of a Female Ethic." In *A Companion to Ethics,* ed. P. Singer (Oxford; Cambridge, MA: Blackwell, 1991). Critically examines the issue of the relation between ethics and gender.

Held. V. "Feminist Reconceptualizations in Ethics." In *Philosophy in a Feminist Voice: Critique and Reconstructions* (Princeton, NJ: Princeton University Press, 1998). Examines the problem of gender bias in the history of ethics and the influence of feminist thinking in society, moral concepts, and theories.

Sarah Lucia Hoagland (1945–)

Sarah Lucia Hoagland teaches philosophy and women's studies at Northeastern Illinois University in Chicago. She identifies herself as a lesbian separatist. She is the author of *Lesbian Ethics: Toward New Value* (1988) and is coeditor, with Julia Penolope, of *For Lesbians Only: A Separatist Anthology* (1988).

By emphasizing the word *lesbian* in the title of her essay "Why *Lesbian* Ethics?," Hoagland is already suggesting the need for an ethics that addresses the particular issues of lesbian existence and morality. For her, lesbians exist within a context of oppression. Thus, as moral agents, lesbians are not free and autonomous—as traditional ethics would assume. Rather, they are coerced into acquiescence, resistance, acts of self-sabotage, and demoralization. Traditional ethical concepts are inadequate because they fail to address this particularity and even contribute to oppression. The context of oppression is determined by heterosexualism—defined as the relationship in which women are dependent upon and subordinate to men. By limiting women's autonomy and possibilities for bonding, heterosexualism undermines female agency and women's community. In refusing to follow the heterosexual model, lesbians can explore new possibilities for lesbian agency and communities. While the heterosexual model of moral agency understands choice as (masculine) entitlement or (feminine) sacrifice, lesbian ethics offers an alternative model of choice as creation. It also offers a middle way between the feminine ethics of dependence and the masculine ethics of independence by stressing the relatedness of self to community and the value of mutual respect of differences among lesbians. However, in breaking away from tradition, it questions the validity of patriarchal notions (such as duty, rule, principle, and free will) while insisting that lesbian moral agency still can and must take place within the context of oppression. The very notion "lesbian" contains the possibility of new forms of existence, new ways of understanding, and a different ethics.

WHY LESBIAN ETHICS?

FOCUSING NOT ON SEXISM, homophobia, or even heterosexism, I consider hetero*sexualism*— a relationship between men and women. "Heterosexualism is men dominating and deskilling women in any of a number of forms, from outright attack to paternalistic care, and women devaluing (of necessity) female bonding as well as finding inherent conflicts between commitment and autonomy and consequently valuing an ethics of dependence" (Hoagland 1988, 29). This undermines female agency.

Further, "heterosexualism is a particular economic, political, and emotional relationship between men and women: men must dominate and women must subordinate themselves to men in any number of ways. As a result men presume access to women while women remain riveted on men and are unable to sustain a community of women" (Hoagland 1988, 29). This undermines women's community.

Thus, two serious problems of heterosexualism for women are female agency and community. By not trying to fit ourselves into a (heterosexual) women's framework and instead recognizing our own, lesbians can discover that from lesbian lives come different conceptual possibilities. . . .

The values assigned to women are the feminine virtues: self-sacrifice, altruism, vulnerability (Hoagland 1988, chap. 2). As a consequence, the healthy and normal woman's actions are to be toward others. If we try to fit that model, it means our actions are away from ourselves, with the result that our ability to act is located in others. And that means that the primary mode of female agency is manipulation.

Under oppression one learns survival skills, including means of manipulation. I have argued (Hoagland 1988, chap. 1) that stereotypical feminine behavior is indicative of sabotage and

resistance (as is stereotypical slave behavior). And I mean for us to herald these actions for what they are, as indications of resistance to domination. Concomitantly I object to academic women's attempt to claim "the feminine" as a balance to the masculine when the feminine was conceived by ecclesiastic and academic men to legitimate male right and was developed by women in resistance and sabotage. Simply championing femininity doesn't change or even acknowledge the fact that men still own the scales. . . .

Thus, I am suggesting that by considering the category "lesbian," not "woman," we discover a different sense of female agency. In lesbian lives we find that choice is creation, not sacrifice. As a result, we can revalue female agency, developing it independently of the manipulation and control from the position of subordination of heterosexualism. Female agency becomes not a matter of sacrifice but a process of engagement and creation. And if we regard choice as creation, not sacrifice, we can regard our ability to make choices as a source of enabling power, rather than as something to avoid because it appears to mean loss. All that is lesbian exists only because we've created it. And realizing this, we can realize that our power lies in choice. . . .

The second problem of heterosexualism is community. As I began writing *Lesbian Ethics,* my initial stress was on sabotage and feminine manipulation. And while unraveling it and honoring it for what it is, I also wanted to move away from it (for sabotage doesn't strictly challenge the system that gave rise to its need, and we too often use manipulation against each other). However, I found that in moving away from feminine agency, I was moving toward its complement, masculine agency, involving those who are egoistic, isolated, aggressive, competitive,

Sarah Lucia Hoagland. "Why Lesbian Ethics?" Hypatia 7, no. 4 (Fall 1992): 195–206. Reprinted with the permission of Indiana University Press.

and antagonistic. Thus, the ethics of duty and of justice are designed to coerce antagonists into "cooperation" (Hoagland 1988, chap. 6). While from femininity we get an ethics of dependence, from masculinity we get an ethics of independence. And I think that from lesbian lives we can find another possibility.

Now while lesbians know all the methods of the feminine, lesbians have also proven quite capable of the masculine, of being arrogant, aggressive, antagonistic, and so on. Just by coming out in a world that says we do not exist, just by breaking away from the central message of heterosexualism, we have needed considerable egoism and aggression, and we have traveled this road in isolation. However, what is interesting to me is that while we broke from heterosexualism and at least to some extent its proponents, we did not break to isolation and independence; we broke to each other—in the bars and the collectives, on the baseball and hockey fields, at the demonstrations. Our desire for and attraction to each other is part of the glue that holds us together.

We have not sought to remain isolated, etc.; we have sought each other out; we have sought community at this level. As I wrote the first draft of *Lesbian Ethics*, an important change washed over me—the importance of our communities and our sense of sharing in creating meaning. Being a lesbian is not a matter of remaining isolated (and thus pursuing masculine agency); it is a matter of recognizing and sharing things with other lesbians, from oppression to recipes, from resistance to outrageousness. That is, considering lesbian lives, we can notice that finding each other in communities is an important part of our lives, a central part of developing and maintaining our sense of our selves.

Now if, as I am claiming, community is an important part of lesbian identity and existence as well as a significant part of the means by which we change and develop as lesbians, what does community mean? Certainly I don't mean by community a lesbian state. I mean something like a context or a place of reference. A context is a source of meaning. And how we understand

our lives is affected by the context to which we refer for meaning. This is true of how we understand even our most inner feelings (Hoagland 1988, chap. 4).

One of the devastating effects of heterosexualism has been the erasure of lesbian meaning. It stifles imagination and blocks memory. When we as lesbians decide we cannot prioritize lesbian visibility and lesbian projects, when we as lesbians attempt to undermine the efforts of those lesbians who do prioritize lesbian contexts, we are displaying continued effects of that erasure. This is one of the reasons I'm a separatist. If we keep focusing on men's meanings, we'll keep focusing on men's meanings. And lesbian imagination and memory dissolves.

Of course, I do not mean that within lesbian communities there is accord of harmony. There isn't, nor should there be. But it is to say that with the festivals, the books, the music, the coffeehouses, the gatherings of all sorts, there is another place of reference, and this place has the possibility of not replicating so readily the values of the brothers. Lesbian spaces, though hardly free of the dregs of heteropatriarchy, are different, are obviously different. And from them emerge the possibility of lesbian agency and the possibilities of lesbian communities.

So what are the possibilities of lesbian communities? One is diversity, for we emerge from everywhere—Palestine and Israel, Argentina and Cherokee Nation, China and India. We have the ready-made possibility of developing concepts of "difference" in a way available to few, if any, other communities.

Under heteropatriarchy, difference is binary, hence oppositional, hence yields dominance and subordination, and hence is a threat: Hegel's master/slave thesis implies that men's interaction is a one-on-one mortal battle for acknowledgment that rationally becomes instead a fight for domination. Behind this argument is the idea that another's perception of me, if through that person's own values and not through mine, is capable of destroying me. Therefore one major message of Hegel's thesis is that difference is a threat (Hoagland 1988, chap. 5).

And, in fact, in community another's perceptions have been capable of threatening us, and so we shut out her world, her values. For example, if I, as a white lesbian, come to know a Latina lesbian and begin to enter her world and understand her life, I begin to understand many things differently. But should I then perceive myself through her values, I might notice something I did as racist. Trying to maintain my sense of self as having integrity against the patriarchal message that I, as a female, was never any good anyway, I shut out her values. Her difference becomes a threat. (We also tend to fear that if we admit differences in our relationships, the relationships will end.) And when we perceive difference as a threat, we try to negate it or deny it exists.

In perceiving ourselves as one among many, we realize we are not destroyed (nor created) by another's reflection, but we also realize that we are not the whole picture. I am suggesting that one's self in relation to others need not be a matter of a polarity. Further, in dealing with differences, no one of us lesbians is purely a dominator, purely from the privileged classes, and no one of us is purely from the subordinate classes. How we live in resistance or acquiescence to any of these classes provides crucial information in community. Thus, as we pursue the work we are doing, we begin to realize that difference is not only not a threat and that difference is more than a gift: difference is at the center of our survival.

Most communities strive to be culturally homogeneous. As lesbians we have the possibility of developing difference in new ways if we consider the reality of our lives. . . .

Now while we have challenged patriarchal politics, we have not challenged patriarchal ethics, fraternal agency. We want the power and control that reside in patriarchal ethics: we want a rule to tell us what to do so that when we act we can rest comfortably in the certainty that we did the right thing no matter the consequences (an ethics of imperialists). We also want rules so we can try to force others to conform. But rules don't tell us when to apply them, and they don't help when all else fails. If we aren't already acting with integrity, then the rules won't guarantee it (Hoagland 1988, introduction).

More significantly, lesbians are an obnoxious, unruly bunch—that's partly how we became lesbians. So any ethics that tries to keep us in line and make us into ladies is not an ethics that suits us. Much of *Lesbian Ethics* involves approaching ethics, including challenges to each other and efforts to change harmful behavior, outside the focus of rules and obligation and duty.

In addition to an obsession with rules and principles, fraternal agency focuses on free will, and we are encouraged to think that to be moral agents we must have free will. Thus, when in understanding ourselves as oppressed we find we don't have free will, we are tempted to think we can't be moral agents and consequently to think of ourselves merely as victims. We get the idea that either we can control a situation or we are helpless victims. Lesbians exist within a context of oppression. Any moral or political theory useful to anyone under oppression must not convince us that either we must be in complete control or we are total victims. While we don't control situations, we do affect them. . . .

If from the reality of our lesbian lives we realize "lesbian" is a category that creates some distinct values and also some distinct possibilities—choice as creation not sacrifice, community as a context of values in which we are one among many, and community as the possibility of difference—then we may approach ethics differently: not trying to control situations but acting within them. Moral agency then becomes a question, not of how am I going to stop all the injustice, but rather what is my part, and what are we going to do next?

Study Questions

1. What traditional ethical concepts does Hoagland specifically challenge, and why? How does a lesbian ethics counter these notions?
2. On what moral principles does Hoagland base her idea of lesbian community? In what ways does this idea criticize and challenge actual lesbian existence and morality?
3. Why must lesbian moral agency take place within the context of oppression? How can that moral agency be realized?
4. Why does Hoagland choose not to categorize her theory as a feminist ethics? Is this an ethics for lesbians only? Does it suggest an ethics for heterosexuals, male and female? for homosexuals?

Suggestions for Further Reading

Frye, M. "A Response to *Lesbian Ethics*." *Feminist Ethics,* ed. C. Card (Lawrence: University Press of Kansas, 1991). A critique of Hoagland's assumption of the need for an ethics for lesbians.

Hoagland, S. L. *Lesbian Ethics: Toward New Value.* (Palo Alto, CA: Institute of Lesbian Studies, 1988). Hoagland develops her theory in eight chapters.

Hypatia. Special Issue in Lesbian Philosophy 7, no. 4 (Fall 1992). Contains seventeen articles on lesbian philosophy, including a section on lesbian community and responsibility where Hoagland's own article appears.

Rich, A. "Compulsory Heterosexuality and Lesbian Existence." *Signs* 5, no. 4 (1980): 631–660. A classical essay arguing for the need to have a feminist critique of the compulsory heterosexual orientation for women in society.

Sara Ruddick (1935–)

Sara Ruddick is the author of *Maternal Thinking: Toward a Politics of Peace* (1989) and co-editor of *Working It Out* (1977) and *Between Women* (1984). She teaches at the Eugene Lang College of the New School for Social Research in New York.

In the following selection, "From Maternal Thinking to Peace Politics," Sara Ruddick outlines an ethics that transforms maternal ways of thinking and being into feminist liberating perspectives and practices. Ruddick characterizes maternal thinking and conduct as "womanly." This points to women's historical roles as caregivers engaged mainly in the task of mothering. It also indicates how these roles generate attitudes, perspectives, and values that focus on caring. However, Ruddick denies that there is something essentially feminine in mothering; it is not the exclusive and natural domain of biological females as opposed to males. There is a contradiction between mothering and violence, particularly in war. There is also a connection between mothering and nonviolence. This connection is a condition for peace. Though Ruddick acknowledges that not all mothers are nonviolent, she emphasizes that the myth of maternal peacefulness is a powerful source for hopes of global peace. Thus, Ruddick develops a project for transforming maternal thinking into a peace politics or feminist ethics of social action.

Ruddick's project is formed by three overlapping "moments," or aspects. The first moment, which she calls a "heuristic representation of the 'womanly' stance," is an interpretation of maternal thinking as if it were ideally peaceful. The purpose of this interpretation is to uncover the potential for peacefulness in maternal thinking. It focuses on the antimilitarist stance of maternal thinking. The second moment provides a critical diagnosis of maternal thinking. The most serious flaw in mothers is found in their militarism or participation in social forms of oppression and violence. This is manifested in forms such as the disciplining of children, patriotism, parochialism, and racism.

The third moment of Ruddick's project is then developed. She labels it the "transformative encounter" of maternal thinking with "feminism and women's politics of resistance." It is a coming to terms between feminism and maternal thinking. Feminism develops an understanding of the positive meaning and significance of mothering. At the same time, maternal thinking opens itself to the critical and liberating perspectives provided by feminism. In this, there is a double movement in thought and action toward what Ruddick calls "lucidity." Through this interaction, mother-respecting feminists and feminist-minded mothers can become compassionate, not only toward each other, but also cross-culturally. They can collectively create a "feminist, maternal peace politics" based on their "decisiveness" or resolution to resist and change the course of global violence and war.

FROM MATERNAL THINKING TO PEACE POLITICS

Mothering/nurturing is a vital force and
    process
establishing relationships through the universe.
Exploring and analyzing the nature of all components involved in a nurturing activity puts
one in touch with life extending itself. . . . We
can choose to be mothers, nurturing and transforming a new space for a new people in a new
    time.   Bernice Johnson Reagon

Peace the great meaning has not been defined.
When we say peace as a word, war
As a flare of fire leaps across our eyes.

We went to this school. Think war;
Cancel war, we were taught.
What is left is peace.
No, peace is not left, it is no cancelling;
The fierce and human peace is our deep power
Born to us of wish and responsibility.
                                        Muriel Rukeyser

In this essay I talk about a journey, a "progress," from a "womanly" practice and way of knowing to a liberatory standpoint. Specifically, I plot a move from maternal thinking to peace politics.

Sara Ruddick, "From Maternal Thinking to Peace Politics." In Explorations in Feminist Ethics: Theory and Practice, *eds. E. Browning Cole and S. Coultrap-McQuin. Bloomington: Indiana University Press, 1992. Reprinted by permission of Indiana University Press.*

First, a word about "war" and "peace." No one can provide easy answers to haunting questions about when and how to fight. I believe that violence is addictive, that the effectiveness of violence is consistently exaggerated, and that the short- and long-term costs of organized violence—economic, social, psychological, and physical—are routinely underestimated. Meanwhile, the multiple rewards and effectiveness of "nonviolence" are underrated, misreported, and misunderstood. But it is arrogant to urge nonviolent confrontation, let alone nonviolent reconciliation and cooperation from a distance, whether in El Salvador, South Africa, Ireland, or Palestine and Israel.

"War" is both the quintessential expression of violence and its most attractive representative. I believe that the ways of thinking that invalidate militarism will also undermine more covert and pervasive violence. "War" is familiar; the myriad forms of nonviolent confrontation, cooperation, and reconciliation that would be "peace" are still to be invented. I believe that to imagine forms of nonviolent resistance and cooperation is to imagine new personal and civic relationships to abuse and neglect. Hence in concentrating on the relationships of mothers to "war," I believe that I am also talking about less dramatic, maternal relationships to closer "enemies."

Although nonviolent action rarely succeeds without global outrage and resources, the conditions of peace and resistance are local. I speak as a citizen of the United States, a nation that, as I see it, frequently, even habitually, enters the social and natural world as an armed, invasive, exploitative conqueror. Within this nation, governments and communities "throw away," quarantine, track, and abuse their more vulnerable, assaulted, or troubled members. Whether moved by outright greed and racist bigotry or paralyzed by passivity, self-preoccupation, and despair, these governments and communities routinely fail to respond to the promise of birth, fail to provide the shelter, healing, and sustenance on which mothering depends. In the midst of this many-faceted violence, maternal thinkers and feminist ethicists can contribute in distinctive ways to imagining and creating "peace."

I begin with a question: How might it be possible to intensify the contradiction between mothering and violence and to articulate the connections between mothering and nonviolence so that mothers would be more apt to move from maternal thinking to peace politics?

The opposition between mothers and war is legendary. Mothering begins with birth and promises life; militaries require organized, deliberate killing. A mother preserves the bodies, nurtures the psychic growth, and disciplines the consciences of children; military enterprises deliberately endanger the bodies, psyches, and consciences that mothers protect. On the face of it, war and other organized violence threaten every aspect of mothering work—sheltering, protecting, attending, feeding, maintaining connections on which children depend. Understandably, the figure of the mater dolorosa—the mother of sorrows—is central to subversive war narrative. Just warriors know that war is hateful and cruel, but it is the mater dolorosa who refuses to subordinate the pain to a warrior's tale of just cause and victory. For her war remains a catastrophe that overshadows whatever purposes lie behind it. The mater dolorosa's vision of war as unredeemed suffering among the ruins takes on new poignancy as nuclear and advanced "conventional" weapons force us to imagine wars that threaten all human and global life.

If military endeavors seem a betrayal of maternal commitments, nonviolent action can seem their natural extension. Maternal "peacefulness" is not a sweet, appeasing gentleness but a way of living in which people demand a great deal of each other. When mothers fight with their children or on their behalf, when they teach their children ways of fighting safely without being trampled on or trampling on others, they engage in nonviolent action. Many individual mothers abuse their children; in most cultures children suffer from accepted but abusive practices; some cultures may legitimate systematic maternal abuse. Nonetheless, some maternal practices are sufficiently governed by principles of nonviolence to offer one model for nonviolent relationships. This does not mean that in these practices mothers achieve the nonviolence to which they aspire. Since children are vulnerable and the vulnerable are subject to abuse and neglect, mothers may be more than usually tempted by sadism, self-indulgent aggression, and self-protective indifference to the real needs of demanding children. It is maternal *commitment* to care for rather than assault or abandon children—whatever failure, guilt, and despair follows in that commitment's wake—that illuminates more public struggles to live nonviolently.

Yet mothers are not "peaceful." Wherever there are wars, mothers support and supply soldiers and, if encouraged, often become fierce and effective fighters themselves. Mothers are as apt as other people to welcome the excitements of violence, rewards of community solidarity, and promise of meaningful sacrifice. War also offers many mothers who suffer from discriminatory economic and social policies distinctive opportunities for adventure and material gain; "peace"-time military service often appears to provide their adolescent children with jobs, social discipline, education, and training that are unavailable or prohibitively expensive in civilian society.

Yet the myth of maternal peacefulness remains alluring. Mothers may be willing warriors, but war is their enemy, nonviolence often their practice. Precisely because mothers have played their supportive parts in military scripts, their refusal to perform might prompt a rewriting of the plot. Hence the urgency of my question: Can the contradictions between mothering and violence, the connections between mothering and nonviolence be made sufficiently visible, audible, disturbing, and promising to turn maternal thinking into an instrument of peace politics?

Different Voices, Standpoints, and "Feminist Ethics"

My particular project, plotting a progress from maternal thinking to peace politics, is an instance of a more general transformative endeavor—namely, the transformation of "womanly" stances into feminist or liberatory standpoints.

Several feminist philosophers have suggested that people who engage in "caring labor" acquire a distinctive epistemological stance, a "rationality of care." Mothering is both an instance of caring labor and intertwined with many other kinds of caring such as homemaking, kin work, nursing, tending the frail elderly, and teaching small children. Hence maternal thinking—a congeries of metaphysical attitudes, cognitive capacities, and values that arises from mothering—is one element of the "rationality of care."

Although societies differ in their ways of distributing the pleasures and burdens of mothering or caring labor, and although individual women and men are variously interested in and capable of these kinds of work, there is nothing distinctively feminine about mothering, nursing, or any other form of caretaking. There is, for example, no reason why men cannot engage in mothering, and many men already do. Nonetheless, maternal work, and more generally caring labor, have historically been the provenance of women. Maternal thinking and the rationality of care are therefore construed—and celebrated or minimized—as "womanly" achievements.

Accordingly, feminist psychologists and critics who identify values or ways of knowing associated with *women* typically attribute the differences they discover at least partly to the effect on women of the caring work they have undertaken. Conversely, certain feminists have cited the value of mothering and caretaking or of maternal thinking and the "rationality of care" in order to argue that women's perspectives offer a "standpoint" from which to criticize dominant values and invent new ones. At the least women's perspectives and voices should be included in any adequate moral or psychological theory. Many feminists make a stronger claim: the destructiveness and "perversion" of dominant values is intertwined with "abstract masculinity," while the values and relationships that would characterize more just and caring societies are intertwined with "caring femininity."

But just as women (and men) who are mothers have not proved "peaceful," women generally have not reliably extended the domain of care beyond class, race, or neighborhood. Nor have they (we) consistently engaged in struggles for political liberty and economic and racial justice. (There are small, fluctuating "gender gaps" between women's and men's support of various progressive issues—perhaps especially peace and ecology. I am not, however, interested in women's possible, marginal superiority to men.) Nor are women's values and relationships reliably feminist. Women's work and stories are not only shaped by, but also often contribute to the exploitation of caretakers and the subordination of women. Women (as well as men) identify care with self-sacrifice, or responsiveness to need with pleasing others. Despite the efforts of feminist and lesbian mothers, women (as well as men) embed the idea of maternity in a heterosexist, sexually conservative ideology. Women have to fight against women (as well as men) to acquire the power to refuse maternal work. If they become mothers, they have to resist women's (as well as men's) reductive definitions of their pleasures and needs as only maternal. Any "feminine" standpoint that feminists might celebrate is yet to be achieved.

Nonetheless, "different voice" critics who set out to identify women's values and perspectives almost always take themselves to be engaged in a feminist project. ("Different voice" theorists is a shorthand label for any critic, reader, or theorist who attempts to identify perspectives or ways of knowing associated with women. The label draws on Carol Gilligan's work *In a Different Voice* and was suggested by Nancy Goldberger, coauthor of *Women's Ways of Knowing*.) Most important, they normally aim to create a liberatory standpoint that at least is compatible with feminism and at best is an extension and expression of militant feminist vision. Their effort to *transform* a "womanly" stance into a liberatory and feminist stand-point is an essay in "feminist ethics."

Although different voice critics may find it impossible to separate their feminist commitments from their respect for women's voices, many of the actual voices currently dominant within North American feminism have serious misgivings about their transformative enterprise.

These skeptical feminists claim that the idea of "womanly" difference will be used against women and is in any case empirically unfounded, exclusionary, ethnocentric, and sentimental. On their view "women" have been historically produced in asymmetrical opposition to a "masculinity" intertwined with racial privilege and defined in conjunction with Reason and Power. Nothing to these women can be named outside of oppressive patriarchal and ethnocentric definitions of "women"—no "womanly" work, "women's" oppression, or female bodily experience. Women might speak and be spoken of once all hierarchical gender distinctions were laid to rest—but then "women's" different voices, if not "women" themselves, would be fading relics that should be buried not resurrected.

I do not directly address these feminist challenges here, but they have prompted me to review my particular project—plotting a progress from maternal thinking to peace politics—and to reread others' essays in transformative "feminist ethics" in order to get a clearer sense of what I (we?) have been about. In retrospect, I now discern three overlapping moments in the transformation of maternal thinking: heuristic representation of the "womanly" stance, which includes antiracist elements; a diagnosis of flaws, including tendencies to racism, within, not apart from, the stance represented; and a transformative encounter with feminism and women's politics of resistance. I also see these moments in others' efforts to transform the "womanly" into the liberatory. . . .

Diagnosis: Maternal Militarism

Heuristic representations of the sort I propose can seem perilously close to mystifying ideology. In order to ward off obfuscation and to insist on the need for change, I try to identify specific sources of maternal militarism within the practices of good enough, potentially peaceful mothers. For example, alongside a "sturdily antimilitarist" conception of bodily life I put a more familiar maternal conception of bodies which is incipiently militarist. A careful, caring welcome of bodily life and respect for bodily integrity is central to maternal nonviolence. Yet even the most benign mother may sometimes take her own and her children's "nature," their willful embodied being, as an enemy to be conquered. In times of rapid change or social crisis, a superstitious terror of the "stranger" can fuel an otherwise temperate mother's rage to control "disorderly," dirty, lustful, bodily life at home. Only in the most malignant forms of maternal thinking are children's bodies conceived as the site of pain and domination, the place where sadistic or terror-driven mothers enact their will. But many ordinary, good enough mothers struggle against their own compulsion for order and their drive to dominate unruly, "disobedient" children.

A maternal struggle to achieve a welcoming response to bodily life is emblematic of struggles to extend publicly maternal nonviolence. Just as mothers have to learn not to hurt or dominate what is strange and threatening in their own children, they also have to *strive* to respect and negotiate with alien and often frightening people outside their "own" circle. This is not surprising. Mothering typically begins with a passionate commitment to particular children and the particular people they live among. Although in a daily way mothers may try to create a peace worth keeping—one that is as free as possible from greed, domination, and injustice—domestic justice does not translate easily beyond the families and cultures in which it originates. Just because they hold themselves responsible for preserving the traditions and integrity, sometimes even the survival, of their social group, many mothers will fiercely support violence against the "enemy" (and therefore against the enemy's children) who seems to threaten their "ways," community, or state. At their not uncommon worst, parochial mothers engage in outright racist battle behind the shield of neighborhood and family.

Some mothers learn to hold their passionate loyalty to particular children in creative tension with a sympathy for other children, including those who are strange or strangers. Even these mothers may nonetheless counsel their children to embrace the violence that their state or political leaders tell them is necessary. Mothers train children in the ways of obedience that enable them at least to survive and at best to flourish—but also to "serve" when "called" by employers or governments. Despite their responsibility for training, many mothers are expected to delegate "difficult" policy decisions to fathers and public officials. To the extent that they have complied with the deauthorization of their authority, they will be ill-prepared for independent-minded resistance to their government's or political group's militarist policies in a time of "emergency." By contrast, committed patriotic sacrifice to the whole nation, to all "our boys," can seem a generous extension of the parochial loyalties of most mothers' lives.

In *Lest Innocent Blood Be Shed*, an account of nonviolent resistance and rescue in a French village during the second world war, Phillip Hallie identified three habits of mind and will that enabled citizens of Le Chambon to appreciate and resist the evils of Nazi racism while many more of their well-intentioned compatriots refused to see or were unable to act. According to Hallie, "lucid knowledge, awareness of the pain of others, and stubborn decision dissipated for the Chambonnais the Night and Fog that inhabited the minds of so many people in Europe, and in the world at large, in 1942." Conversely—adapting Hallie's praise to the purposes of diagnosis—maternal parochialism prevents many mothers from seeing, let alone caring about, the pain of distant or different others. Willingness to abdicate "difficult" decisions to public officials produces ignorance rather than "lucid knowledge" of the real character and motives of war-making and of the painful consequences for "others" of the policies of one's own government. A cultural expectation that mothers will weep for war but can do nothing to stop it makes "stubborn decisiveness" unlikely.

Maternal peacefulness is an empowering myth. At its center is the promise of birth: every body counts, every body is a testament of hope. To violate bodies—to starve, terrorize, mutilate, damage, or abandon them—is to violate birth's promise. At its best, mothering represents a disciplined commitment to the promise of birth and a sustained refusal to countenance its violation. But good enough mothers—like other, good enough women and men—protect themselves from lucidity and therefore from responsibility. The peacefulness of mothering as we know it is entwined with the abstract loyalties on which war depends, the racialism in which war flourishes, and the apolitical privacy that lets dominators and racists have their way. There is no sharp division between the Good Mother of Peace and her fearful, greedy, or dominating sister. The heuristic representation of mothers as peaceful is inseparable from the diagnosis of mothers as militarist. It is the same work, the same thinking, ready for and requiring transformation. It is precisely at the point of felt contradiction, at the intersection of the promise of birth and its violation, that a transformative encounter might occur.

Toward Lucidity, Compassion, and Decision

When I first began thinking about mothers, I was more concerned with what feminists could bring to maternal thinking than with what mothers could bring to the world. I construed mothering and feminism oppositionally. I wrote as a mother who believed that feminism trivialized or simplified the challenges of maternal work. But I also wrote as a feminist daughter who believed that feminism might manage to rescue a damaged and flawed maternity. As a feminist I wrote suspiciously of the very practices and thinking that as a mother I was determined to honor. Yet, so great (at that time) was some feminists' fear of—and other feminists' need of—a mother's voice, that my daughterly suspicion was barely heard.

I am no stranger to feminist fear of mothering. Of all the essentialist identities to which "women" have been subject, the conflation of "the female" with heterosexual (or lesbian?) mothering may well be the most fearsome.

Given a sorry history in which so many women's bodies and dreams have been destroyed by enforced and repressive "motherhood," it is not surprising that feminists have not found it easy to hear, let alone to speak in, a maternal voice. Adrienne Rich may have been the first to name feminist matrophobia and the consequent feminist desire to perform "radical surgery" in order to cut oneself away from the mother who "stands for the victim, the unfree women." Peace activist Ynestra King elaborates this feminist rejection: "Each of us is familiar as daughters with maternal practice, but most of us in becoming feminists have rejected the self-sacrificing, altruistic, infinitely forgiving, martyred unconditionally loving mother—for this is how I saw my mother—have rejected that mother in *ourselves* as the part of ourselves which is complicit in our own oppression."

Feminists have good reason to reject a maternal identity that is still enmeshed in patriarchal and heterosexist institutions and that has often been legally, physically, and psychologically forced on women who would otherwise reject it. This reasoned and conscious resistance to patriarchal institutions of motherhood is intertwined with less conscious fears. As we have learned from Dorothy Dinnerstein and other psychoanalytic feminists, in societies where almost all mothers are women, few people overcome the fears and unfulfilled fantasies of Bad/Good, Devouring/All Providing Maternal Creatures. If, as Marianne Hirsch and others have argued, feminists are especially ambivalent about power, authority, conflict, and anger, they may also be especially liable to what Nancy Chodorow and Susan Contratto have called "The Fantasy of the Perfect Mother," with its attendant fear of maternal power and anger at maternal powerlessness. Like Men of Reason, feminists who honor choice and control may be threatened by the unpredictability and vulnerability of children and by the stark physicality and radical dependencies of birth giving.

Yet, however grounded their (our) rejection or deep their (our) fears, feminists cannot afford to leave mothering alone. Just because "mother" has been a fearsome, crystallized female identity, mothering must be reconstituted as an enabling human work. Moreover, for many women mothering and giving birth are sex-expressive, sex-affirming constitutive identities. To the extent that feminists adopt an exclusively and excluding daughterly stance, these women will either reject feminism or accept their alienation as mothers within feminism just as they accepted their alienation as women within other movements and institutions that ignored or trivialized "womanly" experience. By contrast, a mother-respecting feminism in which mothers (who are also daughter or sons) are speaking subjects, in which daughters (who are sometimes mothers) are attuned to maternal voices, can confront in the name of mothers the damages as well as the pleasures of mothering.

When I now imagine mothers' transformative encounter with feminism, feminism is mother-inclusive, and therefore the meeting is not intrinsically oppositional. A mother-inclusive feminism can avoid the arrogance of setting out to "rescue" militarist mothers from "their" insularity and denial. Various forms of peacefulness are at least as latent in mothering as in feminist practices. Both feminist and mothering practices are drawn to militarist power and domination; each practice has its resources for resisting its own and others' militarism. It is the conjunction of feminist and maternal consciousness, of maternal sympathies and feminist solidarity, that might shift the balance within maternal practices from denial to lucid knowledge, from parochialism to awareness of others' suffering, and from compliance to stubborn, decisive capacities to act.

For example, women and men acquiring feminist consciousness tend to focus on the impact in their lives of norms of femininity and masculinity. They come to recognize that the stories they have been told and tell themselves about what it means to "be a woman" are mystifying and destructive. Central among these stories about women are various tales of female mothering: women are "naturally" suited for maternal work and men cannot be mothers; unless widowed, mothers should be married or at least het-erosexual; mother love is free of anger and ambivalence; good mothers are unselfish; children's demands are consuming and therefore mothers shouldn't, and in a just world needn't, "work"; mothers can't pilot airplanes, don't like to sell or repair heavy machines, can't dedicate themselves to an art or command soldiers in combat . . . and on and on. In unraveling these and other stories, mothers acquiring feminist consciousness may well be prompted to explore undefensively their ambitions and sexual desires and in particular to describe realistically the angers and ambivalences of maternal love. As they ferret out the dominant myths of mothering, they may be able to confront the political conditions—what Adrienne Rich called the "institutions of motherhood"—that exact from them unnecessary sacrifices of pleasure and power.

Whatever the tensions and ambivalence of individual mothers acquiring feminist consciousness, a mother-respecting feminism brings a public and nearly inescapable lucidity to bear on its particular culture's mode of mothering. This feminist-inspired lucidity undercuts many kinds of violence in mothers' lives. Most obviously feminists name the abuses mothers suffer from lovers, employers, husbands, and strangers. Equally important, they recognize mothers' tendencies to "submit" or, even worse, to get their children to submit to or take the blame for the violence they suffer, perhaps especially when that violence is perpetrated by a father or a mother's lover. Feminists also look at *maternal* violence, and name the domineering or sadistic tendencies often barely concealed by the demands of discipline. But mother-respecting feminists look at mothers with a compassionate eye. They acknowledge the complex ambivalences of maternal passion, the poverty and desperation that often lie behind men's or women's maternal abuse or neglect, and the repressive and punitive control of female sexuality and birth giving that squander women's capacity to cherish their own or their children's bodily being. Most important, feminists move on from identifying and analyzing in order to create policies and spaces that offer mothers the minimal economic means and physical safety to take care of themselves and those they care for—to start again.

Mothers who "see" personal violences they previously denied, may find themselves seeing through the fantasies and moralities that justify organized public violence. Feminists have revealed the ways in which the "masculinity" for which men are rewarded is intertwined with the domination and violence that masculinity permits. Militarist discourse is preeminent among the discourses of "masculinity"; as much as men have made war, war has made "men" as we know them. But if war is "manly," it is also "womanly." Many women are thrilled by the armed yet vulnerable Just Warrior who confronts Death on an illusory Battlefield. It is a feminine heroine "behind the lines" who keeps the "home fire burning" and with it the rare and increasingly outdated division between homes and battlefields, civilian and Soldier. A newly perceptive woman may suspect that myths of Heroic Deaths camouflage the realities of war's random, accidental, fratricidal killings as well as the cruelly vicious murder that making war permits. She may recognize that the fiction of a soldier's Battlefield is belied by the myriad soldier–civilian "relationships" created by distant bombings, fire torchings, search and destroy missions, forced relocations, prostitution, rape, torture, and pillage.

Mothers who begin to tease apart the fantasies of hero and battlefield that have buttressed their faith in war, are more likely to suspect the Men in Power and Defense Intellectuals in whom they have trusted. Evil Enemies, National interests, emergencies, conspiracies, and other worst-case scenarios are all vulnerable to the lucid, knowing gaze. When joined with a traditional commitment to protect, lucid knowledge may inspire mothers to protest policies that threaten their own children—thus adding distinctive maternal voices and energies to antinuclear and ecological politics. Increasing *habits* of lucidity might also enable mothers—against the odds of media distortion—to acknowledge the violence of their own government's military and economic policies.

But lucidity alone cannot inspire a maternal compassion that can undercut the ethnic rivalry or racist phobia that fuels violence. Mothers have to learn to apprehend, to appreciate, to identify with the suffering of "other" mothers and children if they are to act against the violence that "others" suffer or to fight the injustices to which violence is so often a response. Imaginative compassion is hard won. Differences among people—of race, class, wealth, gender, sexual preference, nationality, religion, and education—are typically more obvious and almost always more deeply felt than similarities. Of the many differences among people there may be none more painful than the difference between a mother who expects to be able to provide for her children's needs, share in their pleasures, and mitigate their unhappiness and a mother who expects that despite her efforts her children will be hungry, frightened, brutalized by bigotry, or humiliated and disabled by the hidden as well as the evident injuries of class. Moreover, mothers are committed to their children; every fragile, emerging, cross-cultural maternal identification is threatened by any division that sets one people and its children against another. We should read with astonishment the literary and historical record of maternal identification with "other" mothers and their children—including those of the "enemy." Despite the pull of parochial loyalty, fear, and distorting fantasy, at least some mothers can see in "other" and "enemy" mothers a real, particular, and variant form of the passionate attachments and connections that determine the shapes of their own lives.

Interpreted heuristically, cross-cultural maternal compassion is evidence that the difficult discipline of attentive love central to maternal thinking can be tentatively if imperfectly extended. An attentive mother is pained by her children's pain but does not confuse the two separable sufferings or inflict on her child her own distinct, adult and motherly sorrow. She comforts her child and therefore *indirectly* herself. Similarly, cross-cultural mothers do not pretend that they share, or even fully understand, another's suffering. It is sufficient that they imaginatively apprehend another's pain as painful, that they are pained by the other's pain, and that they act to relieve the *other's* suffering and only indirectly their own. Although they may be prompted by shame or guilt, as well as by outrage and sorrow, they do not let their self-preoccupations hinder their power to act.

I believe that a feminist ideal of solidarity with women who struggle against violence can inform and strengthen existing yet fragile maternal compassion. A principal obstacle to compassion for the different "other" is that difference is so often created in a nexus of domination and oppression, outrage and shame. Sympathy is sabotaged by injustice; conversely, to adapt a phrase of Alice Walker's, only justice can stop the curse of mutual hate and fear. Early feminist ideals of sisterhood that assumed a "common" oppression or experience of caretaking mystified real divisions among women and the damages of oppression. A more recent feminist ideal of solidarity aims for a cross-cultural alliance among and identification with just those women who are resisting violence and abuse. Because ideals of solidarity are sex/gender-expressive, mothers would be inspired as women to identify with other women who, as mothers, strive to create for themselves and their children the conditions for dignified work, self-governance, effective love, and pleasure. (Men who are mothers take on themselves something of the feminine condition. . . . They would therefore also identify to some extent with other women mothers.) Because these ideals legitimize women's struggle against specific injustices and abuse (as well as against more "natural" disaster), mothers moved by solidarity could be prompted to move beyond their shame, fear, or even their self-interest. A sex/gender-expressive extension of compassion and action will be more likely if there are actual existing struggles of women in resistance that can call forth and utilize acts of solidarity.

Fortunately in recent years, movements of women in resistance have developed in countries as different as South Africa, Chile, East Ger-many, England, Israel, Palestine, and the United States. A women's politics of resistance begins by affirming "womanly" obligations and then demands that governments or communities respect the conditions necessary for "womanly" work and love. For example, women are responsible for children's health; in the name of their maternal duty they call on their government to halt nuclear testing which, epitomizing its general unhealthiness, leaves strontium 90 in women's milk. Since women feed families, they "riot" for bread. Since (mostly) women actively nurse the sick, women organize not only for better pay but also for conditions that will allow them to do their work effectively. Since women are responsible for protective mothering, in Argentina, Chile and across Latin America, Madres publicly and dramatically protest the "disappearing"—the kidnapping, torturing, mutilating, and murdering—of their children.

Women in resistance create new values of activity and stubborn decisiveness. When women carry pictures of their loved ones in the public plazas of a police state, chain themselves to their capitol building's fence, put pillowcases and photographs up against the barbed-wire fences of missile bases or create open alliances among "enemy" mothers, they translate the symbols of attachment into political speech. Insisting that their governors name and take responsibility for the injuries they risk and inflict, they speak a "woman's language" of loyalty, love and outrage; but they speak with a public anger in a public place in ways they were never meant to do. They are the heirs of the mater dolorosa, taking active, decisive, public responsibility for restoring a world in which their children can survive. As they fulfill expectations of femininity they also violate them, transforming, even as they act on the meanings of maternity and womanliness.

In a utopian mood I have envisioned a "feminist, maternal peace politics" made up of mothers, mother-inclusive feminists, and women in resistance. Feminist, maternal peacemakers draw on the history and traditions of women to create a *politics* of peace. They are inspired by the act and symbol of birth and by the passionate labor of women who throughout most of history have borne the primary responsibility for protection and care. Yet because they are feminists, these peacemakers subvert mythical divisions between women and men, private care and public justice, that hobble both mothering and peacemaking. Men become mothers and mothers invent new models and styles of public, nonviolent resistance and cooperation that are suitable to their particular temperament, personal history, social location, and economic resources.

The forms and ideologies of a feminist, maternal peace politics are various and just being in-vented. Yet even in its inchoate forms this politics is transforming the maternal imagination, creating in mothers new capacities to know, care, and act. This is not to say that feminist mothers or feminist and mother-identified men and women are the only or the loudest voices of peace. Many voices, wills, and projects are needed; there need be no competition for best peacemaker. It is enough that mothers who have hitherto played their parts in the scripts of the violent now move from maternal thinking to peace politics, thus contributing in their own distinctively maternal ways to the many-faceted, polymorphous, collective effort to make a peace worth keeping.

Study Questions

1. What does Ruddick criticize in feminism? in mothering? Why is there a need for a transformation? What kind of transformation is required? What gives impulse for this transformation?

2. In what specific ways can feminists and mothers learn from one another, according to Ruddick? What have been their points of conflict? How would these be resolved in Ruddick's project?

3. Is Ruddick proposing a feminist ethics or a maternal ethics? Why does she retain the ideal of mothering? What roles does she allow for men and fathers?

Suggestions for Further Reading

Ruddick, S. *Maternal Thinking: Toward a Politics of Peace* (Boston: Beacon Press, 1989). Ruddick develops her theory in nine chapters.

Scaltsas, P. W. "Do Feminist Ethics Counter Feminist Aims?" *Explorations in Feminist Ethics: Theory and Practice*, eds. E. B. Cole and S. Coultrap-McQuin (Bloomington: Indiana University Press, 1992). A critique of Ruddick's ethical notion of mothering.

Simons, M. A. "Motherhood, Feminism and Identity." In *Hypatia Reborn: Essays in Feminist Philosophy*, eds. A. Y. Al-Hibri and M. A. Simons (Bloomington: Indiana University Press, 1990). Explores the issue of motherhood from a feminist perspective and considers Ruddick's position, among others.

Treblicot, J., ed. *Mothering: Essays in Feminist Theory* (Totowa, NJ: Rowman and Allanheld, 1983). Contains eighteen essays on mothering, including two by Ruddick.

Rosemary Radford Ruether (1936–)

Rosemary Radford Ruether is Georgia Harkness Professor of Applied Theology at the Garrett-Evangelical Theological Seminary in Evanston, Illinois. She has lectured widely and written extensively on feminist theology. She is the author of many books, including *New Woman/New Earth* (1975), *Sexism and God-Talk: Toward a Feminist Theology* (1983), and *Gaia and God: An Ecofeminist Theology of Earth Healing* (1992). The main focus of her work is an historical exposé and critique of the patriarchal nature of cultural and religious symbols and practices, particularly in Western Judeo-Christian culture and society. As a Christian feminist, Ruether seeks to transform rather than discard the Judeo-Christian tradition by proposing radical changes in our ways of understanding and relating to God, one another, and the earth.

In her essay "Ecofeminism: Symbolic and Social Connections of the Oppression of Women and the Domination of Nature," Ruether develops a critical survey of the patterns of thought and relations that have led to the subjugation of women and the destruction of nature by patriarchal systems. As an alternative, she offers a reconstructed worldview based on ecofeminist principles. Beginning with a definition of ecofeminism that highlights the interconnections between deep ecology and feminism, she examines the linkage between the cultural conceptions of women and nature throughout various historical worlds—pre-Hebraic, Hebraic, Greek, Christian, Protestant Reformation, the Scientific Revolution (where our selection begins), and the ecological crisis that began in the twentieth century. Present-day Western culture suffers from dualist distinctions that split apart matter and mind, nature and consciousness, female and male into opposites. The contemporary scientific, technological perspective views nature as an inexhaustible realm of mere matter. Such realm is known and controlled by an elite male consciousness that transcends or lies beyond it. This worldview has brought about not only the depletion of our resources and the destruction of our environment but also social exploitation and injustice on a global scale. Putting an end to the current social inequalities and the impending ecological debacle requires a complete conversion, a radical change of our worldview into an ecofeminist culture and ethics. Seeing the world as a living, organic, and spiritual whole, ecofeminism is not dualist, hierarchical, anthropocentric, or anthropomorphic in its conceptions and moral values. In affirming the mutual interconnectedness and dependency of all beings, ecofeminism views God, Nature, human, self, male, and female in the transformative light of social and ecological justice.

ECOFEMINISM: SYMBOLIC AND SOCIAL CONNECTIONS OF THE OPPRESSION OF WOMEN AND THE DOMINATION OF NATURE

WHAT IS ECOFEMINISM? Ecofeminism represents the union of the radical ecology movement, or what has been called "deep ecology," and feminism. The word "ecology" emerges from the biological science of natural environmental systems. It examines how these natural communities function to sustain a healthy web of life and how they become disrupted, causing death to the plant and animal life. Human intervention is obviously one of the main causes of such disruption. Thus ecology emerged as a combined socioeconomic and biological study in the late sixties to examine how human use of nature is causing pollution of soil, air, and water, and destruction of the natural systems of plants and animals, threatening the base of life on which the human community itself depends. . . .

Deep ecology takes this study of social ecology another step. It examines the symbolic, psychological, and ethical patterns of destructive relations of humans with nature and how to replace this with a life-affirming culture. . . .

Feminism also is a complex movement with many layers. It can be defined as only a movement within the liberal democratic societies for the full inclusion of women in political rights and economic access to employment. It can be defined more radically in a socialist and liberation tradition as a transformation of the patriarchal socioeconomic system, in which male domination of women is the foundation of all socioeconomic hierarchies. . . . Feminism can be also studied in terms of culture and consciousness, charting the symbolic, psychological, and ethical connections of domination of women and male monopolization of resources and controlling power. This third level of feminist analysis connects closely with deep ecology. Some

would say that feminism is the primary expression of deep ecology. . . .

Yet, although many feminists may make a verbal connection between domination of women and domination of nature, the development of this connection in a broad historical, social, economic, and cultural analysis is only just beginning. Most studies of ecofeminism, such as the essays in *Healing the Wounds: The Promise of Ecofeminism*, are brief and evocative, rather than comprehensive. . . .

Fuller exploration of ecofeminism probably goes beyond the expertise of one person. It needs a cooperation of a team that brings together historians of culture, natural scientists, and social economists who would all share a concern for the interconnection of domination of women and exploitation of nature. It needs visionaries to imagine how to construct a new socioeconomic system and a new cultural consciousness that would support relations of mutuality, rather than competitive power. For this, one needs poets, artists, and liturgists, as well as revolutionary organizers, to incarnate more life-giving relationships in our cultural consciousness and social system.

Such a range of expertise certainly goes beyond my own competence. Although I am interested in continuing to gain working acquaintance with the natural and social sciences, my primary work lies in the area of history of culture. What I plan to do in this essay is to trace some symbolic connections of domination of women and domination of nature in Mediterranean and Western European culture. I will then explore briefly the alternative ethic and culture that might be envisioned, if we are to overcome these patterns of domination and de-

Rosemary Radford Ruether. "Ecofeminism: Symbolic and Social Connections of the Oppression of Women and the Domination of Nature." In Ecofeminism and the Sacred, *ed. Carol. J. Adams. New York: Continuum, 1993.*

structive violence to women and to the natural world. . . .

The view of nature found in Hebrew Scripture has several cultural layers. But the overall tendency is to see the natural world, together with human society, as something created, shaped, and controlled by God, a God imaged after the patriarchal ruling class. The patriarchal male is entrusted with being the steward and caretaker of nature, but under God, who remains its ultimate creator and Lord. This also means that nature remains partly an uncontrollable realm that can confront human society in destructive droughts and storms. These experiences of nature that transcend human control, bringing destruction to human work, are seen as divine judgment against human sin and unfaithfulness to God (see Isaiah 24).

God acts in the droughts and the storms to bring human work to naught, to punish humans for sin, but also to call humans (that is, Israel) back to faithfulness to God. When Israel learns obedience to God, nature in turn will become benign and fruitful, a source of reliable blessings, rather than unreliable destruction. Nature remains ultimately in God's hands, and only secondarily, and through becoming servants of God, in male hands. Yet the symbolization of God as a patriarchal male and Israel as wife, son, and servant of God, creates a basic analogy of woman and nature. God is the ultimate patriarchal Lord, under whom the human patriarchal lord rules over women, children, slaves, and land.

The image of God as single, male, and transcendent, prior to nature, also shifts the symbolic relation of male consciousness to material life. Marduk was a young male god who was produced out of a process of theogony and cosmogony. He conquers and shapes the cosmos out of the body of an older Goddess that existed prior to himself, within which he himself stands. The Hebrew God exists above and prior to the cosmos, shaping it out of a chaos that is under his control. Genesis 2 gives us a parallel view of the male, not as the child of woman, but as the source of woman. She arises out of him, with the help of the male God, and is handed over to him as her Master. . . .

When we turn to Greek philosophical myth, the link between mother and matter is made explicit. Plato, in his creation myth, the *Timaeus*, speaks of primal, unformed matter as the receptacle and "nurse". . . . He imagines a disembodied male mind as divine architect, or Demiurgos, shaping this matter into the cosmos by fashioning it after the intellectual blueprint of the Eternal Ideas. These Eternal Ideas exist in an immaterial, transcendent world of Mind, separate from and above the material stuff that he is fashioning into the visible cosmos.

The World Soul is also created by the Demiurgos, by mixing together dynamics of antithetical relations (the Same and the Other). This world soul is infused into the body of the cosmos in order to make it move in harmonic motion. The remnants of this world soul are divided into bits, to create the souls of humans. These souls are first placed in the stars, so that human souls will gain knowledge of the Eternal Ideas. Then the souls are sown in the bodies of humans on earth. The task of the soul is to govern the unruly passions that arise from the body.

If the soul succeeds in this task, it will return at death to its native star and there live a life of leisured contemplation. If not, the soul will be reincarnated into the body of a woman or an animal. It will then have to work its way back into the form of an (elite) male and finally escape from bodily reincarnation altogether, to return to its original disincarnate form in the starry realm above. . . . Plato takes for granted an ontological hierarchy of being, the immaterial intellectual world over material cosmos, and, within this ontological hierarchy, the descending hierarchy of male, female, and animal.

In the Greco-Roman era, a sense of pessimism about the possibility of blessing and well-being within the bodily, historical world deepened in Eastern Mediterranean culture, expressing itself in apocalypticism and gnosticism. In apocalypticism, God is seen as intervening in history to destroy the present sinful and finite world of human society and nature and to create a new heaven and earth freed from both sin and death. In gnosticism, mystical philosophies chart the path to salvation by way of withdrawal of the soul from the body and its passions and its return to an immaterial realm outside of and above the visible cosmos. . . .

Early Christianity was shaped by both the Hebraic and Greek traditions, including their alienated forms in apocalypticism and gnosticism. Second-century Christianity struggled against gnosticism, reaffirming the Hebraic view of nature and body as God's good creation. The second-century Christian theologian Irenaeus sought to combat gnostic anticosmism and to synthesize apocalypticism and Hebraic creationalism. He imaged the whole cosmos as a bodying forth of the Word and Spirit of God, as the sacramental embodiment of the invisible God.

Sin arises through a human denial of this relation to God. But salvific grace, dispensed progressively through the Hebrew and Christian revelations, allows humanity to heal its relation to God. The cosmos, in turn, grows into being a blessed and immortalized manifestation of the divine Word and Spirit, which is its ground of being. . . .

However, Greek and Latin Christianity, increasingly influenced by Neoplatonism, found this materialism distasteful. They deeply imbibed the platonic eschatology of the escape of the soul from the body and its return to a transcendent world outside the earth. The earth and the body must be left behind in order to ascend to another, heavenly world of disembodied life. Even though the Hebrew idea of resurrection of the body was retained, increasingly this notion was envisioned as a vehicle of immortal light for the soul, not the material body, in all its distasteful physical processes, which they saw as the very essence of sin as mortal corruptibility.

The view of women in this ascetic Christian system was profoundly ambivalent. A part of ascetic Christianity imagined women becoming freed from subordination, freed both for equality in salvation and to act as agents of Christian preaching and teaching. But this freedom was based on woman rejecting her sexuality and reproductive role and becoming symbolically male. The classic Christian "good news" to woman as equal to man in Christ was rooted in a misogynist view of female sexuality and reproduction as the essence of the sinful, mortal, corruptible life. . . .

For most male ascetic Christians, even ascetic woman, who had rejected her sexuality and reproductive role, was too dangerously sexual. Ascetic women were increasingly deprived of their minor roles in public ministry, such as deaconess, and locked away in convents, where obedience to God was to be expressed in total obedience to male ecclesiastical authority. Sexual woman, drawing male seminal power into herself, her womb swelling with new life, became the very essence of sin, corruptibility, and death, from which the male ascetic fled. Eternal life was disembodied male soul, freed from all material underpinnings in the mortal bodily life, represented by woman and nature.

Medieval Latin Christianity was also deeply ambivalent about its view of nature. One side of medieval thought retained something of Irenaeus's sacramental cosmos, which becomes the icon of God through feeding on the redemptive power of Christ in the sacraments of bread and wine. The redeemed cosmos as resurrected body, united with God, is possible only by freeing the body of its sexuality and mortality. Mary, the virgin Mother of Christ, assumed into heaven to reign by the side of her son, was the representative of this redeemed body of the cosmos, the resurrected body of the Church. . . .

But the dark side of Medieval thought saw nature as possessed by demonic powers that draw us down to sin and death through sexual temptation. Women, particularly old crones with sagging breasts and bellies, still perversely retaining their sexual appetites, are the vehicles of the demonic power of nature. They are the witches who sell their souls to the Devil in a satanic parody of the Christian sacraments. . . .

The Calvinist Reformation and the Scientific Revolution in England in the late sixteenth and seventeenth centuries represent key turning points in the Western concept of nature. In these two movements, the Medieval struggle between the sacramental and the demonic views of nature was recast. Calvinism dismembered the Medieval sacramental sense of nature. For Calvinism, nature was totally depraved. There was no residue of divine presence in it that could sustain a natural knowledge or relation to God. Saving knowledge of God descends from on high, beyond nature, in the revealed Word available only in Scripture, as preached by the Reformers.

The Calvinist reformers were notable in their iconoclastic hostility toward visual art. Stained glass, statues, and carvings were smashed, and the churches stripped of all visible imagery. Only the disembodied Word, descending from the preacher to the ear of the listener, together with music, could be bearers of divine presence. Nothing one could see, touch, taste, or smell was trustworthy as bearer of the divine. Even the bread and wine were no longer the physical embodiment of Christ, but intellectual reminders of the message about Christ's salvific act enacted in the past.

Calvinism dismantled the sacramental world of Medieval Christianity, but it maintained and reinforced its demonic universe. The fallen world, especially physical nature and other human groups outside of the control of the Calvinist church, lay in the grip of the Devil. All who were labeled pagan, whether Catholics or Indians and Africans, were the playground of demonic powers. But, even within the Calvinist church, women were the gateway of the Devil. If women were completely obedient to their fathers, husbands, ministers, and magistrates, they might be redeemed as goodwives. But in any independence of women lurked heresy and witchcraft. Among Protestants, Calvinists were the primary witch-hunters. . . .

The Scientific Revolution at first moved in a different direction, exorcizing the demonic powers from nature in order to reclaim it as an icon of divine reason manifest in natural law. . . . But, in the seventeenth and eighteenth centuries, the more animist natural science, which unified material and spiritual, lost out to a strict dualism of transcendent intellect and dead matter. Nature was secularized. It was no longer the scene of a struggle between Christ and the Devil. Both divine and demonic spirits were driven out of it. In Cartesian dualism and Newtonian physics, it becomes matter in motion, dead stuff moving obediently, according to mathematical laws knowable to a new male elite of scientists. With no life or soul of its own, nature could be safely expropriated by this male elite and infinitely reconstructed to augment its wealth and power.

In Western society, the application of science to technological control over nature marched side by side with colonialism. From the sixteenth to the twentieth centuries, Western Europeans would appropriate the lands of the Americas, Asia, and Africa, and reduce their human populations to servitude. The wealth accrued by this vast expropriation of land and labor would fuel new levels of technological revolution, transforming material resources into new forms of energy and mechanical work, control of disease, increasing speed of communication and travel. Western elites grew increasingly optimistic, imagining that this technological way of life would gradually conquer all problems of material scarcity and even push back the limits of human mortality. The Christian dream of immortal blessedness, freed from finite limits, was translated into scientific technological terms. . . .

In a short three-quarters of a century, this dream of infinite progress has been turned into a nightmare. The medical conquest of disease, lessening infant mortality and doubling the life span of the affluent, insufficiently matched by birth limitation, especially among the poor, has created a population explosion that is rapidly outrunning the food supply. Every year 10 million children die of malnutrition. The gap between rich and poor, between the wealthy elites of the industrialized sector and the impoverished masses, especially in the colonized continents of Latin America, Asia, and Africa, grows ever wider. . . .

This Western scientific Industrial Revolution has been built on injustice. It has been based on the takeover of the land, its agricultural, metallic, and mineral wealth appropriated through the exploitation of the labor of the indigenous people. This wealth has flowed back to enrich the West, with some for local elites, while the laboring people of these lands grew poorer. This system of global affluence, based on exploitation of the land and labor of the many for the benefit of the few, with its high consumption of energy and waste, cannot be expanded to include the poor without destroying the basis of life of the planet itself. We are literally destroying the air, water, and soil upon which human and planetary life depend.

In order to preserve the unjust monopoly on material resources from the growing protests of the poor, the world became more and more militarized. Most nations have been using the lion's share of their state budgets for weapons, both to guard against one another and to control their own poor. Weapons also become one of the major exports of wealthy nations to poor nations. Poor nations grow increasingly indebted to wealthy nations while buying weapons to repress their own impoverished masses. Population explosion, exhaustion of natural resources, pollution, and state violence are the four horsemen of the new global apocalypse.

The critical question of both justice and survival is how to pull back from this disastrous course and remake our relations with one another and with the earth. . . .

There are many elements that need to go into an ecofeminist ethic and culture for a just and sustainable planet. One element is to reshape our dualistic concept of reality as split between soulless matter and transcendent male consciousness. We need to discover our actual reality as latecomers to the planet. The world of nature, plants, and animals existed billions of years before we came on the scene. Nature does not need us to rule over it, but runs itself very well, even better, without humans. We are the parasites on the food chain of life, consuming more and

more, and putting too little back to restore and maintain the life system that supports us.

We need to recognize our utter dependence on the great life-producing matrix of the planet in order to learn to reintegrate our human systems of production, consumption, and waste into the ecological patterns by which nature sustains life. This might begin by revisualizing the relation of mind, or human intelligence, to nature. Mind or consciousness is not something that originates in some transcendent world outside of nature, but is the place where nature itself becomes conscious. We need to think of human consciousness not as separating us as a higher species from the rest of nature, but rather as a gift to enable us to learn how to harmonize our needs with the natural system around us, of which we are a dependent part.

Such a reintegration of human consciousness and nature must reshape the concept of God, instead of modeling God after alienated male consciousness, outside of and ruling over nature. God, in ecofeminist spirituality, is the immanent source of life that sustains the whole planetary community. God is neither male nor anthropomorphic. God is the font from which the variety of plants and animals well up in each new generation, the matrix that sustains their life-giving interdependency with one another. . . .

In ecofeminist culture and ethic, mutual interdependency replaces the hierarchies of domination as the model of relationship between men and women, between human groups, and between humans and other beings. All racist, sexist, classist, cultural, and anthropocentric assumptions of the superiority of whites over blacks, males over females, managers over workers, humans over animals and plants, must be discarded. In a real sense, the so-called superior pole in each relation is actually the more dependent side of the relationship.

But it is not enough simply to humbly acknowledge dependency. The pattern of male-female, racial, and class interdependency itself has to be reconstructed socially, creating more equitable sharing in the work and the fruits of work, rather than making one side of the relation the subjugated and impoverished base for the power and wealth of the other.

In terms of male-female relations, this means not simply allowing women more access to public culture, but converting males to an equal share in the tasks of child nurture and household maintenance. A revolution in female roles into the male work world, without a corresponding revolution in male roles, leaves the basic pattern of patriarchal exploitation of women untouched. Women are simply overworked in a new way, expected to do both a male workday, at low pay, and also the unpaid work of women that sustains family life.

There must be a conversion of men to the work of women, along with the conversion of male consciousness to the earth. Such conversions will reshape the symbolic vision of salvation. Instead of salvation sought either in the disembodied soul or the immortalized body, in a flight to heaven or to the end of history, salvation should be seen as continual conversion to the center, to the concrete basis by which we sustain our relation to nature and to one another. In every day and every new generation, we need to remake our relation with one another, finding anew the true nexus of relationality that sustains, rather than exploits and destroys, life. . . .

Finally, ecofeminist culture must reshape our basic sense of self in relation to the life cycle. The sustaining of an organic community of plant and animal life is a continual cycle of growth and dis-integration. The western flight from mortality is a flight from the disintegration side of the life cycle, from accepting ourselves as part of that process. By pretending that we can immortalize ourselves, souls and bodies, we are immortalizing our garbage and polluting the earth. In order to learn to recycle our garbage as fertilizer for new life, as matter for new artifacts, we need to accept our selfhood as participating in the same process. Humans also are finite organisms, centers of experience in a life cycle that must disintegrate back into the nexus of life and arise again in new forms.

These conversions, from alienated, hierarchical dualism to life-sustaining mutuality, will radically change the patterns of patriarchal culture. Basic concepts, such as God, soul-body, and salvation will be reconceived in ways that may bring us much closer to the ethical values of love, justice, and care for the earth. These values have been proclaimed by patriarchal religion, yet contradicted by patriarchal symbolic and social patterns of relationship.

These tentative explorations of symbolic changes must be matched by a new social practice that can incarnate these conversions in new social and technological ways of organizing human life in relation to one another and to nature. This will require a new sense of urgency about the untenability of present patterns of life and compassionate solidarity with those who are its victims.

Study Questions

1. What are the moral principles in Ruether's ecofeminist ethics? In what ways is a conversion of consciousness morally imperative? Is it possible to deliberately undertake such a task?

2. Why must we view all things as interconnected? How do our conceptions change with this view? Why would we still have to retain the concept of God?

3. Do we have a moral obligation to the earth? On what grounds?

Suggestions for Further Reading

Adams. C. J., ed. *Ecofeminism and the Sacred* (New York: Continuum, 1993). A collection of essays on ecofeminism and spirituality. See especially Part 2, "Envisioning Ecofeminism," and Part 3, "Embodying Ecofeminist Spiritualities."

Diamond, I., and G. F. Orenstein, eds. *Reweaving the World: The Emergence of Ecofeminism* (San Francisco: Sierra Club Books, 1990). A collection of essays on various perspectives of ecofeminism. See especially Part 2, "Reweaving the World: Reconnecting Politics and Ethics."

Pearsall, M., ed. *Women and Values: Readings in Recent Feminist Philosophy* (Belmont, CA: Wadsworth, 1986). See Chapter 6 for a sample of critical feminist perspectives in the philosophy of religion.

Plaskow, J., and C. P. Christ, eds. *Weaving the Visions: New Patterns in Feminist Spirituality* (New York: Harper & Row, 1989). A collection of essays on various perspectives of feminist spirituality. See especially Part 4, "Transforming the World."

Index